E–Adoption and Socio–Economic Impacts:

Emerging Infrastructural Effects

Sushil K. Sharma
Ball State University, USA

Senior Editorial Director:	Kristin Klinger
Director of Book Publications:	Julia Mosemann
Editorial Director:	Lindsay Johnston
Acquisitions Editor:	Erika Carter
Development Editor:	Hannah Abelbeck
Production Editor:	Sean Woznicki
Typesetters:	Natalie Pronio, Jennifer Romanchak, Milan Vracarich, Jr.
Print Coordinator:	Jamie Snavely
Cover Design:	Nick Newcomer

Published in the United States of America by
Information Science Reference (an imprint of IGI Global)
701 E. Chocolate Avenue
Hershey PA 17033
Tel: 717-533-8845
Fax: 717-533-8661
E-mail: cust@igi-global.com
Web site: http://www.igi-global.com

Library of Congress Cataloging-in-Publication Data

E-Adoption and Socio-Economic Impacts: Emerging Infrastructural Effects / Sushil K. Sharma, editor.
    p. cm.
  Includes bibliographical references and index.
  Summary: "This book identifies the multidimensional impact of e-adoption and provides theoretical and practical solutions for policy makers, managers, and researchers in government, industry, and academia"--Provided by publisher.
  ISBN 978-1-60960-597-1 (hardcover) -- ISBN 978-1-60960-598-8 (ebook) 1. Customer services--Technological innovations--Management. 2. Internet banking. 3. Knowledge management.
  HF5415.5.E2 2011
  658.8'120285--dc22
                                            2011013283

British Cataloguing in Publication Data
A Cataloguing in Publication record for this book is available from the British Library.

All work contributed to this book is new, previously-unpublished material. The views expressed in this book are those of the authors, but not necessarily of the publisher.

Table of Contents

Introduction

Sushil K. Sharma, Ball State University, USA
Reima Soumi, University of Turku, Finland
Rui Chen, Ball State University, USA

Section 1
Internet Banking Cases

Chapter 1
Modeling User Acceptance of Internet Banking in Malaysia:
Kamel Rouibah, Kuwait University, Kuwait
T. Ramayah, Universiti Sains Malaysia, Malaysia
Oh Sook May, Universiti Sains Malaysia, Malaysia

Chapter 2
M. Makris, Business College of Athens (BCA), Greece
V. Koumaras, Business College of Athens (BCA), Greece
H. Koumaras, Business College of Athens (BCA), Greece
A. Konstantopoulou, Business College of Athens (BCA), Greece
S. Konidis, Business College of Athens (BCA), Greece
S. Kostakis, Business College of Athens (BCA), Greece

Chapter 3
Exploring Antecedents of Behavior Intention to Use Internet Banking in Korea:
Kun Chang Lee, Sungkyunkwan University, Korea
Namho Chung, Kyung Hee University, Korea

Section 2
E-Adoption and Diffusion Among Small and Medium-Size Enterprises (SMEs)

Section 3
E-Commerce and E-Business

Detailed Table of Contents

Introduction

    Sushil K. Sharma, Ball State University, USA
    Reima Soumi, University of Turku, Finland
    Rui Chen, Ball State University, USA

Information and communication technologies (ICT) have made enormous impact on social and economic performance and competitiveness in general, and on productivity, efficiency, and innovation in particular. The literature suggests that ICT has contributed greatly to productivity growth and competitiveness in the developed as well as developing countries in the last decade. This study aims to advance understanding of the social and economic impact of e-adoption. It provides an in-depth understanding through extensive literature survey and analysis of a various success stories. The generalization and conclusions are drawn from documented studies.

Section 1
Internet Banking Cases

Chapter 1
    Kamel Rouibah, Kuwait University, Kuwait
    T. Ramayah, Universiti Sains Malaysia, Malaysia
    Oh Sook May, Universiti Sains Malaysia, Malaysia

This study is the first empirical research that compares three well known technology adoption models in the in the field of e-banking. It aims to determine the dominant factor(s) which influence the user intention to use Internet banking. Three models (TAM, TPB, and TRA) were used to test the impact of five factors (perceived ease of use, perceived usefulness, attitude, subjective norms, and perceived behavioral control) on intention to adopt e-banking by 239 individual bank customers in Malaysia. Survey questions from prior studies were adopted and customized. Partial least Square (PLS) SmartPLS M2

Version 2.0 was used for data analysis. Results reveal that the five factors have a direct positive effect on behavioral intention to use Internet banking. However, attitude toward behavior has the highest beta, followed by perceived usefulness, and subjective norm, while perceived behavioral control exerts the weakest effect. In testing the explanatory power of the different models, results found TAM model has the best explanatory power, followed by TPB and TRA models. Findings of the study should benefit banks in improving their use of e-banking technologies as a strategic weapon, and can be used to target more potential customers.

Chapter 2

   M. Makris, Business College of Athens (BCA), Greece
   V. Koumaras, Business College of Athens (BCA), Greece
   H. Koumaras, Business College of Athens (BCA), Greece
   A. Konstantopoulou, Business College of Athens (BCA), Greece
   S. Konidis, Business College of Athens (BCA), Greece
   S. Kostakis, Business College of Athens (BCA), Greece

A growing phenomenon in the Internet is the rising exploitation of sophisticated security means (e.g. cryptography, digital signatures etc.) toward the development of novel commerce services for providing electronic transactions, collaborating with business partners or serving customers, regardless of geographical and time limitations. This paper discusses, presents and elaborates on the various factors that affect the adaption of Internet banking services in Greece. In particular, it deals with the factors that have been developed within the framework of providing e-banking services over an insecure shared medium like the Internet and affect the Internet Banking customer acceptance. A factor analysis is performed based on the gathered results provided by customer-questionnaires of ALPHA Bank branch in Greece in order to quantify the various parameters that affect the use of an Internet Banking System. The findings of the analysis show that despite the fact that Internet Banking in Greece is steadily increasing its penetration, factors like security, ease of use and perceived usefulness of a system play a major role on the final decision of the customer to adopt an Internet Banking System.

Chapter 3

   Kun Chang Lee, Sungkyunkwan University, Korea
   Namho Chung, Kyung Hee University, Korea

This study is aimed at analyzing adoption and usage behavior within the context of Internet banking services in South Korea. In a country where the penetration rate of the Internet is very high, it seems that the self-efficacy would play a crucial role in affecting the Internet banking adoption. To pursue this research question, this study adopts TAM and incorporates the self-efficacy into TAM as one of antecedent variables such as risk, Internet experience, facilitating conditions. The proposed research model is tested empirically with 185 usable questionnaires and partial least square (PLS) method. Experimental results showed that the self-efficacy plays a prominent role in influencing the Internet banking usage compared to other factors.

Section 2
E-Adoption and Diffusion Among Small and Medium-Size Enterprises (SMEs)

Chapter 4

    Boumediene Ramdani, Cranfield University, UK
    Oswaldo Lorenzo, Instituto de Empresa, Spain
    Peter Kawalek, The University of Manchester, UK

The attention of software vendors has moved recently to Small to Medium-sized Enterprises (SMEs) offering them a vast range of Information Systems' (IS) innovations including enterprise systems (ES), which were formerly adopted by large firms only. Although the number of SMEs adopting new IS innovations has increased over time, strong empirical evidence is still lacking. This paper aims to fill this gap by reporting the findings of a survey on SMEs located in the Northwest of England. The survey results reveal that even more complex IS innovations are increasingly adopted by SMEs. Also, nearly half of the surveyed SMEs are willing to adopt ES in the next three years. These findings suggest that there is a considerable opportunity and a need for further research in the adoption and diffusion of new IS innovations among SMEs.

Chapter 5

    Sim Chia Hua, Swinburne University of Technology, Malaysia
    Modapothala Jashua Rajesh, Swinburne University of Technology, Malaysia
    Lau Bee Theng, Swinburne University of Technology, Malaysia

With a major proportion of research on Electronic Commerce (EC) undertaken on large corporations, and focused primarily on developed countries, little is known about the determinants of EC in Small and Medium-sized Enterprises (SMEs) of developing nations. This chapter explores the extent of EC use by SMEs, and provides some empirical evidence of how internal factors of firm and owner are influencing EC adoption among smaller businesses in Malaysia. The methodology and results of this study may be applicable to other developing countries. Findings confirm the low level of participation in EC by SMEs. The age of enterprise, as well as the owner's gender and education were found to be significant in determining the level of EC adoption. Though some of the results contradict those of previous studies, they may have a greater implication for government authorities in drawing up guidelines, approaches, and formulating more effective frameworks to promote EC use among SMEs in developing countries.

Chapter 6

    Daniel John Doiron, University of New Brunswick Saint John, Canada

Small and medium enterprises (SMEs) have been adopting the internet at a feverish pace. Recent studies have shown that up to 85% of SMEs in industrialized countries have web sites, yet less than half are utilizing these web sites to securely transact with their customers. Consumer media consumption is moving away from traditional media, like newspapers, to the internet. These revelations coupled with the growth of tools and techniques available to support online marketing, make it a perfect time for SMEs to market their web sites and ultimately succeed online. In this chapter we will present and support the hypothesis that SMEs should stop investing in their web site's design and functionality and start investing in efforts to market their web sites online, no matter how *lousy* their web site may be in comparison to today's standards. With the support of two case studies, illustrating the successful utilization of internet marketing by two very different SMEs, we will relate how a SME can effectively market their web site online. We will also discuss the tools and techniques available to help an SME successfully begin a journey of internet marketing.

Chapter 7

Piers Thompson, University of Wales Institute – Cardiff, UK
Robert Williams, National Entrepreneurship Observatory, UK
Gary Packham, University of Glamorgan, UK
Brychan C. Thomas, University of Glamorgan, UK

The potential of the Internet to both geographically expand customer bases and provide a source of sales growth has led to a rapid embracement of the Internet by a majority of small businesses in the United Kingdom. However, many studies suggest that much of this adoption takes the form of simple Web sites representing little more than an electronic brochure. Although theories and models have been proposed suggesting adoption and development of e-commerce takes a staged process, with firms moving to more complex e-commerce processes after first mastering simpler forms of Web site, studies have found mixed evidence with regard to this. This chapter investigates the level of Small and Medium Enterprise (SME) Web site adoption and functionality and how this relates to growth aspirations, specifically the geographical expansion of customer bases. One potential explanation for this slow uptake of true e-commerce is a lack of employees with basic and advanced IT skills. The possibility that Information Technology (IT) skills shortages could explain the gap between the Internet's potential and the extent of involvement by a vast majority of UK SMEs is explored. Discussion within the chapter is complemented with analysis of data from a large survey of SMEs.

Chapter 8

Fiona McMahon, University of Ulster, Northern Ireland
Aodheen O'Donnell, University of Ulster, Northern Ireland

The potential of the Internet to transform marketing practice is well-documented (Hoffman & Novac, 1997; Zineldin, 2000). It is argued that the exploitation of the Internet's interactive and relationship-building properties contribute to customer satisfaction and loyalty and hence, marketing success (Arnott & Bridgewater, 2002). Evidence suggests, however, that small to medium sized enterprises (SMEs) have failed to capitalize on the Internet to facilitate the management of customer relations (e-CRM) and the creation of competitive advantage (Chen & Popovich, 2003; Geiger & Martin, 1999; McGowan et al., 2001; O'Toole, 2001). This is attributed to a lack of influence, time, finance, and specialised knowledge, (Carson & Gilmore, 2003) coupled with the reality that most Information Systems and Technology models and tools have been developed from the perspective of the large firm (Maguire et al., 2007; Poon & Swatman, 1999).

Despite such constraints, it is posited that by exploring the components of e-CRM in the unique context of SME business and marketing practice that a natural synergy exists between e-CRM and SME marketing in the creation of value propositions. Specifically this is addressed through the two contributing constructs of SME marketing; namely entrepreneurial marketing and network marketing (Carson & Gilmore, 2000).

Section 3
E-Commerce and E-Business

Chapter 9

A small but growing body of evidence (SBS, 2004; Beckinsale & Ram, 2006) has indicated that Ethnic Minority Businesses (EMBs) have not adopted Information Communication Technology (ICT) at comparable rates to their non-EMB counterparts, predominantly Small and Medium Sized Enterprises (SMEs). With EMBs accounting for almost 10% of businesses in the UK, the economic impact as ICT adoption continues to further develop across mainstream markets could be highly significant. Existing UK ICT policies also failed to engage with EMBs until the NW ICT Adoption Pilot in 2004. The current, limited body of research is fragmented, provides limited understanding and coherence on reasons of low ICT adoption, and lacks exemplars upon which policy considerations may be made. Firstly, the chapter will examine and review the existing body of literature. Secondly, EMB cases that have developed ICT to a degree where they are engaging in e-business activity are statically and dynamically analysed and discussed. The findings provide a number of options and guidance for EMB owners. Finally, the recommendations point to the need for improved ICT awareness, better business support provision nationally, and the importance of generation and education as key drivers.

Chapter 10

This research reviews studies using the Technology Acceptance Model (TAM) to create a modified model and instrument to study the acceptance of Internet technology by consumers. We developed a modified TAM for the acceptance of Internet-based technologies by consumers. We retained the original constructs from the TAM and included additional constructs from previous literature including gender, experience, complexity, and voluntariness. We developed a survey instrument using existing scales from prior TAM instruments and modified them where appropriate. The instrument yielded respectable reliability and construct validity. The findings suggest that the modified TAM is a good predictor of consumer behavior in using the Internet. We found that attitude toward using the Internet acts as a strong predictor of behavioral intention to use, and actual usage of Internet technologies. Future researchers can use the resultant instrument to test how consumers adopt and accept Internet-based applications.

Chapter 11

Rui Chen, Ball State University, USA
Sushil K. Sharma, Ball State University, USA

Consumer e-commerce extends the marketplace of traditional business and brings in business opportunities in online retailing and service. As a consequence of intensive competition among online vendors, the need to capture customers has become a top priority. Thanks to the wide penetration of Internet, the online consumer group now consists of individuals with diverse cultural values and backgrounds. In the context of ethnic culture, we explore the ways a Web site may attract and accommodate ethnic consumers. Drawing upon existing literature in culture and Web Information System success, we develop a Web-based intercultural accommodation model. This model offers a theoretical explanation of online ethnic consumers' behavioral intention to use e-commerce Web site. The conceptual model recognizes the potential roles of ethnicity attributes of individual consumers as well as the use of ethnic pertaining Web site designs in accommodating ethnic consumers. Future study that validates the theoretical model is discussed as well.

Chapter 12

Nitish Singh, Saint Louis University, USA
John E. Spillan, University of North Carolina, USA
Joseph P. Little, Saint Louis University, USA

The e-commerce industry has experienced spectacular growth, change and development. This situation has initiated an enormous business revolution that has affected the process of globalization tremendously. The goal of this study was to analyze the Web sites of localization companies that provide localization and translation services to other companies and see if they themselves are practicing what they are preaching. The results suggest that localization companies are indeed not practicing what they are preaching. Analysis shows that localization company Web sites are less localized than the Web sites of their clients, the multinational companies. The findings provide some implications to domestic and international marketers who currently operate in or are planning to enter into the global markets in the near future.

Section 4
E-Readiness and E-Government

Chapter 13

A. Seetharaman, Multimedia University, Malaysia
John Rudolph Raj, Multimedia University, Malaysia

Traditional cash has long been envisioned to be replaced with 'virtual' or electronic cash. Electronic money and electronic payment systems for retail transactions are commanding widespread attention. Undeniably, electronic payment cites advantages such as efficiency and convenience to the consumers.

However, with the rapid change and advances in technology, has posed significant risks, related to ensuring security and integrity of electronic payment systems in today's cyber world. Therefore, this study attempts to understand the role of electronic payments for consumers, and to identify the problems and solutions in the emergence of electronic payments. This study also explores the challenges of electronic payments from a security perspective, in particular, and provides preliminary security countermeasures for each of the issues discussed. Beside that, the study also discusses further on the prospects of electronic payment systems. It is essential to put in place an integrated, overall risk-management approach to security, including independent security assessments as one of the components in the use of electronic payment products.

Chapter 14

Sinawong Sang, Seoul National University, Republic of Korea
Jeong-Dong Lee, Seoul National University, Republic of Korea
Jongsu Lee, Seoul National University, Republic of Korea

The purpose of this study is to assess and test the factors that influence user adoption of e-Government services: the Electronic Approval System (EAS). This study uses the Technology Acceptance Model (TAM), the extended TAM (TAM2), the Diffusion of Innovation (DOI), and trust to build a parsimonious yet comprehensive model of factors that influence user acceptance of the EAS. We collected data from a total of 112 public officers in 12 ministries in Cambodia. We assessed the model with regression analyses. The findings in this article show that the determinants of the model (perceived usefulness, relative advantage, and trust) explain 30.5% of the variance in user acceptance of the EAS. At the same time, image, output quality, and perceived ease of use explain 38.4% of the variance in user perception of the usefulness of the EAS. In this article, we discuss our findings, implications, and suggestions for future research.

Chapter 15

Mohammad Reza Hanafizadeh, Islamic Azad University, Iran
Payam Hanafizadeh, Allameh Tabataba'I University, Iran
Abbas Saghaei, Islamic Azad University, Iran

With the advent and evolution of information and communication technologies (ICTs) in general, the Internet, in particular, throughout the world, new terms such as "information society," "digital divide," and "e-readiness" were added to terminologies. Due to the rapid diffusion of the Internet in different aspects of human life, these concepts have attracted many scholars, practitioners, and policy-makers. In addition to much academic research done in these fields, nearly all countries have assessed their e-readiness and compared their digital divide with that of other countries, at least once. Consequently, there have been numerous e-readiness and digital divide models oriented towards certain objectives in recent years. The findings show (1) tremendous importance of the digital divide and e-readiness and (2) their complex and multi-faceted natures. Thus, effective examination and development of digital divide and e-readiness research requires a foundation in several rich literatures. Examining the e-readiness and digital divide literature in terms of their definitions and methodologies, in the current chapter, their strengths and weaknesses were recognized. Moreover, after an extensive literature survey, an integrated model was proposed for assessing e-readiness of small and medium-sized enterprises (SMEs) that can be used as the basis and standard for developing comprehensive models and frameworks in these enterprises. Finally, this chapter contributes to scarce literature on e-readiness/digital divide at micro level and creates additional pool of resources that practitioners and theorists could use to further enrich and extend their analysis of this construct.

Chapter 16

This article proposes a hypothetical model for determining rate of diffusion of an innovation in a system. The model modifies Everett Rogers' S-curve using an index created from Gartner's hype cycle phases. Rogers' model for technology innovation adoption demonstrates that cumulative technology diffusion in a system from zero through the late majority adopters' phase forms a curve resembling the letter "S". Hype cycles analyze the five emotional stages technology adopters go through from over-enthusiasm (hype) though disappointment until it plateaus (beginning of mainstream adoption). When numbers assigned to the phases of adoption from the hype cycle are used as multipliers and applied to the cumulative adoption data of an innovation (Rogers' S-curve), the "S" becomes a "J". With the J-curve you can determine the rate of innovation diffusion in an organization.

Section 5
E-Learning

Chapter 17

In recent years, e-learning technology has been widely used in the academic institutes for supporting the effectiveness and efficiency of the students' learning and the educators' teaching, as a favored approach. However, regarding the student community, the extent to which e-learning technology is used, types of e-learning methods are being mainly used, as well as the barriers for enjoying the advantages of e-technology, remain interesting topics for the educators to explore. This chapter focuses on these issues through an investigation among the students within a higher education institute. The findings give an understanding regarding the usage of e-learning methods and the factors hindering the efficacy of their usage among the students. Also, a primary analysis on the usage difference between undergraduate and postgraduate students is presented.

Chapter 18

Understanding e-learning costs informs decision making on support for the development and implementation of teaching and learning technologies in higher education. This chapter describes costs and processes in a central e-learning support service that is especially applicable to face-to-face universities that use e-learning in a blended or supplemental mode. We differentiate three types of costs: infrastructure costs that are less sensitive to variation in the complexity of e-learning strategies, and e-development and e-delivery costs that are directly related to the nature of the strategies used. Using actual data from a three-year e-learning support project (e3Learning) with 139 sub-projects, the chapter illustrates how the calculations promoted an understanding of e-learning in the following four aspects: 1) total cost of running an e-learning support service, 2) individual costs attributable to each of the sub-projects, 3) 'price-tags' of e-learning strategies, and 4) initial exploration of the cost-effectiveness issue. Institutional decisions made as a consequence of this study are described.

Section 6
E-Adoption and Knowledge Management

Chapter 19

Pei-Di Shen, Ming Chuan University, Taiwan
Tsang-Hsiung Lee, National Chengchi University, Taiwan
Chia-Wen Tsai, Yuanpei University, Taiwan
Yi-Fen Chen, Chung Yuan Christian University, Taiwan

This study is an exploratory investigation of the enabling roles of knowledge management for integrated circuit (IC) Designers, Distributors, and Manufacturers. This study explores the different enabling roles in terms of knowledge creation, storage/retrieval, transfer and application when businesses implement knowledge management in upstream, midstream, and downstream firms in the IC industry. Three cases, Winbond, Worldpeace, and Taiwan Semiconductor Manufacturing Company (TSMC) were studied and analyzed systemically to illustrate the findings and insights in this study. The findings in this study point out that IC designers may focus more on knowledge storage, while IC distributors pay more attention to knowledge application and IC Manufacturers emphasize knowledge creation. The necessity to implement knowledge management in the distribution industry is also emphasized in this study. Moreover, the reasons for the different enabling roles are presented in the 'Insights from Case Studies' section of the paper.

Preface

There is now a great deal of evidence that e-adoption in the form of using the Internet, and information and communications technologies (ICT) over recent decades in various fields have been changing the business landscape and productivity. There is enormous literature appearing on how e-adoption has been changing the work styles, learning paradigms, businesses, and even voting and election campaigns. The E-adoption has a disruptive impact on companies, markets and gross domestic productivity, thus driving innovations. This edited book, *E-Adoption and Socio-Economic Impacts: Emerging Infrastructural Effects,* reports findings of some of the research studies that are conducted for e-adoption.

The book aims to present a various aspects of e-adoption and its socio-economic impact on emerging infrastructure. Information and communication technologies (ICTs) are impacting economic growth and improving governance worldwide. The literature on e-adoption is growing every month as more and more publications on e-adoption are appearing in various refereed journals, handbooks, cases, reports, and monographs.

This book certainly is not intended to cover all the aspects or everything of e-adoption. Rather, this edited book features the ongoing state-of-art research in the e-adoption domain. The book consists of twenty chapters. The introductory chapter provides an overview of e-adoption and its socio-economic impacts.

The first three chapters in the book discuss Internet banking cases in three different countries. The chapters provide insights into the various factors that influence the adoption of Internet Banking Services.

The next five chapters report research on e-adoption and diffusion among Small and Medium-Size Enterprises (SMEs). The literature evidence given by these chapters indicates that a growing number of SMEs around the world are adopting new information systems innovations in the form of e-adoption. Since SMEs are the backbone of an economy in any country, research on e-adoption in the SME sector would be of a great interest to practitioners, policy makers, and researchers around the world. The reported research in these chapters will provide leads to government authorities in drawing up guidelines, approaches, and formulating more effective frameworks to promote e-commerce among SMEs in developing countries.

Chapters nine through twelve are focused on e-commerce and e-business. The research reported in these chapters indicates that the e-commerce industry around the world is growing at an exponential rate, and as a result is helping to expand the gross domestic product (GDP) of the countries.

The next chapter discusses how e-adoption has been helping in creating a newer form of electronic money systems. The research reported in this chapter helps to understand the role of electronic payments for consumers, and the problems and solutions in the emergence of electronic payments.

Chapters fourteen through sixteen report on e-government research. The literature evidence indicates that as Internet user numbers both in developing and developed nations are increasing, more and more citizens and businesses are interacting with e-government websites and adding value to their experiences for quick and better e-government services. E-government implementations are not only making it easier for citizens to obtain service and interact with the government on a 24/7 basis but have been helping to improve government efficiency, effectiveness, and responsiveness to citizens.

A special chapter on e-readiness and the digital divide discusses that despite Internet population growth; there are still huge gaps of digital divide around the world. Many countries worldwide are investing in information and communication technologies infrastructure to improve their e-readiness and minimize the digital divide. The e-readiness condition in every country differs, and every country is trying their best to eradicate digital inequity and the digital divide.

The research reported in chapters seventeen and eighteen on e-learning clearly show that due to its cost efficiency, e-learning is increasing in leaps and bounds around the world. E-learning is flexible, offering self-paced courses at any time and any place. Due to shrinking enrollments, more and more universities and colleges worldwide are embracing e-learning for their advantage and growth. Chapter 19 discusses e-adoption from a knowledge management perspective.

The intended audience of this book will mainly consist of researchers, research students, and practitioners in e-adoption. The book is also of interest to researchers and practitioners in areas such as e-learning, e-government, e-adoption in SMEs, and Internet banking. It is hoped that the diverse and comprehensive coverage of e-adoption in this authoritative edited book will contribute to a better understanding of all topics, research, and discoveries in this evolving, significant field of study. Furthermore, I hope that the contributions included in this edited book will be instrumental in the expansion of the body of knowledge in this vast field. It is my sincere hope that this publication and its great amount of information and research will assist our research colleagues, faculty members, students, and our organizational decision makers in enhancing their understanding of the current and emerging issues in e-adoption. Perhaps this publication will even inspire its readers to contribute to the current and future discoveries in this immense field.

The contents of most of the chapters included in this volume were originally published in the various volumes of *International Journal of E-Adoption*. I am grateful to all authors who updated and enhanced their original papers to make their work current. The whole process of writing, reviewing, rewriting, editing, and proofreading takes a lot of time, and we appreciate all the authors for their efforts and contributions to this project.

Sushil K. Sharma
Ball State University, USA

Introduction
E–Adoption:
Social and Economic Impact

Sushil K. Sharma
Ball State University, USA

Reima Soumi
University of Turku, Finland

Rui Chen
Ball State University, USA

ABSTRACT

Information and communication technologies (ICT) have made enormous impact on social and economic performance and competitiveness in general, and on productivity, efficiency, and innovation in particular. The literature suggests that ICT has contributed greatly to productivity growth and competitiveness in the developed as well as developing countries in the last decade. This study aims to advance understanding of the social and economic impact of e-adoption. It provides an in-depth understanding through extensive literature survey and analysis of a various success stories. The generalization and conclusions are drawn from documented studies.

INTRODUCTION

The rapid development of Information and Communication Technologies (ICTs) continues to have a major influence on the livelihood of people across the world. The literature research shows that e-adoption is a major factor that has fueled social and economic growth throughout the world. Adoption of technologies such as cell phones and Internet services has empowered the individuals and has particularly enhanced education, health care, and general quality of life throughout the world (Bandiera and Rasul 2002). There have been few studies that have highlighted that e-adoption also have created negative impact because it has created digital and knowledge divide workers are displaced, surveillance increases, workers' bargaining power declines, and workers' skills (in many cases) become obsolete, devalued, or constrained by ICT-imposed structures. Some have argued that ICTs cannot possibly benefit poorer people in developing countries, and it is of course true that some ICTs are likely to remain out of the reach of the rural poor, in particular, for many years to come (Adedokun, et al., 2006).

According the Organization for Economic Cooperation and Development (OECD), over 400 local authorities across Europe and North America have implemented or are currently under implementation broadband networks to enhance their e-adoption. Internet has helped creating a huge social capital in the building of social networks. The social networks in turn have created empowered communities that are helping for social and economic development. There have been various studies conducted of examining impact of e-adoption at firm level. Extant literature suggests that e-adoption have has positive impacts improving quality of life, create higher paying jobs and empowered individuals with more opportunity to participate in development (OECD, 2007).

The literature also suggests that profound impact of e-adoption on the economies and societies of the globe has undeniably been on improving economic efficiency, competitiveness and profitability of the enterprises. E-adoption has helped traditional enterprises in developed as well as in developing countries in savings in communications costs, increased availability of information, affordable global reach, reduced transaction costs, lowered barriers to entry and new sources of revenue. ICTs, the Internet and especially electronic commerce has changed the landscape of business environment at national, regional and global levels, and generate major opportunities, and new challenges, for market growth and development of jobs, industries and services. The implementation of ICT in the Organization of Economic and Cooperative Development (OECD) countries points out that it has helped improving living standards, literacy and trade (Anderson, 2009).

A technology is never only a technical artifact but is also a social construction. The use of Internet technology for various kinds of e-adoption has impacted socio-cultural aspects like cultural values, regional priorities, institutional relations,

political dynamics, and educational backgrounds and health standards (Esque, 2009).

LITERATURE REVIEW

Several countries worldwide have started using internet technologies to enhance the services for citizens and businesses to improve internal efficiencies by lowering costs and increasing productivity. Several researchers such as; Grewal, Comer, and Mehta (2001), Mehrtens, Cragg, and Mills (2001), Zheng et al. (2004) J. Zheng, N.D. Caldwell, C.M. Harland, P. Powell, M. Woerndl and S. Xu, Tsikriktisis, Lanzolla, and Frohlich (2004) suggested that e-adoption has contributed positively although e-adoption perceived benefits and motivational factors for e-adoption were different for different organizations. These researchers also concluded that expected performance benefits, access to new markets and external pressures drive the adoption of e-processes (Scupola, 2006).

E-adoption is widely recognized as being a key pillar to enhancing economic growth and national competitiveness. It is also an avenue for fostering social and community development. The growth and development of information and communication technologies (ICTs) and e-adoption has led to increase economic and social impact. There have been variation in e-adoption across and within countries; therefore, socio-economic impact varies across the firms, countries and organizations. However, a recent World Bank study reports indicate that e-adoption had direct correlation with number of performance indicators, including growth in GDP, employment and life styles (Information and Communications for Development Report, 2009).

Through increasing rivalry in the market might drive the E-adoption and innovation, as companies search for new opportunities to cut costs by improving process efficiency or develop new products. Although e-adoption alone will not help bring innovation unless it is supplemented with other changes such as, restructuring, change in workforce skills, and investment in complementary assets in the organizations that are needed. Empirical studies have shown that e-adoption has better positive impact if combined with complementary investments in working practices, human capital, and firm restructuring (Brynjolfsson and Hitt, 2003).

E-adoption has an impact on a company's internal organization, i.e. the structure of and the relationships between departments within an enterprise. Organizational changes has resulted into improving workflows and work efficiencies (Brynjolfsson & Hitt, 2003). E-adoption has enabled inter-organizational integration and collaboration which in turn helped for innovations. E-adoption has also helped integration and optimization of the value chain in order to eliminate the so-called bullwhip effect (Kohli and Devaraj, 2003). The European Commission (2007) highlights that e-adoption in form of use of electronic networks has helped firms to collaborate and innovate which has impacted economic performance overall (European Commission, 2007).

The effects of e-adoption on corporate performance are not clear because not all studies have demonstrated clear payoffs from ICT investments (Kohli and Devaraj, 2003). But work by Koellinger (2004) suggests that e-adoption has in some way helped to drive ICT-enabled innovations. Van Ark (2002) through his work indicate that the countries that have higher e-adoption have shown an upsurge in productivity growth resulting from ICT investment. Similarly, few European authors mention that although productivity growth may be not as compared to U.S. but certainly e-adoption has increased productivity levels in the EU, in particular in service industries like banking, retailing and business services (O'Mahony and Van Ark, eds. 2003; Van Ark, Inklaar, and McGuckin 2003). Despite the different impacts that ICT had in the US and in Europe, it is widely accepted that

e-adoption generally has positive effects on total factor productivity.

Information and Communications for Development 2009: Extending Reach and Increasing Impact report (2009) indicates that information and communication technology (ICT) are impacting economic growth and improving governance worldwide. The report analyzed data measuring ICT in 150 economies and describing the key trends in ICT development (OECD, 2007, 2009). As per report while internet use has not increased as rapidly as mobile communication, it did triple worldwide between 2000 and 2007, while increasing tenfold in developing countries in the same period. This has increased the pace of e-adoption for various applications both at the government as well as organization level. As per report *"Convergence of mobile telephony and the internet is occurring, enabling voice, data, and media services to be transmitted over the same network. Such convergence could have an enormous impact on economic and social development - increasing productivity, lowering transaction costs, facilitating trade, and increasing retail sales and tax revenues."* (Information and Communications for Development Report, 2009). The document concludes that: *"Countries that have taken steps to create a competitive market environment for ICT generally have a larger share of people using ICT services than those that have not"*. However, in some developing countries, trade in ICT goods and services has not only sparked export-led growth and job creation but e-adoption is also transforming how governments deliver public services to citizens and businesses (Dutta & Jain, 2005, Unwin, 2009, UNCTAD, 2008).

Due to e-adoption the academic literature discusses tremendous substantial progress in economic and social development. The United Nations 2010 report indicates that *"e-adoption has enabled better access to government services, the alleviation of fraud and skepticism in elections, increased quantity and quality of training opportunities, a balancing of gender inequalities in access to opportunities, improved delivery of health care services and the education, facilitated broader public goods including improved literacy, civic responsiveness and equitable access to economic opportunity for the full leveraging of economic development potential. E-adoption has created a social inclusion, defined as empowerment and participation of every individual in the Information Society, irrespective of age, gender, socio-economic status or ethnic background."* However, there is no denying fact that there is still a huge digital and knowledge divide that exits in the world (Brown and Licker, 2003, Courtney, 2009, Liu & San, 2006).

METHODS AND DATA SOURCES

Our dataset consists of a many published cases and stories of several countries both developed and developing ones. The data was collected from the published reports between 2000 to 2008. The paper draws and builds on several studies on ICT adoption in small firms (Gibbs et al., 2007; Beckinsale and Ram, 2006; Zappala and Gray, 2006; Manueli et al., 2007), and state and country level case studies. The paper mainly draws inferences from several studies from different countries that include e-government, information technology for health, education and other social and economic factors. Furthermore, it is designed to bring out the details from viewpoints of various studies by using multiple sources of data such as written documents by United Nations, published articles, and books.

SOCIAL AND ECONOMIC IMPACTS

There are various social and economic impacts of e-adoption. The foremost impact is "the connectivity" or the "death of distance" which is resulting to economic and social growth. The E-adoption revolution in form of access to the Internet has become a critical enabler of electronic commerce, e-business, e-learning, e-government and e-health (Esque, 2009). Some electronic commerce applications are emerging as effective means of enhancing the social infrastructure (Bandiera and Rasul 2002). E-adoption in form of using ICTs have begun to make a significant contribution to strengthening the social infrastructure through improvements in education, health, and other aspects of human resource development, including the sense of community (Gibbs et al., 2007). The connectivity has made lifelong learning, continuous upgrading of skills possible for many house makers, retired professionals and even regular college going distance students (Farrell, and Isaacs, 2007, Francis, and Iyare, 2006). The connectivity also has improved access to health related information and in a result has improved health standards. These improved health standards in turn haves contributed significantly to economic prosperity. The virtual worlds, social networks, online communities all have become a reality to strengthen social and economic growth (Crank, 2006).

E-adoption has made businesses possible to transact their business on 24-hour, seven days a week service delivery basis. This has improved the competitiveness of global firms and consumers bargaining power. The use of technologies such as e-mail, Internet discussion groups, social networks have not only improved communication but have resulted to form social groups and geo-political relationships. These technologies are also helping to bring down the gaps among various ethnicity, race, language and disability groups. The Internet and the other e-adoption technologies have allowed small and medium enterprises (SMEs) to collaborate and to extend their geographical reach and secure new customers in ways formerly restricted to much larger firms. In many European countries, recent literature through findings of several case studies indicates that ICT is not only an enabler of innovation and productivity but e-adoption in general has a positive impact on corporate performance, productivity and on economic performance. The literature highlights that ICT adoption, use and diffusion has changed competition levels and value chain characteristics (Beckinsale and Ram, 2006, Blackburn and Smallbone, 2008).

As e-adoption is helping to increase productivity more and more both in developed as well as in developing countries, investments in ICTs have also been increasing (Inklaar and McGuckin 2003). According to the OECD report, the share of ICT capital has increased over the period from 1995 to 2007 particularly in Finland and Korea (UNCTAD, 2008, OECD Report, 2007). E-adoption has also been empowering users of all kinds: citizens, consumers, workers, patients, and students and has been improving the relations between governments and citizens, producers and consumers, doctors and patients, teachers and students etc. It is important to know that the growing use of information and communication technologies in general is linked to the rise of literacy, science and scientific management. Since e-commerce transcend geographical boundaries, many big firms of known brands may not only expand their markets but also may enter into new business activities across the broad spectrum of business activities. This may help to reduce the costs and prices. Some studies credit e-commerce for an increase in the level of GDP by 2-5 per cent (Penbara, 1999, Islam, et al., 2007). The growth of e-commerce has both direct and indirect impacts on labor markets as well as the composition of employment. This has resulted into change in swift labor policies for reallocation of labor to the changing needs of the economy. Electronic commerce is widely expected to improve efficiency due to reduced transaction and search costs, increased competition and more streamlined business processes. Take for instance the case of telecommuting that is becoming a reality. Today many organizations allow their employees to work from their homes. There are some positive aspects of telecommuting to organizations and society. With increased employee autonomy, organizations are able to retain their employees by providing more flexibility in their work schedule. Organizations benefit from fewer costs in recruiting, training, and disability costs. Organizations are also able to locate satellite offices in less densely populated areas. Environmental issues decrease with the elimination of carbon dioxide from commuting cars. Quality of life in general increases where parents are able to spend more time with their children and can play a more dominant role in their community (Zhao, et al., 2007, Unwin, 2009).

DISCUSSION AND SUMMARY

As the use of Internet and e-adoption continues to expand rapidly, it would create both challenges and opportunities to both business and society as a whole. E-commerce has provided opportunity for better interactions with partners, suppliers, and targeted customers for service and relationships. E-commerce is also providing the customers with choice, information, convenience, time, and savings with improvements that add value to their shopping (Zorn, et al., 2008, Zappala and Gray, 2006). However, loss of privacy with e-commerce, security issues, increasingly sophisticated frauds, abuse of personal information, and impact on prices have aroused as the main concerns (Brown and Licker, 2003).

As per the OECD report, e-adoption in terms of the use of ICT by large, medium as well as small and medium enterprises is increasingly common. The widespread uses of ICTs are changing the way people or companies work. For the elderly, disabled or those simply short of time, e-commerce offers the convenience of goods being ordered online and delivered to their doorstep (Ekanem and Smallbone, 2007).

The findings presented in this paper are only based on the several published reports or papers in various journals as well as in trade journals. Future research involving more focused socio-economic variables needs to be conducted to get more detailed insights into e-adoption impact.

REFERENCES

Adedokun, O. A., Tucker, M. A., & Balschweid, M. A. (2006). *Adoption of Information Communication Technologies (ICTs) in Nigeria: Problems and prospects for rural youth.* Paper presented at the annual meeting of the Rural Sociological Society, Seelbach Hilton Hotel, Louisville, Kentucky. Retrieved from http://www.allacademic.com/ meta/p124896_index.html

Anderson, N. (2009). *Equity and Information Communication Technology (ICT) in education.* New York, NY: Peter Lang Publishers.

Bandiera, O., & Rasul, I. (2002). *Social networks and technology adoption in Northern Mozambique,* (p. 49). Suntory and Toyota International Centers for Economics and Related Disciplines (STICERD) – Development Economics Papers, London School of Economics and Political Science.

Beckinsale, M., & Ram, M. (2006). Delivering ICT to ethnic minority businesses: An action-research approach. *Environment and Planning. C, Government & Policy, 24*(6), 847–867. doi:10.1068/c0559

Blackburn, R. A., & Smallbone, D. (2008). Researching small firms and entrepreneurship in the UK: Developments and distinctiveness. *Entrepreneurship Theory and Practice, 32*(2), 267–288. doi:10.1111/j.1540-6520.2007.00226.x

Brown, I., & Licker, P. (2003). Exploring differences in Internet adoption and usage between historically advantaged and disadvantaged groups in South Africa. *Journal of Global Information Technology, 6*(4), 6.

Brynjolfsson, E., & Hitt, L. M. (2003). Computing productivity: Firm-level evidence. [MIT Press.]. *The Review of Economics and Statistics, 85*(4), 793–808. doi:10.1162/003465303772815736

Courtney, L. (2009). Knowledge transfer. In Anderson, N. (Ed.), *Equity and Information Communication Technology (ICT) in education* (*Vol. 6*). New York, NY: Peter Lang.

Crank, L. D. (2006). *The impact of advanced Information and Communication Technology on rural social networks.* Paper presented at the annual meeting of the Rural Sociological Society, Seelbach Hilton Hotel, Louisville, Kentucky. Retrieved from http://www.allacademic.com/ meta/p124902_index.html

Dutta, S., & Jain, A. (2005). The networked readiness index 2003-2004: Overview and analysis framework. In Dutta, S., Lanvin, B., & Paul, F. (Eds.), *The global Information Technology report 2003-2004* (pp. 3–22). New York, NY: Oxford University Press.

Ekanem, I., & Smallbone, D. (2007). Learning in small manufacturing firms: The case of investment decision-making behaviour. *International Small Business Journal, 25,* 107–129. doi:10.1177/0266242607074515

Esque, S. (2009). *Technology in education: Transforming teaching & learning.* Intel Corporation. Global Symposium on ICT in Education. Co-organized by the World Bank, the Korean Ministry of Education, Science, and Technology (MEST) and Korea Education & Research Information Service (KERIS), November 9-11, 2009. Seoul, South Korea.

European Commission Report. (2007). *EU annual report on digital economy highlights benefits of ICT investments.*

Farrell, G., & Isaacs, S. (2007). *Survey of ICT and education in Africa: A summary report, based on 53 country surveys. ICT in education: Catalyst for economic growth in the Congo* (p. 26). Washington, DC: infoDev / World Bank.

Francis, B., & Iyare, S. (2006). Education and development in the Caribbean: A co-integration and causality approach. *Economic Bulletin, 15*(2), 1–13.

Gibbs, S., Sequeira, J., & White, M. M. (2007). Social networks and technology adoption in small business. *International Journal of Globalisation and Small Business, 2*(1), 66–87. doi:10.1504/IJGSB.2007.014188

Grewal, R., Comer, J. M., & Mehta, R. (2001). An investigation into the antecedents of organizational participation in business-to-business electronic markets. *Journal of Marketing, 65*(July), 17–33. doi:10.1509/jmkg.65.3.17.18331

Information and Communications for Development Report. (2009). *Extending reach and increasing impact*, 2009.

Islam, T. S., Wadud, M. A., & Islam, Q. B. (2007). Relationship between education and GDP growth: A multivariate causality analysis for Bangladesh. *Economics Bulletin, 3*(35). Retrieved March 19, 2010 from http://www.accessecon.com/ pubs/EB/2007/Volume3/ EB-07C30001A.pdf

Koellinger, P. (2004). *IT still matters - New evidence on Internet-enabled innovation and financial performance of enterprises. The European e-business report*, (pp. 37-40). Brussels, Belgium: Office of Official Publications of the European Communities, August 2004.

Kohli, R., & Devaraj, S. (2003). Measuring Information Technology payoff: A meta-analysis of structural variables in firm-level empirical research. *Information Systems Research, 14*(2), 127–145. doi:10.1287/isre.14.2.127.16019

Liu, M.-C., & San, G. (2006). Social learning and digital divides: A case study of Internet technology diffusion. *Kyklos, 59*, 307–321. doi:10.1111/j.1467-6435.2006.00329.x

Mehrtens, J., Cragg, P. B., & Mills, A. M. (2001). A model of Internet adoption by SMEs. *Information & Management, 39*, 165–176. doi:10.1016/S0378-7206(01)00086-6

O'Mahoney, C. D. (2009). *Management of education in the information age: The role of ICT. The International Federation for Information Processing.* Boston, MA: Kluwer Academic Publishers.

O'Mahony, M., & Van Ark, B. (2005). Assessing the productivity of the UK retail trade sector: The role of ICT. [July.]. *International Review of Retail, Distribution and Consumer Research, 15*(3), 297–303. doi:10.1080/09593960500119523

OECD. (2007). *Report OECD key ICT indicators.* Directorate for Science, Technology and Industry.

OECD. (2009). *Education at a glance 2009 – Summary of key findings – Embargoed until 11 September 11:00 Paris time.* Retrieved March 17, 2010 from http://www.oecd.org/dataoecd/41/25/43636332.pdf

Ottevanger, W., van den Akker, J., & de Feiter, L. (2007). *Developing science, mathematics, and ICT education in sub-Saharan Africa: Patterns and promising practices.* The world Bank. World Bank Working Paper. No. 101. Africa Human Development Series.

Pohjola, M. (2003). The adoption and diffusion of ICT across countries: Patterns and determinants. In Jones, D. C. (Ed.), *The new economy handbook* (pp. 77–100). San Diego, CA: Academic Press.

Scupola, A. (2006). Factors affecting e-commerce adoption in Danish and Australian SMEs. *The Social Studies of Information Systems Journal, 1*, 7–20.

Seyal, A. H., & Rahman, M. N. A. (2003). A preliminary investigation of e-commerce adoption in small & medium enterprises in Brunei. *Journal of Global Information Technology Management*, *6*(2), 6–25.

Song, K., Heo, H., & Lee, H. (2009). *Measuring ICT in education readiness*. Global Symposium on ICT in Education. Co-organized by the World Bank, the Korean Ministry of Education, Science, and Technology (MEST) and Korea Education & Research Information Service (KERIS), November 9-11, 2009. Seoul, South Korea. ICT in Education: Catalyst for Economic Growth in the Congo 28

Tinio, V. T. (2009). *ICT in education*. New York, NY: United Nations Development Program, Bureau for Development Policy.

Torero, M., & Braun, J. V. (2006). *Information and communication technologies for development and poverty reduction: The potential of telecommunications*. Washington, DC: International Food Policy Research Institute.

Tsikriktsis, N., Lanzolla, G., & Frohlich, M. (2004). Adoption of e-processes by service firms: An empirical study of antecedents. *Production and Operations Management*, *13*(3), 216–229. doi:10.1111/j.1937-5956.2004.tb00507.x

UNCTAD. (2008). *Information economy report 2007-2008. Science and technology for development: The new paradigm of ICT*. Geneva, Switzerland: UNCTAD.

Unwin, T. (Ed.). (2009). *Information and communication technology for development*. Cambridge, UK: Cambridge University Press.

Van Ark, B. (2002). Measuring the new economy: An international comparative perspective. *The Review of Income and Wealth*, *48*(1), 1–14. doi:10.1111/1475-4991.00036

Van Ark, B., Inklaar, R., & McGuckin, R. H. (2003). ICT and productivity in Europe and the United States. Where do the differences come from? *CESifo Economic Studies*, (49)3, 295–318. Retrieved from http://www.eco.rug.nl/ ~inklaar/ papers/ ictdecompositionrev2.pdf

Zappala, S., & Gray, C. W. J. (Eds.). (2006). *Impact of e-commerce on consumers and small firms*. London, UK: Ashgate.

Zhao, H., Kim, S., Suh, T., & Du, J. (2007). Social institutional explanations of global Internet diffusion: A cross-country analysis. *Journal of Global Information Management*, *15*, 28–55. doi:10.4018/jgim.2007040102

Zorn, T., Hector, C., & Gibson, J. (2008). *Perceived effects of Information and Communication Technology adoption on quality of work life: An exploratory study*. Paper presented at the annual meeting of the International Communication Association, TBA, Montreal, Quebec, Canada. Retrieved from http://www.allacademic.com/ meta/ p233009_index.html

Section 1
Internet Banking Cases

Chapter 1
Modeling User Acceptance of Internet Banking in Malaysia:
A Partial Least Square (PLS) Approach

Kamel Rouibah
Kuwait University, Kuwait

T. Ramayah
Universiti Sains Malaysia, Malaysia

Oh Sook May
Universiti Sains Malaysia, Malaysia

ABSTRACT

This study is the first empirical research that compares three well known technology adoption models in the in the field of e-banking. It aims to determine the dominant factor(s) which influence the user intention to use Internet banking. Three models (TAM, TPB, and TRA) were used to test the impact of five factors (perceived ease of use, perceived usefulness, attitude, subjective norms, and perceived behavioral control) on intention to adopt e-banking by 239 individual bank customers in Malaysia. Survey questions from prior studies were adopted and customized. Partial least Square (PLS) SmartPLS M2 Version 2.0 was used for data analysis. Results reveal that the five factors have a direct positive effect on behavioral intention to use Internet banking. However, attitude toward behavior has the highest beta, followed by perceived usefulness, and subjective norm, while perceived behavioral control exerts the weakest effect. In testing the explanatory power of the different models, results found TAM model has the best explanatory power, followed by TPB and TRA models. Findings of the study should benefit banks in improving their use of e-banking technologies as a strategic weapon, and can be used to target more potential customers.

DOI: 10.4018/978-1-60960-597-1.ch001

INTRODUCTION

Banks decide to invest in Internet banking for many reasons; among these are: pressures to cut costs, increase information richness for customers, pressures to produce more without increasing costs, improve the quality of services in order to stay in business or to reach a wider audience. The number of banks adopting Internet banking is increasing over the world even in less developed countries, e.g. but not limited to, Hong Kong (Liao et al. 1999; Wan et al., 2005), Singapore (Tan & Teo 2000; Wang et al., 2003), Malaysia (Ramayah et al., 2006; Ramayah et al., 2008), Finland (Pikkarainen et al., 2004), USA (Lassar et al., 2005), Korea (Suh & Han, 2002), Taiwan (Shih & Fang, 2004, 2006), and Estonia (Erriksson et al., 2005).

This paper focuses on the current state of e-banking in Malaysia. This is an opportunity for banks since the number of Internet users is increasing and represent a growth of 170% between 2005 and 2010. Indeed, the World Stats reported that there are 16.9 million users (representing 64.6% of the population) in 2010, compared to 3.7 million in 2000 (Internet World Stats, 2010). In surfing on the wave of e-banking, all 10 domestic banks and 4 foreign banks among 13 are offering Internet banking services (for details see Goi, 2005). Although huge investments have been spent on building Internet banking systems to grasp potential customers, reports show that potential users may not be using the systems, despite their availability (Wang et al., 2003; Ramayah et al., 2005; Luarn & Lin, 2005), and other studies found that half of the people that have tried Internet banking services would not become active users (Robinson, 2000). Therefore, efforts are needed to understand the determinants of Malaysian users in adopting Internet banking, that we named e-banking. We refer to this concept as the provision of banking services via Internet. Offered services may include, but not limited to, account information and balance enquiry, electronic bill payments, summary reports of transactions, funds transfer, check cancellation, checkbook application, financial planning and analysis, loan application, share margin trading account.

What causes potential customers to adopt these services? Is it merely the instrumental and cognitive complexity beliefs (usefulness and ease of use)? Does it depend on the attitudinal perceptions of customers? Are individuals also influenced by other issues (social pressure or social norm), such as their interaction through a social network, their predisposed tendency to try out a new technology? Does it depend on the behavioral control (capabilities, availability of resources and knowledge)? If these factors are indeed important in the acceptance decisions of potential customers, are they interrelated? If so, how are they related and what are the mechanisms through which they achieve their effects on the acceptance decisions? Such questions have widespread practical as well as theoretical ramifications because the expected benefits from the investments in information and technology are realized only when they are adopted by their intended users and subsequently used. This paper seeks to bring elements of response to these issues from a Malaysian perspective.

There has been little prior research into critical influences on e-banking services adoption in Malaysia. The banking sector in Asia including Malaysia is a rapidly growing market. Many western banking are very interested in establishing in this part of the world and building branches since there are 13 foreign banks among 23 in Malaysia. Therefore, it is important to understand the management actions and investment in e-banking. To achieve this goal, this study reports important empirical data on the adoption of e-banking services. In achieving this goal the study aims to examine the extent to which existing and previous model comparison studies (Davis et al., 1989; Mathieson, 1991; Taylor & Todd, 1995b; Chau & Hu, 2001; Riemenschneider et al., 2003; Celuch et al., 2004; Shih & Fang, 2004) are valid in the e-banking sector. Specifically, this study empirically tests the applicability of three well known models in the technology adoption field: the Technology Acceptance Model (TAM) (Davis, 1989), the Theory of Planned Behavior (TPB) (Ajzen, 1991), and the Theory of Reasoned Action (TRA) (Ajzen & Fishbein, 1980). The main focus is to evaluate to which each model can better explain the customers adoption of e-banking. This is in line with previous studies that called for substantial research to address the limitation of these three models (Chau & Hu, 2001).

The major contributions of this study are as follows. Banking planning to offer e-services or those already established e-banking must be aware of the primary concerns of customers. Such knowledge can help banks to increase the adoption of e-banking services. Additionally, banks can understand the reasons for resistance to e-banking services adoption among potential users since customer acceptance is an important determinant success factor (Delone & McLean, 1992). Banks thus can enhance e-banking services performance based on the user needs identified in the empirical results. Once the critical factors are known, banks can develop new services or improve performance to fit customer needs. Furthermore, marketing staff can understand the critical influences on customer adoption, and then develop an effective marketing strategy to convince customers that e-banking services are a convenient method for them. A good pricing strategy can also be developed accordingly. Based on our findings, marketers should be able to justify expenditures that promote e-banking and how to attract more potential customers.

The remainder of this paper is organized as follows. Section 2 reviews three models related to technology acceptance (TAM, TPB and TRA) as well as a summary of past comparison studies. Next, Section 3 describes the research method. Then, analytical results are reported in Section 4. Finally, section 5 presents conclusions, as well as discussing the implications of the findings of this study.

THEORETICAL BACKGROUND AND RESEARCH MODEL

There are several competing models for IT adoption including TAM, TPB and TRA. The following sections review these models based on two criteria: we included past studies that either compares the three models or focus solely on e-banking.

TRA

TRA is a widely studied model from social psychology (see Figure 1). In TRA, two unique factors that contribute to behavioral intention (noted BI) are determined: attitude toward the behavior (noted ATT) and subjective norm (noted SN). According to Ajzen and Fishbein (1980), in order to gain deeper understanding of the factors influencing behavior, it is required to look into beliefs individuals hold about themselves and their environment. Therefore, beliefs are viewed as underlying a person's attitude and subjective norm, and ultimately determine the intention and behavior. Attitude refers to an individual's positive or negative feeling (evaluative effect) about performing the target behavior. Subjective norm is defined as a person's perception that most people who are important to him or her think that he or she should or should not perform the behavior and his or her motivation to comply with the specific referents. TRA has been widely used over the past (see the meta analysis done by Sheppard et al., 1988). In the IT field, TRA also has been used as the basis to test several technologies and spanning a variety of subject areas, e.g. Word processing (Davis et al., 1989), MS Windows (Karahanna et al., 1999), transactional web site (Rensel et al., 2006), e-commerce (Vijayasarathy, 2004; Grandon, 2005), management information system (Celuch et al., 2004) and e-banking (Shih & Fang, 2004, 2006). A particularly helpful aspect of TRA from an information system perspective is that attitude and subjective norm are theorized to mediate the effect of external variables on intention

Figure 1. The theoretical model of TRA, TPB and TAM

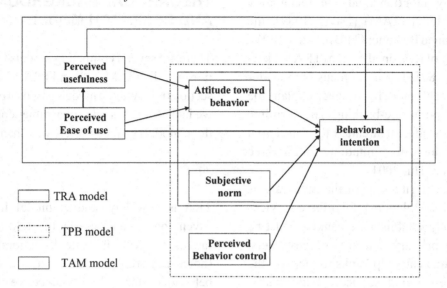

to use new IT (Davis et al., 1989). However three empirical support reported in this study (Davis et al., 1989; Shih & Fang, 2004, 2006) failed to find a significant relationship between SN and BI.

TPB

Grounded in social psychology, TPB is a general model that has been applied in many diverse domains (see Figure 1). TPB is an extension of the TRA (Ajzen, 1991; Fishbein & Ajzen, 1975), due to the limitation of TRA to deal with behavior over which individuals have incomplete volitional control (Ajzen, 1991). It delivers more specific information, giving more insight into why an individual or group might not use a system and was found to be well supported by empirical evidence (Ajzen, 1991) According to TPB, people's actions are determined by their intentions, which are influenced by their *perceived behavioral control*, besides attitude and *subjective norm. Perceived behavioral control* refers to the perception of internal and external resource constraints on performing the behavior. Control beliefs reflect the perceived difficulty (or ease) with which the behavior may be affected with perceived facility

acting as important weighting criteria (Ajzen, 1991). In the case of e-banking, control beliefs refer to knowing how to perform transactions via Internet banking and facility refers to external resource constraints, such as time, money, and resources. Ajzen (2001) collected numerous studies that demonstrated the applicability of TPB to various content domains. These works provide significant support for TPB. In addition, abundant empirical evidence exists that suggests TPB effectively explains individual intentions in adopting of several new information technologies including but not limited to: Computing resource center (Taylor & Todd, 1995a), telemedicine technology (Chau & Hu, 2001), virtual banking (Liao et al., 1999), web site (Riemenschneider et al., 2003), Internet management system (Celuch et al., 2004), e-commerce (Grandon, 2005), and Internet banking (Tan & Teo, 2000; Shih & Fang, 2004).

Empirical findings provide mixed results. Only four studies out of eight that used TPB failed to find a significant relationship between PBC and BI (Liao et al., 1999; Riemenschneider et al., 2003; Celuch et al., 2004; Shih & Fang, 2004; Grandon 2005), in that TPB depend mainly on ATT and SN. Moreover four studies did not found SN to play a role in BI (Mathieson, 1991; Tan & Teo, 2000; Chau & Hu, 2001; Shih & Fang, 2004), while one study (Liao et al., 1999) failed to test the relationship between SN and BI due to the absence of reliable measure.

TAM

Based on the TRA, Davis (1989) developed the TAM model. It states that an individual's system usage is determined by BI, which, in turn, is determined by his attitude toward the behavior, which in turn is determined by two beliefs: perceived usefulness (noted PU) and perceived ease of use (noted PEOU) (see figure 1). PU refers to the extent to which a person believes that using the system will improve his or her job performance. PEOU refers to the extent to which a person believes that using the system will be free of effort. TAM is the most widely applied model that information systems researchers have used to explain or predict the motivational factors underlying user acceptance of technology. Many studies applied TAM to a variety of technologies. To our knowledge, five comparative studies compared TAM to other competing model: e-mail (Davis, 1989), spreadsheet (Mathieson, 1991), university computing resource center (Taylor & Todd, 1995a), telemedicine (Chau & Hu, 2001), and web site usage (Riemenschneider et al., 2003). Moreover, five studies used TAM in the e-banking (Suh & Han, 2002; Wang et al., 2003; Pikkarainen et al., 2004; Lassar et al., 2005; Errriksson et al., 2005). Recently, numerous investigators have modified the initial TAM (e.g. Venkatesh & Davis, 2000; Venkatesh et al., 2003; Yi et al., 2006). The current study will focus on the original TAM. Empirical support was found between different constructs of TAM (see table 1) as well as the state of the art done by Legris et al. (2003).

Past Studies on Model Comparison

Despite that many research that investigated the three models separately, little research has attempted to integrate the three models in IT acceptance (Davis et al., 1989; Mathieson, 1991; Taylor & Todd, 1995a; Chau & Hu, 2001; Riemenschneider et al., 2003; Shih & Fang, 2004; Celuch et al., 2004; Grandon, 2005).

Davis et al. (1989) compared TAM with TRA in studying usage of the word processing program at two different period of time T1 (beginning of the semester) and T2 (14 weeks later from T1). Their data provided mixed support for the two specific theoretical models. They found TRA is partially valid. While ATT had a strong significant influence on BI, SN had no significant effect on BI. With TAM, ATT only partially mediated the effects of beliefs (PU and PEOU) on BI and PU plays the most significant affect on BI. Moreover variance explained by TAM (47% in T1 and 51% in T2) is better than that of TRA (32% in T1 and 26% in T2).

Mathieson (1991) compared TAM with TPB. The results indicated that the TAM and TPB explained BI very well successively R^2 (BI) = 0.697 and 0.621 with TAM slightly better than TPB. In TPB, authors found that the path from SN to BI was not significant.

Taylor and Todd (1995a) decomposed the belief structures in the TPB and proposed the decomposed TPB. They compared this model with TAM and TPB. The results suggested that all three models supported BI as the primary direct determinant of behavior. The addition of SN and PBC and the decomposition of beliefs provided some additional insight into behavioral intention. However, the explained variance of BI in the decomposed TPB (R^2=60%) is greater than the pure TPB (R^2=57%) that is also greater than the variance in TAM (R^2=52%).

Chau and Hu (2001) compared TAM, TPB and decomposed TPB in understanding individual physicians' usage of telemedicine technology.

Table 1. Review of e-banking and comparative studies on technology acceptance (TAM, TRA and TPB) [NS: Not Significant; NT: Not Tested; NA: Not Available]

Studies	IS/IT used	Sample size	TRA			TPB				TAM						
			ATT-BI	SN-BI	R²(BI)%	ATT-BI	SN-BI	PBC-BI	R²(BI)	ATT-BI	PU-BI	PEOU-BI	PU-ATT	PEOU-ATT	PEOU-PU	R²(BI)%
Davis et al.(1989)	MS Word	107 students	0.55(T1), 0.48(T2)	NS	32 (T1), 26(T2)					.27(T1), NS(T2)	.48(T1), .61(T2)	NT	.61(T1), .50(T2)	NS(T1), .24(T2)	NS(T1), .23(T2)	47(T1), 51(T2)
Mathieson (1991)	Spreadsheet	262 students				0.49	NS	0.41	62.1		0.48	NT	0.694	0.22	0.67	69.3
Taylor and Todd(1995a)	IT recourse	786 students				1.15	0.32	0.3	57		1.56	NT	0.79	0.24	0.96	52
Chau and Hu (2001)	Telemedicine	400 physicians				0.63	NS	0.22	32		0.42	NT	0.41	NS	NS	40
Riemenschneider et al. (2003)	Web site	156 executives				0.43	0.39	NS	NA		NS	NT	0.65	0.25	NS	NA
Celuch et al., (2004)	MIS	700 salespersons	0.62	0.24	50	0.35	0.24	NS	58							
Shih and Fang (2004)	E-banking	425 consumers	0.88	NS	46	0.82	NS	NS	54							
Grandon (2005)	E-commerce	N.A		Yes				NS								
Liao et al. (1999)	E-banking	118 consumers				Yes (NA)	NT	Yes (NA)	5.6							
Suh and Han (2002)	E-banking	845 web users								0.48	0.3	NT	0.38	0.71	0.71	74.5
Tan and Teo (2000)	E-banking					Yes (NA)	NS	Yes (NA)	NA							
Wang et al. (2003).	E-banking	123 users								NI	0.18	0.48	NI	NI	0.71	62
Lassar et al., (2005)	E-banking	349 students								NI	Yes(+)	Yes(-)	NI	NI	NA	NA
Pikkarainen et al. (2004)	E-banking	268 consumers								NI	0.23	NS	NI	NI	NT	12
Erriksson et al., (2005)	E-banking	1831 users								NI	0.55	0.07	NI	NI	0.67	NA
Shih and Fang (2006)	E-banking	425 users	Yes (NA)	NS	54											
Lee (2009)	E-banking	368 users				0.25	0.13	0.12	NA		0.21		0.29	0.35	0.68	80
Al-Somali et al. (2010)	E-banking	400 users								0.68	0.85		0.80	0.72	0.77	82.7

The results illustrated that TAM explained the telemedicine adoption (40%) better than does TPB (32%) but less than the decomposed model (42%). PU was found to be the most significant determinant of BI and ATT in both TAM and decomposed models. PEOU was not found not to have any effect on PU or attitude in all models. The findings suggested that instruments that have been developed and repeatedly tested in studies involving end-users and business managers in ordinary business settings may not be equally valid in a professional setting.

Riemenschneider et al. (2003) compared TAM and TPB based on the usage of web site. They conducted a series of models that utilized TAM and TPB to varying degrees in terms of model fit. Specifically, models consisting of TAM and TPB were analyzed separately in addition to models ranging from a loose to a tight integration of the two models. However, the variance explained is not reported in the study.

Celuch et al. (2004) compared TRA and TPB to adopt an Internet management system. They found the two models are comparable in term of variance explained even if TPB (R^2=58%) provides slightly better results than does TRA (R^2=50%).

Shih and Fang (2004) is the only available study that compared TRA with TPB and decomposed TPB in the e-banking. TRA and TPB provide a good fit to the data. In addition authors found that TPB has better explanatory power for BI (R^2= 0.54) than does TRA (R^2= 0.46) and less than does the decomposed TPB (R^2= 0.66). Authors found that the path from SN to BI failed to achieve significance in either models (TPB and TRA).

Grandon (2005) compared TPB and TRA to predict the intention to adopt e-commerce among managers/owners of SMEs in Chile. Findings revealed that TRA proved to be as good as the TPB and could be even preferred for its parsimony. PBC was not a significant predictor.

Other studies compared additional models (e.g. Venkatesh et al., 2003). However, the current study does no aim to test this model. The reason is that in a recent study about e-mail adoption by Lee (2005) done in Malaysia using the UTAUT, it was shown that most of the factors forwarded in this model were insignificant except for performance expectancy which is similar to perceived usefulness and facilitating condition. Moreover, up to date, there are no follow up researches that have been conducted using this model.

Based on the above discussion, we can highlight the following remarks:

First, there are mixed results in the application of TPB. Four comparative studies among seven did not find a significant relationship between PBC and BI against two between SN and BI. Moreover, two studies among three that focused on e-banking successively in Hong Kong and in Taiwan failed to find valid relationship between PBC and BI (Shih & Fang, 2004; Liao et al., 1999); while three other studies found that SN is not a predictor of BI to adopt e-banking (Mathieson, 1991; Tan & Teo, 2000; Shih & Fang, 2004).

Second, two studies that compared TRA with competing models failed to find a significant relationship between SN and BI. In addition, the only study that used TRA in the e-banking (Shih & Fang, 2006) revealed the same result.

Third, Among the six comparative studies that focused on TAM, one study found the path PU-BI was not significant (Riemenschneider et al., 2003), five studies did not test the path PEOU-BI attitude (Davis et al., 1989; Mathieson, 1991; Taylor & Todd, 1995a; Chau & Hu, 2001; Riemenschneider et al., 2003), two studies found the path PEOU-ATT not significant (Davis et al., 1989; Chau & Hu, 2001), and two studies found the path PEOU-PU not significant (Chau & Hu, 2001; Riemenschneider et al., 2003).

Fourth, according to the authors' knowledge, there is no past study that has compared the three models (TRA, TPB and TAM) in the case of e-banking, except the study of Shih and Fang (2004) which focused solely on TRA and TPB in the e-banking sector.

Fifth, there is contradiction about which model is the best in predicting IT acceptance (see table 1). While two studies (Davis et al., 1989; Chau & Hu, 2001) found TAM to have more predicting power than TPB, two other studies (Celuch et al., 2004; Shih & Fang, 2004) found TPB better than TRA, and one study (Taylor & Todd, 1995a) found TPB better than TAM, and one study found TAM and TPB provides the same variance (Grandon, 2005).

As a summary, which model is the best in predicting e-banking requires additional investigation in the case of Malaysia, a vibrant and developing country.

The research model is shown in Figure 1. It involves three research streams (TAM, TPB, and TRA).

RESEARCH METHODOLOGY

To provide insights into the issues, a field study was investigated that consisted of a survey questionnaire.

Construct Measurement

The measures used to operationalize the constructs included in the investigated models and the questionnaires were mainly adapted from previous studies, with minor wording changes to tailor them to the e-banking field. Items for PU and PEOU, and BI were adapted from Davis (1989). Items for attitude, subjective norms, and perceived behavioral control were from Taylor and Todd (1995a). Moreover, constructs common to the examined model were measured using the same scale, an approach suggested by Taylor and Todd (1995a). All items were measured using a 7-point Likert-type scale with anchors on *strongly agree* and *strongly disagree* respectively.

Pretest

A pre-test was conducted prior to the actual data collection by using a collaborative pre-testing procedure. This procedure is where the researcher obtains the consent of the respondents to go through the questionnaire. It was done twice: Once with three respondents who were MBA students at a local university and, and a second one with three customers of a bank located on the campus. Both the pre-tests showed that the respondents were able to understand and answer the questions posed to them without any problem. As such no modification was done to the questionnaire.

Subject, Setting and Procedure

Target subjects were individual customers in Malaysia from the age of sixteen and above who had banking transactions, and who have concerns or taken part in e-banking.

A structured questionnaire was administrated to users over a period of two months. The technique of sampling was non-probability convenient sampling method. It was used because it was a viable alternative and also due to the constraint of time, speed, costs and convenience in order to obtain enough respondents. The questionnaires were distributed to bank branches, factories. Some of the questionnaires were handed over by hand, through e-mail, and also mail to quicken the collection process. The banks' officers were requested to lend a helping hand by placing the questionnaires in the bank branches for customers to fill up willingly. For those questionnaires sent through mail, a cover letter and self-addressed stamped return envelope was also provided. The cover letter stated the purpose of study and ensured confidentiality and anonymity.

Of the 300 questionnaires distributed, 242 were collected and returned back. Three of them were partially completed, and therefore discarded. Thus the effective response rate represents 239,

Table 2. Demographic profile of respondents

Respondents' Demographic		Frequency	Percentage (%)
Gender	Male	121	50.60
	Female	118	49.40
Race	Malay	43	18.00
	Indian	19	7.90
	Chinese	177	74.10
Educational Level	Secondary	19	7.90
	Diploma	54	22.60
	University Degree	145	60.70
	Master & above	21	8.80
Income Level (USD)	<= 400	39	16.30
	401 – 800	95	39.70
	801 – 1200	63	26.40
	1201 – 1600	25	10.50
	Above 1600	17	7.10
Occupation	Private sector	175	73.20
	Government Servant	35	14.60
	Others	29	12.10
Age	Mean Standard Deviation	31.29 7.01	

showing a 79.67% response rate. Table 2 presents the overall profiles of the respondents.

The above table indicates the percentages of genders are almost equal, with an average age of 31 years; the majority of respondents is Chinese and holds a university degree, working in the private sector and having an income level of USD 401 - 800. Besides, 90% of the respondents owned a personal computer and all were aware of e-banking, while 46.0% of them were users of e-banking.

Data Analysis

We tested the research hypotheses based on structural equation modeling using partial least squares (PLS) approach. PLS is a second generation multivariate technique (Fornell & Cha, 1994) which can simultaneously evaluate the measurement model (the relationships between constructs and their corresponding indicators), and the structural model with the aim of minimizing the error variance (Chin, 1998a; Gil-Garcia, 2008).

As proposed by Sang et al. (2010), we also chose PLS as the primary data analysis technique because of the following reasons (Barclay et al., 1995; Chin, 1998b; Fornell & Cha, 1994):

- PLS is a variance-based technique that is oriented towards the predictive aspects (variance explanation) of the model;
- PLS requires minimal demands in terms of sample size; and
- PLS does not assume multivariate normality and it takes into account the measurement error when assessing the structural model.

We used the SmartPLS M2 Version 2.0 to analyze the data. Also following the suggestions

Table 3. Reliability analysis

Variables	Number of items	Item discarded	Cronbach's Alpha	Mean	SD
Attitude (ATT)	3	-	0.83	4.87	1.29
Subjective Norm (SN)	6	-	0.95	*3.96*	1.28
Perceived Behavioral Control (PBC)	4	-	0.94	5.06	1.43
Perceived Usefulness (PU)	6	-	0.93	5.18	1.21
Perceived Ease Of Use (PEU)	6	-	0.95	4.92	1.18
Behavioral Intention (INT)	5	-	0.91	4.32	1.35

of (Chin, 1998b; Gil-Garcia, 2008) we used the bootstrapping method (200 resamples) to determine the significance levels for loadings, weights, and path coefficients

RESULTS

Descriptive and Reliability Analysis

The measurement scales showed high reliability, with Cronbach alpha coefficients for the six variables exceeding 0.80 (see table 3). This pattern of high reliability is consistent with much prior research (Davis, 1989; Mathieson, 1991; Taylor & Todd, 1995a; Chau & Hu, 2001). Table 3 shows that all the six variables had mean values higher than four, indicating that on the average most respondents agreed to the items set in the questionnaire. However, subjective norm had a mean value of 3.96 signifying neutral or neither agree or disagree.

MEASUREMENT MODEL

Convergent Validity

First we tested the convergent validity which is the degree to which multiple items to measure the same concept are in agreement. As suggested by Hair et al. (2010) we used the factor loadings, composite reliability and average variance extracted to assess

convergence validity. The loadings for all items exceeded the recommended value of 0.6 (Chin et al., 1997). Composite reliability values (see Table 4), which depict the degree to which the construct indicators indicate the latent, construct ranged from 0.740 to 0.852 which exceeded the recommended value of 0.7 (Hair et al., 2010). The average variance extracted, which reflects the overall amount of variance in the indicators accounted for by the latent construct, were in the range of 0.905 and 0.959 which exceeded the recommended value of 0.5 (Hair et al., 2010).

Discriminant Validity

Next we proceeded to test the discriminant validity. Discriminant validity is the extent to which the measures is not a reflection of some other variables and it is indicated by the low correlations between the measure of interest and the measures of other constructs (Cheung & Lee, 2010). Discriminant validity can be examined by comparing the squared correlations between constructs and variance extracted for a construct (Fornell & Larcker, 1991). As shown in Table 5, the squared correlations for each construct is less than the square root of the average variance extracted by the indicators measuring that construct indicating adequate discriminant validity. In total, the measurement model demonstrated adequate convergent validity and discriminant validity.

Table 4. Result for measurement model.

Model Construct	Measurement Item	Loading	CR[a]	AVE[b]
Perceived Usefulness	PU1	0.856	0.758	0.949
	PU2	0.828		
	PU3	0.921		
	PU4	0.920		
	PU5	0.861		
	PU6	0.832		
Perceived Ease of Use	PEU1	0.884	0.794	0.958
	PEU2	0.889		
	PEU3	0.888		
	PEU4	0.877		
	PEU5	0.879		
	PEU6	0.927		
Attitude	ATT1	0.820	0.761	0.905
	ATT2	0.927		
	ATT3	0.866		
Subjective Norm	SN1	0.866	0.795	0.959
	SN2	0.870		
	SN3	0.919		
	SN4	0.908		
	SN5	0.892		
	SN6	0.892		
Perceived Behavioral Control	PBC1	0.910	0.852	0.958
	PBC2	0.916		
	PBC3	0.936		
	PBC4	0.929		
Intention	INT1	0.858	0.740	0.934
	INT2	0.838		
	INT3	0.891		
	INT4	0.855		
	INT5	0.857		

Note:

[a] Composite Reliability **(CR)** = (square of the summation of the factor loadings)/{(square of the summation of the factor loadings) + (square of the summation of the error variances)}

[b] Average Variance Extracted **(AVE)** = (summation of the square of the factor loadings)/{(summation of the square of the factor loadings) + (summation of the error variances)}

Structural Model

The structural model indicates the causal relationships among constructs in the model (Sang et al., 2010) which includes the estimates of the path coefficients, and the R^2 value, which determine the prediction power of the model Together, the R^2 and the path coefficients (loadings and significance) indicate how well the data support and hypothesized model (Chin, 1998; Sang et al.,

Table 5. Discriminant validity of constructs.

Constructs	(1)	(2)	(3)	(4)	(5)	(6)
(1) Attitude	**0.872**					
(2) Perceived Behavioral	0.273	**0.923**				
(3) Ease of Use	0.310	0.513	**0.891**			
(4) Intention	0.272	0.153	0.221	**0.860**		
(5) Subjective Norm	0.343	0.137	0.269	0.190	**0.892**	
(6) Perceived Usefulness	0.479	0.406	0.573	0.252	0.264	**0.871**

Note: Diagonals represent the square root of the average variance extracted while the other entries represent the squared correlations

Table 6. Results explaining intention to use, attitude and perceived usefulness

Predicting behavioral intention to use e-banking						
	TRA		TPB		TAM	
	R^2	β	R^2	β	R^2	β
1. ATT--BI		.403**		.337**		.321**
2. SN--BI		.200**		.185**		.
3. PBC--BI		.		.147*		.
4. PU--BI		.		.		.142*
5. PEOU-BI	29.7%	.	31.4%	.	34%	.185**
Predicting attitude toward using e-banking						
6. PU--ATT		.	.	.	.	.638**
7. PEOU--ATT		.	.	.	.	.074+
Predicting perceived usefulness of e-banking						
8. PEOU--PU		.		.		.757**

Note: **p< 0.01, *p< 0.05, +p< 0.1

2010). Table 6 and Figure 2, 3 and 4, show the results of the structural model from the PLS output.

Predicting behavioral intention using TRA: Table 6 indicates that attitude toward behavior and subjective norm have a positive direct effect on behavioral intention to adopt e-banking, successively with (ß = 0.406, p < 0.01) and (ß = 0.200, p < 0.01). Attitude plays a more significant role in predicting behavioral intention than subjective norm. Results also reveal that 29.7% of the variation in the behavioral intention to use e-banking is explained by the two variables. Therefore TRA is still valid in the case of e-banking.

Predicting behavioral intention using TPB: Table 6 shows the three variables (attitude, subjective norm and perceived behavioral control) exert a positive direct effect on behavioral intention, successively with (ß = 0.337, p < 0.01), (ß = 0.185, p < 0.01), and (ß = 0.147, p < 0.05). Moreover, 31.4% of the variation in the behavioral intention was caused by the above three variables. We can observe that TPB and TRA produces the same variance, although TPB is slightly higher than TRA, and attitude plays the strongest direct effect on BI (as in the case of TRA) followed by subjective norm. Accordingly TPB still predicts intention to adopt e-banking very well.

Figure 2. Results for the TRA Model

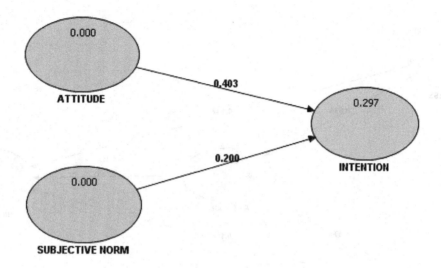

Figure 3. Results for the TPB Model

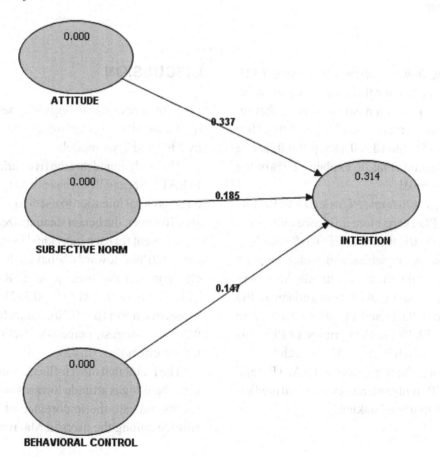

Figure 4. Results for the TAM Model

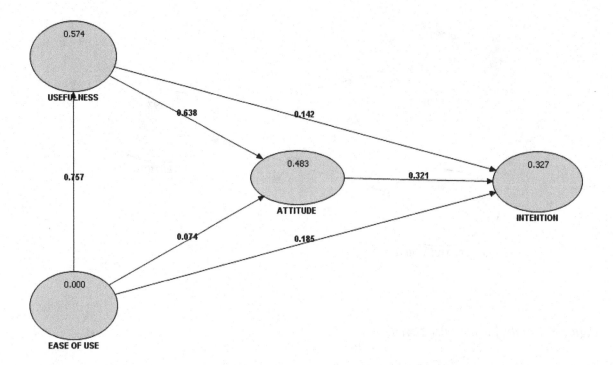

Predicting behavioral intention using TAM: Table 6 indicate that the three variables (attitude, PU and PEOU) exert a positive direct effect on BI successively with (ß = 0.321, p < 0.01), (ß = 0.142, p < 0.05), and (ß = 0.185, p < 0.01). The three variables contribute to explain 32.7% of the total variance in BI.

Predicting attitude and PU using TAM: Results indicate that PU exerts more influence on attitude (ß = 0.638, p < 0.01) than does PEOU (ß = 0.074, p < 0.10). These two variables contribute to explain 48.3% of the total variance in attitude. Moreover results indicate that PEOU is a determinant of PU (ß = 0757, p < 0.01) and PEOU contributes to explain (R²= 57.4%) of the variance of PU. This is in line with much prior TAM research.

In summary, the three models TRA, TPB and TAM have different explanatory power in predicting intention to use e-banking.

DISCUSSION

From the previous findings it appears that TAM model has the best explanatory power; followed by TPB and TRA models.

The study found that the five variables (PEOU, PU, ATT, SN and PBC) have direct positive effect on behavioral intention to use e-banking in Malaysia. However, the betas (standardized coefficient) are different for each individual independent variable. Attitude towards behavior has the highest effect on BI in the three models: TRA (ß = 0.407), TPB (ß =0.337), TAM (ß =0.321), followed by subjective norm (β = 0.20), subjective norm (β = 0.26). In contrast, perceived usefulness has the lowest effect (ß = 0.142).

The factor that most influences the intention to use e-banking is attitude towards behavior. These results indicate the importance of formation of attitude among the users in Malaysia.

These findings support and contradict previous researches both comparative studies as well as those focused on e-banking. With regard to comparative studies that used TRA the current study contrasts with the findings of two studies (Davis et al., 1989; Shih & Fang, 2004) who failed to achieve significance between SN and BI, and support the only study that found both attitude and SN have affect on BI (Celuch et al., 2004). However, this study is in line with all studies that used TRA (Davis et al., 1989; Shih & Fang, 2004; Celuch et al., 2004; Grandon, 2005) in that they found attitude as the most influential factor on BI.

With regard to comparative studies that TPB, this study contracts partially with three studies that failed to find significant relationship between SN and BI (Mathieson, 1991; Tan & Teo, 2000; Chau & Hu, 2001), as well as previous studies which failed to find a significant relationship between PBC and BI (Riemenschneider et al., 2003; Celuch et al., 2004; Grandon, 2005). This study contrasts also with the study of Shih and Fang (2004) who failed to find significance between SN and BI as well as between PBC and BI. This study is different than Liao et al. (1999) in virtual banking who failed to test the relationship between SN and BI due to the absence of reliable measure. With regard to similarities, this study shares two common aspects with previous studies. *First*, the current study supports the only study done by Taylor and Todd (1995a) who found that three components of TPB (attitude, social norm and PBC) have effect on BI. *Second*, it supports all past studies that found attitude has the most influential effect on BI (Mathieson, 1991; Taylor & Todd, 1995a; Chau & Hu, 2001; Riemenschneider et al., 2003; Celuch et al., 2004; Shih & Fang, 2004; Grandon, 2005).

With regard to comparative studies that used TAM this study challenge previous studies. *First,* in particular, all the studies did not test the relationship between PEOU and BI (Davis et al., 1989; Mathieson, 1991; Taylor & Todd, 1995a; Chau & Hu, 2001; Riemenschneider et al., 2003). *Second*, with regard to factors that most affect BI, our

findings are in line with previous studies (Taylor & Todd, 1995a; Riemenschneider et al., 2003) which found that attitude is the most influential factor. Our findings also contrasts with two other studies which found PU as the factor that exerts the strongest effect (Davis et al., 1989; Mathieson, 1991), and the study of Chau and Hu (2001) who found that attitude and PU exerts the same effect on BI. *Finally*, our results also revealed that PEOU has positive effect on PU. This result is in line and consistent with the general trend in TAM (Davis et al., 1989; Taylor & Todd, 1995a; Legris et al., 2003), but contrast with few studies that failed to prove such a link (Chau & Hu, 2001; Riemenschneider et al., 2003).

With regard to which model offers the best explanatory power, the current study reveals that TAM is the best followed by TPB and lastly by TRA, successively by 32.7%, 31.4%, and 29.7%. The findings contrast with previous studies, since it is the only study that compared the three models (TRA, TPB and TAM), and because previous studies found different results. While Davis et al. (1989), Mathieson (1991), and Chau and Hu (2001) found that TAM is better than TRA, Taylor and Todd (1995a) found TPB is better than TAM. Finally, TAM model is proven to have the best explanatory power in our study and it has been already tested and proven its validity in the context of Malaysian environment (Ndubisi & Jantan, 2003; Ramayah et al., 2003). This finding is also similar to Davis et al. (1989), Mathieson (1991) and Chau and Hu (2001), who found that TAM is better than TRA.

With regard to studies in the e-banking, the current study challenge previous studies in many ways. With regards to the two studies that used TRA in the e-banking (Shih & Fang, 2004, 2006), per opposite to our findings, only attitude has positive effect on BI. With regard to past studies that used TPB in the e-banking, two studies failed to find a role for SN on BI (Tan & Teo, 2000; Shih & Fang, 2004). Moreover, only one study (Shih & Fang, 2004) find no role for PBC on BI. However, available data does not allow us to identify which construct exerts the strongest effect on BI since beta values are not reported in these studies. As for past five studies that used TAM as the main basis for e-banking adoption, four studies did not included attitude in their model (Wang et al., 2003; Lassar et al., 2005; Pikkarainen et al., 2004; Erriksson et al., 2005); while one study included attitude and found it the most important factor that affect BI (Suh & Han, 2002), one study found that PEOU exerts the most effect on BI (Wang et al., 2003), while two studies found PU the most important factor on BI (Pikkarainen et al., 2004; Erriksson et al., 2005)

Implications

This research has both perspectives in them of theory and practice.

From a *theoretical perspective*, the results presented contributed to the existing literature in a number of ways. *First*, the article makes a contribution to e-banking literature by providing insights on the factors that seem to affect online banking acceptance. *Second*, this study represents the first comparative study that found all the five variables included in the study to have significance on behavioral intention. It also found that TPB has the best explanatory power. The study proves also that attitude plays a major part in user acceptance of e-banking besides perceived usefulness, and subjective norm. Thus, formation of attitude among the users in Malaysia is pertinent. This is in line with previous studies (Guru et al., 2000), who reported that most Malaysian finds human interaction with bank tellers as important. *Third*, this study is the first rare studies that find social norms and perceived behavioral control to affect e-banking. This is contrary to studies conducted in the past (Shih & Fang, 2004, 2006). *Fourth* the study contributes to the technology acceptance literature by suggesting that PU and PEOU were found to have some effect on technology acceptance (cf. Davis, 1989; Davis et al., 1989; Wang

et al., 2003; Alsajjan & Dennis, 2010; Luo et al., 2010). Furthermore, we found that PU was more influential than PEOU in explaining technology acceptance which is in line with previous studies (Legris et al., 2003).

From a *managerial perspective*, the results of the study provide managers in banks information about the planning of online banking as well as the government and can change the current situation by promoting positive attitudes towards the e-banking technology and its usage. Besides, banks should think of innovative ways that can attract and retain actual and potential customers to use the technology.

In Malaysia customers are driven to adopt e-banking primarily due to their attitude vis-à-vis of e-banking, secondly by the functions it performs for them and thirdly for the social norms factor they receive from peers, friends, family as well for how easy or hard it is to get the system to perform for them. Thus, in designing e-banking system, designer should look at the benefits e-banking can bring to its users. The issue of easy to use is ranked fourth, as it cannot compensate for a system that does not perform useful functions.

Once the attitude has been built then the actual and potential customer will become an effective e-banking user. Marketing can also use the results of the study on how to promote e-banking in Malaysia. People are affected by subjective norms in the form of family members, relatives, friends, superiors and co-workers who always affect users' attitude and behavior. Therefore, actions should be taken to create saleable advertisements, promotional methods that aim to convince about e-banking either in schools, universities, and public places. According to Ajzen and Fishbein (1980), subjective norm may be inferred from the referent's perceived attitude towards performing the action or intention. Therefore, if the referent is perceived to have a favorable attitude toward an intention, subjective norm may be formed among those that related or close with him or her.

Results revealed that the relative strength of the PU-BI compared to PEOU-BI is stronger. Attitude as a mediator acts fully in PU but partially in PEOU. Perceived usefulness was significantly more strongly linked to behavioral intention than was perceived ease of use. Banks can have supporting mechanisms including training to enhance customer's awareness, the convenience and benefits of e-banking. Actual and potential customers need to know what is e-banking, why to adopt it, in which circumstances to perform it and how it benefits their banking transactions.

Research Limitations

The results of this study should be considered in light of the five limitations. *First*, the sample size is small (239) and is limited in scope. It covered respondents from one region in Malaysia (Island of Penang) while other 12 regions were not included due to geographical distance. *Second*, the data of the study was collected conveniently just once, over a period of two months, under the non-contrived setting. This was deemed suitable as it was nearly impossible to a hold of the list of banking customers due to limitations in regulations. Thus, the results obtained are narrowed in term of generalisibility to the whole users in Malaysia as well to other studies in new technologies and systems. *Third*, the study excluded the actual usage behavior in the research models for comparison. However, this is not a serious limitation as previous comparative researchers had substantial empirical support for the causal link between intention and actual behavior (e.g. Taylor & Todd, 1995a; Mathieson, 1991; Chau & Hu, 2001). *Fourth*, as per Wang et al. (2003), since the study was conducted in snapshot, additional research efforts are needed to evaluate the validity of the investigated models and our findings across time. The user acceptance of e-banking is important for further research in the future. Finally, statistical analysis technique used was regression and not simultaneous equation techniques (LISRE or PLS) as opposed to

previous studies (see table 1). Indeed among the eight comparative studies, two used regression against six which used LISREL. However, this is acceptable since four studies in the e-banking used regression while five used LISREL. Finally while the variance explained is in line with previous studies (see table 1), 45%, 46% and 66% in the three models remain unknown and call for substantial research.

Recommendation for Future Research

To overcome the limitations, this study encourages future research to delve into the three following directions.

First, and in order to improve the explanatory power of the three models, future research should incorporate additional constructs. In particular it emphasize the inclusion of trust since results of past studies found it has a direct positive effect on intention to use e-banking adoption (Suh & Han, 2002; Pikkarainen et al., 2004; Erriksson et al., 2005), e-shopping (Gefen et al., 2003), and self-efficacy that has a positive effect on intention to use e-banking over PEOU, PU and trust (Wang et al. 2003), as well as on intention to use Internet information management (Celuch et al., 2004). The study also encourage to test the effect of past experiences in IT and training on e-banking adoption as well as the effect of gender since they affect the intention to use, perceived behavioral control and social norm. Tan and Teo (2000) found that past experience influences positively the intention to use e-banking. Taylor and Todd (1995b) have found that the effect of behavioral intention on actual usage was found to be stronger for the experienced users; while perceived behavioral control was found to be stronger on system usage for inexperienced users. While Venkatesh and Morris (2000) found in the short term (with less experience) social norm for women is positively correlated to intention to use after initial training, but it did not play a significant role in determining intention to use among men. The effect of income on e-banking is another perspective since past studies did also prove that it affects the intention to use e-banking via the mediation of perceived usefulness and perceived ease of use (Lassar et al., 2005).

Second, this study compared solely three models original TAM, TRA, TPB. However, additional and competing models are available including unified model (Venkatesh et al., 2003) where the authors compared it with eight models in the IT acceptance, and the integrated model (Yi et al., 2006) that integrate TAM, innovation diffusion theory and theory of planned behavior. Accordingly the study encourages further studies to compare theses models in order to shed more light on the e-banking acceptance.

Third, we reported earlier that the current study contradicts Shih and Fang (2004). Shih and Fang (2004) is the only study that compared two models in the e-banking in Taiwan, since it found a positive direct effect between SN and BI. Malaysia and Taiwan are two East Pacific Asian countries, which share in common many cultural factors. Further studies are therefore required to investigate why social norm did not play any role in e-banking in Taiwan while it has an effect in Malaysia.

CONCLUSION

This research represents a unique study in the e-banking field that compared three models (TRA, TPB and TAM) adoption in Malaysia. The findings revealed that the five factors included in the three models (attitude, subjective norm, perceived behavioral control, perceived usefulness and perceived ease of use) are significant in affecting users' behavioral intention to use e-banking. Results also revealed that attitude plays the most important role, followed by subjective norm and perceived usefulness. Among the three models,

TAM explains slightly better variance as compared to TPB with TRA producing the lowest variance.

ACKNOWLEDGMENT

This chapter is a revised version of an earlier article, "User Acceptance of Internet Banking In Malaysia: Test Of Three Competing Models" which was published in International Journal of E-Adoption (IJEA)

REFERENCES

Ajzen, I. (1991). The theory of planned behavior. *Organizational Behavior and Human Decision Processes*, *50*, 179–211. doi:10.1016/0749-5978(91)90020-T

Ajzen, I. (2001). Nature and operation of attitudes. *Annual Review of Psychology*, *52*, 27–58. doi:10.1146/annurev.psych.52.1.27

Ajzen, I., & Fishbein, M. (1980). *Understanding attitudes and predicting social behavior*. Englewood Cliffs, NJ: Prentice-Hall.

Al-Somali, S. A., Gholami, R., & Clegg, B. (2009). An investigation into the acceptance of online banking in Saudi Arabia. *Technovation*, *29*(2), 130–141. doi:10.1016/j.technovation.2008.07.004

Alsajjan, B., & Dennis, C. (2010). Internet banking acceptance model: Cross-market examination. *Journal of Business Research*, *63*(9-10), 957–963. doi:10.1016/j.jbusres.2008.12.014

Barclay, D. W., Thompson, R., & Higgins, C. (1995). The partial least squares (PLS) approach to causal modeling: Personal computer adoption and use-An illustration. *Technology Studies*, *2*(2), 285–309.

Celuch, K., Taylor, S. A., & Goodwin, S. (2004). Understanding insurance salesperson Internet information management intentions: A test of competing models. *Journal of Insurance Issues, 27*(1), 22–40.

Chau, P. Y. K., & Hu, P. J. (2001). Information Technology acceptance by professionals: A model comparison approach. *Decision Sciences, 32*(4), 699–719. doi:10.1111/j.1540-5915.2001.tb00978.x

Cheung, C. M. K., & Lee, M. K. O. (2010). A theoretical model of intentional social action in online social networks. *Decision Support Systems, 49*(1), 24–30. doi:10.1016/j.dss.2009.12.006

Chin, W. W. (1998a). Issues and opinions on structural equation modeling. *Management Information Systems Quarterly, 22*(1), 7–16.

Davis, F. D. (1989). Perceived usefulness, perceived ease of use, and user acceptance of Information Technology. *Management Information Systems Quarterly, 13*, 983–1003. doi:10.2307/249008

Davis, F. D., Bagozzi, R. P., & Warshaw, P. R. (1989). User acceptance of computer technology: A comparison of two theoretical models. *Management Science, 35*, 982–1003. doi:10.1287/mnsc.35.8.982

Delone, W. H., & Mclean, E. R. (1992). Information Systems success: The quest for dependent variable. *Information Systems Research, 3*(1), 60–95. doi:10.1287/isre.3.1.60

Eriksson, K., Kerem, K., & Nilsson, D. (2005). Customer acceptance of Internet banking in Estonia. *International Journal of Bank Marketing, 23*(2), 200–216. doi:10.1108/02652320510584412

Fornell, C., & Cha, J. (1994). Partial least squares. In Bagozzi, R. P. (Ed.), *Advanced methods of marketing research* (pp. 52–78). Oxford, UK: Blackwell.

Fornell, C., & Larcker, D. F. (1981). Evaluating structural equation models with unobservable variables and measurement error. *JMR, Journal of Marketing Research, 18*(1), 39–50. doi:10.2307/3151312

Gefen, D., Karahanna, E., & Detmar, W. S. (2003). Trust and TAM in online shopping: An integrated model. *Management Information Systems Quarterly, 27*(1), 51–90.

Gil-Garcia, J. R. (2008). Using partial least squares in digital government research. In Garson, G. D., & Khosrow-Pour, M. (Eds.), *Handbook of research on public Information Technology* (pp. 239–253). Hershey, PA: Idea Group. doi:10.4018/9781599048574.ch023

Goi, C. L. (2005). E-banking in Malaysia: Opportunity and challenges. *Journal of Internet Banking and Commerce, 10*(3). Retrieved June 25, 2006, from http://www.arraydev.com/commerce/JIBC/2006-02 /GOI.htm

Grandon, E. E. (2005). *Extension and validation of the theory of planned behavior: The case of electronic commerce adoption in small and medium-sized businesses in Chile*. Ph.D. thesis Southern Illinois University at Carbondale, 2005, 213 pages.

Guru, B. K., Vaithilingam, S., Ismail, N., & Prasad, R. (2000). Electronic banking in Malaysia: A note on evolution of services and consumer reactions. *Journal of Internet Banking and Commerce, 5*(1). Retrieved June 27, 2006, from http://www.arraydev.com /commerce/jibc/ 0001-07.htm

Hair, J. F., Black, W. C., Babin, B. J., & Anderson, R. E. (2010). *Multivariate data analysis*. Upper Saddle River, NJ: Prentice-Hall.

Karahanna, E., Straub, D. W., & Chervany, N. L. (1999). Information Technology adoption across time: A cross-sectional comparison of pre-adoption and post-adoption beliefs. *Management Information Systems Quarterly, 23*(2), 183–213. doi:10.2307/249751

Lassar, W. M., Manolis, C., & Lassar, S. S. (2005). The relationship between consumer innovativeness, personal characteristics, and online banking adoption. *International Journal of Bank Marketing, 23*(2), 176–199. doi:10.1108/02652320510584403

Lee, B. L. (2005). *Factors influencing e-mail usage: Applying the UTAUT Model.* Unpublished MBA dissertation, Universiti Sains Malaysia, Penang.

Lee, M.-C. (2009). Factors influencing the adoption of Internet banking: An integration of TAM and TPB with perceived risk and perceived benefit. *Electronic Commerce Research and Applications, 8*(3), 130–141. doi:10.1016/j.elerap.2008.11.006

Legris, P., Ingham, J., & Collerette, P. (2003). Why do people use Information Technology? A critical review of the technology acceptance model. *Information & Management, 40,* 191–204. doi:10.1016/S0378-7206(01)00143-4

Liao, S., Shao, Y. P., Wang, H., & Chen, A. (1999). The adoption of virtual banking: An empirical study. *International Journal of Information Management, 19*(1), 63–74. doi:10.1016/S0268-4012(98)00047-4

Luarn, P., & Lin, H. H. (2005). Toward an understanding of the behavioral intention to use mobile banking. *Computers in Human Behavior, 21*(6), 873–891. doi:10.1016/j.chb.2004.03.003

Luo, X., Li, H., Zhang, J., & Shim, J. P. (2010). Examining multi-dimensional trust and multi-faceted risk in initial acceptance of emerging technologies: An empirical study of mobile banking services. *Decision Support Systems, 49*(2), 222–234. doi:10.1016/j.dss.2010.02.008

Mathieson, K. (1991). Predicting user intention: Comparing the technology acceptance model with the theory planned behavior. *Information Systems Research, 2*(3), 173–1991. doi:10.1287/isre.2.3.173

Ndubisi, N. O., & Jantan, M. (2003). Evaluating IS usage in Malaysian small and medium-sized firms using the technology acceptance model. *Logistics Information System, 16*(6), 440–450. doi:10.1108/09576050310503411

Nunnally, J., & Berstein, I. (1994). *Psychometric theory.* New York, NY: McGraw-Hill.

Pikkarainen, T., Pikkarainen, K., Karjaluoto, H., & Pahnila, S. (2004). Consumer acceptance of online banking: An extension of the technology acceptance model. *Internet Research, 14*(3), 224–235. doi:10.1108/10662240410542652

Ramayah, T., Jantan, M., Mohd Noor, M. N., Razak, R. C., & Koay, P. L. (2003). Receptiveness of Internet banking by Malaysian consumers: The case of Penang. *Asian Academy of Management Journal, 8*(2), 1–29.

Ramayah, T., Oh, S. M., & Omar, A. (2008). Behavioral determinants of online banking adoption: Some evidence from a multicultural society. *Journal of Management, 2*(3), 29–37.

Ramayah, T., Taib, M. F., & Koay, P. L. (2006). Classifying users and non-users of Internet banking in Northern Malaysia. *Journal of Internet Banking and Commerce, 11*(2). Retrieved November 25, 2006, from http://www.arraydev.com /commerce/JIBC/2006-08/ Thurasamy.asp.htm

Rensel, A. D., Abbas, J. M., & Rao, H. R. (2006). Private transactions in public places: An exploration of the impact of the computer environment on public transactional Web site use. *Journal of the Association for Information Systems, 7*(1), 19–51.

Riemenschneider, C. K., Harrison, D. A., & Mykytyn, P. P. (2003). Understanding IT adoption decisions in small business: Integrating current theories. *Information & Management, 40*(4), 269–287. doi:10.1016/S0378-7206(02)00010-1

Robinson, T. (2000). Internet banking: Still not a perfect marriage. *Information Week, 17*(782), 104–106.

Sang, S., Lee, J. D., & Lee, J. (2010). E-government adoption in Cambodia: A partial least squares approach. *Transforming Government: People, Process, and Policy, 4*(2), 138–157. doi:10.1108/17506161011047370

Sheppard, B. H., Hartwick, J., & Warshaw, P. R. (1988). The theory of reasoned action: A meta-analysis of past research with recommendations for modifications and future research. *Journal of Consumer Behaviour, 15*(3), 325–343.

Shih, Y., & Fang, K. (2004). The use of a decomposed theory of planned behavior to study Internet banking in Taiwan. *Internet Research, 14*(3), 213–223. doi:10.1108/10662240410542643

Shih, Y., & Fang, K. (2006). Effects of network quality attributes on customer adoption intentions of Internet banking. *Total Quality Management & Business Excellence, 17*(1), 61–77. doi:10.1080/14783360500249661

Suh, B., & Han, I. (2002). Effects of trust on customer acceptance of Internet banking. *Electronic Commerce Research and Applications, 1*(3/4), 247–263. doi:10.1016/S1567-4223(02)00017-0

Tan, M., & Teo, T. S. H. (2000). Factors influencing the adoption of Internet banking. *Journal of the Association for Information Systems, 1*(5), 1–42.

Taylor, S., & Todd, P. A. (1995a). Understanding Information Technology usage: A test of competing models. *Information Systems Research, 6*(2), 144–174. doi:10.1287/isre.6.2.144

Taylor, S., & Todd, P. A. (1995b). Assessing IT usage: The role of prior experience. *Management Information Systems Quarterly, 19*(4), 561–570. doi:10.2307/249633

Venkatesh, V., & Davis, F. D. (2000). A theoretical extension of the technology acceptance model: Four longitudinal studies. *Management Science, 46*(2), 186–204. doi:10.1287/mnsc.46.2.186.11926

Venkatesh, V., & Morris, M. G. (2000). Why don't men stop to ask for directions? Gender, social influence, and their role in technology acceptance and usage behavior. *Management Information Systems Quarterly, 24*(1), 115–139. doi:10.2307/3250981

Venkatesh, V., Morris, M. G., Davis, G. B., & Davis, F. D. (2003). User acceptance of information technology: Toward a unified view. *Management Information Systems Quarterly, 27*(3), 425–478.

Vijayasarathy, L. R. (2004). Predicting consumer intentions to use on-line shopping: the case for an augmented technology acceptance model. *Information & Management, 41*(6), 747–762. doi:10.1016/j.im.2003.08.011

Wang, Y.-S., Wang, Y.-M., Lin, H.-H., & Tang, T.-I. (2003). Determinants of user acceptance of Internet banking: An empirical study. *International Journal of Service Industry Management, 14*(5), 501–519. doi:10.1108/09564230310500192

Yi, M. Y., Jacson, J. D., Park, J. S., & Probst, J. C. (2006). Understanding Information Technology acceptance by individual professionals: Toward an integrative view. *Information & Management, 43*, 350–363. doi:10.1016/j.im.2005.08.006

APPENDIX: QUESTIONNAIRE ITEMS

Behavioral Intention

BI1: If Internet banking were available at your bank(s), how likely would you plan to experiment with or regularly use Internet banking during the next six months?

BI2: If Internet banking were available at your bank(s), how likely would you be interested in using wireless Internet banking (mobile banking) within the next six months?

BI3: If Internet banking were available at your bank(s), how likely would you be interested in using securities trading via Internet banking within the next 6 months?

BI4: If Internet banking were available at your bank(s), how likely would you be interested in using insurance services via Internet banking within the next 6 months?

BI5: If Internet banking were available at your bank(s), how likely would you be interested in using investment fund service via Internet banking within the next 6 months?

Attitude

ATT1: I feel using Internet banking is a wise idea.
ATT2: I feel using Internet banking is a good idea.
ATT3: I like to use Internet banking.

Subjective Norm

SN1: Most people who are important to me would think I should use Internet banking.
SN2: My family who are important to me would think I should use Internet banking.
SN3: My relatives who are important to me would think I should use Internet banking.
SN4: My friends who are important to me would think I should use Internet banking.
SN5: My superiors who are important to me would think I should use Internet banking.
SN6: My co-workers who are important to me would think I should use Internet banking.

Perceived Behavioral Control

PBC1: I would be able to operate Internet banking.
PBC2: I have the resources to use Internet banking.
PBC3: I have the knowledge to use Internet banking.
PBC4: I have the ability to use Internet banking.

Perceived Usefulness

PU1: Using Internet banking would enable me to accomplish task more quickly.
PU2: Using Internet banking would improve the quality of the banking transactions performed.
PU3: Using Internet banking would make it easier to do my banking transactions.
PU4: Using Internet banking would enhance my effectiveness on the transactions.
PU5: Using Internet banking would increase my time availability.
PU6: I find Internet banking useful in my life.

Perceived Ease of Use

PEOU1: My interaction with Internet banking would be clear and understandable.
PEOU2: It would be easy to get Internet banking to do what I want it to do.
PEOU3: Learning to operate Internet banking is easy for me.
PEOU4: I would find Internet banking is flexible to interact with.
PEOU5: It would be easy for me to become skillful at using Internet banking.
PEOU6: I would find Internet banking easy to use.

Chapter 2
Quantifying Factors Influencing the Adoption of Internet Banking Services in Greece

M. Makris
Business College of Athens (BCA), Greece

A. Konstantopoulou
Business College of Athens (BCA), Greece

V. Koumaras
Business College of Athens (BCA), Greece

S. Konidis
Business College of Athens (BCA), Greece

H. Koumaras
Business College of Athens (BCA), Greece

S. Kostakis
Business College of Athens (BCA), Greece

ABSTRACT

A growing phenomenon in the Internet is the rising exploitation of sophisticated security means (e.g. cryptography, digital signatures etc.) toward the development of novel commerce services for providing electronic transactions, collaborating with business partners or serving customers, regardless of geographical and time limitations. This paper discusses, presents and elaborates on the various factors that affect the adaption of Internet banking services in Greece. In particular, it deals with the factors that have been developed within the framework of providing e-banking services over an insecure shared medium like the Internet and affect the Internet Banking customer acceptance. A factor analysis is performed based on the gathered results provided by customer-questionnaires of ALPHA Bank branch in Greece in order to quantify the various parameters that affect the use of an Internet Banking System. The findings of the analysis show that despite the fact that Internet Banking in Greece is steadily increasing its penetration, factors like security, ease of use and perceived usefulness of a system play a major role on the final decision of the customer to adopt an Internet Banking System.

DOI: 10.4018/978-1-60960-597-1.ch002

INTRODUCTION

Communication and computer networks have currently revolutionized and popularized the concept of network-based retail financial services provision among people who are pressed for time and want to accomplish useful tasks in a more efficient and cost-effective manner at any time of day or night regardless of their physical position. Online banking was and remains the B2C e-finance popular application and has been instrumental in developing the stickiness that many business models require in order to prosper.

Especially lately, there is a significant use of the Internet as a shared telecommunication channel for performing financial transactions and offering bank services. The integration of the Internet – as a worldwide network infrastructure – with traditional banking services provided a new class of bank services, which are generally described as "Internet Banking" (IB). For banks, Internet Banking initiative brings: different and arguably lower barriers to entry; opportunities for significant cost reduction; the capacity to rapidly re-engineer business processes and, even greater opportunities to sell cross border (Banks, 2000). Each and all of these potential benefits provide for increased competition and the ability to acquire market leadership from established players. Thus, banks are moving towards the provision of multimodal Internet banking services, offering to customers innovative products with wider choices and at a lower cost.

Conversely, most customers are used to conducting traditional transactions instead of the electronic ones. They are also used to acquiring, touching and examining the transaction receipts after its completion. Moreover, the face-to-face contact is closely related to interpersonal trust in business deals and transactions, while in the new environment of faceless electronic transactions the concept of trust has to be reconsidered on a new basis due to the existence of some security-related limitations, which can be classified into two discrete categories: The technical and non-technical ones.

On the one hand, concerning the technical limitations, since e-banking is based on the technical progress and evolution of the communication networks, respective technical limitations arose, limiting the diffusion of the relevant e-services. When operating in the Internet, a lot of reliability, security and standardization issues appear, mainly due to the fact that the Internet was initially developed for educational purposes, and therefore little attention was paid on how the network can be securely controlled and through this control to reassure the data integrity, confidentiality, authentication and availability for supporting novel business models.

Moreover, the network experiences serious problems of traffic and lack of bandwidth because of the rapid increase of connected users. Even though the networking technologies are advancing fast, the need for more bandwidth is increasing even faster and until this is handled, problems in the quality of service (QoS) remains, causing limited or even low performance (Gritzalis, Katsikas, & Gritzalis, 2003).

This trend can be also addressed by the Internet penetration numbers, which show a relatively limited adoption of e-services. According to Roush (2003), several countries like the Scandinavian countries or the USA have a penetration of the Internet reaching 35-50%. But in most of the other countries (even in western European ones), Internet users reach much smaller numbers. If people don't have access to the Internet, then much of the effort does not actually reach the consumer.

From the enterprise side, many bank branches use IT systems which were developed to support different needs and different kinds of software and applications. These independent but also fragmented systems contain valuable business information but have to be integrated with the new ones; in many occasions, the cost of integrating legacy systems with modern ones may be greater than that of actually scraping them. Although, companies comprehend the importance of e-commerce in the modern business environment, the investment in infrastructure is a factor that needs to be agreed and realized.

On the other hand, the diffusion of the e-banking is limited by some non-technical limitations as well. Beginning from the e-commerce concept itself, it must be noted that it is a rapidly changing field and up to now only speculations concerning its success have been made. There have been some successful examples, like amazon which launched its first webpage in December 1998 or ebay in 1997 through which e-commerce introduced itself to the internet users, but it is only now that we are entering the maturity stage and realizing its implications. Therefore, a lot of organisations are waiting for the situation to stabilize before conducting e-commerce transactions or engaging in e-commerce activities in general.

This immature condition is also evident at the status of the international and national laws, which are slowly adjusting to the changes caused by the appearance of this new kind of commerce (Laudon, & Laudon, 2007). Therefore, a lot of people feel that although there is a lot of enthusiasm there is still undocumented evidence and lack of real and concrete results. Most consumers are used to conducting "look and feel" transactions by touching and examining the product they want to buy, while in the new environment of faceless transactions, the concept of trust has to be reconsidered, especially when people are willing to offer some of their personal data in order to have more personalized e-services. Still, with all the modern technologies and software applications on the one side, and the lack of technical expertise and awareness on the other, the thin and simultaneously sensitive line of privacy might be crossed.

The aim and objectives of this paper are the identification and quantification of the factors that affect the adoption of Internet Banking Services (IBS) in Greece. The rest of this paper is organized as follows: The next section initially presents an extensive literature review about IB acceptance,

followed by data collection analysis, which includes the research aims/objectives, the research design, and the research techniques. Finally, the last section deals with the findings of the paper, providing conclusions and recommendations.

BACKGROUND

The success of e-banking applications requires various network securities issues to be solved or properly managed, fact which will create the basis for loyal users. Focusing on the network security issues that are involved in the IBS, a two-fold view can be considered especially when these issues are examined by the customer or the internet shop side.

From the customer point of view, the network security issues that must be taken under consideration are usually relative to the provision of security over the customer transactions. Since the transactions are performed through the end-user terminal devices, usually all the threats, risks and intrusions have as main aim to infect the end-user's terminal device. Depending on the type of the intrusion or the infection, issues like data privacy and fraud avoidance become very popular among the customers of the online shops (Acquisti, Gritzalis, Lambrinoudakis, & De Capitani di Vimercati, 2007). Typical examples of such security topics are the crackers that act in a malicious manner in contrast to hackers, the viruses or the worms that exploit security leaks in order to create abnormal operations to the terminal devices, the spyware and/or the Trojan horses that are installed on the end-user terminal and through which the intruder gain remote access to end user's terminal without the permission of the owner (Acquisti et al., 2007).

Similar cases are the spoof emails that is often an attempt to trick the user into making a damaging statement or releasing sensitive information (such as passwords) linking the user to sites that look like the original but actually are fake ones. These masqueraded sites are described as phishing, where eBay, PayPal and online banks are common targets. Finally, another common case is the spyware software, which provides to the intruder statistical data information, reveals user's habits, preferences or even sensitive data. Often the efficiency of such malicious software is enhanced by their combined use with key loggers that spy any typed information at the terminal device.

Therefore, for consumers the greatest risks are probably information overload and not understanding with whom they are dealing and on what basis and terms. This can range from dealing with a perfectly respectable and trustworthy company from another country, but not understanding for instance the different legal environment, compensation schemes, through which one might become vulnerable to scams and frauds (Acquisti et al., 2007).

From the bank's branch point of view, security issues are a major source of concern for everyone both inside and outside the industry. E-banking transactions increase security risks, potentially exposing isolated systems to open and risky environments. By this exposure, the likely security breaches essentially fall into three categories: breaches with serious criminal intent (e.g. fraud, theft of commercially sensitive or financial information), breaches by 'casual hackers' (e.g. defacement of web sites or 'denial of service' - causing web sites to crash), and, finally, flaws, also known as bugs, in systems design and/or set up leading to security breaches (e.g. genuine users being able to transact on other users' accounts) (Shukla, & Fui-Hoon 2005).

All of these threats have potentially serious financial, legal and reputational implications, making the IT CIO a. to follow a strategic approach to information security, building best practice security controls into systems and networks as they are developed, b. to follow a proactive approach to information security, involving active testing of system security controls (e.g. penetration testing), rapid response to new threats and vulnerabilities, and regular review of market place developments,

c. to recruit sufficient staff with information security expertise and d. to make active use of system based security management and monitoring tools (Turban, McLean, & Wetherbe, 2001).

Finally, security threats also exist not only at the edges of an electronic transaction (i.e. between the end-user and/or the internet shop), but between the two counterparts as well. During an e-transaction, measures must be taken in order the transmitted data to be treated as sensitive and therefore its disclosure to third persons to be avoided when they travel across the transport network no matter which the communication channel is. Similarly, the truthfulness of the data that is sent to and received from the two parties that are involved in the electronic transaction must be reassured, otherwise corrupted and fake data may be delivered. Finally, the two parties that participate in a transaction must be verified that they actually are the ones that they claim to be, otherwise cases of fraud against third persons might be raised.

Operationally, the intention to transact online is closely related to the significant cut in operational costs, due to the decrease of the branches and the minimization of the staff. It is widely accepted that online banking is the cheapest way for offering banking services once established (Sathye, 1999; Robinson, 2000; Giglio, 2002). More specifically, it has been estimated that the operational cost of a traditional bank transaction is approximately $1.07, while the equivalent cost through a phone transaction is almost the half (*i.e.*, $0.54); if the transaction is performed online, then the cost drops to only $0.001. (Mols, 1998; Robinson, 2000; Sheshunoff, 2000). Moreover, besides IBS being the most profitable and wealthiest segment of bank institutions (Mols, 1998; Robinson, 2000; Sheshunoff, 2000), it has been shown that IB also leads to higher levels of customer satisfaction and retention in comparison to the standard face-to-face financial services. (Polatoglu & Ekin, 2001).

From a business perspective, emphasis has been put on researching the customer acceptance of IBS in correlation to economical, social and psychological issues (Karjaluoto et al., 2002; Waite & Harrison, 2002; Brandley & Stewart, 2003). One of the earliest works in this field was conducted among Denmark citizens and showed that the IBS-registered bank customers are generally more satisfied than non-IBS registered customers for the same bank services (Mols, 1998). Similarly, another early work by Sathye (1999) showed that the main factors for the non-adoption of IBS by Australian customers are (i) security concerns about the Internet, and (ii) the lack of awareness about IBS.

These preliminary outcomes about IBS acceptance motivated the examination also of other aspects/factors that affect IB acceptance, such as compatibility, usefulness and ease of use, as well various demographic data (*i.e.*, gender, age, marital status, ethnic background, and formal instruction of the customer) (Eriksson, Kerem, & Nilsson, 2004; Yoonhee, 2005; Shergil & Bing, 2005; Eun 2001;). Finally, relative advantage, complexity, compatibility, adaptability, and risk tolerance proved to play a crucial role in IB acceptance (Mattila *et al.*, 2003; Kolodinsky, Hogarth, & Hilgert, 2004).

Moreover, another parameter that influences the degree of IB adoption is the customer familiarity with the target-object/service, since it has been proved that experienced customers behave in a more positive way towards IB than inexperienced ones (Karjaluoto *et al.*, 2002). Therefore, customization, personalization, task familiarity, and accessibility seem to have significant influence on perceived usefulness and ease of use, which in turn are important factors in fostering a positive attitude toward accepting the services Therefore, the amount of information that customers receive about IB and its perceived usefulness have been identified as major factors of IB acceptance (Sathye, 1999; Beethika, 2004).

Similarly, security and privacy are considered to be closely related to IB acceptance (Sathye, 1999; Hamlet & Strube, 2000; Tan & Teo, 2000;

Polatoglu & Ekins, 2001; Howcroft *et al.*, 2002; Wu *et al.*, 2006). Exploring the obstacles of IB customer acceptance in Australia, Sathye (1999) found that privacy and security were the major barriers against adoption. On the other hand, we can claim that it does not matter how secure the bank's computer systems are, if the customer's personal computer is infected by malicious software, making the security/privacy issues more fundamental.

From the customer point of view, security remains the vital factor of IB acceptance. Customers still remain skeptic about security, hacking issues and personal data/information misuse by third parties (Kobsa, 2001; Kobsa, 2002; Gupta *et al.,*, 2004). Going to an online/virtual banking environment, in contrast to a face-to-face transaction with a teller, the customer feels that she/he is open to numerous risks. According to a specific study about security, customers want to lead their own acts and to be in the position to know the consequences and causes of their own decisions (Baronas & Louis, 1988; Karvonen, 1999; Schaupp & Belanger, 2005).

However, there are also many other non-psychological factors that may negatively influence IBS adaptation, since a great portion of the potential or existing customers do not have access to the Internet, making impossible for them even to try the online services. Also, another great portion of the customers have Internet access only at work/office, where content/access filtering rules deprive the IB use/acceptance.

A different approach to the IBS customer acceptance is the use of Actor-network theory as a lens to view online banking practices. Actor-network theory, often abbreviated as ANT, is a distinctive approach to social theory and assumes that many relations are both material and 'semiotic' (e.g. the interactions in a bank involve both people and their ideas, and technologies. Together these form a single network). ANT allows exploring the relationship between technology and people, whilst giving insight into the changes enacted

Figure 1. Participants Income Profile

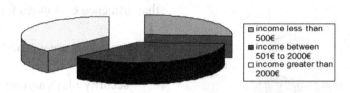

through interactions between them and the bank (Beekhuyzen, 2006).

Another emerging sector of IBS is mobile banking, which is a subset of electronic banking and underlies not only the determinants of the banking business but also the special conditions of mobile commerce. The major goal of the banks is to repeat – and if possible expand – the big success of electronic banking in mobile banking. But the banks have to keep in mind that the usage of mobile banking is taking place under completely different circumstances - under the application of mobile commerce rules. Currently, none of the existing technologies can provide a mobile banking solution that works completely without problems and totally satisfies the customer. The recommendation to the banks by the existing bibliography is not to focus on one technology only, but to combine and use the advantages of different technologies. Only with a respective combination of new technologies it will be possible for banks to achieve success in mobile banking in the long run (Borreguero, 2005).

This paper focuses on researching the customer acceptance of IBS in Greece, where the relevant literature is limited, since the IBS impact in Greece as a member of the EU has not been previously studied. In the next section, we examine the IB acceptance of ALPHA bank in Greece, showing that, using an extended Technology Acceptance Model (TAM), reliable quantitative results can be derived.

Quantifying Factors that Influence IBS in Greece

In order to quantify the factors that influence the acceptance of IBS, we performed a questionnaire survey within ALPHA Bank customers of three different branches in Greece (Chalandri, Spata, and Koropi). ALPHA Bank was founded in 1879 and it is the second largest bank in Greece, after the National Bank of Greece. With more than 450 branches, ALPHA Bank Group is considered a significant international banking player, present from Cyprus and South-eastern Europe to New York, London, and Jersey in the Channel Islands. It is acknowledged as an innovator in introducing new electronic services in the Greek market, such as: Banking services over the phone, PC link, banking services through the Internet and lately banking services over mobile phones.

In order to reassure the selection of a representative population sample, the procedure involved the collection of attitudinal, motivational, behavioural and perceptive primary/personal data from the participants, ensuring higher reliability than other survey techniques. The survey was conducted during the period of January-May 2006 where a total of 200 questionnaires were delivered to respondents, of which 159 were returned, for a response rate of approximately 80%. The mean age of the 159 respondents is 33.2 years and the participants profile is depicted on Figures 1 and 2.

The Likert five-point ranking scale was used, providing adjectival assessment grades, ranging from "*strongly agree*" (i.e. 5) to "*strongly disagree*" (i.e. 1) and the use of Internet Banking was considered in the data analysis as the depen-

Figure 2. Participants Gender Profile

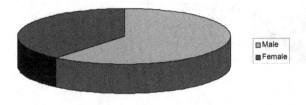

dent variable. The questionnaire included four hypotheses/factors: i. Information, ii. Perceived ease of use, iii. Perceived usefulness, and iv. Security concerns. Beside these hypotheses, some demographic data were included as well, such as background relation with Internet Banking, the familiarity to make online transactions and the frequency and the type of the performed transactions. The questionnaire's validity took its final form after the great contribution and aid of the General Director of the ALPHA bank branch at Spata, Attiki. Then the questionnaire was forwarded by various ALPHA bank branch directors to their customers.

Initially, Bartlett's test of sphericity (BTS) showed that the variables within the same factors are strongly inter-correlated, being used to determine whether the subgroup error variances were homogeneous, which is unlikely that the correlation matrix to be the Identity and thus the variance (and standard deviations) of the groups differ significantly. As null hypothesis was selected the one that supports statistically equal error variances for all the subgroups under test, which is a necessary and often ignored assumption, when moderated multiple regressions are used to evaluate moderating effects of categorical variables. This null hypothesis of BTS is appropriate for determining whether the subgroup error variances are homogeneous (i.e. a stationary process).

Table 1 presents the descriptive statistics for all the variables under investigation. Based on these statistics, the following outcomes can be derived about the statistically important variables that influence customers for or against IB use:

- customers are worried about the security of IBS;
- security plays an important role in accepting IBS; and
- perceived usefulness is an important factor in IB acceptance.

In order to identify and quantify the various parameters, which affect the adoption of IBS, we used the descriptive statistics of Table 1 for factor analysis. From this procedure, the corresponding eigenvalues of the factors were deduced and the Kaiser criterion was applied, which is also known as the "eigenvalue-greater-than-1" method.

Table 2 presents the factors extractable for the analysis along with their eigenvalues, where it can be observed that the first ten factors have eigenvalue greater than 1 and according to Kaiser Criterion these ten factors are retained for the representation of data. The ten factors account for 64.895% of the total variance, with Factor 1 accounting for 8.456%, and Factor 10 for 5.064%. The rest 35.105% of the total variance is attributable to other factors, which demonstrates that these ten factors can satisfactorily represent the data.

Figure 3 indicates the corresponding rotated component analysis, where the factors are reduced on which the variables under investigation have high loadings, making the interpretation of the analysis easier. From the analysis, it can be derived that factors 8 and 10 did not load any parameter on the specific variances, which lead us to exclude them from the specific factor analysis. Elaborating more on the analysis, Factor 1 represents the largest proportion of the total variance (8.456%), which consists of the eight variables with factor loadings ranging from 0.625 to 0.845. Four of the eight items describe perceived usefulness (*i.e.*, Using IB improves my performance at utilizing IBS; Using IB for my banking services increases my productivity; Using IB enhances my effective-

Table 1. Descriptive Statistics

Hypothesis	Item	Mean	Std. Deviation
Information	I have received enough information about IBS	4.0377	0.57243
	I have received enough information about the benefits of IBS	4.5849	0.63944
Perceived Usefulness (PU)	Using IB enables me to utilize services quickly	4.4906	0.72799
	Using IB improves my performance at utilizing IBS	4.7547	0.51209
	Using IB for my banking services increases my productivity	4.7101	0.61533
	Using IB enhances my effectiveness at utilizing IBS	4.8679	0.37506
	Using IB makes it easier for me to utilize IBS	4.7849	0.57701
	Overall, IB is useful for me to utilize IBS	4.7786	0.53229
Perceived ease of use (PEOU)	Learning to use IB is easy for me	3.3082	0.98050
	I find it easy to do what I want to	3.4151	0.90219
	My interaction with IB is clear and understandable	3.9308	1.44134
	I find IB to be flexible to interact with	4.6792	0.69647
	It is easy for me to become skilful at using IB	3.7421	1.07453
	Overall, I find IB easy to use	3.9245	1.38503
Security and Privacy	Using IB is financially secure	3.1698	1.66577
	I trust in the ability of IB to protect my privacy	3.0063	1.41196
	I trust in the technology that IB uses	3.9686	1.43386
	I trust in IB as an actual bank	2.8679	1.27345
	I am worried about the security of IB	4.9371	0.24354
	Matters of security have great influence on me for using IB	4.9308	0.30020

ness at utilizing IBS; Using IB makes it easier for me to utilize IBS), and they suggest that the use of IB improves the performance of bank transactions; three factors are security-related (*i.e.*, I trust in IB as an actual bank, I am worried about the security of IB, Matters of security have great influence on me for using IB), suggesting that a well-secured IBS is a crucial parameter to IB acceptance. Finally, the last factor (*i.e.*, I have received enough information about IBS) regards the amount of information, showing that customers have already received enough information about IBS potentials and security level. Thus, according to this, the factor can be referred to as the *"Amount of information about Perceived Usefulness and Security Level"*.

Factor 2 accounts for 7.646% of the total variance and consists three variables with factor

loadings ranging from 0.584 to 0.711. One factor is related to perceived ease of use (*i.e.*, Overall, I find IB easy to use), while the other two are security-related (*i.e.*, I trust in the ability of IB to protect my privacy, I trust in the technology IB is using), showing the importance of providing, on the one hand, a friendly user interface, and on the other hand, maintaining simultaneously at high levels the trust of the customer regarding privacy and IBS reliability. Thus, this factor can be named *"Friendly user interface, providing privacy and reliability"*.

Similarly, Factor 3 accounts for 7.205% of the total variance and two factor loading are observed: one regarding perceived usefulness (*i.e.*, using IB makes it easier for me to utilize IBS), and one about perceived ease of use (*i.e.*, Learning to use IB is easy for me). Upon this, the factor can

Table 2. Factor Eigenvalues

Component		Initial Eigenvalues		
		Total	% of Variance	Cumulative %
1	I have received enough info about IBS	1.691	8.456	8.456
2	I have received enough info about benefits of IBS	1.529	7.646	16.102
3	Using a IB enables me to utilize services quickly	1.441	7.205	23.308
4	Using a IB improves my performance of utilizing IBS	1.413	7.065	30.372
5	Using a IB for my banking services increase my productivity	1.275	6.373	36.746
6	Using a IB enhances my effectiveness of utilizing IBS	1.216	6.080	42.825
7	Using IB makes it easier for me to utilize IBS	1.199	5.996	48.821
8	Overall, IB is useful for me to utilize IBS	1.144	5.718	54.539
9	Learning to use IB is easy for me	1.058	5.292	59.831
10	I find easy to do what i want to do	1.013	5.064	64.895
11	My interaction in IB is clear and understandable	0.944	4.719	69.614
12	I find IB to be flexible to interact with	0.879	4.395	74.009
13	It is easy for me to become skilful at using IB	0.858	4.290	78.299
14	Overall, I find IB easy to use	0.766	3.830	82.130
15	Using IB is financially secure	0.718	3.592	85.721
16	I trust in the ability of IB to protect my privacy	0.661	3.304	89.025
17	I trust in the technology an IB is using	0.617	3.086	92.112
18	I trust in a IB as a true bank	0.587	2.935	95.047
19	I am worried about the security of an IB	0.531	2.653	97.700
20	Matters of security have great influence on me for using a IB system	0.460	2.300	100.000

be described as *"Easy use of IB and IBS utilization"*, referring to the importance of easy use of the various IBS and their utilization perspectives.

On Factor 4, only one item is loaded about perceived ease of use (*i.e.*, My interaction with IB is clear and understandable), which accounts for 7.065% of the total variance. Thus, this factor is named as *"Clarity between IB and customer interaction"*.

Factor 5 accounts for 6.373% of the total variance. According to Figure 3, this factor consists of two items with loadings ranging from 0.564 to 0.802. One factor is related to perceived ease of use (*i.e.*, I find easy to do what I want to), while the other (*i.e.*, Using IB is financially secure) is security-related. This factor is referred to as

"Easiness to find and run securely a specific IBS financial process".

Factor 6 accounts for 6.080% of the total variance. Table 4 presents the item which loads on this factor at 0.861, describing the amount of information regarding IBS benefits. Thus, this factor is referred to as the *"Amount of information about IBS benefits"*.

Similarly, Factor 7 contains only one item with factor loading of 0.696, which is related to perceived usefulness (*i.e.*, IB is useful for me to utilize IBS) and named *"IB usefulness on IBS utilization"*.

Finally, Factor 8 accounts for 5.292% of the total variance and includes three factors related to security and perceived ease of use. Therefore,

Figure 3. Rotated Component Graph

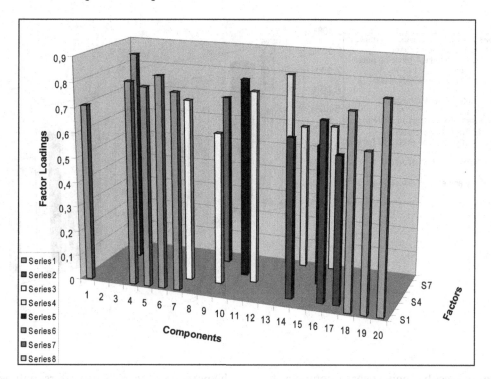

this factor is defined as the *"Flexibility and ease of use of a secure IBS"*.

In summation, the eight factors and their factor names that influence IBS adoption are presented in Figure 4 along with their share in variance. According to the factor analysis of this paper, the key factors towards e-adoption of the IBS seem to be the perceived ease of use and the perceived usefulness in combination with adequate security. Concluding, when customers have received adequate information about the benefits and potentialities of an IB system and realize that the whole service is offered via a friendly, easy, and definitely secure interface, they are more willing to use it. By extrapolating the deduced factors, we can infer that: if customers trust in the security standards of an Internet Banking system and are informed and believe that using it will increase their productivity and effectiveness, then the probability of adopting the particular system is high.

So, bank managers should make efforts towards the following directions:

i.   To improve Security and Privacy standards in order to be trusted by customers while ensuring a continuous improvement of the offered services;

ii. To refer, explicitly analyze and promote the benefits that stem from IBS use/adoption for every end user category;

iii. To increase the amount of information about IB and IBS benefits and made this information easily accessible and fairly understandable;

iv. To offer IB through a graphical, user-friendly and simple IBS interface having always as target market the inexperienced PC user; and

v.   To ensure users of IB services that even in case of problems and potential security issues that are not of user fault, bank will support

Figure 4. Deduced Factors influencing IB Acceptance

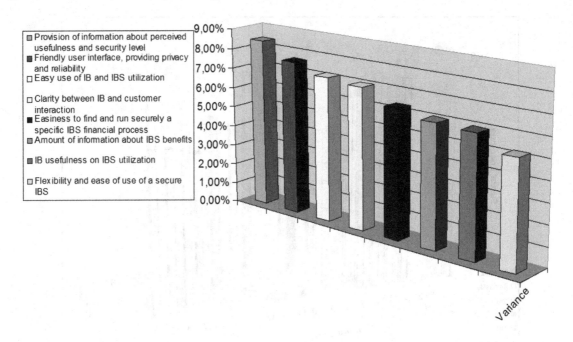

them and resolve their issues (ie compensate them, cancel unauthorized transactions etc).

CONCLUSION

Through this paper we conclude that: when an Internet banking system provides such levels of security that make it trustworthy by its customers, who are also oriented towards the notion that using an IBS will increase their productivity and effectiveness, then the probability of using the particular system is much higher. Based on the presented study of ALPHA Bank IBS customer acceptance in Greece, a factor analysis was performed with a sample of 159 customers. From this, eight different factors were deduced, which are loaded with variables coming from the questionnaires and quantify the IBS customer acceptance. By extrapolating the deduced factors, we reached to the already mentioned conclusion.

Consequently, only if bank institutions take actions that reassure the possible customers about the high standards of the provided security and

the potentials that IBS-use offers, will be able to successfully promote IBS and gain customers acceptance and trust. Within this framework, the provision of consumer reassurance and information by improving IBS security and privacy would be beneficial towards IB acceptance. In order this to be achieved, a first step is that bank IT specialists should be aware of the various security and privacy risks, which will help them to develop even more secure and reliable IB systems. On the other hand, the consumers should be also accurately informed about various available risk-precautions practices and management procedures of an IBS, like not using a public computer to access an IB account, not providing personal data to spoof emails etc, so as to become more cautious on their actions.

Also, another parameter extracted from our quantitative results is that bank institutions should improve the marketing of Internet banking services, in order to eliminate lack of awareness to potential users of IBS. Towards this, various IBS training sessions among customers and bank specialists could be organised in the bank premises for strengthening the confidence of using an IB system, Even more, according to our results, the amount of information that a consumer receives about an IBS plays a major role into adapting its use or not. Thus, by providing informative leaflets and advertisements relative to the alternative services and benefits of using an IBS, new users can be motivated towards IBS adoption with more confidence.

Last but not least, based on the perceived usefulness-related results, it is obvious that customers will accept an IBS only if it is easy for them to use and do not feel that they deal with a complicated computer program that only experienced or even professional IT people can handle. Towards this, the bankers should provide through the IBS an efficient graphical user interface, friendly to the inexperienced end user, which will provide customization/personalization options and ease of access and navigation among the various offered services. The targeted and anticipated user feelings should be confidence and joy of use and not anxiety and suspicion.

REFERENCES

Acquisti, A., Gritzalis, S., Lambrinoudakis, C., & De Capitani di Vimercati, S. (2007). *Digital Privacy: Theory, Technologies, and Practices.* New York: Auerbach Publications, Taylor and Francis Group.

Banks, E. (2000). *e-Finance: The electronic Revolution.* New York: Wiley.

Baronas, A. K., & Louis, M. R. (1998). Restoring a Sense of Control during Implementation: How Users Involvement Leads to System Acceptance. *Management Information Systems Quarterly, 12*(1), 111–124. doi:10.2307/248811

Beekhuyzen, J. P., & Von Hellens, L. A. (2006), An actor-network theory perspective of online banking in Australia, Proceedings of the American Conference on Information Systems

Beethika, S. K. (2004). Consumers Adoption of Online Banking: Does Distance Matters? Economic University of California, Berkeley, Working Paper E04-338

Borreguero, F. J. M., & Pelaez, J. C. (2005), Spanish mobile banking services: an adoption study, International Conference on Mobile Business, 2005. ICMB 2005. 274- 280

Brandley, L., & Stewart, K. (2003). A Delphi Study of the Drivers and Inhibitors of Internet Banking. *International Journal of Bank Marketing, 20*(6), 250–260. doi:10.1108/02652320210446715

Eriksson, K., Kerem, K., & Nilsson, D. (2004). Customer Acceptance of Internet Banking in Estonia. *International Journal of Bank, 23*(2), 200–216. doi:10.1108/02652320510584412

Eun, J. L. (2001). *Customer Adoption and Diffusion of Technological Innovations: A case of E-banking Technologies.* International Journal of Bank Marketing. Emerald Group Publishing Limited.

Giglio, V. (2002). Privacy in the World of Cyberbanking: Emerging Legal Issues and How You Are Protected, The secured lender, March/April 2002, 48-60

Gritzalis, S., Katsikas, S. K., & Gritzalis, D. (2003). *Network Security: Technologies and Services.* Athens, Greece: Papasotiriou Pubs.

Gupta, M., Rao, R., & Upadhyaya, S. (2004). Electronic banking and information assurance issues: survey and synthesis. *Journal of Organizational and End User Computing, 16*(3), 1–21. doi:10.4018/joeuc.2004070101

Hamlet, C., & Strube, M. (2000). Community Banks go Online, ABA Banking journal's 2000 White paper/Banking on the Internet, March, 61-65

Howcroft, B., Hamilton, R., & Hewer, P. (2002). Consumer Attitude and the Usage and Adoption of Home-based Banking in the United Kingdom. *International Journal of Bank Marketing, 20*(3), 111–121. doi:10.1108/02652320210424205

Karjaluoto, H., Mattila, M., & Pento, T. (2002). Electronic Banking in Finland Consumer Beliefs and Reactions to a New Delivery Channel. *Journal of Financial Services Marketing, 6*(4), 346–360. doi:10.1057/palgrave.fsm.4770064

Karvonen, K. (1999). Enhancing Trust Online. Proccedings of PhDIT'99: Ethics in Information Technology Design. Second International Workshop on Philosophy of Design and Information technology, 16-17 December, 1999, Saint-Ferreol, Toulouse, France

Kobsa, A. (2001). Tailoring Privacy to Users' Needs (invited keynote) in Bauer, M., Gmytrasiewicz, P.J. and Vassileva, J.(Eds), Proccedings of the User Modeling 2001: 8th International Conference, Springer Verlag, Berlin and Heidelberg, 303-13

Kobsa, A. (2002). Personalized Hypermedia and International Privacy. *Communications of the ACM, 45*(5), 64–67. doi:10.1145/506218.506249

Kolodinsky, J.M, Hogarth, J.M., & Hilger, M.A (2004). The Adoption of Electronic Banking Technologies by US Customers. The International journal of Bank, 22(4), 238-256

Laudon, K. C., & Laudon, J. P. (2007). *Management Information Systems* (10th ed.). New Jersey: Pearson Prentice Hall.

Mattila, M., Karjaluoto, H., & Pento, T. (2003). Internet Banking Adoption Among Mature Customers: Early Majority or Laggards. *Journal of Services Marketing, 17*(5), 514–526. doi:10.1108/08876040310486294

Mols, N. P. (1998). The Behavioural Consequences of PC Banking. *International Journal of Bank Marketing, 16*(5), 195–201. doi:10.1108/02652329810228190

Polatoglu, V. N., & Ekins, S. (2001). An Empirical Investigation of the Turkish Consumers' Acceptance of Internet Banking Services. *International Journal of Bank Marketing, 19*(4), 156–165. doi:10.1108/02652320110392527

Robinson, T. (2000). Internet Banking: Still not a Perfect Marriage. Informationweek.com April 17, 104-106

Roush, W. (2003, October). The Internet Reborn. [from BCA database.]. *Technology Review*, 10. Retrieved March 08, 2008.

Sathye, M. (1999). Adoption of Internet Banking by Australian Consumers: An Empirical Investigation. International Journal of Bank, 324- 331

Schaupp, L. C., & Belanger, F. (2005). A Conjoint Analysis of Online Consumer Satisfaction. *Journal of Electronic Commerce Research, 6*(2), 95–111.

Shergil, G. S., & Bing, L. (2005). An Empirical Investigation of Customers' Behaviour for Online Banking in New Zealand. Journal of E-business Sheshunoff, A.(2000). Internet Banking –An Update Form the Frontlines. *ABA Banking Journal*, (January): 51–53.

Shukla, S., & Fui-Hoon, N. (2005, August). Web Browsing and Spyware Intrusion. [from BCA database.]. *Communications of the ACM*, 8. Retrieved March 03, 2008.

Tan, M., & Teo, T. S. H. (2000). Factors Influencing the Adoption of Internet Banking. *Journal of the Association for Information Systems, 1*(5), 1–42.

Turban, E., McLean, E., & Wetherbe, J. (2001). *Information Technology for Management* (3rd ed.). New York: Wiley.

Waite, K., & Harrison, T. (2002). Consumer Expectations of Online Information Provided by Bank Websites. *Journal of Financial Services Marketing, 6*(4), 309–322. doi:10.1057/palgrave. fsm.4770061

Wu, J. H., Hsia, T. L., & Heng, M. S. H. (2006). Core Capabilities For Exploiting Electronic Banking. *Journal of Electronic Commerce Research, 7*(2), 111–122.

Yoonhee, T. C. (2005). Dynamics of Internet Banking Adoption MIS Quarterly, 413-443

This work was previously published in International Journal of E-Adoption, Volume 1, Issue 1, edited by Sushil Sharma, pp. 20-32, copyright 2009 by IGI Publishing (an imprint of IGI Global).

Chapter 3
Exploring Antecedents of Behavior Intention to Use Internet Banking in Korea:
Adoption Perspective

Kun Chang Lee
Sungkyunkwan University, Korea

Namho Chung
Kyung Hee University, Korea

ABSTRACT

This study is aimed at analyzing adoption and usage behavior within the context of Internet banking services in South Korea. In a country where the penetration rate of the Internet is very high, it seems that the self-efficacy would play a crucial role in affecting the Internet banking adoption. To pursue this research question, this study adopts TAM and incorporates the self-efficacy into TAM as one of antecedent variables such as risk, Internet experience, facilitating conditions. The proposed research model is tested empirically with 185 usable questionnaires and partial least square (PLS) method. Experimental results showed that the self-efficacy plays a prominent role in influencing the Internet banking usage compared to other factors.

INTRODUCTION

Banking is an information intensive business, and information technology is rapidly changing the way personal banking services are designed and

delivered. For retail banks, the Internet is a new distribution channel, offering less waiting time and high spatial convenience than traditional branch banks. It provides a very effective approach to managing one's finances, as it is easily accessible 24 hours a day. Internet banking allows customers to use the Internet as a transactional, as well

DOI: 10.4018/978-1-60960-597-1.ch003

as an informational medium. Users of Internet banking perform common banking transactions such as ordering checks, paying bills, transferring funds, printing statements, and checking account balances. With the rapid diffusion of the Internet, banking in cyberspace is fast becoming an alternative channel providing banking services and products.

Needless to say, the Internet banking is closely related to the recent trend of the e-commerce. It is widely accepted in literature that in many countries, e-commerce is widening its portion and gaining gravity in commerce activities (Cheng, Lam, & Yeung, 2006). For instance, U.S. B2C e-commerce revenues reached $76 billion in 2002, $90 billion in 2003, $109 billion in 2004, and $133 billion in 2005 (Cheng et al., 2006; Ebusiness Engineering, 2003). In South Korea, the e-commerce transaction reached US$330 billion in 2004, the portion of which in total transactions is almost 19.1% in 2004 (Korea Institute for Electronic Commerce, 2005). Common feature observable in the two countries is that traditional commerce is rapidly either replaced with or backed up by the e-commerce. Therefore, this study also assumes that the Internet banking needs more rigorous empirical analysis from a perspective trying to explain why its adoption rate is so high in a specific country.

In this sense, this study was conducted to investigate the Internet banking environment of South Korea, a country that features outstanding Internet infrastructure. First serviced July 1997, Internet banking is offered by 18 banks in Korea as of September 2005. The number of Internet banking users reached 10 million in November 2001, surpassed the 20 million mark in June 2003, and stands at 24.27 million as of December 2004 (Korea Institute for Electronic Commerce, 2005). The average number of Internet banking transactions such as balance enquiry, fund transfer and loan service is 9 million each day, which is a 24.7% increase from 7.22 million the previous year. Internet banking is now responsible 'for 27.4% of all bank transactions in South Korea.

Although usage of Internet banking in South Korea is substantially higher compared to other Asian economies like Hong Kong and Singapore, studies have yet to be released to describe the South Korean consumer behaviors of adopting and using Internet banking (Chan & Lu, 2004; Cheng et al., 2006; Kim, Shin, & Lee, in press; Lai & Li, 2005, Liao & Cheung, 2002). In turn, this study attempts to analyze the factors that affect the behaviors of consumers who use Internet banking in Korea, placing an emphasis on the importance of self-efficacy because South Korea is one of the highly Internet-driven societies and it is natural for us to believe that many South Koreans are accustomed to using the Internet for various purposes in their daily lives.

Therefore, the research question of study is presented as follows. First, an expanded model is presented that reflects internal constraint and external constraint in the Technology Acceptance Model. Second, this study shall be compared with results from other research activities to provide theoretical and practical suggestions for other countries where Internet banking and its applications have yet to mature. In this paper, we first provide the study's prior literature on Internet banking, and describe the theoretical model and hypotheses. We follow by presenting our research design, methodology and data analysis, results. We conclude with a discussion and suggestions for further research.

PRIOR LITERATURE ON INTERNET BANKING

Since 1999 there have been studies on acceptance of Internet banking conducted by numerous researchers in various countries based on theories such as TAM (Technology Acceptance Model), TRA (Theory of Reasoned Action) and TPB (Theory of Planned Behavior) (Chan & Lu,

2004; Cheng et al., 2006; Hoppe, Newman, & Mugera, 2001; Lai & Li, 2005; Laukkanen, 2007; Liao & Cheung, 2002; Moutinho & Smith, 2000; Sathye, 1999; Tan & Teo, 2000). Table 1 presents the comparison of studies conducted in different countries, that is, Australia, Hong Kong, South Africa, Singapore, and the United Kingdom.

Table 1 indicates that although studies on the acceptance factors of Internet banking use similar variables, their significances vary for some influential relationships. For example, in the case of banking needs and government support, a study performed by Tan and Teo (2000) claims that intention is a variable that has significant effect, whereas a study conducted by Hoppe et al. (2001) states that it is not. In terms of Internet experience, Tan and Teo (2000) and Hoppe et al. (2001) say that it is a factor that affects the intention to use Internet banking, but Liao and Cheng (2002) conclude otherwise. Furthermore, Chan and Lu (2004) claim that the subject norm is a significant factor that affects the intention to use Internet banking, but all the other studies that consider this factor state that it is not. Finally, regarding the correlation between usefulness and intention to use, Chan and Lu (2004) and Chen et al. (2006) mention their significance whereas Lai and Li (2005) conclude that they are not significant.

As explained above, there are diverse factors that influence the acceptance of Internet banking, and it can be determined that some factors vary according to the characteristics of countries in terms of various factors. Some factors even displayed contradicting effects within a country. This indicates that the subject pools and survey methods used in countries with low level of Internet banking acceptance have affected the outcomes. Among the several factors examined in literature about the Internet banking adoption, the self-efficacy becomes important much more as the Internet is adopted widely in work places as well as private lives. Especially, in South Korea where the Internet adoption rate is very high in comparison with other countries, the self-efficacy

would affect the Internet banking adoption significantly compared with other factors. Shih (2006) analyzed the importance of self-efficacy in ERP adoption. However, we will consider a number of additional factors like facilitating conditions, perceived risk, experience as well as self-efficacy so that we can analyze the relative importance of the self-efficacy in affecting the Internet banking adoption.

THEORETICAL MODEL AND HYPOTHESES

Internet banking is a new form of information technology for conducting banking affairs. Analyzing consumer behavior in using Internet banking services from theoretical and practical perspectives is an interesting activity. TAM was chosen as the fundamental framework for this study because it has been sufficiently proven as a tool for analyzing consumer acceptance of information technology. For this study, internal constraints variables (experience, risk, self efficacy) and external constraints (facilitating conditions) in using Internet banking were selected as the trait variables of TAM. The Theoretical model is graphically presented in Figure 1.

Davis (1989) discovered that perceived ease of use acts primarily through perceived usefulness to influence intentions to use. According to TAM, the user's perception about an Internet banking service is defined by beliefs (subjective probability of the consequence if the Internet banking service is used), attitude (positive and negative feelings about the Internet banking service), intention (willingness to use the Internet banking service), and usage. These results were replicated by Mathieson (1991) in a study of intentions to use spreadsheet software and by Adams, Nelson, and Todd (1992) in a series of studies using different end-user productivity software. Taylor and Todd (1995) found that TAM, modified to include subjective norms and perceived behavioral control,

Table 1. Comparison of Internet banking adoption studies among countries

Constructs	Australia Sathye (1999)	Singapore Tan & Teo(2000)	UK Moutinho & Smith (2000)	South Africa Hoppe et al. (2001)	Singapore Liao & Cheung (2002)	Hong Kong Chan & Lu(2004)	Hong Kong Lai & Li (2004)	Hong Kong Cheng et al.(2006)
Independent Variable				Dependent Variable				
Accuracy	-	-	-	-	Intention ◎ (0.50**)	-	-	-
Attitude	-	-	Satisfaction ◎ (0.36**)	-	-	-	Intention ◎	Intention ◎ (0.476*)
Banking Needs	-	Intention ◎ (0.092**)	-	Intention n.s (0.100)	-	-	-	-
Compatibility with Values	-	Intention ◎ (0.149**)	-	Intention ◎ (0.605**)	-	-	-	-
Complexity	-	Intention n.s (-0.029)	-	Intention ◎ (-0.343**)	-	-	-	-
Ease of Use (Convenience)	◎	-	Attitude ◎ (0.43**)	-	Intention n.s (0.04)	Usefulness ◎ (0.48**) Intention n.s	Usefulness ◎ Attitude ◎	Usefulness ◎ (0.878***) Attitude n.s
Facilitating Condition	◎	-	-	-	-	-	-	-
Friendliness	-	-	-	-	Intention ◎ (0.11**)	-	-	-
Government Support	-	Intention ◎ (0.106***)	-	Intention n.s (0.154)	-	-	-	-
Image	-	-	-	-	-	Usefulness ◎ (0.11*)	-	-
Internet Experience	-	Intention ◎ (0.095**)	-	Intention ◎ (0.539**)	Intention n.s (-0.03)	-	-	-
Involvement	-	-	-	-	Intention ◎ (0.08**)	-	-	-
No Resistance to change	◎	-	-	-	-	-	-	-
Reasonable price	◎	-	-	-	-	-	-	-
Relative Advantage	-	Intention ◎ (0.142**)	-	Intention ◎ (0.582**)	-	-	-	-
Result Demonstrability	-	-	-	-	-	Usefulness ◎ (0.40**)	-	-

continued on following page

Table 1. Continued

Constructs	Australia Sathye (1999)	Singapore Tan & Teo(2000)	UK Moutinho & Smith (2000)	South Africa Hoppe et al. (2001)	Singapore Liao & Cheung (2002)	Hong Kong Chan & Lu(2004)	Hong Kong Lai & Li (2004)	Hong Kong Cheng et al.(2006)
Satisfaction	-	-	Switching ◎ (0.20**) Loyalty ◎ (0.49**)	-	-	-	-	-
Security (Risk)	◎	Intention ◎ (-0.081*)		Intention ◎ (-0.221**)	Intention ◎ (0.21**)	Usefulness n.s	-	Attitude n.s Intention ◎ (0.378**)
Self-Efficacy	-	Intention ◎ (0.159**)	-	Intention ◎ (0.500**)		Ease of Use ◎ (0.63**)		-
Speed	-	-	-	-	Intention ◎ (0.19**)	-		
Subjective Norm	-	Intention n.s (0.026)	-	Intention n.s (0.049)		Intention ◎ (0.47**) Usefulness n.s		-
Switching	-	-	Loyalty ◎ (0.41**)	-	-	-	-	-
Technology Support	◎	Intention n.s (-0.021)	-	-	-	-	-	-
Trialability	-	Intention ◎ (0.321**)	-	Intention ◎ (0.197**)	-	-	-	-
Usefulness	◎	-				Intention ◎ (0.53**)	Attitude ◎ Intention n.s	Attitude ◎ (0.574**) Intention ◎ (0.422**)
Sampling Method/# of Samples	Mail/ 589	Internet & E-mail/ 454	Interviews/ 250	E-mail/ 102	Direct survey / 323	Direct survey (Univ. student) / 499	Direct survey (Univ. student) / 241	Mail/ 203

Note: ◎: Significant (*: P<0.05, **: P<0.01), n.s: Not Significant

Figure 1. Proposed research model

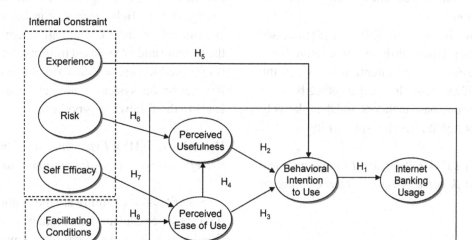

performed adequately in predicting use for both experienced and inexperienced users. Igbaria, Zinatelli, Cragg, and Cavaye (1997) applied an extended version of TAM to study personal computer use in small businesses and obtained support for TAM from the data within and outside the organization. And also, Agarwal and Karahanna (2000) proposed and found empirical support for a minor revision of the technology acceptance model despite some differences in this model from the original conceptualization of TAM. More recently, Gefen, Karahanna, and Straub (2003) proposed an integrated model of trust and TAM, and Venkatesh, Morris, Davis, and Davis (2003) indicated "Unified Theory of Acceptance and Use of Technology (UTAUT)." This theory was developed through a review and consolidation of the constructs of eight models that earlier research had employed to explain information system (IS) usage behavior (theory of reasoned action, technology acceptance model, motivational model, theory of planned behavior, a combined theory of planned behavior/technology acceptance model, model of PC utilization, innovation diffusion theory, and social cognitive theory).

The research model proposed in Figure 1 represents the variable and relationships of TAM, assuming that the user's perceptions are composed of beliefs, attitude, intention, and behavior, and that some external variables influence those user's perceptions enough to accept the IS. Beliefs represent perceived usefulness and perceived ease of use on the assumption that it influences attitude. Among the user's beliefs, perceived usefulness is the degree to which a person believes that a particular IS application would enhance his or her job performance. Perceived ease of use is the degree to which a person believes that using a particular IS would be free of effort (Davis, 1989; Davis, Bagozzi, & Warshaw 1989; Venkatesh, 2000; Horst, Kuttschreuter, & Gutteling, 2007; Venkatesh & Davis, 2000; Venkatesh et al., 2003).

Two other variables in the user's perceptions of TAM are attitude toward use and behavioral intention to use. Attitude toward use is the user's evaluation of the desirability of employing a particular IS. Behavioral intention to use is a measure of the likelihood a person will employ the IS application (Bhattacherjee & Pregmkumar, 2004). The dependent variable of TAM is the actual usage. It has typically been a self-reported measure of time or frequency of employing the IS application.

This study proposes the following hypotheses regarding the relationship between perceived ease of use, usefulness, and intention to use in the context of Web-based Internet banking because of TAM's strong base in theory and the relatively large number of studies that support it:

Hypothesis 1 (H1): *Behavioral Intention to use will have a positive effect on Internet banking usage.*

Hypothesis 2 (H2): *Perceived usefulness will have a positive effect on behavioral intention to use.*

Hypothesis 3 (H3): *Perceived ease of use will have a positive effect on behavioral intention to use.*

Hypothesis 4 (H4): *Perceived ease of use will have a positive effect on perceived usefulness.*

Four external variables, experience, risk, self-efficacy, and facilitating conditions are selected to explain the external influences affecting perceived usefulness and perceived ease of use. Let us investigate the related hypotheses one by one.

It is expected that the more the individual uses the Internet and the more he or she perceives the Internet as compatible with his or her lifestyle, the more likely that the individual will adopt services provided on the Internet (Taylor & Todd, 1995; Venkatesh & Davis, 2000). New technical ideas can be understood, and procedures for their implementation can be developed more easily when the technological knowledge resource exists (Dewar & Dutton, 1986; Hackbarth, Grover, & Mun, 2003). Innovation is facilitated by the diversity of experience in suggesting and proposing more creative ideas. For instance, internal liaison groups play an important role in promoting the adoption of

innovations (Legris, Ingham, & Collerette, 2003; Zmud, 1982). High degrees of in-house experience in information technologies, especially in the Internet and Web-based information systems, is expected to enhance the ease of use for a new Internet-based system—Internet banking. This leads to the following hypothesis:

Hypothesis 5 (H5): *Experience will have a positive effect on behavioral intention to use.*

Security and reliability are the major difficulties for a successful implementation of the Internet (Malhotra, Kim, & Agarwal, 2004; Pavlou, 2003; Pavlou & Gefen, 2004; Suh & Han, 2003). The Internet may not always provide the cheaper alternative medium for transactions due to these security concerns. System vulnerability increases with the growing use of Internet-based applications (Malhotra et al., 2004; Suh & Han, 2003). The flexible design techniques used to build the Internet and the trait of ubiquitous access make it difficult to identify exactly where access and data are coming from or where outgoing data will be going. This security concern also stems from the unprepared legal systems in privacy and security and the potential legal liabilities in the course of electronic transactions (Pavlou & Gefen, 2004; Suh & Han, 2003). A common and widely recognized obstacle to EC adoption has been the lack of security and privacy over the Internet (Malhotra et al., 2004; Suh & Han, 2003; Tan & Teo, 2000). It is difficult for companies to ask customers to do so when the sensitivity or security requirements are great. This has led many to view Internet banking as a risky undertaking. Thus, it is expected that only individuals who perceive using Internet banking service as a low risk undertaking would be inclined to perceive high system usefulness. As such, the security concern of an organization decreases the perceived usefulness of Internet banking. This leads to the next hypothesis:

Hypothesis 6 (H6): *Risk will have a negative effect on perceived usefulness.*

As noted previously, self-efficacy is getting more attention from practitioners and researchers because of the rapid penetration rate of the Internet (Hung, 2003; Shih, 2006; Torkzadeh, Chang, & Demirhan, 2006). Self-efficacy is the judgment the individual makes about his or her ability to execute a particular behavior (Bandura, 1977; Torkzadeh et al., 2006). It is defined as an individual's self-confidence in his or her ability to perform a behavior (Compeau & Higgins, 1995). A model of customer self-efficacy has been developed linking the existing literature regarding customer adoption of new technology and intention to the use of TAM. Bandura's social cognitive theory (Bandura, 1982) suggests that an individual's behavior, environment, and cognitive factors (i.e., outcome expectations and self-efficacy) are all highly interrelated. Self-efficacy judgments also determine how much effort people will spend on a task and how long they will persist with it. People with strong self-efficacy beliefs exert greater efforts mastering a challenge, while those with weak self-efficacy beliefs are likely to reduce their efforts or even quit. It is easily assumed therefore that the higher self-efficacy a use has, the easier the user can use a specific system or technology. Based on the argument so far, another hypothesis can be made between self-efficacy and perceived ease of use.

Hypothesis 7 (H7): *Self-efficacy will have a positive effect on ease of use.*

Self-efficacy is an internal constraint affecting Internet banking service, while facilitating conditions (beliefs about availability of resources to facilitate that behavior) is an external constraint (Bhattacherjee, 2000; Cheung, Chang, & Lai, 2000; Taylor & Todd, 1995; Triandis, 1979) that affects behavioral user's intention to use. The facilitating conditions include management support

of system functionality to induce system usage. Top management support is a key requirement for successful implementation of any system (Lederer & Mendelow, 1988). Given the substantial amount of resources needed for the implementation of Internet banking and its potential, top management should be expected to perform a crucial role, leveraging these resources to expand effectively the system usage. From the customer's perspective, technology deployment determines the customers' impressions about service quality and products and the retailer's coordination with suppliers and distributors. Similarly, users will be more inclined to feel easy using the Internet banking if such technology deployment with plentiful resources is provided on the Internet banking Web site. This leads to the following hypothesis:

Hypothesis 8 (H8): *Facilitating conditions will have a positive effect on ease of use.*

DESIGN AND METHODOLOGY

Research Design

A field study using a survey methodology for data collection was used in this study as the overall approach taken to test empirically the relationships implied by the research model and the research hypotheses. Since it is important to know whether respondents can appropriately answer these items, the survey instrument was verified first by interviewing five IS practitioners working in the field of Internet banking. Wording, interpretation, and item importance were analyzed until the last draft of the questionnaire. This required only minor and very limited number of revisions. Some questions were modified to indicate a more straightforward meaning. Ten interviews with practitioners were conducted, and a final review was then made by three IS professors.

Students (including graduate school students) at Sungkyunkwan University in South Korea were selected as respondents for this study with the following two reasons. First, the Internet banking service is widely available from a number of locations on campus since 2002. Thus, most of the students have been extensively using the Internet banking services on the campus since then. Second, the technology exemplifies the characteristics of contemporary IT that underscores the importance of notions of cognitive absorption (e.g., experience, self-efficacy, etc.).

Participants

The unit of analysis is the individual user of Internet banking. Respondents had conducted numerous offline banking transactions, some of whom had no online banking experience and others of whom had a great deal of online banking experience. Before they answered the questions, the respondents were asked to select one bank with which they did business and to visit its Web site to check out its basic Internet banking functions and services. Since the number of respondents was large and varied in terms of their online banking experience, assistants who had been trained in questionnaire administration answered questions from respondents some of whom needed information on how to locate a specific online banking Web site, join the site as a member and log in. To avoid social desirability response bias, assistants were strictly forbidden to address the characteristics of any online banking service, to click menus or to complete any transactions in lieu of the respondents. Respondents who had experience in online banking were asked to visit their bank Web site first, and then answer the questionnaire. Overall, the exercise took approximately 20 minutes to complete.

This study focuses on banks that provide Internet banking services. Although the range of such services differs from bank to bank, they generally allow customers to access product information, check account balances, make account transfers, receive loan information, open checking accounts, make deposits and receive foreign currency remittances.

Among the distributed 220 questionnaires, 15 were not completed validly, and 20 were not returned, resulting in 185 valid responses. The demographic characteristics of the 185 respondents showed that 67% (124) are male and 33% (61) female. As for age, 55% are 20-29, 35% are 30-39, and 10% are over 40. 57% have online banking experience of below 6 month, including brand new users, 11% 6-12 months, and 32% over 1 year.

Measures

The questionnaire consists of three steps. Step 1 gathers information about the respondents' banking habits and their Internet usage. Step 2 consists of two parts. The first part solicits the respondents' views on their feelings toward external variables of Internet banking service and, the second part seeks the perceptions of the respondents toward using Internet banking service. Finally, step 3 collects demographic information. The seven-point Likert scale is used to elicit responses on the questionnaire. Pre-testing and pilot testing of the measures were conducted by selected users from IS field, as well as experts in the Internet banking area.

The items were measured using a seven-point Likert-type scale anchored between "strongly disagree" and "strongly agree." The assessment was based on the respondent's perception of Internet banking. Eight variables were measured in this study: experience, risk, self-efficacy, facilitating conditions, perceived usefulness, perceived ease of use, intention to use, and usage. These were measured using multiple-item scales, drawn from pre-validated measures in the user acceptance research, and reworded to relate specifically to the context of Internet banking. Table 2 provides the operation of each variable with their operational definitions and sources for the constructs.

Table 2. Measurement of variables

Variable	Item	Description	Reference
Internet Experience	IE1	I am very skilled at using the Internet.	Taylor & Todd (1995), Venkatesh & Davis (2000)
	IE2	I consider myself knowledgeable about good search techniques on the Internet.	
	IE3	I know less about using the Internet than most users. (R)†	
	IE4	I know how to find what I want on the Internet.	
	IE5	Using Internet banking is very interesting.	
Risk	RSK1	I am confident over the security aspects of Internet banking service. (R)	Pavlou (2003), Suh & Han (2003), Tan and Teo (2000)
	RSK2	Information concerning my Internet banking transactions will be not known to others. (R)	
	RSK3	It is easy to cancel the transactions. (R)	
Self Efficacy	SE1	I am confident of using Internet banking if I have only the online instructions for reference.	Bandura (1977), Compeau and Higgins (1995), Tan & Teo (2000), Venkatesh (2000)
	SE2	I am confident of using Internet banking even if there is no one around to show me how to do it.	
	SE3	I am confident of using Internet banking even if have never used such a system before.	
	SE4	I am confident of using Internet banking if I have just seen someone using it before trying it myself.	
	SE5	I am confident of using Internet banking if I have just the online "help" function for assistance.	
Facilitating Conditions	FC1	Advances in Internet security technology provide for safer Internet banking.	Bhattacherjee (2000), Tan and Teo (2000), Triandis (1979)
	FC2	Faster Internet access speed is important for Internet banking.	
Perceived Usefulness	PU1	Using the Internet banking service improves my performance in my finances.	Venkatesh et al. (2003)
	PU2	Using the Internet banking service increases my productivity in my finances.	
	PU3	Using the Internet banking service enhances my effectiveness in my finances.	
	PU4	I find the Internet banking service to be useful in my finances.	
Perceived Ease of use	PEU1	Internet banking makes it easier for me to conduct my banking transactions.	Tan & Teo (2000), Venkatesh et al. (2003)
	PEU2	Internet banking gives me greater control over my finances.	
	PEU3	Internet banking allows me to manage my finances more efficiently.	
	PEU4	Internet banking is a convenient way to manage my finances.	
	PEU5	Internet banking allows me to manage my finances more easily.	
	PEU6	Internet banking is compatible with my lifestyle.	
	PEU7	Using Internet banking fit well with the way I like to manage my finances.	
	PEU8	Using the Internet to conduct banking transactions fit into my working style.	
Intention to Use	ITU1	I think it would be very good to use Internet banking service rather than traditional banking service.	Bhattacherjee & Pregmkumar (2004), Tan & Teo (2000), Venkatesh et al. (2003)
	ITU2	In my opinion it would be very desirable to use Internet banking service rather than traditional banking service.	
	ITU3	Assuming I have access to the Internet stock trading, I intend to use it.	
	ITU4	Given that I have access to the Internet stock trading, I predict that I would use it.	
	ITU5	I plan to use the Internet stock trading in the future.	
Usage	USG1	How many times do you use Internet banking service during a week?	Venkatesh et al (2003)
	USG2	How many hours do you use Internet banking every week?	

†: (R): Reverse scored Item

Table 3. Reliabilities and Correlation of Constructs

Construct	Composite Reliability	Correlation of Constructs and Average Variance Extracted							
		(1)	(2)	(3)	(4)	(5)	(6)	(7)	(8)
(1) Internet Experience	0.892	0.681							
(2) Risk	0.864	0.066	0.682						
(3) Self Efficacy	0.896	0.411**	-0.179*	0.685					
(4) Facilitating Condition	0.842	0.371**	-0.008	0.442**	0.729				
(5) Perceived Usefulness	0.912	0.071	-0.277**	0.207*	0.157**	0.676			
(6) Perceived Ease of Use	0.930	0.383	-0.127	0.531**	0.349**	0.426**	0.654		
(7) Intention to Use	0.927	0.368	-0.287**	0.603**	0.444**	0.329**	0.505*	0.718	
(8) Usage	0.970	0.355**	-0.242**	0.340**	0.164*	0.192*	0.309**	0.380**	0.941

** $p<0.01$, * $p<0.05$

Note: Diagonal elements in the correlation of constructs matrix are the square root of the average variance extracted. For adequate discriminant validity, diagonal elements should be greater than corresponding off-diagonal elements.

DATA ANALYSIS AND RESULTS

Instead of exploratory approaches like regression analysis, this study selected a confirmatory approach using Partial Least Squares (PLS) which allows researchers to integrate measurement and structural model more rigorously. The measurement model examines hypothesized links between indicators and latent constructs, whereas the structural model estimates hypothesized paths between exogenous (independent) and endogenous (dependent) latent constructs (Thatcher & Perrewe, 2002).

MEASUREMENT MODEL

To assess reliability and validity using PLS, researchers typically calculate a block of indicators' composite reliabilities, average variance extracted (AVE). Although many studies employing PLS had used 0.5 as an indication of reliability of measures, a score of 0.7 is a recommended value to be a reliable construct (Chin, 1998). For average variance extracted by measures, a score of 0.5 indicates its acceptable level (Fornell & Bookstein, 1982).

To evaluate discriminant and convergent validity, we examined the correlation of constructs and factor loadings. When the square root of each construct's AVE is greater than the correlation of construct to the latent variables, the correlation of constructs demonstrates discriminant validity. A second way to evaluate discriminant validity is examine each indicator's factor loadings (Chin, 1998). Indicators should load higher on the construct of interest than on any other variable. The correlation of constructs (see Table 3) and factor loading (see Table 4) demonstrate adequate discriminant and convergent validity.

STRUCTURAL EQUATION MODEL

A bootstrapping procedure was used to generate t-statistic and standard errors (Chin, 1998). Interpreted like multiple regression, the R^2 indicates the amount of variance explained by the model. Structural equation model results are presented in Figure 2.

The result of PLS analysis are summarized in Figure 2. The path loadings and R^2 resulting from the PLS model are illustrated. In terms of goodness of fit indicators, the model accounts for 4.8% of the variance in the Internet banking service usage. In addition, experience, perceived usefulness and perceived ease of use account for 32.3%

Table 4. Factor Loadings and Cross Loadings for the Measurement Model

Items	Internet Experience	Risk	Self Efficacy	Facilitating Condition	Perceived Usefulness	Perceived Ease of Use	Intention to Use	Usage
IE1	**0.862**	0.052	0.187	0.032	0.020	0.126	0.145	0.023
IE2	**0.821**	0.030	0.247	0.044	0.025	0.167	0.207	0.088
IE3	**0.735**	0.033	-0.080	0.403	0.036	0.091	0.125	0.034
IE4	**0.647**	0.049	0.065	0.026	-0.125	0.026	0.041	0.036
IE5	**0.668**	-0.149	-0.059	0.006	0.358	0.178	0.086	0.094
RSK1	0.097	**0.842**	-0.183	-0.028	-0.104	-0.005	-0.120	-0.080
RSK2	0.043	**0.826**	-0.084	0.071	-0.128	-0.087	-0.156	-0.097
RSK3	0.007	**0.723**	0.090	0.010	-0.123	-0.024	-0.061	0.118
SE2	0.319	-0.049	**0.736**	0.088	0.012	0.220	0.209	0.062
SE3	-0.024	-0.126	**0.732**	0.200	0.160	0.158	0.154	-0.072
SE4	0.106	0.034	**0.731**	0.041	0.014	0.197	0.288	0.051
SE5	0.308	-0.091	**0.666**	0.125	0.017	0.247	0.352	0.043
FC1	0.102	0.068	0.145	**0.788**	-0.018	0.220	0.162	-0.020
FC2	0.214	-0.010	0.221	**0.741**	0.120	0.026	0.234	0.015
PU1	-0.036	-0.106	0.016	-0.039	**0.839**	0.273	0.112	-0.038
PU2	-0.122	-0.052	0.058	0.098	**0.833**	0.166	0.109	0.028
PU3	-0.068	-0.086	0.093	0.136	**0.816**	0.130	0.126	0.093
PU4	-0.025	-0.080	0.069	-0.059	**0.763**	0.142	0.045	0.011
PEU2	0.026	-0.123	0.130	0.057	0.193	**0.852**	0.151	-0.050
PEU3	-0.043	-0.105	0.009	0.024	0.151	**0.847**	0.106	-0.013
PEU4	0.038	0.042	0.164	0.121	0.206	**0.782**	0.169	0.072
PEU5	0.116	0.054	0.168	0.041	0.184	**0.777**	0.062	0.140
PEU6	0.257	-0.103	0.156	0.065	0.160	**0.662**	0.227	0.028
PEU7	0.381	0.074	0.271	0.155	0.124	**0.591**	0.259	0.032
PEU8	0.465	0.019	0.276	0.025	0.114	**0.583**	0.184	-0.072
ITU1	0.121	-0.016	0.186	0.157	0.034	0.259	**0.808**	0.053
ITU2	0.153	-0.112	0.208	0.143	0.079	0.246	**0.786**	0.064
ITU3	0.122	-0.122	0.160	0.113	0.130	0.140	**0.779**	-0.002
ITU4	0.105	-0.071	0.349	0.232	0.067	0.156	**0.731**	0.018
ITU 5	0.175	-0.228	0.104	-0.094	0.353	0.085	**0.710**	0.056
USG1	0.085	-0.027	0.008	-0.003	0.052	0.063	0.085	**0.965**
USG2	0.051	-0.008	0.029	0.002	0.081	0.032	0.028	**0.964**

Note: SE1, PEU1 was dropped.

Figure 2. Structural Equation Model

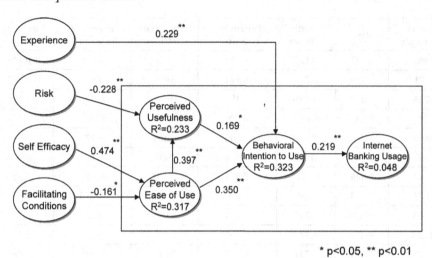

* p<0.05, ** p<0.01

of the variance in intention to use. Risk and perceived ease of use account for 23.3% of the variance in perceived usefulness. Lastly, self-efficacy and facilitating conditions explain 31.7% of the variance in perceived ease of use.

Results provide strong support for the posited relationships between experience, risk, self-efficacy, facilitating conditions, perceived usefulness, perceived ease of use and behavioral intention to use, and usage. The above results can be summarized as follows: Hypothesis H1 examines the link between the behavioral intention to use and Internet banking usage. Behavioral intention to use is significantly related with Internet banking usage ($\beta = 0.219$, $p<0.01$). Therefore, hypothesis H1 is supported.

In terms of the PLS analysis predicting a user's intention, three paths—experience, perceived usefulness and perceived ease of use—are significant. The effect of experience is fairy strong, as indicated by the path coefficient of 0.229 ($p<0.01$). Another path coefficient ($\beta = 0.169$) from perceived usefulness is also statistically significant at $p<0.05$. The other path coefficient ($\beta = 0.346$) from perceived ease of use is also statistically significant at $p<0.01$. These three paths account for approximately 32.3% of the observed variance

for the intention to use. Therefore, hypotheses H5, H2, H3 are not rejected.

Perceived usefulness is statistically significantly related to both perceived ease of use and the risk. The effect of ease of use is strong as indicated by the path coefficient of 0.397 ($p<0.01$). The other path coefficient ($\beta = -0.228$) from risk to perceived usefulness is also statistically significant at $p<0.01$. 23.3% of the observed variance in perceived usefulness can be explained from these two paths. Accordingly, Hypotheses H4 and H6 are confirmed at 0.01 level of significance.

Finally, two paths from self-efficacy and facilitating conditions can statistically significantly predict perceived ease of use. The path coefficients from such paths are 0.474 ($p<0.01$), -0.161 ($p<0.05$), respectively. These two paths account for 31.7% of the observed variance in perceived ease of use. Again, Hypotheses H7 and H8 are confirmed at 0.05 level of significance.

The support for Hypotheses H2 and H3 is expected since users would choose to use Internet banking because of the perceived ease of use and usefulness of the system. The significant relation among perceived usefulness, perceived ease of use and behavioral intention to use, and usage confirms the applicability of TAM in the context of Internet banking, extending the understanding of the behaviors of users of the Internet banking. The support for Hypotheses H1 is consistent with the former literature that has shown the effect of behavioral intention to use and actual usage. That is, the actual system usage is positively related to the extent of behavioral intentions of users.

The significant effect of experience on behavioral intentions to use (Hypothesis H5) indicates that users will consider the usage of Internet banking more positively if they are accustomed to the Internet and information technology. The behavioral intention to use Internet banking is the result of the users' perception of the convenience and promptness of business through Internet. The stronger is the belief in the merits of Internet, the greater is the users' motivation to comply with the perception and the behavioral intention to use the Internet banking.

The significant negative effect of risk on perceived usefulness (Hypothesis H6) indicates that customers do not feel comfortable when they send sensitive information to the Internet banking if the confidentiality and integrity of the communications and transactions are not ensured. When users consider the sensitivity or security requirements of Internet banking greatly, they do not believe much perceived usefulness of Internet banking.

The self-efficacy affects perceived ease of use (Hypothesis H7) and this shows that the users with feelings of self competence will be more likely to consider using Internet banking with less difficulty. Self-efficacy depends on a perception of the availability of skills, resources, and opportunities. It is also termed as perceived control which is defined as the level of one's control over the environment and one's actions. The users of Internet banking demand more control, less effort, and higher efficiency when using Internet banking. The relatively strong path coefficient from self-efficacy to perceived ease of use (0.474) indicates that the self-efficacy, representing how much potential users are accustomed to using IT for various purposes, play more an important

role in influencing the Internet banking usage in comparison to other factors. This is especially true in South Korea where the Internet diffusion and usage rate is top-ranked in the world. Therefore, we recommend that the self-efficacy be given special attention in future studies attempting to tackle the similar research issues.

The significant effect of facilitating conditions on perceived ease of use (Hypothesis H8) indicates that the users of Internet banking may consider it with less difficulty if it provides various useful resources and yields benefits to users including the improvement of work efficiency and effectiveness. Furthermore, the system designers should help users enjoy the visit and cultivate indulgence in the system design by motivating customers to participate, promoting customer excitement and concentration, and including appealing features to attract customers. Web stores have responded to the call for customer control by providing various site features (Koufaris, Kambil, & LaBarbera, 2002). In a similar fashion, the developers of Internet banking should increase the perceived ease of use by providing knowledge of system functions and site features such as search engines, help functions, and recommendation agents to enable users to easily find what they need and learn more about it.

DISCUSSION

This study intends to apply the revised form of TAM to investigate the factors affecting intention to use and the usage of Internet banking. The study provides strong evidence about the strength and relationship between the TAM perception variables and their use. Path analysis is used to assess the causal relations among variables used. The results suggested the general adequacy and applicability of TAM for explaining behavioral attention to use Internet banking as indicated by fairly reasonable path coefficients. Results based on 185 usable questionnaires collected from Korea are as follows:

The experience has a direct effect on the behavioral intention to use, while risk has a negative effect on perceived usefulness. Given the utilitarian nature of online users, they prefer Internet banking that provides less effort and secure transactions during access. The users of Internet banking will demand secure and reliable access to assistance in using it. The self-efficacy and facilitating conditions will have a positive effect on the intention to use Internet banking through their effect on perceived ease of use.

Especially, experimental results showed that self-efficacy plays a prominent role in influencing the Internet banking usage compared to other factors. Its implication is that the Internet banking usage would become more widely accepted in countries like South Korea where individuals are showing high self-efficacy. The user training on Internet banking needs to focus on the steps and procedures of actual use of the technology, as well as on how the technology can help improve the efficiency and effectiveness of the users' transaction process. For the Internet banking to be accepted by users more easily, it will be necessary to satisfy the needs of users by providing the desired functions, and make users familiar with its operation without intense training.

CONCLUSION

The results of this study improve our understanding of the factors affecting the usage of Internet banking. This study was motivated by a broad interest in understanding the user's behavior toward Internet banking and Web-based information technologies that can be easily observed in a specific country. An analyst of the Internet banking industry could use the results of this study to identify dissatisfied users and discover the general nature of their complaints. It can be used to measure general levels of satisfaction across a range of users with diverse interests.

Moreover, the management of business organizations, on decision to adopt Internet banking, should strongly emphasize devising effective means to communicate the utility of the technology to users. Users of Internet banking are relatively "pragmatic" and tend to focus on the perceived usefulness and ease of use of the technology itself. The Web-based Internet banking should provide well designed Web pages and powerful Web features, such as recommended systems and one-click checkouts. It is important to encourage and cultivate a positive attitude toward using the Internet banking to foster individual intentions to use the technology.

While the findings from this study provide some meaningful managerial implications, their generalization should be taken with caution. This study has a number of limitations and, therefore, further development for future study is needed. First, the use of self-report scales to measure the proposed variables suggests the possibility of a common method bias for some of the results. In order to pursue further investigation, it would be appropriate to develop a more direct and objective measure for the variables. Second, the experience, self efficacy and facilitating condition may be influenced by externally controllable factors such as individual lifestyles and Internet environments. Thus, to have a deeper understanding of these variables may require the inclusion of a personal lifestyle and Internet environments factor. Third, we should admit that results from the university students samples used in this study may be somewhat different from the results that would be obtained using general Internet users who are more interested in Internet banking.

ACKNOWLEDGMENT

Kun Chang Lee's work was supported by the MEST (Ministry of Education, Science and Technology), Korea, under the WCU (World Class University) Program supervised by the KOSEF (Korea Science and Engineering Foundation) (No. R31-2008-000-10062-0).

REFERENCES

Adams, D. A., Nelson, R. R., & Todd, P. A. (1992). Perceived usefulness, ease of use, and usage of information technology: A replication. *MIS Quarterly, 16*(2), 227–247. doi:10.2307/249577

Agarwal, R., & Karahanna, E. (2000). Time flies when you're having fun: Cognitive absorption and beliefs about information technology usage. *MIS Quarterly, 24*(4), 665–694. doi:10.2307/3250951

Bandura, A. (1977). Self-efficacy: Toward a unifying theory of behavioral vhange. *Psychological Review, 84*, 191–215. doi:10.1037/0033-295X.84.2.191

Bandura, A. (1982). Self-efficacy mechanism in human agency. *The American Psychologist, 37*(2), 122–147. doi:10.1037/0003-066X.37.2.122

Bhattacherjee, A. (2000). Acceptance of e-commerce services: The case of electronic brokerages. *IEEE Transactions on Systems, Man, and Cybernetics. Part A, Systems and Humans, 30*(4), 411–420. doi:10.1109/3468.852435

Bhattacherjee, A., & Pregmkumar, G. (2004). Understanding changes in belief and attitude toward information technology usage: A theoretical model and longitudinal test. *MIS Quarterly, 28*(2), 229–254.

Burnham, B. (1996). *The Internet's impact on retail banking* (Booz-Allen Hamilton 3rd Quarter Rep.). Retrieved from http://www.strategy-business.com/briefs/96301/

Chan, S. C., & Lu, M. T. (2004). Understanding internet banking adoption and use behavior: A Hong Kong perspective. *Journal of Global Information Management, 12*(2), 21–43.

Cheng, T. C. E., Lam, D. Y. C., & Yeung, A. C. L. (2006). Adoption of internet banking: An empirical study in Hong Kong. *Decision Support Systems, 42*(3), 1558–1572. doi:10.1016/j.dss.2006.01.002

Cheung, W., Chang, M. K., & Lai, V. S. (2000). Prediction of internet and world wide web usage at work: A test of an extended Triandis model. *Decision Support Systems, 30*, 83–100. doi:10.1016/S0167-9236(00)00125-1

Chin, W. W. (1998). The partial least squares approach to structural equation modeling. In G. A. Marcoulides (Ed.), *Modern methods for business research* (pp. 295-336). Mahway, NJ: Lawrence Erlbaum.

Compeau, D. R., & Higgins, C. A. (1995). Computer self-effcacy: Development of a measure and initial test. *MIS Quarterly, 18*(2), 189–211. doi:10.2307/249688

Davis, F. D. (1989). Perceived usefulness, perceived ease of use, and user acceptance of information technology. *MIS Quarterly, 13*(3), 319–339. doi:10.2307/249008

Davis, F. D., Bagozzi, R. P., & Warshaw, P. R. (1989). User acceptance of computer technology: A comparison of two theoretical model. *Management Science, 35*(8), 982–1003. doi:10.1287/mnsc.35.8.982

Dewar, R. D., & Dutton, J. E. (1986). The adoption of radical and incremental innovations: An empirical analysis. *Management Science, 32*(11), 1422–1433. doi:10.1287/mnsc.32.11.1422

Ebusiness Engineering. (2003). *Making sense of US B2C e-commerce findings*. Retrieved from http://www.ebusinessteam.com/

Fornell, C., & Bookstein, F. L. (1982). Two structural equation models: LISREL and PLS applied to consumer exit-voice theory. *JMR, Journal of Marketing Research, 19*, 440–452. doi:10.2307/3151718

Gefen, D., Karahanna, E., & Straub, D. W. (2003). Trust and TAM in online shopping: An integrated model. *MIS Quarterly, 27*(1), 51–90.

Hackbarth, G., Grover, V., & Mun, Y. Y. (2003). Computer playfulness and anxiety: Positive and negative mediators of the system experience effect on perceived ease of use. *Information & Management, 40*(3), 221–232. doi:10.1016/S0378-7206(02)00006-X

Hoppe, R., Newman, P., & Mugera, P. (2001). *Factors affecting the adoption of internet banking in South Africa: A comparative study* (University of Cape Town working paper). Cape Town, South Africa: University of Cape Town.

Horst, M., Kuttschreuter, M., & Gutteling, J. M. (2007). Perceived usefulness, personal experiences, risk perception and trust as determinants of adoption of e-government services in The Netherlands. *Computers in Human Behavior, 23*, 1838–1852. doi:10.1016/j.chb.2005.11.003

Hung, S. Y. (2003). Expert versus novice use of the executive support systems: An empirical study. *Information & Management, 40*(3), 177–189. doi:10.1016/S0378-7206(02)00003-4

Igbaria, M., Zinatelli, N., Cragg, P., & Cavaye, A. (1997). Personal computing acceptance factors in small firms: A structural equation model. *MIS Quarterly, 21*(3), 279–305. doi:10.2307/249498

Kim, G., Shin, B., & Lee, H. G. (in press). Understanding dynamics between initial trust and usage intention of mobile banking. *Information Systems Journal*.

Korea Institute for Electronic Commerce. (2005). *Korea e-business white paper*. Retrieved from http://www.kiec.or.kr

Koufaris, M., Kambil, A., & LaBarbera, P. A. (2002). Consumer behavior in web-based commerce: An empirical study. *International Journal of Electronic Commerce, 6*(2), 115–138.

Lai, V. S., & Li, H. (2005). Technology acceptance model for internet banking: An invariance analysis. *Information & Management, 42*(2), 373–386. doi:10.1016/j.im.2004.01.007

Laukkanen, T. (2007). Internet vs mobile banking: Comparing customer value perceptions. *Business Process Management, 13*(6), 788–797. doi:10.1108/14637150710834550

Lederer, A. L., & Mendelow, A. L. (1988). Convincing top management of the strategic potential of information systems. *MIS Quarterly, 12*(4), 526–536. doi:10.2307/249127

Legris, P., Ingham, J., & Collerette, P. (2003). Why do people use information technology? A critical review of the technology acceptance model. *Information & Management, 40*(3), 191–204. doi:10.1016/S0378-7206(01)00143-4

Liao, Z., & Cheung, M. T. (2002). Internet-based e-banking and consumer attitudes: An empirical study. *Information & Management, 39*, 283–295. doi:10.1016/S0378-7206(01)00097-0

Malhotra, N., Kim, S., & Agarwal, J. (2004). User's information privacy concerns (IUIPC): The construct, the scale, and a causal model. *Information Systems Research, 15*(4), 336–355. doi:10.1287/isre.1040.0032

Mathieson, K. (1991). Predicting user intentions: Comparing the technology acceptance model with the theory of planned behavior. *Information Systems Research, 2*(3), 173–191. doi:10.1287/isre.2.3.173

Moutinho, L., & Smith, A. (2000). Modeling bank customer satisfaction through mediation of attitudes towards human and automated banking. *International Journal of Bank Marketing, 18*(3), 124–134. doi:10.1108/02652320010339699

Pavlou, P. A. (2003). Consumer acceptance of electronic commerce: Integrating trust and risk with the technology acceptance model. *International Journal of Electronic Commerce, 7*(3), 69–103.

Pavlou, P. A., & Gefen, D. (2004). Building effective online marketplaces with institution-based trust. *Information Systems Research, 15*(1), 37–59. doi:10.1287/isre.1040.0015

Sathye, M. (1999). Adoption of internet banking by Australian consumers: An empirical investigation. *International Journal of Bank Marketing, 17*(7), 324–334. doi:10.1108/02652329910305689

Shih, Y. Y. (2006). The effect of computer self-efficacy on enterprise resource planning usage. *Behaviour & Information Technology, 25*(5), 407–411. doi:10.1080/01449290500168103

Suh, B., & Han, I. (2003). The impact of customer trust and perception of security control on the acceptance of electronic commerce. *International Journal of Electronic Commerce, 7*(3), 135–161.

Tan, M., & Teo, T. S. H. (2000). Factors influencing the adoption of internet banking. *Journal of Association for Information Systems, 1*(5), 1–42.

Taylor, S., & Todd, P. A. (1995). Assessing IT usage: The role of prior experiences. *MIS Quarterly, 19*(3), 561–570. doi:10.2307/249633

Thatcher, J. B., & Perrewe, P. L. (2002). An empirical examination of individual traits as antecedents to computer anxiety and computer self-efficacy. *MIS Quarterly, 26*(4), 381–396. doi:10.2307/4132314

Torkzadeh, G., Chang, J., & Demirhan, D. (2006). A contingency model of computer and Internet self-efficacy. *Information & Management, 43*(4), 541–550. doi:10.1016/j.im.2006.02.001

Triandis, H. C. (1979). Values, attitudes and interpersonal behavior. In *Proceedings of the Nebraska Symposium on Motivation, Beliefs, Attitudes and Values,* Lincoln, NE (pp. 195-259). University of Nebraska Press.

Venkatesh, V. (2000). Determinants of perceived ease of use: Integrating control, intrinsic motivation, and emotion into the technology acceptance model. *Information Systems Research, 11*(4), 342–365. doi:10.1287/isre.11.4.342.11872

Venkatesh, V., & Davis, F. D. (2000). A theoretical extension of the technology acceptance model: Four longitudinal field studies. *Management Science, 46*(2), 186–204. doi:10.1287/mnsc.46.2.186.11926

Venkatesh, V., Morris, M. G., Davis, G. B., & Davis, F. D. (2003). User acceptance of information technology: Toward a unified view. *MIS Quarterly, 27*(3), 425–478.

Zmud, R. W. (1982). Diffusion of modern software practices: Influence of centralization and formalization. *Management Science, 28*(12), 1421–1431. doi:10.1287/mnsc.28.12.1421

This work was previously published in International Journal of E-Adoption, Volume 1, Issue 3, edited by Sushil Sharma, pp. 30-47, copyright 2009 by IGI Publishing (an imprint of IGI Global).

Section 2
E–Adoption and Diffusion Among Small and Medium–Size Enterprises (SMEs)

Chapter 4
Information Systems Innovations Adoption and Diffusion Among SMEs:
Current Status and Future Prospects

Boumediene Ramdani
Cranfield University, UK

Oswaldo Lorenzo
Instituto de Empresa, Spain

Peter Kawalek
The University of Manchester, UK

ABSTRACT

The attention of software vendors has moved recently to Small to Medium-sized Enterprises (SMEs) offering them a vast range of Information Systems' (IS) innovations including enterprise systems (ES), which were formerly adopted by large firms only. Although the number of SMEs adopting new IS innovations has increased over time, strong empirical evidence is still lacking. This paper aims to fill this gap by reporting the findings of a survey on SMEs located in the Northwest of England. The survey results reveal that even more complex IS innovations are increasingly adopted by SMEs. Also, nearly half of the surveyed SMEs are willing to adopt ES in the next three years. These findings suggest that there is a considerable opportunity and a need for further research in the adoption and diffusion of new IS innovations among SMEs.

DOI: 10.4018/978-1-60960-597-1.ch004

INTRODUCTION

Small and Medium-sized Enterprises (or SMEs) are considered as major economic players and a potent source of national, regional and local economic growth (Taylor & Murphy, 2004). As described by Diaz and his colleagues (2005), SMEs have been the main creator of new jobs, while on average, large companies have downsized and reduced employment. According to the European Commission (EC, 2003), SME have less than 250 employees. Of 20 million companies in Europe, only 40,000 have more than 249 employees. This implies that 99.8% of all European enterprises are SME. Moreover, European SMEs generate 56.2% of the private sector turnover (Diaz et al. 2005).

The improvement of competitiveness of SMEs is a critical goal for a number of institutions and governments. Microcredits, knowledge transfer, training and venture capital programmes are some of the traditional policies and aids developed to assist SMEs. From the field of management, one of the main debates has been the importance of information systems' (IS) innovations for the survival of SMEs. However, most small firms still under-utilise the potential value of IS innovations by only restricting them to administrative tasks (Brock, 2000). The 'SMB Global Model' study by AMI-Partners (2004) predicts that SMEs' spending worldwide on IT and telecommunications will exceed US$ 1.1 trillion during 2008. Furthermore, it is predicted that the global level of SMEs' spending on CRM software packages alone will double to reach US$ 2 billion by 2008 (Datamonitor, 2004). Although the number of SMEs adopting new IS innovations has increased over time, strong empirical evidence is still lacking (Ordanini, 2006). This study contributes to the understanding of SMEs' adoption and diffusion of IS innovation.

IS INNOVATIONS ADOPTION AND DIFFUSION RESEARCH

Researching IS innovations' adoption and diffusion in SMEs is a challenge not only because smaller firms are more dynamic, innovative and responsive to market changes than their large counterparts (Nolan & O'Donnell, 1991), but also because SMEs are not miniature versions of large firms, they are unique in their own right (Barnett & Mackness, 1983; Westhead & Story, 1996). SMEs differ from large companies in important ways affecting their information-seeking practices (Buonanno et al., 2005; Lang & Calantone, 1997). Thus, the adoption and diffusion of IS innovations in SMEs cannot be a miniaturised version of the larger organisations. Earlier studies suggest that most SMEs avoid the adoption of sophisticated software and applications (Chen & Bernard, 1993; Cragg & King, 1993). More recent studies found that SMEs are more reluctant to spend on technology (Dennis, 2000; Walczuch, Van Braven, & Lundgren, 2000) because most small firms lack the adequate capital to undertake technical investment (Raymond, 2001). SMEs are also found to lack technical expertise (Barry & Milner, 2002) and their decisions are usually made by the owner/manager (Bunker & MacGregor, 2000).

Many theoretical models have been used to examine SMEs' adoption and diffusion of IS innovations: Technology Acceptance Model (TAM) (e.g. Grandon & Pearson, 2004); Theory of Planned Behaviour (TPB) (e.g. Harrison, Mykytyn Jr, & Riemenschneider, 1997); Combined TAM and TPB (e.g. Riemenschneider, Harrison, & Mykytyn Jr, 2003); TAM2 (e.g. Venkatesh, 2000); Innovation Diffusion Theory (e.g. Premkumar, 2003); Resource-Based View (e.g. Mehrtens, Cragg, & Mills, 2001); Stage Theory (e.g. Poon & Swatman, 1999); and Unified Theory of Acceptance and Use of Technology (UTAUT) (e.g. Anderson & Schwager, 2003). From reviewing these models (Ramdani & Kawalek, 2007b), the adoption and diffusion of IS innovations' research

Table 1. E-business index 2006, by firm size (EC, 2007)

	IS Networks[1]	E-Integration of Internal Process[2]	E-Procurement & Supply Chain Integration[3]	E-Marketing & Sales[4]
Micro (0-9)	41	23	34	40
Small (10-49)	60	39	43	54
Medium (50-249)	84	56	56	67

[1] IS Networks (Internet connectivity, LAN, W-LAN, Remote access to company network)

[2] E-Integrated Business Processes (Intranet, ERP systems, Online tracking of production time, e-Invoicing)

[3] E-Sourcing and Procurement (Firms placing orders online, Use of IS systems for sourcing, IS system linked with suppliers, Online inventory management)

[4] E-Marketing and Sales (CRM use, Firms accepting orders online, Use of IS systems for marketing/sales, IS system linked with customers)

[5] All presented figures are percentages

typically evaluate various technological, organisational, and environmental factors that facilitate or inhibit adoption/diffusion. As a generic theory of technology adoption and diffusion, Technology-Organisation-Environment (TOE) framework has also been tested and validated (e.g. Kuan & Chau, 2001).

IS INNOVATIONS ADOPTED BY SMES

Until recently, the software industry was often criticised for failing to provide adequate ES for SMEs. According to the EC (2007), this trend is changing. Driven by market requirements, and enabled by technological advances, software vendors are increasingly addressing the SME market. They are developing affordable ES such as Enterprise Resources Planning (ERP) and Customer Relationship Management (CRM) packages, which can be connected with the more powerful systems of large firms. For example, the German giant SAP offers three different types of solutions to address diverse SMEs' needs. First, *SAP Business One* is ideally for companies from 10 to 100 employees. Second, *SAP Business by Design* is an on-demand (or hosted) solution designed for companies like professional services.

Third, *SAP All-in-One* is suitable for companies with higher operations volume.

The UK has seen significant advancement in the level of IS innovations' adoption and diffusion, particularly amongst smaller businesses. According to former Department of Trade and Industry (DTI, 2004), the digital divide between large and small businesses is closing, with the UK's micro and small businesses showing significant gains in the uptake of websites and trading online. It has been reported that the proportion of small and micro firms with a website has increased by 16% in 2004, compared with a drop of 4% in 2003, driven by lower connectivity costs and more packages tailored to the needs of smaller businesses. In trading online, micro-firms have almost doubled to reach 30% and small firms accounted for 31%.

The adoption of IS innovations in the context of small businesses is considered to be problematic. On the one hand, the 'E-Business Watch' survey by EC (2005), which tracks e-business uptake across 15 industry sectors throughout all EU member states concludes that access to IS innovations is no longer a barrier to e-business uptake by small businesses (Table 1). Simple applications such as email and Web access are virtually ubiquitous. Although this index does not reveal the adoption of specific IS innovations, the sub-groups of IS innovations indicate a higher adoption rate than previously established. On the other hand, SMEs' adoption of applications such as integrated financial ledgers, CRM, Supply Chain Management (SCM) systems and hosted applications is much lower (Lockett, Brown, & Kaewkitipong, 2006). This study aims to shed some light on the current status and future prospects of IS innovations adoption an diffusion among SMEs.

Survey

Using FAME (Financial Analysis Made Easy) database, a random sample of 300 SMEs was chosen in the Northwest of England. SMEs are firms with fewer than 250 employees (DTI, 2004; EC, 2003). This study used direct interviews to collect information from owner/manager or the IS manager in the company. Although the interviewer-administered survey is expensive and time consuming, it was preferred because it allowed us to gain a fairly good response rate. Also, because the questions about ES are of contemporary nature, this technique was useful because it enabled the interviewer to correct any ambiguities and unfold any issues raised by the respondents. In conducting the interviews, letters were sent to all firms in our sample frame, followed by calls to invite them to participate in the study. Firms with positive responses were asked to provide a date for the researcher to visit the company site and conduct the interview. The respondents were informed that their participation was voluntary and the information they provided was confidential. This study ended with 102 usable responses, which means response rate achieved in this study is about 40 percent. Compared to the response rate standard of 60 percent suggested by Curran & Blackburn (2001), this study's response rate is not high but falls inline and even better in some cases than previous studies (e.g. Grandon & Pearson, 2004). The study samples from three industries most reliant on IS innovations.

Table 2. Sample Characteristics (N=102)

Characteristics	Number of Firms	Percent
Number of Employees		
> 10	35	34.3
10-49	34	33.3
50-249	33	32.4
Industry		
Manufacturing	30	29.4
Retail and Wholesale	35	34.3
Real Estate Services	37	36.3

CURRENT STATUS OF IS

Innovations Adoption and Diffusion among SMEs

In assessing the current level of IS innovations' adoption and diffusion, SMEs were asked about different IS innovations adopted in their firms, which are referred to as 'hosted applications' by Lockett et al. (2006). These applications provide e-business functionality ranging from email to contact management and from sales order entry to financial ledgers with report generators. These applications have been classified (Table 3) taking into account the resultant increase in complexity of an IS innovation (Brown & Lockett, 2001; Gillian et al., 1999).

The early analysis of Brown & Lockett (2004) suggested that most SMEs appear to be comfortable with e-mail and Web access (low complexity), are tentative with the use of the Internet for on-line buying and selling (medium complexity), but have little or no engagement in the high or very high complexity applications, such as e-marketplaces, supply chains or inter-organisational collaborative networks.

Compared to the results reported by former DTI (2004), Figure 1 shows that SMEs' uptake of IS innovations is progressing. It can be deduced that some of the survey results are inline with Brown & Lockett's findings. Because of its low complexity, one of the most adopted applications

Table 3. Classification of IS innovations complexity (Lockett, Brown, & Kaewkitipong, 2006)

Classifications	Examples	Complexity
Communication	Email, Web access	Very low
Marketing	Website	Low
Productivity	Microsoft Office, Intranet	Low
E-commerce	Buying and selling online	Medium
Collaborative	Extranet	Medium
Enterprise	Accounting, payroll, vertical applications	High
Marketplace	E-Marketplaces	High
Collaborative Enterprise	Supply chain management, CRM management	Very high
Collaborative Platform	Emerging platforms	Very high

is e-mail & Web access with an adoption rate of 94%. Moreover, 84% of the surveyed SMEs have a website for marketing purposes. Buying and selling online seem to be adopted by around only 31% of the surveyed SMEs, which confirms the tentative nature of SMEs in adopting applications with medium-complexity. Surprisingly, one of the highly adopted IS innovations was accounting &

payroll with an adoption rate of 81%. This might be due the wide availability of these systems. Also, these systems can be considered as IS innovations – Type II according to Swanson's classification (1994), which are applied to the administrative core of the firm. These systems have been found to be operated usually by one person and are becoming easy to operate.

Figure 1. Different IS innovations adopted among SMEs

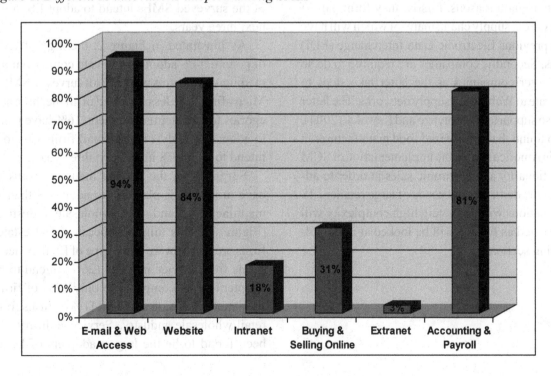

Figure 2. Intended to be adopters/ non-adopters of ES among SMEs, by size

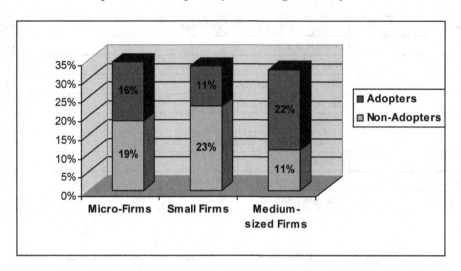

Only 18% of the surveyed SMEs have adopted intranet. Noteworthy, extranet is also marginally adopted. This might be due to investigating SMEs that are wholly-owned (independent) and not part of larger firm. Brown & Lockett (2004) analysis of SMEs' e-business engagement explains that the small number of SMEs engaged in the more complex applications appear to do so for two main reasons. Firstly, they form part of an existing supply chain, many of which will have had previous Electronic Data Interchange (EDI) links. Secondly, companies are required to do so by larger companies as the latter take steps to migrate to Web-based supply networks. The latter is also supported by Lorenzo and Kawalek (2004), who found that a mid-sized food manufacturer in Latin America started the implementation of SCM functionality and electronic sales in order to address the demands and needs of large retailers. IS innovations with high/very high complexity will be treated as ES and will be looked at in the following section.

FUTURE PROSPECTS: SMEs ADOPTION OF ENTERPRISE SYSTEMS

Although ES can be classified as collaborative enterprise applications according to Lockett et al. (2006) classification where complexity is considered to be very high, nearly half (49/102) of the surveyed SMEs intend to adopt ES in the next three years.

As illustrated in Figure 2, the highest level of potential ES adopters seems to come from the medium-sized firms with 22% of surveyed SMEs. Micro-firms, the less expected of all the three categories to be potential adopters, 16% have plans to adopt ES. Only 11% of small firms category intend to adopt ES in the next three years.

Surprisingly, the service industry seems to have more SMEs planning to adopt ES than in manufacturing and retail/wholesale industries (Figure 3). This might be because real estates firms are more aware of the type of ES they need. Firms from service industry (26%) intend to be adopters of ES compared to only 12% of firms from manufacturing and only 11% of firms from retail/wholesale industry. Service industry has been found to be the largest adopters of IS in-

Figure 3. Intended to be adopters/ non-adopters of ES among SMEs, by industry

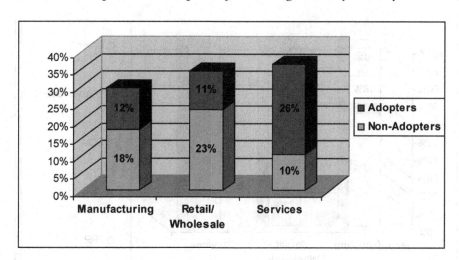

novations, followed by retailers and then manufacturers (Goode & Stevens, 2000).

As shown in Figure 4, the surveyed SMEs will potentially adopt different types of ES. This could be due to offering SMEs component-based solutions (e.g. ERP, CRM, SCM, e-procurement), which allows them to gradually integrate components that are reasonably customised to their needs (Buonanno et al., 2005).

CRM systems are the most intended to be adopted among the surveyed SMEs with 37% of the potential adopters. This may be due to the high percentage of adopters from the service in-

dustry compared to other industries. ERP systems also account for high percentage of the intended to be adopted ES (30%). SCM systems account for 17%. The least intended to be adopted ES among SMEs is e-procurement software with only 4% of the potential adopters. This might be due to investigating SMEs that are wholly-owned (independent) and not part of larger firm. This might also be because SMEs have low level of bargaining to demand their providers to implement an e-procurement system. It is more plausible to think that SMEs are willing to adopt ERP and CRM systems because they are prioritizing their

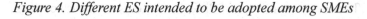
Figure 4. Different ES intended to be adopted among SMEs

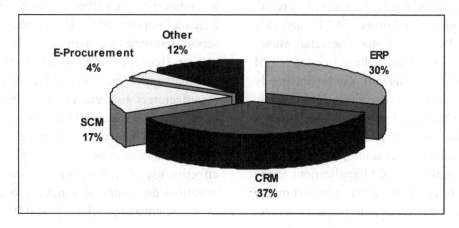

Figure 5. Different ES to be adopted among SMEs, by industry

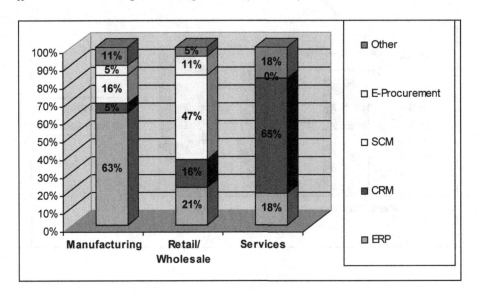

IS innovations' investment in their downstream process in the supply chain. Other system (12%) mostly developed either internally or externally for industry specific usage such as bill-of-material for manufacturing firms.

From Figure 5, it is clear that different ES are intended to be adopted by SMEs from different industries. ERP, SCM and CRM systems are intended to be potentially adopted by firms from manufacturing industry (63%), retail/wholesale industry (47%), and service industry (65%) respectively.

Potential adopters from manufacturing industry (63%) are willing to adopt ERP systems. These systems are also intended to be adopted by retail/wholesale and services' firms with 21% and 18% respectively. Potential adopters from retail/wholesale industry (47%) are willing to adopt SCM systems. These systems will also be potentially adopted by manufacturing firms (16%). Only 10-15% of SMEs are reported to have adopted SCM systems (EC, 2007). However, it is important to mention that other studies have found that the implementation of SCM applications in the retail sector has had high level of impact on the productivity of this sector (Chavez and Lorenzo,

2006). A simple example is the use of scanners that read universal product codes (UPC) and allows companies to reduce checkout costs and easily track inventories. SMEs in this sector have followed this technological trend as it is considered a qualifier capability.

Potential adopters from service industry (65%) are willing to adopt CRM systems. These systems are also intended to be adopted by retail/wholesale firms accounting for 16%. E-procurement software seems to be potentially adopted by retail/wholesale firms with 11%, and only 5% of manufacturing firms. It has been noted that service industries make use of different systems to manufacturing and retail industries (Premkumar & King, 1994; Reich & Benbasat, 1990). These author argues that service industries are often more reliant on information. Hence, CRM as an information-sharing tool may appeal more to service industries than manufacturers and retailers, who are interested in adopting ERP and SCM systems respectively.

Driven by the need for lower costs, faster implementation, easier to use applications and effective use of scarce resources, internal IS innovations development is moving to an external development and provision model (Ward & Peppard, 2002). When SMEs were asked whether they intend to adopt hosted ES in the future, 76% of the responses from potential ES adopters were positive. Only around a quarter of SMEs do not intend to adopt hosted ES applications in the future. This may be due to the complexity level of adopting such systems.

CONCLUSION

In assessing the current level of IS innovations' adoption among SMEs in the Northwest of England, it has been found that compared to the results reported by former DTI (2004) not only less complex IS innovations (e.g. e-mail & Web access), but also more complex IS innovations (e.g. accounting & payroll software) are increasingly adopted by SMEs. These results demonstrate that IS innovation uptake by SMEs is progressing. The future prospects of ES adoption seem to be very positive. Nearly half of the surveyed SMEs intend to adopt ES in the next three years. Surprisingly, the service industry seems to have more SMEs planning to adopt ES then in manufacturing and retail/wholesale industries. ERP, SCM and CRM systems will potentially be adopted by firms from manufacturing industry, retail/wholesale industry, and service industry respectively. Finally, SMEs were found to be attracted to the hosted model of ES.

FUTURE RESEARCH DIRECTIONS

Having assessed the current status and future prospects of IS innovations' adoption and diffusion among SMEs, it is clear that there is a considerable opportunity and a need for further research. Lee (2004) claim that several avenues for future research remain unexplored. He argues that recent research activity in the adoption and diffusion of IS innovations only underscores the importance of this area particularly for small business, where

further research is needed for a range of different IS innovations. Many studies have looked at several variables used to explain, predict, and increase the adoption and diffusion of IS innovations (see Jeyaraj, Rottman, & Lacity, 2006; Ramdani & Kawalek, 2007b). Previous contributions focused not only on a single IS innovation such as Internet adoption (e.g. Mehrtens, Cragg, & Mills, 2001), EDI adoption (e.g. Kuan & Chau, 2001) and e-commerce (e.g. Daniel & Grimshaw, 2002), but also examined a set of IS innovations such as ES (Ramdani & Kawalek, 2008) and communication technologies (Premkumar & Roberts, 1999). Taking the argument that IS innovations are highly differentiated technologies for which there is not a single adoption model (Ramdani & Kawalek, 2007a), it is essential to see whether different types of ES are influenced by different factors. In particular, it would be interesting to investigate the reasons why SMEs favour a particular ES. With the recent popularity of hosted software applications (Lockett, Brown, & Kaewkitipong, 2006), future studies could empirically examine the factors influencing the adoption of these technologies and how they differ from traditional software packages. Future studies may also attempt to examine other phases of adoption and diffusion, and identify factors for each phase.

The data used in this study was collected in 2005. At this time, SMEs in the UK were in the early adoption phase of ES. In our survey, only about half of the respondents intend to adopt ES. This adoption profile is expected to change in the future. Thus, the need for further research to investigate future adoption profiles.

Implications for Software Vendors

There are important implications for software vendors. SMEs represent the majority of businesses in most economies, and consequently represent an important market segment for software vendors or service providers. Brown & Lockett (2004) claim that SMEs have focused primarily on simple applications and that for SMEs to adopt more sophisticated systems, service providers must play a critical role. They further suggest that software vendors' understanding of the nature of SMEs is limited. The results of this survey suggest that a high number of SMEs are planning to adopt ES in the near future. Also, SMEs from different sectors seem to have different software priorities and needs. These insights can be very helpful for software vendors in their future targeting strategies. Although large software vendors seem to be addressing all possible market opportunities, smaller software vendors may decide to develop niche strategies to deal with specific market needs. Finally, because SMEs seem to be attracted to hosted systems, some software vendors may be forced to change their business models to serve the SME market.

REFERENCES

AMI-Partners. (2004). The SMB Global Model [Electronic Version] from http://www.ami-partners.com.

Anderson, J. E., & Schwager, P. H. (2003). *SMEs Adoption of Wireless LAN Technology: Applying UTAUT Model*. Proceedings of the 7th Annual Conference of the Southern Association for Information Systems.

Barnett, R. R., & Mackness, J. R. (1983). *An Action Research Study of Small Firm Management Journal of Applied Systems*, *10*, 63–83.

Barry, H., & Milner, B. (2002). SME's and Electronic Commerce: A Departure from the Traditional Prioritisation of Training? *Journal of European Industrial Training*, *25*(7), 316–326. doi:10.1108/03090590210432660

Brock, J. K. (2000). Information and Communication Technology in the Small Firm. In Jones-Evans, D., & Carter, S. (Eds.), *Enterprise and Small Business: Principles, Practice and Policy* (pp. 384–408). Harlow, England: FT - Prentice Hall.

Brown, D. H., & Lockett, N. (2001). Engaging SMEs in EBusiness: The Role of Intermediaries within eClusters. *Electronic Markets*, *11*(1), 52–58. doi:10.1080/10196780151105429

Brown, D. H., & Lockett, N. (2004). Potential of Critical e-Applications for Engaging SMEs in e-Business: A Provider Perspective. *European Journal of Information Systems*, *13*(1), 21–34. doi:10.1057/palgrave.ejis.3000480

Bunker, D. J., & MacGregor, R. C. (2000). *Small Generation of Information Technology (IT) Requirements for Small/Medium Enterprises (SME's) - Cases from Regional Australia*. Proceedings of SMEs in a Global Economy, Wollongong, Australia.

Buonanno, G., Faverio, P., Pigni, F., Ravarini, A., Sciuto, D., & Tagliavini, M. (2005). Factors Affecting ERP System Adoption: A Comparative Analysis Between SMEs and Large Companies *Journal of Enterprise Information Management*, *18*(4), 384-426.

Chen, J., & Bernard, C. W. (1993). The Impact of Microcomputer Systems on Small Businesses: England, 10 Years Later. *Journal of Small Business Management*, *31*(3), 96–102.

Cragg, P. B., & King, M. (1993). Small-Firm Computing: Motivators and Inhibitors. *Management Information Systems Quarterly*, *17*(1), 47–60. doi:10.2307/249509

Curran, J., & Blackburn, R. (2001). *Researching the Small Enterprise*. Sage Publications.

Daniel, E. M., & Grimshaw, J. (2002). An Exploratory Comparison of Electronic Commerce Adoption in Large and Small Enterprises. *Journal of Information Technology*, *17*(3), 133–147. doi:10.1080/0268396022000018409

Datamonitor. (2004). CRM For Small to Medium Business [Electronic Version] from http://www. datamonitor.com

Dennis, C. (2000). Networking for Marketing Advantage. *Management Decision*, *38*(4), 287–292. doi:10.1108/00251740010371757

DTI (2004). *Business in the Information Age: International Benchmarking Study 2004*. London: Department of Trade & Industry. Retrieved January, 2005

EC. (2003). SME User Guide Explaining the New SME Definition [Electronic Version] from http://ec.europa.eu/enterprise/ enterprise_policy/ sme_definition /index_en.htm.

EC. (2005). The European e-Business Report 2005 [Electronic Version] from http://www.ebusiness-watch.org /key_reports/ synthesis_reports.htm.

EC. (2007). The European e-Business Report 2006/07 [Electronic Version] from http://www. ebusiness-watch.org /key_reports/ synthesis_reports.htm.

Gillian, C., Graham, S., Levitt, M., McArthur, J., Murray, S., & Turner, V. (1999). *The ASPs' Impact on the IT Industry*. IDC Corporation.

Goode, S., & Stevens, K. (2000). An Analysis of the Business Characteristics of Adopters and Non-Adopters of World Wide Web Technology. *Information Technology Management*, *1*(1-2), 129–154. doi:10.1023/A:1019112722593

Grandon, E. E., & Pearson, J. M. (2004). Electronic Commerce Adoption: An Empirical Study of Small and Medium US Businesses. *Information & Management*, *42*(1), 197–216.

Harrison, A. D., Mykytyn, P. P. Jr, & Riemenschneider, K. C. (1997). Executive Decision About Adoption of Information Technology in Small Business: Theory and Empirical Tests. *Information Systems Research*, *8*(2), 171–195. doi:10.1287/isre.8.2.171

Jeyaraj, A., Rottman, J. W., & Lacity, M. C. (2006). A Review of the Predictors, Linkages, and Biases in IT Innovation Adoption Research. *Journal of Information Technology*, *21*(1), 1–23. doi:10.1057/palgrave.jit.2000056

Kuan, K. K. Y., & Chau, P. Y. K. (2001). A Perception-Based Model for EDI Adoption in Small Businesses Using a Technology-Organization-Environment Framework. *Information & Management*, *38*(8), 507–521. doi:10.1016/S0378-7206(01)00073-8

Lang, J. R., & Calantone, R. J. (1997). Small Firm Information Seeking as a Response to Environmental Threats and Opportunities. *Journal of Small Business Management*, *35*(1), 11–23.

Lee, J. (2004). Discriminant Analysis of Technology Adoption Behaviour: A Case of Internet Technologies in Small Businesses. *Journal of Computer Information Systems*, *44*(4), 57–66.

Lockett, N., Brown, D. H., & Kaewkitipong, L. (2006). The Use of Hosted Enterprise Applications by SMEs: A Dual Market and User Perspective. *Electronic Markets*, *16*(1), 85–96. doi:10.1080/10196780500491444

Mehrtens, J., Cragg, P. B., & Mills, A. M. (2001). A Model of Internet Adoption by SMEs. *Information & Management*, *39*(3), 165–176. doi:10.1016/S0378-7206(01)00086-6

Nolan, P., & O'Donnell, K. (1991). Restructuring and the Politics of Renewal: The Limits of Flexible Specialisation. In Pollert, A. (Ed.), *Farewell to Flexibility?* (pp. 158–178). Oxford: Blackwell.

Ordanini, A. (2006). *Information Technology and Small Businesses: Antecedents and Consequences of Technology Adoption.* Cheltenham, UK: Edwaed Elgar.

Poon, S., & Swatman, P. (1999). An Exploratory Study of Small Business Internet Commerce Issues. *Information & Management, 35*(1), 9–18. doi:10.1016/S0378-7206(98)00079-2

Premkumar, G. (2003). A Meta-Analysis of Research on Information Technology Implementation in Small Business. *Journal of Organizational Computing and Electronic Commerce, 13*(2), 91–121. doi:10.1207/S15327744JOCE1302_2

Premkumar, G., & King, W. R. (1994). Organizational Characteristics and Information Systems Planning: An Empirical Study. *Information Systems Research, 5*(2), 75–109. doi:10.1287/isre.5.2.75

Premkumar, G., & Roberts, M. (1999). Adoption of New Information Technologies in Rural Small Businesses. *Omega: The International Journal of Management Science, 27*(4), 467–484. doi:10.1016/S0305-0483(98)00071-1

Ramdani, B., & Kawalek, P. (2007a). *SME Adoption of Enterprise Systems in the Northwest of England: An Environmental, Technological and Organizational Perspective.* Paper presented at the IFIP - Organizational Dynamics of Technology-Based Innovation: Diversifying the Research Agenda, Boston.

Ramdani, B., & Kawalek, P. (2007b). SMEs & IS Innovations Adoption: A Review & Assessment of Previous Research. [Latin American Journal of Management]. *Revista Latinoamericana de Administración, 39*(1), 47–70.

Ramdani, B., & Kawalek, P. (2008). *Predicting SMEs Willingness to Adopt ERP, CRM, SCM & E-Procurement Systems.* Paper presented at the 16th European Conference on Information Systems.

Raymond, L. (2001). Determinants of Website Implementation in Small Businesses. *Internet Research, 11*(5), 411–422. doi:10.1108/10662240110410363

Reich, B. H., & Benbasat, I. (1990). An Empirical Investigation of Factors Influencing the Success of Customer Oriented Strategic Systems. *Information Systems Research, 1*(3), 325–347. doi:10.1287/isre.1.3.325

Riemenschneider, K. C., Harrison, A. D., & Mykytyn, P. P. Jr. (2003). Understanding IT Adoption Decisions in Small Business: Integrating Current Theories. *Information & Management, 40*(4), 269–285. doi:10.1016/S0378-7206(02)00010-1

Swanson, E. B. (1994). Information Systems Innovation Among Organisations. *Management Science, 40*(9), 1069–1092. doi:10.1287/mnsc.40.9.1069

Taylor, M., & Murphy, A. (2004). SMEs and E-Business. *Journal of Small Business and Enterprise Development, 11*(3), 280–289. doi:10.1108/14626000410551546

Venkatesh, V. (2000). Determinants of Perceived Ease of Use: Integrating Control, Intrinsic Motivation, and Emotion into the Technology Acceptance Model. *Information Systems Research, 11*(4), 342–365. doi:10.1287/isre.11.4.342.11872

Walczuch, R., Van Braven, G., & Lundgren, H. (2000). Internet Adoption Barriers for Small Firms in The Netherlands. *European Management Journal, 18*(5), 561–572. doi:10.1016/S0263-2373(00)00045-1

Ward, J., & Peppard, J. (2002). *Strategic Planning for Information Systems* (3rd ed.). West Sussex: John Wiley & Sons.

Westhead, P., & Story, D. J. (1996). Management Training and Small Firm Performance: Why is the Link so Weak? *International Small Business Journal, 14*(4), 13–24. doi:10.1177/0266242696144001

APPENDIX: QUESTIONNAIRE

1. What is the total number of employees?		
☐ (0-9) Employees	☐ (10-49) Employees	☐ (50-249) Employees

2. In which industry does your firm operate?		
	Manufacturing	☐
	Retail/Wholesale	☐
	Services	☐

3. How wide is the market area?			
Local ☐	Regional ☐	National ☐	International ☐

4. What information systems applications has your firm adopted?		
E-mail & Web Access	☐	Buying & Selling Online ☐
Website	☐	Extranet ☐
Intranet	☐	Accounting, Payroll ☐

Overall IS experience:		
Low IT Users ☐	Medium IT Users ☐	High IT Users ☐

5. Which of the following systems does your firm intend to adopt in the next 3 years?

Enterprise Systems	Willing to Adopt (In the next 3 years)
ERP – Enterprise Resource Planning	☐
CRM – Customer Relationship Management	☐
SCM – Supply Chain Management	☐
E-Procurement software	☐
.... Other	☐
I do not intend to adopt any of the mentioned enterprise systems	☐

If you willing to adopt Enterprise Systems in the future, do you intend to adopt a hosted enterprise systems?   Yes ☐   No ☐

This work was previously published in International Journal of E-Adoption, Volume 1, Issue 1, edited by Sushil Sharma, pp. 34-46, copyright 2009 by IGI Publishing (an imprint of IGI Global).

Chapter 5
Determinants of E-Commerce Adoption Among Small and Medium-Sized Enterprises in Malaysia

Sim Chia Hua
Swinburne University of Technology, Malaysia

Modapothala Jashua Rajesh
Swinburne University of Technology, Malaysia

Lau Bee Theng
Swinburne University of Technology, Malaysia

ABSTRACT

With a major proportion of research on Electronic Commerce (EC) undertaken on large corporations, and focused primarily on developed countries, little is known about the determinants of EC in Small and Medium-sized Enterprises (SMEs) of developing nations. This chapter explores the extent of EC use by SMEs, and provides some empirical evidence of how internal factors of firm and owner are influencing EC adoption among smaller businesses in Malaysia. The methodology and results of this study may be applicable to other developing countries. Findings confirm the low level of participation in EC by SMEs. The age of enterprise, as well as the owner's gender and education were found to be significant in determining the level of EC adoption. Though some of the results contradict those of previous studies, they may have a greater implication for government authorities in drawing up guidelines, approaches, and formulating more effective frameworks to promote EC use among SMEs in developing countries.

DOI: 10.4018/978-1-60960-597-1.ch005

INTRODUCTION

The Small and Medium-sized Enterprise (SME) sector plays an important role in the economic development of many countries (Curran & Blackburn, 2001; Simpson & Docherty, 2004). As a major source of income and provider of employment, SMEs account for more than 95 per cent of businesses, generate two thirds of private sector employment (Organisation for Economic Cooperation and Development [OECD], 2005), and contribute between 30 per cent and 70 per cent of the Gross Domestic Product (GDP) of most nations (OECD, 1997). In the United Kingdom, for example, 99.9 per cent of the private sector enterprises are SMEs and they account for 59 per cent of employment in the country (Department for Business Enterprise & Regulatory Reform [BERR], 2007). Similarly, in Malaysia, SMEs form a significant part of the economy, and have evolved to become key suppliers and service providers over the years (United Nations Development Programme [UNDP], Malaysia, 2007). More than 90 per cent of enterprises in Malaysia are SMEs which generate employment for more than half of the work force in the country and contribute 32 per cent to the GDP (Department of Statistics Malaysia, 2005).

With the evolution and widespread use of the Internet, the capability and competitiveness of SMEs have greatly increased. Electronic commerce (EC), in particular, allows buying and selling of products, services, information via computer networks including the Internet (Turban, King, Lee, & Viehland, 2004). Through the use of web sites, email services and web browsers, EC facilitates communication and enables access to large amounts of information. With increased connectivity and flexibility, EC offers new exciting opportunities for firms to improve their business performance (see for example, Tetteh & Burn, 2001). In fact, SMEs are increasingly finding a web presence to be important in building brand/product awareness, and enhancing company im-

age (Gribbins & King, 2004). Others concur that EC brings numerous advantages to firms in terms of lower costs, reduced remittance time, and improved customer service (Wen, Chen, & Hwang, 2001). Through a virtual interactive environment that promotes communication between trading parties, EC also provides SMEs with an effective mechanism for competing with larger organizations worldwide. Hoi, Shim, and Yin (2003) observed that SMEs perceive EC to be beneficial in improving their international exposure and responsiveness. With increased diffusion, EC is expected to remove barriers of culture and national boundaries, leading towards a more unified and globalised economy (Sagi, 2004).

In Malaysia, the SMEs are aware of the importance of Information and Communication Technologies (ICTs) in improving their productivity and business performance (Lim, 2006). However, a review of the literature shows that SMEs in Malaysia have been slow in the uptake of ICTs and EC in particular (Alam, Ahmad, Abdullah, & Ishak, 2007; Alam & Ahsan, 2007; Bolongkikit, Obit, Asing, & Tanakinjal, 2006; Hashim, 2006). In a survey of 12,000 SMEs in the country, only 16 per cent of the firms indicated that they had a web presence, compared to 80 per cent of similar enterprises in Europe and North America (Patrick, cited in UNDP, Malaysia, 2007). Research shows that the slow development of ICTs among Malaysian SMEs may be explained by factors related to technical expertise (Lim, 2006), and security issues (Tan, Chong, Lin, & Eze, 2009). Smaller businesses generally perceive the implementation of ICTs to be risky and technically challenging. Liew (2002) in a study on SMEs concurs that the implementation and maintenance of EC are restricted due to hindrances related to organization, infrastructure and technology.

With limited resources to draw upon, owner-managers of SMEs face a very different world from that of their counterparts in larger enterprises (Beaver, 2007). Due to the dominance of a single owner-manager and factors such as resource constraints, SMEs have their own unique characteristics, and are not simply scaled-down versions of large organizations (Shrader, Mulford, & Blackburn 1989). In many ways, they behave in a distinctly different fashion from their larger counterparts (Hansemark, 1998). However, in the past, considerable research on EC has been conducted on large enterprises or those that are dot.com players. Most of the studies have focused predominantly on SMEs in developed countries. A review on eBusiness/EC research by Parker and Castleman (2007) shows that over half of the journal articles from 2003 to 2006 investigated SMEs in the United Kingdom, United States of America, Australia, Canada and New Zealand. This suggests that there is a need for further study on eBusiness/EC adoption among SMEs in developing countries. While it is important to understand EC in the context of advanced countries, issues faced by SMEs in developing countries may be different from those encountered by their counterparts in developed nations (Elbeltagi, 2007; Sarosa & Underwood, 2005). It is therefore relevant to investigate the issue of EC adoption from the perspective of SMEs in developing economies like Malaysia. In particular, this study aims to fill the knowledge gaps in EC research by attempting to identify some internal factors that are influential in explaining adoption of EC among SMEs in the country.

BACKGROUND

Electronic Commerce

The definitions of E-commerce (EC) are many and varied. The World Trade Organization (WTO) defines EC as "the production, distribution, marketing, sale or delivery of goods and services by electronic means" (Baker & McKenzie, 2001). This basically involves the use of digital devices for gathering information, conducting business communication and ultimately trading with busi-

ness partners. The electronic media involved both 'open' and 'closed' networks like the Internet, the World Wide Web, electronic data interchange (EDI) and intranet. In other words, EC is a concept covering any form of business communication or transaction conducted using ICTs (European Strategic Program on Research in Information Technology, 1997). For the purposes of this study, we have adopted the definition provided by Turban, McLean and Wetherbe (2004) who describe EC as "the process of buying, selling, transferring, or exchanging products, services, and/or information via computer networks, including the Internet". EC is thus not limited to buying and selling of products or services over electronic networks, but is also concerned with transferring or exchanging information and funds such as making orders and payments online.

Small and Medium-Sized Enterprises (SMEs)

There is no one universal definition of an SME. The two common ways of defining SMEs are based on: (i) the financial turnover, and (ii) the number of employees (Curran & Blackburn, 2001). The main criterion that OECD countries use for statistical purposes is the number of persons employed (OECD, 2004). This criterion is considerably more transparent, and objective (Curran & Blackburn, 2001). As in the European Union, the most frequent upper limit designating an SME is 250 employees (OECD, 2005). In Malaysia, SMEs are also defined based on the annual sales turnover and number of full-time employees (National SME Development Council [NSDC], 2005). In general, the Small and Medium Industries Development Corporation (SMIDEC) of Malaysia defined SMEs as enterprises with annual sales turnover not exceeding MYR25 million[1], and full-time employees not more than 150 (cited in UNDP, Malaysia, 2007). For the purposes of this study, the number of employees was adopted as the basis for the definition of an SME, in line with small business research (Analoui & Karami, 2003; Cragg & King, 1993; Smith, 1998). An SME is hereby identified as a firm employing not more than full-time employees 150, and registered under the Malaysian Companies Act 1965 (NSDC, 2005).

RESEARCH OBJECTIVES

The literature shows that there is a number of overlapping divergent models that have been used to predict the decision by SMEs to adopt Internet/EC in Malaysia. Most of the prior studies have attempted to examine the perceived characteristics of the innovation that can potentially explain the Internet/EC adoption rate in the country. For example, perceived usefulness, perceived ease of use, and social influence have been identified as influential in explaining the decision to adopt broadband Internet in Malaysia (Dwivedi, Selamat, Abd Wahab, Mat Samsudin, & Lal, 2008). Other studies found relative advantage, compatibility, complexity, observability, and security issues to be significant in predicting internet-based ICT adoption among SMEs in the country (Tan et al., 2009). In another research to examine the factors affecting EC adoption among electronic manufacturing companies, results suggest that relative advantage and compatibility have significant positive impact on EC adoption in Malaysia, whereas complexity and security were reported to have negative effects (Alam, Khatibi, Sayyed Ahmad, & Ismail, 2007). This is confirmed by Hussin and Mohamad Noor (2005) in a study on CEOs/managers of Malaysian SMEs in the manufacturing sector. Results concur that perceived relative advantage, complexity, and observability significantly affect the adoption of EC. In addition, the study found evidence that the CEO's commitment towards Information Technology (IT) impacted the decision to adopt EC.

Other studies have examined the influence of owner characteristics in explaining the decision to adopt technology in the country. Ramayah,

Dahlan, Mohamad, and Siron (2002) used the Technology Acceptance Model (TAM) along with demographic variables such as gender and educational level of owner-managers to examine technology usage among SME owner-managers in Malaysia. In another study, Jantan, Ismail, Ramayah, and Mohamed Salehuddin (2001) analysed how CEO's characteristics affect the adoption of Advanced Manufacturing Technology among small and medium scale manufacturing industries in the country. Further, Dahlan, Ramayah, and Koay (2002) investigated how individual demographic variables like gender influence the level of data mining readiness within the Malaysian banking industry. Other similar research conducted in the South East Asian region include Teo (2001) who examined the impact of motivational and demographic variables (such as age, gender and education level) on Internet usage.

As this chapter represents a preliminary study of a series of research on the determinants, perceived benefits and barriers of EC use by SMEs, no emphasis is given to the technical aspects or detailed issues surrounding EC adoption. Instead, this study focuses on investigating organisational issues and characteristics of owners involved in the introduction and use of EC. In short, it is an attempt to provide a broader view of the effect of owner and firm characteristics on EC deployment, in the context of SMEs in a developing country.

Alzougool and Kurnia (2008) in a review of EC determinants among SMEs identified various factors that have been studied in developed and developing countries, and classified them into different dimensions. The review shows that the impact of owner's characteristics such as gender, age and educational level have been investigated in the developed world (Chuang, Nakatani, Chen, & Huang, 2007), but not in the developing countries. For SMEs, the decision whether to adopt EC is usually made by the owner-manager, who is often the founder of the firm. As pointed out by Beaver (2007), there is little separation of ownership and control in smaller businesses, and that all corporate

Table 1. EC Adoption by SMEs: Contradictory findings on organisational factors (Adapted fromAlzou-gool & Kurnia, 2008)

Determinants	Context	Significant findings	Insignificant findings
Organisational size & business category	Developed countries	Ling (2001) Zhu & Kraemer (2005) Zhu, Kraemer, & Xu (2003)	Al-Qirim (2007) Chuang, Nakatani, Chen, & Huang (2007) Sparling, Toleman, & Cater-Steel (2007)
	Developing countries	Huy & Filiatrault (2006)	Jeon, Han, & Lee (2006)
Business age	Developed countries		Chuang, Nakatani, Chen, & Huang (2007)
	Developing countries	Hinson & Abor (2005)	

and functional strategies are the concerns of the founder and owner-manager of the enterprise. This is confirmed by Thong and Yap (1995) that CEO's characteristics are important factors in predicting IT adoption by small businesses. It is therefore relevant to investigate how owners' characteristics are influencing adoption of EC among SMEs in a developing economy.

On the other hand, the effects of business attributes like organisational size, category and business age have been studied in both developed and developing nations, but no consistent findings reported (Table 1).

MacGregor and Vrazalic (2008) in another review summarized the business characteristics which have been shown to have an impact on the adoption of EC by SMEs (see Table 2).

From the literature on the effects of business characteristics on EC and prior research on how demographic variables of owner can possibly influence the usage of technology, several determinants are proposed, and arguments provided as to why these variables might play a role in explaining the decisions to adopt EC. Specifically, this study aims to explore the current level of EC adoption by SMEs, and identify which of the attributes of firm and owner is/are influential in explaining the adoption of EC among SMEs in the country.

Table 2. Business characteristics affecting EC adoption by SMEs (Adapted from MacGregor & Vrazalic, 2008)

Business characteristics	Reported by
Business size (number of employees)	Blackburn & Athayde (2000) Fallon & Moran (2000) Matlay (2000)
Age of the business (length of time in operation)	Kai-Uwe Brock (2000) MacGregor, Vrazalic, Carlsson, Bunker, & Magnusson (2002)
Business sector	BarNir & Smith (2002) Blackburn et al. (2000) MacGregor et al. (2002) Matlay (2000) Schindehutte & Morris (2001)

RESEARCH HYPOTHESES

Business Attributes

The introduction of EC into an SME could be affected by features of the firm itself such as its age, size, and nature of business. Prior research shows that the adoption of innovative information systems by an SME in a developing economy is heavily dependent on organisational characteristics such as firm size (Dasgupta, Agarwal, Ioannidis, & Gopalakrishnan, 1999). Teo and Tan (1998) in another study on Internet adoption in Singapore also note that technology adoption can be analyzed according to the physical characteristics of a business. This is supported by Blackburn and Athayde (2000) who show that the adoption of EC technology is associated with business characteristics such as firm size and business type. On the other hand, other studies found contradictory results. Seyal and Rahman (2003) in a research on EC adoption among SMEs in a South East Asian country concluded that organizational characteristics do not have an influential impact on EC adoption. Others noted that firm size had no bearing on implementation of Internet Commerce/EC by SMEs in South Italy (Scupola, 2003), and Canada (Sparling, Toleman, & Cater-Steel, 2007).

Nature of business: Firms in different business sectors have different information processing needs, which in turn affect the adoption of technology (Yap, Soh, & Raman, 1992). It appears that industries with higher information content (such as services) are more likely to adopt IT than those with less information content (such as mining or manufacturing) (Yap, 1990). The impact of business sector is expected to affect EC in a similar manner as with other technologies. Blackburn and Athayde (2000), and Matlay (2000) show that the type of business in which a firm operates is significantly associated with EC adoption. These studies conclude that service organisations tend to adopt EC more than any other industries. It can

therefore be predicted that a tourism enterprise, for example, is more likely to employ EC in its business process than a firm in cement manufacturing or coal mining. Given that EC adoption might be affected by the nature of business activities, it is hypothesized that (H1): the degree to which SMEs adopt EC differs across business sectors.

Size of enterprise: Firm size has often been viewed as one of the important determinants affecting the adoption of new technologies. Prior studies consistently show significant links between business size and the adoption of IT (Chuang, Rutherford & Lin, 2007; Frambach & Schillewaert, 2002; Tiessen, Wright, & Turner, 2001), and the Internet (Fallon & Moran, 2000; Teo & Tan, 1998). Research suggests that as firm size grows, coordination becomes more complicated, and the need for information processing increases. Hence, firms with larger scale of operations are more likely to use IT than smaller firms (Yap, 1990). The impact of firm size is expected to affect EC use in a similar manner as with other technologies. As shown by Huy and Filiatrault (2006), size of the enterprise affects the adoption of EC among SMEs in Vietnam, whereas Matlay (2000) concurs that smaller businesses in the British economy are less likely to adopt EC than larger SMEs. Given that EC applications involve substantial investment in financial, human resource and technological aspects, larger firms which tend to be more resourceful, are more likely to adopt the technology. Small enterprises, on the other hand, often lack resources and face financial constraints (Thong, 1999); therefore they tend to be more cautious with technology adoption. Hence, it is hypothesized that (H2): the extent of EC deployment varies depending on the size of the SMEs.

Age of enterprise: Studies have also shown that EC adoption may be affected by the age of the business (Blackburn & Athayde, 2000; Schindehutte & Morris, 2001). As noted by Daniel, Wilson, and Myers (2002), SMEs which had been in business for a longer period of time were less likely to use EC. The reason might lie with the fact that EC is an innovation to a business. Older businesses with long established rules, procedures and practices tend to be more resistant to change. The long-accepted work norms in established organizations are likely to result in conservative ideas and traditional approaches, and this prohibits the widespread use of EC in business operations. Hence, it is hypothesized that (H3): the involvement of SMEs in EC differs with regards to the age of the enterprise.

Demographic Features of Owners

It is well established that research on SMEs includes an analysis on the roles of the owner-manager. This is attributable to the unique characteristics of SMEs where the business is mostly controlled by a small management team with strong owner influence and centralized power (Reynolds, Savage, & Williams, 1994). As the decision maker, the owner-manager of a SME is inevitably the key person to recognize the relevance and potentials of EC and to adopt it. Bunker and MacGregor (2000) confirm that IT decisions in SMEs are usually made by the owner (cited in MacGregor, 2004). Other research on small businesses also identified a significant link between the gender of the CEO and the level of EC adoption (Mazzarol, Volery, Doss, & Thein, 1999). Age and level of education of the CEO, however, were found to be unrelated.

Age of owner: Prior research has shown that the elderly have a tendency to resist change (Baggozi & Lee, 1999), including changes in work situations and relocation (Kasteler, Gay, & Caruth, 1968; Pollman & Johnson, 1974). Other studies further confirm that the elderly tend to resist adoption of innovation or new technologies (Robertson, 1971; Uhl, Anrus, & Poulson, 1970). This resistance to change could be attributable to the risk-taking attitudes of an individual. Wiersema and Bantel (1992) argue that people's flexibility may decline, and rigidity increase, as they age.

Hence, risk-taking propensity is likely to be lower among older owner-managers. In fact, Xiao, Al-habeeb, Hong, and Haynes (2001) show that age has an impact on risk-taking attitudes and behavior among business owners. In strategic choices made by CEOs, it is observed that the younger ones tend to pursue risky and innovative strategies (Grimm & Smith, 1991; Hambrick & Mason, 1984), and are more positive toward EC (Hunter & Kemp, 2004). Further, research shows that the young to middle-aged have an advantage with respect to technology adoption (Hoffman, Novak, & Schlosser, 2000). Compared to the older generation, young owner-managers tend to be equipped with better education and technical knowledge (Bantel & Jackson, 1989), and hence are more likely to appreciate the potential of innovations like EC. It is therefore proposed that (H4): the extent of EC adoption differs significantly according to the age of the owner-managers.

Gender of owner: Research indicates that gender affects the use of technology like the Internet (Sexton, Johnson, & Hignite, 2002), and EC (Uzoka, Seleka, & Khengere, 2007). Men were reported to make more frequent use of technological products than women (Hoffman et al., 2000). For example, male and female Internet users engage in online activities at different rates. Despite increased awareness and popularity of the Internet, Akhter (2003) observes that men, as consumers, are still more likely to use the Internet for shopping than women. The rationale might lie with the fact that significant differences exist between men and women with respect to the aversion or propensity to risk (Slovic, 1966), and technology in general (Brunner & Bennett, 1998). It is generally believed that risk-averse behavior of women is likely to result in lower rates of technology adoption, especially in developing countries although Ogunlana (2004) argues that women easily adopt innovations that can enhance their economic status. As EC is a special application of IT, it is hypothesized that (H5): the adoption of

EC differs significantly according to the gender of the owner-managers.

Education level of owner: The level of formal education attained by the owner-managers has also been identified to be associated with IT adoption by SMEs (Chuang, Rutherford, & Lin, 2007). Owner-managers with some forms of higher education are likely to generate more creative and innovative solutions in business operations. Hoffman et al. (2000) note that the adopters of IT products like computers and electronic banking tend to have higher levels of education. Hambrick and Mason (1984) add that insufficient education can be an important hindrance to the adoption of new technology. It is believed that owner-managers with some form of higher education tend to have more awareness and understanding of the potential and value of innovations like EC. This is supported by Tabor (2005) who notes that skills beyond simple IT experience are required for successful implementation of EC. Hence, it is proposed that (H6): a firm's involvement in EC varies with the education level of the owner-managers.

METHODOLOGY

Data Collection

The samples of this study were selected from the business directory of the SME Info Portal, which is accessible through the website of the Small and Medium Industries Development Corporation (SMIDEC) of Malaysia. Eight hundred firms were randomly selected from the directory to be surveyed. A questionnaire-based survey of local SMEs was carried out. The questionnaire was checked for content validity with the assistance of academics from both business and IT disciplines. This led to revising and rewording of some items. The revised questionnaire was pilot tested on a sample group. Recommended changes were incorporated into the survey before final distribution. Data collection was performed in two stages. The owner-managers of the selected firms were identified from the directory, and contacted via telephone. To give the subjects a clear understanding of the survey, they were provided with a simplified definition of EC, and an overview of the research aims and design of the survey instrument. Upon receiving the consent from the owner-manager, a cover letter and the questionnaire were sent to them by fax or email. In total, three hundred and thirty four questionnaires were obtained, yielding a response rate of 41 per cent. The response rate is comparable to similar Information Systems (IS) studies on how business characteristics influence adoption of Internet technology (Goode & Stevens, 2000). Due to incomplete data in some questionnaires, only three hundred and twenty nine fully completed responses were used for analysis.

Design of Instrument

The questionnaire consisted of three sections. Section A collects the data about the demographic profile of an SME, covering organizational characteristics, i.e. type, size and age of the business. Business type was categorized in accordance with the definition of the National SME Development Council of Malaysia which groups SMEs into manufacturing, mining and quarrying, services, construction and primary agriculture. As mentioned earlier, the number of employees was used as a measure for the size of an enterprise. The age of a firm was determined using the number of years since the business was in existence. Section B consisted of questions on the managerial profile, i.e. the owner's gender, age in years and education level. Section C measures the extent of EC adoption by SMEs. As identified by Pricewaterhousecoopers (PWC) at the Asia Pacific Economic Cooperation forum (PWC, 1999), the EC capabilities of an SME were measured in four levels as in Table 3.

Table 3. EC capabilities of an SME

Level 1	SME with very basic or no EC capabilities
Level 2	SME with a website but does not carry out online transactions
Level 3	SME takes orders and provides customer service on its website
Level 4	SME completes transactions and receives payment via its website

RESULTS

Sample Characteristics

Results indicated that the majority of the respondents (82 per cent) were from the service industry. This is consistent with the conclusion of Normah (2006) that most of the SMEs in Malaysia are in the service sector, accounting for 86 per cent of total businesses in the country. In terms of size, slightly more than three-fifths (62 per cent) of the respondents were from businesses that had 5 to 50 full-time employees, which are rather small-sized SMEs. In relation to the length of time in business, slightly more than half (52 per cent) of the firms surveyed indicated that they had been operational for more than 10 years. This suggests that the SMEs in this study were more experienced businesses. Only 18 per cent of the firms surveyed were young enterprises which had been operational for less than 5 years.

In terms of owners' characteristics, about three-fifths (58 per cent) of the respondents indicated that they were 45 years or above. Only 14 per cent of them were young entrepreneurs aged below 35. Despite a random selection of sample, the great majority of owner-managers were male (81 per cent). This suggests that females in the country are not playing a key role in owning and managing businesses; or that males tend to show more positive response in IS survey than females. As for the level of education of the owner-managers, about two-thirds (69 per cent) of the owner-managers surveyed had some form of professional qualification. Of this, slightly more than half were bachelor degree or postgraduate degree holders,

while another half were professional certificate or diploma holders. This indicates that the results throughout this study were made by 'informed' respondents.

Analysis and Discussion

Slightly more than three quarters of the respondents (77 percent) indicated that they use computers and Internet connection in daily business operation. Of this, nearly half (47 percent) owned a website but less than one quarter (22 per cent) of them took orders, completed transactions and received payment on their websites. The findings confirm the low level of participation in EC by local SMEs. Instead, SMEs in the country place greater preference on the more familiar regional and international trade shows (UNDP, Malaysia, 2007) to promote their products and services, rather than on EC which could further enhance their competitiveness in the global market. An analysis of ANOVA showed that each level of the EC adoption differs significantly from the total of extent of adoption (Table 4). None of these stages overlapped with one another; hence the model chosen for the study proved satisfactory. This is confirmed by the graphs depicted

Table 4. ANOVA

	F	Sig.
Level 1	4843.909	.000*
Level 2	282.728	.000*
Level 3	273.776	.000*
Level 4	1665.475	.000*
*significant at 0.05 level		

Figure 1. a) Level 1 of EC adoption Vs Degree of EC adoption; b) Level 2 of EC adoption vs Degree of EC adoption; c) Level 3 of EC adoption Vs Degree of EC adoption; d) Level 4 of EC adoption Vs Degree of EC adoption

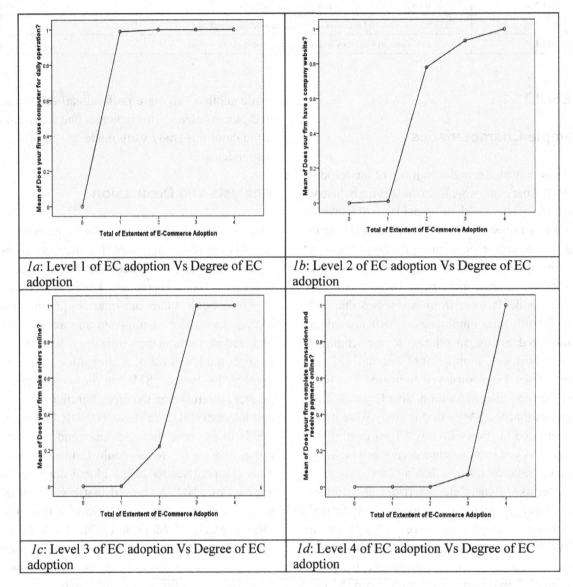

1a: Level 1 of EC adoption Vs Degree of EC adoption

1b: Level 2 of EC adoption Vs Degree of EC adoption

1c: Level 3 of EC adoption Vs Degree of EC adoption

1d: Level 4 of EC adoption Vs Degree of EC adoption

in Figure 1. In particular, Figure 1(d) is a clear inverse replica of Figure 1(a) with no graphical overlapping between the varying levels and the total of extent of adoption.

Further, correlation was performed to measure the relationship between the total extent of EC adoption with each stage of EC adoption. The total of extent of EC adoption in relation to each stage is highly correlated (Table 5). Overall, the results indicate the greater the degree of adoption, the greater the relationship is (+0.07), i.e., the correlation (*r*) increased from level 1 to level 2, and dropped only marginally in level 3.

Table 5. Level of EC adoption Vs. total of extent of EC adoption

	Correlation
Does your firm use the computer and internet for daily operations?	.682**
Does your firm have a company website?	.796**
Does your firm take orders online?	.794**
Does your firm complete transactions and receive payment online?	.725**
** Significant at 0.10 level	

Business Attributes

When analysed with the Chi-square test, the hypothesis (H1) that EC adoption differs across business sectors is supported (p = .09). Among the different types of businesses, the service sector was found to be more likely to adopt EC than manufacturing or agriculture-based SMEs. The result supports the findings of prior research that the decision to adopt EC is significantly associated with the nature of business activities (Matlay, 2000; Schindehutte & Morris, 2001). It is, however, contrary to the findings of Seyal and Rahman (2003); Sparling et al., 2007) who concluded that type of business had no bearing on the adoption of EC. The significant impact of business type on EC adoption could be due to the fact that 21 per cent of the respondents are operating in the mining/construction sector. As compared to services and manufacturing firms,

owner-managers in the mining and construction industries might have not perceived the relevance and value of EC as highly as their counterparts in the other two industries do.

The Chi-square test also shows that the size of enterprise (H2) is significant at the 0.10 level ($\chi2$ = 19.061, d.f = 12, p-value <.087). The result is line with some of the prior research in EC adoption (Huy & Filiatrault, 2006; Uzoka et al., 2007), but contradicts others (Scupola, 2003; Seyal & Rahman, 2003). The finding shows that the degree of EC adoption was greater for larger-sized SMEs. It supports the rationale that having more resources leads to greater EC utilisation. Further, results indicate that the age of the enterprise (H3) is significant at the 0.05 level ($\chi2$ = 26.683, d.f = 16, p-value <.045). The findings support earlier studies (Blackburn & Athayde, 2000; Schindehutte & Morris, 2001) that business age plays an influential role in the decision to adopt EC. The degree

Table 6. EC adoption – Chi-square results

Influence of variables on the extent of EC adoption	Chi-square (p-value)
Nature of Business	.09**
Size of enterprise	.087**
Age of enterprise	.045*
Owner's Age	N.S.
Owner's Education Level	.000*
* Significant at 0.05 level	
** Significant at 0.10 level	
N.S. Not significant	

of EC adoption was lower for firms which had been in business for 20 years or more. This suggests that older businesses with long established rules, procedures and practices might be more resistant to change, which in turn, prohibits the widespread use of EC. The results of Chi-square tests are summarized in Table 6.

Demographic Features of Owners

The hypothesis regarding the effect of owner's age (H4) on the extent of EC adoption is not supported. This result confirmed the findings of Chuang, Nakatani, et al. (2007) that owner's age does not influence the extent of EC adoption in SMEs. It is, however, contrary to the finding of Morris and Ventakesch (2000) that age plays an important role in influencing technology adoption. In this study, there was no significant difference between the older and younger entrepreneurs in terms of EC employment. This could be due to the growing popularity and awareness of EC among various age groups. When the perceived benefits outweigh the cost, owners opt to employ the technology regardless of their age, hence lessening the effect of the variable on the extent of EC adoption.

In contrast, an analysis with the T-test reveals that the owner's gender (p-value = 0.089) is significant on the extent of EC employment. The mean score indicates that greater preference of EC comes from male owners. This supports Hypothesis 5 that males are more open to EC as business owners because they are more willing to adopt the technology as consumers (Akhter, 2003). The findings concur with those of earlier research that that gender affects technology usage (Venkatesh & Morris, 2000; Teo & Lim, 2000), and the intention and ability to adopt EC (Uzoka et al., 2007). On the other hand, the Chi-square test shows that the owner's education level (H6) is significant at 0.05 level ($\chi 2 = 46.722$, d.f = 16, p<.00) (see Table 6). The result is consistent with the finding of Chuang, Rutherford, and Lin

(2007) that owner's education is a significant predictor of IT adoption in SMEs. However, it contradicts with MacGregor and Vrazalic (2008) who found no associations between the level of the CEO's education and EC adoption in SMEs. In this study, owner-managers with a diploma or degree demonstrated a greater extent of EC employment in their business. This supports the rationale that owner-managers with some form of higher education are more likely to recognize and appreciate the values of EC.

CONCLUSION

This study is the first step in a series of research projects that aim at understanding and predicting the adoption of EC technology by SMEs in Malaysia. Owner-managers in this study were informed respondents, with two-thirds of them holding some form of higher qualification. The great majority of them were male, and nearly three-fifths of the respondents were mature and experienced owner-managers aged 45 years and above. They were from the more experienced businesses, which had been operational for more than 10 years. The great majority of the firms surveyed operated in the service industry, with full-time employees not exceeding 50. It was found that three quarters of the firms possessed basic EC applications such as computers and internet connection. However, less than one quarter of them took orders, completed transactions and received payment electronically. The findings confirm the low level of participation in EC by Malaysian SMEs.

Further, the study provides some empirical evidence of the effects of firm and owner attributes on EC adoption by SMEs in the country. Findings on organizational attributes conformed to the features of a developing economy. The age of the enterprise significantly influenced EC employment. The degree of EC adoption was lower for older businesses which had been operational for 20 years or more, implying that older firms with long established rules, procedures and practices might be more resistant to change, which in turn, prohibits the widespread use of EC. Additionally, the degree of EC adoption was greater for larger-sized SMEs. This lends support to the rationale that big firms which tend to be more resourceful are more likely to adopt EC. The findings further confirmed that firms in the service industry were more likely to adopt EC than manufacturing or agriculture-based enterprises. On the influence of owner's attributes, results suggest that gender of owner-manager significantly influenced the extent of EC adoption. A greater preference for EC came from male owner-managers, implying that they might be more open to EC compared to their female counterparts. Additionally, the owner's education level had a significant influence on adoption of EC. Owner-managers with some form of higher qualification seemed to appreciate the value of EC more, and demonstrated a greater deployment of EC in their business. Contrary to prior research, owner's age did not influence the extent of EC adoption. No significant difference was found between the older and younger entrepreneurs in terms of EC employment.

LIMITATIONS OF STUDY

The study focuses on analysing the adoption of E-commerce by SMEs. However, no single definition exists that is universally acceptable for the terms 'E-commerce' or 'SME'. The lack of a single definition for both E-commerce and SME makes comparisons with other studies difficult. Further, the measure of E-commerce adoption extent was created based on the 'Four levels of SME E-commerce capabilities' model (PWC, 1999). With the evolving nature of technology, this model may not be the most accurate reflection of E-commerce behaviour among SMEs. In an exploratory case study using the same staged model, Scupola (2003) argues that the model does not incorporate some of the issues confronting firms

as they proceed to higher levels of E-commerce capability/activity. In particular, it does not take into consideration changes in a firm's capabilities and business processes as it progresses from one stage to the next stage of EC capability/activity (Scupola, 2003). Further, the study is conducted through a survey, and only those interested in the study were likely have responded (Sohal & Ng, 1998). As data was gathered across various business industries, it is not possible to make any sector-specific conclusions.

IMPLICATIONS AND FUTURE RESEARCH

It is hoped that the findings of the study would enrich the IS adoption literature, and provides more insights into EC adoption by SMEs in developing countries. The results may have a greater implication for government authorities responsible in promoting EC adoption and utilization. Given the unique context of SMEs, such an understanding could be useful for governments in drawing guidelines, approaches, and formulating more effective frameworks to promote SME-EC development. It appears that owner's attribute like education drive the adoption and utilisation of EC among smaller businesses in the country. Government agencies, for example, could intensify their efforts to organise seminars or training courses to better equip owner-managers with knowledge of EC, and create a more innovative culture among smaller firms. IT consultants and vendors can direct their marketing efforts at firms which are more likely to adopt EC such as younger enterprises and those operating in the service industry. Future studies may place greater emphasis on developing countries to examine SMEs in different geographic areas, and provide some insights on the factors influencing EC adoption from a cross-country perspective. More comprehensive, prescriptive research could be conducted on a longitudinal approach in terms of case studies.

REFERENCES

Akhter, S. H. (2003). Digital divide and purchase intention: Why demographic psychology matters? *Journal of Economic Psychology*, *24*(3), 321–327. doi:10.1016/S0167-4870(02)00171-X

Alam, S. S., Ahmad, I., Abdullah, Z., & Ishak, N. A. (2007). ICT usage in SMEs: Empirical study of service sectors in Malaysia. In *Proceedings of the 4th SMEs in a Global Economy Conference*, Shah Alam, Malaysia.

Alam, S. S., & Ahsan, M. N. (2007). ICT adoption in Malaysian SMEs from services sectors: Preliminary findings. *Journal of Internet Banking and Commerce, 12*(3). Retrieved May 12, 2009, from http://www.arraydev.com/ commerce/ jibc/2007-12/ Syed_accepted.pdf

Alam, S. S., Khatibi, A., Sayyed Ahmad, M. I., & Ismail, H. (2007). Factors affecting e-commerce adoption in the electronic manufacturing companies in Malaysia. *International Journal of Commerce and Management, 17*(1/2), 125–139. doi:10.1108/10569210710776503

Alzougool, B., & Kurnia, S. (2008). Electronic commerce technologies adoption by SMEs: A conceptual study. In *proceedings of the 19th Australasian Conference on Information Systems*, Christchurch, New Zealand.

Analoui, F., & Karami, A. (2003). *Strategic Management in SMEs*. London: Thomson Learning.

Baggozi, R., & Lee, K. H. (1999). Consumer resistance to, and acceptance of, innovations. *Advances in Consumer Research. Association for Consumer Research (U. S.), 26*, 218–225.

Baker & McKenzie. (2001). *Doing E-Commerce in Europe*. Hong Kong: Baker and McKenzie.

Bantel, K. A., & Jackson, S. E. (1989). Top management and innovations in banking: Does the composition of the top management team make a difference? *Strategic Management Journal, 10*, 107–124. doi:10.1002/smj.4250100709

Beaver, G. (2007). The strategy payoff for smaller enterprises. *The Journal of Business Strategy, 28*(1), 11–17. doi:10.1108/02756660710723161

Blackburn, R., & Athayde, R. (2000). Making the connection: The effectiveness of Internet training in small business. *Education and Training, 42*(4/5), 289–299. doi:10.1108/00400910010373723

Bolongkikit, J., Obit, J. H., Asing, J. G., & Tanakinjal, G. H. (2006). An exploratory research of the usage level of E-commerce among SMEs in the West Coast of Sabah, Malaysia. *Journal of Internet Banking and Commerce, 11*(2).

Brunner, C., & Bennett, D. (1998). Technology perceptions by gender. *Education Digest*, (February): 56–58.

Chuang, T. T., Nakatani, K., Chen, J. C. H., & Huang, I. L. (2007). Examining the impact of organisational and owner's characteristics on the extent of e-commerce adoption in SMEs. *Int. J. Business and Systems Research, 1*(1), 61–80. doi:10.1504/IJBSR.2007.014770

Chuang, T. T., Rutherford, M. W., & Lin, B. (2007). Owner/manager characteristics, organisational characteristics and IT adoption in small and medium enterprises. *International Journal of Management and Enterprise Development, 4*(6), 619–634. doi:10.1504/IJMED.2007.014985

Cragg, P. B., & King, M. (1993). Small-Firm Computing: Motivators and Inhibitors. *MIS Quarterly, 17*(1), 47–60. doi:10.2307/249509

Curran, J., & Blackburn, R. A. (2001). *Researching the Small Enterprise*. SAGE Production, London.

Dahlan, N., Ramayah, T., & Koay, A. H. (2002). Data mining in the banking industry: An exploratory study. In *Proceedings of the International Conference, Internet Economy and Business,* Kuala Lumpur, Malaysia.

Daniel, E. M., Wilson, H., & Myers, A. (2002). Adoption of E-commerce by SMEs in the UK: towards a stage model. *International Small Business Journal, 20*(3), 253–270. doi:10.1177/0266242602203002

Dasgupta, S., Agarwal, D., Ioannidis, A., & Gopalakrishnan, S. (1999). Determinants of Information Technology adoption: An extension of existing models to firms in a developing country. *Journal of Global Information Management, 7*(3), 30–40.

Department for Business Enterprise & Regulatory Reform of UK. (2007). *Small and Medium Enterprise Statistics for the UK and Regions.* Retrieved May 8, 2009, from http://stats.berr.gov.uk/ed/sme/

Department of Statistics Malaysia. (2005). *Census of Establishments and Enterprises 2003.* The Secretariat, Research & Development Division, Department of Statistics, Federal Government Administrative Centre, Putrajaya, Malaysia.

Dwivedi, Y. K., Selamat, M. H., Abd Wahab, M. S., Mat Samsudin, M. A., & Lal, B. (2008). Examining factors influencing the behavioral intention to adopt broadband in Malaysia. In León, G., Bernardos, A., Casar, J., Kautz (Eds), *Open IT-based innovation: Moving towards cooperative IT transfer and knowledge diffusion* (pp. 325-342). Boston: Springer.

Elbeltagi, I. (2007). E-commerce and globalization: An exploratory study of Egypt. *Cross Cultural Management: An International Journal, 14*(3), 196–201. doi:10.1108/13527600710775748

European Strategic Program on Research in Information Technology. (1997). *ESPRIT and ACTS projects related to Electronic Commerce.* Retrieved May 8, 2009, from http://cordis.europa.eu/ esprit/src/ecomproj.htm

Fallon, M., & Moran, P. (2000). Information Communications Technology (ICT) and manufacturing SMEs. In *Proceedings of the 2000 Small Business and Enterprise Development Conference,* University of Manchester (pp. 100–109).

Frambach, R., & Schillweaert, N. (2002). Organizational innovation adoption: A multi-level framework of determinants and opportunities for future research. *Journal of Business Research, 55*(2), 163–176. doi:10.1016/S0148-2963(00)00152-1

Goode, A., & Stevens, K. (2000). An analysis of the business characteristics of adopters and non-adopters of World Wide Web technology. *Information Technology and Management, 1,* 129–154. doi:10.1023/A:1019112722593

Gribbins, M., & King, R. (2004). Electronic retailing strategies: A case study of small businesses in the gifts & collectibles industry. *Electronic Markets, 14*(2), 138–152. doi:10.1080/1019678 0410001675086

Grimm, C. M., & Smith, K. G. (1991). Management and organizational change: a note on the railroad industry. *Strategic Management Journal, 12,* 557–562. doi:10.1002/smj.4250120708

Hambrick, D. C., & Mason, P. A. (1984). Upper echelons: The organization as a reflection of it's top managers. *Academy of Management Review, 9,* 193–206. doi:10.2307/258434

Hansemark, O. C. (1998). The effects of an entrepreneurship programme on need for achievement and locus of control of reinforcement. *International Journal of Entrepreneurial Behaviour and Research, 4*(1), 28–50. doi:10.1108/13552559810203957

Hashim, N. A. (2006). E-commerce adoption issues in Malaysian SME. In *Proceedings of International Conference on E-commerce (ICoEC)*, Penang, Malaysia.

Hoffman, D. L., Novak, T. P., & Schlosser, A. E. (2000). The evolution of the digital divide: How gaps in Internet access may impact Electronic commerce. *Journal of Computer-Mediated Communication, 5*(3).

Hoi, J., Shim, J. P., & Yin, A. (2003). Current Progress of E-commerce adoption: SMEs in Hong Kong. *Communications of the ACM, 46*(9).

Hunter, K., & Kemp, S. (2004). The personality of E-commerce investors. *Journal of Economic Psychology, 25*(4), 529–537. doi:10.1016/S0167-4870(03)00050-3

Hussin, H., & Mohamad Noor, R. (2005). Innovating business through E-commerce: Exploring the willingness of Malaysian SMEs. Retrieved: March 3, 2009, from http://www.it-innovations.ae/iit005/proceedings/articles /I_4_IIT05_Hussin.pdf

Huy, L. V., & Filiatrault, P. (2006). The adoption of E-commerce in SMEs in Vietnam: A study of users and prospectors. *In Proceedings of the 10th Pacific Asia Conference on Information Systems*, Kuala Lumpur, Malaysia (pp. 1335-44).

Jantan, M., Ismail, N., Ramayah, T., & Mohamed Salehuddin, A. H. (2001). The CEO and AMT adoption in Malaysian small and medium scale manufacturing industries. In *Proceedings of the International Conference on Information Technology*, Lausanne, Switzerland.

Kasteler, J. M., Gay, R. M., & Caruth, M. J. (1968). Involuntary relocation of the elderly. *The Gerontologist, 8*(4), 276–279.

Liew, V. K. (2002). *The Prospect of E-commerce for the Small and Medium Enterprises in Malaysia*. Kuala Lumpur, Malaysia: University of Malaya.

Lim, T. M. (2006). *Outsourcings to ensure successful ICT systems implementation and maintenance*. School of Information Technology, Monash University. Retrieved March 20, 2008, from http://www.infotech.monash.edu.my /news/media.html

MacGregor, R. C. (2004). The role of small business strategic alliances in the adoption of E-commerce in small-medium enterprises (SMEs). Retrieved June 6, 2008, from http://ro.uow.edu.au/cgi/ viewcontent.cgi?article=1303&context=theses

MacGregor, R. C., & Vrazalic, L. (Eds.). (2008). *E-commerce in regional Small to Medium Enterprises*. Hershey, PA: IGI Publishing.

Matlay, H. (2000). Training in the small business sector of the British Economy. In S. Carter & D. Jones (Eds.), *Enterprise and small business: Principles, policy, and practice*. London: Addison Wesley Longman.

Mazzarol, T., Volery, T., Doss, N., & Thein, V. (1999). Factors influencing small business start-ups. *International Journal of Enterpreneurial Behaviour and Research, 5*(2), 48–63. doi:10.1108/13552559910274499

Morris, M., & Ventakesch, V. (2000). Age differences in technology adoption decisions: Implications for a changing work force. *Personnel Psychology, 53*(2), 375–403. doi:10.1111/j.1744-6570.2000.tb00206.x

National SME Development Council of Malaysia. (2005). *Definitions for small and medium enterprises in Malaysia*. Secretariat to National SME Development Council, Bank Negara Malaysia, Kuala Lumpur. Retrieved May 3, 2009, from http://www.smeinfo.com.my/ pdf/sme_definitions _ENGLISH.pdf

Normah, M. A. (2006). *SMEs: Building blocks for economic growth*. Paper presented at the National Statistical Conference, Kuala Lumpur, Malaysia.

Ogunlana, E. A. (2004). The technology adoption behavior of women farmers: The case of alley farming in Nigeria. *Renewable Agriculture and Food Systems, 19*, 57–65. doi:10.1079/RAFS200057

Organisation for Economic Co-operation and Development. (1997). *Globalisation and Small and Medium Enterprises (SMEs).* Paris, France: OECD Publications Service.

Organisation for Economic Co-operation and Development. (2004). *SME Statistics: Towards a more systematic statistical measurement of SME behaviour.* Background report for the 2nd OECD Conference of Ministers Responsible for Small and Medium Enterprises (SMEs), Istanbul, Turkey. Retrieved May 3, 2009, from http://www.oecd.org/dataoecd /6/6/31919286.pdf

Organisation for Economic Co-operation and Development. (2005). *OECD SME and Entrepreneurship Outlook - 2005 Edition.* Paris, France: OECD Publications Service. Retrieved May 3, 2009, from http://www.oecd.org/document /15/0,2340,en_2649_33956792_35096847_1_1_1_1,00.html

Parker, C., & Castleman, T. (2007). New directions for research on SME-eBusiness: Insights from an analysis of journal articles from 2003-2006. *Journal of Information Systems and Small Business, 1*(1), 21–40.

Pollman, A., W., & Johnson, A. C. (1974). Resistance to change, early retirement and managerial decisions. *Industrial Gerontology, 1*(1), 33–41.

Pricewaterhousecoopers (1999). *Asia Pacific Economic Cooperation (APEC): SME Electronic Commerce Study - Final Report September 24, 1999.* Retrieved May 12, 2009, from http://www.apec.org/apec/ publications/free_downloads/1999.MedialibDownload.v1.html ?url=/etc/medialib/ apec_media_library/downloads/working-groups/telwg/pubs /1999.Par.0001.File.v1.1

Ramayah, T., Dahlan, N., Mohamad, O., & Siron, R. (2002). Technology usage among owners/managers of SME's: The role of demographic and motivational variables. In *Proceedings of the 6th Annual Asian-Pacific Forum for Small Business on Small and Medium Enterprises Linkages, Networking and Clustering,* Kuala Lumpur, Malaysia.

Reynolds, W., Savage, W., & Williams, A. (1994). *Your own business: A practical guide to success.* New York: Thomson Learning Nelson.

Robertson, T. S. (1971). *Innovative behavior and communication.* New York: Holt, Rinehart and Winston, Inc.

Sagi, J. (2004). ICT and business in the new economy: Globalization and attitudes towards eCommerce. *Journal of Global Information Management, 12*(3), 44–65.

Sarosa, S., & Underwood, J. (2005). Factors affecting IT adoption within Indonesian SMEs: manager's perspectives. In *Proceedings of the 9th Pacific Asia Conference on Information Systems,* Bangkok, Thailand.

Schindehutte, M., & Morris, M. H. (2001). Understanding strategic adaptation in small firms. *International Journal of Entrepreneurial Behaviour and Research, 7*(3), 84–107. doi:10.1108/EUM0000000005532

Scupola, A. (2003). The adoption of Internet commerce by SMEs in the South of Italy: An environmental, technological and organizational perspective. *Journal of Global Information Technology Management, 6*(1), 52–71.

Sexton, R. S., Johnson, R. A., & Hignite, M. A. (2002). Predicting internet/EC use. *Internet Research: Electronic Networking Application and Policy, 12*(5), 402–410. doi:10.1108/10662240210447155

Seyal, A. H., & Rahman, M. N. A. (2003). A preliminary investigation of E-commerce adoption in small & medium enterprises in Brunei. *Journal of Global Information Technology Management, 6*(2), 6–26.

Shrader, C., Mulford, C., & Blackburn, V. (1989). Strategic and operational planning, uncertainty, and performance in small firms. *Journal of Small Business Management, 27*(4), 45–60.

Simpson, M., & Docherty, A. J. (2004). E-commerce adoption support and advice for UK SMEs. *Journal of Small Business and Enterprise Development, 11*(3), 315–328. doi:10.1108/14626000410551573

Slovic, P. (1966). Risk-taking in children: Age and sex difference. *Child Development, 37*, 169–176. doi:10.2307/1126437

Smith, J. A. (1998). Strategies for start-ups. *Long Range Planning, 31*(6), 857–872. doi:10.1016/S0024-6301(98)80022-8

Sohal, A. S., & Ng, L. (1998). The role and impact of Information Technology in Australian Business. *Journal of Information Technology, 13*, 201–217. doi:10.1080/026839698344846

Sparling, L., Toleman, M., & Cater-Steel, A. (2007). SME Adoption of e-Commerce in the Central Okanagan Region of Canada. *In Proceedings of the 18th Australasian Conference on Information Systems*, Toowoomba, Australia (pp. 1046-1059).

Tabor, S. W. (2005). Achieving significant learning in E-Commerce education through small business consulting projects. *Journal of Information Systems Education, 16*(1).

Tan, K. S., & Chong, S., C., Lin, B., & Eze, U. C. (2009). Internet-based ICT adoption: Evidence from Malaysian SMEs. *Industrial Management & Data Systems, 109*(2), 224–244. doi:10.1108/02635570910930118

Teo, T. S. H. (2001). Demographic and motivational variables associated with Internet usage activities. *Internet Research: Electronic Networking Applications and Policy, 11*(2), 125–137. doi:10.1108/10662240110695089

Teo, T. S. H., & Lim, V. K. G. (2000). Gender differences in Internet usage and task preferences. *Behaviour & Information Technology, 19*(4), 283–295. doi:10.1080/01449290050086390

Teo, T. S. H., & Tan, M. (1998). An Empirical Study of adopters and non-adopters of Internet in Singapore. *Information & Management, 34*, 339–345. doi:10.1016/S0378-7206(98)00068-8

Tetteh, E., & Burn, J. (2001). Global strategies for SME-business: Applying the SMALL framework. *Logistics Information Management, 14*(1-2), 171–180. doi:10.1108/09576050110363202

Thong, J. Y. L. (1999). An integrated model of information systems adoption in small businesses. *Journal of Management Information Systems, 15*(4), 187–214.

Thong, J. Y. L., & Yap, C. S. (1995). CEO characteristics, organizational characteristics and information technology adoption in small business. *Omega International Journal of Management Science, 23*(4), 429–442.

Tiessen, J., Wright, R., & Turner, I. (2001). A model of E-commerce use by internationalizing SMEs. *Journal of International Management, 7*, 211–233. doi:10.1016/S1075-4253(01)00045-X

Turban, E., King, D., Lee, K. J., & Viehland, D. (2004). *Electronic Commerce: A Managerial Perspective*. New Jersey: Pearson Prentice Hall.

Turban, E., McLean, E., & Wetherbe, J. (2004). *Information Technology for management: Transforming organizations in the digital economy*. Hoboken, NJ: John Wiley & Sons.

Uhl, K., Anrus, R., & Poulson, L. (1970). How are laggards different? An empirical inquiry. *JMR, Journal of Marketing Research*, *7*, 51–54. doi:10.2307/3149506

United Nations Development Programme. Malaysia. (2007). *Small and Medium Enterprises: Building an enabling environment*. Retrieved May 12, 2009, from http://www.undp.org.my/uploads /UNDP_SME_Publication.pdf

Uzoka, F. M. E., Seleka, G. G., & Khengere, J. (2007). E-commerce adoption in developing countries: A case analysis of environmental and organizational inhibitors. *International Journal of Information Systems and Change Management*, *2*(3), 232–260. doi:10.1504/IJISCM.2007.015598

Venkatesh, V., & Morris, M. G. (2000). Why don't men ever stop to ask for directions? Gender, social influence, and their role in technology acceptance and usage behavior. *MIS Quarterly*, *24*(1), 115–139. doi:10.2307/3250981

Wen, H. J., Chen, H. G., & Hwang, H. G. (2001). E-commerce web site design: Strategies and models. *Information Management & Computer Security*, *9*(1), 5–12. doi:10.1108/09685220110366713

Wiersema, M. F., & Bantel, K. A. (1992). Top management team demography and corporate strategic change. *Academy of Management Journal*, *35*, 91–121. doi:10.2307/256474

Xiao, J. J., Alhabeeb, M. J., Hong, G. S., & Haynes, G. W. (2001). Attitude toward risk and risk-taking behavior of business-owning families. *The Journal of Consumer Affairs*, *35*(2), 307–325.

Yao, J. D., Liu, C., Xu, X., & Lu, J. (2003). Organizational size: a significant predictor of IT innovation and adoption. *Journal of Computer Information Systems*, *43*(2), 76–82.

Yap, C. S. (1990). Distinguishing characteristics of organizations using computers. *Information & Management*, *18*(2), 97–107. doi:10.1016/0378-7206(90)90056-N

Yap, C. S., Soh, C. P. P., & Raman, K. S. (1992). International systems success factors in small business. *Omega International of Management Science*, *5*(6), 597–609. doi:10.1016/0305-0483(92)90005-R

ENDNOTE

[1] In June 2009, the exchange rate for the Malaysian Ringgit (MYR) is approximately MYR3.54 to USD1.00.

This work was previously published in International Journal of E-Adoption, Volume 1, Issue 4, edited by Sushil Sharma, pp. 1-18, copyright 2009 by IGI Publishing (an imprint of IGI Global).

Chapter 6
Internet Marketing and SMEs

Daniel John Doiron
University of New Brunswick Saint John, Canada

ABSTRACT

Small and medium enterprises (SMEs) have been adopting the internet at a feverish pace. Recent studies have shown that up to 85% of SMEs in industrialized countries have web sites, yet less than half are utilizing these web sites to securely transact with their customers. Consumer media consumption is moving away from traditional media, like newspapers, to the internet. These revelations coupled with the growth of tools and techniques available to support online marketing, make it a perfect time for SMEs to market their web sites and ultimately succeed online. In this chapter we will present and support the hypothesis that SMEs should stop investing in their web site's design and functionality and start investing in efforts to market their web sites online, no matter how lousy their web site may be in comparison to today's standards. With the support of two case studies, illustrating the successful utilization of internet marketing by two very different SMEs, we will relate how a SME can effectively market their web site online. We will also discuss the tools and techniques available to help an SME successfully begin a journey of internet marketing.

INTRODUCTION

Internet marketing can be simply described as marketing or advertising a web site online. This is accomplished through the use of a number of tools and techniques, which are readily available on the internet. These tools tend to be relatively inexpensive and fairly easy to use for any business no matter its size or stature. Why then, aren't more SMEs actively marketing their web sites? The answer partially lies in understanding what motivates an SME to venture into the realm of the internet in the first place, or more importantly, what factors are inhibiting them from initiating this journey. Recent research is shedding important light on this question. With this information in hand, we can

DOI: 10.4018/978-1-60960-597-1.ch006

more readily discuss how SMEs should approach the tremendous opportunity of internet marketing. One thing we know for sure is that the internet is going to play an increasingly important role for all enterprises, big or small, in the way they market their products or services, given the rapid rate at which consumers are transitioning away from traditional media. In fact, media consumption is moving to the internet from more traditional channels at an unprecedented pace. This is good news for SMEs as they are not as disadvantaged when it comes to marketing online, as they have been with more traditional mediums, like television.

Once there is an appreciation that SMEs need to be fully engaged in internet marketing, the question shifts to how they should approach this opportunity. SMEs tend to lean towards spending their limited resources in making more attractive, more functional web sites under the notion that "if my web site is *better* than my competitors then it will attract more potential customers." The pressure to do this can be enormous, driven primarily by the seemingly endless advances in internet (or HTML) technology. This approach bears little fruit and often increases the mystic of internet marketing when few gains are achieved. We will present and support a hypothesis suggesting SMEs should spend all their resources marketing their current web sites, before they undertake any efforts to update or add functionality to their online presence.

We will look at some of the most popular tools and techniques available to help SMEs market their web sites. This will include discussing analytics, search engine optimization, search engine advertising, e-mail and social media marketing.

Throughout the chapter we will reinforce the notion that SMEs need to look at internet marketing from a strategic point of view. Implementing tactical internet marketing initiatives can indeed have short term positive results, but it will be highlighted that a strategic approach to internet marketing is the only way to achieve sustained, long term results.

After reviewing this chapter the reader will better understand why internet marketing can be so attractive to SMEs, how they should approach their engagement with it, and which tools and techniques are available for them to utilize on this transformational journey. Finally, much of what a SME puts into place with regards to its internet marketing must be strategically planned and critically evaluated to achieve the desired result of business growth. .

BACKGROUND

Davis et al (2004, 2005) in their studies of Atlantic Canadian SMEs in both 2004[1] & 2005[2] showed, among other things, that SMEs are adopting the internet at a record pace. However, they identified a large gap in the number of SMEs who have web sites and the number of SMEs who are actually securely transacting on those web sites. Other recent studies of SMEs and internet adoption would support these findings and also suggest that *facilitators* play a primary role in moving SMEs to the internet or to use advanced internet technology. This seems to be true with internet marketing as well. It could even be suggested that Google, in fact, sees their role as *the* facilitator of internet marketing. Google, while profit motivated, has, nonetheless, been primarily responsible for enabling the SME market to engage in internet marketing through the introduction of tools and services like Google Analytics™ and Google Adwords™.

There is no better time than the present for SMEs to close this gap. Media consumption is moving to the internet at a rapid pace, while at the same time the tools and techniques available to help a small business market their web site online are relatively inexpensive to use and increasingly accessible and abundant online.

OPENING CASE STUDY: AIDEN'S DEEP SEA FISHING[3] (WWW.PEIFISHING.COM)

When a family business that is steeped in 50 years of proud history trials a progressive, modern-day internet marketing strategy, new opportunities for growth come to light that can position the company for another 50 years of business success. Aiden's Deep Sea Fishing of North Rustico PEI, Canada is successfully defying a two-year, 25% downturn in the provincial tourism industry by creating a new market of customers through their Google Adword™ advertising campaign. While competitors are forced to cancel tours, or send their boats out without a full complement of customers, Aiden's two boats continue to sail three tours a day, many times at or near capacity.

Aiden's Deep Sea Fishing is owned and operated by Paul and Colleen Doiron, who, in 2005, invested in the development of a website to profile the business, like many other tour operators around the province. Given that Paul's father Aiden, the company founder, was credited with pioneering the deep sea fishing industry in PEI, the company enjoys a solid business reputation amongst the over 40 competitors throughout the province. However, in an effort to attract customers, service or product differentiation in the industry is very difficult, and as such, marketing plays a key role to ensure maximum boat capacity for each of the day's scheduled tours. The competition is stiff: within 20 miles of North Rustico, there are twelve competitors, four of whom offer tours from the same location along the picturesque wharf of North Rustico's inner harbour. The company's reputation serves them well, but a competitive advantage would also provide a critical edge over the competition.

During the website development, the company was able to secure the URL *peifishing.com,* a desirable address that could attract many visitors to their site when searching for a "PEI fishing" experience. While searches amongst MSN and Yahoo portals provided a top-ten search ranking for the company, inquiries on the most popular search engine, Google, did not bring up the new site. In an effort to get Google working for them, the company made the decision to trial one of Google's own offerings – Google Adwords™. The strategy was straight forward: a Google Adwords™ advertisement could drive traffic to their site by giving them a "virtual" number one ranking when customers search one of over 20 keyword phrases. Among other advantages, this will also enable the Google spiders to notice the increased activity to the URL and a higher search engine ranking may be achieved. Today, even when the Adwords™ campaign is paused during the off season, Aiden's Deep Sea Fishing enjoys a "first page" ranking on a Google search for deep sea fishing.

In 2007, the company celebrated its 50th Anniversary, and to mark the occasion, Aiden's offered a prize package promotion to every customer who sailed with them during the season. In completing the ballot, customers responded to the question "Where did you hear about us?" and were asked to include their email address. Valuable insight from the customers' responses was gained. With 39% of customers indicating that a referral was their primary reason for choosing Aiden's, there is no doubt that the business relies on this traditional means of promotion. However, after their first full season with a Google Adword Campaign, 11% of the customer base indicated that they had they had found the company through the internet. This customer segment was an important driver to helping Aiden's succeed in a down market. Given the total cost of the Adword Campaign was less than $200, yet supported a rate of 11% of customers converting to purchase, a significant opportunity exists to expand the customer base and maximize revenues through this highly cost effective, targeted and less labour-intensive effort than some traditional marketing channels.

Aiden's marketing efforts have typically focused on print advertising in a variety of tourism brochures, the selective distribution of their own brochure though partnerships with local accommodation providers and the effective visibility of their onsite signage at the wharf. Road and highway signage, some radio advertising and a link to the provincial tourism website is also a part of the marketing mix. However, like many small businesses, measuring the effectiveness of any individual marketing strategy proves to be difficult, and as such, advertising expenditures are made on some anecdotal information and intuition. During the tourism season of 2007, Aiden's took another step toward better understanding their market by turning on Google Analytics capability within their website. This is a free service offered by Google. The data that is available to Aiden's from tracking its website traffic allows for detailed information such as the number of new and previous customers that are accessing the site, what information customers are most interested in reading, and the hometown from where they are making the inquiry. By their own admission, Paul and Colleen have yet to fully utilize the power and information available through their Google Analytics reports, but through future evaluation, Aiden's will be able to target a prospective new customer base, and even support the level of referrals to the business which represents their largest group of customers. They have already made changes to their website to more efficiently push their prospective customers to their "reservation" page. By setting goals within Analytics they will be able to better understand how users are finding their way to this page.

They started the 2008 tourism season off with an email newsletter campaign which drove a number of online bookings prior to the season opening. Although 2008 was another down year in tourism for PEI, Aiden's saw their online orders almost double. The effectiveness of their internet marketing activities was really starting to pay off. At the end of 2008 they implemented a "fishing blog" and are excited by the prospect of extending their reach to increase their referral business.

Aiden's Deep Sea Fishing has successfully adopted a progressive internet marketing strategy that has provided them with a competitive edge during negative market conditions, which will position them for future seasons of maximum growth in this competitive industry.

THE INTERNET AS A MARKETING TOOL

Many SMEs in today's marketplace have adopted web sites to market their products or services. In fact, in some industrialized countries, up to 85%[4] of SMEs currently have functioning web sites (Davis et al., 2005). The sad anecdote to this, however, is that very few of them are actually transacting online. For the most part, SME's web sites are not really working as sales and marketing tools. One set of benchmark studies in Atlantic Canada, taken from 2004 through to 2007[5] (Davis et al, 2004; Davis et al., 2005; Fleet, 2007), would suggest that only 35% of SMEs currently provide the capability to execute secure transactions online. While this has been climbing at a rate of approximately 10% per year, the overall low adoption of this capability is indicative of how these SMEs view their web sites; as electronic brochures and not as a true opportunity to sell products or services through secure online transactions. Further, the research indicates that only 58.8% of SMEs with web sites are not treating the internet as a true marketing channel. Most SMEs would disagree and suggest the reason they have a web site is to market their products or services and their web sites are functionally designed for this purpose. What, then, does this statement really suggest?

To explore this apparent division in intent versus reality, we would like to propose a simple hypothesis, which is aimed at uncovering the underlying issues and challenges facing SMEs as they attempt to leverage the internet.

SMEs should not spend their efforts and resources enhancing their web site designs or even on enhancements for enabling secure online transactions. Instead, they should spend their efforts and the associated costs on MARKETING their current web sites, no matter the current design.

This notion immediately raises a number of concerns and objections when presented to SMEs. For one, most businesses would think that a *"lousy"* or old web site will not be appealing to their target customers and thus the argument for updating their web sites frequently. Clearly, this argument is strengthened with the move to a more interactive web (Web 2.0) and the popular theory that the internet is changing quickly and businesses have to change with it.

However, there is a powerful argument for another, better approach, whose foundation rests in one of the basic tenants of marketing – understanding your customers! If businesses don't understand their customers' reactions to their web site, how will they know what is or isn't working, and more importantly, what will work. A second driver for this approach is that web sites need to be part of a marketing mix, not an adjunct advertising channel. This notion has not been overwhelmingly adopted in the business community and even less so in the SME sector. Most SMEs do not have a detailed marketing strategy, treating all advertising channels equally as incremental opportunities to sell products or build awareness. SMEs rarely measure the incremental effectiveness of the money spent on advertising and their web sites are no exception. For the most part, web sites are knee jerk reactions to the opportunity to sell products or services outside of traditional selling territory, a way to circumvent traditional distribution channels or utilized because their competitors are also online. The irony is that web sites and customers' interaction with them are infinitely measurable. In fact, understanding customer's interaction with web sites is remarkably easy and for the most part, free. Yes that is right, free! Marketing a web site

is relatively inexpensive and this has been made possible by the explosion of internet marketing capabilities, services and tools, for which any small or large business should thank Google.

The approach which supports the hypothesis is actually quite simple. It goes something like this – promote your web site, regardless of how bad it is against today's current standards, measure what potential customers who respond to this marketing do on the web site, regardless of how much or little time they spend on it, then and only then, make adjustments to the site to *incrementally* improve its effectiveness. The notion of "incrementality" is critical to understand and is somewhat analogous to a "virtual flywheel". The momentum created by a flywheel as it begins to spin is fed back into the underlying propulsion system, which in turn allows it to drive the flywheel even faster. The net effect of this is to use the energy created to create and sustain even more energy. By measuring how customers interact with a web site, any SME can introduce incremental changes based on what they learn and then implement further changes as customer interactions dictate. Through this iterative process any SME can dramatically improve the effectiveness of their web site, as it relates to their business goals; in effect creating a virtual flywheel.

As simple as it sounds, this approach is a hard sell to SMEs. And, to be fair, this approach would not even have been possible a few years ago, given the state of the tools and capabilities available on the internet to market and measure web site effectiveness. However, now is a great time to execute this approach, due mainly to the accessibility of cost effective tools that are exploding at an exponential pace. This has turned the traditional marketing equation on its head and provided a strong argument that if SMEs don't adopt internet marketing as part of their marketing mix, they will quickly fall behind and lose ground to competitors. If you buy into this notion, then the hypothesis isn't really a hypothesis at all; it is a fact of doing business in an internet enabled world.

Figure 1. U.S. media spend[6] (©2007, UNB Saint John. Used with permission.)

	2006	2007	2008	2009
Newspapers	21.4	19.8	18.1	16.8
TV	22.1	20.8	21.2	19.1
Cable Network Television	10.1	10.5	10.5	10.4
Branded Ent. /Product Placement	2.4	3.2	3.9	4.9
Videogame Advertising	0.1	0.2	0.5	0.7
Cinema Advertising	0.3	0.3	0.3	0.4
Terrestrial Radio	9.4	9	8.6	8
Satellite Radio	0.1	0.1	0.2	0.2
Magazines (consumer and business)	18.4	19.3	19.2	19.3
Online / Internet	6.2	7.2	8.4	10.5
Out-of-Home/Place-Based (excl. Cinema)	2.9	3	3.1	3.1
Mobile Advertising	0.2	0.2	0.4	1
Yellow Pages-Print	6.4	6.3	5.8	5.5

There is however, one fundamental tenant which all SMEs must embrace prior to setting out on this journey. It is the creation of a well defined marketing plan, or in the very least, a set of goals and objectives which will drive their internet marketing activities.

INTERNET MARKETING AS PART OF SMES MARKETING MIX?

The 4 P's of marketing, product, pricing, promotion and placement (or distribution) are evolving in today's internet world as a more complex, internet-centric model. This is being driven, in part, by the effectiveness of the internet as a marketing and promotion channel. We need only look at recent trends to better understand what the future holds.

The internet today represents the second most popular media in terms of consumption. In the United States, 21% of "media" consumption currently takes place on the internet, with television at 50% and radio at 20%[3]. With the first internet-savvy generation about to take over the workplace, one can only assume media consumption will continue to move in the internet's favor. The irony is that ad spending in the United States

has the internet projected to be a paltry 10.5% in 2009 as noted in Figure 1; half of its current consumption. However, the rapid decline of relative advertising spending in more traditional channels, like newspapers, is indicative of the inevitable shift to the internet. Plainly, consumers are using it. For businesses, the potential reach of internet advertising solves the traditional richness vs. reach conundrum and most importantly, customer interaction and reactions are measurable and directly attributable to sales.

One way to exemplify the changes the internet is driving is to look at the extreme shift it has imposed on traditional communication models. Figure 2 highlights this shift.

Essentially, communication models have evolved from a push model with the advertisers in control to a pull model with consumers in control. The fundamental differences in these models are highlighted in Figure 3.

All of this would suggest that internet marketing should be included in a firm's marketing mix. However, a more appropriate way to think about the changes being driven by the capacity of internet marketing is that the marketing mix itself needs to evolve to reflect the new marketing re-

Figure 2. Communications model evolution[7] (Adapted from Jarboe, 2007. © 2007, UNB Saint John. Used with permission.)

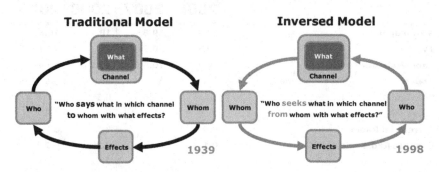

alities brought about by the internet. This is best reflected in Figure 4.

The new marketing mix will take into consideration the broader notions of interactivity and individualization, along with leveraging the new communities of interest that are available only on the internet. The power of communicating with interactive communities, made possible by sites like *Facebook*, exemplifies this notion. *Twitter* is a more recent phenomenon which takes this notion of communities of interest to a real time standard. Imagine launching a product in real time to an expressed group of interested or passionate customers or stakeholders!

An example of the power of utilizing this evolved marketing mix can be illustrated through the case presented at the start of the chapter, Aiden's Deep Sea Fishing. Through a traditional promotion, Aiden's found that 39% of their customers found them through referrals. How could they leverage this new found knowledge? A traditional marketing approach would have led them to a rather expensive promotion or referral program: refer customers and earn a chance to win a prize or a free trip. These kinds of programs are often difficult to execute, where the expensive component isn't the prize, its promoting the promotion.

A SME's marketing plan that embraces an internet marketing mix would address this op-

Figure 3. Old versus digital media

Old Media	Digital Media
One-to-many communication model	One-to-one or many-to-many communication model
Mass-marketing push model	Individualized marketing or mass customization (pull model for web)
Monologue	Dialogue
Branding	Communication
Supply-side thinking	Demand-side thinking
Customer as a target	Customer as a partner
Segmentation	Communities

Figure 4. Evolution of the marketing mix[8] (© 2007, UNB Saint John. Used with permission.)

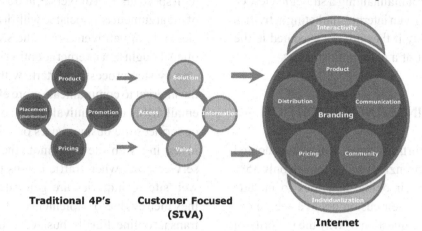

Traditional 4P's   **Customer Focused (SIVA)**   **Internet**

portunity differently. In our example, Aiden's would purchase digital cameras for each of their boats and the captain or crew would take pictures of the customers catching their fish and having fun, much like the photos in Figure 5.

On completion of the trip they would post these pictures on their blog, which is free to build (and host) and linked to their web site. They would encourage their customers to visit their web site and blog to view and download pictures from the trip. This will create an opportunity for their customers to refer their friends, relatives and colleagues to Aiden's through what is called "e-mail viral marketing"- a fancy way of saying they will send an e-mail with a link to the blog to all their friends suggesting they "look at the huge fish my son caught during our visit to PEI!". This is a very effective means of building a rich referral network by taking full advantage of the interactivity of the internet at no cost to the business as your customers are promoting your products or services for you! This represents the evolved internet marketing mix. The incremental costs of this program would be two digital cameras, which have a pay back of one referral. Everything else is free; as it should be on the internet.

The simple message this example highlights is that a marketing mix for an SME needs to properly allow for the opportunities the internet represents. Later in this chapter we will discuss

Figure 5. Fishing & fun with Aiden's Deep Sea Fishing[9]

the importance of maintaining a strategic view of these activities. Even internet marketing activities fizzle out quickly if they are not executed in the broader context of a marketing strategy.

SMEs AND INTERNET ADOPTION

As noted earlier in this chapter, SMEs have adopted the internet at a frenzied pace, although only 35% have evolved their online activities to include transacting with their customers in a secure on-line fashion. The question of why the majority of SMEs have not been more successful in growing their business via the internet can be more easily answered by studying those who have been successful. A study in Atlantic Canada, by Davies & Vladica in 2004, provides some important clues to help answer this question. In this study, they contacted over 450 SMEs through an extensive questionnaire, with the intent to understand the factors affecting e-business adoption. When the data was analyzed for the causal factors affecting success, it presented some startling findings. The measure for success was defined as an SME successfully utilizing e-business, which was more broadly defined as selling online and/or using internet based tools to drive productivity within their businesses. The two most surprising findings of the study were:

1. Having a broadband or high speed internet link into the business had zero causal effect on successful e-business adoption.
2. Having a web site had zero causal effect on successful e-business adoption.

This research suggests that the adoption of a web site or broadband link are not enabling factors in moving SMEs to the next level of e-business effectiveness. This is truly surprising as most industry stakeholders push for the universal availability of these capabilities. Governments around the world are spending billions of dollars to make

high speed internet universal, and a consistent part of the argument is associated with driving efficiencies and competitiveness into the SME sector. It is often thought that internet adoption is a sequential, step by step process that starts with SMEs using the internet to communicate more effectively (via email, MSN or an equivalent) to source products or services the business uses or sells. They then invest in a web site to promote their products or services, and when traffic begins to flow to the web site or inquiries are generated through it, they then evolve to implement the functionality to transact online. Finally, businesses begin to utilize the internet as a core productivity tool through the use of an intranet or CRM system. Well, this sequential process does not hold. It seems there is no link to having a web site and then moving on to more complex e-business type applications.

To better understand this we need to explore the third and most revealing finding from the research:

3. The one major defining factor in driving e-business success, by far, was the presence of a "facilitator".

Facilitators played the defining factor in enabling these SMEs to adopt e-business in their firms. When Davies et al dug a little deeper they found that facilitators are more loosely defined by the SMEs as "someone, from within or outside the firm, who is trusted and understands this crazy internet stuff". A facilitator could be a front desk employee who embraces the internet, a relative with an internet background, or they could be the consultant who helped build the company's web site. The important factor is facilitators are a *trusted* source of knowledge and posses the capability to help the SME wade through the complexity of the internet.

This is an extraordinary piece of information to understand why, or more importantly how, SMEs move to the next level of internet activity. We also believe facilitators to be important catalysts when it comes to helping SMEs build and execute internet marketing strategies as well. This was true in the case of Aiden's Deep Sea Fishing as the owners didn't implement all the internet marketing activities discussed, their cousin did. He was not associated with the business; he and his family owned a cottage nearby where they spent the summer months and they loved to go fishing!

LEVELING THE PLAYING FIELD WITH INTERNET MARKETING

Internet marketing represents a significant opportunity for SMEs, primarily due to the fact that it levels the playing field and in some cases, provides an advantage over larger competitors. So why aren't more SMEs succeeding on the internet today, especially when up to 85% of them have web sites?

One of the challenges for a SME utilizing the internet is the inherent belief that if the site is there, customers will find you. This is the internet communication model discussed earlier; consumers are in control, they instigate finding the business, and if they choose, interact with the company.. However, the complexity starts with how the consumer approaches finding a business. The internet is a very crowded place with more and more businesses turning to it as a marketing and promotion channel, coupled with the fantastic growth of social media. However, this growth area can be a double edge sword. If consumers are spending all of their time on Facebook™, they are not looking for your web site, and thus, SMEs must spend energy and resources attracting customers to their site. This is really what internet marketing is all about. Once a potential customer has found a website, the SME must work diligently in the opportunity to build a relationship with them and eventually close a sale.

The good news surrounding internet marketing, as exemplified in the case studies presented in this chapter, is that it can be inexpensive and very effective. The best and cheapest way to have

a potential customer find an SME's web site is through effective search placement, which is the practice of ensuring the SME's website appears on the first page of a Google search. If the company's web site can achieve this kind of search placement against the important key words for their product or service, they will drive traffic to their web site. While this is ideal, it is also very hard to achieve. Search Engine Optimization is an art and a very complex one at that. An easier way to drive traffic to a web site is through pay-per-click (PPC) advertising. Google's PPC product is called Adwords™. This tool entails paying for small text based ads which typically present on the right hand side of a search page. This service offering is the bread and butter of Google's $21.8B U.S[10]. in revenue and represents the majority of internet marketing spending by companies ("Google Investor Relations," 2008). The good news for SMEs is that the service is simple to engage and very cost effective as Google only charges for the click-throughs[11] to a business's web site that were generated from the advertisement. As such, the SME is effectively only paying for a somewhat qualified lead.

Once a customer "finds" a SME's web site, the focus should be to convert them to a paying customer. The most important tool to help achieve this is the deployment of *analytics*. This is the art of measuring what customers are doing on a web site. Google's product, called Google Analytics™, is free and discussed at greater length later in this chapter.

These tools support the hypothesis presented at the beginning of the chapter, that SMEs should essentially spend all of their available resources directing potential customers to their web site and then measure what they are doing on the site, prior to making adjustments. Studying customer usage and behavior patterns will allow SMEs to make informed decisions as to what changes will be most effective for their website.

The important message here is that internet marketing is not difficult to execute, it is relatively

Figure 6. Internet marketing at a glance[13] (© 2007, UNB Saint John. Used with permission.)

- **Search engine marketing**
- **Search engine optimization**
- **Social media marketing**
- **Display advertizing**
- **E-Mail marketing**
- **Blog marketing**
- **Mobile marketing**
- **In-game (in-world) marketing**
- **Widget marketing**
- **Viral marketing (Word-of-mouse)**
- **Online PR**

inexpensive and in some cases free. This gives SMEs an opportunity to more directly compete with larger competitors. Historically, this was not possible within the confines of traditional media, as only the large companies could afford to fund media placement in channels such as television for example. SMEs were effectively shut out of this marketing channel, or those that tried, did so with relatively poor results; remember those car dealer commercials of yesteryear! Thus, only larger companies had access to powerful marketing channels with broad reach that deployed rich messages while SMEs were relegated to newspaper, radio or direct mail advertising and promotions. This is all changing as media consumption moves to the internet. SMEs can now promote their services as effectively as large companies, by using the internet. In fact, due to their size, they can in most cases move more quickly to engage in new opportunities, like Twitter or Adwords™ campaigns.

The playing field is leveling, or as Thomas Friedman so eloquently put it, *"the world is flattening"* (Friedman, 2005)[12], and internet marketing is not exception to this new reality.

INTERNET MARKETING TOOLS

The execution of an internet marketing strategy is really a function of utilizing one or multiple tools and techniques available on the internet through providers like Google. As mentioned earlier, these tools are being developed at a tremendous pace with some defining this pace as "internet time". Samples of key internet marketing tools are highlighted in Figure 6:

It is fairly straight forward for an SME to utilize these tools and achieve positive results. However, without strategic forethought it is difficult to achieve sustained long term results over time. The notion of strategic internet marketing will be discussed further in the next section of this chapter.

A brief overview of five of the most common internet marketing tools and techniques will follow. These are:

1. Analytics
2. Search Engine Advertising (SEA)
3. Search Engine Optimization (SEO)
4. Email Marketing
5. Social Media Marketing

Figure 7. Google analytics html tracking code[14]

```
<script type="text/javascript">
var gaJsHost = (("https:" == document.location.protocol) ?
"https://ssl." : "http://www.");
document.write(unescape("%3Cscript src='" + gaJsHost +
"google-analytics.com/ga.js'
type='text/javascript'%3E%3C/script%3E"));
</script>


<script type="text/javascript">
try{
var pageTracker = _gat._getTracker("UA-xxxxxx-x");
pageTracker._trackPageview();
} catch(err) {}
</script>
```

Analytics

If you don't measure it, you can't manage it! This is a common phrase, often heard in management circles and goes hand-in-hand with the earlier hypothesis. Promote the web site to attract customer visits, measure what they are doing on the site, and make adjustments accordingly. The measurement is made possible through analytics. Google offers a tremendous analytics tool, which is free to use. Google understands the value in offering this free service as it helps to drive AdWords™ revenue. Turning on analytics is the first step in journeying into the world of internet marketing. It is straight forward only requiring three simple steps. First, an SME needs to create a Google account and register their web site for analytics. Secondly, the SME needs to attach a "tag" or tracking code to the bottom of each page of their web site. Tags are essentially HTML commands; shown in Figure 7 below. It should take a web designer less than 15 minutes to make this modification to a typical SME web site.

The final step is to submit the web site to Google. This is an option available to anyone with a Google account. Once a web site is submitted, it may take a few hours or days for the Google Analytics to start working effectively, so a little patience is required.

Setting up analytics is the easy part. SME's then need to begin to utilize the plethora of information Google Analytics provides. Some important highlights are:

Visits and Bounce Rate

Visits to a web site are fairly self explanatory and represent the number of people who open the site whether for the first time or as a repeat visitor. Bounce rate represents a percentage of visitors who come to a web site and then leave the site immediately from the entry page without clicking through to another page. The assumption in this case is that nothing really caught their eye or the site was not what they were looking for. Bounce rate is a key measure within internet marketing. Clearly, if SMEs are going to spend a fair amount of effort attracting potential customers to a web site, they do not want them "bouncing". The other important thing to understand is that bounce rate is a relative measure, where some industries have extremely high bounce rates and others are relatively low. Bounce rates can be more easily understood by benchmarking a web site against others in the SME's sector. Google Analytics allows you to do this.

Figure 8. Google analytics dashboard[15]

Traffic Sources

Analytics will capture where traffic to a site originates from; either by the customer typing in the URL directly, from a search engine, a referring site or from a search engine ad if the SME is running an AdWords™ campaign. While it is optimal to have potential customers find a web site directly through a search engine, this will not always be the case and successful internet marketing will attract traffic through a combination of these and other sources. Analyzing traffic sources and how they are changing or evolving over time is essential to effective internet marketing.

Goals

Setting goals within analytics (which may be, as an example, the desire to create an order page on the web site) allows an SME to understand how potential customers either find their way to a goal

page - or not. Setting goals and then managing the effectiveness of the web site to achieve these goals is paramount to effective internet marketing. Analytics offers a tremendous amount of information to help an SME manage to their goals.

Key Words

Analytics will also highlight the key words that are being used to find their web sites. This makes good sense for Google as it will enhance the effectiveness of their AdWords™ system by driving more focused and presumably successful, AdWords™ advertising. By analyzing what words potential customers are using in their searches to find a web site, SME's are then able to turn around and advertise against those words with the goal of driving more traffic to their web site.

Analytics is clearly a critical first step in adopting internet marketing. Used correctly it can help drive small, incremental changes to a web site which can have a material impact on a firm's bottom line via online originated sales. An important rule of thumb with the deployment of analytics is that it is an investment in human capital first and foremost and technology second. This will be an ongoing investment of time spent digesting information about the site and then acting upon it. Analytics helps an SME understand their customer's behavior and gives them the opportunity to react to it in near real time.

Search Engine Advertising (SEA)

Search engine advertising is the most utilized internet marketing technique available. Adwords™, Google's primary search engine advertising service, is the bread and butter of Google's success. SEA has a number of key features of which a SME should be aware. First and foremost, the company only pays for click-throughs. Unlike more traditional media, where payment is based on *potential* exposure to an ad, the internet allows for a more targeted, measurable service. By paying for click-throughs the SME is ensured of an opportunity to turn a visitor into a customer. In other words, it is in their hands once the potential customer hits their web site.

One little known fact about Google Adwords™ is the logic behind how Google sets the rate for a click-through. One of the defining factors is Google's view of how successful the web site will be in turning a potential customer into a sale. They will analyze a web site for its effectiveness and set the click-through rate accordingly. The more effective they view the web site to be, the cheaper the rate. The less effective they consider the web site in their conversion to sales, the higher the rate. Obviously, they want successful customers for their Adwords™ service who will continue to use this means of internet marketing. Another interesting factor is that the SME chooses how much they want to spend and against which key words. Google takes this information and displays the Adwords™ message based on these criteria.

If a lower spending limit is indicated, the ad will not be shown every time a key word is searched, thus balancing the amount of advertising spend against the broader number of searches on a desired set of keywords. Setting up an SEA account with Google is quite simple; a menu pick within a Google account.

Search Engine Optimization (SEO)

A highly desirable result for any company is to appear on the first page of a search against relevant key words. This is effective search engine placement and is accomplished through search engine optimization. If this can be achieved, then the requirement to use Adwords™ for example diminishes and internet marketing becomes much cheaper. But SEO is an art as much as a science and is best left to the experts. SEO is more generally defined as:

a structured approach used to increase the position of a company or its products in natural or organic search engine results listings for selected keywords or phrases.

In a nutshell, effective SEO can be broken down into two distinct categories:

- On the page (inherent in the SME's site)
    ○ Optimization and coding standards
    ○ Relevant content, keyword phrases and cross-links
- Off the page (recognized affiliations with other sites)
    ○ Link building strategy

It is the art of building web pages which are searchable against certain keywords and building content and links which meet certain search criteria. Links are extremely important in Google's world, and the nature of links represents the very foundation for which Google built their search engine. Changing content is also an important

Table 1. Search engine optimization – avoiding the common mistakes[16] (© 2007, UNB Saint John. Used with permission.)

Common Mistakes	Best Practices
Same title, meta description and keywords on every page	Cerate standardized but unique titles for every page Use distinct but relevant description and keyword phrases on every page
Insufficient or poor body content	No content = no ranking Be relevant and proofread content
Poor cross-linking	Add relevant cross-links (body and image links, secondary navigation, breadcrumbs, site maps, etc) Avoid link over kill
Inexistent or poor incoming links	No incoming links = no ranking Create a link strategy based on context, relevancy and quality of placement Avoid link farms, link networks, poorly ranked or banned sites
Duplicate content	Avoid duplicate body content Avoid multiple domain names for same site Avoid circular navigation and inconsistent cross-linking Exclude duplicate pages
Un-crawlable navigation	Avoid problematic technologies (Flash, JavaScript, DHTML) if possible Add a second navigation schemes
Invalid HTML	Fix the errors! Validate to standards
No site map	Create one! (Google site map makes it easy)
No alt text on images	Add alt text to images
Improper link anchor text	Be relevant Avoid generic "click here"
No use of heading tags	Use H1, H2 . . . H6 properly
No exclusions	Robots.txt is a must Exclude the appropriate pages
Over optimization	Design for users, not search engines
Mass submission	Avoid using automated submission services Don't manually submit to crawlers

aspect of successful SEO and one reason why more and more web sites are building in blogs. Blogs represent user-based, dynamically changing content, and Google likes that. Some of the common mistakes and related best practices for effective search engine optimization are listed in Table 1. In part, this is meant to illustrate the complexities in effective SEO and why it is best left to the professionals.

E-Mail Marketing

E-mail marketing is a form of direct marketing that uses electronic mail to build relationships with current and prospective customers, increase sales and improve customer retention. Put another way, e-mail marketing represents an important step in internet marketing and can be the delivery engine behind effective database marketing. Building a database of users, through online and more traditional means and then effectively communicating with them, on their terms, is central to good marketing. A key understanding here is the notion that e-mail communication needs to be offered on the customer's terms and is not all about sales. It can strengthen an SME's database marketing and can be used to engage customers

Figure 9. Customer life cycle and engagement tactics[17] (© 2007, UNB Saint John. Used with permission.)

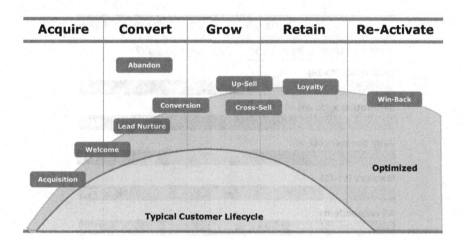

across the entire customer life cycle as depicted in Figure 9.

E-mail marketing engines are readily available, inexpensive and can be quite effective. One thing to look for in an e-mail marketing tool is the reporting ability which allows the SME to know, among other things, *who opened what e-mail when*. Most e-mail marketing tools also include "opt out" capability for customers and will report on which links (assuming there are multiple links in the message) the customers choose.

Social Media Marketing

Social Media Marketing (SMM) is the form of internet marketing which seeks to achieve branding and marketing communication goals through the participation in various social media networks and online communities by encouraging brand feedback and dialogue. Some SMEs may question "Why does it matter?" The simple answer, which is highlighted in Figure 10, is that more and more on-line time is spent on "user-generated" sites, like Facebook™, MySpace™ and LinkedIn™. Internet evolution seems to be moving at the fastest speed within these social media networks.

SMEs who engage in social media sites and product/service specific blogs have, in some cases, shown a tremendous ability to engage with customers and ultimately drive sales. The important nuance of social media marketing is it has to be indirect. This approach takes a fair amount of patience, something that SMEs cannot always afford in terms of their development. Slapping up a Facebook™ site is not effective social media marketing. Engaging in discussion forums, bringing product expertise to relative blog sites, working to build an online reputation and understanding the issues facing potential customers are all facets of social media marketing. Undoubtedly, social media marketing will consume a significant amount of the entrepreneurs' time. The closing case study of Abbyshot Clothiers effectively illustrates the potential of social media marketing.

There are many other and evolving forms of internet marketing but the commonality is such that results are measurable and can be immediate, and one reason why internet marketing is growing at an accelerated pace. However, a caution flag needs to be raised surrounding the longer term implications of effective internet marketing. Internet marketing tactics left alone are just that, tactics. They will be copied, lose relevance and essentially become less effective over time. Internet marketing tactics executed within the context

Figure 10. Why does it matter? (© 2007, eMarketer.com, Used with permission.)

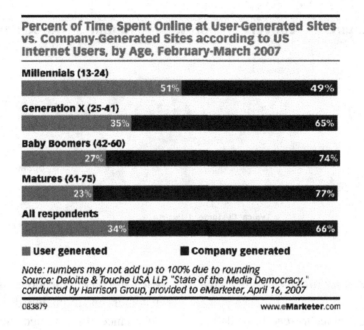

Percent of Time Spent Online at User-Generated Sites vs. Company-Generated Sites according to US Internet Users, by Age, February-March 2007

Millennials (13-24)
51% | 49%

Generation X (25-41)
35% | 65%

Baby Boomers (42-60)
27% | 74%

Matures (61-75)
23% | 77%

All respondents
34% | 66%

■ **User generated**   ■ **Company generated**

Note: numbers may not add up to 100% due to rounding
Source: Deloitte & Touche USA LLP, "State of the Media Democracy," conducted by Harrison Group, provided to eMarketer, April 16, 2007

083879   www.e**Marketer**.com

of a strategic marketing plan can, however, have long lasting effects.

STRATEGIC INTERNET MARKETING

Internet marketing, when guided by fundamental marketing practices, can provide desirable, extraordinary results over long periods of time. It is the integration and focused execution of multiple internet marketing tactics which, when driven by a broader set of objectives and goals, can lead to great results. Our case study at the beginning of the chapter on Aiden's Deep Sea Fishing, exemplifies this very notion.

In summary, Aiden's customer database drives e-mail campaigns which helps customers learn of their fishing blog, driving voluntary, customer-originated viral e-mail marketing which may enhance customer referrals. These tactics are tied to the effective use of analytics to understand key word search and goal conversion, ultimately driving an increasingly more effective spend in search engine advertising. All of this activity is focused on the goal of growing the strength of their referral-originated business, which currently represents just under half of their total customers with online-originated new customers more than doubling annually. The irony is the referral business is measured by asking the simple question – *How did you find out about us?* – at dockside when customers show up to go fishing. This exemplifies, in a simple way, how Aiden's is tying old marketing techniques, with new internet marketing tactics, to leverage their current strengths in their market and deal with challenging market conditions. Aiden's started their internet marketing journey by running a simple Adwords™ campaign and turning on Google Analytics which was quickly copied by their prime competitor in the region, and represents a key downfall of internet marketing. In its simplest forms it can be easily replicated, yet when woven into a broader marketing approach can become more strategic, less tactical and much harder to copy.

When building a marketing mix to leverage the power of the internet, it is important to build in the notions of interactivity, measurability, community and communication. This expanded view of the four P's will set the stage for an internet marketing strategy designed to be sustainable over the long run. The challenge for SMEs, as with more traditional marketing, will be to take the time and effort to set their goals and objectives properly; ones which are reflective of the opportunities facing them and realistic as to the challenges of their particular markets.

FUTURE RESEARCH DIRECTIONS

Further benchmark research needs to be conducted to provide an understanding of the adoption rates of internet marketing in the global SME market. This research should also focus on the factors driving internet adoption and the use of internet marketing. A strong understanding of these driving factors can help policy makers and internet marketing providers make informed decisions as to the most effective way to build adoption of internet technologies and internet marketing efforts within the SME sector. Through these policy and commercial efforts, SMEs can become comfortable in adopting the internet in greater numbers, which will result in leveling the playing field with their larger competitors and reaching out to a broader set of global growth opportunities. Internet marketing is the future marketing engine of the SME sector, the sooner, and better we understand the factors affecting successful adoption of internet marketing and related technologies the sooner we can help this sector use this understanding to grow and thrive in a global marketplace.

CONCLUSION

In this chapter we learned how small and medium sized businesses can utilize internet marketing to level the playing field with their larger competitors. And, that internet marketing must come before web site changes or renewal. We took the view

that long term success with internet marketing is predicated on a more integrated strategic approach, versus a non-integrated tactical approach. Two small businesses were profiled that used various internet marketing tools and techniques to successfully build online sales and referral programs. We have a better sense of a number of key internet marketing tools, like analytics, search engine advertising, search engine optimization, email marketing and social media marketing and we understand how cost effective and thus attractive these tools can be to the SME sector.

We better understand why it is an opportune and encouraging time for SMEs to engage in internet marketing, with media consumption moving quickly away from traditional media outlets and over to the internet. Finally, we have also gained a sense of how the internet is changing the marketing mix with the introduction of measurable interactivity and accessible communities of interest.

CLOSING CASE STUDY: ABBYSHOT CLOTHIERS – A DEEP APPRECIATION FOR THEIR CUSTOMERS (WWW. ABBYSHOT.COM)[18]

What happens when a smash hit movie creates a loyal, if not cult-like following? A niche market for screen accurate, movie inspired clothing is created. Armed with the basic premise that fans would crave the likeness of their favorite movie character, independent web consultant Adam Bragg and classically trained seamstress Bonnie Cook, created AbbyShot Clothiers.

From the beginning, this creative team had the intuitive sense to present their website as a customer-focused interface, catering to the response and feed back of their clients. The humble, single item clothing line which was presented on a single-page site in 2002, has grown to become an eight-page site featuring 41 product items with sales in over 28 countries around the globe. Their successful growth is attributable to the carefully cultivated customer relationships that have been a function of segmenting their customer base and having a rich understanding of their customer profile.

Appreciate your Customer Demographic

Fans are a dedicated and "fanatical" bunch. Across sporting, music or movie genres, you can find the subculture of on-line communities where fans gather. Adam was a fan of the original 1999 Matrix movie that spurred the entire business concept for Abbyshot. While surfing the net, he came across others who were enthralled with the movie, and who, would even like to wear the same coat as their favorite movie character. His research revealed that "no one else on the planet" was offering these unique, customized overcoats. In that moment he saw an opportunity.

Initially, Abbyshot would visit the fan websites and movie review sites, posting comments about their company, soliciting feedback. "We knew that to connect with the fans of the movie, we would want to express interest in their "fandom" and let them know that we like it too, and are willing to invest in their interests." Within 3 months they had added 4 more styles to their product offering and in their first year of business exceeded $150,000 in revenues.

Reviewing the source material (such as the movies or hit shows) is important for product development, but even more so is understanding the inherent differences that exist between the "fandoms" and keeping up to speed with their customers. Abbyshot continues to visit the fan discussion forums of the various movies which serve as the catalysts for their screen-accurate wares. This provides valuable insight into potential customer preferences, and also ensures that they can talk sensibly about the products they consider producing. From these forums, different opportunities for each product may arise. One

on-line fan community allowed them to promote their products to their membership, where another supported a "peer review" prior to a product's release. "The fans will know if a lapel is 3 degrees off-center, and they are telling us!"

Create a Dialogue with your Customer

It became evident that customers in this niche market would willingly offer direction, create demand, and support the venture. The key would be to continue to manage the customer relationship, engaging knowledgeable fans, their customers, in dialogue which would support their business.

A primary tool of their customer engagement is their company newsletter. In 2002, it was a simple, text-based email announcement of new product releases to a very small distribution list of a few hundred. If recipients clicked on the link, they would land on the website. With the addition of product photography to their newsletter, the response rate, as measured by click-throughs and open rates began to grow. The addition of a "subscribe now!" button captured even more names and contributed to growing the distribution list. Finally, embedding their newsletter within the format of the email message has successfully garnered a 30% open rate and a click-through rate as high as 40%. Today, Abbyshot engages a newsletter management service enabling them to track statistics and generate reports which reflect who is opening it, how quickly upon receipt, and what articles or areas in the newsletter are of interest. There is now an appreciation for the increase in the click-through rate when their newsletter announces a product debut. Understanding their customer from all angles is the cornerstone of their marketing strategy.

The solid relationship and dialogue that Abbyshot has created with its customers has also provided leads to broader markets through other websites that Abbyshot has not been aware of. It is market information directed by their customers.

However, lessons are to be learned in the process, and customer comments and suggestions also require a degree of management and evaluation. In early 2007, the company closed its own customer forum as it started to become less of a product development tool, and more of a chat room with less useful product information provided by fans and customers. This has prompted the creation of a blog to augment the company's efforts to speak to its customer base.

Manage your Customer Relationship for Future Growth

Of course, new movie releases, sequels, DVD and video game launches provide ongoing product development opportunities and a shot in the arm for revenue for the company. However, it has been Abbyshot's commitment to profiling and engaging their customer base that has reaped the rewards. With only 6-7,000 customers within their current niche market, the company relies on the constant "back and forth" with their customers, valuing their comments and suggestions, and enjoying a healthy 30% "second" purchase rate amongst customers who have already invested in one of Abbyshot's products.

The company so values the relationships created with the "fandoms" that have become their customer base, that they have donated garments for charity fundraisers to the fan clubs. The mutual respect has been established, and fandoms link to Abbyshot as well.

While the company's first five years were intensely product-quality focused given the savvy fan knowledge, Abbyshot now looks forward to continued growth as their reputation has been established as the leading world-wide producer of screen-accurate movie clothing. With over 9,000 unique views per month, and total revenues having grown by 100% in five years, to over $300,000/year, Abbyshot will continue to closely follow its customers' direction, expand its newsletter reach, and begin to focus more closely on target-ing website visitors to ensure maximum sales are achieved. Abbyshot Clothiers believes in its own credo that "No longer are we using marketing to attract customers, our marketing strategies should support what the customer demands from the company. Ignore at your peril!"

ADDITIONAL READING

A significant amount of information on the world of internet marketing and its implications is available through traditional published sources and of course, on the internet. If you like to read, I would suggest the following:

- *Web Analytics: An Hour a Day* (Avinash Kaushik & Jim Sterne)
- *33 Million People in a Room: How to Create, Influence, and Run a Successful Business with Social Networking* (Juliette Powell)
- *Purple Cow: Transform Your Business by Being Remarkable* (Seth Godin)
- *The World is Flat* (Thomas Friedman)
- *Ultimate Guide to Google AdWords: How to Access 100 Million People in 10 Minutes* (Perry Marshal and Bryan Todd)
- *Internet Marketing: Integrating Online and Offline Strategies* (Mary Lou Roberts)
- *Creative Marketing for SMEs* (Ian Fillis)

Not to be overlooked is the immediate, real time way to capture insight on this topic: engage with Twitter. If this is of interest, a first step could be to ask Radian6[19] to allow you to follow them into the world of real time social media marketing; a fantastic way to relish the possibilities that are present within the scope of internet marketing.

ACKNOWLEDGMENT

I would like to acknowledge all the contributors to this chapter, including the UNB Saint John Electronic Commerce Research and Training Center for their willingness to share information from their *Marketing on the Internet* training seminar, with special thanks to Louis Philippe Gauthier for his expertise, knowledge and passion for internet marketing. I would also like to acknowledge Catherine Connolly for her editing help and of course Jackie for her support and patience throughout the learning and writing process.

REFERENCES

Davis, C., Lin, C., & Vladica, F. (2005). *State of e-Business in SMEs in Atlantic Canada in 2005*. Paper presented at the annual Atlantic Schools of Business conference, Halifax, N.S., Canada.

Davis, C., & Vladica, F. (August 2004). *Adoption of Internet Technologies and e-Business Solutions by Small and Medium Enterprises (SMEs) in New Brunswick*. Saint John, Canada: University of New Brunswick Saint John, Electronic Commerce Centre.

Dev, C.S., & Schultz, D.E. (2005, January/February). In the Mix: A Customer Focused Approach Can Bring the Current Marketing Mix into the 21st Century. *Marketing Management, 14*(1).

Electronic Commerce Research & Training Centre (ECRTC). (2008). *Marketing on the Internet Training Program*. University of New Brunswick Saint John, Saint John, N.B., Canada.

Fleet, G. (November 2008). *Export and the role of the Internet for SMEs in Atlantic Canada*. Paper presented at the International Council for Small Business (ICSB) 2008 World Conference, Halifax, N.S., Canada.

Friedman, T. (2005, April). The World is Flat: A Brief [st Century. New York: Farrar, Straus & Giroux.]. *Histoire (Paris)*, 21.

Google Investor Relations – Financial Tables. (2008). Retrieved March 18, 2009, from http://investor.google.com /fin_data.html

Jarboe, G. (March 16, 2007). *Boosting PR results with SEO and RSS*. Retrieved March 18, 2009 from www.ipressroom.com/pr/ SchwartzmanPR/info/document/ JarboeBulldogChicago2007.ppt

McCarthy, E. J. (1960). *Basic Marketing: A Managerial Approach*. Homewood, IL: Irwin.

Report, J. M. M. B. *US Advertising Forecast*. (November 2007). Retrieved November 2008 from http://www.jackmyers.com

ENDNOTES

1. Davis, Vladica (2004)
2. Davis, Lin, Vladica (2005)
3. This case was built for the UNBSJ Electronic Commerce Research & Training Centre *Marketing on the Internet* training program by Catherine M. Connolly, L. Philippe Gauthier and the author.
4. Davis, Lin, Vladica (2005)
5. Including the two studies from Davis et al in 2004 & 2005, plus the subsequent study by Fleet in 2007
6. Information retrieved from Jack Myers Media Business Report (November 2007)
7. Greg Jarboe (March 16, 2007). Illustration created by L. Philippe Gauthier for the UNBSJ Marketing on the Internet training seminar.
8. Information sourced from McCarthy E.J., & Dev, C. S., Schultz, D.E. Illustrated by L. Philippe Gauthier for the UNB Saint John *Marketing on the Internet* training program.

9   Photos provided with permission from the author.

10   Google Investor Relations – 2008 earnings report.

11   Click-through's refer to when an ad is clicked on and the user is brought to the company's web site

12   Friedman, T. The World is Flat

13   Compliments of the UNBSJ Marketing on the Internet training seminar

14   Tracking html code information sourced from www.google.com

15   Take from the authors Google account.

16   Sourced from UNB Saint John *Marketing on the Internet* training program. This table was compiled for UNB Saint John by L. Philippe Gauthier.

17   Adapted from information on Bronto.com – List Management essential to Email marketing (2007). Illustrated for the UNB Saint John *Marketing on the Internet* training seminar by L. Philippe Gauthier.

18   This case study was written for the UNBSJ *Marketing on the Internet* training program by Catherine Connolly and L. Philippe Gauthier.

19   Radian6 is a social media monitoring company

Chapter 7

SME Characteristics and the Use of the Internet to Expand the Scale and Geographic Scope of Sales:
Evidence from the United Kingdom

Piers Thompson
University of Wales Institute – Cardiff, UK

Robert Williams
National Entrepreneurship Observatory, UK

Gary Packham
University of Glamorgan, UK

Brychan C. Thomas
University of Glamorgan, UK

ABSTRACT

The potential of the Internet to both geographically expand customer bases and provide a source of sales growth has led to a rapid embracement of the Internet by a majority of small businesses in the United Kingdom. However, many studies suggest that much of this adoption takes the form of simple Web sites representing little more than an electronic brochure. Although theories and models have been proposed suggesting adoption and development of e-commerce takes a staged process, with firms moving to more complex e-commerce processes after first mastering simpler forms of Web site, studies have found mixed evidence with regard to this. This chapter investigates the level of Small and Medium Enterprise (SME)

DOI: 10.4018/978-1-60960-597-1.ch007

Web site adoption and functionality and how this relates to growth aspirations, specifically the geographical expansion of customer bases. One potential explanation for this slow uptake of true e-commerce is a lack of employees with basic and advanced IT skills. The possibility that Information Technology (IT) skills shortages could explain the gap between the Internet's potential and the extent of involvement by a vast majority of UK SMEs is explored. Discussion within the chapter is complemented with analysis of data from a large survey of SMEs.

INTRODUCTION

The increasing accessibility of the Internet for SMEs has led to a massive surge in the level of UK e-commerce sales in recent years. Sales of goods and services over the Internet for SMEs have risen from £11.6 billion in 2004 to 48.5 billion in 2008 (ONS, 2009). The total contribution to the UK economy was estimated to be £100 billion or 7.2 per cent of GDP in 2009, making it more important to the economy than the construction, transportation or utilities industries (Kalapesi et al., 2010). This is not just a reflection of customers becoming familiar and comfortable with accessing the Web sites of large established businesses within the UK, but also the increasing number of smaller businesses which have taken advantage of the potential of the Internet to cheaply advertise, market and sell their products to a wide range of customers (O'Keefe et al., 1998; Simmons et al., 2008; Kalapesi et al., 2010). As well as more traditional business models being augmented with the addition of a Web site there are new businesses reliant entirely on the Internet for their sales although many of these collapsed when the dot.com bubble burst in the early 2000s (Drew, 2003). Again Web only activity has not just been restricted to the larger, now household names, such as Amazon. Relatively low fixed costs and perceived risk has led to an explosion of entrepreneurial activity by individuals often alongside other economic activity such as salaried employment (O'Keefe, et al., 1998). There is an extensive literature examining the possible determinants for firms choosing to develop Web

sites, which includes not only the opportunities created (Stockdale and Standing, 2004), but also the threats that Internet usage brings (Kleindl, 2000). Whatever the driving forces by the beginning of the present century the unavoidability of the Web meant that e-commerce in its broadest sense has become an imperative rather than an alternative (Wen et al., 2001).

Whilst a vast majority of firms have or will develop their own Web presences, there is a greater variation in the speed, depth and form that involvement will take (Wen et al., 2001). It has also been suggested that Web site development is a staged process often driven by the availability of resources, particularly knowledge (Levy & Powell, 2003; Rao et al., 2003; Lee, 2004). Not all researchers are convinced of the merit of simpler staged models given the existence of early adopters and heterogeneity of small businesses (Martin & Matlay, 2001; Alonso Mendo & Fitzgerald, 2005a).

This study concentrates on the functions included in the Web sites of UK SMEs, and how these different levels of functionality relate to the perceived benefits of the Internet in providing growth potential and in particular access to markets beyond their local core market (Lawson et al., 2003). This would mean that greater adoption of e-commerce would lead to higher sales growth (Raymond et al., 2005; Kalapesi et al., 2010), even providing a relatively cheap method of internationalizing client bases (Kula and Tatoglu, 2003). These opportunities are particularly pertinent to SMEs who often may operate in niche markets, relying on a thinly but widely distributed customer base (Napier et al., 2005; Galloway et al., 2008). Whether, UK SMEs can fully take advantage of the opportunities open to them seems questionable given that their Web sites are often little more than product brochures (Levy and Powell, 2003; Crespi et al., 2004).

Given the potential of the Internet to not only grow the firm, but also to simply allow the firm to compete in a rapidly globalizing marketplace, it seems strange that studies have found little sign of true e-commerce adoption. One explanation comes from those studies examining the choice to adopt, which find a link to the perceived ease of use (Grandon & Pearson, 2004). Potential skills shortages for owners/managers and their staff could clearly hold back greater functionality of Web sites (Mehrtens et al., 2001; Mirchandani & Motwani, 2001; Robertson et al., 2007; Weltevreden & Boschma, 2008).

When discussing the issues raised by UK SME Web site functionality, analysis of data from the Federation of Small Business (FSB) 'Lifting the Barriers to Growth' survey is used to complement the findings of the existing literature. The next section discusses studies that have examined the decision to adopt and develop a Web presence and what role growth plays in this decision. Since one of the main growth prospects derived from the internet for SMEs is to break out of their traditional markets, attention is then turned to the possibility of geographical expansion and internationalization through Web site functions. The role IT skills shortages play in low Web site functionality is explored in the fourth section before considering future routes for research, and drawing conclusions in the last section.

GROWTH, WEB SITE ADOPTION AND FUNCTIONALITY

The latter part of the 20th century saw a rapid resurgence of small business activity in the form of a 'third industrial revolution' (Audretsch &

Thurik, 2001). Explanations for this include: the emergence of new industries, such as software and biotechnology; deregulation and privatization of many sectors; a greater emphasis on core competences for large firms; new demand for more varied products; greater prosperity leading to a greater desire for self-realization from work; and finally a greater emphasis on services (Carree et al., 2002). Given the increasing need for flexibility and reduced scale (Arbore & Ordanini, 2006), advances in information and communications technology (ICT) such as e-commerce become essential tools for remaining competitive in the modern economy (Rogers, 1995; Poon & Swatman, 1999; Fillis et al., 2004).

As the Internet has become more widely accessed by the world's population its commercial potential has exploded. Although, both stock and order models of technology adoption suggest that the benefits of adoption decline with the number of firms already using the technology and the order in which firms adopt technology, the adoption rate is positively related to the expected number of future users (Crespi et al., 2004). This means that given the potential for further expansion of the Internet there is still a strong incentive for SMEs to set up their own Web sites. In addition, access to a larger variety of suppliers and ease of comparison mean positive network externalities exist, generating more online sales for both firms creating new and those with existing Web presences (Elliot & Fowell, 2000). This means that a presence on the Internet is becoming more and more of a competitive necessity, if only to keep up with competitors and enhance survival prospects (Wen et al., 2001; de Búrca et al., 2005; Bruque & Moyano, 2007). This is reflected in the FSB data with 77.3 per cent of firms responding that they have a Web site of some kind (see the data appendix for greater explanation of the FSB data and Web site functionality measures).

The benefits of Internet adoption and barriers to adoption are likely to vary greatly between different groups of SMEs depending on their characteristics. One such characteristic is firm size, with larger firms generally deemed to have the resources to pursue adoption at all stages of Web site development (Dutta & Evrard, 1999; Love & Irani, 2004; Bengtsson et al., 2007; Bhagwat & Sharma, 2007). This relationship between firm size and Web site development has not been universally found to exist (Daniel et al., 2002). These conflicting results may reflect higher levels of adoption positively influenced by the greater flexibility of smaller firms but also by the superior resource availability of larger firms. Using the FSB data to provide insights into those characteristics associated with the decision to adopt a Web site, a logit regression is run with presence of a firm Web site as the dependent variable. Clearly the availability of resources plays an important role with larger firms both in terms of employment and turnover significantly more likely to have a Web site (Table 1). While only 72.1 per cent of businesses with turnover of less than £100,000 a year have a Web site, 90.2 per cent of those with a turnover of more than £1 million have a Web site. Employment shows a similar pattern with 69.6 per cent of those with no employees having a Web site compared to 88.8 per cent of those employing ten or more people. The relationship between employment and Web site presence is perhaps the most telling as those businesses with fewer employees are more likely to have to draw on outside expertise to develop and maintain a Web site (Cragg & Zinatelli, 1995).

Clearly the importance of a Web presence will vary between firms operating in different industry sectors, with service industries suggested to benefit more from closer relationships to their clients (O'Keefe et al., 1998). The tourist trade has been singled out as one industry where the Web could play a valuable role in generating a competitive edge (McQuade et al., 1996). The reliance of the business on the tourist trade understandably increases the probability of having a Web site as sales are more likely to be non-repeat sales and therefore greater market presence will be required.

The age of the firm is likely to have a complicated relationship with Web site adoption. Given that studies suggest there may be a minimum level of resources required to produce a Web site, this may prevent adoption by the youngest firms (Dutta & Evrard, 1999). A pattern apparent in the FSB data. Equally though, older and larger established firms that have been successfully trading may not see the fit with their existing business models (Fariselli et al., 1999; Darch & Lucas, 2002), explaining why firms in the FSB data over 9 years of age are no more likely to have Web sites than those just formed.

Even after controlling for industry sectors and size, UK SMEs are not homogeneous, but also differ greatly in terms of their aims, objectives and cultures. Whilst it is difficult if not impossible to produce a perfect understanding of all these potential influences through a survey instrument, the central figure of a majority of SMEs is the owner-manager (Fuller-Love, 2006). Whilst imperfect the characteristics of the owner-manager are likely to be strongly related to the business's raison d'être. For instance the age of the entrepreneur themselves is likely to have major influence on the strategic aims of a business, with businesses owned by older entrepreneurs perhaps less likely to seek growth and expansion, which will obviously impact on Web presence. As firms' ITC competencies are positively correlated with the extent to which managers champion new technologies, older entrepreneurs less familiar with the latest technologies may act as a brake on the firm's progress in adopting Internet related technologies (Eurostat, 1996; Bassellier et al. 2003). Fundamentally the more knowledgeable and comfortable the owner-manager is with IT in general and the Internet specifically (Iacovou et al., 1995), the more likely the firm is to have a Web site. It is clear that younger entrepreneurs brought up using the Web will be more likely to push their firms towards adoption and better integration of Web sites, although this is likely to lead to higher levels of business failure where untried

Table 1. Logit of Website Usage and Active Website Usage

		Website		Active Website	
Employment (Base category – owner only)	2 - 4 Employees	**0.2468**	(0.020)	0.1852	(0.164)
	5 - 9 Employees	**0.4384**	(0.003)	0.0722	(0.668)
	10 - 19 Employees	**0.7244**	(0.000)	0.1405	(0.499)
	20+ Employees	**0.7819**	(0.003)	0.1018	(0.681)
Turnover (Base category – less than £25,000)	£25K - £50K	0.0874	(0.576)	0.1106	(0.556)
	£500k - £100K	0.1156	(0.457)	-0.1284	(0.504)
	£100K - £200K	**0.3747**	(0.024)	0.0354	(0.857)
	£200K - £300K	**0.3923**	(0.040)	0.0941	(0.672)
	£300K - £500K	**0.5675**	(0.005)	0.2637	(0.246)
	£500K - £1m	**0.7877**	(0.000)	0.1839	(0.429)
	£1 million	**1.3001**	(0.000)	0.4720	(0.071)
Tourist Trade (Bc – no involvement)	Direct Tourist Trade	**1.1470**	(0.000)	**0.4021**	(0.015)
	Indirect Tourist Trade	0.2291	(0.078)	0.2062	(0.110)
Firm Age (Base category – less than 3 years old)	4 - 9 years	**0.4661**	(0.004)	**0.4202**	(0.017)
	10 to 19 years	0.1442	(0.416)	**0.4677**	(0.014)
	20 or more years	-0.2313	(0.235)	**0.4814**	(0.025)
Entrepreneur's Age (Base category – younger than 35 years)	35 to 44 years old	**-0.5419**	(0.014)	0.1952	(0.330)
	45 to 54 years old	**-0.5612**	(0.009)	0.0043	(0.983)
	55 to 64 years	**-0.6134**	(0.006)	0.1346	(0.513)
	Over 65 years old	**-0.6605**	(0.010)	0.1577	(0.517)
Entrepreneur's educational attainment (Base category A-levels)	Postgraduate	**0.3777**	(0.024)	0.1853	(0.279)
	Bachelors Degree	**0.2839**	(0.039)	0.0632	(0.667)
	Professional Qualifications	-0.0265	(0.839)	-0.0856	(0.557)
	GCSE/O level	-0.2198	(0.123)	0.0981	(0.532)
	Vocational Qualifications	**-0.3803**	(0.027)	-0.0185	(0.932)
	No Formal Qualifications	-0.0768	(0.686)	0.1570	(0.454)
Gender of owners (Bc – equal male & female)	Male Majority	-0.0018	(0.983)	-0.0906	(0.351)
	Female Majority	**-0.2947**	(0.019)	-0.1283	(0.366)
Hours committed to business (Bc – 30 to 48 hours)	Less than 30 hours	**-0.5236**	(0.002)	0.1851	(0.368)
	49 to 60 hours	-0.0987	(0.288)	0.0722	(0.495)
	More than 60 hours	-0.1032	(0.377)	0.1010	(0.424)
Change in sales volume over last 12 months (base category – decreased by 0% to 5%)	Decreased by 20%+	0.2805	(0.140)	0.0231	(0.919)
	Decreased by 10%-20%	0.1672	(0.355)	-0.1411	(0.511)
	Decreased by 5%-10%	-0.0358	(0.844)	0.1119	(0.602)
	Increased by 0%-5%	-0.0118	(0.937)	-0.0515	(0.778)
	Increased by 5%-10%	0.1748	(0.263)	-0.1396	(0.454)
	Increased by 10%-20%	0.0961	(0.563)	-0.0771	(0.683)
	Increased by 20%+	0.2817	(0.111)	0.2325	(0.232)

continued on following page

Table 1. continued

		Website		Active Website	
Objectives for business over next two years (base category – remain same size)	Grow turnover 20%+	**0.9703**	(0.000)	**0.6440**	(0.000)
	Expand up to 20%	**0.6795**	(0.000)	**0.3229**	(0.010)
	Downsize business	-0.0292	(0.883)	0.2118	(0.444)
	Sell or close business	-0.0540	(0.701)	0.1896	(0.308)
	Hand on business	0.4367	(0.145)	0.5220	(0.123)
N		5089		3938	
R²		0.204		0.2368	
Hosmer-Lemeshow		12.46	(0.132)	10.61	(0.225)

Notes: p-values in parenthesis

entrepreneurs combine with untested business models (Howcroft, 2001). Confirming this, the FSB data finds those firms owned by the youngest group of business owners (aged under 35 years) are significantly more likely to have Web sites.

Owner-managers with higher levels of education are more likely to have firms with Web sites. Although this represents a crude measure of IT skills and usage, higher formal education qualifications may indicate an ability to understand and foresee the potential of Web site facilities for achieving growth. This comes from a greater familiarity with the Internet from their studies and previous work experience, thus increasing the owner-managers' perceived capability levels (Dutta & Evrard, 1999).

Whilst a large body of work has examined the differences between male and female entrepreneurs (Carter & Bennett, 2006), work looking at the impact of gender on SME adoption of the Web is relatively sparse (Chuang et al., 2007). The motivations and measures of success may differ considerably between male and female business owners, with non-pecuniary factors playing a more important role for women (Walker & Brown, 2004). For example, the greater autonomy of self-employment can make it attractive given that childcare and other domestic chores, traditionally place a greater burden on women, meaning that

they need more flexibility in their employment (Carter & Allen, 1997). Given this it is perhaps of little surprise that the FSB data indicates that those firms majority owned by women are less likely to have Web sites. Emphasizing this, those firms in which, a lower level of hours are committed by the owner, are also less likely to have Web sites.

A recent study of the Internet in the UK by Kapaseli et al. (2010) found that SMEs with greater Web site functionality experienced considerably higher growth in sales during the period 2006 to 2009. They found that those with no online sales capacity saw turnover grow by 0.6 per cent annually compared to 4.1 per cent for those with active Web sites allowing online sales. However, it is difficult to separate the direction of causality in these results. It may be that more growth orientated firms will undertake greater Web site development (Levy et al., 2002). Equally the Internet provides firms with the opportunity to reach more customers, a theme returned to later in this chapter. The FSB data suggests that actual growth of firms is not connected to the decision to adopt a Web site. Turning attention towards those firms which are intending to grow their businesses over the next two years there is more likely to be a Web site present. Raymond et al. (2005) indicate that the strategic position of a firm substantially changes the likelihood of a firm having a Web site. The likelihood of owning a Web site for those firms intending to expand rapidly is two and half times that of those intending to maintain turnover at current levels (odds ratio of 2.633). Even those intending to grow turnover more modestly (up to 20 per cent) are twice as likely to have a Web site as those taking a more conservative approach (odds ratio of 1.973). Clearly the desire to grow the firm has a strong influence on Web site adoption. Whether this is sustaining existing growth (85.4 per cent adoption), or new growth (81.9 per cent adoption) the proportion of SMEs adopting a Web site is much higher than for those firms not intending to grow in the future, whether growth was previously present (68.5 per cent adoption), or the firm has no intention to grow and has not previously grown (64.8 per cent adoption).

It is worth noting that those firms included in the FSB data are primarily traditional bricks and mortar SMEs. This means that the drive of growth may be under-estimated due to a possible under-representation of pure play Web-based firms, as these firms may be more focused on expansion than their more traditional counterparts.

Clearly the Internet has potential to provide the next opportunities for economic growth and expansion for those small businesses embracing new business practices based around the Internet. However, for all its potential, only 9.8 per cent of UK sales of non-financial business take place through the Internet, although this has risen rapidly from 1.1% in 2002 (ONS, 2009), with business to business usage likely to be an even smaller proportion of total activity. One explanation for the conflicting facts of high UK SME Web site adoption and relatively low e-commerce sales is that many Web sites take the form of simple brochures. These simple Web sites without functions for interaction do not fully exploit the potential of a Web presence (Levy & Powell, 2003; Crespi et al., 2004). This is a feature found for many IT investments in SMEs where the capabilities are not present to fully exploit the new technology (Bhagwat & Sharma, 2007). It may also reflect

the fact that competitive pressures drive SMEs to adopt and develop their own Web sites, but these pressures do not provide clear goals for the technology's purpose other than not being left behind (Sellitto et al., 2003; de Búrca et al., 2005; Bruque & Moyano, 2007). The FSB data indicates that when considering those firms with Web sites nearly one in four have nothing more than basic contact information available (24.3 per cent). In addition, an even larger proportion is found in the next level up with just information provided to advertise their products (49.3 per cent). This means that roughly only a quarter of those firms with Web sites utilize their Web sites in an active manner. It is found that 21.3 per cent of firms have Web sites providing facilities to sell their products online to customers. A much smaller proportion of firms use their Web sites as a method of connecting with their suppliers alone (1.5 per cent), although a further 3.6 per cent of firms with Web sites use these as tools to interact with both suppliers and customers.

This low level of active Web site development may be driven by a number of issues. Included within these are: resource restrictions; complementaries of available Web site and software solutions with the firms' businesses; and security issues. Although the Internet has often been seen as having the potential to provide a level playing field for SMEs to compete with large firms (Howcroft, 2001; Bayo-Moriones & Lera-López, 2007), the limited time SMEs have to spend on future business development can result in under exploitation of opportunities presented by technological developments (Irani et al., 1997; Levy et al., 1998). Use of resources such as management time can see indirect costs of adoption increasing rapidly (Cohen & Kallirroi, 2006). This leads to the 'bare minimum' brochure Web site being developed to allow customers to contact the firm, but little more. Daniel and Wilson (2002) also find that the highest rated motivations for adoption of e-commerce relate to keeping up with competitors. This means that adoption decisions are taken with a desire to not fall behind rather than consideration of what needs to be undertaken to ensure any ITC investment is value adding. Where benefits are considered these are not necessarily considered in relation to existing organization goals marginalizing e-commerce as a sideshow of the firm (Lin et al., 2007).

As champions of new technology, the manager's IT skills are found to play an important role increasing the likelihood that a firm will possess a sophisticated interactive Web site (Damanpour, 1991; Fichman & Kemerer, 1997). However, one problem that can often exist is that while top management is enthusiastic about new technology they do not consider the desires and preferences of their staff. The extent that innovations are embraced by those who use them may influence the extent of adoption within the firm's processes. Thus, where enthusiastic managers do not consult their work forces, they run the risk of reduced development of Web site functions and weaker integration of Web sites with existing business functions (Lin et al., 2007).

Most enterprise software has been designed for and marketed towards larger organizations, who have the budgets, processes and technical skills required to deploy it. Since SMEs come in all shapes and sizes enterprise software suppliers have struggled to develop e-commerce software for the SME sector, which would attract sufficient sales to justify its development. The high cost of marketing to, and then servicing, hundreds of thousands of small companies compared to servicing a relatively small number of very large clients means the SME sector has been neglected. The SME sector is also unique in terms of its business style, with higher risk awareness, plus a lack of confidence and trust in new technologies. There is also often a lack of relevant experience, education and understanding of the e-commerce opportunities available (Kadlec & Mareš, 2003; Acar et al., 2005).

The security of those transactions undertaken through Web sites also forms a barrier to greater

Web site development, with both SMEs and their customers displaying a degree of distrust towards online payments (Yeung & Lu, 2004). In fact although not sufficient to ensure the success of a Web site, security, trust and the use of appropriate technologies are necessary conditions for development of a successful Web site (Liu & Arnett, 2000; Holsapple & Sasidharan, 2005).

All these factors mean that the adoption processes relating to IT within SMEs is different from that in larger businesses. The limited resources of SMEs available for managing the IT adoption process mean, SMEs need to be more conservative in their IT investment. Investment decisions have to pass through a number of stages. The process therefore consists of: assessing the SME's IT requirements (step 1), assessment of organization's IT maturity (step 2), evaluation of available IT solutions in the market (step 3), matching the available solutions with the SME's IT requirements and SME's IT maturity and readiness (step 4), implementation of the selected IT solution (step 5), and post adoption evaluation (step 6). Even though the guidelines appear to be a sequential process, it is possible to use the guidelines as an iterative process (Sarosa & Zowghi, 2003).

In combination these barriers to Web site development mean that SMEs' level of adoption is restricted by the availability of resources within the firm. These resources take the form of time, capital and knowledge. This has led to a number of models being developed with Web site and e-commerce development occurring in stages as enough resources are acquired to move to the next stage. To an extent this implies Web site development is a natural process which gradually takes place over time. Although the timing of any business model adaptation is likely to be influenced by internal life-cycle developments within the firm as well as competitive pressures coming from outside the firm (Andries & Debackere, 2006). Daniel et al. (2002) identify four clusters of firms moving from development of e-commerce tools, to communication through email, through informative

Table 2. Example of e-commerce Adoption Ladder

Step	Title	Description
0	**Not started yet**	The business does not have Internet access.
1	**E-Mail**	Accesses information and services on-line and uses e-mail. Does not have web-site, or surfs the Web, but has an efficient internal and external communications structure.
2	**Web-site**	Business has web-site but contains only basic information about business, relies on customer initializing contact for further information. Can buy services and supplies on-line.
3	**E-Commerce**	Customers have access to more information (catalogue) about products/services. On-line ordering and payment (store) system. Reduced costs and higher levels of accessibility and speed. Web-site not linked to internal systems and orders are processed manually.
4	**E-Business**	Have integrated supply chain, ordering, manufacture, delivery, accounts and marketing to other business systems (seamless processing). Minimum (reduction of) waste regarding resources between supply chain stages.
5	**Transformed Organizations**	Open information systems for customers, suppliers and partners. Internet technology drives both external and internal processes more effectively and efficiently (enabled). Based on networking between firm and other organizations/individuals.

Adapted from: Cisco led Information Age study on E-commerce and Small Business (Martin and Matlay, 2001)

non-interactive Web sites, to the adoption of true e-commerce tools of online selling in the final cluster. The adoption ladder developed under the UK Department for Trade and Industry, provides an alternative hierarchy of stages of ITC adoption and integration within SMEs.

Ultimately, this assumes that the Web site decisions of business owners, take the form of two distinct and sequential decisions (Daniel et al., 2002; Rao et al., 2003). Initially the decision to develop a Web presence is taken. At a later date a decision is taken to develop e-commerce facilities within the Web-page of increasing complexity as time progresses.

Under the staged models firms over time learn the skills required to add additional features to the Web site, gradually progressing up a hierarchy of interactivity and functionality (Daniel et al., 2002). Obviously this progression is associated with acquired knowledge from experience of possessing a Web presence, rather than business experience in general (Levy & Powell, 2003; Rao et al., 2003; Lee, 2004). Even so it would be expected that newer firms would be at lower levels of Web site functionality, particularly as ambiguity and uncertainty will prevent most firms from defining a viable business model from

the outset (Andries & Debackere, 2006). Using a multi-nominal logit regression it is found that older firms in the FSB data are significantly more likely to have developed an active Web site rather than simple brochure style Web site (Table 3), similar results were found when using an ordered logit (Williams et al., 2010). Staged models have been criticized as unrealistic given the existence of early adopters and heterogeneity of small businesses (Martin & Matlay, 2001; Alonso Mendo & Fitzgerald, 2005a). This has led to the development of a number of alternative models examining the e-commerce adoption process of SMEs from a number of perspectives, although the decisions made are likely to require a combination of many models to truly do justice to the adoption process (Alonso Mendo & Fitzgerald, 2005b).

As well as acquiring knowledge about Web technologies it would be natural to expect as Arnott and Bridgewater (2002) find that larger firms have more sophisticated Web sites in terms of their informational, relationship and transactional functions, due to the various resources available to them. This may not necessarily relate to just financial resources, but also managerial resources (Del Aguila-Obra & Padilla-Meléndez, 2006). This is supported by both a logit of active

Table 3. Multinominal Logit of Non-active and Active Website

		Website		Active Website	
Employment (Base category – owner only)	2 - 4 Employees	**0.2210**	(0.040)	**0.4086**	(0.008)
	5 - 9 Employees	**0.4352**	(0.003)	**0.4815**	(0.018)
	10 - 19 Employees	**0.7093**	(0.000)	**0.7946**	(0.003)
	20+ Employees	**0.7652**	(0.004)	**0.8525**	(0.011)
Turnover (Base category – less than £25,000)	£25K - £50K	0.0749	(0.637)	0.1921	(0.382)
	£500k - £100K	0.1351	(0.390)	0.0266	(0.905)
	£100K - £200K	**0.3823**	(0.023)	0.4300	(0.064)
	£200K - £300K	**0.3902**	(0.044)	0.4713	(0.075)
	£300K - £500K	**0.5376**	(0.008)	**0.8232**	(0.003)
	£500K - £1m	**0.7761**	(0.000)	**0.9873**	(0.001)
	£1 million	**1.2535**	(0.000)	**1.7628**	(0.000)
Tourist Trade (Bc – no involvement)	Direct Tourist Trade	**1.0960**	(0.000)	**1.4774**	(0.000)
	Indirect Tourist Trade	0.1956	(0.142)	0.4416	(0.008)
Firm Age (Base category – less than 3 years old)	4 - 9 years	**0.3944**	(0.017)	**0.7843**	(0.000)
	10 to 19 years	0.0670	(0.708)	**0.5105**	(0.031)
	20 or more years	-0.3262	(0.099)	0.1557	(0.556)
Entrepreneur's Age (Base category – younger than 35 years)	35 to 44 years old	**-0.5687**	(0.010)	-0.3931	(0.160)
	45 to 54 years old	**-0.5553**	(0.011)	**-0.5805**	(0.035)
	55 to 64 years	**-0.6248**	(0.005)	-0.5378	(0.058)
	Over 65 years old	**-0.6744**	(0.009)	-0.5318	(0.105)
Entrepreneur's educational attainment (Base category A-levels)	Postgraduate	**0.3502**	(0.038)	**0.5503**	(0.013)
	Bachelors Degree	0.2704	(0.053)	0.3571	(0.053)
	Professional Qualifications	-0.0247	(0.852)	-0.0829	(0.644)
	GCSE/O level	-0.2470	(0.089)	-0.0582	(0.762)
	Vocational Qualifications	-0.3929	(0.025)	-0.3070	(0.219)
	No Formal Qualifications	-0.1079	(0.577)	0.1250	(0.627)
Gender of owners (Bc – equal male & female)	Male Majority	0.0160	(0.858)	-0.1039	(0.389)
	Female Majority	**-0.2773**	(0.031)	**-0.3764**	(0.029)
Hours committed to business (Bc – 30 to 48 hours)	Less than 30 hours	**-0.5568**	(0.001)	-0.3578	(0.126)
	49 to 60 hours	-0.1059	(0.260)	-0.0377	(0.771)
	More than 60 hours	-0.1145	(0.333)	-0.0236	(0.881)
Change in sales volume over last 12 months (base category – decreased by 0% to 5%)	Decreased by 20%+	0.2705	(0.161)	0.3353	(0.209)
	Decreased by 10%-20%	0.1951	(0.288)	0.0786	(0.757)
	Decreased by 5%-10%	-0.0558	(0.764)	0.0536	(0.833)
	Increased by 0%-5%	-0.0054	(0.972)	-0.0541	(0.800)
	Increased by 5%-10%	0.1809	(0.252)	0.0812	(0.714)
	Increased by 10%-20%	0.0973	(0.564)	0.0499	(0.828)
	Increased by 20%+	0.2346	(0.191)	**0.4841**	(0.044)

continued on following page

Table 3. continued

		Website		Active Website	
Objectives for business over next two years (base category – remain same size)	Grow turnover 20%+	**0.8844**	(0.000)	**1.4624**	(0.000)
	Expand up to 20%	**0.6502**	(0.000)	**0.9384**	(0.000)
	Downsize business	-0.0349	(0.862)	0.0570	(0.854)
	Sell or close business	-0.0757	(0.598)	0.1257	(0.548)
	Hand on business	0.3691	(0.228)	**0.8646**	(0.035)
N		5089			
R^2		0.221			
Hosmer-Lemeshow					

Notes: p-values in parenthesis

versus non-active Web sites (Table 1) and a multi-nominal logit of Web site functionality (Table 3). However, Williams et al. (2010) using a probit model incorporating a Heckman (1979) selection model (Van de Ven & Van Praag, 1981), which separates the adoption and development decisions indicates that it is the adoption decision that drives this relationship with firm size. This perhaps represents the fact that resource in shortest supply for SMEs is often time rather than finance, of which Web site development can be particularly draining (Cohen & Kallirroi, 2006; McConville, 2009). Direct involvement in the tourist trade increases the probability of having an active rather than non-active Web site, as customers will frequently be at a distance from the firm's base and is identified as a tool capable of expanding such businesses' reach (Lituchy & Rail, 2000).

Interestingly the characteristics of the business owner have little further influence on the probability of greater Web site functionality. This is quite striking given the role that age and education played in initial Web site adoption. Whilst a young dynamic entrepreneur may see the benefits of a Web presence and may even know enough to develop a basic Web site this may be the point that the skills of the owner and his workforce are restricted to. Any further work will involve bringing in talent from outside, either as new employees, training of existing employees, or outside contractors. The alternative suggested by the staged models will require experience to be acquired gradually over time, with no shortcuts available. However, there could be communication problems between the owner-manager and the other employees, so that information is hoarded rather than disseminated throughout the workforce. Where managers take this approach Martin (2005) finds firms struggle to reach higher levels of e-commerce adoption. It may also be that once the decision to adopt has been taken, business experience plays a greater role in the success of this adoption, by bringing together all elements of the business (Wilson & Daniel, 2007).

Raymond et al. (2005) find that those firms with more aggressive strategies towards new markets are more likely to be utilizing e-commerce. This is reflected in the FSB data (Table 1), with those firms intending to grow moderately are around forty per cent more likely to have active rather than non-active Web sites than those not intending to grow their firms (odds ratio = 1.381). Those with the strongest growth ambitions encompassing those intending to expand turnover by more than 20 per cent a year are approaching twice as likely to have active Web sites (odds ratio = 1.904). The multi-nominal logit of Web site functionality further emphasizes this with active Web sites significantly associated with those owner-manager characteristics associated with greater growth ambitions, youth and higher levels of education. As with adoption, businesses with a majority of female owners are less likely to have active Web sites, potentially reflecting the importance of non-pecuniary measures of success.

Again it is the ambition to grow which is more strongly linked to Web site functionality rather than the growth itself. Discriminant analysis finds this to be the case with those firms without Web sites being those without the objective to grow in the next two years (Table 4 function 1). Moderate growth ambitions are most strongly associated with non-active Web sites (Table 4 function 2). A resource-based explanation for the lack of connection between Web site functionality and growth achieved is that it is not the presence of e-commerce tools that is important in improving firm performance, but rather the performance of the firm's e-commerce strategy which is important. E-commerce performance success requires the presence of complementary business resources without these e-commerce resources will not guarantee e-commerce success (Zhuang & Lederer, 2006). However,

Drew (2003) in his study of firms in the East of England found that active Web sites and e-business are important for supporting major growth thrusts of firms. The multi-nominal logit (Table 3), which separates the adoption and development decisions found more rapid growth of turnover over the previous two years was significantly linked to development of Web sites with greater functionality.

GEOGRAPHICAL SCOPE, INTERNATIONALIZATION AND WEB FUNCTIONALITY AND INTEGRATION

A major difficulty faced by SMEs attempting to grow beyond their core market is a lack of knowledge of new markets (Petersen et al., 2002).

Whilst particularly important for breaking into international markets, this is also true of moving from a local to regional or national scale (Gorton, 1999). Frequently this can result in the need for partners or intermediaries who possess greater knowledge of the market to be engaged (Johanson & Vahlne, 1977). This may result in increased costs and reduced margins and leads to a continuing principal-agent problem. One of the early expectations of e-commerce was to decrease the cost for both buyers and sellers by the elimination of intermediaries within the electronic value chain (O'Keefe et al., 1998), however, research suggests that intermediaries remain important in providing value-added linkages and therefore cannot be easily substituted by the direct supplier-buyer e-commerce relationship (Howcroft, 2001; Giaglis et al., 2002). However, Mansor and Abidin (2010) argue that when SMEs adopted e-commerce, they indirectly removed or partly removed the need for intermediary distribution channels, while at the same time extending the global distribution of sales. They argue that these intermediaries were no longer needed, because the monopoly on information that they previous held will no longer be meaningful as connectivity increases.

Yet, authors including Lawson et al. (2003); Kula and Tatoglu (2003) and Galloway et al. (2008) have suggested that the Web provides an opportunity to grow beyond local markets and even internationalize client bases at a relatively low cost. In general there has been a reduction in the physical and psychical barriers to commerce allowing for greater internationalization (Wen et al., 2001). UK business appears to be taking advantage of these opportunities with the UK a net exporter of e-commerce goods and services, so that in 2009 £9.5 billion of e-commerce goods and services were exported compared to imports of only £3.4 billion (Kalapesi et al., 2010). For SMEs the reduction in barriers, due to the advent of e-commerce, has been predicted to increase the linkages between entrepreneurial activity and international trade which was previously the

Table 4. Discriminant Analysis of Firms by Website Functionality

		Function 1	Function 2
Employees	Owner Only	-0.128	0.059
Turnover	£100,000 or less	-0.194	0.128
	£500,000 or more	0.303	-0.094
Tourist Trade	Direct	0.363	0.183
	Indirect	0.105	0.085
Firm Age	4 to 9 years	0.151	-0.070
	Over 20 years	-0.108	0.165
Owner's qualifications	GCSE	-0.093	0.141
	Vocational Qualifications	-0.186	0.113
Objective for next two years	Grow Rapidly 20%+	0.579	0.110
	Grow Moderately up to 20%	0.477	-0.151
Geographical Variation	Yorkshire and Humber	-0.091	0.111
	South East	0.048	-0.199
	Northern Ireland	-0.102	-0.105
Industry	Agriculture	-0.215	0.119
	Mining and Construction	-0.310	-0.137
	Motor Vehicle Sales and Repair	-0.174	0.051
	Financial Services	-0.143	0.026
	Business Services	0.126	-0.218
	Retail and Wholesale	0.077	0.729
	Eigenvalue	0.141	0.057
	Percentage of Variance	71.391	28.609
		Functions 1 and 2	**Function 2**
	Wilks' Lambda	0.829	0.946
	Chi-square	940.767	276.712
	df	[40]	[19]
	Sig.	(0.000)	(0.000)
		Function 1	**Function 2**
	No Website	-0.649	0.152
At Group Centroides	Non-Active Website	0.102	-0.197
	Active Website	0.437	0.377
Percentage correctly classified		49.90%	

sole domain of large businesses (McDougall and Oviatt, 2000). A couple of notes of caution need to be highlighted, large trans-national corporations may use market power to ensure that e-commerce develops in a fashion, which in turn favours their requirements rather than SMEs (Fariselli et al., 1999; Howcroft, 2001). In addition, although a basic Web site is relatively cheap to develop a more comprehensive offering is not and leaves SMEs disadvantaged in the global cyber-market place as well as in the conventional market place (Samiee, 1998).

A further mistake that may be made by SMEs is to regard online customers as a more distant version of their traditional offline customers. This may be far from the case with online customers having quite different characteristics to online customers requiring adjustments of marketing practices, pricing and even product ranges (Chen et al., 2003). This type of adaptation may be much easier for larger businesses more familiar with accommodating the needs of diverse client groups, but for SMEs dependant on local specific niches this may not be the case.

The experience of economic downturns is that often SMEs can be adversely affected by localized business failures, where a more diversified client base would allow the firm to survive (Packham, 2002; Packham et al, 2005). For those firms operating in more peripheral regions being effective beyond the local market is the only way to achieve growth (Gorton, 1999). The reliance on local markets is observable in the FSB data with firms that have no Web sites reporting that local markets account for 59.2 per cent of sales. This falls to only 32.7 per cent and 34.7 per cent of sales for those firms with on-line sales facilities and fully integrated facilities on their Web sites, respectively. Non-active Web sites again tend to be associated with a more confined geographical spread of sales with those only providing contact details relying on local markets for around half their sales (50.1 per cent), whilst advertising products on-line only lowers this reliance to 41.7 per cent.

Many of the characteristics associated with greater Web site functionality are also likely to be associated with greater geographical spread. For example, larger firms with higher turnover will tend to place less reliance on local markets. This will especially be the case where firms have grown rapidly or intend to grow swiftly, in fact this may be a necessary condition for growth (O'Farrell et al., 1995). Equally those involved in the tourist trade will tend to draw custom from outside the local area, and it is for this reason that the tourist industry

is often cited as a possible source of growth for marginalized and peripheral areas (Briedenhann & Wickens, 2004). When moving beyond a core market, human capital has an important role to play, especially the decision-makers' knowledge of internationalization which has been linked to educational attainment and foreign market experience (Simpson & Kujawa, 1974; Langston & Teas, 1976). Equally, information systems and information technology (IS/IT) may be used to leverage existing capabilities (Duhan et al., 2001; Zhang & Lado, 2001), those with the most experience will see the greatest creation of value from such investments. The FSB data confirms these characteristics are negatively associated with reliance on the local market when using a multi-nominal logit of sales from local markets (Table 5)

One of the expectations of owner-managers in the late 1990s was that the Internet would allow them to increase the geographical scope of their customer bases (Dutta & Evrard, 1999). This is seen as particularly important for growth if the firm is reliant on a thinly spread customer base (Levy et al., 2002). Although attracting new customers was a major incentive for adoption of Internet related activities Daniel and Wilson (2002) found that firms felt e-commerce under performed in terms of achieving this type of benefit. From the FSB data it appears that this is particularly salient for those firms using active rather than non-active Web sites. For example those with non-active Web sites are more than 60 per cent more likely to rely on local markets for less than a quarter of their turnover compared to those without Web sites (relative risk of 1.634), on the other hand, those with active Web sites are two and half times as likely to have reduced their reliance on local markets to this level compared to those without Web sites (relative risk of 2.532). The importance of an active Web site in reducing reliance on the local market to the lowest level is confirmed by discriminant analysis (Table 7, function 1).

Table 5. Multinominal Reliance of Customers within Local Area

		0-25%		26-50%		51-75%	
Website (Bc – No Website)	Non-Active Website	**0.4912**	(0.000)	**0.3560**	(0.005)	**0.5562**	(0.000)
	Active Website	**0.9288**	(0.000)	**0.6347**	(0.000)	**0.4649**	(0.012)
Turnover (Bc – less than £25,000)	£25K - £50K	0.3044	(0.058)	0.1958	(0.321)	0.4039	(0.054)
	£500k - £100K	**0.7549**	(0.000)	0.2272	(0.241)	0.3457	(0.096)
	£100K - £200K	**0.5918**	(0.000)	0.0518	(0.793)	0.2887	(0.165)
	£200K - £300K	**0.7924**	(0.000)	0.1394	(0.536)	**0.5876**	(0.010)
	£300K - £500K	**0.7230**	(0.000)	0.3632	(0.095)	0.3848	(0.100)
	£500K - £1m	**1.2988**	(0.000)	**0.4959**	(0.031)	**0.6873**	(0.004)
	£1 million	**1.8761**	(0.000)	**0.7337**	(0.004)	**0.9216**	(0.000)
Tourist Trade (Bc – none)	Direct	**1.7164**	(0.000)	**1.5659**	(0.000)	**0.6964**	(0.007)
	Indirect	**-0.2547**	(0.048)	**0.4189**	(0.004)	0.1042	(0.488)
Firm Age (Bc – less than 3 years old)	4 - 9 years	0.3073	(0.052)	**0.4812**	(0.020)	0.1397	(0.482)
	10 to 19 years	0.1519	(0.376)	**0.5827**	(0.010)	-0.1177	(0.592)
	20 or more years	-0.1244	(0.519)	0.2788	(0.272)	-0.0153	(0.950)
Entrepreneur's Age (Bc – younger than 35 years)	35 to 44 years old	-0.1451	(0.451)	**-0.4579**	(0.037)	**-0.4208**	(0.051)
	45 to 54 years old	0.2063	(0.275)	-0.3263	(0.131)	-0.3564	(0.094)
	55 to 64 years	**0.5644**	(0.004)	-0.2521	(0.268)	-0.3760	(0.097)
	Over 65 years old	**0.7794**	(0.001)	-0.3893	(0.177)	**-0.7578**	(0.012)
Entrepreneur's educational attainment (Bc A-levels)	Postgraduate	**0.7478**	(0.000)	0.2954	(0.145)	**0.5259**	(0.013)
	Bachelors Degree	0.2082	(0.114)	-0.2805	(0.091)	-0.0550	(0.752)
	Professional	-0.0921	(0.476)	-0.2103	(0.184)	0.0889	(0.589)
	GCSE/O level	0.0159	(0.911)	-0.1636	(0.351)	0.0406	(0.823)
	Vocational	-0.3403	(0.060)	-0.1948	(0.376)	0.1707	(0.442)
	No Formal	**-0.5168**	(0.008)	-0.0541	(0.812)	0.0876	(0.712)
Owners' gender (Bc – equal)	Male Majority	0.0952	(0.260)	**0.2293**	(0.037)	0.1134	(0.304)
	Female Majority	-0.0802	(0.523)	0.1624	(0.301)	0.0699	(0.658)
Hours committed to business (Bc – 30 to 48 hours)	Less than 30 hours	0.1224	(0.477)	-0.2468	(0.304)	-0.2996	(0.251)
	49 to 60 hours	0.0205	(0.822)	-0.0850	(0.464)	0.1561	(0.186)
	More than 60 hours	0.0406	(0.719)	0.0324	(0.818)	0.0443	(0.763)
Objectives for business over next two years (Bc – remain same size)	Grow 20%+	**0.3248**	(0.014)	0.0996	(0.558)	**0.3651**	(0.038)
	Expand up to 20%	0.0989	(0.325)	0.1105	(0.386)	**0.3758**	(0.005)
	Downsize business	-0.0162	(0.939)	-0.0974	(0.728)	-0.0490	(0.872)
	Sell or close	-0.1413	(0.353)	-0.2885	(0.156)	0.0906	(0.657)
	Hand on business	-0.1943	(0.508)	-0.8408	(0.077)	0.2664	(0.470)
	N	5056					
	R^2	0.117					

Notes: p-values in parenthesis

Where the Web is seen as emerging in importance is in terms of breaking into international markets. Whilst SMEs are often felt to be able to grow organically and acquisitively within national markets, they are often felt to be incapable of breaking into international markets (Fariselli et al., 1999). SMEs considering internationalization may not dive in straight away, but rather take a staged approach, with traditional internationalization models such as the Uppsala process suggesting a depth of involvement based upon the extent of market knowledge and commitment (Johanson & Vahlne, 1977). Commitment is incrementally increased as market knowledge is deepened moving from no exports through exports via independent agents and offshore sales subsidies to overseas production facilities. The rate of internationalization depends on the speed that market risk falls, which is related to changes in uncertainty and commitment. In spite of this, the process of internationalization may differ between firms depending on their products and characteristics. For example, those with innovative goods and services may prefer to sell to a greater number of markets, whilst maintaining a single source of production for economies of scale. Those firms with less innovative products may not have the margins to cover freight costs, and need to rely on speed of delivery to a greater extent to win customers, and therefore develop production facilities in other countries. It is likely that the Internet will be of aid in internationalizing for both these groups, as far as it provides information via a 'sow and reap' approach. Firms will have a presence in more countries and can identify those which are most promising for further exploitation (Chetty & Campbell-Hunt, 2003).

The advent of e-commerce and the opportunities to service international markets in different ways might be expected to alter the traditional patterns of internationalization. The relatively low infrastructure costs of entering new markets, for example, may increase the speed that new markets of a similar nature are entered. Some

patterns are found to continue with firms more likely to enter those markets with the lowest psychic distance first, and local partners often are involved in localizing the Web site (Kim, 2003). This indicates that some barriers such as cultural and language differences still remain even in the Internet age (Jaw & Chen, 2006). Evidence also suggests that entry normally takes the lower risk exporting route as previously, but later stages may be jumped (Jaw & Chen, 2006).

A study of SMEs in the North American hospitality industry found that a large proportion of respondents saw the Internet as being an effective tool to expand their international trade, in spite of this, an early study, like many others, found Web site functionality to be relatively low (Lituchy & Rail, 2000). This means that often firms will limit themselves to the advantages of advertising internationally without putting the means to undertake transactions internationally in place (Poon & Swatman, 1999). The average scale of the firms included in the FSB data means that relatively few sales are obtained overseas, so that the average percentage of all sales that are outside the UK is 7.6 per cent. In results similar to those found by Kapaseli et al. (2010), the FSB data indicates that firms with fully integrated Web sites obtained more than twice the proportion of sales from outside the UK (11.6 per cent) to those firms with no Web site (4.6 per cent). Nevertheless, these figures if anything, overstate the sales overseas as 66.4 per cent of firms obtain none of their sales from outside the UK. This again varies from 80.7 per cent of firms without Web sites who make no sales outside the UK, to only 44.3 per cent of firms with fully integrated Web sites having no non-UK sales. A majority of those firms with just on-line sales facilities are found to obtain some of their sales from outside the UK. Brochure style Web sites have less influence in increasing international presence as would be expected with 74 per cent of those with just contact details and 64.8 per cent using their Web sites simply as a method of advertising their products having no international sales. This comes as no surprise given that Sinkovics and Penz (2005) find online transactions to be one of the factors identified when establishing the effectiveness of Web sites. Firms may not actually intend to internationalize when developing a Web presence, rather it is a side-effect and may lead to the firm receiving its first overseas orders unsoliciting (Oviatt & McDougall, 1999). Since unsolicited orders from international markets are found to be one of the strongest stimuli to exporting (Simpson & Kujawa, 1974), the development of Web sites may increase the likelihood that SMEs will start to internationalize their sales.

Using a multi-nominal logit of the proportion of sales from international markets the FSB data provides evidence that greater Web site integration is positively associated with increased probability of exporting (Table 6). For the highest level of exports those with non-active Web sites are half as likely again to belong in this category as those with no Web site (relative risk of 1.504). Those with active Web sites are over twice as likely to be exporting more than 20 per cent of their sales (relative risk of 2.175). This is similar to the results found by Daniel et al. (2002) suggesting that one of the primary discriminants between those at an early 'stage' and those at a later 'stage' of e-commerce adoption was the proportion of sales outside the UK.

Interestingly, the presence of a firm Web site increases the probability of exporting, but the coefficients do not appear to show the increase in probability for those firms with active Web sites that might be expected for those categories representing a larger proportion of sales. This is confirmed by discriminant analysis (Table 7), which indicates that both active and non-active Web sites play a role in generating non-UK sales (function 1), but both types of Web site are also linked with the separating out of lower levels of exports (function 2). This means that whilst the Web increases the probability of internationalizing, for UK SMEs at this point in time there is

little influence on expanding international sales to a point where they contribute a large proportion of sales. This is likely to be once again a reflection of the relatively low level of reliance on the Internet by UK SMEs, where even those firms using more integrated Web sites, e-commerce sales are in general dominated by their bricks and mortar sales.

Obviously the links between Web site adoption and greater geographical distribution of the customer base may run in both directions. Those firms with customers further from the firm's home base may feel that the Internet may provide an efficient means of communicating with their customers. Similarly the influence of greater integration may in part reflect the requirement to sell to customers further a field, consistent with the findings that a firm's use of the Web will relate to the fit with the firm's existing business model. Consistent with this Arnott and Bridgewater (2002) found that those firms selling to international markets used higher levels of facilities within their Web sites, but no significant difference was found between those firms using the Web to internationalize and those that internationalized before developing a Web site.

SHORTAGES OF IT SKILLS AND WEB SITE FUNCTIONALITY AND INTEGRATION

Although Web site functionality is associated with greater growth ambitions particularly through increased geographical spread of customer bases, Web sites of UK SMEs remain mainly in the form of electronic brochures with few, if any, interactive functions. Even when firms acknowledge the benefits and potential of the Web for growth and internationalization, the level of functionality is generally low, with a fear of technology leading to a suboptimal usage of the Web (Lituchy & Rail, 2000).

Table 6. Multinominal Logit of Sales to Customers Outside the UK

		1-5%		6-20%		21-100%	
Website (Bc – No Website)	Non-Active Website	**0.5266**	(0.000)	0.2722	(0.059)	**0.4079**	(0.007)
	Active Website	**0.8024**	(0.000)	**0.7216**	(0.000)	**0.7772**	(0.000)
Turnover (Bc – less than £25,000)	£25K - £50K	0.2745	(0.243)	0.0544	(0.797)	0.3939	(0.091)
	£500k - £100K	0.3930	(0.085)	0.3745	(0.058)	**0.8019**	(0.000)
	£100K - £200K	**0.6169**	(0.006)	0.2273	(0.268)	**0.5768**	(0.011)
	£200K - £300K	0.3181	(0.205)	0.0858	(0.712)	0.4805	(0.057)
	£300K - £500K	0.3016	(0.235)	0.2328	(0.309)	**0.7532**	(0.002)
	£500K - £1m	**0.6251**	(0.011)	**0.4514**	(0.047)	**0.9712**	(0.000)
	£1 million	**0.9476**	(0.000)	**0.8693**	(0.000)	**1.2739**	(0.000)
Tourist Trade (Bc – none)	Direct	**1.1599**	(0.000)	**1.4219**	(0.000)	**0.9779**	(0.000)
	Indirect	0.2211	(0.140)	0.1052	(0.501)	-0.0185	(0.913)
Firm Age (Bc – less than 3 years old)	4 - 9 years	0.3735	(0.088)	0.1321	(0.503)	0.2789	(0.215)
	10 to 19 years	**0.7267**	(0.002)	0.0867	(0.682)	**0.6920**	(0.003)
	20 or more years	**0.5457**	(0.038)	0.3293	(0.163)	**0.6671**	(0.012)
Entrepreneur's Age (Bc – younger than 35 years)	35 to 44 years old	-0.1911	(0.388)	-0.1176	(0.612)	0.3097	(0.276)
	45 to 54 years old	-0.2041	(0.348)	-0.0223	(0.921)	**0.6163**	(0.025)
	55 to 64 years	-0.2348	(0.303)	0.0147	(0.950)	**0.7840**	(0.005)
	Over 65 years old	-0.3284	(0.250)	0.4381	(0.108)	**1.1904**	(0.000)
Entrepreneur's educational attainment (Bc A-levels)	Postgraduate	0.3140	(0.103)	**0.7456**	(0.000)	**0.8351**	(0.000)
	Bachelors Degree	0.0495	(0.759)	**0.3717**	(0.029)	**0.3656**	(0.029)
	Professional	-0.2189	(0.174)	0.0611	(0.719)	-0.1906	(0.273)
	GCSE/O level	-0.2899	(0.100)	0.1154	(0.525)	**-0.4444**	(0.025)
	Vocational	-0.3104	(0.192)	0.0413	(0.861)	**-0.6558**	(0.017)
	No Formal	-0.4262	(0.087)	-0.1759	(0.482)	-0.3680	(0.150)
Owners' gender (Bc – equal)	Male Majority	-0.0631	(0.565)	0.1363	(0.210)	-0.1645	(0.130)
	Female Majority	0.2104	(0.178)	0.2791	(0.073)	-0.1502	(0.379)
Hours committed to business (Bc – 30 to 48 hours)	Less than 30 hours	-0.1325	(0.593)	-0.1901	(0.425)	**0.5405**	(0.011)
	49 to 60 hours	-0.1224	(0.295)	-0.0272	(0.817)	0.0869	(0.483)
	More than 60 hours	-0.1048	(0.469)	0.0740	(0.598)	0.2520	(0.088)
Objectives for business over next two years (Bc – remain same size)	Grow 20%+	-0.2369	(0.191)	0.1482	(0.369)	0.2360	(0.160)
	Expand up to 20%	0.2076	(0.119)	0.0781	(0.552)	0.0359	(0.791)
	Downsize business	-0.5097	(0.135)	-0.4030	(0.181)	-0.0668	(0.810)
	Sell or close	0.0029	(0.988)	-0.1695	(0.391)	-0.1420	(0.480)
	Hand on business	0.0500	(0.900)	0.3574	(0.294)	-0.2070	(0.626)
	N	5056					
	R²	0.124					

Notes: p-values in parenthesis

Table 7. Discriminant Analysis of Firms by Reliance on Local and Non-UK Markets

		Reliance on Local Sales		Reliance on non-UK Sales	
		Function 1	Function 2	Function 1	Function 2
Website	No Website	-0.273	0.471		
	Non-Active Website			0.278	-0.126
	Active Website	0.297	0.018	0.581	-0.270
Turnover	£500,000 or more	0.307	0.035	0.146	0.024
Tourist Trade	Direct	0.351	-0.176	0.400	-0.386
	Indirect	-0.098	-0.360		
Firm Age	Less than 4 years			-0.199	0.014
	4 to 9 years	0.152	-0.101	-0.121	-0.058
Owner's Age	16 to 34 years	-0.146	-0.327		
	35 to 44 years	-0.281	-0.091		
	45 to 54 years	-0.171	-0.120		
	Over 64 years	0.074	0.208	0.114	0.235
Experience	10 to 19 years	0.121	0.066		
Owner's Qualifications	Postgraduate	0.239	0.043	0.283	0.352
	Bachelors Degree	0.143	0.334	0.175	0.273
Sales growth	5% to 10% Growth	-0.121	-0.129		
Objective for next two years	Grow Rapidly 20%+	0.133	-0.011		
	Grow up to 20%	0.052	-0.272	0.056	-0.307
Geographical Variation	North West	-0.141	0.182		
	Yorkshire and Humber	-0.107	-0.006	-0.117	-0.059
	London	0.132	-0.070	0.169	-0.046
	Wales			-0.098	-0.227
	Northern Ireland			0.146	-0.064
Industry	Mining & Construction	0.189	-0.066		
	Manufacturing	0.555	0.185	0.570	0.361
	Transport and Utilities	0.196	0.235	0.155	0.256
	Hotels & Restaurants	0.141	0.191	0.298	0.185
	Business Services	0.447	0.162	0.248	0.310
	Retail and Wholesale			0.329	-0.220
	Health & Social	-0.044	0.293		
	Eigenvalue	0.199	0.023	0.175	0.013
	Percentage of Variance	89.6	10.4	93.3	6.7
		Func 1 & 2	Function 2	Func 1 & 2	Function 2
	Wilks' Lambda	0.815	0.977	0.840	0.987
	Chi-square	1021.742	114.401	869.917	62.989
	df	[50]	[24]	[38]	[18]
	Sig.	(0.000)	(0.000)	(0.000)	(0.000)

continued on following page

Table 7. continued.

		Reliance on Local Sales		Reliance on non-UK Sales	
		Function 1	Function 2	Function 1	Function 2
	0 - 25% Local 0% Non-UK	0.473	0.071	-0.294	0.008
At Group Centroides	26 - 75% Local 1 – 20% Non-UK	-0.097	-0.251	0.541	-0.152
	76 - 100% Local 21 – 100% Non-UK	-0.573	0.118	0.687	0.260
Percentage correctly classified		50.3%		57.0%	

Research repeatedly indicates that one of the primary barriers to adoption of technology, such as the Internet and the Web, is the lack of IT and IS capabilities within the business (Drew, 2003; Bhagwat & Sharma, 2007). In the late 1990s a lack of understanding of the potential benefits and costs of new technology was identified as one of the major barriers to full embracement of the Web (Dutta & Evrard, 1999). This may even turn into resistance to new technology if improvements to existing business practices cannot be observed (Anderson & Huang, 2006; Bruque & Moyano, 2007). This means that once a decision to adopt has been made research also suggests that it is important that relevant skills are in place before implementation, so that staff have the confidence to overcome the barriers they encounter during the implementation process (Love et al., 2001). A lack of Web site development skills is likely to be common within SMEs preventing inexpensive improvements of Web site functionality (Darch & Lucas, 2002; Lawson et al., 2003). This comes as no surprise as most SMEs will be reliant on basic skills of staff specializing in other tasks, with more complex tasks subcontracted to expensive external consultants. This will be especially a problem for the smallest firms where managerial capabilities will be absent, leading to a greater reliance on external expertise (Del Aguila-Obra & Padilla-Meléndez, 2006). A further problem is that many SMEs lack a formal ITC adoption strategy (Ballantine et al., 1998). This means that it is also

unlikely that a complementary training strategy will be in place to develop the skills required.

Table 8 shows the raw percentages of firms indicating that they had experienced a shortage of basic and advanced IT skills in relation to their level of Web site integration. As would be expected those firms with higher levels of Web site functionality are more likely to have encountered both basic and advanced IT skills shortages. It appears that those firms least likely to encounter shortages are those with no Web sites at all, the group of employees in which shortages of skills are most frequently reported is the older employee group, so that of those firms with no Web sites 8.7 per cent have reported a shortage of basic IT skills and 9.1 per cent a shortage of advanced IT skills. Less than one in twenty firms with no Web site reported a shortage of basic and advanced IT skills when considering potential recruits.

At the other end of the spectrum those businesses with fully integrated Web sites appear to be most likely to encounter IT skills shortages from current and potential employees. Again, it is older workers that are most likely to display IT skills shortages for this group of firms, so much so, that nearly one in five firms (19.0 per cent) reported encountering a shortage of basic IT skills in employees aged over 25 years, with a shortage of advanced IT skills reported by 17.0 per cent of firms with fully integrated Web sites for this group of workers. For younger workers (those less than 25 years of age) the percentage of fully inte-

Table 8. Shortage of Staff IT Skills by Website Facilitation

		No	Basic Information	Advertise Products	Sell on-line	Link to Suppliers	Sell on-line and link to suppliers	All	Pearson Chi-Square		
Employees younger than 25 years of age	Shortage of Basic IT Skills	6.9%	8.1%	9.3%	9.7%	11.9%	16.3%	8.8%	18.198	[5]	(0.003)
	Shortage of Advanced IT Skills	4.2%	8.9%	8.5%	9.3%	11.9%	17.7%	8.0%	46.327	[5]	(0.000)
Employees older than 25 years of age	Shortage of Basic IT Skills	8.7%	10.5%	12.8%	12.6%	13.6%	19.0%	11.6%	22.580	[5]	(0.000)
	Shortage of Advanced IT Skills	9.1%	12.9%	12.8%	11.7%	13.6%	17.0%	11.9%	15.556	[5]	(0.008)
In potential staff recruits	Shortage of Basic IT Skills	4.4%	8.0%	8.8%	8.4%	15.3%	14.3%	7.8%	35.187	[5]	(0.000)
	Shortage of Advanced IT Skills	3.7%	6.9%	8.3%	7.5%	11.9%	13.6%	7.0%	36.769	[5]	(0.000)
Staff recruitment and training decisions	New staff	22.3%	33.0%	41.7%	34.6%	49.2%	48.3%	34.8%	140.993	[5]	(0.000)
	Increasing in Staff Training	11.7%	18.6%	23.6%	19.5%	28.8%	25.2%	19.4%	74.450	[5]	(0.000)

Notes: degrees of freedom shown in square brackets; p-values in parenthesis

grated Web site firms encountering a shortage of IT skills drops to 16.3 per cent for basic skills and 17.7 per cent for advanced skills. The lower shortages reported regarding recruitment may be in part misleading as many firms may not have attempted to recruit during the last two years.

The need to keep Web sites updated and relevant makes true e-commerce either impractical or more commonly simply out of the price range of most UK SMEs. Consequently, this has made it highly important that firms ensure that the staff and management receive training in the usage of new IT developments (Dutta & Evrard, 1999; Fariselli et al., 1999). No significant differences in the probability of encountering basic IT skills shortages are found between firms with active and non-active Web sites (Table 10). Using logit regressions with greater division of Web site functionality it is found that those firms with fully integrated Web sites are twice as likely to encounter basic IT skills shortages when recruiting (odds ratio = 2.051) compared to those without Web sites. Interestingly, the probability of encountering a basic IT skills shortage when recruiting for those firms using Web sites to connect primarily with suppliers is approaching three times that of those without Web sites (odds ratio = 2.778). This means that those firms which have moved to the highest levels of Web site functionality are not able to bring in the talent they require. Knowledge of this is likely to put firms operating with more basic Web sites off further development unless they already have employees with the skills required. In fact Thompson et al. (2010) find that basic IT shortages have the greatest constraining effect on achieving the firm's objectives when the firm sells some goods online, but these sales account for no more than 10 per cent of the total.

Using a resource-based theory approach Caldeira and Ward (2003) highlight the importance of IT skills being developed in-house to ensure they fit with the requirements of the firm, where possession of IT skills can form an important competitive advantage in itself. However, when considering advanced IT skills it appears those with more sophisticated Web sites do not appear to have developed these skills in-house. Table 11 provides evidence of this with firms utilising fully integrated Web sites found to be three times as likely to encounter advanced IT skills shortages in younger workers than those firms with no Web sites at all (odds ratio = 3.139). Searching for new talent may not solve the problem either as those with fully integrated Web sites are twice as likely to encounter advanced IT skills shortages when attempting to recruit as those with no Web site (odds ratio = 2.060). Again this appears to be where firms with greater Web site integration are attempting to bring in employees with the skills that they require, or looking to younger employees to take on responsibilities associated with newer technological advances. It should be noted that the severity of the constraints imposed by such advanced IT skills shortages may also increase with the sophistication of the firm's Web site as the firm becomes more reliant on the Internet within its business model (Thompson et al., 2010).

CONCLUSION AND FUTURE RESEARCH DIRECTIONS

Building on existing literature this chapter has used data from a relatively large sample of SMEs from the UK to examine the links between the level of Web site integration and turnover growth in general, and more specifically through increased geographical scope. The data examined here has confirmed the findings of previous studies such as Levy and Powell (2003) and Crespi et al. (2004) in that Internet adoption in general in the UK appears to be high and many firms have their own Web sites. As in previous studies however, the average level of functionality and integration is low in UK SMEs. Whilst Web site functionality is not significantly linked to the growth rates achieved by firms over the past two years, it is linked per-

haps more tellingly to aspirations of growth, so that those firms whose objectives are to grow in the future are much more likely to develop their Web sites so they have higher levels of facilities incorporated.

The percentage of firms adding active elements to their Web sites is still relatively low, which is surprising given the links found between Web site functionality and the escape from reliance on local markets. Those firms with greater Web site functionality are both found to be more likely to export and are less likely to draw a majority of their sales from local markets.

It was suggested that given the importance of IT self-efficacy in the adoption of newer technologies (Lee, 2004), a shortage of IT skills was likely to be one of the factors holding back greater Web site development (Drew, 2003). The percentage of firms encountering shortages of basic and advanced IT skills was found to be much higher for those firms with higher levels of Web site integration. Whilst much of this appears to be related to firm and entrepreneurial characteristics associated with both Web site adoption and skills shortages it does appear that those firms with the Web sites of greatest functionality are significantly more likely to be hindered by a lack of availability in advanced IT skills.

Whilst IT skills shortages are most commonly found for older workers it is the skills shortages associated with younger workers and potential employees when attempting to recruit that are linked to Web site functionality. It does seem therefore that those firms that have brochure style Web sites are unlikely to naturally follow the staged models of Web site development (Daniel et al., 2002), if those firms that have already followed this path are frequently baulked in their ambitions by a lack of available talent.

The findings suggest that SMEs that understand the potential of the Web are prepared to embrace the potential of e-commerce. This reduces the reliance on local markets which in times of economic difficulty can be essential. Nonetheless,

Table 9. Shortage of Staff IT Skills by Presence of Non-Active and Active Website

		No Website	Non-Active Website	Active Website	All	Pearson Chi-Square		
Employees younger than 25 years of age	Shortage of Basic IT Skills	6.9%	8.9%	10.7%	8.8%	9.975	[2]	(0.007)
	Shortage of Advanced IT Skills	4.2%	8.6%	10.6%	8.0%	34.122	[2]	(0.000)
Employees older than 25 years of age	Shortage of Basic IT Skills	8.7%	12.1%	13.5%	11.6%	14.128	[2]	(0.001)
	Shortage of Advanced IT Skills	9.1%	12.9%	12.5%	11.9%	12.063	[2]	(0.002)
In potential staff recruits	Shortage of Basic IT Skills	4.4%	8.5%	9.6%	7.8%	25.782	[2]	(0.000)
	Shortage of Advanced IT Skills	3.7%	7.8%	8.6%	7.0%	26.390	[2]	(0.000)
Staff recruitment and training decisions	New Staff	22.3%	38.8%	37.3%	34.8%	104.843	[2]	(0.000)
	Increase in staff training	11.7%	22.0%	20.8%	19.4%	58.877	[2]	(0.000)

Notes: degrees of freedom shown in square brackets; p-values in parenthesis

as has been found previously a large proportion of SMEs do not desire or seek growth (Levy & Powell, 2003). This may reflect differing objectives and ambitions. However, the extent to which firms understand the ramifications of not adopting and embracing technological advances is not clear. Whilst business advice services are provided from a variety of sources, it is likely that all too often owners of SMEs will seek this advice at a point when it is too late to change the course of the firm, and resources are not available. It would appear therefore that trade associations and local community intermediaries have an important role to play in educating their members/ local business community to the benefits and threats that technological advancements such as the Web bring (Lockett & Brown, 2006). Matlay and Westhead (2005) highlight the emergence of e-entrepreneur networks and that entrepreneurship plays a central role in the adoption of information technologies by small business. Given that the strategic importance of functionality and integration appears to be recognized or acted upon by relatively few firms (Lee, 2004), and given the increase in globalization, UK SMEs need to be made aware of these issues to ensure competitiveness is maintained. Fundamentally the Internet provides not just opportunities but also is a source of threats to existing sales (Drew, 2003). Therefore, Government Internet policies will play a significant role in adoption rates and role of e-business (Simmons et al., 2008).

Against a backdrop of low interest in growth, firms that would gladly use Web site functionality as a method of not only growing, but also expanding their customer base, even achieving international sales growth, may not be able to do so. A considerable barrier to this may be the lack of IT skills present in the UK labour force. Clearly any scheme to increase the awareness of UK SMEs to the Web will be limited if the skills are not available in the workforce. Whilst training can be provided directly to SMEs the shortage of more advanced IT skills appears to be fairly

Table 10. Logits of Shortages of Basic IT Skills encountered

		Younger Employees (Under 25 years)		Older Employees (Under 25 years)		Recruitment	
Website (Bc – No Website)	Non-Active Website	-0.1441	(0.333)	-0.0412	(0.756)	0.2477	(0.155)
	Active Website	-0.0731	(0.701)	0.0029	(0.986)	0.3550	(0.101)
Employment (Bc – owner only)	2 - 4 Employees	**0.6823**	(0.001)	**1.1095**	(0.000)	**0.7632**	(0.001)
	5 - 9 Employees	**1.0305**	(0.000)	**1.5871**	(0.000)	**1.3498**	(0.000)
	10 - 19 Employees	**1.5384**	(0.000)	**1.7826**	(0.000)	**1.5566**	(0.000)
	20+ Employees	**1.8602**	(0.000)	**2.1079**	(0.000)	**2.0074**	(0.000)
Turnover (Bc – less than £25,000)	£25K - £50K	0.2313	(0.487)	0.0299	(0.915)	0.1236	(0.737)
	£500k - £100K	0.3684	(0.244)	0.0958	(0.717)	0.2027	(0.561)
	£100K - £200K	0.4798	(0.133)	0.1904	(0.475)	0.6420	(0.061)
	£200K - £300K	0.5477	(0.106)	0.3255	(0.249)	0.4900	(0.183)
	£300K - £500K	0.6030	(0.077)	0.3170	(0.267)	**0.7236**	(0.048)
	£500K - £1m	0.5265	(0.133)	0.4743	(0.103)	0.6268	(0.095)
	£1 million	0.6834	(0.063)	**0.6062**	(0.049)	**0.8287**	(0.034)
Tourist Trade (Bc – none)	Direct	0.3749	(0.089)	0.0556	(0.785)	-0.1484	(0.564)
	Indirect	0.1182	(0.477)	-0.0596	(0.694)	0.0789	(0.656)
Firm Age (Bc – less than 3 years old)	4 - 9 years	-0.0909	(0.673)	-0.1467	(0.428)	-0.0528	(0.815)
	10 to 19 years	-0.0008	(0.997)	-0.2723	(0.178)	-0.2052	(0.404)
	20 or more years	-0.1336	(0.611)	-0.3187	(0.167)	-0.1952	(0.489)
Entrepreneur's Age (Bc – younger than 35 years)	35 to 44 years old	-0.1366	(0.546)	0.0388	(0.853)	-0.1231	(0.592)
	45 to 54 years old	**-0.4883**	(0.032)	-0.1593	(0.446)	-0.4317	(0.061)
	55 to 64 years	**-0.8060**	(0.001)	**-0.4842**	(0.030)	**-0.7356**	(0.003)
	Over 65 years old	**-0.6577**	(0.030)	-0.4532	(0.104)	-0.5954	(0.067)
Entrepreneur's educational attainment (Bc A-levels)	Postgraduate	0.2185	(0.314)	0.2883	(0.132)	0.2360	(0.280)
	Bachelors Degree	0.1721	(0.354)	**0.3496**	(0.030)	0.1888	(0.316)
	Professional	0.2655	(0.142)	0.1420	(0.382)	0.0089	(0.962)
	GCSE/O level	0.1490	(0.454)	0.0946	(0.591)	-0.0050	(0.981)
	Vocational	0.2611	(0.302)	-0.0206	(0.930)	-0.1170	(0.678)
	No Formal	0.0944	(0.728)	-0.0308	(0.900)	**-0.8054**	(0.028)
Owners' gender (Bc – equal)	Male Majority	-0.0388	(0.742)	0.1643	(0.119)	0.0669	(0.600)
	Female Majority	**0.3557**	(0.036)	**0.4912**	(0.001)	**0.6598**	(0.000)
Hours committed to business (Bc – 30 to 48 hours)	Less than 30 hours	-0.2175	(0.524)	0.3046	(0.220)	-0.1780	(0.634)
	49 to 60 hours	**0.4725**	(0.001)	**0.3178**	(0.010)	**0.4546**	(0.003)
	More than 60 hours	**0.8920**	(0.000)	**0.8231**	(0.000)	**1.0356**	(0.000)
Objectives for business over next two years (Bc – remain same size)	Grow 20%+	0.2641	(0.159)	0.0833	(0.618)	0.3026	(0.135)
	Expand up to 20%	0.1570	(0.312)	0.1292	(0.338)	0.2242	(0.189)
	Downsize business	0.0903	(0.777)	-0.1726	(0.579)	-0.0819	(0.826)
	Sell or close	**0.5270**	(0.012)	0.3126	(0.102)	0.2673	(0.274)
	Hand on business	-0.1238	(0.777)	-0.4759	(0.268)	0.2205	(0.610)

continued on following page

Table 10. continued

	Younger Employees (Under 25 years)		Older Employees (Under 25 years)		Recruitment	
N	5056		5056		5056	
R^2	0.105		0.106		0.131	
Hosmer-Lemeshow	10.6	(0.226)	2.88	(0.942)	6.22	(0.623)

Notes: p-values in parenthesis

chronic for those firms with the highest levels of Web site integration. This would suggest that there needs to be an emphasis on providing IT skills of this level to young people in full time education. It is surprising that given the role that IT/IS equipment and applications play in the modern workplace that a vast majority of further and higher education courses are limited to basic PC applications with Web skills learnt in an ad hoc and informal manner.

Web site integration may currently be the preserve of those firms wishing to grow rapidly. Given the rapid integration of global markets and growth of online sales this may not remain the case for much longer. The ability of the Web to help firms grow beyond their core local markets will become more and more of a necessity for survival. If this is the case it is important that SME owners are educated to make them aware of the threats and opportunities this engenders. Growth orientated firms and more and more frequently those firms with aspirations simply to survive will be hamstrung unless more advanced IT skills are added to the curriculum of students as standard.

It is important to acknowledge the limitations of the data in terms of investigating issues relating to e-commerce given the survey's more general purpose and clearly there is a need for further quantitative and qualitative work to be undertaken. For example, firms with Web sites more fully integrated into their businesses are more likely to be growth orientated but there is no strong link between previous growth and Web site functionality. Future work needs to ascertain what these growth orientated businesses hope to achieve through their greater integration of their Web sites, and also why in retrospect this did not occur. Ideally such work would be longitudinal in nature to follow businesses through their adoption, and integration decisions, keeping track of their expectations and desires at all points. Obviously focused research projects such as this could examine the functions of Web sites in much greater detail to obtain a fuller and more precise measure of integration. Similarly when looking for explanations as to why a greater number of UK SMEs do not develop their Web sites beyond basic brochure style Web sites the FSB data is limited in asking indirect questions in relation to shortages of IT capabilities. Clearly there does seem to be an issue of IT shortages which may hinder growth orientated businesses from increasing their geographical scope, but whether this is the reason for lower levels of commitment to the Web by UK SMEs in general needs to be investigated more thoroughly through questionnaire and interview approaches specifically looking to answer these questions. Overall there seems to be an acceptance that although SME Web site adoption and functionality is relatively low and a number of potential answers to why this might be the case, no conclusive work has so far been conducted. This means that policy responses will have to be made to a large extent in the dark, possibly costing the UK in terms of lost opportunities for growth and employment.

Table 11. Logit of Shortages of Advanced IT Skills encountered

		Younger Employees (Under 25 years)		Older Employees (Under 25 years)		Recruitment	
Website (Bc – No Website)	Non-Active Website	**0.3384**	(0.050)	0.0272	(0.835)	0.1528	(0.412)
	Active Website	**0.5181**	(0.014)	-0.0551	(0.748)	0.2437	(0.288)
Employment (Bc – owner only)	2 - 4 Employees	**0.7077**	(0.001)	**0.8025**	(0.000)	**0.9060**	(0.000)
	5 - 9 Employees	**1.1395**	(0.000)	**0.8916**	(0.000)	**1.2441**	(0.000)
	10 - 19 Employees	**1.4141**	(0.000)	**0.9907**	(0.000)	**1.4263**	(0.000)
	20+ Employees	**1.7359**	(0.000)	**1.2297**	(0.000)	**1.5788**	(0.000)
Turnover (Bc – less than £25,000)	£25K - £50K	0.4593	(0.171)	0.1441	(0.535)	-0.5228	(0.134)
	£500k - £100K	0.3153	(0.338)	0.0302	(0.894)	-0.2438	(0.435)
	£100K - £200K	**0.6439**	(0.049)	0.1591	(0.491)	0.1542	(0.618)
	£200K - £300K	0.4040	(0.252)	0.0555	(0.830)	-0.0748	(0.827)
	£300K - £500K	0.4929	(0.163)	0.3147	(0.220)	0.2433	(0.471)
	£500K - £1m	0.6552	(0.067)	0.4459	(0.090)	0.4741	(0.166)
	£1 million	0.4852	(0.203)	**0.6631**	(0.019)	0.6179	(0.091)
Tourist Trade (Bc – none)	Direct	-0.0620	(0.810)	0.2301	(0.264)	0.0185	(0.947)
	Indirect	0.0818	(0.641)	0.1477	(0.317)	0.2320	(0.223)
Firm Age (Bc – less than 3 years old)	4 - 9 years	0.0360	(0.874)	-0.1816	(0.309)	0.5359	(0.038)
	10 to 19 years	-0.0523	(0.827)	-0.3079	(0.117)	0.3025	(0.273)
	20 or more years	-0.3220	(0.232)	-0.2488	(0.270)	0.2121	(0.502)
Entrepreneur's Age (Bc – younger than 35 years)	35 to 44 years old	**-0.4500**	(0.043)	-0.0141	(0.943)	-0.3052	(0.205)
	45 to 54 years old	**-0.8542**	(0.000)	-0.3810	(0.054)	-0.3456	(0.146)
	55 to 64 years	**-1.1537**	(0.000)	**-0.7551**	(0.000)	**-0.8436**	(0.001)
	Over 65 years old	**-1.2892**	(0.000)	**-0.7138**	(0.008)	**-0.9879**	(0.006)
Entrepreneur's educational attainment (Bc A-levels)	Postgraduate	**0.6675**	(0.002)	**0.4827**	(0.007)	**0.6941**	(0.003)
	Bachelors Degree	0.3665	(0.057)	**0.3615**	(0.021)	**0.6047**	(0.004)
	Professional	0.2125	(0.270)	0.1055	(0.507)	0.3167	(0.138)
	GCSE/O level	0.0512	(0.811)	-0.1223	(0.498)	0.0170	(0.944)
	Vocational	-0.1002	(0.736)	-0.4228	(0.106)	-0.0042	(0.990)
	No Formal	0.0279	(0.925)	-0.1571	(0.537)	-0.0625	(0.861)
Owners' gender (Bc – equal)	Male Majority	-0.0539	(0.653)	**0.2055**	(0.049)	-0.0005	(0.997)
	Female Majority	-0.0791	(0.683)	**0.3245**	(0.030)	0.3063	(0.117)
Hours committed to business (Bc – 30 to 48 hours)	Less than 30 hours	0.4373	(0.133)	**0.5966**	(0.007)	-0.2685	(0.494)
	49 to 60 hours	**0.3832**	(0.009)	**0.4127**	(0.001)	**0.2947**	(0.057)
	More than 60 hours	**0.8515**	(0.000)	**0.7154**	(0.000)	**0.8315**	(0.000)
Objectives for business over next two years (Bc – remain same size)	Grow 20%+	0.0706	(0.713)	0.3157	(0.053)	**0.5482**	(0.008)
	Expand up to 20%	0.0164	(0.918)	**0.2727**	(0.044)	0.2114	(0.245)
	Downsize business	-0.0629	(0.852)	0.2774	(0.315)	0.1211	(0.749)
	Sell or close	**0.5262**	(0.015)	0.3823	(0.053)	0.3018	(0.264)
	Hand on business	-0.7484	(0.177)	-0.7797	(0.147)	0.2454	(0.608)

continued on following page

Table 11. continued

	Younger Employees (Under 25 years)		Older Employees (Under 25 years)		Recruitment	
N	5056		5056		5056	
R^2	0.112		0.0857		0.1406	
Hosmer-Lemeshow	21.31	(0.006)	2.86	(0.943)	23.05	(0.003)

Notes: p-values in parenthesis

Whilst the work discussed within this chapter has concentrated upon the use of the Web site for the purposes of e-commerce, the final stage of development is seen as the complete integration of the businesses operations to form an e-business, clearly as time goes on similar issues to those raised above will need to be investigated in terms of the full development of e-businesses. Similarly certain under-researched groups such as pure-play Web-based firms need to also be captured in surveys as these are often under-represented in existing data sources, and may provide many of the new opportunities for employment growth in the SME sector in the future.

ACKNOWLEDGMENT

The authors wish to thank the Federation of Small Business for their support and the opportunity to use the data from the "Lifting the Barriers to Growth Survey" of their members. Without this support it would not have been possible to complete the work within this chapter.

REFERENCES

Acar, E., Koçak, I., Sey, Y., & Arditi, D. (2005). Use of information and communication technologies by small and medium-sized enterprises (SMEs) in building construction. *Construction Management and Economics*, *23*(7), 713–722. doi:10.1080/01446190500127112

Alonso Mendo, F., & Fitzgerald, G. (2005a). A multidimensional framework for SME e-business progression. *Journal of Enterprise Information Management*, *18*(6), 678–696. doi:10.1108/17410390510628382

Alonso Mendo, F., & Fitzgerald, G. (2005b). Theoretical approaches to study SMEs e-business progression. *Journal of Computing and Information Technology*, *13*(2), 123–136. doi:10.2498/cit.2005.02.04

Anderson, R., & Huang, W.-Y. (2006). Empowering salespeople: Personal, managerial, and organizational perspectives. *Psychology and Marketing*, *23*(2), 139–159. doi:10.1002/mar.20104

Andries, P., & Debackere, K. (2006). Adaptation in new technology-based ventures: Insights at the company level. *International Journal of Management Reviews*, *8*(2), 91–112. doi:10.1111/j.1468-2370.2006.00122.x

Arbore, A., & Ordanini, A. (2006). Broadband divide among SMEs: The role of size, location and outsourcing strategies. *International Small Business Journal*, *24*(1), 83–99. doi:10.1177/0266242606059781

Arnott, D. C., & Bridgewater, S. (2002). Internet interaction and implications for marketing. *Marketing Intelligence & Planning*, *20*(2), 86–95. doi:10.1108/02634500210418509

Audretsch, D. B., & Thurik, A. R. (2001). What is new about the new economy? Sources of growth in the managed and entrepreneurial economies. *Industrial and Corporate Change, 10*(1), 17–34. doi:10.1093/icc/10.1.267

Ballantine, J., Levy, M., & Powell, P. (2005). Evaluation Information Systems in small and medium-sized enterprises: Issues and evidence. *European Journal of Information Systems, 7*(4), 241–251. doi:10.1057/palgrave.ejis.3000307

Bassellier, G., Benbasat, I., & Reich, B. H. (2003). The influence of business managers' IT competences on championing IT. *Information Systems Research, 14*(4), 317–336. doi:10.1287/isre.14.4.317.24899

Bayo-Moriones, A., & Lera-López, F. (2007). A firm-level analysis of determinants of ICT adoption in Spain. *Technovation, 27*(6/7), 352–366. doi:10.1016/j.technovation.2007.01.003

Bengtsson, M., Boter, H., & Vanyushyn, V. (2007). Integrating the Internet and marketing operations: A study of antecedents in firms of different size. *International Small Business Journal, 25*(2), 27–48. doi:10.1177/0266242607071780

Bhagwat, R., & Sharma, M. K. (2007). Information System architecture: A framework for a cluster of small and medium-sized enterprises (SMEs). *Production Planning and Control, 18*(4), 283–296. doi:10.1080/09537280701248578

Briedenhann, J., & Wickens, E. (2004). Tourism routes as a tool for the economic development of rural areas – Vibrant hope or impossible dream? *Tourism Management, 25*(1), 71–79. doi:10.1016/S0261-5177(03)00063-3

Bruque, S., & Moyano, J. (2007). Organisational determinants of Information Technology adoption and implementation in SMEs: The case of family and cooperative firms. *Technovation, 27*(5), 241–253. doi:10.1016/j.technovation.2006.12.003

Caldeira, M. M., & Ward, J. M. (2003). Using resource-based theory to interpret the successful adoption and use of Information Systems and Technology in manufacturing small and medium-sized enterprises. *European Journal of Information Systems, 12*(2), 127–141. doi:10.1057/palgrave.ejis.3000454

Carree, M., van Stel, A., Thurik, R., & Wennekers, S. (2002). Economic development and business ownership: An analysis using data of 23 OECD countries in the period 1976-1996. *Small Business Economics, 19*(3), 271–290. doi:10.1023/A:1019604426387

Carter, N. M., & Allen, K. R. (1997). Size determinants of women-owned businesses: Choice or barriers to resources? *Entrepreneurship and Regional Development, 9*(3), 211–220. doi:10.1080/08985629700000012

Carter, S., & Bennett, D. (2006). Gender and entrepreneurship. In Carter, S., & Jones-Evans, D. (Eds.), *Enterprise and small business: Principles, practice and policy*. London, UK: FT Prentice-Hall.

Chen, L.-D., Haney, S., Pandzik, A., Spigarelli, J., & Jesseman, C. (2003). Small business Internet commerce: A case study. *Information Resources, 16*(3), 17–41. doi:10.4018/irmj.2003070102

Chetty, S., & Campbell-Hunt, C. (2003). Paths to internationalisation among small- to medium-sized firms: A global versus regional approach. *European Journal of Marketing, 37*(5/6), 796–820. doi:10.1108/03090560310465152

Chuang, T.-T., Nakatani, K., Chen, J. C. H., & Huang, I.-L. (2007). Examining the impact of organisational and owner's characteristics on the extent of ecommerce adoption in SMEs. *International Journal of Business and Systems Research, 1*(1), 61–80. doi:10.1504/IJBSR.2007.014770

Cohen, S., & Kallirroi, G. (2006). E-commerce investments from a SME perspective: Costs, benefits and processes. *Electronic Journal of Information Evaluation, 9*(2), 45–56.

Cragg, P., & Zinatelli, N. (1995). The evolution of IS in small firms. *Information & Management, 29*(1), 1–8. doi:10.1016/0378-7206(95)00012-L

Crespi, G., Mahdi, S., & Patel, P. (2004). *Adoption of e-commerce technology: Do network and learning externalities matter? Draft Final Report for the Department of Trade and Industry.* London, UK: HMSO.

Damanpour, F. (1991). Organizational innovation: A meta-analysis of effects of determinants and moderators. *Academy of Management Journal, 34*(3), 555–590. doi:10.2307/256406

Daniel, E., & Wilson, H. (2002). Adoption intentions and benefits realised: A study of e-commerce in UK SMEs. *Journal of Small Business and Enterprise Development, 9*(4), 331–348. doi:10.1108/14626000210450522

Daniel, E., Wilson, H., & Myers, A. (2002). Adoption of e-commerce by SMEs in the UK: Towards a stage model. *International Small Business Journal, 20*(3), 253–270. doi:10.1177/0266242602203002

Darch, H., & Lucas, T. (2002). Training as an e-commerce enabler. *Journal of Workplace Learning, 14*(4), 148–155. doi:10.1108/13665620210427276

de Búrca, S., Fynes, B., & Marshall, D. (2005). Strategic technology adoption: Extending ERP across the supply chain. *Journal of Enterprise Information Management, 18*(4), 427–440. doi:10.1108/17410390510609581

Del Aguila-Obra, A. R., & Padilla-Meléndez, A. (2006). Organizational factors affecting Internet technology adoption. *Internet Research, 16*(1), 94–110. doi:10.1108/10662240610642569

Drew, S. (2003). Strategic uses of e-commerce by SMEs in the East of England. *European Management Journal, 21*(1), 79–88. doi:10.1016/S0263-2373(02)00148-2

Duhan, S., Levy, M., & Powell, P. (2001). Information Systems strategies in knowledge-based SMEs: The role of core competencies. *European Journal of Information Systems, 10*(1), 25–40. doi:10.1057/palgrave.ejis.3000379

Dutta, S., & Evrard, P. (1999). Information Technology and organisation within European small enterprises. *European Management Journal, 17*(3), 239–251. doi:10.1016/S0263-2373(99)00003-1

Elliot, S., & Fowell, S. (2000). Expectations versus reality: A snapshot of consumer experiences with Internet retailing. *International Journal of Information Management, 20*(5), 323–336. doi:10.1016/S0268-4012(00)00026-8

Eurostat. (1996). *Enterprises in Europe*, 4th report.

Fariselli, P., Oughton, C., Picory, C., & Sugden, R. (1999). Electronic commerce and the future for SMEs in a global market-place: Networking and public policies. *Small Business Economics, 12*(3), 261–275. doi:10.1023/A:1008029924987

Fichman, R. G., & Kemerer, C. F. (1997). The assimilation of software process innovations: An organizational learning perspective. *Management Science, 43*(10), 1345–1363. doi:10.1287/mnsc.43.10.1345

Fillis, I., Johannson, U., & Wagner, B. (2004). Factors impacting on e-business adoption and development in the smaller firm. *International Journal of Entrepreneurial Behaviour and Research, 10*(3), 178–191. doi:10.1108/13552550410536762

Fuller-Love, N. (2006). Management development in small firms. *International Journal of Management Reviews, 8*(3), 175–190. doi:10.1111/j.1468-2370.2006.00125.x

Galloway, L., Deakins, D., & Sanders, J. (2008). *The use of Internet portals by Scotland's rural business community*. Paper presented at the 31st Institute for Small Business and Entrepreneurship (ISBE) Conference, Belfast, Northern Ireland. November.

Giaglis, G. M., Klein, S., & O'Keefe, R. M. (2002). The role of intermediaries in electronic marketplaces: Developing a contingency model. *Information Systems Journal, 12*(3), 231–246. doi:10.1046/j.1365-2575.2002.00123.x

Gorton, M. (1999). Spatial variations in markets served by UK-based small and medium sized enterprises (SMEs). *Entrepreneurship and Regional Development, 11*(1), 39–55. doi:10.1080/089856299283281

Grandon, E. E., & Pearson, J. M. (2004). Electronic commerce adoption: An empirical study of small and medium US businesses. *Information & Management, 42*(1), 197–216.

Heckman, J. J. (1979). Sample selection bias as a specification error. *Econometrica, 47*(1), 153–161. doi:10.2307/1912352

Holsapple, C. W., & Sasidharan, S. (2005). The dynamics of trust in online B2C e-commerce: A research model and agenda. *Information Systems and E-business Management, 3*(4), 377–403. doi:10.1007/s10257-005-0022-5

Howcroft, D. (2001). After the goldrush: Deconstructing the myths of the dot.com market. *Journal of Information Technology, 16*(4), 195–204. doi:10.1080/02683960110100418

Iacovou, C. L., Benbasat, I., & Dexter, A. S. (1995). Electronic data interchange and small organizations: Adoption and impact of technology. *Management Information Systems Quarterly, 19*(4), 465–485. doi:10.2307/249629

Irani, Z., Ezingeard, J.-N., & Grieve, R. J. (1997). Integrating the costs of a manufacturing IT/IS infrastructure into the investment decision-making process. *Technovation, 17*(11/12), 695–362. doi:10.1016/S0166-4972(97)00060-6

Jaw, Y.-L., & Chen, C.-L. (2006). The influence of the Internet in the internationalization of SMEs in Taiwan. *Human Systems Management, 25*(3), 167–183.

Johanson, J., & Vahlne, J.-E. (1977). The internationalization process of the firm - A model of knowledge development and increasing foreign market commitments. *Journal of International Business Studies, 8*(1), 23–32. doi:10.1057/palgrave.jibs.8490676

Kadlec, P., & Mareš, M. (2003). B2B e-commerce opportunity for SMEs. In *Proceedings of the 11th International Conference on Systems Integration,* Prague, Czech Republic (pp. 537-544).

Kalapesi, C., Willersdorf, S., & Zwillenberg, P. (2010). *The connected kingdom: How the Internet is transforming the U.K. economy*. Boston, MA: Boston Consulting Group.

Kim, D. (2003). The internationalization of US Internet portals: Does it fit the process model of internationalization? *Marketing Intelligence & Planning, 21*(1), 23–36. doi:10.1108/02634500310458126

Kleindl, B. (2000). Competitive dynamics and new business models for SMEs in the virtual marketplace. *Journal of Developmental Entrepreneurship, 5*(1), 73–85.

Kula, V., & Tatoglu, E. (2003). An exploratory study of Internet adoption by SMEs in an emerging market economy. *European Business Review, 15*(5), 324–333. doi:10.1108/09555340310493045

Langston, C. M., & Teas, R. K. (1976). *Export commitment and characteristics of management.* Paper presented at the Annual Meeting of the Midwest Business Association, St Louis, MO.

Lawson, R., Alcock, C., Cooper, J., & Burgess, L. (2003). Factors affecting adoption of electronic commerce technologies by SMEs: An Australian study. *Journal of Small Business and Enterprise Development, 10*(3), 265–276. doi:10.1108/14626000310489727

Lee, J. (2004). Discriminant analysis of technology adoption behaviour: A case of Internet technologies in small businesses. *Journal of Computer Information Systems, 44*(4), 57–66.

Levy, M., & Powell, P. (2003). Exploring SME Internet adoption: Towards a contingent model. *Electronic Markets, 13*(2), 173–181. doi:10.1080/1019678032000067163

Levy, M., Powell, P., & Yetton, P. (1998). SMEs and the gains from IS: From cost reduction to value added. In Larsen, T., Levine, L., & DeGross, J. (Eds.), *Information Systems: Current issues and future changes* (pp. 377–392). Amsterdam, The Netherlands: Kluwer Academic Publishers.

Levy, M., Powell, P., & Yetton, P. (2002). The dynamics of SME information systems. *Small Business Economics, 19*(4), 341–354. doi:10.1023/A:1019654030019

Lin, C., Huang, Y.-A., & Tseng, S.-W. (2007). A study of planning and implementation stages in electronic commerce adoption and evaluation: The case of Australian SMEs. *Contemporary Management Research, 3*(1), 83–100.

Lituchy, T. R., & Rail, A. (2000). Bed and breakfasts, small inns, and the Internet: The impact of technology on the globalization of small business. *Journal of International Marketing, 8*(2), 86–97. doi:10.1509/jimk.8.2.86.19625

Liu, C., & Arnett, K. P. (2000). Exploring the factors associated with Web site success in the context of electronic commerce. *Information & Management, 38*(1), 23–33. doi:10.1016/S0378-7206(00)00049-5

Lockett, N., & Brown, D. H. (2006). Aggregation and the role of trusted third parties in SME e-business engagement: A regional policy issue. *International Small Business Journal, 24*(4), 379–404. doi:10.1177/0266242606065509

Love, P. E. D., & Irani, Z. (2004). An exploratory study of Information Technology evaluation and benefits management practices for SMEs in the constructing industry. *Information & Management, 42*(1), 227–242.

Love, P. E. D., Irani, Z., Li, H., Cheng, E. W. L., & Tse, R. Y. C. (2001). An empirical analysis of the barriers to implementing e-commerce in small-medium sized construction contractors in the state of Victoria, Australia. *Construction Innovation, 1*(1), 31–41.

Mansor, N., & Abidin, A. F. A. (2010). The application of e-commerce among Malaysian small medium enterprises. *European Journal of Scientific Research, 41*(4), 591–605.

Martin, L. (2005). Internet adoption and use in small firms: Internal processes, organisational culture and the roles of the owner-manager and key staff. *New Technology, Work and Employment, 20*(3), 190–204. doi:10.1111/j.1468-005X.2005.00153.x

Martin, L. M., & Matlay, H. (2001). "Blanket" approaches to promoting ICT in small firms: Some lessons from the DTI ladder adoption model in the UK. *Internet Research, 11*(5), 399–410. doi:10.1108/EUM0000000006118

Matlay, H., & Westhead, P. (2005). Virtual teams and the rise of e-entrepreneurship in Europe. *International Small Business Journal, 23*(6), 279–302. doi:10.1177/0266242605052074

McConville, A. (2009). *Impact of ICT on SMEs in the South East: Report prepared for the South East of England Development Agency.* Birmingham, UK: BMG Research.

McDougall, P. P., & Oviatt, B. M. (2000). International entrepreneurship: The intersection of two research paths. *Academy of Management Journal, 43*(5), 902–906. doi:10.2307/1556418

McQuade, S., Waitman, R., Zeisser, M., & Kierzkowski, A. (1996). Marketing to the digital consumer. *The McKinsey Quarterly, 3*, 5–21.

Mehrtens, J., Cragg, P. B., & Mills, A. M. (2001). A model of Internet adoption by SMEs. *Information & Management, 39*(3), 165–176. doi:10.1016/S0378-7206(01)00086-6

Mirchandani, D. A., & Motwani, J. (2001). Understanding small business e-commerce adoption: An empirical analysis. *Journal of Computer Information Systems, 41*(3), 70–73.

Napier, H. A., Rivers, O. N., Wagner, S. W., & Napier, J. B. (2005). *Creating a winning e-business.* Boston, MA: Thompson Course Technology.

O'Farrell, P. N., Hitchens, D. M., & Moffat, L. A. R. (1995). Business service firms in two peripheral economies: Scotland and Ireland. *Tijdschrift voor Economische en Sociale Geografie, 86*(2), 115–128. doi:10.1111/j.1467-9663.1995.tb01351.x

O'Keefe, R. M., O'Connor, G., & Kung, H.-J. (1998). Early adopters of the Web as a retail medium: Small company winners and losers. *European Journal of Marketing, 32*(7/8), 629–643. doi:10.1108/03090569810224038

Office for National Statistics. (2009). *E-commerce and information and communication Technology (ICT) activity, 2008.* Newport, UK: ONS.

Oviatt, B. M., & McDougall, P. P. (1999). Accelerated internationalization: Why are new and small ventures internationalizing in greater numbers and with increasing speed? In Wright, R. (Ed.), *Research in global strategic management* (pp. 23–40). Stamford, CT: JAI Press.

Packham, G. (2002). Competitive advantage and growth: The challenge for small firms. *International Journal of Management and Decision-Making, 3*(2), 165–179. doi:10.1504/IJMDM.2002.002471

Packham, G., Brooksbank, D., Miller, C., & Thomas, B. (2005). Climbing the mountain: Management practice adoption in growth oriented firms in Wales. *Small Business and Enterprise Development, 12*(4), 482–497. doi:10.1108/14626000510628171

Petersen, B., Welch, L. S., & Liesch, P. (2002). The Internet and foreign market expansion by firms. *Management International Review, 42*(2), 207–221.

Poon, S., & Swatman, P. M. C. (1999). An exploratory study of small business Internet commerce issues. *Information & Management, 35*(1), 9–18. doi:10.1016/S0378-7206(98)00079-2

Rao, S. S., Metts, G., & Monge, C. A. M. (2003). Electronic commerce development in small and medium sized enterprises: A stage model and its implications. *Business Process Management Journal, 9*(1), 11–32. doi:10.1108/14637150310461378

Raymond, L., Bergeron, F., & Blili, S. (2005). The assimilation of e-business in manufacturing SMEs: Determinants and effects on growth and internationalization. *Electronic Markets, 15*(2), 106–118. doi:10.1080/10196780500083761

Robertson, A., Lockett, N. J., Brown, D. H., & Crouchley, R. (2007). *Entrepreneur attitude towards the computer and its effect on e-business adoption.* Paper presented at the 30th Institute for Small Business and Entrepreneurship (ISBE) Conference, Glasgow. November.

Rogers, E. M. (1995). *Diffusion of innovations.* New York, NY: Free Press.

Samiee, S. (1998). Exporting and the Internet: A conceptual perspective. *International Marketing Review, 15*(5), 413–426. doi:10.1108/02651339810236452

Sarosa, S., & Zowghi, D. (2003). Strategy for adopting information technology for SMEs: Experience in adopting email within an Indonesian furniture company. *Electronic Journal of Information Systems Evaluation, 6*(2), 165–176.

Sellitto, C., Wenn, A., & Burgess, S. (2003). A review of the websites of small Australian wineries: Motivations, goals and success. *Information Technology Management, 4*(2/3), 215–232. doi:10.1023/A:1022954429432

Simmons, G., Armstrong, G. A., & Durkin, M. G. (2008). A conceptualization of the determinants of small business website adoption: Setting the research agenda. *International Small Business Journal, 26*(3), 351–389. doi:10.1177/0266242608088743

Simpson, C. L. Jr, & Kujawa, D. (1974). The export decision process: An empirical inquiry. *Journal of International Business Studies, 5*(1), 107–117. doi:10.1057/palgrave.jibs.8490815

Sinkovics, R. R., & Penz, E. (2005). Empowerment of SME websites – Development of a Web-empowered scale and preliminary evidence. *Journal of International Entrepreneurship, 3*(4), 303–315. doi:10.1007/s10843-006-7858-8

Stockdale, R., & Standing, C. (2004). Benefits and barriers of electronic marketplace participation: An SME perspective. *Journal of Enterprise Information Management, 17*(4), 301–311. doi:10.1108/17410390410548715

Thompson, P., Williams, R., Thomas, B. C., & Packham, G. (2010). *Shortages of IT Skills in UK SMEs.* Paper presented at the 33rd Institute for Small Business and Entrepreneurship (ISBE) Conference, London. November.

Van de Ven, W. P. M. M., & Van Praag, B. M. S. (1981). The demand for deductibles in private health insurance: a probit model with sample selection. *Journal of Econometrics, 17*(2), 229–252. doi:10.1016/0304-4076(81)90028-2

Walker, E., & Brown, A. (2004). What success factors are important to small business owners? *International Small Business Journal, 22*(6), 577–594. doi:10.1177/0266242604047411

Weltevreden, J. W. J., & Boschma, R. A. (2008). The influence of firm owner characteristics on Internet adoption by independent retailers: A business survey. *International Journal of Internet Science, 3*(1), 34–54.

Wen, H. J., Chen, H.-G., & Hwang, H.-G. (2001). E-commerce Web site design: Strategies and models. *Information Management & Computer Security, 9*(1), 5–12. doi:10.1108/09685220110366713

Williams, R., Packham, G. P., Thomas, B. C., & Thompson, P. (2010). Small business sales growth and internationalization links to Web site functions in the United Kingdom. In Thomas, B., & Simmons, G. (Eds.), *E-commerce adoption and small business in the global marketplace: Tools for optimization* (pp. 139–173). Hershey, PA: Business Science Reference. doi:10.4018/978-1-60566-998-4.ch008

Wilson, H., & Daniel, E. (2007). The multi-channel challenge: A dynamic capability approach. *Industrial Marketing Management, 36*(1), 10–20. doi:10.1016/j.indmarman.2006.06.015

Yeung, W. L., & Lu, M.-T. (2004). Functional characteristics of commercial Web sites: A longitudinal study in Hong Kong. *Information & Management, 41*(4), 483–495. doi:10.1016/S0378-7206(03)00086-7

Zhang, M. J., & Lado, A. A. (2001). Information Systems and competitive advantage: A competency-based view. *Technovation, 21*(3), 147–156. doi:10.1016/S0166-4972(00)00030-4

Zhuang, Y., & Lederer, A. L. (2006). A resource-based view of electronic commerce. *Information & Management, 43*(2), 251–261. doi:10.1016/j.im.2005.06.006

ADDITIONAL READING

Al-Qirim, N. (2005). An empirical investigation of an e-commerce adoption-capability model in small businesses in New Zealand. *Electronic Markets, 15*(4), 418–437. doi:10.1080/10196780500303136

Beynon-Davies, P. (2007). eBusiness maturity and regional development. *International Journal of Business Science and Applied Management, 2*(1), 9–20.

Bharati, P., & Chaudhury, A. (2006). *Small and medium enterprises (SMEs) adoption of technology along the value chain.* Paper presented at the European and Mediterranean Conference on Information Systems (EMICS), Alicante. July.

Brynjolfsson, E., & Kahin, B. (Eds.). (2000). *Understanding the Digital Economy: Data, Tools and Research.* Cambridge, MA: MIT press.

Bui, T. X., Sankaran, S., & Sebastian, I. M. (2003). A framework for measuring national e-readiness. *International Journal of Electronic Business, 1*(1), 3–22. doi:10.1504/IJEB.2003.002162

Dos Santos, B. L., & Peffers, K. (1998). Competitor and Vendor influence on the adoption of innovative applications in electronic commerce. *Information & Management, 34*(3), 175–184. doi:10.1016/S0378-7206(98)00053-6

Harland, C. M., Caldwell, N. D., Powell, P., & Zheng, J. (2007). Barriers to supply chain information integration: SMEs adrift of eLands. *Journal of Operations Management, 25*(6), 1234–1254. doi:10.1016/j.jom.2007.01.004

Jutla, D., Bodorick, P., & Dhaliwal, J. (2002). Supporting the e-business readiness of small and medium-sized enterprises: approaches and metrics. *Internet Research Electronic Working Applications and Policy, 12*(2), 139–164. doi:10.1108/10662240210422512

MacGregor, R. C., & Vrazalic, L. (2005). A basic model of electronic commerce adoption barriers: a study of regional small businesses in Sweden and Australia. *Journal of Small Business and Enterprise Development, 12*(4), 510–527. doi:10.1108/14626000510628199

Marasini, R., Ions, K., & Ahmad, M. (2008). Assessment of e-business adoption in SMEs: A study of manufacturing industry in the UK North East region. *Journal of Manufacturing Technology Management, 19*(5), 627–644. doi:10.1108/17410380810877294

Mohamad, R., & Ismail, N. A. (2009). Electronic commerce adoption in SME: the trend of prior studies. *Journal of Internet Banking and Commerce, 14*(2).

O'Regan, N., Ghobadian, A., & Gallear, D. (2006). In search of the drivers of high growth in manufacturing SMEs. *Technovation, 26*(1), 30–41. doi:10.1016/j.technovation.2005.05.004

Parker, C. M., & Castleman, T. (2007). New directions for research on SME-eBusiness: insights from an analysis of journal articles from 2003 to 2006. *Journal of Information Systems and Small Business*, *1*(1-2), 21–40.

Pavic, S., Koh, S. C. L., Simpson, M., & Padmore, J. (2007). Could e-business create a competitive advantage in UK SMEs. *Benchmarking: An International Journal*, *14*(3), 320–351. doi:10.1108/14635770710753112

Poon, S. (2000). Business environment and internet commerce benefit-small business perspective. *European Journal of Information Systems*, *9*(2), 72–81.

Quayle, M. (2002). E-commerce: the challenge for UK SMEs in the twenty-first century. *International Journal of Operations & Production Management*, *22*(10), 1148–1161. doi:10.1108/01443570210446351

Rickards, R. C. (2007). BSC and benchmark development for an e-commerce SME. *Benchmarking: An International Journal*, *14*(2), 222–250. doi:10.1108/14635770710740413

Steinfield, C., & Whitten, P. (1999). Community level socio-economic impacts of electronic commerce. *Journal of Computer-Mediated Communication*, *5*(2).

Van Beveren, J., & Thompson, H. (2002). The use of electronic commerce by SMEs in Victoria, Australia. *Journal of Small Business Management*, *40*(3), 250–253. doi:10.1111/1540-627X.00054

Wagner, B. A., Fillis, A., & Johannson, U. (2003). E-business and e-supply strategy in small and medium-sized businesses (SMEs). *Supply Chain Management: An International Journal*, *8*(4), 343–354. doi:10.1108/13598540310490107

Yasin, M. M., Czuchry, A. J., Gonzales, M., & Bayes, P. E. (2006). E-commerce implementation challenges: Small to medium-sized versus large organisations. *International Journal of Business Information Systems*, *1*(3), 256–275. doi:10.1504/IJBIS.2006.008599

DATA APPENDIX: OPERATIONALIZATION OF WEB SITE FUNCTIONALITY

The data used in this study is drawn from the Federation of Small Business (FSB) Lifting the Barriers to Growth Survey 2008. The survey is distributed to the members of the FSB through postal questionnaires and electronically through the FSB Web site, with the questions identically phrased in the two formats. The questionnaire was originally mailed early in 2008 with a number of reminder emails sent out directing respondents to the FSB Web site where the electronic version of the questionnaire was accessible. For the purposes of the work studied here 5,089 usable responses were available.

Although the FSB survey was not designed to examine Web site functionality specifically, it does include a question which allows a measure of understanding of the level of Web site development by respondent firms:

"Does your business have a Web site, and if yes, what is it used for?"

The respondents are asked to select one of the options from those listed below that best describes their current Web presence.

1. No
2. Yes, but only for basic contact information
3. Yes and it is used to advertise our products
4. Yes and it is used to advertise and sell our products on-line
5. Yes and it is used to link to suppliers
6. Yes and it is used to link to suppliers and sell our products on-line

In general the options can be thought of as increasing in Web presence from a complete absence through brochure style non-active Web sites to e-commerce capable Web sites with links to customers and suppliers. In terms of ranking responses as lesser or greater Web site integration it is perhaps only options 4 and 5 which are difficult to rank relative to one another.

As a vast majority of those with Web sites are in the lower orders of Web site functionality it is often necessary for analysis to aggregate groups by Web site functionality into non-adopters (those with no Web presence at all, group 1), non-active Web site users (those with Web sites simply providing contact details, or simple brochure Web sites advertising products, groups 2 and 3), and active Web site users (those using Web sites for some form of e-commerce, either to link to customers, suppliers, or both, groups 4 to 6).

The more general nature of the FSB survey means that the no specific question is asked linking Web site adoption or functionality and a lack of IT skills. On the other hand, if a shortage of IT skills is an important barrier to greater functionality it would be expected that those firms with greater functionality would be more likely to report that they had encountered shortages in IT skills in the previous two years. Questions are asked in relation to whether basic and advanced IT skills shortages have been encountered in younger employees (less than 25 years of age), older employees (25 years and over), and when attempting to recruit.

In addition to the reported coefficients in order to control for geographical and industry heterogeneity all binary logistic, multi-nominal logistic regressions and discriminant analysis is conducted with regional and industry dummies included. For geographical variation, controls are made on the basis of the UK government office regions (GOR) definition of the 12 English regions and devolved territories. The industry controls are based on the standard industrial classification (SIC). Variables are selected to enter the discriminant analysis via a staged process based on Wilks' lambda.

Chapter 8
Exploring the Potential of e–CRM in SME Marketing Practice

Fiona McMahon
University of Ulster, Northern Ireland

Aodheen O'Donnell
University of Ulster, Northern Ireland

ABSTRACT

The potential of the Internet to transform marketing practice is well-documented (Hoffman & Novac, 1997; Zineldin, 2000). It is argued that the exploitation of the Internet's interactive and relationship-building properties contribute to customer satisfaction and loyalty and hence, marketing success (Arnott & Bridgewater, 2002). Evidence suggests, however, that small to medium sized enterprises (SMEs) have failed to capitalize on the Internet to facilitate the management of customer relations (e-CRM) and the creation of competitive advantage (Chen & Popovich, 2003; Geiger & Martin, 1999; McGowan et al., 2001; O'Toole, 2001). This is attributed to a lack of influence, time, finance, and specialised knowledge, (Carson & Gilmore, 2003) coupled with the reality that most Information Systems and Technology models and tools have been developed from the perspective of the large firm (Maguire et al., 2007; Poon & Swatman, 1999).

Despite such constraints, it is posited that by exploring the components of e-CRM in the unique context of SME business and marketing practice that a natural synergy exists between e-CRM and SME marketing in the creation of value propositions. Specifically this is addressed through the two contributing constructs of SME marketing; namely entrepreneurial marketing and network marketing (Carson & Gilmore, 2000).

DOI: 10.4018/978-1-60960-597-1.ch008

INTRODUCTION

More than a decade on from the dotcom boom and burst, debate continues as to the influence of e-business and the Internet upon contemporary marketing practice and business performance (Brodie et al. 2007; Day & Bens, 2005). Whilst it is accepted that the use of the Internet has become widespread amongst businesses, the *extent* of its use and subsequent impact remains unclear (Drennan & McColl-Kennedy, 2003; Gilmore et al. 2007). Potential benefits including reduced market research and entry costs; customer service efficiencies; and improved customer satisfaction and retention via two-way personalized interactions, are well-documented in the extant literature (Arnott & Bridgewater, 2002; Day & Hubbard, 2003; Ibeh et al., 2005; Martin & Matlay, 2001; Rowley 2004;). Yet there is a dearth of scholarly evidence linking Internet usage to improved sales, profits and customer satisfaction levels (Bitner et al., 2000; Drennan & McColl-Kennedy, 2003; Feinberg & Kadam 2002; Kula & Tatoglu, 2003). Indeed, recent research suggests that in reality, most firms will fail to capitalize on Internet–related opportunities (Day & Bens, 2005). In order to address this dichotomy between theory and practice, there is a need for specific tools and techniques to be developed to help the small firm identify and capitalise upon the opportunities offered by the Internet to create business value (Downie, 2003; Maguire et al. 2007; Sands, 2003). A conceptual framework is therefore proposed that models how particular small firm characteristics might be exploited to counteract the inherent difficulties associated with SME Internet adoption for relational purposes.

For the SME in particular, the ability to successfully engage with and optimise Internet technologies is considered particularly essential. Harrigan et al. (2009; p.457) suggest that for the small firm e-CRM may be 'the single most important means of competing with larger organizations either locally or globally. By widening customer access and pro-

viding equal exposure to prospects, the efficiency, interactivity and immediacy of the Internet can level the playing field for the smaller organization (Drennan & McColl-Kennedy, 2003; Simmons et al, 2008). The integration of the Internet with strategic thinking is considered critical to SME value propositions, both online and offline and their overall competitiveness (Ab Hamid, 2005; Day & Hubbard, 2003; Martin & Matlay, 2003; Simmons et al. 2008). Competitive advantage is realised through the sustained creation and delivery of customer value (Porter, 2001). The Internet supports this process by providing access to a range of performance and profit-enhancing tools (Drennan & McColl-Kennedy, 2003). Firms that fail to engage strategically are considered to be at a distinct disadvantage (Bohling et al., 2006; Egan et al., 2003).

Grönroos (2004) contends that the principles of relationship marketing should underpin any value-adding strategy, and the Internet itself has been hailed as the ultimate relationship marketing tool (Geller, 1998; Zineldin, 2000) In relationship marketing, profits are maximised by attaining, maintaining and enhancing mutually beneficial relationships with specific customers and other partners in order to increase their lifetime value (Gummesson, 2004). Establishing and retaining relationships with customers is considered key to profitability, as 'relationship customers' are likely to be less price sensitive, more loyal, and prove less costly to sell to than new customers (Bull, 2003; Reichheld & Sasser, 1990;).

While it is recognised in the literature that the purported benefits of e-CRM are unlikely to be realised through software implementation alone, (Doherty & Lockett, 2008) there is a lack of consensus as to how best to approach e-business adoption from a small firm perspective (van der Veen, 2004). For the small business, typified by inherent resource constraints and their close, personal relationships with customers, (Gilmore & Carson, 1999; Xu et al., 2007) it is therefore posited that e-CRM; the use of Internet technologies to facilitate the management of customer relationships (Chanston & Mangles, 2003) may act as a natural complement to SME business and marketing practice. By exploring the components of e-CRM, in the unique context of SME entrepreneurial marketing and network marketing practice, it is proposed by way of a conceptual model that a natural synergy exists between e-CRM and SME marketing in the creation of value propositions.

The proposed conceptual model attempts to align small firm characteristics, resources and practices with the more formal organisational and resource requirements associated with successful e-CRM adoption. By modelling the potential relationships and synergies between e-CRM success factors and SME business and marketing practice, its purpose is to help the SME owner better identify and strategically assess opportunities to leverage their existing capabilities and characteristics in order to successfully implement e-CRM; and to compensate in instances where there are none. It is hoped that this model will help reduce the 'expectations gap' typically experienced by SME owner/managers upon adoption of new technologies (Doherty & Lockett, 2008; Ortega et al., 2008) by providing a tool which will enable a more strategic and informed approach to e-CRM, resulting in the creation of added value. Suggestions also follow as to how researchers might use this model to support qualitative research into e-CRM practice by SMEs, with the intention of developing an empirically validated model to further inform academia, small business practice and government policy.

BACKGROUND

The Rise of e-CRM

In the last decade, the rapid advancement of e-business technologies have combined with the key concepts of relationship marketing to produce a new 'core communications strategy' typically referred to as customer relationship management (CRM) (Buttle, 2004). CRM is a combination of people, processes and technology intended to increase a firm's competitiveness via increased operational efficiency and improved customer satisfaction and loyalty (Chen & Popovich, 2003). Crucially, technology facilitates the management of customer relationships by linking front and back office business functions and all customer 'touch-points' to provide a unified, enterprise-wide customer view.

CRM traditionally involved the purchase and hosting of specific software (Buttle, 2004). However, the rise in web-based applications has led to the evolution of e-CRM, (Iyer & Bejou, 2003). E-CRM extends connectivity among a business, their customers and stakeholders by integrating Internet technologies with existing e-business applications (Pan & Lee, 2003). The superior analytical, interactive and personalisation capabilities of Internet technologies can offer firms real sources of competitive advantage (Chanston & Mangles, 2003; Kennedy, 2006; Romano & Fjermestad, 2003).

Competitive advantage in e-CRM is realised through the 'dual creation' of both firm and customer value (Boulding et al., 2005). This concept of value creation is derived from relationship marketing; a strategy developed to defend against purely price-based competition (Chanston & Mangles, 2003). Core to e-CRM therefore, are the practice and principles of relationship marketing (Doherty & Lockett, 2008). The relationship marketing paradigm emphasises long-term partnering with customers and other stakeholders as providing more value-adding opportunities than the classic product and sales, transactional, 'marketing mix' approach (Boulding et al. 2005; Grönroos 2004; Gummesson, 2004). Value added by e-CRM includes the provision and management of detailed customer knowledge, more targeted, personalised and real-time customer interaction, cost savings, mass-customisation and customer empowerment

(Buttle, 2004: Chen & Chen, 2004; Frieldlein, 2001; Peppers at al 1999).

E-CRM fosters relationship building and customer loyalty in an increasingly competitive and dynamic market by facilitating the effective interactive exchange of information between a firm and its customers (Sands, 2003). The Internet has contributed to heightened customer knowledge and expectations by allowing the easy search, research, and comparison of alternative offerings on a global scale (Ab Hamid & Kassim, 2004; Srirojanant & Creswell, 1998; Zineldin, 2000). Organisations that fail to capitalise on the relational and informational properties of the Internet and pursue a transactional strategy may be at risk of reduced margins, commoditisation of their product range and temporal customer loyalty (Chanston and Mangles, 2003; Day & Hubbard, 2003; Grönroos, 2004).

To date, academic research into e-CRM is fragmented. In particular, the literature refers to the marketing benefits and Information Technology (IT) challenges of e-CRM somewhat independently. As a result, there is an increasing body of research critical of e-CRM's ability to deliver upon the associated benefits of relationship marketing (Adebanjo, 2003; Rigby et al. 2002). This failure is often attributed to an unrealistic expectation on the part of an organisation that technology implementation alone should suffice (Doherty & Lockett, 2008). However, the lack of empirical research exploring both the process and outcome perspectives of e-CRM makes it difficult for organizations to understand how to improve effectiveness in a more holistic manner (Kennedy, 2006; Romano and Fjermestad, 2003). In addition, most IT techniques and business models have been developed from the perspective of the large firm, further highlighting the difficulty for SMEs to leverage e-CRM to gain competitive advantage (Maguire et al., 2007). However, there is an increasing body of literature which recognizes e-CRM as a natural extension of SME marketing practice, and therefore e-CRM's potential as a viable competitive strategy for the smaller firm (Harrigan et al. 2009).

SME Marketing

There is growing recognition of the importance of research into SME business activities and practice due to their combined economic weight and unique business context (Hill, 2001). Some literature exists detailing the parallels between relationship marketing and small business practice (Zotanos & Anderson, 2004) and the potential of the Internet within it (Geiger & Martin, 1999; O'Toole, 2001; McGowan et al, 2001). However, there is little firm evidence to suggest that SMEs have managed to utilise the Internet in order to add value and competitive advantage through the management of customer relationships (Pavic et al. 2007). Indeed much of the extant literature points to the small firm failing to capitalise on the Internet by continuing to use it for basic, informational rather than advanced, relational purposes, which assumes interactivity and data processing opportunities (Ab Hamid, 2004; Bengtsson et al. 2007; Harrigan et al., 2008; Kennedy, 2006).

Despite illustrating that small business relationships can be improved by an electronic dimension, O'Toole (2001) suggests that a relationship approach may not always the most suitable marketing strategy for SMEs. This may be due to SMEs' marketing orientation, which tends to be more operational and concerned with short-term profits (Carson & Gilmore 2000; Gilmore et al., 2006). Interestingly, research is emerging however to suggest that Internet technologies can be used to complement and positively contribute to a transactional marketing strategy (Brodie et al, 2007). Indeed, Thomas (2001) reminds that before a relational strategy can be deployed it is firstly necessary to acquire a customer base. Therefore, customer acquisition and retention are not mutually exclusive (Johnson & Selnes, 2004). Brodie et al. (2007) clearly evidence this link through their empirical research study which demonstrates a positive relationship between the extent of Internet usage and customer acquisition performance; which in turn positively influences retention.

SME marketing practice does not adhere to traditional, large-firm marketing theory, (Blankson & Stokes, 2002; Hill, 2001). but rather is limited by inherent resource constraints, and dominated by owner/manager characteristics (Carson & Gilmore, 2000). The small business owner/manager must therefore rely upon, and leverage their unique competencies in an effort to remain competitive (Gilmore et al, 2006). In recent years a number of concepts have been applied in an attempt to better understand and explain the nature of SME marketing. In order to further explore the potential for e-CRM in SME marketing practice, the two contributing constructs of entrepreneurial marketing and network marketing, (Carson & Gilmore, 2000) are considered.

Entrepreneurial Marketing

While it is acknowledged that entrepreneurial marketing is not exclusive to the small firm, (Runyan et al, 2008) for many, its practice has become 'second-nature' (Collinson & Shaw, 2001). This is due to the flatter, cross-functional structure of the SME; its natural customer intensity and the necessity of an intuitive, creative approach to marketing in order to leverage limited resources and remain competitive (Morris et al. 2002). Despite many small firms not having a specified marketing function, these dual processes of customer intensity and value creation indicate a market orientation (Collinson & Shaw, 2001; Jaworski & Kohli, 1993). The conceptual overlap between market orientation and relationship marketing is clear. Market orientation, like relationship marketing, is essential to the acquisition and long-term maintenance of profitable customer relationships (McNaughton et al., 2002). As with relationship marketing, market orientation emphasises a customer-centric focus, and also involves the afore-

mentioned dual-creation of firm-customer value (Shah et al., 2006). A customer-centric approach anticipates and exceeds customer expectations, and is therefore deemed a sustainable strategy in an increasingly competitive marketplace. Crucially, it can be challenging for larger organizations to implement and maintain (Shah et al. 2006).

E-CRM technologies are considered to be particularly aligned to supporting and augmenting a market-orientation and customer-centric focus (Schoder & Madeja, 2004). Advances in Internet technology will increasingly facilitate strategic market-orientation, as new ways of interacting with customers and documenting such interactions become available (Shah et al. 2006). A market orientation, in which firms are closely connected to the needs of their customers, positively contributes to the successful implementation of e-business technologies (van der Veen, 2004). The ability to create value through the innovative exploitation of the Internet opportunity is 'shaped by the adopting organisation' and the extent to which they are entrepreneurial in business practice (van der Veen, 2004, p.18).

A 'hands-on' management approach typifies the entrepreneurial culture and the term 'entrepreneurial marketing' acknowledges the dominating influence of the entrepreneurial owner/manager upon SME marketing activities, (Stokes, 2000) and IT adoption decisions (Riemenschneider et al., 2003). McGowan et al. (2001) characterise entrepreneurs as 'constantly innovative, continuously opportunity focused and comfortable with change' (pg.2). This practice of innovation and change is considered core to entrepreneurial marketing (McGowan & Durkin 2002) and is in keeping with the following definition:

"Entrepreneurial marketing is defined as the proactive identification and exploitation for acquiring and retaining profitable customers through innovative approaches to risk management, resource leveraging and value creation" (Morris et al. 2002; p.5).

'Innovative approaches' therefore, do not solely relate to new product development, but rather extend to new ways of doing business (Gilmore et al. 2001; McGowan & Durkin, 2002). Indeed with less bureaucracy than the large organisation and a resulting lack of constraint on creativity, flexibility and responsiveness (Coviello & Munro, 1997; Storey, 1994) the entrepreneurial small firm is ideally placed to inherently incorporate added value across their business and marketing activities to create competitive advantage (Gilmore et al. 1999).

Morris et al. (2002) describe innovative value creation as the focal point of entrepreneurial marketing. Innovation alone however, does not automatically result in value creation (van der Veen, 2004). Rather, it is the 'entrepreneurial perspective' that leads to value-adding opportunities for both firm and customer. This perspective differentiates entrepreneurship from innovation by framing the e-business technology within a specific external market context (van der Veen 2004 p.69). Interestingly, this entrepreneurial concern with creating and eliciting value across all business functions is also in keeping with the relationship marketing perspective (Zontanos & Anderson, 2004). The entrepreneurial small firm, naturally closer to their customers than their larger counterparts, can better identify and understand their customers' needs (Gilmore et al. 1999). This closeness allows SMEs to provide added value through customized offerings (Gilmore et al., 1999) leading to more satisfied, loyal and profitable customers in the long term. Maximising the lifetime value of customers through tailored products and services is an outcome that is associated in the literature with both entrepreneurial marketing (Morris et al. 2002) and relationship marketing (Grönroos, 2004) respectively.

Ragins and Greco (2003) identify industries that have close customer contact, are competitive and innovative as best placed to implement e-CRM; qualities inherent in the entrepreneurial small firm. Morris et al. (2002) identify a number of

creative and alternative marketing approaches that have emerged in recent years as being particularly suited to the smaller firm. Radical, viral and buzz marketing, amongst others, naturally complement the tactical, creative and visceral entrepreneurial marketing approach and crucially are enabled by Internet technologies. In a recent investigation into small firm advanced Internet usage, it was the companies that had management, technical and entrepreneurial support which were mostly likely to succeed (Bengtsson et al., 2007).

Network Marketing

Just as the creation of value is integral to small firm marketing activity, networking is also considered an inherent part of this process (Hill and McGowan, 1996; Gilmore & Carson, 1999). McGowan and Durkin, (2002) identify the maintenance of close networked relations by the entrepreneur as key to continuous development and growth of the small firm. Small firms form networks to increase their value offering and market influence (Eikebrokk & Olsen, 2007). Carson et al. (1995) define networking as:

an activity in which the entrepreneurially orientated SME owners build and manage personal relationships with particular individuals in their surroundings (p.201).

The forging of relationships between the entrepreneur and their networks helps the small firm to compensate for lack of market knowledge by accessing accurate market, technical and scientific information, as well as sharing resources and business opportunities (Shaw, 1999). In order to innovate and remain competitive SMEs increasingly leverage their networks to provide access to market information, know-how and new technologies (Lal, 2002; OECD, 2005). An SME's marketing network extends to both potential and existing customers and suppliers, competitors, business friends and colleagues, government agencies and employees of the firm (O'Donnell, 2004). The innate networking of the small firm owner/manager is in keeping with relationship marketing practice, whereby the emphasis is upon establishing, developing and maintaining relational exchanges for the creation of added value and attainment of mutual goals (Hunt & Morgan, 1994).

This small firm networking approach to marketing is indicative of Vargo & Lusch's (2006) concept of 'service dominant logic', which describes marketing as a series of social as well as economic processes. Arguably an extension of relationship marketing, service dominant logic defines value as reciprocal and co-created both *'indirectly through interaction with goods in their use, as well as through direct interaction between suppliers, customers and other parties'* (Ballantyne et al., 2008, p.). Ballantyne and Varey (2006) define the value-creating activities underpinning service dominant logic as knowledge generation and application; relationship development; and communicative interaction. Similarly, it is only through strategic integration into a firm's communication and information management processes that the value-adding relational benefits of e-CRM are realised (Harrigan et al. 2009).

Innovation in both products and processes is a recognised outcome of recurrent interaction between firms and their customers (Håkansson & Snehota, 1995). Vargo and Lusch (2006) refer to their 'service-centred view of marketing' as both customer-centric and market-driven. They emphasise continual customer collaboration and the dynamic adaption of products and services to meet individual customer needs. Small firm owner-managers typically engage in extensive networking with existing and potential customers (O'Donnell, 2004, McGowan & Durkin, 2002). The close customer relationships maintained by small firms can create strategic value and loyalty opportunities. In line with both relationship marketing and service dominant logic principles, a customer becomes a 'co-producer' rather than

a receiver of the product or service (Rothwell, 1992; McGowan & Durkin, 2002; Vargo & Lusch, XXXX).

Competitive advantage may also be gained through the structure of the owner/manager's network and the location of their contacts within it (van der Veen, 2004). Recent research into 'scale-free' networks highlights the potential benefits of dominant 'hubs', (nodes within a network with a disproportionately high number of connections) to business and marketing practice (Barabasi, 2003). As with entrepreneurial marketing, the level of networking activity is related to individual owner/manager characteristics and ability (O'Donnell, 2004; Stokes, 2000).

By identifying conceptual linkages between key elements of SME marketing and business practice and components of e-CRM, the next section endeavours to explore the existence of synergies which may enable SME owner-managers to more fully exploit the interactive potential of the Internet for the creation of added-value for customers and themselves.

E-CRM AND SME MARKETING; ISSUES, PROBLEMS, CONTROVERSIES

Successful e-CRM implementation involves the integration of 'hardware, software, processes, applications and management commitment' (Romano & Fjermestad, 2003). However, SMEs' inherent lack of influence, time, finance and specialised knowledge (Carson & Gilmore, 2000) makes them particularly vulnerable when attempting to avail of knowledge management processes such as e-CRM (Maguire et al. 2007). Furthermore, a perceived lack of applicability and uncertain profitability prevents the small firm from adopting and eliciting value from new technologies as readily as their larger counterparts (OECD, 2005; Poon & Swatman, 1999).

The somewhat limited research in this area suggests that in instances where SMEs are implementing e-CRM, their approach is somewhat 'ad hoc' and lacking in strategic planning (Harrigan et al, 2007). While this is typical of the SMEs' more informal, tactical approach to business and marketing management (Carson & Gilmore, 2000; McCole & Ramsey, 2004; McGowan & Durkin, 2002) there is consensus in the literature that a well-planned strategy is a prerequisite to successful e-business practice (Chen & Chen, 2004; Coltman, 2007; Day & Hubbard, 2003; Lin et al. 2006, Pavic et al., 2007). Without prior development of a strategy dedicated to improved identification, understanding and retention of the most profitable customers, purely technical e-CRM application is likely to meet with failure, negatively impacting upon the business as a whole (Ab Hamid, 2005; Lin et al, 2006; Ramsey et al. 2003; Rigby et al, 2002). Without planning, Pavic et al. (2007) contend that 'it is difficult for SMEs to succeed and create competitive advantage in this new virtual environment.' (p.323)

Relating to the above discussion, there is clearly confusion present in the extant literature in relation to e-CRM and its relevance to SMEs in affording competitive advantage. This is not surprising given the lack of empirical research pertaining to the use of the Internet for marketing purposes by SMEs, (Dandridge & Levenburg, 2000) and the generally discursive and dichotomous nature of the literature detailing its importance (Downie, 2003). In addition there is limited, in-depth research into the relevance and practice of CRM by SMEs and the role that technology plays, (Harrigan et al. 2009; McGowan & Durkin, 2002). While some models have been developed detailing the factors that contribute to e-CRM success (Chen & Chen, 2004; Day & Hubbard, 2003; Lin et al. 2006; Romano & Fjermestad, 2003) with the exception of that of Doherty & Lockett (2008) they have been developed with the larger organisation in mind. There is a need, therefore, for 'models, tools, techniques and methodologies' (Maguire et

al. 2007) to be developed for the entrepreneurial small firm with its unique characteristics, to help enable it to derive sustainable competitive advantage from e-business strategies such as e-CRM (Downie, 2003; Harrigan et al. 2008; Haynes et al. 1998; Sands, 2003).

A review of the literature pertaining to e-CRM implementation and practice identifies several factors as fundamental to e-CRM success. Romano & Fjermestad (2003) categorise the five key e-CRM influences as: 'Markets, Business Models, Human Factors, e-CRM Technology and Knowledge Management'. Change and knowledge management processes are considered necessary to ensure employee buy-in and a market-orientated organisational culture (Bradshaw and Brash, 2001; Chen & Chen, 2004; Doherty & Lockett, 2008; Lin et al. 2006; Romano & Fjermestad, 2003). Adequate resources and infrastructure are required to support the alignment and integration of e-CRM technologies with existing Information Systems and business strategies (Doherty & Lockett, 2008; Lin et al. 2006, Chen & Chen, 2004; Romano & Fjermestad, 2003; Bradshaw and Brash, 2001). Finally, senior management leadership and commitment is considered core to the success of e-CRM operations (Bengtsson, 2007; Buttle, 2004; Chen & Chen, 2004; Lin et al. 2006).

At first, these proposed frameworks appear to conflict with the characteristics of SME marketing, suggesting that fully integrated e-CRM requires significant competencies and resources and may therefore be beyond the reach of the small firm. For example, the small firm has limited capabilities when it comes to accessing and processing information (McGowan & Durkin, 2002). A recent study by Maguire et al. (2007) cited financial constraints and a lack of technical and business expertise as barriers to SMEs effectively implementing IT/IS strategies to gain competitive advantage.

Much of SME marketing practice is unplanned and deficient of a long-term market-orientated focus (Blankson & Stokes, 2002, pg.49). This somewhat contradicts the formal, planned approach required for e-CRM. In relation to the use of the Internet for relational purposes specifically, McGowan et al, (2001) conclude that even when an owner-manager has technological competence and an awareness of the importance of the Internet, they are often unable to appreciate the valuable contribution it can make to their business relationships and treat it instead as an informational tool.

However, despite these obvious restrictions in relation to the implementation of e-CRM and the practice of marketing in general, SMEs do manage to survive and grow. Indeed the above critique is based upon models mainly developed for large firm practice, which clearly do not make allowances for the unique context of the smaller firm. If taken instead from the perspective of SME marketing; there are natural linkages with relationship marketing (Zotanos & Anderson, 2004; McGowan et al. 2001). Furthermore, whilst acknowledging the necessity of the adequate provision of resources to develop and support CRM initiatives, Day and Bens (2005) claim that this does not automatically translate into the purchase or pioneering use of Information Technology. Rather, they emphasise that it is companies who already excel at managing customer relationships and whose customers perceive significant differences in their value offering that are best positioned to gain from e-CRM. Those companies with a 'relationship leader' are better not only at anticipating how to exploit the Internet but also deploy it more quickly and effectively. It could be argued, therefore, that the entrepreneurial SME with a marketing orientation (Bengtsson, 2007; Blanskon & Stokes, 2002) will be ideally positioned to gain from the competitive opportunities offered by e-CRM (Baumeister, 2002; Sands, 2003). This is in keeping with Day & Bens' (2005) findings which suggest that smaller firms more readily recognize the Internet as an additional channel with which to reach their customers.

SME/e-CRM Synergy: Opportunities and Implications

While the SME's focus on short term profits could be considered a somewhat transactional approach to marketing, from the above discussion it is apparent that they inherently practice relationship marketing through their entrepreneurial and networking endeavours. E-CRM should therefore be viewed as a natural complement to SME marketing activity (Harrigan et al. 2009). E-CRM provides SMEs with the opportunity to enhance, not replace, existing communications channels and practices by improving the management of customer information and the delivery of value through increasingly personalised, two-way interactions (Kennedy, 2006; Scullin et al. 2004; Swatman, 2000).

In the case of the SME, trust and credibility between external network partners is intrinsically linked to interpersonal interactions (McGowan & Durkin, 2002). Research by Geiger & Martin (1999) suggests a preference on the part of both the small firm owner/manager and their customers for face to face contact. The social relationship with customers differentiates SME business practice from that of the larger firm and can provide them with a competitive edge (Ragins & Greco, 2003). Economic opportunities can be realized through the exchange of knowledge, learning and problem-solving endeavours between inter-firm relationships characterized by trust (Uzzi, 1997). However, SME owner managers should be able to leverage the high levels of intimacy and trust they enjoy as a result of their extensive, proactive networking (O'Donnell, 2004) to introduce an additional electronic dimension to the relationship. Indeed, Bauer et al. (2002) contend that the use of Internet technologies is most appropriate in established face-to-face relationships, where trust is already established. When used creatively, personalisation and on-line interactivity has been shown to help forge emotional connections with customers in ways that no other medium can (Weiss, 1999). Research by Brodie et al. (2007) reveals that despite an increase in Internet penetration amongst businesses, face to face, personal contact remains core to fostering customer relationships and encouraging retention. Recognising and accepting the Internet as a channel to supplement, rather than substitute, existing relationships is therefore crucial. Furthermore, a more in-depth understanding of customer behaviour, buying patterns and profitability as a result of e-CRM technology and practice can inform the allocation of resources, both *off-line* as well as on. (Buttle, 2004)

There are a number of online e-CRM methods and tools that small business managers can use to add value and enhance competitiveness, of which many are tactical in nature (Morris et al., 2002). In addition to a web presence, assessing interest or increasing awareness of products and services can be addressed via on-line mailing lists, participation in discussion groups and the organisation of on-line focus groups (Dandridge and Levenburg, 2000). By participating in online industry forums, browsing competitor web sites or signing-up to government portals, small firms could easily and effectively supplement information that they would normally gather from trade shows and business seminars (Sands, 2003). Existing customer relationships may benefit from e-bulletins, personalised web pages, or the opportunity to customise products or services online (Sands, 2003). In relationships with potential customers the electronic personalisation of the relationship via relevant and timely emails may help encourage purchase and strengthen relationship ties (Chanston & Mangles, 2003). Such online tools and applications enable small firms to firstly 'experiment' at relatively low cost and risk, in order to learn how e-CRM can contribute to, and augment existing business relationships, before investing resources in specialised database technologies.

Ultimately, the successful integration of online and offline channels in the management of network relationships will rely upon the ability of the entrepreneur to appropriately balance personal relationships with more remote electronic relationships (McGowan & Durkin, 2002). Both the owner/manager and the networks members' acceptance or resistance to online channels could impede first level adoption of the Internet (Howcroft and Durkin, 2000) and consequently its advanced usage for relational, interactive purposes. Prowess with Internet technologies (Day & Hubbard, 2003) or in the case of the small firm an 'Internet champion' (Mehrtens et al., 2001; Bengtsson, 2007) is required if e-CRM is to be successfully integrated with existing business routines. Management leadership and employee support are incremental to e-CRM, with the small firm's close workforce ties considered an added advantage (Bengtsson, 2007; Doherty & Lockett, 2008). Finally, before implementing Internet technologies all firms regardless of size must identify how e-CRM can be utilised to augment their value proposition, by carefully considering the product or service offering and the market environment in which they operate (Day and Hubbard, 2003; Howcroft & Durkin, 2000).

SME/e-CRM Synergy: A Conceptual Model

In light of the above discussion, is posited that there is a synergy between e-CRM and the entrepreneurial and networking components of SME marketing for the creation of added value. While it also acknowledges that there are inherent characteristics of the small firm that conflict with the factors considered to contribute to successful e-CRM integration and implementation; one should not necessarily negate the other.

In keeping with Sadowaski et al.'s (2002, p.90) assertion that research into SME Internet adoption should focus on *'the exploitation and leveraging of pre-existing, complementary human assets and business resources'*, the following conceptual model (Figure 1) developed from the

Figure 1. Synergy for the creation of added value

E-CRM Success Factors	SME Characteristics	SME *Opportunities*
Conditions	**Conditions**	
• Customer-centric culture ⟶	⟵ • Customer intensity/close customer ties	
• Top management leadership/support ⟶	⟶ • Lack of perceived efficacy/ Preference for face-to-face contact	*Emphasis on 'Relationship Leadership'*
• Nature of product service offering ⟶	⟵ • Creativity, flexibility and innovation via entrepreneurial and network marketing	
• Market environment ⟶	⟵ • Creativity, flexibility and innovation via entrepreneurial and network marketing	
Processes	**Processes**	*Processes*
• Strategic Planning ⟶	⟶ • Informal, tactical approach	*Experiment with online tools*
• Change Management (Internal & External network) ⟶	⟵ • Networking ability (strong internal and external network ties)	
• Knowledge management (IS/IT integration) ⟶	⟶ • Lack of formal structures	*'Engage Internet Champion'*
Resources	**Resources**	*Resources*
• Technological ⟶	⟶ • Constrained	*Leverage entrepreneurial/ network ability/ Engage Internet Champion/ Experiment with Online tools*
• Informational ⟶	⟶ • Constrained	
• Financial ⟶	⟶ • Constrained	
• Human ⟶	⟶ • Constrained	
• Time ⟶	⟶ • Constrained	

SYNERGY FOR THE CREATION OF ADDED VALUE

extant literature, interprets the potential synergy between more formal e-CRM approaches and informal SME characteristics. The factors detailed in the literature as critical to the success of e-CRM, (Bengtsson, 2007; Day and Hubbard, 2003; Day & Lockett, Chen & Chen, 2004; Lin et al. 2006, Romano & Fjermestad, 2003) were combined and categorised, and an attempt made to align them with SME characteristics to illustrate where a natural synergy may or may not exist. 'Conditions' refers to the organisational culture or climate necessary for e-CRM to flourish. 'Processes' recognises the formal business strategies and approaches required for successful e-CRM, and 'resources' identifies the individual resource requirements needed to implement e-CRM. These success factors mostly relate to the larger organization and the implementation of specific e-CRM software. The model therefore attempts to incorporate both the small business context and the potential offered by the Internet, which is comparatively lower risk and lower cost than specific e-CRM software applications.

As discussed in the literature, the 'outcome' of successful e-CRM is added value. Therefore the conditions, processes and resources categorised as formal e-CRM success factors positively contribute to the creation of added value. In the conceptual model this is illustrated by arrows pointing inwards. In the case of the SME, the characteristics associated with the creation of added value, and which naturally complement the more formal components of successful e-CRM, have also been attributed inward-pointing arrows.

In instances whereby SME characteristics conflict with elements of the formal e-CRM approach, and thus hinder the creation of value, the arrows point away from the central line of synergy. The third column makes tentative suggestions, again drawn from the literature reviewed, as to how entrepreneurial capabilities, online tools and additional human resources may be leveraged further by the SME to lessen the potential 'risk' areas associated with small firm e-CRM implementation.

The model goes some way to illustrate where natural synergies, and therefore opportunities, may exist for SMEs to leverage their unique characteristics to optimise the Internet for competitive impact. Furthermore, it highlights the potential 'risk' areas such as lack of perceived efficacy; (OECD, 2005; Poon & Swatman, 1999) preference for face to face contact; (Geiger & Martin, 1999; McGowan & Durkin, 2002) informal, unstructured approach to business processes (Carson & Gilmore, 2000; McCole & Ramsey, 2004) and lack of resources (Maguire et al., 2007) which could perhaps inhibit or undermine the successful implementation of e-CRM in SMEs. There is a suggestion in the literature that existing theoretical frameworks, and the extension thereof, no longer adequately address the competitive complexities of the contemporary marketplace (Morris et al. 2002). In the SME context, Harrigan et al. (2008) suggest that in order to capitalize upon the Internet for the management of customer relationships, small firms must draw upon their own 'entrepreneurial style' to develop suitable strategies. By introducing the constructs of network and entrepreneurial marketing in relation to e-CRM, it is therefore proposed that the more inherent and developed the entrepreneurial and networking ability of the small firm, the better placed they are to develop unique Internet strategies which will positively impact upon the creation and maintenance of valuable customer relationships (e-CRM).

Finally, it is generally accepted that E-business adoption is a continuous process (Wu et al., 2003).

The more a firm engages in Internet activities, even at a tactical level, the greater the perceived performance (Drennan & McColl-Kennedy, 2003; Morris et al.) and the increased likelihood of advanced Internet usage (Dholakia & Kshetri (2004). It is proposed by way of the conceptual model therefore, that the small firm which displays a willingness to experiment by seeking advice from an Internet champion (Bengtsson, 2007; Merhtens et al. 2001) via their networks, or by proactively appointing one, is more likely to overcome the difficulties associated with small firm e-CRM adoption and implementation.

CONCLUSION AND FUTURE RESEARCH

While there is a growing body of literature concerning the use of the Internet as a strategic customer relationship management tool, there is little empirical evidence linking Internet usage amongst small firms with improved customer retention and profitability (Ab Hamid & Kassim, 2004; Dandridge & Levenburg, 2000; Drennan & McColl-Kennedy, 2003). Consequently, this first-stage model is proposed as a means to explore both how, and to what extent SMEs are using the Internet to augment their value proposition and facilitate customer relationships, retention and loyalty.

In particular, this model not only identifies the organisational conditions, processes and resources necessary for successful e-CRM implementation, but also anticipates the small firm characteristics and opportunities that can best support the use of the Internet for advanced relational purposes. It is proposed that this conceptual model can be further developed and used in longitudinal case studies of SMEs to explore if, and how, they leverage their unique capabilities and characteristics to support these 'natural synergies' by incorporating e-CRM into their existing business practices; and compensate in the instances where there are none.

Brodie et al. (2008) call for in-depth, qualitative research with exemplar firms to help better understand how and under what conditions the Internet can optimally influence business and marketing practice. A purposive sample of 'brick and click' SMES is therefore proposed, whereby firms are selected based upon their level of integration of Internet technologies with existing processes. Further, it would be of interest to apply the model to firms from less technologically advanced regions with those from 'first wave' adopter countries, (Fletcher et al. 2004) or to compare firms from differing industry sectors. The desired outcome of such research would be to establish an empirically validated framework, specific to SMEs. This would allow small form owner/managers to understand through the experiences of their peers, Internet usage patterns to become more competitive through the development of successful e-CRM strategies (Downie, 2003; Haynes et al, 1998; Sands 2003).

REFERENCES

Ab Hamid, N. R. (2005). E-CRM: Are we there yet? *The Journal of American Academy of Business, 6*(1), 51–57.

Ab Hamid, N. R., & Kassim, N. (2004). Internet technology as a tool in customer relationship management. *The Journal of American Academy of Business, 4*(1/2), 103–108.

Adebanjo, D. (2003). Classifying and selecting e-CRM applications: An analysis-based proposal. *Management Decision, 41*(6), 570–577. doi:10.1108/00251740310491517

Arnott, D. C., & Bridgewater, S. (2002). Internet, interaction and implications for marketing. *Marketing Intelligence & Planning, 20*(2), 86–95. doi:10.1108/02634500210418509

Barabasi, A. L., & Bonabeay, E. (2003, May). Scale-free networks. *Scientific American, 288*(5), 60–70. doi:10.1038/scientificamerican0503-60

Bauer, H. H., Gretner, M., & Leach, M. (2002). Building customer relations over the Internet. *Industrial Marketing Management, 31*(2), 155–163. doi:10.1016/S0019-8501(01)00186-9

Baumeister, H. (2002, October). Customer Relationship Management for SMEs, e2000 e-business & e-work. *Proceedings of the E2002 Conference*, Prague.

Bengtsson, M., Boter, H., & Vanyushyn, V. (2007). Integrating the Internet and marketing operations: A study of antecedents in firms of different size. *International Small Business Journal, 25*(1), 27–48. doi:10.1177/0266242607071780

Berry, L. L. (1995). Relationship marketing of services – Growing interest, emerging perspectives. *Journal of the Academy of Marketing Science, 23*, 236–245. doi:10.1177/009207039502300402

Bitner, M. J., Brown, S. W., & Meuter, M. L. (2000). Technology infusion in service encounters. *Journal of the Academy of Marketing Science, 28*(1), 138–149. doi:10.1177/0092070300281013

Blankson, C., & Stokes, D. (2002). Marketing practices in the UK small business sector. *Marketing Intelligence & Planning, 20*(1), 49–61. doi:10.1108/02634500210414774

Boulding, W., Staelin, R., Ehret, M., & Johnston, W. J. (2005). A customer relationship management roadmap: What is known, potential pitfalls, and where to go. *Journal of Marketing, 69*(4), 155–166. doi:10.1509/jmkg.2005.69.4.155

Bradshaw, D., & Brash, C. (2001). Managing customer relationships in the e-business world: How to personalise computer relationships for increased profitability. *International Journal of Retail & Distribution Management, 29*(11/12), 520. doi:10.1108/09590550110696969

Brodie, R. J., Winklhofer, H., Coviello, N. E., & Johnston, W. J. (2007). Is E-marketing coming of age? An examination of e-marketing and firm performance. *Journal of Interactive Marketing, 21*(1), 3–21. doi:10.1002/dir.20071

Bull, C. (2003). Strategic issues in customer relationship management (CRM) implementation. *Business Process Management Journal, 9*(5), 592–602. doi:10.1108/14637150310496703

Buttle, F. (2004). *Customer relationship management, concepts and tools.* Oxford, UK: Elsevier, Butterworth, Heinemann.

Carson, D., Cromie, S., McGowan, P., & Hill, J. (1995). *Marketing and entrepreneurship in SMEs.* Englewood Cliffs, NJ: Prentice-Hall.

Carson, D., & Gilmore, A. (2000). Marketing at the interface: Not 'what' but 'how.'. *Journal of Marketing Theory and Practice, 8*(2), 1–8.

Chanston, I., & Mangles, T. (2003). Relationship marketing in online business-to-business markets: A pilot investigation of Small UK manufacturing firms. *European Journal of Marketing, 37*(5/6), 753–773. doi:10.1108/03090560310465134

Chen, I. J., & Popovich, K. (2003). Understanding customer relationship management (CRM) people, process and technology. *Business Process Management Journal, 9*(5), 672–688. doi:10.1108/14637150310496758

Chen, Q., & Chen, H. (2004). Exploring the success factors of e-CRM strategies in practice. *Database Marketing & Customer Strategy Management, 11*(4), 333–343. doi:10.1057/palgrave.dbm.3240232

Collinson, E., & Shaw, E. (2001). Entrepreneurial marketing- A historical perspective on development and practice. *Management Decision, 39*(9), 761–766. doi:10.1108/EUM0000000006221

Coviello, N., & Munro, H. (1997). Network relationships and the internationalisation process of the small software firm. *International Business Review, 6*(4), 361–386. doi:10.1016/S0969-5931(97)00010-3

Dandridge, T., & Levenburg, N. M. (2000). High-tech Potential? An exploratory study of very small firms' usage of the Internet. *International Small Business Journal, 18*(81), 81–91. doi:10.1177/0266242600182004

Day, G. S., & Bens, K. F. (2005). Capitalizing on the Internet opportunity. *Journal of Business and Industrial Marketing, 20*(4/5), 160–168. doi:10.1108/08858620510603837

Day, G. S., & Hubbard, J. K. (2003). Customer relationships go digital. *Business Strategy Review, 14*(1), 17–26. doi:10.1111/1467-8616.00240

Dholakia, R. R., & Kshetri, N. (2004). Factors impacting the adoption of the Internet among SMEs. *Small Business Economics, 23*(4), 311–322. doi:10.1023/B:SBEJ.0000032036.90353.1f

Doherty, N., & Lockett, N. (2008). Mind the gap: Exploring the links between the expectations of Relationship marketing and the reality of electronic-CRM. *International Journal of e-Business Management, 2*(2), 1-17.

Downie, G. (2003). Internet marketing and SMEs. *Management Services, 47*(7), 8–11.

Drennan, J., & McColl-Kennedy, J. R. (2003). The relationship between Internet use and perceived performance in retail and professional service firms. *Journal of Services Marketing, 17*(3), 295–311. doi:10.1108/08876040310474837

Egan, T., Clancy, S., & O'Toole, T. (2003). The integration of e-commerce tools into the business processes of SMEs. *Irish Journal of Management, 24*(1), 139–153.

Feinberg, R., & Kadam, R. (2002). E-CRM Web service attributes as determinants of customer satisfaction with retail Web sites. *International Journal of Service Industry Management, 13*(5), 432–451. doi:10.1108/09564230210447922

Fletcher, R., Bell, J., & McNoughton, R. (2004). *International e-business marketing.* London, UK: Thomson.

Freidlein, A. (2001, February). *CRM meets E-CRM: An executive briefing.* Wheel Consultancy. Retrieved 4ᵗʰ February, 2008, from www.e-consultancy.com

Geiger, S., & Martin, S. (1999). The Internet as a relationship marketing tool – Some evidence from Irish companies. *Irish Marketing Review, 12*(2), 24–35.

Geller, K. (1998). The Internet: The ultimate relationship marketing tool. *Direct Marketing, 61*(5), 36–39.

Gilmore, A., & Carson, D. (1999). Entrepreneurial marketing by networking. *New England Journal of Entrepreneurship, 2*(2), 31–38.

Gilmore, A., Carson, D., & Grant, K. (2001). SME marketing in practice. *Marketing Intelligence & Planning, 19*(1), 6–11. doi:10.1108/02634500110363583

Gilmore, A., Carson, D., Grant, K., O'Donnell, A., Laney, R., & Pickett, B. (2006). Networking in SMEs: Findings from Australia and Ireland. *Irish Marketing Review, 18*(1/2), 21–29.

Gilmore, A., Carson, D., O'Donnell, A., & Cummins, D. (1999). Added value: A qualitative assessment of SME marketing. *Irish Marketing Review, 12*(1), 27–36.

Gilmore, A., Gallagher, D., & Henry, S. (2007). E-marketing and SMEs: Operational lessons for the future. *European Business Review, 19*(2), 234–247. doi:10.1108/09555340710746482

Grönroos, C. (1994). From marketing mix to relationship marketing: Towards a paradigm shift in marketing. *Management Decision, 32*(2), 4–22. doi:10.1108/00251749410054774

Grönroos, C. (2004). The relationship marketing process: Communication, interaction, dialogue, value. *Journal of Business and Industrial Marketing, 19*(2), 99–113. doi:10.1108/08858620410523981

Gummesson, E. (1994). Making relationship marketing operational. *International Journal of Service Industry Management, 5*(5), 5–20. doi:10.1108/09564239410074349

Gummesson, E. (2004). Return on relationships (ROR): The value of relationship marketing and CRM in business-to-business contexts. *Journal of Business and Industrial Marketing, 19*(2), 136–146. doi:10.1108/08858620410524016

Håkansson, H., & Snehota, I. (1995). *Developing relationships in business networks.* London, UK: Routledge.

Harrigan, P., Ramsey, E., & Ibbotson, P. (2008). E-CRM in SMEs: An exploratory study in Northern Ireland. *Marketing Intelligence & Planning, 26*(4), 385–404. doi:10.1108/02634500810879296

Haynes, P. J., Becherer, R. C., & Helms, M. M. (1998). Small and mid-sized businesses and Internet use: unrealized potential? *Internet Research: Electronic Networking Applications and Policy, 8*(3), 229–235. doi:10.1108/10662249810217786

Hill, J. (2001). A multidimensional study of the key determinants of effective SME marketing activity: Part 1. *International Journal of Entrepreneurial Behaviour & Research, 7*(5), 171–204. doi:10.1108/EUM0000000006006

Hill, J., & McGowan, P. (1996). Marketing development through networking: A competency based approach for small firm entrepreneurs. *Journal of Small Business and Enterprise Development, 3*(3), 148–157. doi:10.1108/eb020974

Hoffman, D. L., & Novak, T. P. (1997). A new paradigm for electronic commerce. *The Information Society, 13*, 43–54. doi:10.1080/019722497129278

Howcroft, J. B., & Durkin, M. (2000). Reflections on bank-customer interactions in the new millennium. *Journal of Financial Services Marketing, 5*(1), 9–20. doi:10.1057/palgrave.fsm.4770002

Hunt, S. D., & Morgan, R. M. (1994). Relationship marketing in the era of network competition. *Marketing Management, 3*(1), 18–28.

Ibeh, K. I., Luo, Y., & Dinnie, K. (2005). E-branding strategies of Internet companies: Some preliminary insights from the UK. *The Journal of Brand Management, 12*(5), 355–373. doi:10.1057/palgrave.bm.2540231

Iyer, R., & Bejou, D. (Eds.). (2003). *Customer relationship management in electronic markets.* Binghamton, NY: Hawthorne Press.

Jaworski, B. J., & Kohli, A. J. (1993). Marketing orientation: Antecedents and consequences. *Journal of Marketing, 57*, 53–70. doi:10.2307/1251854

Johnson, M. D., & Selnes, F. (2004). Customer portfolio management: Toward a dynamic theory of exchange relationships. *Journal of Marketing, 68*, 1–17. doi:10.1509/jmkg.68.2.1.27786

Kennedy, A. (2006). Electronic customer relationship management, (e-CRM): Opportunities and challenges in a digital world. *Irish Marketing Review, 18*(1/2), 58–69.

Lal, K. (2002). E-business and manufacturing sector: A study of small and medium-sized enterprises in India. *Research Policy, 31*, 1199–1211. doi:10.1016/S0048-7333(01)00191-3

Lin, C., Lin, K., Huang, Y., & Kuo, N. (2006). Evaluation of electronic customer relationship management: The critical success factors. *Business Review (Federal Reserve Bank of Philadelphia), 6*(2), 206–212.

Maguire, S., Koh, S. C. L., & Magrys, A. (2007). The adoption of e-business and knowledge management in SMEs. *Benchmarking: An International Journal, 14*(1), 37–58. doi:10.1108/14635770710730928

Martin, L., & Matlay, H. (2001). "Blanket" approaches to promoting ICT in small firms: Some lessons from the DTI ladder adoption model in the UK. *Internet Research, 11*(5), 399–410. doi:10.1108/EUM0000000006118

Martin, L., & Matlay, H. (2003). Innovative use of the Internet in established small firms: The impact of knowledge management and organisational learning in accessing new opportunities. *Qualitative Market Research: An International Journal, 6*(1), 18–26. doi:10.1108/13522750310457348

McCole, P., & Ramsey, E. (2004). Internet-enabled technology in knowledge-intensive business services: A comparison of Northern Ireland, the Republic of Ireland and New Zealand. *Marketing Intelligence & Planning, 22*(7), 761–779. doi:10.1108/02634500410568

McGowan, P., & Durkin, M. (2002). Toward an understanding of Internet adoption at the marketing/entrepreneurship interface. *Journal of Marketing Management, 18*, 361–377. doi:10.1362/0267257022872451

McGowan, P., Durkin, M., Allen, L., Dougan, C., & Nixon, S. (2001). Developing competencies in the entrepreneurial small firm for the use of the Internet in the management of customer relationships. *Journal of European Industry Training, 25*(2/3/4), 126-36.

Mehrtens, J., Cragg, P. B., & Mills, A. M. (2001). A model of Internet adoption by SMEs. *Information & Management, 39*(3), 165–176. doi:10.1016/S0378-7206(01)00086-6

Morris, M. B., Schindehutte, M., & Laforge, R. W. (2002). Entrepreneurial marketing: A construct for integrating emerging entrepreneurship and marketing perspectives. *Journal of Marketing Theory and Practice, 10*(4), 1–19.

O'Donnell, A. (2004). The nature of networking in small firms. *Qualitative Market Research: An International Journal, 7*(3), 206–217. doi:10.1108/13522750410540218

O'Toole, T. (2001). E-relationships – Emergence and the small firm. *Marketing Intelligence & Planning, 21*(2), 115–122. doi:10.1108/02634500310465434

OECD. (2005). SME and entrepreneurship outlook. Retrieved November 6th, 2007, from www.oecd.org

Pan, S. L., & Lee, J. (2003). Using e-CRM for a unified view of the customer. *Communications of the ACM, 46*(4), 95–99. doi:10.1145/641205.641212

Pavic, S., Koh, S. C. L., Simpson, M., & Padmore, J. (2007). Could e-business create a competitive advantage in UK SMEs? *Benchmarking: An International Journal, 14*(3), 320–351. doi:10.1108/14635770710753112

Peppers, D., Rodgers, M., & Dorf, B. (1999). Is your company ready for one-to-one marketing? *Harvard Business Review, 77*(1), 151–160.

Peppers, D., Rodgers, M., & Dorf, B. (1999). Is your company ready for one-to-one marketing? *Harvard Business Review, 77*(1), 151–160.

Poon, S., & Swatman, P. M. C. (1999). An exploratory study of small business Internet commerce issues. *Information & Management, 35*(1), 9–18. doi:10.1016/S0378-7206(98)00079-2

Porter, M. E. (2001). Strategy and the Internet. *Harvard Business Review, 79*(3), 62–78.

Ragins, J. E., & Greco, J. A. (2003). Customer relationship management and e-business: More than a software solution. *Review of Business, Cambridge, 24*(1), 25–30.

Ramsey, E., Ibbotson, P., Bell, J., & Gray, B. (2003). E-opportunities of service sector SMEs: An Irish cross-border study. *Journal of Small Business and Enterprise Development, 10*(3), 250–265. doi:10.1108/14626000310489709

Reichheld, F. F., & Sasser, J. W. E. (1990). Zero defections: Quality comes to services. *Harvard Business Review, 68*(5), 105–111.

Riemenschneider, C. K., Harrison, D. A., & Mykytyn, P. P. Jr. (2003). Understanding IT adoption decisions in small business: Integrating current theories. *Information & Management, 40*, 269–285. doi:10.1016/S0378-7206(02)00010-1

Rigby, D. K., Reichheld, F. F., & Schefter, P. (2002). Avoid the four perils of customer relationship marketing. *Harvard Business Review, 80*(2), 101–199.

Romano, N. C. Jr, & Fjermestad, J. (2003). Electronic commerce customer relationship management: A research agenda. *Information Technology Management, 4*, 233–258. doi:10.1023/A:1022906513502

Rothwell, R. (1992). Successful industrial innovation: Critical factors for the 1990s. *R & D Management, 22*(3), 221–239. doi:10.1111/j.1467-9310.1992.tb00812.x

Rowley, J. (2004). Partnering paradigms? Knowledge management and relationship marketing. *Industrial Management & Data Systems, 104*(2), 149–157. doi:10.1108/02635570410522125

Runyan, R., Droge, C., & Swinney, J. (2008). Entrepreneurial orientation versus small business orientation: What are their relationships to firm performance? *Journal of Small Business Management*, *46*(4), 567–588. doi:10.1111/j.1540-627X.2008.00257.x

Sadowski, B. M., Maitland, C., & van Dongen, J. (2002). Strategic use of the Internet by small-and medium-sized companies: An exploratory study. *Information Economics and Policy*, *14*, 75–93. doi:10.1016/S0167-6245(01)00054-3

Sands, M. (2003). Integrating the Web and e-mail into a push-pull strategy. *Qualitative Market Research*, *6*(1), 27–37. doi:10.1108/13522750310457357

Scullin, S. S., Fjermestad, J., & Romano, N. C. Jr. (2004). E-relationship marketing: Changes in traditional marketing as an outcome of electronic customer relationship management. *The Journal of Enterprise Information Management*, *17*(6), 410–415. doi:10.1108/17410390410566698

Shaw, E. (1999). Networks and their relevance to the entrepreneurial/marketing interface: A review of the evidence. *Journal of Research in Marketing & Entrepreneurship*, *1*(1), 24–40. doi:10.1108/14715209980001554

Simmons, G. (2008). Marketing to postmodern consumers: Introducing the Internet chameleon. *European Journal of Marketing*, *42*(3/4), 294–310. doi:10.1108/03090560810852940

Simmons, G., Armstrong, G., & Durkin, M. (2008). A conceptualization of the determinants of small business Web site adoption. *International Small Business Journal*, *26*(3), 351–389. doi:10.1177/0266242608088743

Srirojanant, S., & Cresswell-Thirkell, P. (1998). Relationship marketing and its synergy with Web-based technologies. *Journal of Market Focused Management*, *3*, 23–46. doi:10.1023/A:1009790421951

Stokes, D. (2000). Entrepreneurial marketing: A conceptualisation from qualitative research. *Qualitative Market Research: An International Journal*, *3*(1), 47–54. doi:10.1108/13522750010310497

Storey, D. J. (1994). *Understanding the small business sector*. London, UK: Routledge.

Subba Rao, S., Metts, G., & Monge, C. A. M. (2003). Electronic commerce development in small and medium sized enterprises. *Business Process Management Journal*, *9*(1), 11–33. doi:10.1108/14637150310461378

Swatman, P. (2000). Internet for SMEs: A new Silk Road? *International Trade Forum*, *3*, 22–24.

Uzzi, B. (1997). Social structure and competition in interfirm networks: The paradox of embeddedness. *Administrative Science Quarterly*, *42*(1), 35–67. doi:10.2307/2393808

Van der Veen, M. (2004). *Explaining e-business adoption: Innovation and entrepreneurship and in Dutch SMEs*. Unpublished doctoral dissertation, University of Twente, Holland.

Weiss, T. J. (1999). Cyber-relationships and brand building. *Integrated Marketing Communications Research Journal*, *5*, 19–22.

Wu, F., Mahajan, V., & Balasubramanian, S. (2003). An analysis of e-business adoption and its impact on business performance. *Academy of Marketing Science Journal*, *31*(4), 425–448. doi:10.1177/0092070303255379

Zineldin, M. (2000). Beyond relationship marketing: Technological ship marketing. *Marketing Intelligence & Planning*, *18*(1), 9–23. doi:10.1108/02634500010308549

Zontanos, G., & Anderson, A. R. (2004). Relationships, marketing and small business: An exploration of links in theory and practice. *Qualitative Market Research: An International Journal*, *7*(3), 228–236. doi:10.1108/13522750410540236

Section 3
E–Commerce and E–Business

Chapter 9

eBusiness Among Ethnic Minority Businesses:
Ethnic Entrepreneurs' ICT Adoption and Readiness

Martin Beckinsale
De Montfort University, UK

ABSTRACT

A small but growing body of evidence (SBS, 2004; Beckinsale & Ram, 2006) has indicated that Ethnic Minority Businesses (EMBs) have not adopted Information Communication Technology (ICT) at comparable rates to their non-EMB counterparts, predominantly Small and Medium Sized Enterprises (SMEs). With EMBs accounting for almost 10% of businesses in the UK, the economic impact as ICT adoption continues to further develop across mainstream markets could be highly significant. Existing UK ICT policies also failed to engage with EMBs until the NW ICT Adoption Pilot in 2004. The current, limited body of research is fragmented, provides limited understanding and coherence on reasons of low ICT adoption, and lacks exemplars upon which policy considerations may be made. Firstly, the chapter will examine and review the existing body of literature. Secondly, EMB cases that have developed ICT to a degree where they are engaging in e-business activity are statically and dynamically analysed and discussed. The findings provide a number of options and guidance for EMB owners. Finally, the recommendations point to the need for improved ICT awareness, better business support provision nationally, and the importance of generation and education as key drivers.

INTRODUCTION

The role of Information Communication Technology (ICT) is viewed as critical within the economic challenges faced by government and businesses, whether small or large. ICT's importance is often

conflated with viable and competitive businesses (Levy et al., 2003). Only recently has government policy considered Ethnic Minority Businesses (EMBs) within ICT and economic policy. Most notably the North West ICT Adoption Pilot supported by the DTI, SBS and The North West Development Agency (Beckinsale & Ram, 2006). The

DOI: 10.4018/978-1-60960-597-1.ch009

pilot confirmed that Ethnic Minority Businesses (EMBs) are not utilising ICT to the same degree as other small businesses (Foley and Ram, 2002; Beckinsale and Ram, 2006). The gap was widest in the area of website adoption and eCommerce suggesting a more potentially significant economic weakness amongst EMBs.

The difficulty for both policy makers and deliverers is the lack of data, detail and understanding of ICT amongst Ethnic Minority Business communities. There have been significant assumptions that the gap in ICT adoption is significantly influenced by culture or language. There is some truth in the fact that these are factors but are only two in a list of factors relevant to all SMEs. Therefore, the chapter reviews existing data (Foley & Ram, 2002; SBS 2004) along with research carried out (Beckinsale & Ram, 2006) across a year-long DTI-supported pilot initiative that aimed to address the lack of utilisation of ICT by EMBs and stimulate the adoption of ICT and electronic commerce (e-commerce) amongst EMBs.

The main objectives of the following discussion and analysis are: to provide a review and critical understanding of Ethnic Minority Business issues in the context of Information Communication Technology (ICT, eCommerce and eBusiness); to discuss those issues in the wider context of SME literature including growth, ICT adoption, ICT readiness, new business opportunities and entrepreneurial activity; and to provide simple steps and guidelines developed from a critical examination of identified exemplar entrepreneurial EMBs.

In achieving the objectives the interplay of insights from relevant literatures on ICT, EMBs, entrepreneurship, and actual elements that impact on adoption will be examined. Further to developing the insight is the examination of entrepreneurial EMB owners. The chapter critically examines two cases relating to 2nd or 3rd generation Ethnic Minority Businesses owners that are leaving behind the traditional view of EMB business owners. The cases focused upon have either developed traditional businesses into online brands or op-

erating in sectors not traditionally considered or perceived to be EMB related and invested in ICT with varying degrees of success. The discussion will examine: How they developed their vision?; What made the entrepreneurs different?; Causal Mechanisms - Inhibitors and enablers; Business Support and Policy engagement; and good practice and why and how this may be applied in a wider EMB context.

SUMMARY OF ICT ADOPTION AND eBUSINESS

ICT is defined as 'any technology used to support information gathering, processing, distribution and use' (Beynon-Davies, 2004, pp. 7-8). ICT has also become synonymous with the areas of eCommerce and eBusiness and Chaffey (2007) states that ICT is 'used to create eBusiness systems' (p. 14). Chaffey (2007) defines eCommerce as all electronically mediated information exchanges between an organisation and its external stakeholders and significantly distinguishes eBusiness by including additional exchanges within the organization that support a range of business processes (p. 5). The definitions are clear but the ICT adoption literature has generally been viewed as fragmented (Galloway, 2006) and lacking cohesion in the understanding of issues (p. 140) especially relating to SMEs, entrepreneurs and EMBs.

Though wide-ranging, research interest in the use of ICT within SMEs can arguably be classified in four ways although not mutually exclusive. First, there is a stream of research that tends to concentrate upon ICT adoption (Levy & Powell, 2003; Mehrtens et al., 2001; Levy et al., 2005). The ICT adoption literature tends to focus on technology use based upon the purchase of computer hardware, software, data and communications technology. In some instances this has focused upon the differences between adopters and non-adopters (Thong & Yap, 1995) but government literature tends to be concerned with benchmarking adoption rates in the UK against other G7 countries (DTI, 2004). A second group of studies examine how ICT is actually used in SMEs (Foley, Watts & Wilson, 1993; Lunati, 2000) concentrating, in particular, on the key factors that influence the success of ICT in SMEs. This research tends to focus on the development of the information system, rather than its effects on the business. Third, studies have also investigated the degree to which ICT is used within SMEs as a strategic tool, with particular reference to the necessary intent, capabilities and structures required within a small firm to exploit the technology (Levy et al., 2005; Beckinsale & Levy, 2002). Finally, and perhaps most pertinently, some studies have endeavoured to embed ICT firmly within the small firm context (Beckinsale et al., 2006; Blackburn & McClure, 1998; Southern & Tilley, 2000). The SME ICT literature has predominantly focused on the stages of Internet adoption. Suggesting SMEs move through various stages of adoption that can be categorised (Chaffey, 2007; Willcocks et al., 2000; Poon & Swatman, 1999). These have their critics (Levy et al., 2001; Martin & Matlay, 2001; Storey, 1994). The developed frameworks/models are helpful in classifying the stage or stages at which individual SMEs are currently at the ICT adoption cycle but are far less helpful in moving them forward as circumstances/drivers and influences vary. Tending to be linear models they over simplify a variety of complex issues and over generalise circumstances and economic issues (Fallon & Moran, 2000; Kai-Uwe Brock, 2000). Recently, the ICT strategic vision literature has begun to provide a more dynamic view of strategic ICT adoption. Dyerson and Spinelli (2010) have developed a framework that considers how senior management views ICT opportunities (ICT strategic vision) and the ICT infrastructure and applications of the firm (ICT maturity), They suggest that these are 'the two key factors which determine the ICT readiness of the firm (p.3).

However, this research explicitly recognises the heterogeneity of the small firm sector and questions the presumption that the use of ICT will benefit all businesses, and how, in some inevitable way, all small and micro businesses will profit.

To summarise, the ICT adoption literature provides a number of frameworks to bring mutually exclusive issues for adoption together. Within the ICT adoption literature the factors/drivers for ICT adoption have tended to be focused around: perceived benefits (Dyerson & Harindranath, 2007; Mehrtens et al., 2001; Poon & Swatman, 1999; Windrum & de Berranger, 2003) often focused on efficiency improvements, organisational/operational effectiveness and new business opportunities (Levy et al., 2005) and SME promotion; organisational readiness (Levy et al., 2005; Levy & Powell, 2003; Merhtens et al., 2001) and external pressures (Merhtens et al., 2001). As Merhtens et al. (2001) and Levy et al. (2005) point out, these factors along with strategic intent influence the decisions to invest in eBusiness.

The inhibitors are especially prevalent in micro (1-9 employees) and small firms (10-49 employees) as well as limiting development beyond email and basic web sites. The literature (Levy et al., 2005; Poon & Swatman, 1999; Straub et al., 2002; Van Akkeren & Cavaye, 2000) identifies a number of inhibitors including: culture, government policies; cost of implementation; the need for immediate return on investment; considered complexity of technologies like EDI which could require new skills; lack of organisational readiness with many SMEs having limited existing IT resources; a lack of perceived benefits; and a lack of assertiveness by the owner/manager.

The summary of ICT adoption enablers and inhibitors among SMEs since the work of Poon and Swatman (1999) highlights the fragmented nature of the literature and how it has concentrated on generic groups of SMEs, has failed to develop an holistic view of adoption among SMEs and has considered a variety of sectors (Food, Agriculture, IT, Manufacturing ect.). However, one fragment missing, until only recently, has been EMBs. The examination of ICT adoption and eCommerce/eBusiness is documented across a handful of academic papers to varying degrees of understanding and insight.

ICT Adoption and Use by EMBs

The ICT literature (Beckinsale et al., 2006; Levy et al., 2005; Poon & Swatman, 1999) has dealt with SMEs examining the areas or adoption, resources, inhibitors, enablers, commerce, sector and size variations, growth, strategy and entrepreneurial activity. However, the literature relating to SMEs and ICT has a major flaw EMBs have been conspicuous by their absence. According to Deakins & Freel (2009) ethnic immigrants are of importance to the UK's economic development. Through history they have brought new skills, practices and developments in markets and sectors (restaurants and retail) that have been ignored. Figures from Ram and Jones (2008) show, that in 2004, EMBs in the UK contributed at least £15 billion (€19 billion) to the UK economy.

The labour survey for Spring 2004 to Winter 2004/5 highlights the variation between full-time and self-employment among various ethnic groups and compared to non-ethnic groups. Across all ethnic groups, including Indian, Pakistani, Bangladeshi, Caribbean, African, and Chinese the rate of self-employment is 16.7%. The highest rate by ethnicity is the Pakistani community with 25.6% and lowest being African at 9.3%. Being self-employed does not in itself indicate growth or entrepreneurial activity. The figures are comparable with the data and findings of the ONS survey (2004). The ONS survey also provides population size by ethnicity. The ONS survey (2004) states that ethnic minorities account for 7.9% of the UK population. That figure suggests a significant economic population that has been ignored in terms of ICT policy development and delivery.

Ram & Smallbone (1999) were, amongst the first researchers to identify a limited use of ICT amongst Ethnic Minority Businesses. They noted that EMBs were significantly less likely to be users of ICT than white owned firms. Only 64% of EMBs used ICT for some purpose (such as for accounts, stock control or 'general purpose' computing) compared with 89% of white owned firms. Their findings also identified 82% of white owned micro enterprises were using computers for some purpose compared with just 54% of EMBs in this size group (Ram & Smallbone, 1999, p.16).

Foley and Ram (2002) undertook the first major study, commissioned by the Small Business Service (SBS), into the use of ICT and EMBs in the UK. Their findings identified a lower adoption rate than in the non-EMB population. The adoption level differed significantly with only 37% of micro EMBs having Internet access compared to 75% of micro non-EMBs. The Small Business Service survey (SBS, 2004), undertook one of the most comprehensive studies comparing almost 5000 EMBs and non-EMBs. However, specific research into industry or sector effects was remiss. The survey noted a smaller disparity with 65.8% of micro EMBs now using ICT compared to 81.9% of non-EMBs. Uniquely, the SBS (2004) survey also identified differences between ethnic groups. African Caribbean businesses adoption rates were comparable or exceeded their non-EMB counterparts; but Chinese business owners, at 32.9%, were the least likely to use ICT. Pakistani and Bangladeshi EMBs had a higher rate of use at 57%. Furthermore, ICT use by EMBs was confined to lower level functions such as PC use for word processing or accounts and email. As stated 'Record keeping, accounts, word processing, email communication and research are the five most common uses of ICT among EMBs with employees' (SBS, 2004, p. 2).

Moving from lower to higher-level ICT adoption the gap continues to remain significant. EMBs with a website were in low single figures (Chinese – 3.4%, Pakistani – 3.5% and Bangladeshi – 5.4%) compared to over 22% of non-EMBs. eCommerce is even less evident across the variety of EMBs surveyed by the SBS. In the SBS (2004) survey

Table 1. Rate of eCommerce amongst Ethnic Groups (adapted from SBS, 2004)

	Sales via internet- %	Sales via other e-networks - %
Indian	5.6	4.2
Pakistani	6.6	3.3
Other Asian (incl. Bangladeshi)	2.4	3
Black	14.4	0.6
Chinese	0.5	1.7
Other	2.3	0.1
Total (All)	7.6	1.1

eCommerce was treated as sales via the Internet or via other e-Networks. As table 1 shows the adoption of eCommerce was highest in Black businesses and in all other ethnic groups was less than 7% for sales via the Internet. In relation to selling via other networks (such as B2B portals, eMarketplaces and government engagement) the figures dropped even further. With regards to government engagement electronically only 2.5% of all ethnic minority businesses interacted whilst the figure was 4% for non-ethnic minority businesses. Neither figure is high but the evidence points to a gap between ethnic and non-ethnic groups. Of the 2.5% of ethnic minority businesses the majority of interaction was identified between Indian and Black (BME) owned businesses. The later actually accounting for 3.5% of all electronic government interactions and Michaelis *et al.*, (2003) examined the national e-procurement picture and found that of total spending, 0.3%

was with ethnic minority businesses and according to SBS (2004) only 0.6% of BMEs engaged in e-networks a potentially important technology in the context of e-procurement and developing UK economic policy in this area.

Beckinsale & Ram's (2006) findings, in relation to the NW ICT Adoption Pilot initiative, also support the previous discussed data (SBS, 2004). The pilot, unlike the SBS (2004) survey, focused on two ethnic communities in a single region of the United Kingdom. The two ethnic communities were Chinese and Pakistani EMBs. Table 2 provides a summary of the findings from almost 200 EMBs

Beckinsale & Ram's (2006) examination of ICT beyond basic PC use begins to provide a picture further supporting the SBS (2004) survey. The data did suggest higher levels of email and website adoption compared to the SBS (2004) survey. However, there is a clear pattern of reducing ICT adoption rates and use between PC use and Sales via Internet. Most notable was the extremely limited sales via the Internet and the low adoption of business websites especially in the Pakistani business community. Interestingly however where a website was adopted in the Pakistani community this appeared to develop into selling online especially in the retail sector where as Chinese retail had adopted websites at the rate of 20% but none of these where converted into online retail.

The gap between EMBs and non-EMB ICT adoption has evidently reduced since 1999. However, the reduction appears to mainly be

Table 2. Summary of ICT use in NW ICT Adoption Pilot

Business Community	PC use	Email	Website	Purchasing	Online Sales
Chinatown	52.5%	45%	27.5%	20%	0%
Retail	15%	12.5%	20%	10%	0%
Restaurant	37.5%	32.5%	7.5%	10%	0%
Rusholme	92.3%	84.6%	6%	5%	3.5%
Retail	69%	69%	3.5%	3.5%	3.5%
Restaurant	23.3%	15.4%	2.5%	1.5%	0%

due to low-level ICT adoption i.e. PC use, record keeping and limited email. This is very much in keeping with evidence from the United States that although not as detailed in terms of ethnic groups, highlights a significant closing of the ICT adoption gap between 2002 and 2007 amongst non-EMBs, Hispanic and African-Americans (Laudon & Traver, 2008 pp. 340-341). International studies that offer a comparable examination are extremely limited. The focus in the UK has been Pakistani, Bangladeshi and Chinese business where as US studies focus on Hispanic and African Americans (Laudon & Traver, 2008). From other areas of the Globe studies focus on Chinese SMEs in China (Yu et al., 2008) and Indian SMEs in India. Therefore, the context is different again making comparisons very problematic.

Ethnic Minorities account for at least 8% of the UK population (Smallbone et al., 2010) and EMBs represent a significant and increasing slice of the economic business population having a considerable prominence in government policy towards Small and Medium-sized Enterprises (SMEs). However, the question still remains as to why EMBs have not played a role in ICT policies delivered and not adopted ICT to the levels of their non-EMB counterparts. Policy makers, according to Ram & Smallbone (2003), are increasingly turning to small firms to tackle myriad economic challenges, from the creation of a 'knowledge-driven economy' to the regeneration of depressed 'inner-cities'. The role of ICT in SMEs is critical within this discourse, since it is often conflated with viable and competitive businesses already engaging in policy. This suggests that to develop policy and detailed understanding champions or exemplars may prove beneficial.

Reason for Lower ICT Adoption Among EMBs

The ICT adoption rate variation amongst ethnic groups raises a number of questions that may identify explanations that are in inline with SME

findings but also outside the traditional ICT literature view. The studies outlined in the previous section (SBS, 2004; Foley & Ram, 2002; Ram & Smallbone, 1999), have suggested reasons why the ICT adoption disparity between EMBs and non-EMBs may exist but have not examined or explained them. The existing suggestions for the disparity appear to include size, sector, clustering, family support, culture and age of business owner. These possible reasons outlined in the existing studies are examined.

Firstly, Ram & Smallbone (1999) suggest that the lower level of computer use by EMBs could not be explained by their smaller average size. Which taking the general SME ICT literature suggests that firm size is not the predominant issue but may play some role. The research however was not focused on causal effects of ICT adoption and therefore did not consider other factors or a detailed examination of firm size. It is widely accepted that most EMBs are not just small, but very small firms. ICT adoption may be more difficult for micro-businesses given their shortage of resources (Premkumar & Roberts 1999) and lack of capacity to view ICT strategically (Levy et al., 2001). Therefore, other factors may be at play in influencing or inhibiting ICT adoption. Differences between what are by any definition SMEs go to highlight the possible failings of the ICT adoption literature and support the Windrum & de Berranger (2003) criticism. With the SBS (2004) data showing significant differences between cultural groups this heterogenic view of the factors may have even less credence in the case of EMBs.

Secondly, in respect to EMBs the argument may not simply be age as a factor but generation. Allinson et al. (2004) suggest that second generation business owners are more likely to be receptive to ICT than their first generation counterparts; recent surveys of EMBs support this observation (CEEDR, 2001; Ram et al., 2003). The children of immigrant entrepreneurs now tend to shy away from the self-denying life-style demanded by self-employment, with increasing numbers of second generation South Asians opting for higher education and a professional trajectory (Jones & Ram, 2003; Ram et al., 2003). This statement may well indicate a greater awareness by second and third generation business owners of technology, computers and ICT. Where the second generation does opt for business, its members are now increasingly to be found in pioneering areas, higher up the entrepreneurial food chain and far away from the stereotypical corner shop and sweat shop activities that traditionally sustained their parents. (Ram et al., 2003, pp. 5-6). Such changes may also account for the obvious reduction in the ICT gap between the Ram & Smallbone (1999) study and the SBS (2004) study.

Thirdly, the tendency for EMBs to cluster in particular sectors and, as stated by Ram and Jones (2008, p. 64), that EMBs are 'lamentably skewed towards a narrowly constricted range of poorly rewarded and fiercely competitive sectors.' is advanced as an explanatory factor as ICT is not seen to be used. Allinson et al. (2004), drawing on evidence from focus groups conducted with ethnic minority business owners, points to this as a significant reason for low ICT adoption. The suggestion is that with the focus on traditional businesses such as restaurants there is less inclination by EMB business owners to view ICT as an integral factor to the business. The internal drive of the business owner is viewed as critical to adoption and success amongst EMBs (Levy et al., 2005).

Fourthly, culture, according to Straub et al. (2002) can have both positive and negative influences on ICT adoption. Given Yap et al.'s (1992) identification of social networks as a critical influence to ICT adoption, the expectation is that particular specific cultural traits may influence ICT adoption to varying degrees and vary by ethnicity if culture is a factor. An example of such an influence may relate to finance issues in the Chinese business community where access to investment predominantly is via the family.

Therefore, a particular cultural trait to resource and investment is likely to influence ICT adoption investment. Specific ICT research relating to this factor in relation to EMBs is non-existent, although a number of information systems studies have introduced the cultural characteristic (Checchi et al., 2002; Straub et al., 2002). Culture specific beliefs and values, including hierarchical social structures and preference for personal contact (Checchi et al., 2002, p. 7) are viewed to be inhibiting factors where such cultural beliefs are strong. Such a factor may well account for differences between EMB groups.

Finally, Deakins & Freel (2006) point out that the ethnic minority enterprise development literature has tended to point to the accessing of resources (finance and labour), the accessing markets and motivation. The first, accessing of resources, may well be a significant issues in the context of ICT take-up as well as for policy development. If the use of family and co-ethnic labour is important to EMB development then it may well be that this is the very issue that limits ethnic business owners accessing business support or being aware of the business potential of ICT. Deakins and Freel, (2009) suggest that EMBs, when and if, engaging in policy activity have suffered from the mechanisms in place, the delivery approach and the lack of support for specific policy initiatives. The business support issue raises a further question as to whether contextually appropriate support can influence ICT adoption in EMBs. Yap et al. (1992) and CLES (2003) addressed this question in relation to non-EMBs concluding that business support can influence adoption but the examination from a contextual and holistic perspective has been limited. Beckinsale & Ram (2006) examined the EMB context. The research findings relating to the North West ICT Pilot found that less than 2% of EMBs had engaged with traditional business support. Importantly 75% of businesses identified business support as important but were unsure of what support was needed other than finance.

Awareness of initiatives or areas of support appropriate to ICT development and adoption was non-existent, until the pilot, amongst EMBs.

From the foregoing discussion and existing data, it is clear that EMBs are less likely to utilise ICT than their non-EMB counterparts. A variety of reasons have been identified many of which are represented in the general small firm ICT literature as inhibitors to adoption but also those that are more significant to EMBs. The limitation of this current understanding is the lack of data or as Deakins et al. (2003, p. 857) states there is a 'widespread lack of intelligence on the characteristics and needs of EMBs'. This lack of data adds to the consistent difficulty in identifying generalisable causal factors amongst EMBs. As Ram & Smallbone (2002) point out there is an absence of comprehensive, large-scale business databases. The ethnicity variable in current data sets makes it impossible to paint a totally accurate picture. Ram & Jones (2008) suggest that this contributes to the failure of policy development, support and solutions.

THEORETICAL FRAMEWORK

To better form solutions and develop intelligence with a focus on ICT adoption, use and development, two exemplar cases (Beckinsale and Ram,
2006) are examined. The cases are examined and analysed utilising Yap et al. (1992) framework/schema, developed by Windrum and de Berranger (2003) for the examination of SMEs and ICT adoption. To summarise, the framework clusters successful and limiting adoption factors discussed earlier for ICT in SMEs under a set of five factors. The factors are summarised in table 3.

The Yap et al. (1992) schema is potentially useful in understanding the majority of key elements that influence ICT adoption. However, there has been criticism of the frameworks (Windrum & de Berranger, 2003). One of the major criticisms of the use of these factors has been the lack of heterogeneity between SMEs. Especially under the category of SME as highlighted by Windrum and de Berranger (2003) with many studies categorising SMEs based on 'nearly all conceivable dimensions' (Windrum and de Berranger, 2003, p. 186). Another key criticism is the lack of contextually specific categorisations of ICT adoption and a lack of a dynamic understanding of the contextually appropriate enablers and inhibitors Therefore, the dynamic view will be provided by Dyerson and Spinelli's (2010) ICT readiness matrix (see figure 1). This framework may be most agreeable in the context of EMBs given the lower level of ICT adoption and the limited research into the reasons. The value of the framework is the ability to map the paths (summarised in

Table 3. Summary of Yap et al.'s (1992) Five Factors (adapted from Windrum and de Berranger, 2003, p. 184-188)

Organisational Characteristics	Organisational Action	System Characteristics	Internal Expertise	External Expertise
The key characteristics highlighted by Yap et al. (1992) are company size, ICT experience and in-house capabilities, ICT training, financial resources, managerial resources and time.	The focus is the relationship between the CEO (Business Owner) and support for ICT. Palvia and Palvia (1999) suggested that age and experience are critical factors in ICT adoption success that has been suggested in terms of generation for influencing ICT adoption amongst EMBs.	Examines and identifies the relationship between particular ICT systems and 'decisional and functional problems' (Windrum and de Berranger, 2003, p. 186).	Daft (1998) points to the exploitation of internal expertise such as systems analysts to ensure plans/strategy fit with ICT adoption strategy. However, finding a systems analyst inside many SMEs or EMBs is unlikely.	External expertise can be utilised to overcome internal weaknesses. Yap et al.'s (1992) research highlighted successful ICT adoption is related to the quality of external advice provided by consultants and social networks.

Figure 1. The dynamic paths on the readiness matrix (Dyerson and Spinelli, 2010, p.7)

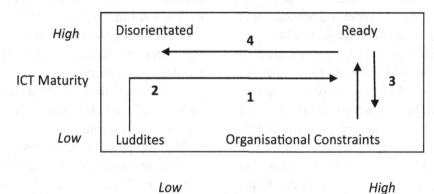

CASE STUDIES

Case 1: SimplyIslam Background

Table 4) that a firm or case can follow as its vision and maturity change. As Dyerson and Spinelli (2010, p. 7) state 'This is important because, as previously discussed, assuming implicitly that small firms follow a linear development path has been criticised.'

The two frameworks also provide a systematic ability, to develop this lack of contextually specific understanding and to go beyond the quantitative approaches of the existing research. The focus on more detailed cases offers a qualitative insight and intelligence that is also remiss in the current EMB–ICT literature. The cases where identified as exemplars for reasons that they had begun to adopt and had utilised and engaged with systems, policies that as Deakins et al. (2003) and Ram and Jones (2008) suggest are unusual in the examination of EMBs.

Rolex Books (Four Corners) began selling Islamic books to the Islamic community. The business began trading in 1962 from its origins in Bradford and was the very first Islamic/Asian bookstore in the UK. Currently, the business imports goods from across the globe. Countries include: Turkey, Dubai, South Africa, India, Malaysia, Hong Kong and it has offices in Pakistan. In November 2001 Rolex Books began to trade online as SimplyIslam. com (http://www.SimplyIslam.com). The online store offers and continues to offer a broad range of Islamic products including books, tapes and CDs, clothing and Muslim toothbrushes. These

Table 4. Summary of Dyerson and Spinelli's (2010, p.7) Dynamic ICT Readiness Pathways

Path 1	Path 2	Path 3	Path 4
A firm starts as a luddite with low ICT maturity and strategic vision. However, as knowledge of the strategic potential of ICT evolves and develops the strategic vision increases. In this case structural changes and investment in ICT occur due to and not despite of strategy.	Unlike Path 1 the firm would invest in ICT and increase its ICT maturity before strategic awareness evolves or develops. The strategic path is 'more emergent' Dyerson and Spinelli (2010, p.7)	The firm has a clear strategic vision in such cases but is unable to keep up with changes or the pace of technological development. Such firms will end up lagging behind their peers. Dyerson and Spinelli (2010) point out that such a path highlights the value in continuous investment and sustaining readiness is a continuous task.	Like Path 3 there is a decrease in value of one of the factors. In this case strategic vision decreases. The reasons suggested are internal or external changes. These might include changes in senior management, new policy o investment, and new competitive environment. Ultimately the firm is unable to manage its ICT equipment.

products, as Amazon has proven, can be sold over the Internet.

SimplyIslam ICT Adoption

Rolex Books stood still whilst SimplyIslam made a significant leap into ICT adoption. Importantly the new business and business model was the idea of the Son (< 30 years of age) of the owner of Rolex Books. The Father was happy with the sate of the business prior to the consideration of ICT adoption. However, he was supportive of his Son's ideas. Investment was made in a single PC, email and website development.

The ICT developments that SimplyIslam undertook focussed on software, at the expense of the necessary hardware. Accounting software, stock control packages and web design packages were the main investments along with third party payment services. "We work with an online Internet payment service provider, which deals with all the payments for the goods, but our customer database, and access to our products is vital to our trading. If we lose data, it would be very damaging to our bottom line." The Son added, "The IT system we had was adequate, but in need of updating, and security was negligible – which was dangerous when you consider we are transacting online," (SimplyIslam.com, Business Owner).

Importantly, SimplyIslam's market went beyond the local community selling globally with its largest market, outside the UK, being the US. Significantly this eCommerce activity was predominantly with customers in the U.S. rather than the UK. Trade was in Islamic goods. Figure 2 plots SimplyIslam's ICT adoption stages.

SimplyIslam ICT Drivers

The Son, a second generation Pakistani, educated to degree level in Computer Science saw an opportunity in growing the business beyond its' local community based market. This drive with the support on his Father was key to ultimately moving Rolex books forward. Marketing undertaken by the Son was also influential in the rapid adoption to eCommerce activity. "Our marketing suggests that in the US there are very few Islamic

Figure 2. A summary of the ICT adoption stages of SimplyIslam (adapted from Martin and Matlay, 2001, p. 400)

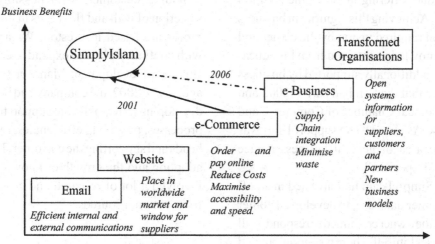

merchants. Therefore the online store provides an opportunity to offer those wishing to purchase Islamic products a channel to do so." (SimplyIslam, Business Owner). A risk aversion strategy was also adopted. The businesses although based on the same premises trades as a separate organisations. As stated by the Son "The potential risk of failure in 2001 and my Father concerned it could have an adverse effect on the original business meant Simplyislam.com began as a separate business entity and ran parallel to Rolex Books."

The Son was very clear about his reasons for the online element of his business, alluding to a generational gap and the view that business must develop and evolve. "Although I am a business owner I now have a family and enjoy other areas in my life. This business is not the be all and end all. The business potentially could run itself and therefore I would have a lot more time away from the business whilst still reaping the rewards." He continued, "My father has worked tirelessly on his business but it runs his life. I do not want that."

SimplyIslam eBusiness Success and Limitations

The owner was very clear about his reasons for the business and its continued development and evolution. This was notably evident in 2007 when the product offering included the addition of downloads. Achieving this significant business transformation required vision by the owner and importantly knowledge obtained from his education. This was additionally supported by business support advice that the Son had sort in 2002 and 2004 from his local Chamber of Commerce and Business Link. As stated "The support I sort was mainly in the area of general business advice rather than ICT specific."

Although SimplyIslam had invested in an off the shelf customer database, to develop customer relationships, the owner continued to respond to all customer queries himself. There was no automated system in place. A very time consuming activity

that as the business continued to grow, the more difficult that personal service response became. Also, suppliers were not fully, e-procurement automated. There was some spot sourcing e-procurement (Beynon-Davies, 2004) but traditional purchasing methods are the norm due to suppliers not being ready. The majority of suppliers to SimplyIslam.com are EMBs themselves.

In 2005 Simply Islam looked to further business advice and specifically ICT support. When they engaged with the NW ICT pilot initiative the hardware was out-of-date, and no longer capable of dealing with the volume of sales that the business was turning over. The IT system, that is one PC, had everything attached to it, the printers, Internet etc. If anything failed, employees had to stop working. The pilot provided a funding opportunity to move hardware development and improvements providing more robust internal back-office ICT developments, wireless stock control and electronic customer relationship. This now supports the eCommerce activities allowing for new offerings online but also the inclusion of Rolex Books.

Case 2: Tile Mart Background

Tile Mart was founded in 1994 as a family run business. In 10 years it grew to employ 32 staff, providing customers with possibly the largest selection of wall and floor tiles in the North West. Stores are based in Preston, Wigan and Bolton with continued plans to expand. According to the Business Development Manager (< 30 years of age), since 2002, the company had been internally developing its use of ICT to support the businesses processes, providing efficiencies, reducing overheads and supporting the customer. The process of adoption and the growth of knowledge in house involved a lot of research and accessing advice from external sources.

Tile Mart ICT Adoption

Initially two PCs and email were installed and a software based systems were put in place to undertake accounts and stock control. The initial investment was aimed at supporting internally communications of the business. The business then developed, utilising third party web developers, a website (www.tilemart.co.uk) to aid the marketing of Tile Mart and with the potential to sell online. In 2004 the company's web site was launched (http://www.tilemart.co.uk). Since 2005 the business had attempted, to varying success, engage in eProcurement activity. Figure 3 plots Tile Mart's ICT adoption stages.

Tile Mart ICT Drivers

Tile Mart's Business Development Manager, with the support of the business owner, had driven the developments. The decision to develop ICT was focused around clear strategic intent including co-ordination, growth and access to new markets

(Levy et al., 2005). This internal support identified early on the need for external help, advice and support. The Business Development Manager made a conscious decision in 2002 to access their local Business Link advisors. They had been contacted via a Business Link outreach advisor, prior to 2002, and followed up this original contact. As stated by the Business Development Manager about the Outreach Worker "…..he was from and is based in the community."

Advice was taken, by the Business Development Manager, on how to move forward with the development of the web site. Based on a lack of in house web site development skills and a need for a professional online site a third party web design company was approached. The company was one of many on the Business Link preferred provider list. Through the outreach advisor, in 2005 the Business Development Manager was made aware of possible e-procurement activity within the region (Lancashire).

Figure 3. A summary of the ICT adoption stages of Tile Mart (adapted from Martin and Matlay, 2001, p. 400)

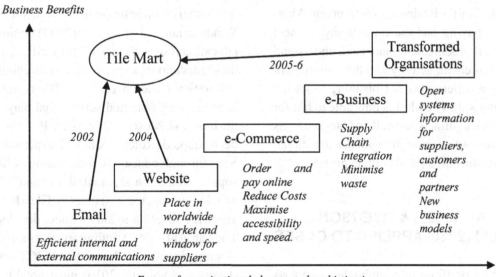

Tile Mart eBusiness Success and Limitations

Prior to Tile Mart's awareness of local council eProcurement opportunities, the Business Development Manager had examined placing bids in local council regeneration projects and had bid and won a contract with Preston North End Football Club. He stated, "The process and submission of the tender was complicated and at times frustrating......... The experience from prior tender failures had helped in understanding the process and delivering improved tender submissions."

The pilot required limited ICT (email and web access only) by the participating firms. Tile Mart had previously developed ICT well in excess of the requirements plus, had a level of skills and knowledge of the potential that ICT could provide the business. The Business Development Manager was trained in accountancy packages and stock control utilising Microsoft Excel. This prior training provided them with the knowledge, tools and a degree of understanding required to make full use of the e-procurement system offered.

Important to engaging with local councils and potentially securing eProcurement contracts was the service and products that fit the council requirements. The potential was identified early on by Tile Mart's Business Development Manager who, having had the opportunity to meet with council procurement managers, understand their eProcurement activity and the requirement of potential sellers, was not planning to let the opportunity slip. Tile Mart is now able to bid for local council contracts and sell and buy products and supplies online through regional and national business-to-business (B2B) online portals.

YAP ET AL. (1992) & DYERSON & SPINELLI (2010) APPLIED TO CASES

The product portfolio of SimplyIslam supports a positive organisational characteristic for ICT adoption and potential value and benefits to engage with a wider market as argued by Windrum and de Berranger's (2003). The understanding and knowledge of the market beyond that of Rolex Books was critical to visioning an opportunity. Further supporting a positive set of organisational characteristics (Yap et al., 1992). The Son also had time unlike his Father who was running Rolex Books day to day (Yap et al., 1992). Tile Mart has moved away from traditional EMB retail markets and provides products and services that are not ethnically specific. Interestingly, Tile Mart had adopted a Business Development Manager within its small firm structure. The role significantly driving business development focused on growth, efficiency and effective activities that offered opportunities and value through ICT adoption (Windrum & de Berranger, 2003).

Simply Islam's owner drove organisational action. As CEO he was singularly making the decisions based on Yap et al. (1992) and Palvia and Palvia (1999) findings. In terms of leveraging ICT adoption the SimplyIslam findings are supported by Levy et al.'s (2005) concept of 'strategic intent' in relation to ICT adoption and eBusiness development. Although, unlike Tile Mart there was no formal strategy their was strategic vision and the objectives of selling Islamic merchandise online supports Yap et al.'s (1992) and Windrum and de Berranger's (2003) findings. The educational experiences of both differ however their educational experience and 'technological culturation' (Checchi et al., 2002) was significant in identifying potential actions that may benefit the business. Most notably where ICT has not yet been adopted (Rolex Books), IT experience (The Son) through education and training is likely to support adoption and potential success (Windrum and de Berranger, 2003) or as in Tile Mart's case argue for adoption to aid business development. The Yap et al. (1992) finding suggests a high level of strategic vision in the context of ICT readiness (Dyerson &Spinelli, 2010) most notably in the context of SimplyIslam.

The system characteristics factor relates to both cases in very differing ways. Positive system characteristics are evident in SimplyIslam. The systems (ICT adoption) being driven by a different way of operating and running a business compared to the Father. After the initial adoption weaknesses in the initial systems and the day-to-day running of the business outgrew the initial investments meant development was required to continue growth. The finding supports, in a limited way, the disorientated element of the Dyerson and Spinelli (2010) framework whilst providing evidence of a rapid development of ICT maturity. Functional weaknesses in existing technology drove the owner to identify solutions (Yap et al., 1992) just as in the case of Tile Mart except it was activities rather than technology. Tile Mart's case the key system characteristics related to a realisation that the business functions in the back office may benefit and add value from the adoption of ICT (Windrum and de Berranger, 2003; Beckinsale et al., 2006).

SimplyIslam's owner appeared to have greater expertise in relation to ICT in comparison to Tile Mart. This internal expertise meant that the owner was able to significantly rely on the knowledge, understanding and any expertise he had in the early adoption stage. Evidently the Father lacked any of these in relation to ICT and its application. Supporting Yap et al. (1992) view that a lack or limited internal expertise whether of the owner or of the employees will limit and likely stifle ICT adoption. The Son is the antithesis of his Father and the fact that expertise is evident leads to ICT adoption although not necessarily success. Tile Mart's Business Development Manager had knowledge of back office software packages. The understanding and knowledge was important in stimulating the identification of limited internal expertise (including his own) and begin to identify other sources of expertise. Comparing the two cases indicates the move from low ICT maturity to high ICT maturity was influenced in terms of

speed and development by an increased level of knowledge.

External expertise relates to a resounding concern amongst EMB scholars (Deakins et al., 2003; Ram & Jones, 2008). The use of external expertise outside of the family structures is argued to potentially limit business development and possibly ICT adoption. In order to develop organisational learning and therefore internal expertise it can be argued that external sources are required. Both cases, to varying degrees, engaged with external business support with some success. The findings show Tile Mart using this method most significantly as part of evolving its strategic vision (Dyerson & Spinelli, 2010). The findings of both cases support the argument that business support can assist the development of the business (Windrum & de Berranger, 2003; Yap et al., 1992) and in this case the ICT infrastructure of the original ICT adoption. Significantly, the role of outreach in the Tile Mart case assisting across a wide spectrum of business issues over time has led to a strong relationship and trust between the two parties.

CRITICAL VIEW OF THE CASES & SOLUTIONS

The two cases highlight the possibilities of developing and breaking out of the traditional and expected EMB activity to the extent that the business is able to grow and offer new opportunities not available prior to the investment in ICT. Both cases support the findings of Jones and Ram (2003) and the 'technological culturation' theory developed by Checchi et al. (2002) that suggests exposure to technology through education and use is likely to act as an enabler to ICT adoption. The introduction to ICT and its potential provides a view of the family business not conceived in the previous generation. A lack of drive and knowledge are two key inhibitors throughout the ICT literature (Poon & Swatman, 1999; Levy et al.,

2005) for SMEs but both EMBs have either an Owner or a Champion (Business Development Manager) driving adoption and ICT development.

Strategically, both cases are examples of very different paths to ICT adoption and relative success. The cases highlight an evolutionary/systematic approach but SimplyIsalm was far more risk taking and direct. Investing in ICT Maturity and going direct to market before realizing fully the ICT strategic vision. Tile Mart took a more strategic and progressive strategy and invested based on developing the ICT strategic vision first. Therefore, in terms of Dyerson and Spinelli's (2010) classification of ICT readiness Tile Mart was Path 1 and SimplyIslam Path 2 (see Figure 4). The later case reduced the risks to Rolex Books seeing success early with online growth. However, the limited strategic planning (Levy et al., 2005) saw technological problems and significant impact on investment for the owner 4 years on from initial investment. Tile Mart's evolutionary approach has meant planned investment within budget and developments based on actual business benefits.

The tendency for EMBs to utilise business support less than the wider SME population is documented (Deakins et al., 2003). Deakins et al. (2003) have argued the case of EMBs to engage with and be engaged by appropriate business support. Evidence, from the Tile Mart case suggests there is an emphasis to developing relationships with ethnic minorities that may have been under-represented among business support clients in the past. From an ICT adoption perspective, Yap et al. (1992) first raised the significant issues of appropriate business support or networks. Both cases, although using business support for very different requirements have gained through those relationships. It must be said that SimplyIslam's owner was a rare EMB case in the North West region for seeking business support. Where as in Tile Mart's case business support took a pro-active approach to engagement across SMEs and EMBs. The reasons for and use of business support seen by both entrepreneurs, although more so in Tile Mart's case, as important to developing their ICT strategic vision. Outreach was common in their particular region and the support agencies in the area undertook significant steps to raise awareness among a wide variety of business including EMBs. Business support in the case of Tile Mart has not only supported ICT awareness raising and advice but acted as an intermediary/broker between local councils and the EMB to facilitate a relationship.

The cases and the findings of the review of ICT adoption amongst EMBs highlights a number of potential opportunities, options and recommen-

Figure 4. The dynamic paths SimplyIslam and Tile Mart took

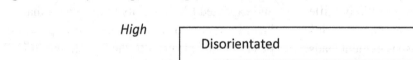
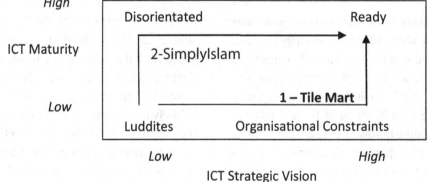

dations to consider for EMB owners. Business context will be important in the final decision-making process but understanding and awareness of a number of avenues and options could enable a serious consideration for adopting ICT.

1. With family connections more often than not being the focus for help and advice amongst EMBs the use of increasingly IT and ICT literate children to, at the minimum, build awareness of ICT and possible applications is likely to foster a raising of internal expertise within a business.

2. The strategic perspective seen in case 1 follows a low risk strategy (Chaffey, 2007). Rather than implementing ICT formally in Rolex Books the approach is to have a new business running in parallel therefore reducing the costs and risks to the existing offline brand and importantly allowing a trial or pilot of the business model in an online context. A note in doing this the online context could develop beyond the existing brand limiting the traditional businesses opportunities. This has not been seen in the cases outlined.

3. The adoption of ICT is not simply about having a web site and selling products on line. EMB owners should be aware that ICT could be utilised to improve the day-to-day performance of business activities. Most notably in cost savings, and efficiencies in areas where paper based systems add time to a process. By identifying those activities decisions can be made on areas of investment (e.g. accounts, stock & inventory control, invoicing and more developed payment systems).

4. Solutions can be obtained through a range of private third party support and solution providers. Case 1 uses Google's own check out system for payments. Reducing the need for complex, costly systems and infrastructure. Be aware to take advice from the experience of other business owners. Where business

owner experience is lacking then business support is available. EMB owners must be aware of where their local Chamber of Commerce or Business Link is. A simple phone call (number available in Yellow Pages under business centres, business enterprise agencies) can identify avenues of assistance not just in terms of ICT but other business areas including marketing, finance and law. There are also business support third parties such as Enterprise4all (www.enterprise4all. co.uk) that take a greater EMB focus but are open to all.

5. There is also a need for business support agencies to ensure that EMB owners are aware that they exist. Learning from the Tile Mart case, findings from CLES (2003) and Beckinsale & Ram (2006) offers a precedence supporting personal contact through Outreach that builds relationships between EMBs and traditional business support and can stimulate ICT adoption. The relationship developed between the cases and business support highlights the importance of trust. Windrum and de Berranger (2003, p. 188) state that 'Trusted external sources may to some extent offset constraints of SMEs arising from limited time, financial and other resources'. In relation to the external support provided trust was, on a number of occasions, raised as important for third party engagement similar to the findings of Lockett and Brown (2006).

6. From applying the Dyerson and Spinelli (2010) ICT readiness matrix to the examination of the EMBs the findings and evidence suggests the importance of business support to the development of a firms and entrepreneurs ICT strategic vision.

7. The application of the stages model suggests that engagement in business support should not end after ICT adoption. Each business context will differ but the cases highlight that, as time progresses, the original adoption may

no longer deliver in relation to its original objectives and new opportunities may well be considered like ecommerce, eMarketing and eProcurement activity. If the case, as the two cases here highlight, business support should be considered seriously as an avenue for ICT and eBusiness development.

CONCLUSION

The chapter has presented an overview and review of the current ICT literature. The review has provided an insight into the well-developed causal mechanisms for why SMEs adopt ICT as well as the factors that inhibit adoption. The review then indicates the limited insight of EMBs within the ICT literature but importantly provides unquestionable evidence that EMBs are adopting ICT to a lesser extent than their non-EMBs counterparts. The focus then turned to EMBs and clear indicators as to why the ICT adoption gap currently continues to exist albeit slowly reducing. Evident, is the dearth of qualitative based data and literature. The data have not offered examples or exemplars that are representative of the potential of ICT adoption (Beckinsale & Ram, 2006). For this reason there is a lack of contextually appropriate detailed data and understanding (Deakins et al., 2003).

The examined cases indicate that EMBs can successfully adopt ICT and move beyond the PC use and email options. Importantly, in understanding factors that are perceived as inhibitors there is evidence they can potentially be enablers. The range of ICT drivers and inhibitors are relevant in the EMB sector. Although not an exhaustive list, the critical drivers in ICT adoption are: the owner; the strategic intent; education; family support; and business support. The experiences reported on here are not unique but, as the data suggests, they are certainly not the norm amongst EMBs. The often-noted reluctance of EMBs to use formal sources of business support (Ram & Smallbone, 2003) was not evident in the two cases. It appears that sufficient time and resources for contextually appropriate awareness-raising activities had been built into local business support activities and programmes. Across the two cases business support was not seen as a choice between family support or a third party support option. They appear to have complemented each other assisting the development of their ICT strategic vision (Dyerson and Spinelli, 2010) and the success of their readiness, adoption, understanding, knowledge and application of ICT. From a policy perspective generation and education are critical to the perceived view of ICT adoption allowing, as EMB owner's Sons and Daughters enter the employment market, to see ICT from a very different perspective. The generation factor is where ICT and eBusiness policy and awareness raising needs to focus, with significant improvements, nationally to business support awareness raising and delivery within EMB sectors.

REFERENCES

Allinson, G., Braidford, P., Grewer, N., Houston, M., Orange, R., Leigh Sear, R., & Stone, I. (2004) *Ethnic minority businesses and ICT, focus group research*. Durham Business School for SBS. Retrieved May 2, 2008, from http://www.sbs.gov.uk/SBS_Gov_files/researchandstats/EMB_and_ICT.pdf

Beckinsale, M. J. J., & Levy, M. (2002). *Hi-tech entrepreneurs and the Internet*. Paper presented at the 10th Annual International Conference High Technology Small Firms Conference, Twente University, 10-11 June 2002, Netherlands.

Beckinsale, M. J. J., Levy, M., & Powell, P. (2006). Exploring Internet adoption drivers in SMEs. *Electronic Markets – International Journal (Toronto, Ont.)*, *16*(4), 361–370.

Beckinsale, M. J. J., & Ram, M. (2006). Delivering ICT to ethnic minority businesses: An action research approach. *Environment and Planning. C, Government & Policy, 24*(6), 847–867. doi:10.1068/c0559

Beckinsale, M. J. J., & Ram, M. (2008). *SME/ EMB action research: A framework for ICT policy driven initiatives ®*. Paper presented at the 31st Institute for Small Business and Entrepreneurship, Nov 5th-Nov 7th, Belfast, Ireland.

Beynon-Davies, P. (2004). *E-business*. New York, NY: Palgrave Macmillan. Blackburn, R., & McClure, R. (1998). *The use of Information Communication Technologies (ICTs) in small business service firms*. Small Business Research Centre, Kingston Business School.

CEEDR. (2001). *Researching business support needs of ethnic minority owned businesses in Coventry and Warwickshire*. Coventry and Warwickshire Chamber of Commerce, Training and Enterprise, Centre for Enterprise and Economic Development Research, Middlesex University.

Chaffey, D. (2007). *E-business and e-commerce management* (3rd ed.). London, UK: Pearson Education.

Checchi, R. M., Sevcik, G. R., Loch, K. D., & Straub, D. D. (2002). An instrumentation process for measuring ICT policies and culture. *Proceedings of International Conference on Information Technology, Communications and Development* (pp. 1-17). Kathmandu, Nepal.

CLES (Centre for Local Economic Strategies) Consulting. (2003). *EMBs and ICT services*. Retrieved June 14, 2005, from http://cles.live. poptech.coop/C2B/document_tree/ ViewACategory.asp?CategoryID=1

Coghlan, D., & Brannick, T. (2004). *Doing action research in your own organization* (2nd ed.). London, UK: Sage Publications.

CREME. (2009). *The Minority Ethnic Enterprise Centre of Expertise*. Retrieved February 25, 2009, from http://www.dmu.ac.uk/faculties/business_and_law/business/research/creme/meecoe/index.jsp

Deakins, D. a&nd Freel, M. (2009). Entrepreneurship and small firms, 5th edition. Berkshire, UK: McGraw-Hill Education.

Deakins, D., & Freel, M. (2006). *Entrepreneurship and small firms* (4th ed.). Berkshire, UK: McGraw-Hill Education.

Deakins, D., Ram, M., & Smallbone, D. (2003). Addressing the business support needs of ethnic minority firms in the United Kingdom. *Environment and Planning. C, Government & Policy, 21*(6), 843–859. doi:10.1068/c0305

DTI. (2004). *International bench marking survey for ICT use*. UK Department of Trade and Industry. Retrieved July 28, 2006, from http://www2.bah.com/dti2004/main/mr_86.htm

Dyerson, R., & Harindranath, G. (2007). ICT adoption & use by SMEs in the UK: A survey of South East. *Management of Engineering and Technology, 5*(9), 1756–1770.

Dyerson, R., & Spinelli, R. (2010). The evaluation and impact of ICT readiness in SMEs: Constructing a new framework. Paper presented at the 33rd Institute of Small Business and Enterprise Conference, 3rd-4th November, 2010, London.

Eden, C., & Huxham, C. (1996). Action research for the study of organisations. In Clegg, S., Hardy, C., & Nord, W. (Eds.), *Handbook of organisation studies* (pp. 526–542). London, UK: Sage.

ESRC. (2008). Society today – Business engagement scheme for ESRC centres. Retrieved June 25, 2008, from http://www.esrcsocietytoday.ac.uk/ESRCInfoCentre/opportunities/current_funding_opportunities/business_engagement.aspx?ComponentId=18191&SourcePageId=15428

European Commission. (2007). *ICT- Information and Communication Technologies – Work programme 2007-8*. Cordis. Retrieved May 3, 2008, from ftp://ftp.cordis.europa.eu/pub/fp7/ict/docs/ict-wp-2007-08_en.pdf

Foley, P., & Ram, M. (2002). *The use of online technology by ethnic minority businesses: A comparative study of the West Midlands and UK*. De Montfort University monograph. Retrieved February 3, 2008, from http://www.sbs.gov.uk/contents/research/EMB-IT.pdf

Foley, P., Watts, H. D., & Wilson, B. (1993). New technology, skills shortages and training strategies. In Swann, P. (Ed.), *New technology and the firm* (pp. 279–289). London, UK: Routledge.

Galloway, L. (2006). Information and Communications Technologies and e-business. In Deakins, D., & Freel, M. (Eds.), *Entrepreneurship and small firms* (4th ed., pp. 139–156). Berkshire, UK: McGraw-Hill.

Jones, T., & Ram, M. (2003). South Asian businesses in retreat? The case of the United Kingdom. *Journal of Ethnic and Migration Studies, 29*(3), 485–500. doi:10.1080/13691830305611

Kai-Uwe Brock, J. (2000). Information and technology in the small firm. In Carter, S., & Jones-Evans, D. (Eds.), *Enterprise and the small business* (pp. 384–408). Prentice Hall, Pearson Education.

Laudon, K. C., & Traver, C. G. (2008). *E-commerce business, technology, society* (4th ed.). London, UK: Pearson.

Levy, M., & Beckinsale, M. J. J. (2004). *SMEs and Internet adoption strategy: Who do SMEs listen to?* Paper presented at the 12th European Conference on Information Systems, June 14-16, 2004, Turku, Finland.

Levy, M., & Powell, P. (2003). Exploring SME Internet adoption: Towards a contingent model. *Electronic Markets, 13*(2), 173–181. doi:10.1080/1019678032000067163

Levy, M., Powell, P., & Worrall, L. (2005). Strategic intent and e-business in SMEs enablers and inhibitors. *Information Resources Management Journal, 18*(4), 1–20. doi:10.4018/irmj.2005100101

Levy, M., Powell, P., & Yetton, P. (2002). SMEs: The dynamics of IS development, small business economics.

Lunati, M. (2000). *SMEs and electronic commerce: An overview*. OECD, Directorate for Science, Presented to the Technology and Industry Committee, DST/IND/PME.

Martin, L. M., & Matlay, H. (2001). "Blanket" approaches to promoting ICT in small firms: Some lessons from the DTI ladder adoption model in the UK. *Internet Research, 11*(5), 399–410. doi:10.1108/EUM0000000006118

Mehrtens, J., Cragg, P., & Mills, A. (2001). A model of Internet adoption by SMEs. *Information & Management, 39*, 165–176. doi:10.1016/S0378-7206(01)00086-6

Migration Policy Group. (2002). *Supplier diversity: The case of immigrant and ethnic minority enterprise*. Background paper prepared for the Transatlantic Round Table, Brussels, 15 January 2002.

Mingers, J. (2002). Realizing Information Systems: Critical realism as an underpinning philosophy for Information Systems. *Proceedings from the International Conference on Information Systems*, (pp. 295-303). Association of Information Systems, Barcelona.

Papazafeiropoulou, A., Pouloudi, A., & Doukidis, G. (2002). A framework for best practices in electronic commerce awareness creation. *Business Process Management Journal, 8*(3), 233–245. doi:10.1108/14637150210428943

Poon, S. (2000). Business environment and Internet commerce benefit- Small business perspective. *European Journal of Information Systems, 9*(2), 72–81.

Poon, S., & Swatman, P. (1999). An exploratory study of small business Internet commerce issues. *Information & Management, 35,* 9–18. doi:10.1016/S0378-7206(98)00079-2

Premkumar, G., & Roberts, M. (1999). Adoption of new Information Technologies in rural small businesses. *Omega International Journal of Management Science, 27*(4), 467–484. doi:10.1016/S0305-0483(98)00071-1

Ram, M., Gilman, M., Arrowsmith, J., & Edwards, P. (2003). Once more into the sunset? Asian clothing firms after the national minimum wage. *Environment and Planning. C, Government & Policy, 21,* 71–88. doi:10.1068/c0136

Ram, M., & Jones, T. (2008). Ethnic minority business: An overview. Retrieved February 26, 2009, from http://www.oi.acidi.gov.pt/docs/Revista_3_EN/Migr3_Sec1_Art3_EN.pdf

Ram, M., & Smallbone, D. (1999). *Ethnic minority enterprises in Birmingham.* Paper presented to the 2nd Ethnic Minority Enterprise Seminar, London, November 1999.

Ram, M., & Smallbone, D. (2002). Ethnic minority business support in the era of the small business service. *Environment and Planning. C, Government & Policy, 20*(2), 235–249. doi:10.1068/c0050

Ram, M., & Smallbone, D. (2003). Policies to support ethnic minority enterprise: The English experience. *Entrepreneurship and Regional Development, 15*(2), 151–166. doi:10.1080/0898562032000075177

Sanderson, I. (2002). Evaluation, policy learning and evidence-based policy making. *Public Administration, 80*(1), 1–22. doi:10.1111/1467-9299.00292

SBS (Small Business Service). (2004). *SBS booster survey.* Retrieved July 7, 2005, from http://www.sbs.gov.uk/sbsgov/action/layer?r.l2=7000000243&r.l1=7000000229&r.s=tl&topicId=7000011759

Smallbone, D., Lyon, F., & Li, X. (2006). Trust, co-operation and networking in an immigrant business community: The case of Chinese-owned businesses in the UK. In Hohmann, H. H., & Welter, F. (Eds.), *Trust and entrepreneurship: A West-East perspective.* Cheltenham, UK/ Brookfield, USA: Edward Elgar.

Southern, A., & Tilley, F. (2000). Small firms and information and communication technologies (ICTs): Toward a typology of ICT usage. *New Technology, Work and Employment, 15*(2), 138–154. doi:10.1111/1468-005X.00070

Straub, D. W., Loch, K. D., Evaristo, R., Karahanna, E., & Strite, M. (2002). Toward a theory-based measurement of culture. *Journal of Global Information Management, 10*(January), 13–23. doi:10.4018/jgim.2002010102

Thong, J. Y. L., & Yap, C. S. (1995). CEO characteristics, organisational characteristics and Information Technology adoption in small businesses. *International Journal of Management Science, 23*(4), 429–442.

Van Akkeren, J. K., & Cavaya, A. L. M. (2000). Factors affecting entry-level Internet technology adoption by small firms in Australia – Evidence from three cases. *Journal of Systems and Information Technology*, 3(2), 33–47. doi:10.1108/13287269980000747

Windrum, P., & de Berranger, P. (2003). The adoption of e-business technology by SMEs. In Jones, O., & Tilley, F. (Eds.), *Competitive advantage in SMEs: Organising for innovation and change* (pp. 177–201). England: Wiley.

Yap, C. S., Soh, C. P. P., & Raman, K. S. (1992). Information Systems success factors in small businesses. *Omega International Journal of Management Science*, 20(5), 597–609. doi:10.1016/0305-0483(92)90005-R

Yu, L., Suojapelto, K., Hallikas, J., & Tang, O. (2008). Chinese ICT industry from supply chain perspective - A case study of the major Chinese ICT players. *International Journal of Production Economics*, 115(2), 374. doi:10.1016/j.ijpe.2008.03.011

ADDITIONAL READING

Costello, F. J. (2000). An exemplar model of classification in simple and combined categories in Gleitman, L. R. & Joshi, A. K. (eds) Proceedings of the Twenty-Second Annual Conference of the Cognitive Science society (pp. 95-100) Mahwah, N. J.: Erlbaum

Cragg, P., & King, M. (1993). Small Firm Computing: Motivators and Inhibitors. *Management Information Systems Quarterly*, 17(1), 47–60. doi:10.2307/249509

Fallon, M., & Moran, P. (2000). Information Communication technology (ICT) and manufacturing SMEs, paper presented at The 2000 Small Business and Enterprise Development Conference, pp. 100-109, Manchester University, Manchester

Fuller, T., & Southern, A. (1999). Small Firms and Information and Communication Technologies: Policy issues and some words of caution. *Environment and Planning. C, Government & Policy*, 17, 287–302. doi:10.1068/c170287

Jones, T., & Ram, M. (2007). Re-embedding the Ethnic Business Agenda. *Work, Employment and Society*, 21(3), 439–457. doi:10.1177/0950017007080007

Keindl, B. (2000). Competitive Dynamics and New Business Models for SMEs in the Virtual Marketplace. *Journal of Developmental Entrepreneurship*, 5(1), 73–85.

Levy, M., Powell, P., & Yetton, P. (2001, September). SMEs: Aligning IS and the Strategic Context. *Journal of Information Technology*, 16, 133–144. doi:10.1080/02683960110063672

Oc, T., & Tiesdell, S. (1999). Supporting ethnic minority business: a review of business support for ethnic minorities in city challenge areas. *Urban Studies (Edinburgh, Scotland)*, 36(10), 1723–1746. doi:10.1080/0042098992791

OGC. (2002) Office of Government Commerce, *Review of Major Government IT Projects*, Retrieved July 11, 2005, from http://www.ogc.gov.uk/embedded_object.asp?docid=2634

Papazafeiropoulou, A., Pouloudi, A., & Doukidis, G. (2002). A framework for best practices in electronic commerce awareness creation. *Business Process Management Journal*, 8(3), 233–245. doi:10.1108/14637150210428943

Ram, M., Edwards, P., & Jones, T. (2007). Staying underground: informal work, small firms and employment regulations in the United Kingdom. *Work and Occupations*, 34, 318–344. doi:10.1177/0730888407303223

Ram, M., & Jones, T. (1998). *Ethnic minorities in business*. Small Business Research Trust.

Ram, M., Smallbone, D. and Deakins, D. (2002). *The Finance and Business Support Needs of Ethnic Minority Firms in Britain*, British Bankers Association Research Report

Saunders, M., Lewis, P., & Thornhill, A. (2007). *Research Methods for Business Students* (4th ed.). London: Prentice Hall.

Sergeant, J. (2000). Presentation by the e-envoy of UK Online, British Academy of Management Conference, Aston University Business School, Birmingham cited in Martin, L. M. and Matlay, H. (2001). "Blanket" approaches to promoting ICT in small firms: Some lessons from the DTI ladder adoption model in the UK. *Internet Research, 11*(5), 399–410.

Smallbone, D., Kitching, J., & Athayde, R. (2010). Ethnic diversity, entrepreneurship and competitiveness in a global city. *International Small Business Journal, 28*, 174–190. doi:10.1177/0266242609355856

Smallbone, D., Lyon, F., & Li, X. (2006). Trust, Co-operation and Networking in an Immigrant Business Community: the Case of Chinese-Owned Businesses in the UK. In *Small Business and Enterprise Research Group, 2001 Barriers and Drivers for Ethnic Minority Businesses in the East Midlands, Report for East Midlands Observatory, November 2001*. Leicester: De Montfort University, Leicester Business School.

Steeples, C. (2004). *Using Action-Oriented or participatory Research Methods for Research on Networked Learning*, in Banks, S. Goodyear, P., Hodgson, V., Jones, C., Lally, V., McConnel, D., and Steeples, C. (eds). Proceedings of the Fourth International Conference on networked learning 2004: a research based conference on e-learning in higher education and lifelong learning. (pp. 113-118) Lancaster University and University of Sheffield

Storey, D. (1994). *Understanding the Small Business Sector*. London: Routledge.

Willcocks, L., Sauer, C., & Associates. (2000). *Moving to E-Business: The Ultimate Practical Guide to Effective E-Business*, Published: Century Press, ISBN 0712669833

Zuber-Skerritt, O. (1996). Emancipatory action research for organisational change and management development. In Zuber-Skerritt, O. (Ed.), *New Directions in Action Research* (pp. 83–105). London: Falmer.

Chapter 10
Model for Understanding Consumer Adoption of Online Technologies

Donald L. Amoroso
Kennesaw State University, USA

Scott Hunsinger
Appalachian State University, USA

ABSTRACT

This research reviews studies using the Technology Acceptance Model (TAM) to create a modified model and instrument to study the acceptance of Internet technology by consumers. We developed a modified TAM for the acceptance of Internet-based technologies by consumers. We retained the original constructs from the TAM and included additional constructs from previous literature including gender, experience, complexity, and voluntariness. We developed a survey instrument using existing scales from prior TAM instruments and modified them where appropriate. The instrument yielded respectable reliability and construct validity. The findings suggest that the modified TAM is a good predictor of consumer behavior in using the Internet. We found that attitude toward using the Internet acts as a strong predictor of behavioral intention to use, and actual usage of Internet technologies. Future researchers can use the resultant instrument to test how consumers adopt and accept Internet-based applications.

INTRODUCTION

This research develops measures for the acceptance of Internet technologies by consumers. Organizations spend millions of dollars annually on the development and enhancement of their Web sites to attract new customers and retain current customers (Amoroso, 2002). By investing in Web-based technologies, firms become more sophisticated by building Web sites with advanced capabilities and greater levels of personalization

DOI: 10.4018/978-1-60960-597-1.ch010

and functionality available to their customers (Amoroso & Gardner, 2003). But are consumers accepting these technologies as evidenced by their usage? This paper describes the development and testing of an instrument designed to measure the acceptance of Internet technologies by consumers. We designed this instrument to serve as a tool for the study of the acceptance of Internet-based applications by individuals and an indication of the Internet technology's diffusion from the organization to the consumer.

Researchers made significant progress over the last decade in explaining and predicting user acceptance of information technologies. In particular, substantial theoretical and empirical support accumulated for the Technology Acceptance Model (TAM) (Davis, Bagozzi, & Warshaw, 1989). Numerous studies found that the TAM consistently explains a substantial proportion of variance in usage intentions and behavior, among a variety of technologies. TAM performs well against alternative models such as the Theory of Reasoned Action (TRA) and the Theory of Planned Behavior (TPB) (Mathieson, 1991; Sun, 2003). TAM theorizes that two beliefs determine an individual's behavioral intention to use a technology: perceived usefulness and perceived ease of use. TAM serves as a well-established and robust model for predicting user acceptance. TAM functions as one of the most influential research models in studies of determinants of information systems/ information technology acceptance (Chau & Hu, 2001).

While increasing numbers of empirical studies on Internet technologies have appeared recently, few studies on determinants of Internet usage and acceptance appeared. Only a small number of these studies focused on Internet technology (Agarwal & Karahanna, 2000; Gefen, Karahanna, & Straub, 2003; Koufaris, 2002; Van der Heijden, 2000, 2003). Much of the research appeared in the marketing area, studying the Internet from the consumer side from the studies using the technology acceptance model. Most studies examined very

specific factors, rather than a more comprehensive acceptance model. The current work examines the following objectives:

1. **To review the existing user acceptance models:** This research reviews the current literature on technology acceptance by users and assesses the current state of knowledge with respect to understanding individual acceptance with new information technologies. While some studies look at similarities and differences across acceptance models, this review examines the technologies from which the studies examine findings. We selected studies that contain analyses relevant to Internet technology and constructs appropriate for our technology. We present a review of acceptance literature in the second section.

2. **To develop a model and metrics for Internet-based technologies:** Based upon the theory developed and empirically tested, we create a model that shows the impacts of the TAM constructs and external variables on consumer-based adoption patterns. We developed hypotheses from the theoretical foundation and empirical results of the studies that impact the consumer acceptance of Internet technologies. We subsequently developed and pre-tested an instrument by using and modifying the Technology Acceptance Model. We tested the instrument scales for reliability and validity and used factor analysis as an assessment of construct validity. We present the development of the model, metrics, instrument, and validation in the third and fourth sections.

3. **To empirically validate the TAM for Internet-based technologies:** An empirical test of the TAM for Internet-based technologies provides preliminary support for the hypotheses of the constructs measuring acceptance by users. Correlational analysis determined the significance of independent

relationships of items. Multiple regression analysis helped to ascertain the cumulative effects of items on constructs. We present the empirical validation of the research model in the Analysis section.

THEORETICAL BACKGROUND

In this section, we focus on a key set of studies centered on online consumer behavior and technology acceptance constructs. While we realize that a wider set of studies reference technology assimilation and technology acceptance, we focus on those that advance or modify the Technology Acceptance Model for specific technologies. We report the results of those studies as well as show the models. Based upon this theory, we propose and test a model of customer acceptance of Internet technologies.

Considerable research currently examines consumer behavior on the Web and use of Internet-based technologies. Given the strong growth in e-commerce and Web-based transactions in the past decade, online consumers are becoming more commonplace. Many studies have examined online consumers' behavior. These studies have determined that a variety of factors often influence consumers' intentions to purchase online. In preparing our model, we reviewed numerous articles concerning online consumer behavior to better understand which factors have shown significance in previous work.

In their research, Kim, Chan, and Gupta (2007) empirically analyzed the adoption of mobile Internet in terms of value to the consumer, suggesting that intention to adopt mobile Internet is directly related to the consumers' perception of the value of mobile Internet. The purpose of this study was to better analyze perceptions of mobile Internet. The findings of the study conducted confirmed that consumers' perception of the value of mobile Internet is a principal determinant of adoption in-

tention, and the other beliefs are mediated through perceived value. Findings concluded that value perception is a key determinant role in mobile Internet adoption. The results determined that a mobile Internet service that combines customer's benefit and sacrifice beliefs would ultimately benefit mobile Internet adoption. It is proposed that acceptance of mobile Internet service is the first step toward understanding customer perception and adoption of mobile-commerce.

Lin and Wang (2006) examined the factors that contributed to customer loyalty in mobile commerce. This study evaluated the factors that determine or affect repeat purchases within the mobile commerce industry. Variables, such as perceived value and trust, were found to be directly related to customer satisfaction and customer loyalty; customer satisfaction was also suggested to positively affect customer loyalty; and habit was proposed to determine customer loyalty. Results found that customer loyalty was directly affected by perceived value, trust, habit, and customer satisfaction. Customer loyalty was evaluated to be a strong determining factor in acceptance of mobile commerce.

Pavlou, Lie, and Dimoka (2007), attempted to understand what drives consumers to participate in mobile commerce by examining three interrelated behaviors including getting information, giving information, and purchasing with mobile devices. Two independent studies of approximately 700 mobile users in the U. S. and the Republic of China were used to corroborate the integrative model of m-commerce adoption. Getting information associates the transfer of information between the seller and mobile user. Giving information associates transmit of information from consumers to sellers. Mobile purchasing involves a satisfying exchange relationship between products/ services offered and the mobile device that uses WAP (Wireless Application Protocol).

Kuo, Wu, and Deng (2009) proposed the relationships that existed between service quality, perceived value, customer satisfaction, and post-purchase intention in mobile services. The purpose of their research was to understand the effect that such factors as service quality and perceived value had on post-purchase intention in online shopping in Taiwan. They found that service quality positively influences both perceived value and customer satisfaction. Perceived value positively influenced both customer satisfaction and post-purchase intention. It was found that customer satisfaction positively influenced post-purchase intention. Service quality had an indirect positive influence on post-purchase intention through customer satisfaction or perceived value. The findings concluded that service quality directly impacted customer satisfaction and perceived value. Perceived value was also determined to positively impact customer satisfaction. Finally, both perceived value and customer satisfaction determined post-purchase intention. The authors did not find that service quality had any direct influence on post-purchase intention.

For the purposes of this research, the online consumer can also be considered a user of technology. Assimilation is defined as the extent to which the use of a technology diffuses across organizational processes of society and becomes an integral part of the tasks associated with those processes (Cooper & Zmud, 1990; Gefen & Straub, 1997). Many researchers have focused on the importance of the causality between the adoption of an information technology and its impacts on business performance. The Technology Acceptance Model (TAM) is an adaptation of TRA specifically tailored for modeling user acceptance of information systems (Davis et al., 1989). The model provides a basis for tracing the impact of external factors on internal beliefs, attitudes, and intentions.

The two main constructs of TAM are perceived usefulness and perceived ease of use. Perceived usefulness is defined as the extent to which a person believes that using a technology will enhance her/his productivity and perceived ease of use is the extent to which a person believes that using a technology will be free of effort. TAM posits that behavioral intention determines actual systems use and behavioral intention is determined by both attitude and perceived usefulness. Perceived usefulness and perceived ease of use have both been found to have an effect on behavioral intention. Perceived ease of use also affects perceived usefulness. Behavioral intentions are influenced indirectly by external variables through perceived usefulness and perceived ease of use (Davis et al., 1989). The relative strength of the usefulness-usage relationship versus the ease of use-usage relationship is a significant finding and particularly important for designers. Users need to perceive the system as being useful or they will not attempt to use it regardless of how easy or difficult it is to use. Ease of use is less important because difficulty in using a system can be overcome if the user thinks that the system will be useful to them. Overall the model explained 47% of the overall model's variance. Davis modified his original TAM model (corroborating the finding of Mathieson (1991) where he found a stronger support of perceived ease of use construct with perceived usefulness rather than with intention to use.

Several earlier studies examined online payments, but not mobile payment systems.

He and Mykytyn (2007) examined the factors for consumer adoption of online payment systems. Findings in this study evaluated consumers' intent to adopt the concept of online payments. They found that a majority of participants favored the concept of online payments with the primary consideration of risk being associated with making online payments. The primary motive for adopting such a system would be to meet payment deadlines. The customers' willingness to adopt online payments methods included three primary factors: the vendor's transaction network is secure; the online payment methods are easy to learn; and the vendor's online payment system offers customers the option feature of recurring automatic deductions, as it is viewed as the most time- and cost-effective way to avoid past-due late penalties.

Rigopoulos and Askounis (2007) developed a model to examine users' attitude towards adopting online payments and proposed a revised version of the TAM for evaluating consumers' adoption of proposed technology. They found perceived usefulness, perceived ease of use, and intention to use were all positively associated with consumers' actual usage of online payments.

Luo, Li, Zhang, and Shim (2010) examined multi-dimensional trust and risk perceptions in the adoption stage of the wireless Internet platform. The suggested research model was established to suggest factors such as trust, risk, self-efficacy, and performance expectancy to essentially drive the consumer acceptance of mobile banking services. Variables such as performance expectancy, trust belief, perceived risk, and structural assurance determined behavioral intention of accepting emerging technologies. It was also suggested in the research model that self-efficacy influences both perceived risk and structural assurance and disposition to trust impacted structural assurance. Furthermore, the study proposes that perceived risk is directly influenced by eight variables, all of which are strong determinants of technology acceptance. Risk was found to have eight components, including performance risk, financial risk, time risk, psychological risk, social risk, physical risk, and privacy risk.

Deng, Lu, and Chen (2010), used the TAM model to study trust to assess what influences the adoption of mobile banking in China. The model had three new constructs including perceived credibility, SMS usage, and perceived service cost. Perceived credibility was one of the few extensions to the TAM model that was presumed to reflect the specific influences of technological and usage context factors that impact user acceptance. In China, mobile banking is primarily managed via SMS usage that includes specific coded numbers to assist in checking bank accounts and transfers of money; thus, SMS usage was expected to have a significant effect on the dependent variables. Perceived cost (service cost) was determined to have an immense effect on whether or not consumers would adopt mobile banking. Neither perceived ease of use, perceived credibility, nor perceived cost were found to have significant effects on user's behavioral attitude toward mobile banking.

RESEARCH MODEL

The Technology Acceptance Model has tested the degree of acceptance of a wide variety of technologies. It could be argued that TAM provides a better overall fit with certain technologies than with others. Overall, the relationships may differ between constructs in TAM based upon the technology being studied. Gefen et al. (2003) argue that a Web site is, in essence, an information technology and therefore TAM can explain online purchase intentions. Also shown in previous research (Gefen et al., 2003; Koufaris, 2002), the paths predicted by TAM also apply to e-commerce. The more useful and easy to use a Web site in enabling consumers to accomplish their tasks, the more it will be used. Based upon the empirical research of TAM constructs, a model is proposed from which to study the impacts of these constructs on the consumer-based adoption patterns. The research model (see Figure 1) consists of the original TAM with the external variables broken down into four items: (1) perceived complexity, (2) experience, (3) gender, and (4) voluntariness. We hypothesize that each of the four items will have a significant effect on Internet usage. Prior studies (Davis, 1986; Gefen & Straub, 1997; Taylor & Todd, 1995b; Venkatesh & Davis, 2000) showed the individual influence of each of these items (Davis et al., 1989; Gefen & Straub, 1997; Taylor & Todd, 1995a; Venkatesh & Davis, 2000).

Figure 1. Research model for Internet-based Applications

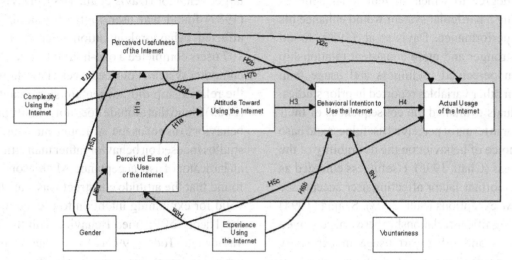

The considerable amount of research conducted on TAM varies in scope from extensions of the model to specific applications of the model. We present a modified research model for studying Internet-based applications. We offer the following related hypotheses based on the TAM theoretical foundation of research.

Perceived Ease of Use of the Internet

Perceived ease of use is defined as the degree to which an individual believes that using a particular system would be free of physical and mental effort. Previous studies suggest that perceived ease of use influences usefulness, attitude, intention, and actual use (Chau, 1996). Davis et al. (1989) found that perceived ease of use directly and indirectly affects usage through its impact on perceived usefulness through the attitude toward using the Internet. Davis et al. also found that perceived ease of use is a significant secondary determinant of people's intentions to use computers. Chau's study (1996) also showed that perceived ease of use significantly affected near-term usefulness, but did not significantly affect intention to use. Venkatesh and Davis (2000) discovered that TAM2 retains perceived ease of use from TAM

as a direct determinant of perceived usefulness. The importance of perceived ease of use increased (Gefen & Straub, 1997) when an online shopper buys a product online as opposed to just gathering information about a product. Van der Heijden (2004) found that perceived ease of use strongly determines intention to use a hedonic Web site. Lohse and Spiller (1998) stated that consumers prefer easy-to-navigate Web sites. Interestingly, Wu and Wang (2005) found that perceived ease of use did not significantly affect behavioral intention in a study concerning the acceptance of mobile commerce. However, we still propose that perceived ease of use remain an important variable in our study.

H1: *Perceived ease of use of the Internet is positively and significantly correlated to perceived usefulness of the Internet and attitude toward using the Internet.*

Perceived Usefulness of the Internet

Perceived usefulness, based on expectancy theory, is concerned with an individual's beliefs in the decision making process (Venkatesh & Davis, 2000). Perceived usefulness is defined as the degree to which an individual believes that using a particular system would enhance his or her performance. Davis et al. (1989) found that a stronger and more consistent relationship between perceived usefulness and usage than between other variables reported in prior studies. Individuals evaluated the consequences of their behavior in terms of perceived usefulness and base their choice of behavior on the desirability of the usefulness (Chau, 1996). Usefulness emerged as most important factor affecting user acceptance with few exceptions (Sun, 2003). Szajna (1994) found a significant relationship between perceived usefulness and self-report usage in her study of 61 graduate business students, however not hypothesized in her revised TAM. In studying personal computing acceptance in small firms, Igbaria, Zinatelli, Cragg, and Cavaye (1997) found that perceived usefulness exerted a strong direct effect on usage. Sun (2003) found perceived usefulness to emerge as the most important factor affecting the constructs related to user acceptance of a variety of technologies. Pikkarainen, Pikkarainen, Karjaluoto, and Pahnila (2004) found that perceived usefulness was one of the main factors influencing acceptance of online banking. Carey and Day (2005) found a strong relationship between perceived usefulness and attitude. Van der Heijden (2004) found that perceived usefulness loses its predictive power for hedonic Web sites, however.

H2: Perceived usefulness of the Internet is positively and significantly correlated to attitude toward using the Internet, behavioral intention to use the Internet, and actual usage of the Internet.

Attitude Toward Using the Internet

Attitude toward using is defined as the user's evaluation of the desirability of his or her using the system. The attitude toward using is an individual's positive or negative feelings about performing the target behavior (Davis et al., 1989). Davis et al. (1989) found that user's attitudes significantly affected behavioral intention after a group of 107 users completed a one-hour introduction to a computer system. Fourteen weeks later, however, the relationship did not remain significant. Sun (2003) found that attitude does not reliably predict behavior to use or usage. Although many previous studies focused on behavior rather than attitude as an indicator of user acceptance, Mathieson (1991) found that the attitude construct was statistically valid for explaining intention to use, comparing the Theory of Planned Behavior with the TAM. Taylor and Todd (1995a) found that attitude is not a significant determinant of behavioral intention although the relationship between attitude and behavioral intention is more significant for experienced users. Chau and Hu (2001) reported perceived usefulness to be a significant determinant of attitude as well as behavioral intention. These findings show that users are likely to have a positive attitude if they believe that usage of a technology will increase their performance and productivity. Wu (2003) found that consumers who shop online have higher attitude scores, which are directly related to online purchase decisions. Athiyaman (2002) found that consumers may avoid online purchasing items such as airline tickets because of their attitudes concerning the security of the Internet. Since we are measuring the experience with which users interact with the Internet, we include attitude toward using in our modified TAM.

H3: Attitude toward using the Internet is positively and significantly correlated to behavior toward using the Internet.

Behavioral Intention to Use the Internet

Behavioral intention is defined as a measure of the strength of one's intention to perform a specified behavior. Sun and Zhang (2003) reported that behavioral intention does well in predicting actual usage of a technology. Prior studies also report similar findings (Davis et al., 1989; Taylor & Todd, 1995b; Venkatesh & Davis, 2000).Intentions predict people's computer use reasonably well from (Davis et al., 1989). Therefore, any factors that influence behavior act as indirect influences through behavioral intention. The results of Taylor and Todd's study (1995b) of inexperienced and experienced users confirmed a stronger correlation between behavioral intention and behavior (usage) for experienced users.

H4: *Behavioral intention toward using the Internet is positively and significantly correlated to actual usage of the Internet.*

Gender

Gender differences exist in many disciplines, including technology. In studying the gender differences in the perception and use of e-mail, Gefen and Straub (1997) found that women's and men's perceptions of technology differ. Women view e-mail as higher in social presence than men, and women placed a higher value on perceived usefulness than men. Also, their study supported the idea that men tend to feel more comfortable with computers. In another study by Venkatesh and Morris (2000),perceptions of usefulness strongly influenced men's decisions, whereas perceptions of ease of use and subjective norm affected women more. However, they concluded that men consider perceived usefulness to a greater extent than women in making their decisions regarding the use of a new technology. This study showed that men perceive that more experience with the system makes it easier to use. Sun (2003) found that gender mediates perceived usefulness and user acceptance. Stafford, Turan, and Raisinghani (2004) found no differences between men's and women's involvement in online shopping across the United States, Finland, and Turkey, however.

H5: *Gender will significantly influence the perceived use of the Internet, perceived usefulness of the Internet, and actual usage of the Internet.*

Experience

Prior research suggests that experience is a determinant of behavior (Ajzen & Fishbein, 1980). Significant differences exist between experienced users and inexperienced users. For experienced users, a stronger link between intentions and usage exists (Taylor & Todd, 1995a). Also, perceived usefulness emerged as the strongest predictor of intention for the inexperienced group in the same study. The results of Taylor and Todd's study (1995a) of inexperienced and experienced users confirmed a stronger correlation between behavioral intention and behavior (usage) for experienced users. Venkatesh and Morris (2000) found that as direct experience with technology increases over time, individuals possess a better assessment of the benefits and costs associated with using that technology. They suggested that in the absence of direct behavioral experience with the target object, individuals anchor their perceptions to general abstract criteria, which in this case is the perceived usefulness of the Internet. Igbaria, Guimaraes, and Davis (1995) found that computer experience will directly and indirectly affect usage through beliefs. They found that individual skills and expertise relate to user beliefs and usage. They found computer experience and user training positively associated with perceived ease of use and perceived usefulness. Igbaria, Parasuraman, and Baroudi (1996) found that the use of computer technology depends on the technology itself and the level of skill or expertise of the individual using it. Mathieson's study empirically supported the relationship between experience, expressed as skills or expertise (Mathieson, 1991). Venkatesh and Davis (2000) found that the perceived ease of use of a system measured after hands-on experience will be system specific and hence, significantly different from measures taken before hands-on experience. Agarwal and Prasad (1999) reported a strong relationship between an individual's prior experience with similar technologies and her/his behavior to use that technology. Szajna (1994) found that as an individual becomes more experienced with the information technology, usefulness directly determines not only intentions to use but also the usage behavior. Miyazaki and Fernadez (2001) found that higher levels of Internet experience lead to lower risk perceptions regarding online shopping. Sun (2003) found experience to mediate the relationships between ease of use and perceived usefulness.

H6: *Experience using the Internet will be positively and significantly correlated to perceived usefulness of the Internet and the behavioral intention to use the Internet.*

Complexity

Complexity is defined as the degree to which the user expects the technology to be free of effort. Perceived complexity is defined as the degree to which computer technology is perceived as relatively difficult to understand and use (Pitt, Berthon, & Watson, 1996). Davis et al. (1989) and Igbaria et al. (1996) measured complexity in terms of time taken to perform tasks, integration of computer results into existing work, and vulnerability. Igbaria et al. (1996) found strong relationships between perceived complexity and perceived usefulness and with usage. Chau and Hu (2001) reported that the more complex the technology, the less relevant experience and subsequently a weaker link exists between perceived usefulness and behavioral intention to use. We hypothesize a negative relationship between complexity and Internet usage.

H7: *Perceived complexity of using the Internet will be negatively and significantly corre-*

lated to perceived usefulness of the Internet and the actual usage of the Internet.

Voluntariness

The level of voluntariness is defined as the extent to which potential adopters perceive the adoption decision to be non-mandatory (Venkatesh & Davis, 2000). Organizations often require their employees to use a certain technology. However, some people will not agree to follow such regulations. In the Venkatesh and Davis study (2000), they found that voluntariness moderates the relationship between subjective norm and intention to use. Therefore, behavioral intentions vary between mandatory and voluntary usage (Sun & Zhang, 2003). Moore and Benbasat (1991) suggested that it is not necessarily actual voluntariness which will influence behavior, but rather a perception of voluntariness. Innovations diffuse because of the cumulative decisions of individuals to adopt them. It is not the potential adopters' perception of the innovation itself but their perceptions of using the innovation that are key to how rapidly the innovation diffuses. Venkatesh and Morris (2000) found that in the context of technology acceptance in voluntary usage settings, the influence of other users will diminish to non-significance over time with increasing experience with the target system. Sun and Zhang (2003) found that voluntariness is considered a moderating factor in shaping behavioral intention to use.

H8: *Voluntariness of using the Internet is positively and significantly related to the behavioral intention to use the Internet.*

Actual Usage of the Internet

Straub, Limayen, and Karahanna-Evaristo (1995) found that system usage demonstrates a notable practical value for managers interested in evaluating the impact of information technology. Igbaria et al. (1995) defined perceived usage as the amount of time interacting with a technology and the frequency of use. They found strong relationships with behavioral intent to use the technology. Igbaria et al. (1997) found individuals likely to use a system if they believe it is easy to use and will increase their performance productivity. Actual usage, as originally conceptualized in the Davis et al. study (1989), is measured by the frequency of use and the length of time of use. It is difficult to obtain objective measures of actual use for Internet-based technologies; consequently, many of the TAM studies either left out usage as a dependent variable, focusing solely on behavioral intention or else moved to perceived usage. Szajna (1994) recommended the examination of self-reported usage.

RESEARCH DESIGN

Measurement Scales

We operationalized theoretical constructs for the revised TAM based upon Internet technologies by using validated items from prior research. After extensive research of TAM, we found that prior TAM studies used several commonscales (Agarwal & Karahanna, 2000; Chau, 1996; Davis et al., 1989; Igbaria et al., 1996, 1997; Legris, Ingham, & Collerette, 2002; Van der Heijden, 2000; Venkatesh & Davis, 2000). We measure perceived usefulness, perceived ease of use, and behavioral intention using scales adapted from Davis et al. (1989) and Chau (1996). Perceived usefulness of the Internet included measuring the enablement of the ability to accomplish tasks more quickly, improvement in performance, using the Internet to increase productivity and enhancing effectiveness. Perceived ease of use measured easiness to learn to use the Internet, getting what is needed, interacting with the Internet in a clear and concise manner, ease of flexibility, and respondents' ease to become skillful. We derived measures of attitude toward using the Internet primarily from

the Agarwal and Karahanna study (2000) where they looked at fun and enjoyment interacting with the technology. We examined the behavioral intention to use the Internet as a combination of carrying out the task and planned utilization in the future (Agarwal & Prasad, 1999; Chau, 1996). To examine behavioral inclinations now (T1) and in the future (T2), we used the Venkatesh and Davis (2000) measures.

The external variables include the perceived complexity using the Internet, experience, voluntariness using the Internet, and gender. We derived the perceived complexity construct from Igbaria et al. (1997) where they measured the amount of time it takes to perform a task, the integration of the results into existing work, and the exposure of the Internet to the vulnerability of computer breakdowns and a loss of data. We operationalized the experience construct from the research of Venkatesh and Davis (2000) and Legris et al. (2002) where the perceived experience using the Internet is measured in conjunction with the number of years using the Internet. We derived voluntariness using the Internet from the Venkatesh and Davis (2000) research where they looked at the requirement to use the technology for work or school and where it enhances tasks where there is not a requirement to use it. We measured gender as a single-item as suggested by Gefen and Straub (1997). We used a perceptual measure for the actual usage variable for this technology due to the difficulty in obtaining actual logged data. Though some research suggests that self-reported usage measures are biased (Moore & Benbasat, 1991), other research suggests that self-reported usage measures correlate well with actual usage measures (Taylor & Todd, 1995a, 1995b; Venkatesh & Davis, 2000). As suggested by Venkatesh and Davis (2000), we minimized this potential problem by using the common-method variance resulting from measuring both self-reported usage and its determinants (intention, perceived usefulness, etc.) with single-item measures.

Survey Instrument

We developed a survey instrument for pre-test to ensure content validity. Davis et al. (1989) pointed out that psychometricians emphasize the validity of a measurement scale is built from the outset (Davis, 1986). To ensure content validity of the scales, the items selected must represent the concept about which generalizations are to be made. First, all items identified in existing instruments were categorized according to the various TAM scales published in the literature. This generated an initial item pool for each construct. To keep the length of the instrument reasonable, we selected three to six scales for the measurement of each of the constructs, keeping the wording similar to the original studies. The typical item in previous instruments tended to ask respondents to indicate a degree of agreement. We used this approach for this study, with a five-point Likert scale ranging from "strongly disagree" to "strongly agree" chosen as the response format. After creating the item pools for each construct, we re-evaluated these items to eliminate those that appeared redundant or ambiguous, which might load on more than one factor in subsequent research. We pre-tested the instrument with a respondent pool of 30 students. As appropriate, we modified the question formats based upon the statistical results of their responses and a set of interviews.

Data Sample

Subjects for this study included 192 students who were using Internet technologies in classes across four different departments at a major university in the United States. The sample included a fairly broad range of departments including management, computer science, geological science, and arts and letters. Of the 240 students requested to participate in this study, 192 agreed to complete the survey instrument, yielding a response rate of 80%.

Assessing Reliability and Validity

We found strong support for construct validity and reliability by examining Cronbach alpha reliability coefficients and by factor analysis using principal components measures. The measurement scales for this instrument showed strong psychometric properties. All measurement scales showed relatively high Cronbach alpha coefficients (see Table 1) at $\alpha>=0.80$ for all the measures with the exception of perceived complexity which is slightly below the lower bounds set for this study, near the $\alpha>=0.70$ (Moore & Benbasat, 1991). This pattern of high scale reliability is consistent with much of the prior research dealing with the technology acceptance model.

We used factor analysis as an assessment of construct validity. Moore and Benbasat state that, where possible, data analysis ought to be grounded in a strong a priori theory set (1991). This research fits the approach where the constructs related to the acceptance of Internet technologies by consumers are based on a substantial body of prior research and where the scale development fits the construct's conceptual meaning as a method of ensuring construct validity. We conducted principal components analysis with varimax rotation yielding a seven-factor solution (see

Table 1. Cronbach alpha coefficients

Variable	Alpha	Standardized item alpha
Perceived Usefulness	0.909	0.909
Perceived Ease of Use	0.928	0.929
Attitude Toward Using	0.931	0.931
Behavioral Intention	0.874	0.901
Perceived Complexity	0.678	0.682
Voluntariness	0.846	0.848
Actual Usage	0.818	0.817

Table 2) with eigenvalues greater than 1.0, explaining 72.2% of the variance in the data set.

We examined the rotated factor matrix (see Figure 2) for items that did not load strongly on any factor (<0.40), that loaded on another factor greater than the intended component, or that loaded relatively equally on more than one factor. All of the items from the perceived usefulness construct loaded cleanly on a factor with all loadings >= 0.621. Perceived ease of use items all loaded at or above 0.677 showing strong excellent factor patterns. Actual utilization of Internet technologies showed loadings about 0.591 with all items remaining in the various scales loading together. The construct known as attitude toward using the Internet also showed strong component cohesion with all items loading together on the same factor, with loadings at or exceeding 0.727 in general, with the item where the "Web bores me" to have an expected negative loading at -0.540. We found behavioral intention to use the

Table 2. Principal components analysis

Componenet	Total	% of Variance	Cumulative %
1	13.114	38.571	38.571
2	3.155	9.279	47.850
3	2.604	7.659	55.508
4	1.909	5.614	61.123
5	1.606	4.725	65.848
6	1.108	3.260	69.108
7	1.066	3.136	72.244

Internet to have performed in general as good with loadings above 0.587, while one item, "I always try to use the Internet in as many case/ occasions as possible" loaded on another factor to a greater degree that the one that contained the other relative factors. The voluntariness construct showed strong construct validity with each item loading above 0.822. Finally, the construct revolv-

Figure 2. Principal components analysis – factor loadings

	1	2	3	4	5	6	7
Using the Internet can enable me to accomplish tasks more quickly	0.726	0.243	-0.049	0.228	0.151	0.056	0.145
Using the Internet can improve my performance	0.820	0.116	0.184	0.119	0.125	-0.026	0.062
Using the Internet can make it easier to do my tasks	0.798	0.200	0.026	0.168	0.231	-0.005	0.117
Using the Internet in my job/school can increase my productivity	0.786	0.147	0.053	0.133	0.145	-0.097	0.085
Using the Internet can enhance my effectiveness	0.839	0.200	0.077	0.126	0.072	-0.082	0.166
I find the Internet useful in my job/school	0.621	0.139	0.011	0.402	0.322	0.097	0.091
Learning to use the Internet is easy for me	0.132	0.766	0.276	0.111	0.270	0.066	0.114
I find it easy to get what I need from the Internet	0.424	0.677	0.024	0.198	0.159	0.068	0.156
My interaction with the Internet is clear and understandable	0.251	0.752	0.271	0.081	0.176	0.115	0.137
I find the Internet to be flexible to interact with	0.442	0.691	0.111	0.270	0.082	0.029	0.111
It is easy for me to become skillful at using the Internet	0.194	0.767	0.363	0.104	0.207	0.057	0.094
I find the Internet easy to use	0.103	0.811	0.233	0.127	0.169	0.101	0.108
How often do you use the Internet	0.137	0.207	0.672	0.300	0.197	-0.113	0.117
On average, how frequently do you use the Internet	0.006	0.321	0.591	0.346	0.020	-0.095	0.069
Indicate how frequently you use the Internet	0.104	0.219	0.718	0.164	0.081	-0.060	0.077
How many different Websites do you visit	0.027	0.124	0.707	0.119	0.005	0.004	-0.011
Number of different Internet tasks used	0.169	0.224	0.596	0.200	0.083	-0.066	-0.047
I have fun interacting with the Internet	0.335	0.315	0.246	0.727	0.208	-0.007	0.120
Using the Web provides me with a lot of enjoyment	0.286	0.277	0.279	0.746	0.122	-0.037	0.095
I enjoy using the Web	0.292	0.127	0.316	0.772	0.211	-0.013	0.055
Using the Web bores me	-0.330	-0.006	-0.273	-0.540	-0.090	-0.027	-0.292
I always try to use the Internet in as many cases/occassions as possible	0.437	0.273	0.113	0.330	0.347	-0.042	0.331
I always try to use the Internet to do a task whenever it has a feature to help me perform it	0.252	0.361	0.065	0.357	0.587	-0.048	0.210
I plan to use the Internet in the future	0.270	0.217	0.243	0.092	0.833	-0.065	-0.025
I intend to continue using the Web in the future	0.331	0.317	0.179	0.211	0.780	-0.051	-0.042
I expect my use of the Web to continue in the future	0.274	0.292	0.236	0.166	0.833	-0.019	-0.046
Using the Internet is voluntary as far as work/school is concerned	-0.157	0.108	0.089	0.037	0.062	0.822	0.001
I am not required to use the Internet for work/school	0.031	0.087	-0.089	0.003	-0.049	0.890	-0.031
While the Internet enhances my effectiveness, it is not required that I use it	0.049	0.040	-0.084	-0.070	-0.097	0.875	-0.042
Using the Internet can take up too much of my time when performing many tasks	-0.201	-0.213	-0.061	-0.307	0.053	0.109	-0.747
When I use the Internet, I find it difficult to integrate the results into my existing work	-0.031	-0.316	-0.124	-0.146	-0.166	0.114	-0.749
Using the Internet exposes me to the vulnerability of computer breakdowns and loss of	-0.245	-0.007	-0.054	0.047	0.093	-0.082	-0.622

ing around the perceived complexity all showed negative loadings less than -0.622, as expected.

We then looked at the construct correlation matrix among the item in a particular construct (see Figure 3). We examined the correlations for each of the constructs in the study and found relatively good cohesiveness for most of the items. Moore and Benbasat (1991) suggested that a "good" range for a set of items in a factor cluster should be at 0.55 or higher, but at least 0.45 to be considered "fair" and reasonable for measuring new constructs. Perceived usefulness and perceived ease of use exhibited strong correlations between the items, with the lowest correlationat0.565 and 0.586, respectively. The attitudes toward using items were also strongly related, with the lowest correlation of 0.797. In the behavioral intent to use items, BI3 appears to more strongly correlated with BI4 (r =.849) and BI5 (r =.922) rather than with BI1 (r =.493) and BI2 (r=.436). This seems logical since BI4 and BI5 also concern the future usage of the Internet. The perceived complexity items were not all strongly related as the PC3 variable on the vulnerability of using the Internet was suggested by Igbaria et al. (1997) as a measure of complexity was supported in their research. The voluntariness items all appeared to be strongly correlated with each other, where the lowest correlation is 0.594. The actual correlation items tended to be strongly correlated with the exception of AU4 (r =0.417) where the respondent was asked how many Web sites they had visited.

Figure 3. Construct correlation matrices

Perceived Usefulness Correlation Matrix

	PU1	PU2	PU3	PU4	PU5
PU1	1.000				
PU2	0.565	1.000			
PU3	0.738	0.700	1.000		
PU4	0.619	0.619	0.673	1.000	
PU5	0.603	0.726	0.713	0.713	1.000

Perceived Ease of Use Correlation Matrix

	PE1	PE2	PE3	PE4	PE5	PE6
PE1	1.000					
PE2	0.613	1.000				
PE3	0.680	0.693	1.000			
PE4	0.586	0.685	0.731	1.000		
PE5	0.737	0.624	0.771	0.682	1.000	
PE6	0.771	0.584	0.692	0.628	0.795	1.000

Attitude Toward Using Correlation Matrix

	AT1	AT2	AT3
AT1	1.000		
AT2	0.824	1.000	
AT3	0.797	0.836	1.000

Behavioral Intention Correlation Matrix

	BI1	BI2	BI3	BI4	BI5
BI1	1.000				
BI2	0.687	1.000			
BI3	0.493	0.436	1.000		
BI4	0.592	0.516	0.849	1.000	
BI5	0.542	0.470	0.922	0.941	1.000

Perceived Complexity Correlation Matrix

	PC1	PC2	PC3
PC1	1.000		
PC2	0.674	1.000	
PC3	0.310	0.265	1.000

Voluntariness Correlation Matrix

	VU1	VU2	VU3
VU1	1.000		
VU2	0.612	1.000	
VU3	0.594	0.745	1.000

Actual Usage Correlation Matrix

	AU1	AU2	AU3	AU4
AU1	1.000			
AU2	0.552	1.000		
AU3	0.745	0.535	1.000	
AU4	0.433	0.483	0.417	1.000

RESULTS

Descriptive Statistics

Figure 4 presents the descriptive statistics for the constructs and the statistics for individual items. An examination of perceived usefulness shows extremely strong scores on all items. It appears that most of the respondents in this study felt the Internet is useful in enabling them to accomplish tasks more efficiently (μ=4.48) and making it easier to do tasks in general (μ=4.34). We also found that the Internet is useful in the workplace to increase respondents' productivity (μ=4.35). We found that the Internet is extremely useful in the job or at school by the respondents in this study (μ=4.54).

Most of the items related to perceived ease of use showed strong means. The respondents found it relatively easy to use the Internet (μ=4.24) and easy to learn to use the Internet (μ=4.30). In the same way that learning to use the Internet was

Figure 4. Descriptive statistics

Perceived Usefulness	Mean	Median	Std. Dev.	Skewness	Minimum	Maximum
PU1 Using the Internet can enable me to accomplish tasks more quickly	4.48	5	0.898	-1.584	1	5
PU2 Using the Internet can improve my performance	4.17	4	0.786	-0.942	1	5
PU3 Using the Internet can make it easier to do my tasks	4.34	4	0.735	-1.201	1	5
PU4 Using the Internet in my job/school can increase my productivity	4.35	4	0.752	-1.136	1	5
PU5 Using the Internet can enhance my effectiveness	4.18	4	0.790	-0.736	1	5
PU6 I find the Internet useful in my job/school	4.54	5	0.662	-1.688	1	5

Perceived Ease of Use	Mean	Median	Std. Dev.	Skewness	Minimum	Maximum
PE1 Learning to use the Internet is easy for me	4.30	4	0.827	-1.570	1	5
PE2 I find it easy to get what I need from the Internet	3.95	4	0.902	-1.150	1	5
PE3 My interaction with the Internet is clear and understandable	4.03	4	0.869	-0.930	1	5
PE4 I find the Internet to be flexible to interact with	3.90	4	0.935	-0.732	1	5
PE5 It is easy for me to become skillful at using the Internet	4.07	4	0.855	-0.856	1	5
PE6 I find the Internet easy to use	4.24	4	0.841	-1.279	1	5

Attitude Toward Using	Mean	Median	Std. Dev.	Skewness	Minimum	Maximum
AT1 I have fun interacting with the Internet	3.97	4	0.892	-0.924	1	5
AT2 Using the Web provides me with a lot of enjoyment	3.71	4	0.966	-0.413	1	5
AT3 I enjoy using the Web	3.91	4	0.902	-0.645	1	5
AT4 Using the Web bores me	2.07	2	1.058	0.986	1	5

Behavioral Intention to Use	Mean	Median	Std. Dev.	Skewness	Minimum	Maximum
BI1 Use the Internet whenever there is a feature to help	4.04	4	0.873	-1.082	1	5
BI2 Use the Internet in as many cases/occassions as possible	3.66	4	0.975	-0.628	1	5
BI3 Plan to use the Internet in the future	4.57	5	0.618	-1.692	1	5
BI4 Will continue using the Web in the future	4.59	5	0.608	-1.760	1	5
BI5 Expect use of the Web to continue in the future	4.60	5	0.608	-1.814	1	5

Perceived Complexity	Mean	Median	Std. Dev.	Skewness	Minimum	Maximum
PC1 Using the Internet can take up too much of my time	2.80	3	1.141	0.118	1	5
PC2 Difficulty integrating Internet into work tasks	2.34	2	0.969	0.764	1	5
PC3 Exposure to Internet vulnerabilities	3.02	3	1.076	0.036	1	5

Voluntariness	Mean	Median	Std. Dev.	Skewness	Minimum	Maximum
VU1 Using the Internet is voluntary as far as work/school is concerned	3.02	3	1.162	-0.083	1	5
VU2 I am not required to use the Internet for work/school	2.62	2	1.102	0.355	1	5
VU3 It is not required to use the Internet to complete tasks	2.77	3	1.081	0.015	1	5

Actual Usage	Mean	Median	Std. Dev.	Skewness	Minimum	Maximum
AU1 How often do you use the Internet?	4.23	4	0.904	-1.109	1	5
AU2 On average, how frequently do you use the Internet?	3.45	3	0.966	0.281	1	5
AU3 Indicate how frequently you use the Internet	4.23	5	0.999	-1.161	1	5
AU4 How many different Websites do you visit?	3.81	4	0.854	-0.027	1	5

Internet Tasks	Mean	Median	Std. Dev.	Skewness	Minimum	Maximum
e-mail	0.950	1	0.216	-4.217	0	1
Research for papers	0.930	1	0.257	-3.379	0	1
School assignments	0.840	1	0.370	-1.839	0	1
Information gathering	0.830	1	0.380	-1.735	0	1
Searching	0.820	1	0.389	-1.638	0	1
News	0.710	1	0.457	-0.915	0	1
Entertainment	0.600	1	0.491	-0.426	0	1
Work-related	0.480	0	0.501	0.088	0	1
Shopping	0.520	1	0.501	-0.066	0	1
Instant messaging	0.460	0	0.499	0.198	0	1
Auctions	0.220	0	0.417	1.343	0	1
Chat rooms	0.080	0	0.274	3.084	0	1
Tasks TOTAL	7.410	7	2.298	-0.395	1	12

easy for the sample respondents, so was the ease at which they were skillful using the Internet (μ=4.07). Flexibility with Internet interaction (μ=3.90) also led respondents to find it easy to get what they need from the Internet (μ=3.95). The items associated with attitude toward using mean responses were around the 3.7-3.9 range. Most of the respondents reported having fun using the Internet (μ=3.97). With respect to enjoyment, respondents enjoyed using the Internet (μ=3.71, μ=3.91). Asking about the boredom using the Internet yielded a relatively low mean (μ=2.07), as expected.

Most of the scores related to behavioral intention to use came in relatively high. The items related to the behavioral usage in the future elicited fairly high responses, such as planning to use the Internet in the future (μ=4.57), will continue to use the Web in the future (μ=4.59), and expect one's use of the Web to continue in the future (μ=4.60). The items related to using the features of the Internet (μ=4.04) and using the Internet in as many cases as possible (μ=3.66) were significantly lower as individual indicators of a user's behavioral intention to use. The items related to perceived complexity using the Internet were lower than most of the other items in the survey, as expected. All of the items in this category contained questions that were negative in connotation; nevertheless if they are reversed out, the means are still much lower than other items.

The Internet was found not to take up too much of the respondent's time, with a moderate response (μ=2.80). Difficulty integrating the Internet into work tasks was not seen as too significant in this study (μ=2.34) and exposure to Internet vulnerabilities, such as security and virus protection, was not considered significant (μ=3.02). This last finding surprised us given the growth of online viruses and worms. The voluntariness items all appear to contain only a moderate degree of required usage when it came to using the Internet for school or work. Using the Internet is deemed voluntary (μ=3.02), not being required to use the Internet for work/ school (μ=2.52), and not being required to use the Internet to complete tasks (μ=2.77). We can only conclude here that a majority of the respondents in this study felt that using the Internet was required in order to complete their work and/or school tasks. This finding is not unusual given that although use of the Internet was not deemed to be explicitly mandatory with most of the respondents, they felt that not using the Internet would not allow them to complete their tasks.

The actual usage variable was measured in terms of frequency of use and amount of use. Both frequency of use (μ=4.23) and amount of Internet usage (μ=4.23) were both relatively high. Respondents in our study reported visiting between 5-10 Web sites per day and using the Internet between two to three hours per day on average. Most of the respondents in the study used the Internet for e-mail (95%) and research (93%), while surprisingly only a small number of respondents reported using the Internet for chatting (8%).

Inter-Correlation Analysis

We noticed a significant number of independent two-tailed correlations among the constructs as we initially found in the literature (see Figure 5). This is in keeping with other studies that demonstrated similar correlational patterns (Agarwal & Karahanna, 2000; Agarwal & Prasad, 1999; Igbaria et al., 1996, 1997; Szajna, 1994). We used the correlations to examine the independent relationships between the constructs and to get an initial feeling for how well the hypotheses were supported in the original model.

Hypotheses Testing

Hypothesis 1: *Perceived ease of use of the Internet is positively and significantly correlated to perceived usefulness of the Internet and attitude toward using the Internet.*

Figure 5. Inter-correlations among study variables

		Perceived Usefulness	Perceived Ease of Use	Attitude Toward Using	Behavioral Intention to Use	Perceived Complexity	Voluntariness	Experience	Gender
Perceived Ease of Use	Pearson Correlation	.523**							
	Sig. (2-tailed)	0.000							
	N	192							
Attitude Toward Using	Pearson Correlation	.467**	.522**						
	Sig. (2-tailed)	0.000	0.000						
	N	192	192						
Behavioral Intention to Use	Pearson Correlation	.566**	.566**	.497**					
	Sig. (2-tailed)	0.000	0.000	0.000					
	N	192	192	192					
Perceived Complexity	Pearson Correlation	-.368**	-.418**	-.264**	-.245**				
	Sig. (2-tailed)	0.000	0.000	0.000	0.001				
	N	192	192	192	192				
Voluntariness	Pearson Correlation	-0.069	0.085	-0.061	-0.101	0.123			
	Sig. (2-tailed)	0.344	0.240	0.405	0.166	0.091			
	N	191	191	191	191	191			
Experience	Pearson Correlation	0.132	.379**	.235**	.389**	-.183**	-0.053		
	Sig. (2-tailed)	0.068	0.000	0.001	0.000	0.011	0.462		
	N	191	191	191	191	191	191		
Gender	Pearson Correlation	-0.112	-0.282**	-0.121	-0.131	0.164	-0.014	-0.168	
	Sig. (2-tailed)	0.131	0.000	0.131	0.076	0.026	0.847	0.023	
	N	184	191	184	184	184	184	184	
Actual Usage	Pearson Correlation	.276**	.473**	.499**	.463**	-.289**	-.149**	0.49	-0.227**
	Sig. (2-tailed)	0.000	0.000	0.000	0.000	0.000	0.039	0.000	0.002
	N	191	191	191	191	191	191	191	184

We found support for H1 where a strong correlation exists between perceived usefulness and perceived ease of use ($r=.523$) as purported by Venkatesh and Davis (2000). Szajna (1994) also reported a strong correlation between these variables ($r=.48$). Van der Heijden, Verhagen, and Creemers (2003) ($r=.48$) and Gefen (2003) ($r=.55$) have reported similar correlations.

Hypothesis 2: *Perceived usefulness of the Internet is positively and significantly correlated to attitude toward using the Internet, behavioral intention to use the Internet, and actual usage of the Internet.*

The relationships between perceived usefulness and attitude toward using ($r=.467$), behavioral intention to use ($r=.566$), and actual usage ($r=.276$) are all statistically significant, supporting H2.

Chau (1996) found a strong relationship between perceived near-term usefulness and perceived long-term usefulness and behavioral intention to use. Igbaria et al. (1997) found that perceived usefulness directly impacts system usage. Sun (2003) reported that after looking at 13 studies examining the relationship between perceived usefulness and behavioral intention to use that all of the studies found statistical significance with that relationship. Pikkarainen et al. (2004) found perceived usefulness to be a main factor influencing online banking acceptance. Carey and Day (2005) found a strong relationship between perceived usefulness and attitude.

Hypothesis 3: *Attitude toward using the Internet is positively and significantly correlated to behavior toward using the Internet.*

The relationship between attitude toward using the Internet and behavior toward using is also supporting H3 (r = .497). Taylor and Todd (1995b) did find this relationship as significant in their study where they integrated experience, as we have. Chau and Hu (2001) found the relationship between attitude and behavioral intention to be significant in all three of their models. Wu (2003) found that online shoppers have higher attitude scores, which are directly related to online purchase decisions.

Hypothesis 4: *Behavioral intention toward using the Internet is positively and significantly correlated to actual usage of the Internet.*

We also found a significant relationship between behavior toward using and actual usage of the Internet (r = .463), giving support to H4. Davis et al. (1989) found that behavioral intention to use the Internet strongly affected actual usage in both models, taking into effect direct belief-intention relationships.

Hypothesis 5: *Gender will significantly influence the perceived use of the Internet, perceived usefulness of the Internet, and actual usage of the Internet.*

We did not find that gender impacts perceived usefulness (r = -0.112) as we initially thought yielding mixed results for H5. However, gender was correlated to actual usage (r = -0.227) and perceived ease of use (r = -.0282). Venkatesh and Morris (2000) found that ease of use was not a significant determinant for behavioral intent for men, whereas women weighted ease of use more strongly in determining behavioral intent than did men. They also found that men consider perceived usefulness to a greater extent than women in making their decisions regarding the use of a new technology. Gefen and Straub (1997) found that gender impacts perceived usefulness and perceived ease of use in their study of 392 respondents. Surprisingly, they did not find a relationship between gender and actual usage. Sun (2003) found that gender has a mediating effect on perceived usefulness on user acceptance.

Hypothesis 6: *Experience using the Internet will be positively and significantly correlated to perceived usefulness of the Internet and the behavioral intention to use the Internet.*

We did not find a significant relationship between experience and perceived usefulness (r = .132) although Taylor and Todd (1995b) found a strong differentiation between experienced and inexperienced users and their perceived usefulness variable of information technologies. Szajna (1994) reported a strong relationship between perceived usefulness and experience using. Igbaria et al. (1995) found a strong relationship between experience and behavioral intent (as measured by variety of use), similar to the study (r = .389). Agarwal and Prasad (1999) found a strong relationship between experience and their behavioral intent to use the technology. Sun (2003) found experience to have mediating effects between the relationships of ease of use and perceived usefulness. The findings supported part of H6, while other portions require further investigation.

Hypothesis 7: *Perceived complexity of using the Internet will be negatively and significantly correlated to perceived usefulness of the Internet and the actual usage of the Internet.*

We found a strong correlation between perceived complexity and perceived usefulness (r = -.368) and with perceived complexity and actual usage (r = -.289). This finding shows support for H7 and corroborates the results from Igbaria et al. (1996) and Davis et al. (1989).

Hypothesis 8: *Voluntariness of using the Internet is positively and significantly related to the behavioral intention to use the Internet.*

In this study, we did not find a strong relationship between voluntariness and behavioral intent to use (r=-.101) and therefore could not support H8. Venkatesh and Davis (2000) found a significant correlation between voluntariness and intention to use in their study looking longitudinally across four organizations (n=156). Sun and Zhang (2003) found that voluntariness moderates behavioral intention to use. The testing of the hypotheses in this section is intended to demonstrate further validation of the instrument, as discussed earlier. If the constructs perform as predicted by theory, then we can infer that the measurement of the constructs is nomologically valid. In testing the model, we wanted to see the difference in explanatory power between the part of the model that considers the perceived usefulness and perceived ease of use and that which considers interaction with actual use of the Internet. Table 7 shows the linear regression models for dependent variables. While not originally hypothesized, three external variables explain a large percentage of variance ($R^2=0.371$). The coefficients for gender (p=.007), perceived complexity (p =.000) and experience (p =.000) are all statistically significant. We only hypothesized the relationship of gender to impact

Figure 6. Linear regression model for the dependent variables

Dependent Variable	R Square	F-value (sig)	Independent Variable	B	Std. Error	Stand Beta	t	Signif
Perceived Ease of Use	37.1%	35.406	Gender	-0.241	0.088	-0.165	-2.723	0.007
		0.000	Perceived Complexity	-0.377	0.054	-0.427	-7.025	0.000
			Experience	0.263	0.057	0.280	4.609	0.000
			Constant	4.730	0.283		16.716	
Dependent Variable	R Square	F-value (sig)	Independent Variable	B	Std. Error	Stand Beta	t	Signif
Perceived Usefulness	31.5%	20.539	Perceived Complexity	-0.148	0.054	-0.196	-2.730	0.007
		0.000	Perceived Ease of Use	0.403	0.067	0.473	6.056	0.000
			Gender	0.049	0.080	0.039	0.606	0.545
			Experience	-0.069	0.054	-0.087	-1.287	0.200
			Constant	3.227	0.404		7.997	
Dependent Variable	R Square	F-value (sig)	Independent Variable	B	Std. Error	Stand Beta	t	Signif
Attitude Toward Using	32.4%	46.312	Perceived Ease of Use	0.281	0.052	0.383	5.450	0.000
		0.000	Perceived Usefulness	0.238	0.063	0.267	3.797	0.000
			Constant	1.235	0.244		5.072	
Dependent Variable	R Square	F-value (sig)	Independent Variable	B	Std. Error	Stand Beta	t	Signif
Attitude Toward Using	39.5%	40.746	Perceived Ease of Use	0.175	0.053	0.239	3.286	0.001
		0.000	Perceived Usefulness	0.220	0.059	0.246	3.702	0.000
			Actual Usage	0.231	0.047	0.319	4.931	0.000
			Constant	0.841	0.244		5.072	
Dependent Variable	R Square	F-value (sig)	Independent Variable	B	Std. Error	Stand Beta	t	Signif
Behavioral Intention to Use	47.4%	41.830	Perceived Usefulness	0.412	0.058	0.423	7.054	0.000
		0.000	Attitude Toward Using	0.262	0.067	0.241	3.938	0.000
			Experience	0.204	0.041	0.275	5.010	0.000
			Voluntariness	-0.026	0.033	-0.042	-0.791	0.430
			Constant	1.245	0.283		4.402	
Dependent Variable	R Square	F-value (sig)	Independent Variable	B	Std. Error	Stand Beta	t	Signif
Actual Usage	31.7%	12.366	Perceived Usefulness	-0.040	0.100	-0.034	-0.403	0.688
		0.000	Behavioral Intention to Use	0.357	0.113	0.262	3.146	0.002
			Perceived Complexity	-0.232	0.065	-0.263	-3.558	0.000
			Gender	-0.223	0.098	-0.153	-2.278	0.024
			Constant	3.519	0.587		5.990	
Dependent Variable	R Square	F-value (sig)	Independent Variable	B	Std. Error	Stand Beta	t	Signif
Actual Usage	41.3%	15.395	Gender	-0.125	0.088	-0.086	-1.423	0.157
		0.000	Attitude Toward Using	0.358	0.096	0.259	3.726	0.000
			Perceived Usefulness	-0.080	0.092	-0.069	-0.873	0.384
			Perceived Ease of Use	0.146	0.085	0.146	1.699	0.091
			Behavioral Intention to Use	0.317	0.110	0.313	4.156	0.000
			Perceived Complexity	-0.123	0.061	-0.140	-2.021	0.045
			Experience	0.297	0.061	0.318	4.857	0.000
			Voluntariness	-0.098	0.044	-0.132	-2.219	0.028
			Constant	2.337	0.585		3.996	
Dependent Variable	R Square	F-value (sig)	Independent Variable	B	Std. Error	Stand Beta	t	Signif
Actual Usage	44.0%	24.072	Attitude Toward Using	0.393	0.093	0.285	4.210	0.000
		0.000	Perceived Ease of Use	0.137	0.079	0.136	1.735	0.084
			Behavioral Intention to Use	0.355	0.092	0.292	3.261	0.000
			Perceived Complexity	-0.059	0.056	-0.065	-1.053	0.294
			Experience	0.299	0.058	0.318	5.177	0.000
			Voluntariness	-0.084	0.044	-0.109	-1.906	0.048
			Constant	1.037	0.442		2.347	

perceived ease of use (H5a). We analyzed the relationships for perceived usefulness (see Figure 6). The linear regression model showed a relatively strong percentage of variance explained ($R^2 =$ 0.315).Only the coefficients related to perceived complexity (p =.007) and perceived ease of use (p =.000) are statistically significant supporting H1a and H7a. We did not find experience or gender to be significant; therefore hypotheses H5b and H6a are not supported.

The variance explained is relatively strong (R^2 = 0.324) with both coefficients found to be statistically significant at p =.000 for perceived usefulness and perceived ease of use. Therefore, the findings support hypotheses H1b and H2a. Venkatesh et al. (2003) discussed the underlying theory and resulting constructs of user acceptance models, purporting that the actual use of information technologies could affect individual reactions and attitudes toward using those technologies. We tested that relationship finding an increase in variance explained (R^2 = 0.395) where the coefficient for actual usage (p =.000) was found to be significant. This could explain why a user's attitude toward using Internet technologies is partially influenced by his or her current utilization of that technology. The linear regression model showed a stronger amount of variance explained (R^2 = 0.474). The coefficients for attitude toward using (p =.000), perceived usefulness (p =.000), and experience (p =.000) were all statistically significant supporting hypothesesH3, H2b, and H6b. However the coefficient from voluntariness (p =.430) was not significant, removing support for hypothesis H8. The amount of variance explained (R^2 = 0.317) by this model is significantly lower than expected. The coefficients that were found to be statistically significant include behavioral intention to use (p =.002) and perceived complexity (p =.000) supporting hypotheses H4 and H7b. Gender is also significant at the p < 0.05 level, supporting H5c. Surprisingly, we did not find perceived usefulness to be significant (p=.688). The summary of our hypotheses, show-

ing both the correlational analysis and regression analysis, is displayed in Table 8.

DISCUSSION

The technology acceptance model (TAM) serves as one of the most accepted theories for explaining the assimilation of technologies, where we defined assimilation in this study as the extent to which the use of technology diffuses in an organization and within a society. The technology acceptance model is an adaptation of the theory of reasoned action model specifically tailored for modeling user acceptance of information systems. This study analyzed existing research using the TAM in order to develop a reasonably grounded modified model for testing the acceptance of Internet technology by consumers. We analyzed studies using the TAM for model definitions, constructs, and scales in order to assess the construct validity of scale items. The technologies for which the TAM was used in previous studies were examined and the statistically significant correlations analyzed. Analyses of TAM studies by Legris et al. (2002), Sun (2003), and Venkatesh et al. (2003) showed significant relationships between each of the constructs. Based upon existing theory and the findings from those studies, we developed a modified technology acceptance model for Internet-based applications. In this model, we analyzed the constructs and their underlying theory including relevant findings as well as relationships between these constructs as related to the Internet-based applications. We retained the basic constructs of perceived ease of use, perceived usefulness, attitudes toward using, behavioral intention to use, and actual use in this study. We included external variables in the survey instrument based upon the relevance of the construct and the impact of the variables on the Internet technology, to include complexity using the Internet, gender, experience using the Internet, and voluntariness using the Internet. This research purported a set of hypotheses resulting from established theory.

The development process also helped to clarify and refine some of the definitions used by a variety of researchers using the technology acceptance model. During the development of the instrument, the pre-test data showed the importance of experience using the Internet as a variable affecting both the perceived usefulness of the Internet and the behavioral intention to use the Internet. We found correlation between voluntariness and behavioral intention to use the Internet. Perceived complexity using the Internet may be significantly related to the perceived usefulness (as is the perceived ease of use) and directly impact perceived use. Finally, we concluded during development that gender may play an important role in the both of the "belief" variables as well as directly on perceived use of the Internet. The results showed very strong relationships between the main constructs of the TAM. We found the relationship between attitude toward using and behavioral intention to be surprising. Sun (2003) found, in a comparative analysis of TAM study results, that this relationship was only statistically significant 43% of the times it had been studied. We measured attitude toward using in this study by assessing the enjoyment, fun, and boredom using the Internet, as suggested by Agarwal and Karahanna (2000). This corroborates the finding by Koufaris (2002)

where he found a predictive relationship between enjoyment and intent to return to a specific Web site. Wu (2003) also found that consumers who shop online possess higher attitude scores, which are directly related to online purchase decisions. We also found a relationship between complexity using the Internet and the perceived ease of use construct. Although not hypothesized, this finding appears to indicate that Internet users in our study found complexity, measured in loss of time, vulnerability, and difficulty integrating results, as suggested by Igbaria et al. (1996), affected their perception of ease of use. We feel that complexity could exist as a sub-component of the ease of use perceptual construct.

We were surprised by the extent to which experience using the Internet tended to affect not only perceived ease of use and behavioral intent, but also directly with actual usage. While the relationship of experience with ease of use perceptions seems logical and intuitive, the link to actual usage suggests that enhanced education and hands-on exposure to Internet tools can potentially increase an individual's usage of the Internet. This corroborates Holland and Baker (2001), whose model suggests that creating site loyalty leads repeat visits and more positive attitudes toward the site. This also validates the prior research on experience and its impact on TAM variables (Legris et al., 2002).

Figure 7. Summary of support for hypotheses

Hypothesis	Variable 1 (independent)	Variable 2 (dependent)	Correlational Analysis	Significance	Support (sig <=0.01)	Regression Analysis	Significance	Support (sig <=0.01)
1a	Perceived ease of use	Perceived usefulness	r = -0.523	p = 0.000	yes	β = 0.403	p = 0.000	yes
1b	Perceived ease of use	Attitude toward using	r = 0.522	p = 0.000	yes	β = 0.281	p = 0.000	yes
2a	Perceived usefulness	Attitude toward using	r = 0.467	p = 0.000	yes	β = 0.238	p = 0.000	yes
2b	Perceived usefulness	Behavioral intention to use	r = 0.566	p = 0.000	yes	β = 0.412	p = 0.000	yes
2c	Perceived usefulness	Actual usage	r = 0.276	p = 0.000	yes	β = -0.040	p = 0.898	no
3	Attitude toward using	Behavioral intention to use	r = 0.497	p = 0.000	yes	β = 0.262	p = 0.000	yes
4	Behavioral intention to use	Actual usage	r = 0.463	p = 0.000	yes	β = 0.357	p = 0.000	yes
5a	Gender	Perceived ease of use	r = -0.282	p = 0.000	yes	β = -0.241	p = 0.007	yes
5b	Gender	Perceived usefulness	r = -0.112	p = 0.131	no	β = 0.049	p = 0.546	no
5c	Gender	Actual usage	r = -0.227	p = 0.002	yes	β = -0.223	p = 0.024	no
6a	Experience using the Internet	Perceived usefulness	r = 0.132	p = 0.068	no	β = -0.069	p = 0.200	no
6b	Experience using the Internet	Behavioral intention to use	r = 0.389	p = 0.000	yes	β = 0.204	p = 0.000	yes
7a	Perceived complexity of using	Perceived usefulness	r = -0.368	p = 0.000	yes	β = -0.148	p = 0.007	yes
7b	Perceived complexity of using	Actual usage	r = -0.289	p = 0.000	yes	β = -0.232	p = 0.000	yes
8	Voluntariness of using	Behavioral intention to use	r = -0.101	p = 0.166	no	β = -0.026	p = 0.430	no

Voluntariness is not significantly related to behavioral intent as was originally proposed in H8. While the theory tends to show strong support for voluntariness and its moderating effect on intention to use by Venkatesh and Davis (2000), we only a significant relationship to actual usage. This could account for the indirect effect on intention to use that Venkatesh and Davis reported. We also discovered by examining the qualitative data that Internet users in the study did not possess a clear understanding of mandatory use of the Internet, rather more of a perception, as suggested by Moore and Benbasat (1991). Some of the respondents said that mandatory use of the Internet was not "explicitly" stated; however the fact that Internet research, for example, was conducted more efficiently on the Internet created an implied mandatory usage that, in turn, impacted actual usage.

Although previous studies reported gender differences impact the assimilation of technologies (Gefen & Straub, 1997; Venkatesh & Morris, 2000), we did not find significant statistical relationships with either perceived usefulness or actual usage. This finding is similar to what Stafford et al. (2004) discovered in their study of men's and women's involvement in online shopping across the United States, Finland, and Turkey. We can report, and did expect, a strong relationship to exist between gender and perceived ease of use, confirming prior research. We ran another model where all of the variables were added in order to assess changes in the amount of variance explained and to potentially uncover relationships that may have missed. We created a multiple linear regression model for actual usage with all of the coefficients entering the model. We found a substantial increase in the amount of variance explained ($R^2 = 0.413$). However, only attitude toward using (p =.000), behavioral intention (p = .000), and experience (p = .000) emerged as significant coefficients. It is interesting to note that these coefficients are different than the earlier model and that two of these variables had not

been theoretically hypothesized. Voluntariness (p = .028) and perceived complexity (p = .045) were also significant at the $p < 0.05$. Continuing to search for the best linear regression model, we produced a set of regression models and generated a final model to predict actual usage. The coefficients statistically significant at $p < 0.05$ include attitude toward using (p = .000), experience (p = .000), and voluntariness (p = .048). Using this final model, we have generated two additional relationships, between experience and actual usage and between attitude toward using and actual usage.

CONCLUSION

Many individual and environmental factors exist that can determine a consumer's emotional and cognitive responses to using the Internet. We did not consider physical stimuli variables such as colors and personality traits in this research data (Koufaris, 2002). In fact, we did not include individual differences in the acceptance of Internet-based technologies, investigated by several studies examining the implications of users in specific Web site applications (Gefen, 2003; Van der Heijden, 2000). This study examined the technology users' perceptions of Internet-based technologies to help them accomplish activities and tasks, rather than rating an individual Web site or measuring individuals' perceptions of a specific Web site.

We administered the survey instrument in both paper and electronic formats (Excel via e-mail) to respondents in this study. Unfortunately, we did not prepare the Web survey in a browser-based technology, which may be more relevant to the sample under study. In the future, we might want to analyze the bias toward "older-generation" assessment instruments versus Web-enabled surveys.

This study investigated experienced consumers who were working on undergraduate or MBA degrees at a major university in the United States. To the extent that these consumers are typical of online consumers, the results will hold Across more general populations (Gefen, 2002). Gefen et al. (2003) found that, although Remus used business students as good surrogates for managers, students were good subjects for studying Internet-based shopping behaviors and that their status as "student" did not impact the validity of their study.

One of the variables missing from the research framework in this study includes planned purchases of first-time online consumers. Rather than study a consumer's propensity to either visit or return to a specific Web site for purposes of shopping, we focused on the acceptance of consumers to use the Internet generally for a variety of purposes, including shopping. However, Koufaris (2002) stated the importance of capturing data on consumers' planned purchases to shop comparing both their purchase pattern as first-time consumers and returning customers. Another variable that might be influential in adopting a wide variety of technologies is the trust construct. Gefen et al. (2003) suggests that there might be different conceptualizations of trust and those may be useful in defining the model of acceptance for Internet-based technologies. The applicability of the TAM to specific technologies is an important consideration as a potential limitation to this study. While we tried to specifically capture the variables that might impact actual usage of Internet-based technologies, we realize that the behavior of users toward different technologies may ultimately create models that have different nomological structures.

Research Contribution

An important contribution of our study includes the testing and validation of metrics for understanding consumer behavior on the Internet. In addition to high scale reliability, the main constructs of the technology acceptance model also demonstrated high nomological validity, demonstrating behavior as expected in past studies. Therefore, we believe

that future research measuring the acceptance of Internet technology by consumers can use these metrics with some assertion. Related is the creation of an overall instrument to measure the various perceptions in the adoption of Internet-based technologies. The creation process included surveying known existing instruments, choosing appropriate items, revising items as necessary, and then undertaking an extensive scale development process. It is believed that the method of developing the scales will result in a high degree of confidence in their content and construct validity for measuring the acceptance of Internet technology by consumers. This instrument, comprising all of the original TAM constructs (including attitude toward using) and additional external variables, antecedents, and moderators related to the technology in study can now be used to investigate how consumers adopt and accept Internet-based applications.

In recommending this instrument to researchers investigating the acceptance of Internet-based technologies, we caution that its use is tailored for Web-enabled applications. Therefore the wording of the scales reflects our specificity toward this type of technology. As the business world continues to change, it is necessary for companies to adapt to the new environment. With more and more businesses going online, e-business is an appropriate area to focus the attention. For centuries, businesses have attempted to sell their products or services by providing what the customers want or need. Businesses still do this today, but their efforts have moved online. By examining TAM and supported results, we can better understand how to meet the needs of the e-business customer.

Implications

It is believed that results from this study also provide managers with a framework for which areas they need to focus when launching new online products, such as shaping and/or changing their consumers' attitude toward using the Internet, making their Web site easier to use, and enhancing the perceived usefulness of the technologies that enable consumers to get at their products online. The framework we tested and refined in this paper also serves as an important first step toward subsequent predictive modeling with critical marketing variables.

FUTURE RESEARCH

Future research includes validation of an expanded model for mobile technologies by testing the model relationships with organizational samples. While many of the studies we investigated had small sample sizes, in future research we plan to test and validate the model using the instrument in this research with organizations that are developing Internet-based solutions for their customers. Future research also includes testing this modified model with the instrument created to ascertain how consumers can more effectively assimilate Web-base technologies in a global setting. We feel that this research could enhance an organization's ability to determine how well its consumer base will accept their Internet initiatives. Additional variables could be considered in future research to enhance the overall predictability usefulness in Internet-based situations, such as performance expectancy and effort expectancy. These variables could provide further explanatory power of the TAM to better understand how online consumers use Internet technology to facilitate a number of activities.

REFERENCES

Agarwal, R., & Karahanna, E. (2000). Time flies when you are having fun: Cognitive absorption and beliefs about Information Technology usage. *Management Information Systems Quarterly, 24*(4), 665–694. .doi:10.2307/3250951

Agarwal, R., & Prasad, J. (1999). Are individual differences germane to the acceptance of new Information Technologies? *Decision Sciences, 30*(2), 361–391. doi:10.1111/j.1540-5915.1999.tb01614.x

Ajzen, I., & Fishbein, M. (1980). *Understanding attitudes and predicting social behavior*. Englewood Cliffs, NJ: Prentice-Hall.

Alba, J. W., Lynch, J., Weitz, B., Janiszewski, C., Lutz, R., & Sawyer, A. (1997). Interactive home shopping: Consumer, retailer, and manufacturer incentives to participate in electronic marketplaces. *Journal of Marketing, 61*(3), 38–53. doi:10.2307/1251788

Amoroso, D. (2002). Successful penetration into the e-business environment: An empirical study. In *Proceedings of the 36th Annual Hawaii International Conference on System Sciences,* Kona-Kailua, HI (vol. 8, pp. 257). Washington, DC: IEEE Computer Society.

Amoroso, D., & Gardner, C. (2003, January). Development of an instrument to measure the acceptance of Internet technology by consumers. In *Proceedings of the 37th Annual Hawaii International Conference on System Sciences,* Big Island, HI (vol. 8, pp.80260c). Washington, DC: IEEE Computer Society.

Anderson, R., & Srinivasan, S. S. (2003). E-satisfaction and e-loyalty: A contingency framework. *Psychology and Marketing, 20*(2), 123–138. doi:10.1002/mar.10063

Athiyaman, A. (2002). Internet users' intention of purchase air travel online: An empirical investigation. *Marketing Intelligence & Planning, 20*(3-4), 234–243.doi:10.1108/02634500210431630

Bauer, H. H., Grether, M., & Leach, M. (2002). Building customer relations over the Internet. *Industrial Marketing Management, 31*, 155–163. doi:10.1016/ S0019-8501(01)00186-9

Berthon, P., Pitt, L., & Watson, R. (1996). The World Wide Web as an advertising medium: Toward an understanding of conversion efficiency. *Journal of Advertising Research, 36*(1), 43–54.

Bhatnagar, A., Misra, S., & Rao, H. R. (2000). On risk, convenience, and Internet shopping behavior. *Communications of the ACM, 43*(11), 98–105. doi:10.1145/353360.353371

Burke, R. R. (2002). Technology and the customer interface: What consumers want in the physical and virtual store. *Academy of Marketing Science, 30*(4), 411–432.doi:10.1177/009207002236914

Carey, J. M., & Day, D. (2005). *Cultural aspects for technology acceptance: Asian perspectives and research techniques.* Paper presented at the Americas Conference on Information Systems, Omaha, NE.

Cenfetelli, R. T. (2004). *An empirical study of the inhibitors of technology usage.* Paper presented at the International Conference on Information Systems, Washington, DC.

Chakraborty, I., Hu, P. J.-H., & Cui, D. (2005). *Examining effects of cognitive style on technology acceptance decisions.* Paper presented at the Pacific Asia Conference on Information Systems, Bangkok, Thailand.

Chau, P. (1996). An empirical assessment of a modified technology acceptance model. *Journal of Management Information Systems, 13*, 185–204.

Chau, P., & Hu, P. (2001). Information Technology acceptance by individual professionals: A model of comparison approach. *Decision Sciences, 32*(4), 699–719. doi:10.1111/j.1540-5915.2001.tb00978.x

Chin, W., & Todd, P. (1995). On the use, usefulness, and ease of use of structural equation modeling in MIS research: A note of caution. *Management Information Systems Quarterly, 19*(2), 237–246. doi:10.2307/249690

Compeau, D., Higgins, C., & Huff, S. (1999). Social cognitive theory and individual reactions to computing technology: A longitudinal study. *Management Information Systems Quarterly, 23*(2), 145–158. doi:10.2307/249749

Cooper, R., & Zmud, R. (1990). Information Technology implementation research: A technological diffusion approach. *Management Science, 36*(2), 123–139. doi:10.1287/mnsc.36.2.123

Dasgupta, S., Granger, M., & McGarry, N. (2002). User acceptance of e-collaboration technology: An extension of the technology acceptance model. *Group Decision and Negotiation, 11*, 87–100. doi:10.1023/A:1015221710638

Davis, F. (1986). *A technology acceptance model for empirically testing new end-user information systems: theory and results.* Unpublished doctoral dissertation, Massachusetts Institute of Technology.

Davis, F., Bagozzi, R., & Warshaw, P. (1989). User acceptance of computer technology: A comparison of two theoretical models. *Management Science, 35*, 982–1003. doi:10.1287/mnsc.35.8.982

Deng, Z., Lu, Y., & Chen, Z. (2010). Exploring Chinese user adoption of mobile banking. *International Journal of Information Technology and Management, 9*(3), 289–301. doi:10.1504/IJITM.2010.030945

Dennis, C., Harris, L., & Sandhu, B. (2002). From bricks to clicks: Understanding the e-consumer. *Qualitative Market Research, 5*(4), 281–290. doi:10.1108/13522750210443236

Dishaw, M. T., Strong, D. M., & Bandy, D. B. (2004). *The impact of task-technology fit in technology acceptance and utilization models.* Paper presented at the Americas Conference on Information Systems, New York.

Dutt, A., & Srite, M. (2005). *A cultural perspective on technology acceptance*. Paper presented at the Americas Conference on Information Systems, Omaha, NE.

Featherman, M. S. (2001). *Extending the technology acceptance model by inclusion of perceived risk*. Paper presented at the Americas Conference on Information Systems, Waltham, MA.

Gammack, J., & Hodkinson, C. (2003). Virtual reality, involvement and the consumer interface. *Journal of End User Computing, 15*(4), 78–96. doi:10.4018/joeuc.2003100105

Gefen, D. (2002). Customer loyalty in e-commerce. *Journal of the Association for Information Systems, 3*, 27–51.

Gefen, D. (2003). TAM or just plain habit: A look at experienced online shoppers. *Journal of End User Computing, 15*(3), 1–13. doi:10.4018/joeuc.2003070101

Gefen, D., Karahanna, E., & Straub, D. (2003). Trust and TAM in online shopping: An integrated model. *Management Information Systems Quarterly, 27*(1), 51–90.

Gefen, D., & Straub, D. (1997). Gender differences in the perception and use of e-mail: An extension to the technology acceptance model. *Management Information Systems Quarterly, 21*(4), 389–400. doi:10.2307/249720

Girard, T., Korgaonkar, P., & Silverblatt, R. (2003). Relationship of type of product, shopping orientations, and demographics with preference for shopping on the Internet. *Journal of Business and Psychology, 18*(1), 101–119. doi:10.1023/A:1025087021768

Goodhue, D. L., & Thompson, R. L. (1995). Task-technology fit and individual performance. *Management Information Systems Quarterly, 19*(2), 213–236. doi:10.2307/249689

Gribbins, M. L., Shaw, M. J., & Gebauer, J. (2003). *An investigation into employees' acceptance of integrating mobile commerce into organizational processes*. Paper presented at the Americas Conference on Information Systems, Tampa, FL.

Hampton-Sosa, W., & Koufaris, M. (2005). The effect of Web site perceptions on initial trust in the owner company. *International Journal of Electronic Commerce, 10*(1), 55–81.

Heijden, H., Verhagen, T., & Creemers, M. (2001, January). Predicting online purchase behavior: Replications and tests of competing models. In *Proceedings of the 34ᵗʰ Hawaii International Conference on Systems Sciences,* Maui, Hawaii (vol. 7, pp.7068). Washington, DC: IEEE Computer Society.

Holland, J., & Baker, S. M. (2001). Customer participation in creating site brand loyalty. *Journal of Interactive Marketing, 15*(4), 34–45. doi:10.1002/ dir.1021

Hwang, Y. (2005). *An empirical study of online trust and consumer behavior: Cultural orientation, social norms, and personal innovativeness in Information Technology*. Paper presented at the International Conference on Information Systems, Las Vegas, NV.

Igbaria, M., Guimaraes, T., & Davis, G. (1995). Testing the determinants of microcomputer usage via a structural equation model. *Journal of Management Information Systems, 11*(2), 87–114.

Igbaria, M., Parasuraman, S., & Baroudi, J. (1996). A motivational model of microcomputer usage. *Journal of Management Information Systems, 13*(2), 127–143.

Igbaria, M., Zinatelli, N., Cragg, P., & Cavaye, A. (1997). Personal computing acceptance factors in small firms: A structural equation model. *Management Information Systems Quarterly, 21*(3), 279–305. doi:10.2307/249498

Javenpaa, S., & Todd, P. (1997). Consumer reactions to electronic shopping on the World Wide Web. *International Journal of Electronic Commerce, 1*(2), 59–88.

Kau, A. K., Tang, Y. E., & Ghose, S. (2003). Typology of online shoppers. *Journal of Consumer Marketing, 20*(2), 139–156. doi:10.1108/07363760310464604

Kim, E., Nam, D.-I., & Stimpert, J. L. (2004). Testing the applicability of Porter's generic strategies in the digital age: A study of Korean cyber malls. *The Journal of Business Strategy, 21*(1), 19–45.

Kim, H., Chan, H., & Gupta, S. (2007). Value-based adoption of mobile Internet: An empirical investigation. *Decision Support Systems, 43*(1), 111–126. doi:10.1016/j.dss.2005.05.009

Kim, H. W., & Xu, Y. (2004). *Internet shopping: Is it a matter of perceived price or trust?* Paper presented at the International Conference on Information Systems, Washington, DC.

Koufaris, M. (2002). Applying the technology acceptance model and flow theory to online consumer behavior. *Information Systems Research, 13*(2), 205–223. doi:10.1287/isre.13.2.205.83

Krishnamurthy, S. (2002). An empirical study of the causal antecedents of customer confidence in e-tailers. *First Monday, 6*(1), 1–13.

Kuo, Y. F., Wu, C. M., & Deng, W. J. (2009). The relationships among service quality, perceived value, customer satisfaction, and post- purchase intention in mobile value- added services. *Computers in Human Behavior*, 887–896. doi:10.1016/j.chb.2009.03.003

Legris, P., Ingham, J., & Collerette, P. (2002). Why do people use Information Technology? A critical review of the technology acceptance model. *Information & Management, 40*, 191–204. doi:10.1016/ S0378-7206(01)00143-4

Liaw, S. S., & Huang, H.-M. (2003). An investigation of user attitudes toward search engines as an information retrieval tool. *Computers in Human Behavior, 19*(6), 751–766. doi:10.1016/ S0747-5632(03)00009-8

Lohse, G., & Spiller, P. (1998). Electronic shopping. *Communications of the ACM, 41*(7), 81–86. doi:10.1145/278476.278491

Long, K. (2004). Customer loyalty and experience design. *Design Management Review, 15*(2), 60–67. doi:10.1111/j.1948-7169.2004.tb00163.x

Luo, X., Li, H., Zhang, J., & Shim, J. P. (2010). Examining multi-dimensional trust and multi-faceted risk in initial acceptance of emerging technologies: An empirical study of mobile banking services. *Decision Support Systems*, 222–234. doi:10.1016/j.dss.2010.02.008

Ma, Q., & Liu, L. (2003). *The role of internet self-efficacy in accepting Web-based medical records.* Paper presented at the Americas Conference on Information Systems, Tampa, FL.

Mahinda, E., & Whitworth, B. (2005). *The Web of system performance: Extending the TAM model.* Paper presented at the Americas Conference on Information Systems, Omaha, NE.

Mathieson, K. (1991). Predicting user intentions: Comparing the technology acceptance model with the theory of planned behavior. *Information Systems Research, 2*(3), 173–191.doi:10.1287/ isre.2.3.173

Mathwick, C. (2002). Understanding the online consumer: A typology of online relational norms and behavior. *Journal of Interactive Marketing, 16*(1), 40–55. doi:10.1002/dir.10003

Methlie, L. B., & Nysveen, H. (1999). Loyalty of online bank customers. *Journal of Information Technology, 14*, 375–386. doi:10.1080/026839699344485

Miyazaki, A. D., & Fernadez, A. (2001). Consumer perceptions of privacy and security risks for online shopping. *The Journal of Consumer Affairs, 35*(1), 27–44. doi:10.1111/j.1745-6606.2001.tb00101.x

Moore, G., & Benbasat, I. (1991). Development of an instrument to measure the perceptions of adopting new Information Technology innovation. *Information Systems Research, 2*(3), 192–222. doi:10.1287/ isre.2.3.192

Morrisette, S., McQuivey, J., Maraganore, N., & Lampher, G. (1999). *Are net shoppers loyal?* Boston, MA: Forrester.

Muthitacharoen, A., & Palvia, P. C. (2003). *Explaining alternative behaviors of online consumers: An integration of the technology acceptance model to preferential decision*. Paper presented at the Americas Conference on Information Systems, Tampa, FL.

Noor, N. L. M., Hashim, M., Haron, H., & Sriffin, S. (2005). *Community acceptance of knowledge sharing system in the travel and tourism Web sites: An application of an extension of TAM*. Paper presented at the European Conference on Information Systems, Regensburg, Germany.

Novak, T., Hoffman, D., & Yung, Y. (2000). Measuring the customer experience in online environments: A structural modeling approach. *Marketing Science, 19*(1), 22–42. doi:10.1287/ mksc.19.1.22.15184

Park, C.-H., & Kim, Y.-G. (2003). Identifying key factors affecting consumer purchase behavior in an online shopping context. *International Journal of Retail & Distribution Management, 31*(1), 16–29. doi:10.1108/09590550310457818

Parsons, A. G. (2002). Non-functional motives for online shoppers: Why we click. *Journal of Consumer Marketing, 19*(4-5), 380–392. doi:10.1108/07363760210437614

Pavlou, P. A., Lie, T., & Dimoka, A. (2007). An integrative model of mobile commerce adoption. *JMR, Journal of Marketing Research*, 1–18.

Peterson, R., Balasubramanian, S., & Bronnenberg, B. (1997). Exploring the implications of the Internet for consumer marketing. *Academy of Marketing Sciences Journal, 25*(4), 329–346. doi:10.1177/0092070397254005

Pikkarainen, T., Pikkarainen, K., Karjaluoto, H., & Pahnila, S. (2004). Consumer acceptance of online banking: An extension of the technology acceptance model. *Internet Research, 14*(3), 224–235. doi:10.1108/10662240410542652

Pitt, L., Berthon, P., & Watson, R. (1996). From surfer to buyer on the WWW: What marketing managers might want to know. *Journal of General Management, 22*(1), 1–13.

Reichheld, F. F., & Schefter, P. (2000). E-loyalty: Your secret weapon on the Web. *Harvard Business Review*, 105–113.

Rigopoulos, G., & Askounis, D. (2007). A TAM framework to evaluate users' perception towards online electronic payments. *Journal of Internet Banking and Commerce, 12*(3).

Sánchez-Franco, M. J., & Roldán, J. L. (2005). Web acceptance and usage model: A comparison between goal-directed and experiential Web users. *Internet Research, 15*(1), 21–48. doi:10.1108/10662240510577059

Speier, C., & Poston, R. (2001). *Web site acceptance: The effects of task type*. Paper presented at the Americas Conference on Information Systems, Waltham, MA.

Stafford, T. F., Turan, A., & Raisinghani, M. S. (2004). International and cross-cultural influences on online shopping behavior. *Journal of Global Information Technology Management, 7*(2), 70–87.

Straub, D., Limayem, M., & Karahanna-Evaristo, E. (1995). Measuring system usage: Implications for IS theory testing. *Management Science, 41*(8), 1328–1342. doi:10.1287/mnsc.41.8.1328

Sun, H. (2003). *An integrative analysis of TAM: Toward a deeper understanding of technology acceptance model*. Paper presented at AMCIS '03, Tampa, FL.

Sun, H., & Zhang, P. (2003). *A new perspective to analyze user technology acceptance.* (Working paper).

Szajna, B. (1994). Software evaluation and choice: Predictive validation of the technology acceptance instrument. *Management Information Systems Quarterly, 18*(3), 319–324. doi:10.2307/249621

Taylor, S., & Todd, P. (1995a). Assessing IT usage: The role of prior experience. *Management Information Systems Quarterly, 19*(2), 561–570. doi:10.2307/249633

Taylor, S., & Todd, P. (1995b). Understanding Information Technology usage: A test of competing models. *Information Systems Research, 6*(4), 144–176. doi:10.1287/isre.6.2.144

Thorbjornsen, H., & Supphellen, M. (2004). The impact of brand loyalty on Web site usage. *The Journal of Brand Management, 11*(3), 199–209. doi:10.1057/palgrave.bm.2540166

Torkzadeh, G., & Dhillon, G. (2002). Measuring factors that influence the success of Internet commerce. *Information Systems Research, 13*(2), 187–204. doi:10.1287/isre.13.2.187.87

Van der Heijden, H. (2000). *Using the technology acceptance model to predict Web site usage: Extensions and empirical test.* Series Research Memoranda.

Van der Heijden, H. (2003). Factors influencing the usage of Web sites: The case of the generic portal in the Netherlands. *Information & Management, 40,* 541–549. doi:10.1016/S0378-7206(02)00079-4

Van der Heijden, H. (2004). User acceptance of hedonic Information Systems. *Management Information Systems Quarterly, 28*(4), 695–704.

Van der Heijden, H., Verhagen, T., & Creemers, M. (2003). Understanding online purchase intentions: Contributions from technology and trust perspectives. *European Journal of Information Systems, 12,* 41–48. .doi:10.1057/palgrave.ejis.3000445

Venkatesh, V., & Davis, F. (2000). A theoretical extension of the technology acceptance model: Four longitudinal field studies. *Management Science, 46*(2), 186–204. doi:10.1287/mnsc.46.2.186.11926

Venkatesh, V., & Morris, M. (2000). Why don't men ever stop to ask for directions? Gender, social influence, and their role in technology acceptance and usage behavior. *Management Information Systems Quarterly, 24*(1), 115–139. doi:10.2307/3250981

Venkatesh, V., Morris, M., Davis, G., & Davis, F. (2003). User acceptance of Information Technology: Toward a unified view. *Management Information Systems Quarterly, 27*(3), 425–478.

Vijayasarathy, L. R. (2003). Shopping orientations, product types and Internet shopping intentions. *Electronic Markets, 13*(1), 67–79. doi:10.1080/1019678032000039903

Wang, W., & Benbasat, I. (2004). *Trust and TAM for online recommendation agents*. Paper presented at the Americas Conference on Information Systems, New York.

Wilson, E. V., Mao, E., & Lankton, N. K. (2005). *Predicting continuing acceptance of IT in conditions of sporadic use*. Paper presented at the Americas Conference on Information Systems, Omaha, NE.

Wolfinbarger, M., & Gilly, M. C. (2001). Shopping online for freedom, control, and fun. *California Management Review, 43*(2), 34–55.

Wu, J.-H., & Wang, S.-C. (2005). What drives mobile commerce? An empirical evaluation of the revised technology acceptance model. *Information & Management, 42*(5), 719–729. doi:10.1016/j.im.2004.07.001

Wu, S.-L. (2003). The relationship between consumer characteristics and attitude toward online shopping. *Marketing Intelligence & Planning, 21*(1), 37–44. doi:10.1108/02634500310458135

Xia, L., & Sudharshan, D. (2000). *An examination of the effects of cognitive interruptions on consumer online decision processes*. Paper presented at the 2nd Marketing Science Internet Conference, Los Angeles.

Yoon, S. J. (2002). The antecedents and consequences of trust in online-purchase decisions. *Journal of Interactive Marketing, 16*(2), 47–63. doi:10.1002/ dir.10008

Yu, J. L. C.-S., Liu, C., & Yao, J. E. (2003). Technology acceptance model for wireless internet. *Internet Research, 13*(3), 206–233. doi:10.1108/10662240310478222

Chapter 11
Cultural Accommodation in Consumer E-Commerce:
A Theoretical Exploration in the Context of Ethnic Culture

Rui Chen
Ball State University, USA

Sushil K. Sharma
Ball State University, USA

ABSTRACT

Consumer e-commerce extends the marketplace of traditional business and brings in business opportunities in online retailing and service. As a consequence of intensive competition among online vendors, the need to capture customers has become a top priority. Thanks to the wide penetration of Internet, the online consumer group now consists of individuals with diverse cultural values and backgrounds. In the context of ethnic culture, we explore the ways a Web site may attract and accommodate ethnic consumers. Drawing upon existing literature in culture and Web Information System success, we develop a Web-based intercultural accommodation model. This model offers a theoretical explanation of online ethnic consumers' behavioral intention to use e-commerce Web site. The conceptual model recognizes the potential roles of ethnicity attributes of individual consumers as well as the use of ethnic pertaining Web site designs in accommodating ethnic consumers. Future study that validates the theoretical model is discussed as well.

DOI: 10.4018/978-1-60960-597-1.ch011

INTRODUCTION

The growth of the World Wide Web and its user groups has paved a way to the rise of Web-based consumer e-commerce (Gupta & Sharma, 2003). Such web-based information system represents a new frontier for business to establish an online presence by launching virtual stores, which exist in the cyberspace offering merchandise and services. Due to the low setup cost, transaction cost, maintenance cost, and increasing business opportunities (24/7), the prevalence of the e-commerce Web sites on retailing and services has been stimulated. US online retailing, for example, grew 11% in 2009 to reach $155 billion and the revenue has been expected to reach $248 billion by 2014 (Mulpuru, Hult, Evans, Sehgal, & McGowan, 2010). The Web creates business opportunities for companies ranging from small start-ups to Fortune 100 giants. This prosperity in consumer e-commerce Web sites, however, introduces enormous competition into the online market. Meanwhile, the higher availabilities of broadband Internet access and personal computers have granted online users with capabilities and convenient access to online shopping. Customers have grown to be powerful, demanding, and utilitarian in their online shopping (Koufaris & Hampton-Sosa, 2004) which shifts the locus of power from vendors to customers (Raman, 1997). As more and more business opportunities have been brought to the Internet, how to fully utilize Web site to attract customers has become a major issue. Not only does this capture immediate business opportunities (Longwell, 1999), it also casts great impact on customers' return purchases in the future and the buildup of their loyalty, which is poor in consumer e-commerce nowadays (Morrisette, McQuivey, Maraganore, & Lanpher, 1999).

The consumer group has grown culturally diverse (Sudweeks & Simoff, 2001). Take national culture for example, online consumers from Africa, Asia, Europe, Middle East, North America, Latin America, and Ocean/Australia represent 5.6%,

42%, 24.2%, 3.2%, 13.5%, 10.4%, and 1.1%. This diversity is further complicated by the different values that consumers keep with respect to religious culture, political culture, and ethnic culture systems. When culture groups interact, acculturation takes place which leads to the acquisition and adoption of new culture values. With this observation, online firms have begun to recognize consumer cultural difference for its strategic impact on sales and customer retention. Failure to recognize and respect cultural differences may, on the other hand, lead to struggled e-commerce business. The e-commerce's modest success in China was attributed to the fact that the prototypical Amazon experience lacked one or more ingredients important for China's online shoppers (Wolf, 2010). While cultural implications have been explored in prior literatures (Krishna, 2004; Moffett, Mcadam, & Parkinson, 2002; Quaddus & Tung, 2002), it has not been understudied in the context of e-commerce. It remains largely unknown how online vendors may attract users through an accommodation of their cultural values for business advantage.

In this article we investigate e-commerce Web site design and management through cultural perspective. To explore this topic, we focus on ethnic culture since it is one of the most prominent culture values (Ayouby & Croteau, 2008). Drawing upon the relevant literature in linguistic, sociology, and web information system success, we uncover the theoretical underpinning of ethnicity involving consumer e-commerce phenomena. The paper presents the Web-based Intercultural Accommodation Model, a conceptual framework that explains the relationships among individual ethnic attribute, intercultural accommodation reaction, and e-commerce consequence. We propose that the extent of ethnic designs on a Web site may positively affect an online user's attribution affects. This relationship however is contingent upon the strength of consumer ethnic identification. The attribution affects may further increase the personal attitude to Web site as well as the perception on Web site information quality, which jointly influence the individual's intention to use the e-commerce Web site. This model is subject to empirical validation. The rest of the paper is organized as follows. The first section presents a literature review of the key research issues, followed by the research model and propositions. We then lay out the proposed research method and discuss the paper's limitations. Finally, we conclude the paper with a discussion and future research.

LITERATURE REVIEW

A few streams of literature yield key insights regarding the cultural implications in consumer e-commerce. In this section, we present an overview of these literatures and discuss how they contribute to the theoretical development of our research model.

Cultural Theory

Culture theories have underlined the importance of culture value in social systems (Harris, 1994; Robey & Azevedo, 1994).In general culture value refers the customs and beliefs of a group of people who share the same identification (Oetting, 1993). Culture value is cultivated and shaped by ethnic, religious, politics, and social traditions (Leidner & Kayworth, 2006). Prior studies have examined national culture (Hofstede, 1993; Trompenaars, 1996), organizational culture (Robey & Azevedo, 1994; Robey & Boudreau, 1999), and ethnic/racial culture (Ainsworth-Darnell & Downey, 1998; Nagel, 1994). Culture is important to IS research. Walsh and Kefi suggested that the issue "'*lack of IS/culture fit' has generated a wide range of studies trying to understand cultural influences on IT adoption and usage*" (Walsh & Kefi, 2008). Leidner and Kayworth found that culture aspects have an impact on information system development, adoption and diffusion,

use and use outcomes, and management strategies (Leidner & Kayworth, 2006). The existing literature has also suggested that similar cultural values between business partners may facilitate their interactions while discrepancies in cultural values between the transacting partners may hinder the process of inter-firm collaboration. In the context of supply chain management systems, Hult et al. (Hult, Ketchen, & Nichols, 2002) found that similar cultural values among members contribute to greater levels of supply chain system success. Using structuration analysis, Walsham (Walsham, 2002) also found that transacting parties with cultural value discrepancies experienced conflicts and contradictions during the course of business engagements.

Few studies have explored cultural implications in e-commerce context. Cyr et al studied the perception of human images on e-commerce Web site and explored the perception differences across Canada, Germany, and Japan national cultures (Cyr, Head, Larios, & Pan, 2009). Zaoui examined the trust perception of e-commerce vendors and technologies between Tunisians and French cultures (Zaoui, 2008). Zaoui found that only technological trust has an effect on French citizens' intentions to buy online whereas, technological trust, vendor trust and previous online purchase influence Tunisians' intention to buy online. Sia et al found that the impact of customer endorsements on e-commerce Web site trust perceptions was stronger for individuals in Hong Kong than Australia and that portal affiliation was effective only in the Australian sites (Sia et al., 2009). Sudweeks and Simoff suggested that "*To have cultural appeal, an e-commerce site must localise the content for each culture*" (Sudweeks & Simoff, 2001). Consequently this will reflect in the different, culturally adapted website design. When e-commerce Web site designs are not aligned with cultural values of their intended customers, however, the site may fail to capture business opportunities. To improve our understanding of culture and to involve them into e-commerce, new research endeavor is very much warranted.

Ethnic Culture

Ethnic culture is a prominent culture value and we focus on ethnic culture in the current study. Conzen et al. recognized ethnic culture as a dynamic process of "construction or invention which incorporates, adapts, and amplifies preexisting communal solidarities, cultural attributes, and historical memories" (Conzen, Gerber, Morawska, Pazzetta, & Vecoli, 1992). Due to the demographic shift and changes of immigrant policy, the minority groups in the United States have kept growing. Data from the U.S. Census Bureau shows that, between 1990 and 2000, the minority population (e.g., Hispanics, African Americans, and Asian Americans) grew by approximately 34% while the white population grew by 5.9% (Cotton, 2002). The current U.S. population is over 289 million, over 30% of which is made up of minority ethnic groups. The growing influence of the minority population is also reflected in their buying power. Between 1990 and 2000, the household income growth for African, Hispanic, and Asian American households was 32.5%, 24.3%, and 23.1%, respectively. The speed of growth surpasses that for white households at 14.2%. Consequently, it is important that online product and service venders attend to the minority groups and adopt successfully strategies to attract them as customers. In the context of e-commerce, companies rely heavily on the Web site designs to accomplish this goal. Therefore, it is of a high priority for researchers and practitioners to study the Web site design options that may attract more ethnic consumers.

In the United States, business research of ethnic groups has experienced three major stages (Holland & Gentry, 1997). Prior to the 1960s, ethnic groups were largely ignored due to their lack of influences. Between mid-1960s and 1980, more studies were conducted and they were centered on African Americans. The differences between the black and white consumers were examined with respect to their consumption patterns, media habits, and reactions to advertising (Sturdivant, 1973). Since the 1980s to present, research has extended to all the ethnic groups such as Hispanic and Asian Americans. The existing studies suggest that new immigrants as well as the generations of earlier immigrants are in active pursuit of their ethnic values which are embodied by cultural symbols and traditions (Holland & Gentry, 1999). When information systems are concerned, little is known about how we may attract the ethnic groups through information technology such as Web site. Cole and O'Keefe conceptualized the dynamics of globalization and investigated the role of ethnicity in e-commerce (Cole & O'Keefe, 2000). Chau, Cole, Massey, Montoya-Weiss, and O'Keefe explored how the variety of ethnic groups perceive and use the Web site in e-commerce (Chau, Cole, Massey, Monyota-Weiss, & O'Keefe, 2002).

Speech Accommodation Theory

Giles et al developed the Speech Accommodation Theory (SAT) (Giles, Coupland, & Coupland, 1991). SAT is grounded on similarity-attractiveness research (Byme, 1961; Simons, Berkowitz, & Moyer, 1970) to investigate socio-linguistic domains in verbal and non-verbal behaviors. In its essence, SAT suggests that the similarity between two persons, either in speech rate (Webb, 1970) or length of utterance (Giles, 1973), may cultivate favorable evaluations one will hold towards the other. That is, an individual in a conversation may adjust his/her speech patterns to resemble the other party, with an attempt to seek approval or improved communication. On the contrary, a pattern of divergence may arise when communicator employs communication schemes that are sharply differ. In the context of intercultural communication, therefore, companies may accommodate their targeted audience by adapting messages to the receivers' culture. Specifically, companies may modify speech or language styles and utilize cultural symbols so as to become similar to and gain the approval of their audience. When e-commerce is considered, Web sites typically utilize text, graphics, and animation as preferred media in communication with their targeted consumers. Following the tenets of SAT, e-commerce Web site may strategically adopt communication designs and seek resemblance with the value systems of the ethnic groups.

Holland and Gentry extended SAT to propose the Intercultural Accommodation Model (IAM) (Holland & Gentry, 1997). In the context of target marketing, IAM measures both affective and cognitive response from the ethnic consumers. IAM consists of five constructs: strength of ethnic identification, attribution affect, attitude toward the AD, attitude toward the brand, and message recall. Strength of ethnic identification of a consumer is suggested to influence his or her attribution affect to a target marking commercials. The attribution affect may later casts impact over the affective, cognitive, and behavioral activities of the consumer. That is, the attribution affect may influence the evaluation of the company and its products as well as the effectiveness of the communication. Ultimately, it may result in accommodative behaviors of the consumer. IAM broadens the traditional domain of SAT and measures the communication effectiveness and reciprocal behavioral responses of accommodation. It also examines a wide range of ethnic symbols in addition to social-linguistic areas. In the domain of intercultural accommodation, ethnic symbols may include spokespersons and salespersons of the target ethnic groups, in addition to ethnic language, music, art, national flags, or other cultural symbols. With respect to e-commerce, IAM provides some theoretical explanation to the consumer behaviors of ethnic groups. First, it recognizes the ethnic identification as an important antecedent to ethnic behaviors. Second, it highlights the channels, such as attribution affect, through which ethnic factors may affect an impact a consumer's affective and cognitive behaviors.

Web Information System Success

Prior information system literature has examined the success of web information systems in consumer e-commerce through the lens of Technology Acceptance Model (TAM) and DeLone and McLean Model (D&M). TAM (Davis, 1989) is based on Fishbein and Ajzen's Theory of Reasoned Action (Fishbein & Aizen, 1975) to explain the individual's IT acceptance behaviors. This model postulates that technology usage is influenced by behavioral intention to use the technology, which is itself influenced by the attitude of the users on Web sites. It is also suggested that user perceived usefulness and perceived ease of use are the two major determinant factors to the user attitude. The DeLone and McLean Model (D&M) (DeLone & McLean, 1992) is mainly based on the communication research of Shannon and Weaver (Shannon & Weaver, 1949) as well as Information Influence theory of Mason (Mason, 1978). In D&M Model, construct "system quality" measures technical success and "information quality" measures semantic success. In addition, "user satisfaction," "individual impacts," and "organizational impacts" measure system success when the system "use" is executed.

Both TAM and D&M have been empirically validated in the context of consumer e-commerce (DeLone & McLean, 2004; Shen & Eder, 2009). They are used to examine the quality of Web sites and consequently the Web site usage. It remains, however, largely unknown to what extend do these models capture the behaviors of ethnic consumers on the Internet and how we may better involve the ethnic consumers into the e-commerce.

RESEARCH MODEL AND HYPOTHESES

Drawing upon the literature discussed above, we develop the conceptual research model that examines the online ethnic consumers' behavior

Figure 1. Consumer E-Commerce Web Site Intercultural Accommodation Model in the Context of Ethnic Culture

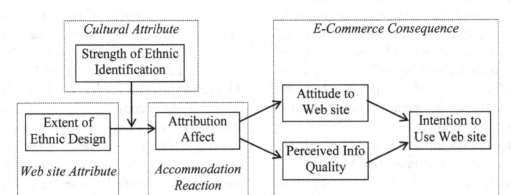

towards Web site. As in Figure 1, this Web-based Intercultural Accommodation Model (hereafter referred to as WIAM) portrays the likely interactions among Web site design, personal attribute, and consumer response to the e-commerce Web site.

We define the extent of ethnic design as the level of e-commerce Web site in its use of ethnic design elements. IAM suggests the use of ethnic language, symbol, music, and art to improve communications between vendors and consumers. As a consequence, a consumer e-commerce Web site may strategically incorporate these cultural elements into the Web site interface design. A retailing Web site, for instance, may display the image of a minority American model wearing the appeal products. Similarly, a Web site may offer contents through multi-language versions. Theory of Attribution posits that the use of ethnic symbols is likely to invoke attribution affect from ethnic consumers (Harvey & Weary, 1985). Attribution theory argues that "people try to determine why people do what they do." During this process, a person seeking to understand the others' behavior may attribute positive or negative causes to the behavior under question. One may perceive favorable affective effects when he or she receives kind attention or helping behaviors from the others. Weiner stressed that such attribution affect an important construct to influence user behaviors

(Weiner, 1989). That is, the cognitive interference acts as a factor contributing to the attributive predispositions and it consequently functions as a major determinant of affective reactions. When an e-commerce Web site adopts ethnic designs, ethnic group members are likely to have a positive emotional response to the use of their cultural symbols. The greater the use of ethnic designs (e.g., language and picture) on a Web site, the higher the attribution affect may rise from an ethnic consumer. Therefore we propose:

Proposition 1: The extent of ethnic design will positively correlate with attribution affects towards the ethnic design.

Strength of ethnic identification measures the consumer's strength of identification with his or her ethic background (Holland & Gentry, 1997). The strength of ethnic identification is reflected by the person's sense and attachment to his or her ethnic group and community (Ayouby & Croteau, 2008). Prior studies have pointed out that ethnic group members vary in their strengths of ethnic identification (Deshpande, Hoyer, & Donthu, 1986; O'Guinn & Faber, 1985; Whittler, 1989). A number of factors may alter the strength of ethnic identification. Examples are such as an individual's development environment and his/her education experience. For consumers with great strength of ethnic identification, they may highly appreciate the ethnic designs on an e-commerce Web site. Consequently, the presence of ethnic designs on an e-commerce Web site may arouse strong attribution affect from the customers. On the contrary, individuals with low strength of ethnic identification may less value the designs that are tied with their ethnicity. As a result, the relationship between the extent of ethnic design and the attribution affects is likely to reduce. Hence we posit below:

Proposition 2: The strength of ethnic identification will positively moderate the relationship between extent of ethnic design and attribution affect.

Attribution affects may result in favorable evaluation of the others (Riggins, 1992). When an individual is entrenched with positive attribution affects, he/she tends to develop an obligation to the party from whom he/she benefits. As a consequence, his or her viewpoint towards the others is likely to be biased and this individual may develop favorable attitude toward the others. In the context of e-commerce, positive evaluative response from the consumers can be operationally defined as their attitude toward the service or retailing Web sites. Holland and Gentry found that attribution affect positively influences a consumer's attitude to the brand (Holland & Gentry, 1997). E-commerce Web site sells services or products to the online users; Web sites therefore carry their own brands and images. Following this thought, we expect that users who maintain a favorable attribution affect of the ethnic designs on a Web site may also keep favorable attitude toward the Web site. In their development of *"e-commerce framework,"* Sudweeks and Simoff suggested argued that cultural appeal with cultivate attitude towards e-commerce Web site (Sudweeks & Simoff, 2001). We postulate:

Proposition 3: Attribution affects will positively correlate with consumer attitude to a Web site.

TAM suggests that attitude impacts user behavioral intentions of a given technology (Davis, 1989). The higher positive attitude a user has, the more likely he or she would prefer to use the technology. Within the context of consumer e-commerce, likewise, we propose that similar relationship between user attitude and the system use intention still holds. That is, the attitude toward a Web site will positively affect the user's intention to use the Web site (e.g., making a purchase). Since customers have grown to be powerful, demanding, and utilitarian in their online shopping (Koufaris, 2002), the locus of power has been shifted from vendors to customers (Raman, 1997). Therefore, a high level of user intention to use Web site greatly determines the business opportunities that an e-commerce Web site may capture. We therefore posit:

Proposition 4: Attitude to Web site will positively correlate with the intention to use a Web site.

Information quality has been identified as an essential quality of web systems in that it measures the quality of the information delivered to the online customers (Chen, 2007; DeLone & McLean, 2003). Unfortunately, an individual's perception of information quality may be easily comprised. An average online user is likely to be burdened by information overload and exhausts his or her cognitive resources that are necessary to process purchasing related information on a Web site. The poor designs of interconnected Web pages and navigation structures further discourage an online consumer from fully engaging in reading the Web site contents. Therefore the Web site information may not be fully comprehended and the quality of information not well and fairly recognized. IAM suggests that positive attribution affect may lead to reciprocal accommodative behaviors. In this context, the attribution affect to a Web site's use of ethnic components may lead to reciprocal behaviors such as paying more attention to the Web site content. When attending to the Web site carefully, a potential consumer may recognize the useful information of products and services that otherwise may be omitted during a regular Web site visit. Prior studies have present preliminary evidence. Holland and Gentry, for example, found that attribution affects increase message recall. We posit:

Proposition 5: Attribution affects will positively correlate with perceived information quality of a Web site

Quality information helps customers capture product and service information and enhances the efficiency of decision making and purchasing tasks. Meanwhile, quality information affects customers' perceptions of the quality of products and services (Wang & Strong, 1996). In their IS Success Model, DeLone and McLean suggested that information quality positively influence the user behavioral intention to use information systems. And thus we posit:

Proposition 6: Perceived information quality will positively correlate with the intention to use a Web site.

PROPOSED RESEARCH METHODOLOGY

The research model is to be tested using a survey-based approach. Multiple versions of one single e-commerce Web site are to be created with differences in their richness of ethnic elements. The ethnic groups may include African, Hispanic, and Asian American. The ethnic elements to be employed include ethnic language, ethnic group picture, and traditional icons (e.g., food, clothes, and holiday) of cultures. The other parts of the Web sites remain the same, such as the interface and content.

To ensure that the content of acceptable for every participant, the Web site will have no content of violence, sex, prejudice, political preference. The Web site will also be simple in its design in order to eliminate the difficulty in use. Subsequent manipulation check is required in the analysis stage to verify that the use of cultural symbols on the Web site do, in fact, makes draw attentions of the respondents. The manipulation question is listed in Table 1.

Experiment subjects from African, Hispanic, and Asian Americans are to be recruited. They will be assigned to surf the Web site that is designed with elements from their corresponding ethnicity groups. Prior to the experiment, participants will be informed that the purpose of the study is to learn more about the types of Web sites they like best, which would enable researchers to improve the look, style, and the content of Web site design. They will be asked to spend 30 minutes on the Web site and complete a questionnaire pertaining to the Web site at the end of the experiment. Participants are guaranteed anonymity and the results are kept confidential.

The measurements of the principal constructs are borrowed from prior studies to ensure validity. Strength of ethnic identification is measured using items by Roberts et al (Roberts, Phinney, Masse, Chen, Roberts, & Romero, 1999). This questionnaire has been proved accurate in measuring strength of ethnic identification. Respondents who do not designate themselves as being African, Hispanic, or Asian Americans or identified with more than one racial or ethnic group will be removed from analysis. Attribution affect to ethnic symbols is measured by three items. They are in five-point semantic differential scales: strongly negative, negative, natural, positive, strongly positive. Attitude toward Web site employs measurements adapted from previous research (McMillan, Hwang, & Lee, 2003). Four items are used in five-point semantic differential scales. Perceived information quality measurements are adapted from (Muylle, Moenaert, & Despontin, 2003). Four items are used in five-point semantic differential scales. Intension to use Web site employs measurements adapted from previous research (Chen & Cheng, 2009). Three items are employed in seven-point semantic differential scales. Measurements of ethnic design are not available in the literature and new items are created on the basis of prior literature (Holland & Gentry, 1997).

Table 1. Principal Construct Measurement

Manipulation Check Question Have you noticed the cultural elements (e.g., language or picture) on the Web site? Yes: _____ No: _____
Extent of Ethnic Design Use the numbers below to indicate how much you agree or disagree with each statement. (4) Strongly agree (3) Agree (2) Disagree (1) Strongly disagree 1- The Web site has a great deal of symbols that reflect my ethnic group 2- The Web site has an extensive amount of content pertaining to my ethnicity
Strength of Ethnic Identify: Use the numbers below to indicate how much you agree or disagree with each statement. (4) Strongly agree (3) Agree (2) Disagree (1) Strongly disagree 1- I have spent time trying to find out more about my ethnic group, such as its history, traditions, and customs. 2- I am active in organizations or social groups that include mostly members of my own ethnic group. 3- I have a clear sense of my ethnic background and what it means for me. 4- I think a lot about how my life will be affected by my ethnic group membership. 5- I am happy that I am a member of the group I belong to. 6- I have a strong sense of belonging to my own ethnic group. 7- I understand pretty well what my ethnic group membership means to me. 8- In order to learn more about my ethnic background, I have often talked to other people about my ethnic group. 9- I have a lot of pride in my ethnic group. 10- I participate in cultural practices of my own group, such as special food, music, or customs. 11- I feel a strong attachment towards my own ethnic group. 12- I feel good about my cultural or ethnic background. 13- My ethnicity is (1) Asian or Asian American, including Chinese, Japanese, and others (2) Black or African American (3) Hispanic or Latino, including Mexican American, Central American, and others
Attribution Affect Use the numbers below to indicate how much you agree or disagree with each statement. (5) Definitely agree (4) Agree (3) Neutral (2) Disagree (1) Definitely disagree 1- I am happy to see the cultural elements on the Web site 2- I am relaxed to see the cultural elements on the Web site 3- I am comfortable to see the cultural elements on the Web site
Attitude to Web Site Use the numbers below to indicate how much you agree or disagree with each statement. (5) Definitely agree (4) Agree (3) Neutral (2) Disagree (1) Definitely disagree 1- This Web site makes it easy for me to build a relationship with this company 2- I'm satisfied with the service provide by this Web site 3- I feel comfortable in surfing this Web site 4- I feel surfing this Web site is a good way for me to spend my time
Perceived Information Quality Use the numbers below to indicate how much you agree or disagree with each statement. (5) Definitely agree (4) Agree (3) Neutral (2) Disagree (1) Definitely disagree 1- The information in the Web site does not help me at all (reversed coded) 2- I can rely on the information in the Web site 3- The information in the Web site is presented clearly 4- The information in the Web site is sufficiently detailed
Intention to Use the Web Site (7) Strongly agree to (1) Strongly disagree 1- I will regularly use the shopping Web site in the future 2- I will continue using the shopping Web site in the future 3- I intend to continue using the shopping Web site rather than discontinue its use

The model is to be tested using structural equation modeling approach. We will employ partial least squares (PLS) to examine the significance of path coefficients in the conceptual model. PLS employs a component-based approach for estimation and places minimal restrictions on sample size and residual distributions. It is best suited for testing complex relationships by avoiding inadmissible solutions and factor indeterminacy (Chin, 1998). PLS also supports exploratory research. Our paper studies an important yet understudied research perspective in the context of e-commerce; PLS is therefore appropriate. Accordingly, a sample size over 130 is deemed appropriate to achieve satisfactory level of statistical power (Gefen, Straub, & Boudreau, 2000).

CONCLUSION, LIMITATION, AND FUTURE STUDY

The online market has become more culturally diverse than ever before. With the assistance of Internet, individuals with varying cultural background actively participate in e-commerce. The existing literature in culture has attested to the importance of cultural implications on business strategy and consumer behavior (Cyr, Larios, & Pan, 2009; Sia, Lim, Leung, Lee, Huang, & Benbasat, 2009). It is therefore important that e-commerce vendors adjust their strategies to appropriate Web sites in attracting and retaining users with culture backgrounds. Walsh and Kefi developed an extended "*virtual onion*" model of culture and suggested culture values such as religion, ethnic group, national, professional/occupational, organizational, and workgroup (Walsh & Kefi, 2008). The current study focus on ethnic culture that is most prominent. As ethnic groups keep expanding with respect to population and purchasing power, they also present opportunities to the e-commerce Web sites. Venders who are able to cater to these populations are likely to make direct sales and generate revenue.

In particular, we study the ethnic factors that may influence the ethnic consumers in their Web site usage. The Web-based intercultural accommodation model is a conceptual model that theorizes the potential implications of Web site attribute, ethnicity attribute, accommodation reaction, and e-commerce consequence on ethnic consumers' behavioral intention to use the Web site. Drawing upon prior literature, the research model predicts how the ethnic consumers may react to the e-commerce Web site that employs ethnic designs. The study attempt to contribute to the culture aspects in information systems research and it may benefit the practitioners to better attract the ethnic consumers through proper use of ethnic designs.

This conceptual paper is subject to a number of limitations which also serve as directions for future research. First, the theorization of ethnic consumers' behavioral intention is subject to rigorous empirical validation before it can serve as a referent framework to guide the practitioners of e-commerce. Second, the research article does not project the potential backslash when Web sites misuse the ethnic designs. For instance, consumers from one ethnic group may respond negatively to the excessive exposure of a different ethnicity. This is a likely case when a Web site cannot properly profile and personalize its diversified consumers. Future research needs to investigate into this important issue. Future study may also adapt the model to other cultural value systems such as religious and political.

REFERENCES

Ainsworth-Darnell, J. W., & Downey, D. B. (1998). Assessing the oppositional culture explanation for racial/ethnic differences in school performance. *American Sociological Review*, 63(4), 536–553. doi:10.2307/2657266

Ayouby, R., & Croteau, A. M. (2008). *Acculturation to the global culture, ethnic identification and the adoption of social computing.* Paper presented at the Americas Conference on Information Systems.

Byme, D. (1961). Interpersonal attraction and attitude similarity. *Journal of Abnormal and Social Psychology, 62*, 713–715. doi:10.1037/h0044721

Chau, P. Y. K., Cole, M., Massey, A. P., Monyota-Weiss, M., & O'Keefe, R. M. (2002). Cultural differences in the online behavior of consumers. *Communications of the ACM, 45*(10), 138–143. doi:10.1145/570907.570911

Chen, C.-W. D., & Cheng, C.-Y. J. (2009). Understanding consumer intent in online shopping. *Behaviour & Information Technology, 28*(4), 335–345. doi:10.1080/01449290701850111

Chen, R. (2007). *Consumer's initial acceptance of e-commerce Web site: A contingency approach.* Paper presented at the The 13th Americas Conference on Information Systems, Keystone, CO.

Chin, W. (1998). Issues and opinions on structural equation modeling. *MIS Quarterly, 22*(1), 7, 10.

Cole, M., & O'Keefe, R. M. (2000). Conceptualizing the dynamics of globalisation and culture in electronic commerce. *Journal of Global Information Technology Management, 3*(4), 4–17.

Conzen, K. N., Gerber, D. A., Morawska, E., Pazzetta, G. E., & Vecoli, R. J. (1992). The invention of ethnicity: A perspective from the U.S.A. In R. C. Monk (Ed.), *Taking sides: Clashing views on controversial issues in race and ethnicity* (pp. 64-66). Guilford, CT: Dushkin Publishing Group.

Cotton. (2002). Understanding the multicultural consumer base. *Textile Consumer,* (Winter 2002).

Cyr, D., Head, M., Larios, H., & Pan, B. (2009). Exploring human images in Web site design: A multi-method approach. *Management Information Systems Quarterly, 33*(3), 530–566.

Davis, F. D. (1989). Perceived usefulness, perceived ease of use, and user acceptance of Information Technology. *Management Information Systems Quarterly, 13*(3), 318. doi:10.2307/249008

DeLone, W. H. &. McLean, E.R. (2003). The DeLone and McLean Model of Information Systems success: A ten year update. *Journal of Management Information Systems, 19*(4), 9, 22.

DeLone, W. H., & McLean, E. R. (1992). Information Systems success: The quest for the dependent variable. *Information Systems Research, 3*(1), 60. doi:10.1287/isre.3.1.60

DeLone, W. H., & McLean, E. R. (2004). Measuring e-commerce success: Applying the DeLone & McLean Information Systems success model. *International Journal of Electronic Commerce, 9*(1), 31–47.

Deshpande, R., Hoyer, W. D., & Donthu, N. (1986). The intensity of ethnic affilation: A study of the sociology of Hispanic consumption. *The Journal of Consumer Research, 13*(September), 214–220. doi:10.1086/209061

Fishbein, M., & Aizen, I. (1975). *Belief, attitude, intention, and behavior: An introduction to theory and research.* Addison-Wesley.

Gefen, D., Straub, D. W., & Boudreau, M.-C. (2000). Structural equation modeling and regression: Guidelines for research practice. *Communications of the Association for Information Systems, 4*(7).

Giles, H. (1973). Accent mobility: A model and some data. *Anthropological Linguistics, 15*(87).

Giles, H., Coupland, N., & Coupland, J. (1991). Accommodation theory: Communication, context, and consequences. In H. G., et al. (Eds.), *Contexts of acommodation: Developments in applied sociolinguistics* (pp. 1-68). Cambridge, UK: Cambridge University Press.

Gupta, J. N. D., & Sharma, S. K. (2003). Creating business value through e-commerce. In Shin, N. (Ed.), *Creating business value with Information Technology*. Hershey, PA: Idea Group Inc. doi:10.4018/9781591400387.ch007

Harris, S. G. (1994). Organizational culture and individual sensemaking: A schema-based perspective. *Organization Science, 5*(3), 309–321. doi:10.1287/orsc.5.3.309

Harvey, J. H., & Weary, G. (1985). *Attribution: Basic issues and applications*. San Diego, CA: Academic Press.

Hofstede, G. (1993). Cultural constraints in management theories. *The Academy of Management Executive, 7*(1), 81.

Holland, J., & Gentry, J. W. (1997). The impacts of cultural symbols on advertising effectiveness. *Advances in Consumer Research. Association for Consumer Research (U. S.), 24*, 483–489.

Holland, J., & Gentry, J. W. (1999). Ethnic consumer reaction to targeted marketing. *Journal of Advertising, 28*(1), 65.

Hult, G. T. M., Ketchen, D. J., & Nichols, E. L. (2002). An examination of cultural competitiveness and order fulfillment cycle time with supply chain. *Academy of Management Journal, 45*(3), 557–586. doi:10.2307/3069382

Koufaris, M. (2002). Applying the technology acceptance model and flow theory to online consumer behavior. *Information Systems Research, 13*(2), 205. doi:10.1287/isre.13.2.205.83

Koufaris, M., & Hampton-Sosa, W. (2004). The development of initial trust in an online company by new customers. *Information & Management, 41*(3), 377–397. doi:10.1016/j.im.2003.08.004

Krishna, S., Sahay, S., & Walsham, G. (2004). Managing cross-cultural issues in global software outsourcing. *Communications of the ACM, 47*(4), 62–66. doi:10.1145/975817.975818

Leidner, D. E., & Kayworth, T. (2006). A review of culture in Information Systems research: Toward a theory of Information Technology culture conflict. *Management Information Systems Quarterly, 30*(2), 357.

Longwell, F. (1999). Effective Web sites can facilitate worksite sales. *National Underwriter, 103*(49), 27–29.

Mason, R. O. (1978). Measuring information output: A communication systems approach. *Information & Management, 1*(5), 219–234. doi:10.1016/0378-7206(78)90028-9

McMillan, S. J., Hwang, J.-S., & Lee, G. (2003). Effects of structural and perceptual factors on attitudes toward the Web site. *Journal of Advertising Research, 43*, 400–409.

Moffett, S., Mcadam, R., & Parkinson, S. (2002). Developing a model for technology and cultural factors in knowledge management: A factor analysis. *Knowledge and Process Management, 9*(4), 237–255. doi:10.1002/kpm.152

Morrisette, S., McQuivey, J. L., Maraganore, N., & Lanpher, G. (1999). *Are net shoppers loyal*? The Forrester Report.

Mulpuru, S., Hult, P., Evans, P. F., Sehgal, V., & McGowan, B. (2010). *U.S. online retail forecast 2009 to 2014*. Forrester Research.

Muylle, S., Moenaert, R., & Despontin, M. (2003). The conceptualizatioin and empirical validatiion of Web site user satisfaction. *Information & Management, 41*(5), 543–560. doi:10.1016/S0378-7206(03)00089-2

Nagel, J. (1994). Constructing ethnicity: Creating and recreating ethnic identity and culture. *Social Problems, 41*(1), 152–176. doi:10.1525/sp.1994.41.1.03x0430n

O'Guinn, T. C., & Faber, R. J. (1985). New perspectives on acculturation: The relationship of general and role specific acculturation with Hispanics' consumer attitudes. In Hirschman, E. C., & Holbrook, M. B. (Eds.), *Advances in consumer research* (*Vol. 12*, pp. 113–117). Provo, UT: Assocation for Consumer Research.

Oetting, E. R. (1993). Orthogonal cultural identification: Theoretical links between cultural identification and substance use, drug abuse among minority youth: Methodological issues and recent research advances. In De La Rosa, M. (Ed.), *NIDA research monograph* (pp. 32–56). Rockville.

Quaddus, M. A., & Tung, L. L. (2002). Explaining cultural differences in decision conferencing. *Communications of the ACM, 45*(8), 93–98. doi:10.1145/545151.545157

Raman, N. V. (1997). A qualitative investigation of Web browsing behavior. *Advances in Consumer Research. Association for Consumer Research (U. S.), 24*, 511–516.

Riggins, S. H. (1992). The media imperative: Ethnic minority survival in the age of mass communication. In Riggins, S. H. (Ed.), *Ethnic minority media, an international perspective* (pp. 1–20). Newbury Park, CA: Sage.

Roberts, R. E., Phinney, J. S., Masse, L. C., Chen, Y. R., Roberts, C., & Romero, A. (1999). The structure of ethnic identity of young adolescents from diverse ethnocultural groups. *The Journal of Early Adolescence, 19*(3), 301–322. doi:10.1177/0272431699019003001

Robey, D., & Azevedo, A. (1994). Cultural analysis of the organizational consequences of Information Technology. *Accounting, Management and Information Technologies, 4*(1), 23–27. doi:10.1016/0959-8022(94)90011-6

Robey, D., & Boudreau, M. (1999). Accounting for the contradictory consequences of Information Technology: Theoretical directions and methodological implications. *Information Systems Research, 10*(2), 167–185. doi:10.1287/isre.10.2.167

Shannon, C. E., & Weaver, W. (1949). *A mathematical model of communication*. Urbana-Champaign, IL: University of Illinois Press.

Shen, J., & Eder, L. (2009). *Determining factors in the acceptance of social shopping Web sites*. Paper presented at the Determining Factors in the Acceptance of Social Shopping Websites.

Sia, C. L., Lim, K. H., Leung, K., Lee, M. K. O., Huang, W. W., & Benbasat, I. (2009). Web strategies to promote Internet shopping: Is cultural-customization needed? *Management Information Systems Quarterly, 33*(3), 491–512.

Simons, H. W., Berkowitz, N. N., & Moyer, R. J. (1970). Similarity, credibility and attitude change: A review and a theory. *Psychological Bulletin, 73*(1). doi:10.1037/h0028429

Sturdivant, F. D. (1973). Subculture theory: Poverty, minorities, and marketing. In Ward, S., & Robertson, T. S. (Eds.), *Consumer nehavior: Theoretical sources* (pp. 469–521). Englewood Cliffs, NJ: Prentice-Hall, Inc.

Sudweeks, F., & Simoff, S. (2001). *Culturally commercial: A cultural e-commerce framework*. Paper presented at the OzCHI2001, Edith Cowan University, Perth.

Trompenaars, F. (1996). Resovling international conflict: Culture and business strategy. *Business Strategy Review, 7*(3), 51–68. doi:10.1111/j.1467-8616.1996.tb00132.x

Walsh, I., & Kefi, H. (2008). *Developing the concept of individual IT-culture: The spinning top metaphor*. Paper presented at the Americas Conference on Information Systems.

Walsham, G. (2002). Cross-cultural software production and use: A structurational analysis. *Management Information Systems Quarterly, 26*(4), 359–380. doi:10.2307/4132313

Wang, R. Y., & Strong, D. M. (1996). Beyond accuracy: What data quality means to data customers. *Journal of Management Information Systems, 12*(4), 5–33.

Webb, J. T. (1970). *Interview synchrony: An investigation of two speech rate measures in the automated standardized interview.* Paper presented at the Research Conference on the Interview, Elmsford, NY.

Weiner, B. (1989). An attributional theory of motivation and emotion. *Psychology and Marketing, 6*(Winter), 287–309.

Whittler, T. E. (1989). Viewers' processing of actor's race and message claims in advertising stimuli. *Psychology and Marketing, 6*(Winter), 287–309. doi:10.1002/mar.4220060405

Wolf, D. (2010). *Culture is overlooked in e-commerce.* Seeking Alpha.

Zaoui, I. (2008). *Which kind of trust for buying online? An intercultural study.* Paper presented at the Mediterranean Conference on Information Systems, Hammamet, Tunisia.

Chapter 12
Web Site Localization Practices:
Some Insights into the Localization Industry

Nitish Singh
Saint Louis University, USA

John E. Spillan
University of North Carolina, USA

Joseph P. Little
Saint Louis University, USA

ABSTRACT

The e-commerce industry has experienced spectacular growth, change and development. This situation has initiated an enormous business revolution that has affected the process of globalization tremendously. The goal of this study was to analyze the Web sites of localization companies that provide localization and translation services to other companies and see if they themselves are practicing what they are preaching. The results suggest that localization companies are indeed not practicing what they are preaching. Analysis shows that localization company Web sites are less localized than the Web sites of their clients, the multinational companies. The findings provide some implications to domestic and international marketers who currently operate in or are planning to enter into the global markets in the near future.

INTRODUCTION

From the mid-1990s to the present day, the e-commerce industry has experienced spectacular growth, change and development. The global online population is estimated to reach 1.8 billion by 2012 (Jupiter Research, 2008). In 2008 North

America accounted for only 17.5% of the online population and that percentage is in decline as countries such as China, Brazil, India, and Russia show the highest level of online population growth (Internet World Stats, 2008). This situation has initiated an enormous business revolution that has affected the process of globalization tremendously (Cyr & Lew, 2003). During the past several years an entire industry (the localization industry) has

DOI: 10.4018/978-1-60960-597-1.ch012

grown up around helping companies design multilingual Web sites and software applications for different countries. An industry report estimates the size of the worldwide translation and localization services market at US$ 8.8 billion (DePalma & Beninatto, 2006). According to this report the commercial market for localization services is estimated at US$6 billion and the government market at US$ 2.8 billion worldwide.

Localization is the process of adapting products and services (Web sites, manuals and software) in accordance to linguistic, cultural, technical and other locale-specific requirements of the target market (Localization Program at California State University, Chico, College of Business, 2008). Localization is now being seen by multinationals as a necessary process to develop multilingual and multicultural content to effectively tap global markets. Forester research estimates put the 2006 global e-commerce revenues at around $12.6 trillion. Furthermore, research has shown that consumers prefer Web sites in their native language and Web sites that reflect their local preferences (Singh, Furrer, & Ostinelli, 2004). Thus, companies around the world are creating multilingual Web sites to tap this vibrant online market. Companies like IBM, Oracle, Intel and other have almost 90 international sites to take advantage of the global online markets and communicate with their global customers. This surge in creating multilingual online content and software has also led to the growth of the localization industry which is helping these companies by effectively translating their Web sites, user interfaces, software, and manuals. Beyond translation the localization companies are also involved in the following (Esselink, 2000):

- Making visual or graphics, technical and textual modifications to the site content.
- Rewriting the text, translating the text, and ensuring translation, idiomatic, and conceptual equivalence of the translated text.

- Modifying graphics, data fields, tables, forms, layout, colors and tables etc.
- Modifying the cultural content of the site or software to be congruent to the local culture.
- International e-commerce readiness for multi-country transactions.
- Web site navigational modifications to meet local preferences.

This study analyzes the Web sites of localization service providers in order to understand to what extent these companies are translating and localizing their own sites, and modifying graphics, layout, colors, text, policies, navigation, and cultural content. The study then compares the localization efforts of the localization vendor company with their clients, who are generally multinational companies. This analysis will reveal if the companies that are preaching localization are also effectively implementing it on their own Web sites. After all, the localization service providers should set the benchmarks for their clients to follow. Moreover, the companies that will be the winners in this fast growing and consolidating localization industry will be the ones that are able to highlight and exemplify the need for Web site localization. What is a localization service provider telling their current clients along with potential future clients if their own Web sites are not sufficiently localized? The goal of this article is to gain understanding of the localization processes used in the localization industry and to focus on the current trends in the localization industry.

This article is composed of seven sections. The first section presents and introduces a review of the globalization and localization literature. Section two explains the research methodology. Section three provides a presentation of the analysis. Section four provides a discussion of the results, section five describes some managerial implications, section six explains some limitations along with future research ideas, and finally section seven provides a conclusion.

LITERATURE REVIEW

Globalization and the Localization Industry

Increased ownership of computers and Internet usage is growing every day. Throughout the world the Internet is rapidly becoming the main source for information, shopping and services. Furthermore, computer and Internet users are increasingly from non-English speaking countries. One estimate indicates that 32% of Internet users are non-native English speakers. This number is increasing. The result of this huge Internet expansion motivated businesses to recognize the value of Website localization (Kwintessential, 2009). Moreover, the unending process of globalization is fundamentally altering the manner in which enterprises do business. When businesses globalize their e-business, there is a great need recognize that language, cultural expectations and trust play a huge role when building online Web capabilities (Culnan & Armstrong, 1999; Jarvenpaa, Tractinsky, & Vitale, 2000; Singh & Pereira, 2005; Violino, 2001). For an organization to be successful in this demanding setting, they must adjust their offerings so that their products and services present the appearance and feel of being produced locally. The process of localization begins with an understanding of a wide range of linguistic, cultural, content, and technical issues. A product or service presentation has to be tailored to the local customs and practices of a country or region. For example, producing a Web site in only the English language is not sufficient because the majority of the world does not understand English. Furthermore, even if consumers do understand English research has shown that they prefer Web sites in their native language (Singh et al., 2004). While many companies use machine translations to adapt the language used on their Web sites (Singh & Boughton, 2002), this type of translation is not sufficient either. Languages not only differ in their use of characters or syntax, but also

their use of rhetorical style and use of metaphors. Therefore, a simple machine translation, without an understanding of a culture and its language, may result in a cultural faux pas (Singh et al., 2004). Beyond linguistics companies also need to consider such culturally sensitive areas such as persuasion techniques, colors, icons, signs, Web page layout, and cultural values when localizing Web sites (Singh & Pereira, 2005).

Previous research has shown that culturally sensitive Web content enhances the site's usability (Fock, 2000; Luna, Peracchio, & de Juan, 2002; Singh & Pereira, 2005; Simon, 2001). So, in order to effectively communicate to foreign online consumers it is beneficial for a firm to adapt their Web sites to the targeted market. Furthermore, research has shown that not only does Web site localization enhance usability but also attitude towards the Web site, perception of the ease of site navigation, and ultimately purchase intention (Singh et al., 2004).

The cultural impact is substantial and Hall (1976) believes that it is very difficult to act or interact in any meaningful way if they do not understand language and culture. The consequence of not including language and culture, when considering global Web presence, is discarding profitable global online consumer. The Internet, similar to any other advertising document, is a replica of the culture of the country or locale (Cyr & Trevor-Smith, 2004; Hermeking, 2005; Singh & Matsuo, 2004). According to Mooij (1998) advertising mimics a society's values. It can only be effective when it is inseparably connected to the primary culture of the group for which it is targeted. Studies have demonstrated that advertising that is harmonious with local cultural values is significantly more compelling than standardized advertising. Several researchers, therefore, have emphasized the use of country-specific cultural values appeal when developing international advertising campaigns and communication material (Albers-Miller & Gelb, 1996; Han & Shavitt, 1994). Research indicates that Web site localization and cultural customization promotes a better opinion regarding the site ultimately influencing people's purchase intentions (Singh & Pereira, 2005). Luna et al. (2002) discovered that culturally harmonious Web content creates a more user friendly environment where the user has clear instructions and comes away from the Website with a better attitude about the content that is presented. Consequently, the localization of Web sites also necessitates culturally tailoring the Web sites to be congruent with the cultural requirements of the local environment. Miscommunications, in the international context, generally take place when the message is seemingly mismatched with the local culture and does not produce the response that was expected towards the businesses products or services. The foreign language, signs and symbols, and Web content that is culturally different, creates confusion, frustration, offensiveness and in the long run a loss of business (Luna et al., 2002).

While company Web sites provide a major opportunity to impart and promote a corporate image and to sell products and services, the effectiveness of the Website depends almost exclusively on the value of its content (Pollach, 2005). An effective Web site is the one where the consumers invest a considerable amount of time reviewing the content of interest, requesting more information, and buying the goods or services offered (Liu, Marchewka, & Ku, 2004). As such, the quality and value of a Web site will be influenced by how the Web site mirrors the culture of the nation for which it has been designed (Fletcher, 2006; Singh & Pereira, 2005).

Culture influences just about everything we do, say, read, hear and think. Web sites are not immune to the affect of culture (Kwintessential, 2009). Those companies that are able to develop, manage and customize their business Web sites to the culture of the country they are doing business, will generate more interest in their company and ultimately increase the sales of their products and services.

The differences in cultures require international businesses to find ways to make their Web sites communicate with different cultures in different parts of the world. As such, the key acronym that has emerged in this new arena of business operation is GILT or Globalization, Internationalization, Localization and Translation (Lommel, 2003). Globalization addresses the enterprise issues associated with making a company truly global. So, for products and services this means integrating the internal and external business functions with marketing, sales, and customer support in the world market (The Localization Industry Standards Association, 2008). More specifically, Web site globalization includes two complementary processes: Internationalization and Localization.

Internationalization is the process of generalizing a product so that it can handle multiple languages and cultural conventions without the need for redesign. In more technical terms, it is the process through which back-end technologies are used to create modular, extendible, and accessible global Web site templates that support front-end customization (Singh & Boughton, 2005). This process enables company Web sites to be locally responsive to the end-user through front-end customization. Internationalization takes place at the level of program design and Web document development (Singh & Little, 2009).

Localization and translation is the process of adjusting a product or service and making it linguistically and culturally appropriate to the target locale. More specific to the current study, Web site localization is the process of the front-end customization, whereby Web sites are adapted to meet the needs of an international target market (Singh & Boughton, 2005; Singh & Little, 2009).

The localization industry can trace back its roots to early 1980's when the software industry was emerging as an upcoming sector of the US economy, and felt a need to translate software products in multiple languages (Globalization Industry Primer (LISA), 2007). As the application of software grew across a cross-section of industries and with the growth of the Internet, the localization industry also saw sustained growth. Now the localization industry is seeing a growth phase with the need for translation and localization of software, manuals, packaging, and most importantly multilingual Web sites. The industry is also undergoing considerable consolidation. During the 1990's the trend toward industry consolidation started with small vendors joining hands to offer "one-stop shopping" for large software developers like Microsoft, Oracle, and IBM who needed translation and localization services in multiple languages (Cyr & Lew, 2003). The industry consolidation leads to the emergence of multi-language vendors (MLVs) which specialized in completing multi-language, multi-service localization/translation projects. These MLVs also used an outsourcing model where they outsourced the core translation services to single-language vendors (SLVs); Single Language Vendors normally work into one target language only, from one or more source languages (Esselink, 2000). The acquisition of Bowne Global Solutions by Lionbridge Technologies in 2005 lead to the emergence of Lionbridge as one of the largest Globalization and off-shoring companies in the industry. Similarly, SDL International, another major player in the localization industry, enhanced its portfolio by acquiring Trados Inc., which was a major translation technology solution provider. As the localization industry grows, and serves new and bigger clients across a cross-section of industries, it will need localization vendor companies to invest in process and product innovations and R&D to be competitive. In order for these large investments and comprehensive solutions to be provided, vendors will need to be backed by substantial capital investments. However, Leon Z. Lee (2005), an industry expert, warns that the current focus of large and small localization companies toward primarily cost leadership, automated enterprise workflows, and technology integration from corporate consolidations is not a recipe for long term growth and sustainability of this industry.

Lee (2005) recommends that for the localization industry to be viable it needs to expand its role from just a translation or technology-solution provider to truly embracing the wider concept of localization by providing international marketing expertise. This international marketing orientation will then help the localization companies to expand their offerings by delivering localized information and comprehensive resident knowledge in designing marketing campaigns for geopolitical and ethnographic regions in areas of print advertisement, online brand valuation, and Website usability analysis (Lee, 2005).

The next sections of this article will detail the methodology, sample, and the analyses used in this study. Additionally, insights into the current level of localization practiced by localization vendors and their multinational clients are presented.

METHODOLOGY

To analyze the quality and extent of localization depicted on the localization vendor Web sites, the study conducted a content analysis of the vendor Web sites and Web sites of multinational companies. More specifically, content analysis methodology was used and a coding system was developed to measure various facets of the localization efforts. The coding system used in this study was adapted from Singh, Toy and Wright (2009). The coding sheet included items like:

- Ease of finding global gateway on the Web site
- Use of country code domain names of ccTLD
- Translation depth
- Local customer support
- E-commerce information and policies
- Navigational outlay
- Web site page structure/layout
- Use of Locale-specific graphics, colors and values.

To perform the content analysis two coders were trained in the coding scheme and jointly coded several Web sites. The inter-coder reliability on the sample of vendor and multinational client Web sites ranged from .82 to .86. It is suggested that inter-coder reliability needs to be above .80 in order to be acceptable (Grant & Davis, 1997). Thus, the coder reliability exceeded the suggested threshold.

SAMPLE

Analyzing all country sites (which can range from 10-90 and may include more than 2000 pages) to measure localization efforts was beyond the scope of this study. Thus, the study measured the localization efforts on the German and Spanish Web sites of each vendor company. German and Spanish have been forecasted as some of the top languages in which multinationals are localizing their sites.

To find a sample of localization vendor company Web sites the study used the vendor company data base provided at the Globalization and Localization Association Web site. In total the study was able to include only 53 localization vendor company Web sites in the sample, as these were the only companies we found having international Web sites for Germany and Spain. Thus, 53 companies and their German and Spanish sites served as the final sample, which included almost 106 Web sites and more than a thousand Web pages. The study also analyzed the company home site (mostly in English) to see the structure of the global gateway, Web page structure, and Web content

depth and navigation. The sample of multinational company Web sites was selected from Forbes top 500 international company list. 100 multinationals were identified that had international Web sites and Web sites specifically for both Germany and Spain. Thus, a total of 100 multinationals with 300 country sites (U.S. English, Germany and Spain) were analyzed for this study.

RESULTS AND ANALYSIS

Number Unique Languages Supported

The purpose of finding the number of unique languages was to understand how many languages is the company providing its services in. The results show that on average a vendor company site had about 7 unique languages depicted. On the other hand the Vendor clients, such as Multinational company Web sites had on average 19 unique languages supported. This shows that Localization vendors are far behind their clients in terms of languages supported on the site (see Table 1). In fact the mean number of languages depicted by multinational Web sites (19.38) exceeded the maximum depicted (16) by the vendor sites. An independent sample t-test indicates the means are significantly different ($F = 37.708$, $p = .000$).

Ease of Finding Global Gateway

The aim here is measure how visible the link for international sites is from the company's U.S. English home page. Based on the comparison

Table 1. Number of languages used

	N	Minimum	Maximum	Mean	Std. Dev.
Vendor No. of Languages	53	3	16	7.11	3.06
Multinational No. Of Languages	102	5	38	19.38	7.44

data between the vendor and client Web site, it seems 30 percent of client (Multinational) sites have a dedicated global gateway page compared to which only about 9 percent of vendor sites have a dedicated gateway page (see Table 2). The results of a chi-square test for two independent samples indicates there is a significant difference in the presentation of a global gateway page between vendor and multinational sites ($\chi^2 = 22.191$, $p = .000$). However, it seems both vendor and client sites are lacking quality gateway pages, which are crucial to drive international online traffic to country-specific sites.

Use of Country-Specific Domain

The goal here is to see if the company has invested in buying the country code top level domains also called cctld for the country. The use of ccTLD helps in international search engine optimization and also shows commitment of the company to that country market (see Table 3). The analysis shows that no vendor site was using ccTLD exclusively

to create international sites. Most vendors were using some extension of .com/Spain of .com/Germany. The client multinational Web sites did relatively better in terms of use of ccTLD. About 26 percent of multinational sites were fully using ccTLD for their international Web sites. The results of a chi-square test for two independent samples indicates there is a significant difference in the use of ccTLD between vendor and multinational sites ($\chi^2 = 20.346$, $p = .000$).

Localization Assessment of Country-Specific Web Sites (Germany and Spain)

- Translation Depth: Translation depth was measured to see to what extent are the companies translating their Web pages relative to U.S. English Web pages. To measure translation depth the study counted the number of English page and local language primary links or main links on the home page of English and local language site.

Table 2. Web site global gateway page

	Vendor Frequency	Multinational Frequency	Vendor %	Multinational %
No Link	0	7	0	6.80
Not Easy to Locate	6	20	11.32	19.42
Located at Middle Third	18	12	33.96	11.65
Located at Upper Right Corner	24	33	45.28	32.04
A Dedicated Global Gateway Page	5	31	9.43	30.10
Total	53	103	100.00	100.00

Table 3. Web site use of country-specific domain

	Vendor Frequency	Multinational Frequency	Vendor %	Multinational %
No ccTLD	22	20	42.31	19.80
Not Fully Using ccTLD	30	54	57.69	53.47
ccTLD Used	0	27	0.00	26.73
Total	52	101	100.00	100.00

The results, in Table 4, show that on vendor Web sites about 85 percent of English pages links were translated. On the other hand in terms of Multinational sites, on average about 67 percent of English page links were translated.

- Content Localization: This Category measures to what extent the company has localized its Web site content in terms of local support, e-commerce related information, and navigational ease.
  - Local Customer Support and Contact: By analyzing the level of local customer support it can be measured to what extent is the company localizing its customer service efforts for a specific-locale (see Table 5). The results show that while both the vendors and the client multinationals are not fully localizing their sites, the vendor sites depict far less degree of localization efforts. Only about 4 percent of vendor sites had local support pages which were equivalent to

their US Web site, compared to 24 percent by multinationals. The results of a chi-square test for two independent samples indicates there is a significant difference in the use of local customer support between vendor and multinational sites (χ^2 = 21.200, p = .000).

  - Availability of all policies and e-commerce information such as shipping policy, return, privacy, terms of use, copyright etc.

Under this category the results for vendor and client sides were very different. Almost 70 percent of vendor sites did not have policies related to e-commerce and information use (see Table 6). This shows that most vendors are not very global in terms of conducting e-commerce. On the other hand, almost 47 percent of multinational sites had all the policies available. These results suggest that at least half the multinationals are localizing their site in terms of e-commerce readiness. The results of a chi-square test for two

Table 4. Web site English vs. local language links

	N	Minimum	Maximum	Mean	Std. Dev.
Vendor - English	53	5	92	28.51	20.04
Multinational - English	101	4	299	56.08	47.10
Vendor - Local Language	102	2	96	24.23	19.01
Multinational - Local Language	202	3	177	39.73	30.55

Table 5. Web site level of customer support

	Vendor Frequency	Multinational Frequency	Vendor %	Multinational %
No Online Support	6	14	5.94	6.93
Basic Support	15	20	14.85	9.90
Basic Support - Customer Contact	38	68	37.62	33.66
Several Pages of Support	38	51	37.62	25.25
Equivalent to English Site	4	49	3.96	24.26
Total	101	202	100.00	100.00

Table 6. Web site e-commerce and information use policies

	Vendor Frequency	Multinational Frequency	Vendor %	Multinational %
Not Available	70	26	69.31	12.87
Only One or Two of the Policies	2	30	1.98	14.85
2-3 Policies Available	3	18	2.97	8.91
Most Policies Available	4	32	3.96	15.84
All Policies Available	22	96	21.78	47.52
Total	101	202	100.00	100.00

independent samples indicates there is a significant difference in the availability of policies between vendor and multinational sites ($\chi^2 = 101.136$, $p = .000$).

- Navigational ease in terms of sitemap, local search, navigation buttons etc (see Table 7): Analysis of navigation revealed that only about 8 percent of local vendor sites had navigational elements that were equivalent to their US home pages. On the other hand the 26 percent of the multinational client site had navigational elements equivalent to the US English pages. In general, both Vendor and Client Web sites were not highly localized in terms of navigation. However, the results of a chi-square test for two independent samples indicates there is a significant difference in the navigational ease between vendor and multinational sites ($\chi^2 = 18.085$, $p <= .001$).

- Layout and cultural adaptation
  ○ Web Page Structure (see Table 8): The Overall Look of the Site and Design: Under this category the objective is to measure to what extent the look and the layout of the Web site has been localized for a specific-locale. Surprisingly, almost 92 percent of vendor international sites for Spain and Germany were basically standardized templates of their US site. Multinational sites also did not seem to achieve much localization under this category with almost 45 percent international sites being standardized. The results of a chi-square test for two independent samples indicates there is a significant difference in the structure of the Web pages between vendor and multinational sites ($\chi^2 = 66.671$, $p = .000$) **(see**Table 9).

Table 7. Web site navigational ease

	Vendor Frequency	Multinational Frequency	Vendor %	Multinational %
Very Poor	6	7	5.94	3.47
Poor	24	27	23.76	13.37
Few Navigational Elements	35	54	34.65	26.73
Navigational Elements Seen	28	61	27.72	30.20
Navigation Elements Equivalent to English Site	8	53	7.92	26.24
Total	101	202	100.00	100.00

Table 8. Web site page structure

	Vendor Frequency	Multinational Frequency	Vendor %	Multinational %
Standardized	96	92	92.31	45.10
Mostly Standardized	5	27	4.81	13.24
Some Differences	3	37	2.88	18.14
Localized	0	28	0.00	13.73
Highly Localized	0	20	0.00	9.80
Total	104	204	100.00	100.00

Table 9. Web site local culture

	Vendor Frequency	Multinational Frequency	Vendor %	Multinational %
Standardized	97	72	93.27	35.29
Mostly Standardized	4	52	3.85	25.49
Some Differences	1	38	0.96	18.63
Localized	0	34	0.00	16.67
Highly Localized	2	8	1.92	3.92
Total	104	204	100.00	100.00

○ Use of local models, graphics, colors and other cultural markers. Under this category the study measures if the site uses local models, different colors more appropriate for the country, and cultural symbols. The results show that only about 2 percent of vendor sites are localized or highly localized, compared to 20 percent of multinational sites. It seems neither vendors or multinational clients are truly focusing their efforts to culturally customize their sites, even though a growing body of evidence is suggesting that cultural customization of sites leads to better attitude and intentions to buy online (Singh & Pereira, 2005). The results of a chi-square test for two independent samples indicates there is a significant difference in the use of local culture between vendor and multinational sites ($\chi^2 = 95.101, p = .000$).

DISCUSSION

The results clearly show that companies (localization vendors and multinationals) are currently not fully localizing their sites in terms of using country code top level domains, global gateway pages, customer support, e-commerce and information use policies, navigation, Web site structure, layout, colors, and graphics. It is even more concerning that companies selling localization services are actually localizing their own sites to a much lesser extent than multinational companies, the firms that tend to be their clients. The localization industry is not practicing what they preach.

In every single category examined in this study the multinational Web sites were shown to be more localized than the vendor Web sites.

A telling comparison is the number of distinct languages used. Vendor sites average using seven different languages compared to multi national sites that average nineteen different languages. This result exemplifies the lack of localization practices being used by the vendors themselves. Furthermore, over 93 percent of vendor sites are culturally standardized.

None of the vendor sites were found to be using a ccTLD which is surprising as international domains are crucial for international search engine optimization. This may be due to the fragmented nature of the localization industry wherein small localization vendors from a specific country tend to serve their own local market and are content with their local customer base. However, large localization vendor Web sites also seemed to show lack of ccTLD use and an overall low level of localization on various parameters we used in this study. So, do these vendors really believe that Web site localization practices are important? From this study's results, the picture we get is that vendor sites are lacking commitment toward localization. However, before reaching any conclusion we should consider a bigger picture and understand what are the reasons for localization vendors to not sufficiently localize their sites? In the limitations and future research section we discuss some of these issues.

MANAGERIAL IMPLICATIONS

With few large localization vendors like Lionbridge Technologies, SDL International, and Translations.com holding the top positions there seems to be a large segment of niche markets that small localization vendors or single language vendors are able to serve without much competition. However, as the localization industry consolidates and matures, it will be difficult for small localization vendors to remain competitive and profitable by just providing generic translation/localization services to niche markets or local country markets. Even large sized localization vendors risk losing their competitive position due to industry consolidation, over-reliance on generic translation services, and cut throat price-based competition. If the localization industry wants to keep its competitive position and provide a healthy industry environment for both small and large localization vendors to grow, it must go beyond generic product offerings in the form of translation services, and expand the definition of localization to include not just translation but to also offer:

- Localization of the Website lay out and navigation based on locale-specific requirements.
- Cross-cultural Web site and user interface usability research.
- Country-market analysis
- Cultural customization of Web sites to specific locales
- International online business strategy and marketing expertise
- Online branding and advertising localization
- International search engine optimization and search engine marketing

These are just some ways the industry can expand the definition of localization and offer complementary services that can help companies differentiate their offerings from their competitors and stay profitable.

Localization services firms, in order to be profitable in the future, must practice what they preach. They must practice not only to exemplify their services being sold, but also to appeal to an international market. Research has shown that individuals prefer Web sites that are localized to their own language and culture (Singh et al., 2004).

LIMITATIONS AND FUTURE RESEARCH

The current study is an exploratory study focusing on the amount of Web site localization used by vendors offering Web site localization services compared to their clients level of Web site localization (multinational company Web sites). So, the data analysis here is a simple frequency examination. The goal of this study was to examine the use of localization practices frequency and that goal was met. However, further, more in-depth data analysis could be used in the future. Another limitation to this study was the sample used. The vendor Web sites may not be intended for an international audience. As stated earlier, many of the smaller localization firms are serving single, niche markets. On the other hand, multinational company Web sites, by their nature, are meant for international consumption. Therefore, it is expected that vendor sites may be less localized than their client's sites. However, the results show that even the large localization services firms lack localized content on their Web sites to meet the needs of an international market. Furthermore, even the smaller firms should aspire to exemplify the practices that they preach.

Future research directions should include a closer examination of localization practices within the localization industry. A comparison between the large localization service firms Web sites and their smaller, niche market, counterparts is needed. Also, a longitudinal study examining the increased amount of localization used on the internet is warranted. Is the trend to localize Web sites to a greater extent, or are more Websites trying to serve a smaller, local niche market instead of an international market? If the trend is to serve international markets then are the localization practices keeping up with international expansion?

To further shed light into why localization vendors are not actively localizing their sites we need further research to investigate their overall globalization strategy by asking questions such as:

- Are the localization vendors just targeting some large multinational companies from predominantly English speaking countries (U.S., U.K., Australia etc.) and a few other non-English speaking countries?
- What resource and marketing constraints do these vendor companies face?
- Another interesting question to investigate is to understand the top management willingness to globalization and their vision for globalization. It seems several small and medium sized localization companies are run by top management which has primarily a translation background. So is it the lack of business education background that is restricting the global expansion of localization vendors?

Thus, to get a full picture of Web globalization efforts of localization vendors, we should not lonely study localization vendors Web sites but also understand their overall globalization strategy and how it has evolved over time.

CONCLUSION

The findings of this research suggest that both localization vendor and multinationals are barely localizing their Web site offerings. This may not be all bad news, as more multinationals seek to tap online markets and compete for them, the winner will be the multinational sites that are truly localized and speak to their international customers in their language and culture. Localization service sales may be increased by simply practicing what they preach.

Not only has research shown that consumers prefer localized Web site content, but research has also shown that by localizing you can increase traffic to Web sites (Ferranti, 1999), and increase willingness to purchase (Singh et al., 2004). Localization services vendors may be missing out on increased sales by simply preaching and not practicing. Actually, applying what they preach to their own Web sites, according to research, should increase the amount of traffic to their sites while also increasing the willingness to purchase their localization services. This means that the localization industry can look forward to significant growth, but only if it can educate its multinational clients about the importance of localization and the best way to do that is to practice what they preach.

ACKNOWLEDGMENT

The data collection for this study was supported by students and Gary Muddyman, CEO of Conversis Global.

REFERENCES

Albers-Miller, N., & Gelb, B. (1996). Business advertising appeals as mirror of cultural dimensions: A study of eleven countries. *Journal of Advertising, 25*(Winter), 57–70.

Culnan, M. J., & Armstrong, P. K. (1999). Information privacy concerns, procedural fairness and impersonal trust: An empirical investigation. *Organization Science, 10*, 104–115. doi:10.1287/orsc.10.1.104

Cyr, D., & Lew, R. (2003). Emerging challenges in the software localization industry. *Thunderbird International Business Review, 45*(3), 337–358. doi:10.1002/tie.10077

Cyr, D., & Trevor-Smith, H. (2004). Localization of Web design: An empirical comparison of German, Japanese and United Stats Web site characteristics. *Journal of the American Society for Information Science and Technology, 55*(13), 1199–1208. doi:10.1002/asi.20075

DePalma, D., & Beninatto, R. (2006). Language services 2006: Supply-side outlook. *Research Report by Common Sense Advisory*. Retrieved July 28 2008, from www.commonsenseadvisory.com

Esselink, B. (2000). *A practical guide to localization (Language International world directory)*. Philadelphia: John Benjamins Publishing Co.

Ferranti, M. (1999). From global to local. *InfoWorld, 21*(41), 36–37.

Fletcher, R. (2006). The impact of culture on Web site content, designs, and structure: An international and a multicultural perspective. *Journal of Communication Management, 10*(3), 259–273. doi:10.1108/13632540610681158

Fock, H. (2000, September). *Cultural influences on marketing communication on the World Wide Web*. Paper presented at the Multicultural Marketing Conference, Hong Kong.

Globalization Industry Primer (LISA). (2007). Globalization industry primer. *LISA*. Retrieved April 3, 2009, from http://www.lisa.org/ Globalization-indust. 468.0.html#c261.

Grant, J., & Davis, L. (1997). Selection and use of content experts for instrument development. *Research in Nursing & Health, 20*, 269–274. doi:10.1002/(SICI)1098-240X(199706)20:3<269::AID-NUR9>3.0.CO;2-G

Hall, E. T. (1976). *Beyond culture*. Garden City, NY: Doubleday & Company.

Han, S. P., & Shavitt, S. (1994). Persuasion and culture: Advertising appeals in individualistic and collectivistic societies. *Journal of Experimental Psychology, 30*, 8–18.

Hermeking, M. (2005). Culture and Internet consumption: Contributions from cross-cultural marketing and advertising research. *Journal of Computer-Mediated Communication, 11*(1). Retrieved April 3, 2009, from http://jcmc.indiana.edu/ vol11/issue1/ hermeking.html.

Internet World Stats. (2008). World Internet users and population stats. *Internet World Stats*. Retrieved July 28, 2008, from http://www.internetworldstats.com /stats.htm.

Jarvenpaa, S. L., Tractinsky, N., & Vitale, M. (2000). Consumer trust in an Internet store. *Information Technology Management, 1*(1-2), 45–71. doi:10.1023/A:1019104520776

Jupiter Research. (2008). Jupiter research. *Jupiter Research*. Retrieved July 28, 2008, from http://www.jupiterresearch.com /bin/item.pl/home/.

Kwintessential (2009). Culture and Web site localization. *Kwintessential*. Retrieved April 3, 2009, from http://www.kwintessential.co.uk /translation/articles/ culture-Website-localization.html.

Lee, L. Z. (2005). Evolving localization and its brand extension. *Galaxy Newsletter, Q4*. Retrieved April 3, 2009, from http://www.gala-global.org/ newsletters/ newsletter_3516.html.

Liu, C., Marchewka, J., & Ku, C. (2004). American and Taiwanese perceptions concerning privacy, trust, and behavioral intentions in electronic commerce. *Journal of Global Information Management, 12*(1), 18–40. doi:10.4018/jgim.2004010102

Localization Program at California State University. Chico, College of Business (2008). What is localization? *The Localization Program*. Retrieved November 26, 2008, from http://www.csuchico.edu/localize/ whatislocalization.html.

Lommel, A. (2003). LISA, The localization industry primer, 2nd edition. *LISA*. Retrieved July 28, 2008, from http://www.lisa.org/ Globalization-Indust.468.0.html?&no_cache=1&sword_list[]= industry&sword_list[]= localizatio&sword_list[]=primer.

Luna, D., Peracchio, L. A., & de Juan, M. D. (2002). Cross-cultural and cognitive aspects of Web site navigation. *Journal of the Academy of Marketing Science, 30*(4), 397–410. doi:10.1177/009207002236913

Mooij, M. D. (1998). *Global marketing and advertising. Understanding cultural paradox.* Thousand Oaks, CA: Sage Publications.

Pollach, I. (2005). Corporate self-presentation on the WWW: Strategies for enhancing usability, credibility and utility. *Corporate Communications, 10*(4), 285–301. doi:10.1108/13563280510630098

Simon, S. J. (2001). The impact of culture and gender on Web sites: An empirical study. *The Data Base for Advances in Information Systems, 32*(1), 18–37.

Singh, N., & Boughton, P. (2002). *Measuring Web site globalization: A cross-sectional country and industry level analysis. Proceedings from American Marketing Association Educators' Conference (Winter), Austin, TX.* Chicago: American Marketing Association.

Singh, N., & Boughton, P. (2005). Measuring Web site globalization: A cross-sectional country and industry level analysis. *Journal of Website Promotion, 1*(3), 3–20. doi:10.1300/J238v01n03_02

Singh, N., Furrer, O., & Ostinelli, M. (2004). To localize or to standardize on the Web: Empirical evidence from Italy, India, Netherlands, Spain, and Switzerland. *Multinational Business Review, 12*(1), 69–88.

Singh, N., & Little, J. (2009). Culturally customizing international Web sites. In Shareef, M. A., Dwivedi, Y. K., Williams, M. D., & Singh, N. (Eds.), *Proliferation of the Internet economy: E-commerce for global adoption, resistance, and cultural evolution.* Hershey, PA: IGI Global.

Singh, N., & Matsuo, H. (2004). Measuring cultural adaptation on the Web: A study of U.S. and Japanese Web sites. *Journal of Business Research, 57*(8), 864–872. doi:10.1016/S0148-2963(02)00482-4

Singh, N., & Pereira, A. (2005). *The culturally customized Web site: Customizing Web sites for the global marketplace.* Burlington, MA: Elsevier.

Singh, N., Toy, D. R., & Wright, L. K. (2009). A diagnostic framework for measuring Web site localization. *Thunderbird International Business Review, 51*(3), 281–295. doi:10.1002/tie.20265

The Localization Industry Standards Association. (2008). What is globalization? *The Localization Industry Standards Association.* Retrieved July 28, 2008, from http://lisa.org/ What-Is-Globalization.48.0.html.

Violino, B. (2001). E-business lurches abroad. *Internet Week, March 19th.* Retrieved July 28, 2008, from http://www.internetweek.com.

This work was previously published in International Journal of E-Adoption, Volume 1, Issue 2, edited by Sushil Sharma, pp. 36-54, copyright 2009 by IGI Publishing (an imprint of IGI Global).

Section 4
E–Readiness and E–Government

Chapter 13
Evolution, Development and Growth of Electronic Money

A. Seetharaman
Multimedia University, Malaysia

John Rudolph Raj
Multimedia University, Malaysia

ABSTRACT

Traditional cash has long been envisioned to be replaced with 'virtual' or electronic cash. Electronic money and electronic payment systems for retail transactions are commanding widespread attention. Undeniably, electronic payment cites advantages such as efficiency and convenience to the consumers. However, with the rapid change and advances in technology, has posed significant risks, related to ensuring security and integrity of electronic payment systems in today's cyber world. Therefore, this study attempts to understand the role of electronic payments for consumers, and to identify the problems and solutions in the emergence of electronic payments. This study also explores the challenges of electronic payments from a security perspective, in particular, and provides preliminary security countermeasures for each of the issues discussed. Beside that, the study also discusses further on the prospects of electronic payment systems. It is essential to put in place an integrated, overall risk-management approach to security, including independent security assessments as one of the components in the use of electronic payment products.

INTRODUCTION

Money in retail transactions is becoming electronic, transformed into information and stored on a computer chip in a plastic card or on a personal computer so that it can be transmitted over open information systems, such as the Internet. An electronic payment is characterized as a substitute for physical currency. It is a replacement for currency like other payment mechanisms such as credit cards, checks, traveler's checks, and debit cards. Electronic payment is a direct substitute for traditional cash, where value is transferred electronically to pay for goods and services at vending

DOI: 10.4018/978-1-60960-597-1.ch013

machines, retail establishments, over networks, or through direct person-to-person exchange medium. The goal of electronic payment is to make purchasing simpler. For example, stored-value cards let consumers transfer cash value to a card. They are commonly used in public transportation, at colleges and universities, at petrol stations, and for prepaid mobile phone usage.

The potential benefits of e-money to consumers include:

- faster, more efficient transactions
- less need to carry pocket money
- loyalty and frequent user plans
- automatic personal financial record-keeping
- possible financial anonymity
- possible security from theft
- access to electronic commerce
- more personalized banking services and instruments

The potential benefits of e-money to businesses are extensive, which include:

- instant transactions
- substantial cost savings because of the reduction in the physical handling of currency
- easier collection of marketing information on customers; and promotion of 'free banking'

The explosion of electronic payment technology raises a number of security issues. Security factors are perhaps the biggest deterrent for individuals interested in making on-line purchases. Most people fear giving their credit card numbers, phone numbers or addresses not knowing who will be able to retrieve that information without their consent. It is interesting to note that most people don't even give it a second thought when purchasing items with a credit card over the phone, but to ask them to do it from the networks will make them very uncomfortable and unsecured.

From an operator's view, the cost of installing any technological infrastructure with the current equipment will need a significant financial outlay. There is always the barrier of compatibility of the methods of payment being used currently with the adaptation of a new system. Besides that, operators have to find ways and means to limit costs of using the new system than utilizing the current ones. It may be a daunting task of re-engineering the system into converting itself into the electronic money world, but undoubtedly, it is possible to do so in order to keep up with the current trend.

RESEARCH PROBLEM

The emergence of electronic payments can be expected to work just like paper money without the risk, convenience and cost associated with handling, administering and safeguarding traditional currency. It plays a key role in today's global economies. But, there are also obstacles in the widespread use of electronic payments that can slow down its growth in the marketplace. This is compounded by the fact that consumers lack confidence in the potential use of electronic payment systems.

Objectives of the Research

The objectives of the research are:

a. To understand the role of electronic payment and analyze its related problems

b. To identify the evolution and growth of the technologies needed for electronic payment systems.

c. To analyze the security framework to prevent crimes and fraud and to reduce its risks.

d. To analyze the solutions and the potential development and growth of electronic payments in the marketplace.

Scope of Study

The term "electronic payment" has been used in different settings to describe a wide variety of payment mechanism systems and technologies. The research study was set up to provide a comprehensive panorama of the position of the electronic payments. A thorough investigation was needed to address issues that could hamper the growth of electronic commerce. Next, the study also focused on the computer network or development of telecommunication technologies playing a key role in the electronic payment systems. The study also highlighted on the security framework of electronic payment systems. In addition, this study will discuss the problems and solutions of electronic payments. By assessing the problems and preferences, the research study will further analyse the potential of electronic payments in the marketplace.

LITERATURE SURVEY

Allen, Helen (2003), mentioned that the innovative products in retail payments are based on e-payments. Their usage has increased quite rapidly over the years. The authors found that the main access channel of e-payments services is based on the Internet, mobile phones and prepaid card or e-purses. According to Allen, in the United Kingdom, 90% of online purchases are through credit cards. The cards nowadays are being adapted, for the purpose of being more secure and convenient for the Internet users. Pre-paid airtime on mobile phones are suitable for lower value purchases. This is to aim at the specific market segment, such as younger users who do not own a credit card or operate a bank account. In addition, the authors found that using e-payments, may affect the frequency of transaction and cause substitution in the new market. The authors say that, in order to establish this new service, there has to be sufficient end-users carrying the cards, retailers who are ready to accept cards, and facilities to load cards are the basic requirement for this new service in the market. Technical security, consumer protection and regulation are the main policy issues in e-payments service too. Inadequate securities can have adverse effects on users' confidence across this new service. The authors too discuss that there are two main areas of interest for e-payment. Firstly, we need to tackle transactions that could move outside the existing payments systems. The second area of interest is where e-payment services interact with existing payments systems. However, the article does not cover the prospect of e-payments driving the economy and increasing transactional efficiencies and economic growth in the country. The concept of a cashless society is a tantalizing prospect for the twenty-first century.

Richard Crone (2003) mentioned that on a daily basis, there are more than 100,000 customers enrolling directly with recurring billings to manage their accounts online. It is due to the fact that online billing offers virtually a 'no cost and low risk 'way of service. It can be projected that, the growth of the number of users activating direct electronic billing and payment will be five times faster than online bill payment option or any other internet banking. The most attractive advantages of recurring billings are cost savings from reduced printing, mailing, and processing paper payments. The consumers can individually access the billing agency's website on their own and can view their statement online. The author also found that, the number of customers who agree to pay "electronically" is much less then the total number of consumers who enroll to view their accounts online. Almost all the purchases made through the internet are consummated with a card-based payment. Billing agencies know that accepting card payments can streamline the electronic payment processes, because the input request only requires the card number and expiration date only. Card based input is much easier and faster than prompting a consumer for the routing and transit number that appear in the

Magnetic Ink Character Recognition (MICR) line at the bottom of a paper check. The author explains the benefits of all the parties that use and accept card-based payments for recurring bills. The cash flow of billing agencies will improve since e-payments typically transfer to account faster than other form of payments. Beside that, all parties can benefit from the decrease in cost per payment process by over 50 percent. The new revenue potential from increased cross-sell and affiliate marketing is another benefit of using electronic payments. The author did not touch on why the consumers mostly view their account statements online instead of making transactions online. He also did not explain the ways that can make the consumers fully accept and trust this new service in the future.

Lafferty Ltd (2005) is of the opinion that the payments industry today is facing an attack from online criminals. In the last few months, well over 40 million credit cards were potentially exposed to fraudulent transactions. Obviously, the global payment industry was now facing a potential security threat. There are a few branded cards in the market, like MasterCard, Visa, American Express and Discover cards. The secret code numbers printed on the card itself is the main stolen data from others. It is easier to produce a counterfeit version. MasterCard spokeswoman Jessica Antle said that, "proportionally very small incidences of fraud have been detected". She did not mention whether this security breach was an inside job or from the external hacker. The author also mentions that, the online phishing attacks have prompted four of the UK's largest banks to delay intra-bank online payments between accounts. According to a study by technology research consultancy Gartner, estimates that 2.4 million US online consumers lost their money directly because of receiving phishing attacks emails in the 12 months to May 2005. Since the online attack, Gartner found that 30 percent of 5000 internet users were less frequently using online purchases and 14 percent have stopped using electronic payment

services due to security fears. The author says that, banks and financial institutions involved in online payments should increase internet security measures. CEO of Net 1 UEPS Technologies, Serge Belamat says that passwords and other forms of identity verification always remain on customers' computers and are the basic problem with secure payments. The hacker will always find a best way to gain access to this. EPN's Universal Payment Identification Code (UPIC) becomes an organization's permanent electronic payment address. In this article, the author had not covered what the internet users should do when facing online fraud. It just mentions the new approach of the online security, without guiding the users on the features and benefits of using the new approach. This will cause the users to lose confidence in using the approaches suggested.

Will Wade (2004), indicated that many corporations have realized the value of electronic payments. Government agencies that process large numbers of taxpayer remittances have been less eager to install similar systems. As a result, some agencies that do accept electronic payments use a vendor that charges consumers a "convenience fee" to cover both the processing costs and its own profit margin. The in-house electronic payments systems offer a huge potential for increased operational efficiencies and faster settlement, said Gary Grippo, the assistant commissioner for federal finance in the Treasury Department's financial management service, "There is a major shift going on in the reasons why agencies are adopting electronic payment technologies," said Mr. Gentile. In the past, he said, offering electronic payment options typically meant allowing individuals to use credit cards and was considered a convenience for the person making a payment. Mr. Grippo, who oversees the federal government's multitrillion-dollar revenue collection process, agrees. Not to charge people a fee for paying various fees or taxes is one of those incentives to attract more people using electronic payments. The fee applies only to credit card payments, which are outsourced to two vendors, Official Payments Corp. and Link2Gov Corp., because of a law prohibiting the government from accepting credit card payments on federal tax payments. All other federal agencies can accept card payments directly, without charging a convenience fee. Because of the huge number of electronic payments the federal government receives from businesses for such items as payroll withholding taxes, 80% of the dollar value of incoming payments arrived in a digital format in fiscal 2003, though the number of electronic transactions initiated by individuals is far lower. Jim Weaver, the chairman and chief executive officer of Tier Technologies Inc., the parent company of Official Payments, says these fees are not deterring people from making payments electronically. Official Payments, which manages card payment systems for local, state, and federal agencies, says it processes 72% of all IRS card payments. Despite the fees, Mr. Weaver said, the number of card payments to government agencies is surging; the value of traffic fines paid electronically through Official Payments has risen 12% in the past year, and property tax payments has grown 39%. For starters, he said, paper checks must be manually keyed into the system, and that labor-intensive processes can generate a lot of mistakes; the error rate is 30 times higher for paper payments than it is for e-payments. Electronic transactions can be filed into the government's books as much as a month sooner than paper payments.

Money laundering is defined as the act of disguising the origin or ownership of illegally gained funds to make them appear legitimate. The huge sum of money is obtained through illegal activities and has been linked to nearly all kinds of crime for profit including organized and white collar crimes. There was a growing concern on money laundering as it is often associated with drug trafficking, bank savings abuses, real estate fraud, and tax evasion. Money laundering was first declared as a crime under the Money Laundering Control Act of 1986 of the U.S Code. Under this act, the penalties include 10 to 20 years in prison and substantial fines. The money laundering comprised three steps, namely placement, layering, and integration. Cash will be introduced into the banking systems in order to fulfill the placement step. The layering process will then take place where the money will be separated from its criminal origins by means of financial transactions. Such transactions include bank accounts, travelers' checks, and cashiers' checks. The aggregations of funds with money owned legally through false explanation for its ownership will complete the final integration step in money laundering. The author has successfully elaborated on the background of money laundering including its history and how it is being carried out in the modern era today. The technical aspects of money transfer and transaction has also been covered tactfully. However, the only shortcoming of the article is that the author failed to provide substantial explanation on how this matter should be tackled and curbed.

Ovum said that, *"Electronic payments are the way to the heart of your e-commerce customers"*. It is very easy to make payments for the goods and services through the advance technologies. The buyer and seller will be feeling secure, affordable and flexible by using electronic payments. The author suggests that traditional credit cards can be replaced by the second-generation electronic payment methods. *"Credit cards are necessary for e-commerce, but not sufficient,"* said Duncan Brown. From the research of Ovum, there are five different types of new electronic payment methods. First is a metered payment, which are the electronic transactions that appear as itemized entries on a bill. Second is an Optimized card payment. This method is more secure, because it has built-in payment card enhancements, such as smart card, virtual cards. Third method is E-checks. This method is based on online transaction between the buyer and seller bank account. Next method is E-cash such as micropayments for digital goods. The last method is alternative currencies. It is non-cash initiatives that used to replace traditional currencies. Payment Service Providers (PSPs) is one type of electronic payments which was discovered by Ovum. The PSPs is bringing the convenience for the sellers and buyers. It also can be a central broker of electronic payments. The role of players in the electronic payment area is to enhance the services and develop the transaction to facilitate the payments, such as provide brokerage, optimization, aggregation, internationalization, and billing services. This can displace banks as well. Brown said, *"They run the risk of complacency, and may run themselves out of the market eventually through their own egos"*. This article had covered many new methods of electronic payments. Unfortunately, the author has not clearly explained the threats that will emerge from using the new methods of electronic money.

Daniel Thomas (2002) in his article mentioned that the UK retailers start to pay attention to online credit card verification scheme which could help them to save millions of pounds a year from the lost of online fraud. The launching of Visa online payment authentication service in April will be able to reduce the number of e-commerce disputes by 80%, and UK retailers could save up to £55m a year. The cardholders will be able to use personalized passwords to verify their identities when shopping online. Unfortunately, after a few months the scheme was launched, the response was very poor. However, this slow trend changed when HSBC became the third acquiring bank to sign up for this service. A numbers of major online retailers had signed up for this service after HSBC. *"Our effort so far has been with the acquirers such as Barclaycard and Royal Bank of Scotland, which cover 80% of all Visa's e-commerce volume,"* said Sandra Alzetta, senior vice-president at Virtual Visa. Interactive Media in Retail Group (IMRG) had launched an industry-wide-fraud database, which is designed to allow retailers to safely share lists containing data about fraudsters, including their names, credit card numbers and address details. Beside that, CyberSource also allow e-retailers to check

the names, postcodes and addresses of online buyers suspected of fraud. Bill Briggs, chairman of the data and information group at the British Retail Consortium, said *"Selling for profit is a competitive issue but protecting our profit from crime should not be."* James Roper, chief executive of online trade body IMRG is confident that the warm card file service together with Visa and MasterCard's new services, will able to reduce the online fraud cases. But it is very difficult to convince e-retailers to sign up for these services. As we know internet network is the future and we want it to be safe, but it looks like moving slow, and people are not willing to change their status quo. The author had covered various ways to protect the retailers from online fraud. The collaboration of people is also an important element to make these services a success, but the author failed to cover the ways and means to eliminate the resistance.

Peter Buck (1996) mentioned that there is an explosive increase in the use of the Internet, mail-order and catalog based services. Newspapers have already expanded into online editions too. The successful use of the Internet will impose a payment mechanism. The distinction between services and digital products has become difficult to determine in the cyber world. The online users rely on credit and debit mechanisms for payment transactions. *"Much of the literature to do with electronic payment mechanisms, whether on the Internet, ISH or elsewhere, has been dominated by academics and mathematicians,"* the author said. All payment mechanisms involved three parties: users, issuers and regulators. The security requirements fall into three categories, which is safety of the payment itself, privacy of the consumers, and trustworthiness of all participants. The author also explained some constraints including integration, acceptability and portability. Today, there are various types of payment mechanisms on the internet, such as credit or debit card, prepaid tokens like phone cards and traveler's checks. Some Internet banks have started offering electronic bank on the Internet. This service includes electronic cheques and BankNet. Cyber-Cash provides free client software to users and merchants, implementing their Secure Internet Payment Service™. A token-based mechanism, such as Digicash system involves the creation of "electronic coins" in the form of digitally signed numbers in exchange for money from the user's bank account. In this smart environment, there are many payment mechanisms being proposed for the Internet. Most are being proposed by technologists and concentrate on overcoming the insecurity of the Internet to enable existing credit/debit card mechanisms to be used. Electronic commerce on the Internet needs payment mechanisms that can cater for as much diversity as commerce in the real world. The author had covered most of the payment mechanisms; however, he has not addressed the negative effects of online payment.

Elliott C McEntee (2000) discussed the dynamic evolution of payment systems from barter to coins to paper currencies to checks and to electronic payments. Today commerce continues to migrate to a more automated and electronic environment, so too must payments. NACHA had developed the Automated Clearing House (ACH) for safety, secure, and low cost of electronic payment method. Credit cards became one of the mechanism payment methods for B2C in the US. An obvious payment method is to allow consumers to authorize debits to their bank account in two ways. First, it uses the ACH Network, second is to debit a consumer's account through an electronic funds transfer (EFT) Network. Under this method, consumers widely use ATM card for online purchasing, but instead of using a Personal Identification number (PIN), consumer used the digital signature to verify. Besides that, Direct Pay has allowed consumers to checkout their financial institution's website and to identify their financial status. NACHA had developed a web site – eBilling.org, to encourage electronic billing and payment. The ACH Network is already widely used for B2B commerce. The author said

that electronic payment can greatly reduce the administrative burden in digital marketplaces. The demand for cross-border payments has increased due to the growth in global commerce. In 1999, NACHA had created WATCH (Worldwide Automated Transaction Clearing House) to process cross-border payments. Innovations in electronic payments are growing rapidly in the marketplace. ACH Network is a secure and reliable payments system for conducting e-commerce. This article explains that NACHA developed many solutions to improve the payment systems in the US; nevertheless, the author did not specify which payment system is the most secure for consumers.

The survey of the art in payment technologies and emerging development has been elaborated by N. Asokan and friends (1997). Electronic means of payment suffer security issues and risks. Today, the flow of money from payer via the issuer and acquirer to the payee has been implemented by electronic payment. Security requirements of electronic payment systems are based on their features. A payment system with integrity disallows money to be taken from a user without explicit authorization by that user. Confidentiality is another requirement for security. The identity of payer or payee, purchase content, and amount must be restricted only to the parties involved. Networking services and all software and hardware components should be reliable and available. The techniques used for authorizing money transfer can be categorized as online and offline. Mondex and CAFÉ (Conditional Access for Europe) are offline systems. Tamper-resistant hardware can be used to prevent double spending. Thus for true security, trusted input/output channels between the user and the smart card must exist. Beside that, cryptographic techniques are essential tools in building secure payment systems over open networks. First Virtual is a cryptofree system, which relies on out-band security. Generic payment switch is an online payment system that implements both the prepaid and pay-later models. According to the author, *"Authentication based on shared-key cryptography requires that the prover (the payer) and a verifier (the issuer) both have a shared secret."* Complete payment systems using public-key cryptograph include e-cash, NetCash, CyberCash, the 3KP variant of iKP, and Secure Electronic Transactions (SET). The payment systems should provide payer anonymity and untraceable with respect to the privacy of the payee. Micropayment techniques must be both inexpensive and fast, because it is a low-value payment. The European Standardization Organization (CEN), Europay, MasterCard, and Visa (EMV) are working on standards for smart-card-based electronic payment systems. Today, the electronic payment technology exists to prevent and to secure the payment over the Internet. The author had covered the issues of security for electronic payment, but he did not mention other issues that electronic payment will encounter, such as policy and regulations issues.

Setsuya Sato and John Hawkins (2001) mentioned the current and potential changes in exchanges and trading systems, payment systems and financial institutions were greatly affected by the internet and other innovative information technology. Korea has higher usage of high-tech equipment and e-finance. The author said the future growth of e-finance is hard to predict. Online day traders have emerged in United States retail broking market. Electronic systems have made far less impact on transaction between banks and their customers. E-trading is now predominant in many equity and future markets, it can cut trading costs. E-banking services need high initial set-up costs. E-finance has the potential to create new and radically different business models for banks used for evaluating and pricing loans for customers. In an e-finance world, cross-border expansion becomes cheaper and less risky, but it is harder for an offshore bank to build up trust, because of non-familiarity with the market conditions. *"Increased competitive pressures and the speed of technology changes are leading to rapidly increasing outsourcing relationships."* the authors

said. Internet users do not trust E-banking due to an important factor - security concerns. Besides that, other public policy issues also emerge as a risk of E-finance. E-banking could facilitate money laundering, privacy, and other consumer issues. Banks are not integrating retail payments into their systems. According to Forrester Research, in the US, the average income of people using e-banking services is twice that of people not online. E-banking services need high investment but lower marginal cost and over time it will speed up bank consolidation. According to the authors, today, the key challenge for the central banks is e-finance risks. Development of e-finance will be affected by monetary policy. Privately issued e-money on the internet is another new challenge. This article had not covered the ways to increase the number of people using internet payments for trading.

Benjamin J. Cohen (2001) stated that people are now doing business in cyberspace, across the internet, and World Wide Web. Electronic money is an effective means of payment to expanding e-commerce. The era of e-money is a natural development of globalizing world economy. There are two basic forms of e-money: smart cards and network money, but both are also still in their infancy. The emergence of e-money creates some critical issues, such as tricky technical issues, security, anonymity, portability and trust. The obstacle to the success of electronic money is the conservative bias of the marketplace. The most critical question of all is the question of value. According to many economies in the world, central bankers had experienced increased difficulty in controlling monetary aggregates, owing to accelerating cross-border competition among currencies. The major problem of monetary policy is that not all of the money stock can be controlled directly, so the challenge for central banks is the deterritorialization which represents a fundamental change in the nature of monetary governance. *"The effect of electronic money will be to expand the population of currencies circulating within each country further eroding an already increasingly tenuous connection between nominal demand and supply of national money,*" the author explained. In U.S, Europe, and Japan, there is greater online access than in other countries. So if electronic money is to gain widespread acceptance anywhere, it will mostly start in these areas.

The question "Will the creation of electronic money be acceptable as a new form of money and become the new medium of exchange to take over traditional money ", had been elaborated by Edward W. Kelley Jr. (1997) There are three functions of traditional money: (i) money is a unit of account, or a method to measure and record value, (ii) money is a way to store value conveniently for future use, (iii) money is a medium of exchange. The use of modern electronics and computers enable money to be transferred virtually instantaneously. Electronic cash serves better functions then the historic money; it is very convenient for consumers. Privacy is the tricky issue as consumers wish to keep the transaction details privately, so merchants and issuers should ensure they keep an appropriate record of their transactions.

The electronic banking products designed to improve access to existing retail banking functions will almost certainly soon find a place in our financial activities. The stored-value or e-money products could at the least evolve to serve a special niche in small transactions. Innovation of the financial system may lead to noteworthy new efficiencies for payment system. *"One thing I will predict with confidence: the forms of money will continue to evolve, as scientists and engineers continue to advance the applicable technologies,"* the author said. This article covered most of the benefits of electronic money; however, it lacks solid examples to prove to consumers on the efficiency and effectiveness of this new payment system.

Ed Stevens (2002) mentioned the prospect of new forms of electronic money holdings and suggested new challenges that could make central banks obsolete and reduce their power to control inflation. Electronic Funds Transfer (ETF) has replaced paper checks and currency with purely paperless electronic payments. The automated clearinghouse (ACH) is being used for retail payments for sending and receiving routine debits. *"Today, Fedwire, the Reserve Banks' wire transfer service, and CHIPS, another private service, handle about $2 trillion in electronic payments daily,"* the author said. If one day, electronic money were to replace today's currency holdings, the Federal Reserve Banks would lose nearly $30 billion in annual revenue, the central bank might be left with no customers for its deposit facilities. However, electronic money can allow banks to track actual versus expected inflows and outflows and manage their end-of-day balance at the Federal Reserve more precisely.

The advances of computer and telecommunication technology facilities allows depository institutions to avoid reserve requirement, so too many it will reflect the holding of bank deposits and stimulate the regulator to cut reserve requirements. Charles Freedman has argued that stored value cards will influences the development of network money and the policy rate. Another debating issue is demand to hold central bank base money may dry up longer. Lombard facility and conduct open market operations in the money markets are the ways the central bank could influence the price at the balance trade. The European Central Bank (ECB) ensures the safety of the public's money holdings and the control of the price level. The competing private suppliers of payments services will emerge if government did not preserve the roles of currency and central bank deposits, and users stop using central bank money and settlement accounts. The author argued that most monetary instruments might some day be issued by institutions other than depository institutions, since there is ample evidence of a shrinking demand for deposits at the central bank. The author had discussed the future of the central bank; nevertheless he had not covered the prospect of the development and growth of electronic money to the society in the marketplace.

S. Peter Buck (1997) identifies the different types of payment mechanisms that are being used. Today, everyone need services, this has caused the increase in the use of the commercial online services such as CompuServe, Prodigy, America Online, eWorld, CIX and so on. The future Information Super Highway (ISH) is as significant now as it ever will be. There were two key problems in the electronic marketplace: (i) protecting property rights, (ii) making payments. Most transactions are now conducted in the cyberspace of banking computers and communications networks, cash were a small component of money. There are several types of payment mechanisms schemes in the real world, such as credit mechanisms (e.g. Email, First Virtual, Cybercash, Visa/Master cards), debit mechanisms (e.g. BankNet, FSTC Electronic Checks), token (e.g. Digicash), and cash (e.g. Mondex). Although in the marketplace emergence many types of electronic payment mechanisms, but the most essence part is left, lack of attention to what the potential users actually want from such a mechanism. Any payment mechanisms will involve three significant parties; there are the users, issuers, and regulators. All users also required the flexible, ease for use, no additional transaction cost, and effectiveness payment schemes. *"Collecting small payments (micropayments) for each item of "information" as it is bought /used may be much simpler (cheaper) than maintaining billing or invoicing systems and recovering fees for total usage after the event."* the author said. Beside that, credit cards are not suitable for retailers used for low value transactions, because may be the cost of transaction is greater than their profit margin. From a user point of view, security of electronic money is the main obstacle. The privacy of the consumer, the trustworthiness of the retailers, and the safety of the payment itself is the issues the users always need to consider twice before they make transactions. Electronic commerce on the internet needs payment mechanisms that can cater for as much diversity as commerce in the real world. However, in this smart environment, must concentrate on overcoming the insecurity of the internet to enable existing credit /debit card mechanisms to use in the global cyber world. This article had covered many different types of payment mechanisms and security requirement needed, however the author did not clearly classify the types of payment mechanisms which are appropriate and used by different kind of users.

Ian Christie and friends (1999) mentioned that, recently Europe had begun to deploy digital money on a large scale: GeldKarte in Germany, Proton in Belgium, CASH in Switzerland and so on. Emergence of the Net has revitalized the digital money scene, and consumer can place their trust on this service. Prepaid mobile phone was one of the success examples. Electronic money enables to settle and clear so instantaneously, and it is cheaper to use because it is anonymously. In the new networked environment, wherever the IP goes, the money can go. Technology is the power of real drive towards the digital money. The issue of regulating digital money will be recognized as crucial. Glyn Davies has argued, "Money innovations have always tended to diminish state control over the monetary system." To prevent new forms of systematic social disadvantage arising, government should create "social inclusion" from the outside in the development of e-cash networks wherever feasible. E-cash systems raise issues about the protection of commercial and personal privacy, such as fraud and laundering. The main goals for a regulatory framework are: (i) measuring and controlling the money supply, (ii) avoiding negative impacts on public finance, (iii) protecting personal and organizational privacy, (iv) securing public trust in e-cash issuers, (v) preventing e-cash from exacerbating social exclusion. The authors also highlighted the importance of innovation by industry, cooperation as the basis for competition and the creation of a regulatory framework by government. The regulating authorities need to ensure that economically disadvantaged groups are not excluded from the digital money environment. The authors had elaborated most of the government regulatory issues of digital money, but had avoided the users point of view in digital money, although users were playing a key role in the expansion of this new money.

Isabelle T.D. Szmigin and friends (1999) had come out with a qualitative assessment of electronic cash. A paperless and cashless society had led to a decreased use of the cheque payment method. Debit card payments are widely used in the market due to cheaper processing cost. Credit card cardholders may receive over 50 days of free credit from the date of purchases. Besides that, smart cards are used as an electronic purse which offers benefits to cardholders and retailers in terms of security, convenience and to issuers in reduced handling costs. *"The future of retail financial services is the changing nature of consumer behavior and an increase in consumers discriminating between different service providers,"* Lewis said. The author found that all students like to make comparison of performance between electronic cash and the traditional form of cash. A qualitative study of students' use of a specific form of electronic cash, know as Mondex, which behaves like cash. Beside that, this card acts as the university identity and library card in Exeter University campus since 1996. It is because this card enables ease of loading, outlets acceptability and security of the card is reliable. The survey indicated that one of the problems encountered by students are that they did not know how much money they actually had on their Mondex card unless they used the separate "reader". According to the author, the advantages of Mondex is compatibility, communicability, complexity and risk, but to gain more general acceptance, it must match customers' functional and emotional requirements and it must encourage further use by point of sale incentives that give consumers real perceived value. The number of consumers using different types of card as payment method is dramatically increasing in the market today. The author had covered the advantages and limitation of Mondex, but unfortunately the survey was only concentrated on the students based group. So the findings of this research study were restrictive.

Nick Lockett (1999) had discussed the main legal issues on digital money. Money is a mechanism for value transfer. EFTPOS transaction is closest to cash because it is transferred instantaneously and satisfying the customer's liability to pay the merchant immediately. European Commission (EC) realized that, the success of electronic money is dependent on the level acceptance of consumers. The four main areas to boost consumer confidence: (i) proper supervisory framework is to ensure the constancy and soundness in the issuance of electronic money, (ii) the precision, liability and regulatory procedures for issuers and users, (iii) the emphasis by EC competition rules to achieve a proper balance between interoperability and competition in these markets, (iv) Security is vital to tackle the risks of fraud and counterfeit. Electronic money had some specific issues such as discharge of liability and digital discharge of debt. An operation of electronic money is to avoid deposit taking regulations by not lending out the deposits to other parties. Another issue is the increase in tax avoidance due to the possibility that electronic money can flow invisibly through the globe. Employee earnings, royalties, intellectual property income, capital gains, etc., can be paid in cash via unregulated networks to offshore banking havens, thus evading tax at source. Anonymous electronic money provides more opportunity for money laundering. According to the author, even though electronic money cannot yet function like "real" money, it has additional features over cash. "If security concerns are overcome, the electronic money market is bound to be lively and progressive and we can only hope that legal issues do not hinder or distort the market", the author explained. This article had covered up many issues of electronic money, but regrettably, the author did not point out the ways to avoid these security risks.

The technical security of electronic money products are the critical issues discussed by Heidi Richards (1997). New retail payment technologies, such as stored-value cards and electronic purses were designed to substitute cash. According to Heidi, an electronic money product was predictable as the target for fraud and theft. Smart card chip has been used in the design of tamper-resistant hardware to prevent technical threats. Besides that, electronic "note-based" systems are able to identify and have been assigned a specific, indivisible dollar value. The electronic money product developers used Cryptography to defend verification of the authenticity and integrity of messages and devices engaged in transactions. The implementation of low balance limits on cards or on transactions is one of the simplest and perhaps most effective means of deterring fraudulent attacks. The author mentioned that a task force would generate an electronic record of each transaction of electronic money products. Peer-to-peer payments may raise security concerns if it prevents a large amount of transaction information from getting through a security monitoring point. Non-technical threats and money laundering are other security issues that need to be addressed. The main differences between electronic money and physical currency are that electronic money products lack legal-tender status, a well-established legal basis, general acceptability, and government backing. However, electronic payment products have other features which are more useful to the range of payment options suitable for the current market. As a conclusion, the author had discussed many different approaches to electronic money products security designs to reduce fraudulent and other security risks most effectively. However, he was unable to point out which of the approaches would be absolutely immune to fraudulent attack.

Santosh K. Misra and friends (2004) stated that the digital technology has fostered innovation in electronic money and payment systems. Electronic money is the substitute of cash, tokens and banknotes in the new era. This medium of exchange will create a paperless or cashless society. The digital form of money can be used for transactions in the borderless business environment. The devices of e-money include a smart card, computer memory, mobile phone, magnetic swipe card, or personal digital assistant. Electronic money is useful for individuals who do not own credit cards to making payments over the internet. There are a few characteristics of electronic payment system, such as identifiability, scalability, consistency, interoperability, vulnerability, reliability, durability, and transaction costs. The legal and regulatory issues are the major concerns related to electronic money. The security of consumers, merchants and the robustness of financial markets necessitate protection against criminal abuse. Besides that, privacy is another vital concern of electronic payment system. The system must install safeguards to make total privacy; and all the transaction must be memory-free and anonymous. *"Protection of privacy must also apply to keeping one's information private from various governments"*, said the author. Electronic money transactions are an innovation that has made a major impact on the business value chain. The inadequacy of technological infrastructure is one of issues faced by both business and consumers. Cultural complexities pose an obstacle to the introduction of electronic money products into the country, especially new products requiring a change in existing behavior patterns. However, this electronic money will have the ability to drive the global economy. The author had discussed many critical issues in the development of electronic money, unfortunately, he did not point out his views on the growth potential of this new product.

Simon S.M. Ho and Victor T.F. Ng (1994) mentioned Hong Kong was the first in the world to launch the operation of an Electronic Fund Transfer at Point-of-sale (EFTPoS) system. This system was supported by all banks in Hong Kong and as an alternative payment system. Consumers can make purchase payments at the merchant's location by transferring funds from consumer's bank account to the shop's account immediately by using EFTPoS system. This kind of transactions can reduce bank paperwork, decrease the volume of fraud and result in fewer delinquent accounts because of bad cheques and credit cards. However, there are some barriers to EFTPoS adoption, so it takes time for this innovation to grow in the commercial environment. This study also includes the risk perceptions of consumers in different payment methods. The main risk is from consumer behaviors, which include financial risk, performance risk, physical risk, psychological risk, social risk and time-loss risk. According to the research findings, EFTPoS payments have a higher performance risk, particularly in large purchases, because such methods of payment are less acceptable to retailers. Therefore, EFTPoS terminals should expand their coverage more widely. In addition, credit cards have the lowest psychological risk and highest time loss risk, while cash has highest physical risk and lowest performance risk. The difference risk perception between users and non-users are psychological risk, time loss risk and financial risk. Today, the success of new electronic bank products needs to address adequately the crisis of technology feasibility, marketing and promotion efforts. The bank's marketers should launch some promotion programs to attract more consumers' acceptance of EFTPoS. Furthermore, the banks should recommend some risk reduction techniques to reduce their customers' fears and worries. The techniques include endorsement by key people, money back guarantee, live demonstration and free trial. To increase the number of consumers using of EFTPoS, it must create its own identity as a low risk, but high performance payment method within the new electronic money products. This article had pointed out many risk perception of various types of payment methods, but did not touch upon the classification and assessment of those risk reduction techniques introduced by banks.

Tomas Sander and Amnon Ta-Shma (1999) studied the approaches on solving criminal abuse which might be posed by anonymous electronic cash systems. In fact anonymity features of electronic payment systems play a vital role in protecting privacy in an electronic world. However, the monitoring of financial transactions and money trail is prevented by this complete anonymity, and perhaps, might thus forbid the job of triggering suspicion as well as combating serious crime activity such as money laundering and blackmailing. In the author's opinion, the major attacks on electronic cash systems are caused not by the anonymity feature but rather of the signature-based scheme that have been used to implement them Therefore, to solve these problems, escrowed cash systems with anonymity given to the users can be lifted by trustees, are brought out by the author. Nonetheless, several weaknesses in this escrowed cash systems are discussed. According to the author, to overcome these flaws, the following technical features should be employed in the electronic cash systems, which comprise of: (1) amount-limited anonymity where users whose transactions exceeding a certain amount do not enjoy the anonymity protection; (2) non-transferability where payment can only be made by the sole user who withdraws a coin; and (3) auditability where there should be a one-to-one correspondence between the withdrawal records and valid coins. By using the amount-limitedness and non-transferability, money-laundering and tax evasion can be addressed while auditability is used to address issuer related attacks, blackmailing and bank robbery. Besides that, two approaches are suggested in order to limit prospective abuses of anonymous electronic cash systems. Firstly, by using the banking system as the intermediary in monitoring financial transactions to ensure the safety and soundness of the financial system. Secondly, by targeting the large value transactions monitoring by the law enforcement agencies, instead of small value transactions. The restriction of this article is that there is a scarcity of practical studies by the author concerned with the prospective security issues and solutions of crimes caused by anonymous electronic cash.

RESEARCH METHODOLOGY

All resources for this research topic were collected from various sources of secondary data. The databases like EBSCO host research database, Proquest, Emerald-library, and InderScience had been widely used to gather most of the research articles. The various articles were published in the Journal of Finance, Journal of Logistics Information Management, and International Journal of Bank Marketing, and the Journal of International Finance. Beside that, the research was also conducted by using internet search engines such as Yahoo, Google, AltaVista, and Lycos which offered excellent search facilities for locating on-line articles. Additional information was also found from various chapters of relevant E-commerce and financial textbooks. The research framework developed was as in Figure 1.

DISCUSSION, ANALYSIS AND FINDINGS

The Study of the Evolution and the Growth of Electronic Payment Technologies

An electronic payment is defined as a payment service that utilizes information and communication technologies including integrated circuit (IC) card, cryptography, and telecommunication networks. The need for electronic payment technologies is to respond to fundamental changes in socio-economic trends. The payment system is the infrastructure which comprise of institutions, instruments, rules, procedures, standards, and technical features established to affect the transfer of monetary value between all parties concerned.

An efficient payment system reduces the cost of exchanging goods and services, and is indispensable to the functioning of the inter-bank, money, and capital markets. However, a weak payment system may severely affect the stability and development capacity of an economy. Its failures can result in inefficient use of financial resources, inequitable risk-sharing among agents, actual

Figure 1. Research framework

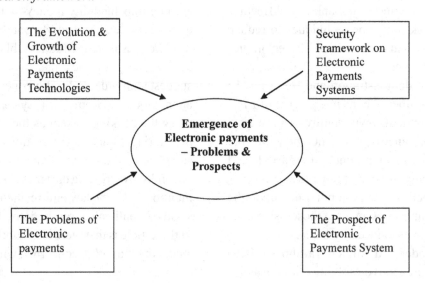

losses for participants, and loss of confidence in the financial system and in the very use of money. The task to design payment system infrastructure can become more complex as competition and innovation push constantly the search for better combination of efficiency, reliability, safety, and system stability in the provision of payment services to larger numbers of individual users and institutions.

Currently, there are more than thirty systems and technologies that are being proposed and tested for electronic payments. They differ in a number of ways such as size of payment; whether the system is closed (e.g. a specific system for a specific purpose such as a pre-paid phone card), or open (a generic system for a wide variety of uses such as a stored value card); degree of anonymity; level of security and consumer protection; and type of payment (credit, debit or electronic cash). A plethora of new electronic technologies are emerging, opening up new transaction opportunities. Microchip-based payment devices, such as chip cards and other new technologies, such as transponders, are being tested in many parts of the globe. The potential of digital wireless transactions remains untapped, yet it is very likely to emerge as telecommunications and computer technologies converge in devices. New technologies supporting the electronic storage, transfer, and use of money could have significant implications for consumers, merchants, governments and financial institutions.

The Security Framework of Electronic Payments Systems

In analyzing security risks, the focus is primarily on those aspects of electronic money products that are different from conventional payment instruments such as credit and debit cards and electronic funds transfers. At the core of the electronic payments network is the ability to conduct transactions efficiently, reliably, and in a secure environment. Protection of cardholder information is intrinsic to the success and continued growth of electronic

payments around the world. Without the implicit trust that information will be transmitted in a secure and reliable manner, the integrity of electronic payments would be in question. Payment card organizations are vigilantly committed to protecting cardholder information and ensuring the future integrity of the payment card system. Visa Canada for instance, has taken a number of steps to ensure transactions flow seamlessly and securely.

Fraud Risk

"The global networks, credit, debit and charge cards can never avoid the risk of crime entirely", said Michael Levi (2000). According to the author, individual crime victims, merchant service providers and retailers have always encountered conflict of interest. After sloping by around half between 1991 and 1995, plastic fraud losses have risen steadily and an estimate indicates that plastic fraud would be doubling in the next two years and with recorded fraud statistics rising. The pattern of fraud is changing. Electronic payment frauds are rapidly emerging in the organization. It becomes a major problem for business today. As organizations struggle to remain competitive in a global marketplace, the business is more complex, systems are left open to employee manipulation and without a finely tuned internal control system, and the opportunity for significant loss is always present. How serious is this problem of electronic money fraud in the workplace?

Electronic payment fraud and computer crime are not limited to the USA. KPMG Canada found that Canada's largest companies reported an average loss of $1.3 million to fraud in 1997 (KPMG Fraud Survey Report, 1998). The same survey reported that 47 percent of people believe fraud will increase in 1998, and only 11 percent of survey participants believe the Internet is a secure way to doing e-business transactions. From the finding, there are several internal forces which can make electronic money fraud more likely in the organization, such as poor internal controls, poor personnel policies and practices, and poor examples of honesty at the top levels of an organization (Bologna, 1993).

Money Laundering

Money laundering is defined as the act of disguising the origin or ownership of illegally gained funds to make them appear legitimate. The huge sum of money is obtained through illegal activities and has been linked to nearly all kinds of crime for profit including organized and white collar crimes. This money must be laundered in order to avoid being seizing by the law enforcement agency and handed to the government. There is a growing concern on money laundering as it is often associated with drug trafficking, bank savings abuses, real estate fraud, and tax evasion. Money laundering was first declared as a crime under the Money Laundering Control Act of 1986 of the U.S Code. The process of transferring funds through electronic messages between banks is known as wire transfers. It acts as the prime step in money laundering where the profits from organized crimes, for instance drugs, gambling, racketeering, and prostitution must be somehow slipped into the banking systems before it can be safely spent. It is the duty of the bank staff to report any detection of potential money laundering via direct telephone notification to the bank regulators and financial enforcers. The high number of transaction and the flow of wire transfer through fully automated systems have made it hard for it to be detected by law enforcement agencies.

Privacy and Anonymity

With the increasing usage of the Internet, the fears of privacy abuse have become a top concern of most of the Internet users. In fact anonymity features of electronic payment systems play a vital role in protecting privacy in an electronic world, and as a safeguard for a privacy-protecting

Internet. Nonetheless, the anonymity of an Internet user is mainly compromised through the payment method that is employed widely on the Internet – credit card, since most of the information is being collected on the Internet when users enter their credit card purchasing details. As consumers prefer to keep the details of their transaction private, conversely merchants and issuers are in favor to ensure they capture and possess enough and appropriate records of their transactions. Then privacy may become a thorny issue here. For instance, the Financial Crimes Enforcement Network (FinCEN), the Secret Service, and other Treasury law enforcement bureaus have participated in an wide-ranging look at the issues of the emerging e-money technologies, by examining the potential impact of e-cash systems on the Treasury's law enforcement responsibilities. Last but not least, privacy must be regarded as a political right that consumers enjoy and ought to be respected. At the same time, precautions need to be put in place to ensure that electronic money systems are not used as a means to thwart existing laws.

The Problems of Electronic Payments

Electronic payments bring greater efficiencies for businesses. It can eliminate the costs of handling coin and currency., which includes costs associated with the processing and accounting of money, as well as storage, transport, and security. Electronic money brings greater efficiency to those tasks, offering substantial cost savings. Electronic payment networks have the potential to provide cost savings of at least 1 percent of GDP annually over paper-based systems through increased velocity, reduced friction and lower costs. Acceptance of electronic payments would allow merchants to move more commerce from the physical world to the Internet, which offers access to global markets at lower cost.

The continuing rapid decline in the cost of technology will increase the extent of these cost savings, enhance innovation, and further increase the attraction of electronic money and finance. To the extent electronic payments displaces checks, moreover, check fraud, may be reduced. For example, retailers could track customer activities to discern buying patterns and offer buyer-specific discounts and loyalty programs. These targeted promotions, also known as "micromarketing," are generally viewed as more efficient than the mass-marketing techniques currently used. One of the biggest advantages of electronic payments is convenience of global acceptance, a wide range of payment options, and enhanced financial management tools. It is faster and easier than exchanging cash and making change, writing a check, or getting a credit card authorization.

Despite these benefits, uncertainties on the part of consumers and merchants about the underlying technology could slowdown the widespread use and acceptance of electronic payment systems. Some of these uncertainties focus on how well the technology secures personal transaction information over the Internet from theft and related forms of abuse such as false or non-authentic commitments. Other uncertainties arise from concerns about whether or not competing forms

of electronic-money for use outside the Internet will require idiosyncratic computer hardware and software. Still others arise from the fact that innovation is often fast-paced, creating doubts about how long any particular technology will be at hand. Lack of consumer acceptance has retarded the spread of debit cards and may also slow further advances in electronic payments means.

Another obstacle is authentication. If consumers are to use electronic money over the Internet they must have confidence in the issuers of the electronic money and the merchants who accept it. Consumers may demand that a trusted third party certify or authenticate the legitimacy of both those parties. Confidence is particularly important for the development of Internet commerce with its virtual shopkeepers that consumers cannot see and evaluate in the traditional way. Besides that, technology issues also make people slow in acceptance of electronic payment. Most observers agree that electronic money will not find widespread use until technical experts solve the problem of interoperability. In the context of electronic money, the term interoperability captures the extent to which debit cards and store value cards from different issuers use a common set of standards. These standards govern such issues as the size of the cards (length, thickness,

Figure 2. Future of consumer payments

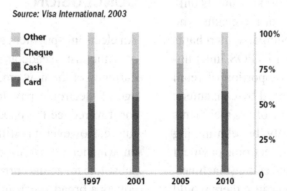

Source: Visa International, 2003

Data is only Consumer to Business Spending ($21.5 T in 2001) – does include non PCE spend, such as repayment of interest on debt – est. at $2.5T

and width) the location and size of the magnetic strip or computer chip, and the coding technology, manufacturers use to store information on the magnetic strip or computer chip. They also cover other matters such as the design and workings of devices that "read" the cards. Anonymity and privacy of personal information are always the concern of the consumers on e-money practices, in both online and offline electronic cash payment systems.

The Prospect of the Electronic Payments

Innovation in payment systems, made possible by electronic technology is transforming the monetary landscape of many countries. Electronic payments have introduced a new era of convenience and opportunity. Businesses today recognize the inherent value of electronic payments in reducing their costs and controlling expenses. Payment cards allow companies to reduce processing costs, increase management control, and negotiate better supplier pricing. While some of the value of payment card programs is attributable to "soft" costs savings (e.g. personnel), the net impact on the bottom line is tangible. Adoption of a 'network good' such as a new payments medium in an economy depends on mutual expectations of providers and users of the goods. Thus, against the status quo of a fully versatile currency, consumers will be encouraged to adopt card payments only if they expect a critical mass of merchants who will accept it in lieu of cash. Similarly, merchants will hesitate to subscribe to EFTPOS links unless they expect a growing proportion of retail expenditures to be card-financed by consumers. In the future, electronic money offers merchants increasing safety and security by eliminating some opportunities for theft. Electronic payment could help curtail vandalism of vending machines, public phones, and the like, because there would be no coin or currency to steal. Similarly, owners and employees of retail establishments and

other service providers who handle cash, such as taxicab drivers, could be much less vulnerable to robbery. Furthermore, in a cashless society, people will not encounter problems such as searching for exact change for parking, fumbling with foreign currency, pay exorbitant foreign exchange commissions, trying to cash a cheque in another country, or been concerned about carrying a large roll of banknotes.

Limitation

In this study, it is concluded that electronic payments play a vital role in the new marketplace. The limitation of this research is that it is only concentrated in the European economy. As such the study is not comprehensive enough as the Asian and other economies are left out. In addition, there are no articles which can provide and measure the cost of developing an electronic payment system in a country. Electronic payments face a myriad of problems, especially in respect of security issues, even though; there are many ways to reduce those crimes. However, no articles can suggest the best fool-proof mechanism to combat security breaches in electronic payment systems. There is no one best solution to electronic payments and this must be addressed in a comprehensive manner before digital money can become a success.

CONCLUSION

An electronic payment system has slowly grown over the last decade and it is fast becoming the currency of the new era. With the increasing usage of electronic payment, it is not impossible for it to reduce the paper currencies in the near future. However it is still early to make judgment on whether electronic payment will become a substitute for actual currency. Electronic payment covers a broad spectrum of different objectives, markets, and tools. However in any new product or service, the basic rules for it to succeed are the

time consuming and several fruitless attempts in order to seek for the best solutions to fulfill the needs of all parties involved. It would be crucial to ensure the reliability and safety of the electronic system. In order for the corporations, institutions and individuals to gain confidence and feel secure in the electronic business world, the marketplace should be controlled by a clear set of rules and regulations. Without a doubt, electronic payment plays a vital role in the criminal offenses and national securities issues. The technology also raises other policy issues such as erosion of the tax base and privacy concerns. Rather than existing money-related crimes such as fraud and counterfeiting, is it possible that the primary problem created by e-payments will be in its use to support other kinds of crime. Issues related to electronic payment should be addressed and resolved. Despite the impending issues, electronic payment systems are being utilized at an accelerated rate. In the borderless world, electronic payment continues to drive the global economy.

REFERENCES

Asokan, N. Janson, Phillipe A., Steiner, Michael, Waidner, Michael (1997). The State of the Art in Electronic Payment Systems, from http://www.semper.org/sirene/publ/AJSW_97PayOver.IEEE.pdf

Buck, P. S. (1996). Electronic commerce – would, could and should you use current Internet payment mechanisms. *Internet Research*, 6, 5–18. doi:10.1108/10662249610127283

Buck, P. S. (1997). From Electronic money to electronic cash: payment on the Net. *Logistic Information Management.*, 10(6), 289–299. doi:10.1108/09576059710187429

Cohen, B. J. (2001). Electronic Money: new day or false dawn. *Review of International Political Economy*, 8(2), 197–225. doi:10.1080/09692290010033376

Crone, R. (2003). The Future of Electronic Billing lies in "electronic" payments. *ProQuest*, from http://proquest.umi.com/pqdweb?did=283552781&sid=2&Fmt=3&clientId=24792&RQT=309&VName=PQD

Department of Justice Canada and Solicitor General Canada, (1997). Electronic money laundering: An environmental scan. 1-22

Helen, A. (2003). Innovation in retail payments: e-payments. From http://www.findarticles.com/p/articles/mi_qa3774/is_200301/ai_n9180494

Ho, S.M., & Simon, T.F.Ng Victor. (1994). Customers' risk perceptions of Electronic payment systems. *International Journal of Bank Marketing*, 12(8), 26–38. doi:10.1108/02652329410069029

Ian, D., & Christie, G.-S. (1999). E-cash is more interesting than you think: what are the key issues. *European Business Review*, 99(4), 207–210. doi:10.1108/09555349910281379

Kelley, J. R., & Edward, W. (1997). The future of Electronic money: a regulator's perspective. *IEEE Spectrum, 34, Issue: 2*, from http://140.98.193.112/xpls/abs_all.jsp?isnumber=12295&arnumber=570822&count=17&index=5

Lafferty Ltd. (2005). Payments industry facing a rapidly growing menace from online criminals, from http://proquest.umi.com/pqdweb?did=862647621&sid=12&Fmt=3&clientId=24792&RQT=309&VName=PQD

Lockett, N. (1999). Legal Perspective on Digital money in Europe. *European Business Review*, 99(4), 235–241. doi:10.1108/09555349910281423

McEntee, E. C. (2000). Connecting e-payment to e-commerce, from http://www.bankingmm.com/e-Commerce/e-payments.htm

Misra, S. K. Rajshekhar (Raj) G. Javalgi and Robert F. Schere (2004), "Global Electronic Money and Related Issue" http://www.findarticles.com/p/articles/mi_go2233/is_200403/ai_n6545665

Ovum, "E-payments are the way to E-commerce success" URL: http://techtalk.appssolutions.com/viewcontent.asp?article_id=56

Richard, H. (1997). New Electronic Payment Technologies: A Look at Security Issues. *Journal of Retail Banking Services.*, *XIX*(3), 41.

Sander, Ta-Shma, Tomas, Amnon (1999). On Anonymous Electronic Cash and Crime. 202-206.

Sato, S., & Hawkins, J. (2001). Electronic Finance: an overview of the issues, from http://www.paris-europlace.net/files/dossier059034.pdf

Stevens, E. (2002). Electronic money and the future of Centrals Banks. From http://www.cleve-landfed.org/research/com2002/0301.pdf

Szmigin, I. T. D., & Humphrey, B. (1999). Electronic Cash: A qualitative assessment of its adoption. *International Journal of Bank Marketing*, *17*(4), 192–202. doi:10.1108/02652329910278888

Thomas, D. (2002). Retailers and Card Issuers step up fight against online fraud. *Computer Weekly*, from http://www.computerweekly.com/Articles/2002/10/17/190338/Retailersandcardis-suersstepupfightagainstonlinefraud

Wade, W. (2004). Government's New Stance on E-Payments. *American Banker*, *169*(Iss. 165), 1–4.

This work was previously published in International Journal of E-Adoption, Volume 1, Issue 1, edited by Sushil Sharma, pp. 77-95, copyright 2009 by IGI Publishing (an imprint of IGI Global).

Chapter 14
Adoption of E-Government Services:
The Case of Electronic Approval System

Sinawong Sang
Seoul National University, Republic of Korea

Jeong-Dong Lee
Seoul National University, Republic of Korea

Jongsu Lee
Seoul National University, Republic of Korea

ABSTRACT

The purpose of this study is to assess and test the factors that influence user adoption of e-Government services: the Electronic Approval System (EAS). This study uses the Technology Acceptance Model (TAM), the extended TAM (TAM2), the Diffusion of Innovation (DOI), and trust to build a parsimonious yet comprehensive model of factors that influence user acceptance of the EAS. We collected data from a total of 112 public officers in 12 ministries in Cambodia. We assessed the model with regression analyses. The findings in this article show that the determinants of the model (perceived usefulness, relative advantage, and trust) explain 30.5% of the variance in user acceptance of the EAS. At the same time, image, output quality, and perceived ease of use explain 38.4% of the variance in user perception of the usefulness of the EAS. In this article, we discuss our findings, implications, and suggestions for future research.

INTRODUCTION

Since the adoption of a liberal political system and market economy in the late 1990s, Cambodia, a developing nation with an emerging economy,

has enthusiastically pursued various political, economic, social, and public administration reforms to accelerate its economic growth and help alleviate poverty. As a reform measure, the government has implemented e-Government, in a form known as the Government Administration Information System (GAIS). GAIS is intended as

DOI: 10.4018/978-1-60960-597-1.ch014

a tool to improve the process of government in order to meet a variety of challenges, including corruption, poor public administration, and lack of adequate transparency and accountability in the exercise of public decision-making powers and the delivery of public services. The GAIS was to connect and computerize the government with four core practical applications: the Electronic Approval System (EAS), the Real Estate Registration system, the Resident Registration system, and the Vehicle Registration system, as well as the presence of the government on the World Wide Web.

The real estate, resident, and vehicle registration systems are in operation and are widely used. However, the EAS is not yet widely used (Phu, 2003).

Indeed, the main purpose of the EAS is to allow ministries to exchange documents both internally and externally. It incorporates all traditional manual functions to allow users to use the system with ease (Phu, 2003). It allows users to send, approve, store, and retrieve documents electronically, in order to replace manual processing of paper and signatures. This is because most problems that previously arose at government offices, departments, or ministries were caused by a complicated maze of administrative processes. Paper forms are the main way to collect routine administrative approvals. Every day, government employees roll paper forms into manual typewriters to record the basis of an administrative approval. After typing, the forms are reviewed, checked, signed, transported, entered in computer databases, filed, retrieved, archived, shredded, dumped, and burned. The workload of paper forms is considerable. Frequently, agencies lose documents without knowing who was responsible, and documents are unreasonably delayed without reasonable cause (Phu, 2003).

The functions of the EAS include:

- Approval: The Approval features include reporting processes such as drafting, sub-

mitting, approving, sending, receiving, and accepting electronic documents. The approval process is restricted by an individual's position and permissions granted: thus, a user can only do what he or she is allowed to do. The drafter can draft, submit, send, and resend the document. The approver can approve, modify, suspend, and examine the draft. The Document Manager can accept and distribute the document. Aside from these basic approval processes, the system offers many other features to facilitate electronic document approval.

- Mail: The system lets users exchange messages, not only with other members of their organization but also with people outside the system. It offers an easy-to-use HTML editor as well as a plain text pad, so that users can create vivid messages with just a few clicks.

- Bulletin board: The system offers versatile bulletin boards that can be used for such purposes as sharing ideas or making announcements. It offers several types of boards, such as public announcement boards, department boards, and secured boards. Bulletins can have an unlimited number of attachments for easy distribution of documents, software, or patches. The board has another distinctive feature called "Reservation Posting". This feature allows users to set the post date, so that the bulletin will be posted automatically at the designated time.

- User and organization chart: The system offers an easy way to search for members of the system. The internal search offers detailed information on departments and users, and the external search lets users search other organizations through a central database server. Users can search using keywords or by navigating through the organizational chart.

• Document management: This feature lets users effectively manage documents and approve them electronically. Approved documents will be registered to the document folder automatically after the final approval process or the acceptance process is completed. Documents can be divided between the registered document folder and the received document folder. The first is for documents produced by the department that owns this folder; the second is for documents that have arrived from other departments or ministries.

• Administration tool: The system provides administrative functions.

Recall that the EAS does not yet enjoy wide use, even though the EAS has many useful functions mentioned above that replace manual processing of paper and signatures for office automation. Only a few technical documents or reports have been sent using the EAS. Users still prefer the traditional means of processing for other administrative documents (Phu, 2003).One of the key reasons for the infrequent use of the EAS is the lack of awareness of public officers that can help users use it (Phu, 2003; Sang, 2008). Thus, the government needs research that identifies the factors that influence user adoption of the EAS. The objective of this study, therefore, is to assess and test the factors that influence the adoption of the EAS in the public sector.

The remainder of this article is organized as follows. It begins with theoretical background, followed by a description of the proposed research model and hypotheses. Next, it describes the research method and presents the analytical results of the study. Then, it discusses these results. Finally, it concludes by examining implications and suggestions for future research.

THEORETICAL BACKGROUND

Technology Acceptance Model

Many information technology (IT) researchers have used the Technology Acceptance Model (TAM) to better understand IT adoption and its use in organizations (Gefen et al., 2000; Legris et al., 2003; Venkatesh & Bala, 2008). This model has been used in very different settings: for example, to test the acceptance of: computer technology (Davis et al., 1989), online shopping (Gefen et al., 2000; Van Slyke et al., 2004), mobile computing (Wu et al., 2007), e-commerce (Pavlou, 2003), and e-Government services (Carter & Bélanger, 2005).

The theoretical foundation for TAM lies in Fishbein and Ajzen's (1975) Theory of Reasoned Action (TRA). The TAM proposed that two particular beliefs have the strongest effect on technology acceptance and use: *perceived usefulness* and *perceived ease of use* (see Figure 1). Perceived usefulness is defined as "the degree to which a person believes that using a particular system would enhance his or her job performance" (Davis, 1989, p.320), while *perceived ease of use* is defined as "the degree to which a person believes that using a particular system would be free of physical and mental efforts" (Davis, 1989,

Figure 1. Technology acceptance model (Davis et al., 1989)

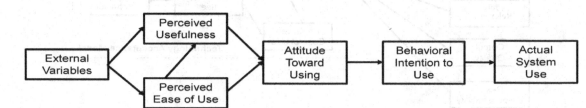

p.320). *Perceived usefulness* and *perceived ease of use* influence one's *attitude towards system usage*, which influences one's *behavioural intention to use* a system, which, in turn, determines *actual system usage* (Davis et al., 1989). The external variables that impact the *perceived usefulness* and *perceived ease of use* are not completely explored in the TAM. Davis et al. (1989) also found that *attitude* did not fully mediate *perceived usefulness* and *perceived ease of use*. Based on these findings, other scholars have suggested a more parsimonious TAM that does not include the *attitude towards usage* construct (Carter & Bélanger, 2005; Davis et al., 1989).

Technology Acceptance Model 2

Venkatesh and Davis (2000) proposed an extension of the TAM (TAM2) by adding more important determinants of *perceived usefulness*, that is, *subjective norm, image, job relevance, output quality, result demonstrability*, and *perceived ease of use*, as well as two moderators, *experience* and *voluntariness*. In addition to this, TAM2 omits *attitude toward using* because of weak predictors of either *behavioral intention to use* or *actual system usage* (Venkatesh & Davis 2000; Wu et al., 2007).

The TAM2 (Venkatesh & Davis, 2000) takes social influence and cognitive instrumental processes as the determinants of *perceived usefulness* (see Figure 2). The social determinants are *subjective norm* (a "person's perception that most people who are important to him think he should or should not perform the behaviour in question" (Fishbein & Ajzen, 1975, p.302)) and *image* ("the degree to which use of an innovation is perceived to enhance one's... status in one's social system"(Moore & Benbasat, 1991, p.195)). The cognitive determinants are: *job relevance* ("an individual's perception regarding the degree to which the target system is applicable to his or her job performance" (Venkatesh & Davis, 2000, p. 191), *output quality* (the degree to which an individual believes that the system performs his or her job tasks well (Venkatesh & Davis, 2000, p. 191), and *result demonstrability* ("the tangibility of the results of using the innovation"(Moore & Benbasat, 1991, p. 203). *Experience* and *voluntariness* were included as moderating factors of *subjective norm* (Venkatesh & Davis, 2000).

Diffusion of Innovations

Rogers, a sociologist, developed the theory of Diffusion of Innovations (DOI) to explain how

Figure 2. Technology acceptance model 2 (Venkatesh & Davis, 2000)

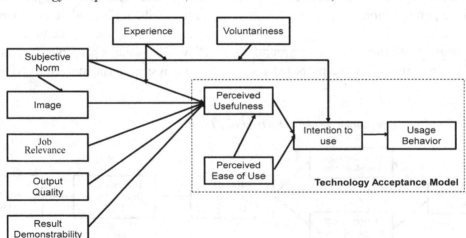

Figure 3. The research model

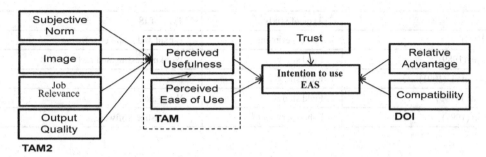

an innovation spreads through a society (Rogers, 2003). It has been used extensively to explain the adoption of IT innovations in an organization or society (Carter & Bélanger, 2005). Innovation here is defined as "an idea, practice, or object perceived as new by an individual or another unit of adoption" (Rogers, 2003, p.36), while diffusion is "the process by which an innovation is communicated through certain channels over time among the members of a social system" (Rogers, 2003, p.35).

Five factors affect the rate of adoption of innovations (Rogers, 2003, pp.265-266): *relative advantage* ("the degree to which an innovation is perceived as better than the idea it supersedes"), *compatibility* ("the degree to which an innovation is perceived as consistent with the existing values, past experiences, and needs of potential adopter"), *complexity* ("the degree to which an innovation is perceived as relatively difficult to understand and to use"), *triability* ("the degree to which an innovation may be experimented with on a limited basis"), and *observability* ("the degree to which the results of an innovation are visible to others"). These characteristics strongly affect acceptance behavior (Agarwal & Prasad, 1997; Rogers, 2003).

Trust

Trust is a central defining aspect of many economic and social interactions in which uncertainty is present (Pavlou, 2003; Warkentin et al., 2002). Trust is defined as a set of beliefs that other people would fulfil their expected commitments under conditions of vulnerability and interdependence (Rousseau et al., 1998). Lack of trust in online transactions has been identified as one of the major obstacles in the adoption of e-Government services (Carter & Bélanger, 2005; Horst et al., 2007), since transactions over the Internet entail a great deal of uncertainty and risk (Bélanger & Carter, 2008). Therefore, the government needs to establish trust in the online services they provide or will be providing (Warkentin et al., 2002).

RESEARCH MODEL

Based on the preceding theoretical background, we integrate TAM, TAM2, DOI, and *trust* to form a model of user acceptance of the EAS in the public sector (see Figure 3).

The EAS and TAM Relationship

Many empirical studies have shown that the TAM is a parsimonious and robust model (Adams et al., 1992; Davis et al., 1989; Davis, 1989; Gefen and Straub, 1997). Moreover, many researchers have found that *perceived usefulness* and *perceived ease of use* explain a large portion of the variance in *intention to use* IT (Davis et al., 1989; Gefen et

Table 1. Some empirical studies testing TAM

Study	Type of study	Type of IS
Davis (1989)	Lab experiment	E-mail and graphics software
Davis et al. (1989)	Field study	Word processing and text editor
Thompson et al. (1991)	Field study	PCs
Straub et al. (1995)	Field study	Voice-mail
Mathieson (1991)	Lab experiment	Spreadsheet software

al., 2000). Table 1 lists some of the many studies that have tested TAM empirically.

Users will find the EAS useful if it helps them to find the information that they want or helps them to perform administrative transactions. Thus, a high level of usefulness is likely to increase user acceptance of the EAS. Moreover, users will perceive the EAS as easy to use when they find it clear and understandable and when they do not have to expend a lot of mental effort to interact with it (in, for example, website content, information surfing, and online administrative processes). Thus, ease of use is likely to strengthen users' intentions to use the EAS. As such, we propose the following hypotheses:

H1. Perceived usefulness is positively related to intention to use the EAS.
H2. Perceived ease of use is positively related to intention to use the EAS.

In their evaluation of TAM2, Chismar and Patton (2003) found that only two of the three cognitive instrumental determinants of *perceived usefulness, job relevance* and *output quality*, were significant. However, if top management is committed to providing support and a positive environment that encourages participation in the EAS, then most users will use the system and take into consideration what tasks a system is capable of doing, how those match to their job, and how well the system does these tasks. Moreover, in the Cambodian context, public officers who adopt a new innovation like the EAS may impress others

who have not adopted it. This may enhance the adopters' social status. Hence, a public officer who has a higher need for social recognition and a clear understanding of the e-Government system is likely to perceive the usefulness of the system. We omitted the construct *voluntariness* from our model because the use of e-Government services, particularly in the Cambodian context, was not being mandated, nor was there any expectation that it would be mandated in the future. Hence, *subjective norm* had no direct effect on *intention*, because *subjective norm* significantly and directly affect *intention* only when usage is mandatory (Venkatesh & Davis, 2000). Moreover, we also omitted the construct *experience*, since it was intended to measure the adoption of existing technology (i.e., EAS).

H1a. Subjective norm is positively related to perceived usefulness.
H1b. Image is positively related to perceived usefulness.
H1c. Job relevance is positively related to perceived usefulness.
H1d. Output quality is positively related to perceived usefulness.
H1e. Perceived ease of use is positively related to perceived usefulness.

The EAS and Trust Relationship

One of the main important factors in the adoption of e-Government services is trust (Bélanger and Carter, 2008; Horst et al., 2007; Warkentin et al.,

2002; West, 2008), because when public officers browse governmental Web sites or perform administrative transactions, they expect the information on the Web site to be accurate, reliable, and timely. Trust is defined as "an expectancy that the promise of an individual or group can be relied upon" (Rotter, 1971). In the EAS context, the issue of trust is very important, since the EAS involves approval signatures, the protection of personal information that the government collects about individuals, and the protection of EAS sites from attack and misuse. Hence, trust encompasses the intention to make public officers to receive information, to provide information, and to request e-Government services. Moreover, the need for trust in the maintenance of accurate public information in the EAS will increase because government agencies may be required by law to share information with other agencies or with public officers (Wang and Liao, 2008). "Visible statements outlining how a site insures visitors' privacy and security are valuable assets for encouraging people to use e-Government services and information" (West, 2008, p. 7). Therefore, we propose the following hypothesis:

H3. Trust is positively related to intention to use the EAS.

The TAM and the DOI Relationship

Several empirical studies suggest the need to integrate TAM with other theories (for example, DOI, or DeLone and McLean's IS Success Model) in order to improve its specificity and explanatory power (Carter & Bélanger, 2005; Legris et al., 2003; Wang & Liao, 2008).

Some scholars have modified the TAM by adding the DOI theory as a factor affecting the *intention to use* technology, and they found that *relative advantage*, *compatibility* and *complexity* are more important than others in predicting *intention to use* a technology (Carter & Bélanger, 2005; Agarwal & Prasad, 1998; Tornatzky &

Klein, 1982). In addition to this, they suggested that the *complexity* construct in the DOI is often considered as a *perceived ease of use* construct in the TAM (Agarwal & Prasad 1997; Moore & Benbasat, 1991). Hence, we included *relative advantage* and *compatibility* constructs in the research model. However, we ignored *triability* and *observability*, since the previous research found no strong correlations between them and *users' attitude* toward IT adoption (Agarwal & Prasad, 1998). We propose the following hypotheses:

H4. Compatibility is positively related to intention to use the EAS.
H5. Relative advantage is positively related to intention to use the EAS.

METHODOLOGY

Subjects

We collected the data for the study via a survey questionnaire that was divided into two sections. The first section captured demographic information about each participant and each participant's experience using the Internet. The second section captured the subject's perception of each variable in the model.

Since the study focused on the EAS, the target participants were Cambodian public officers who have experience using the Internet. We administered a survey to 112 public officers within 12 ministries in Cambodia (see Table 2). Of the 112 surveys administered, all were complete and used in the analyses.

Measurements

All of the items used in this survey were adapted from previous studies (Davis, 1989; Carter & Bélanger, 2005; Venkatesh & Davis, 2000; Van Slyke et al., 2004) with minor changes to the context of the EAS. The measurements of *intention to use, perceived ease of use,* and *perceived usefulness*

Table 2. Number of participants in each ministry

No.	Ministry	Participants
1	Office of the council of ministers	10
2	Secretariat of public service	10
3	Ministry of water resources	10
4	National audit authority	10
5	Ministry of agriculture	10
6	Ministry of economy and finance	10
7	Ministry of planning	10
8	Ministry of vocations & training	10
9	Ministry of national defense	5
10	Ministry of environment	5
11	Ministry of information	10
12	Ministry of posts & telecommunication	12
Total		112

were adapted from the studies of Davis (1989) and Carter & Bélanger (2005). The measurements of *subjective norm, image, job relevance,* and *output quality* were adapted from the study of Venkatesh & Davis (2000). The measurements of *relative advantage* and *compatibility* were adapted from the study of Carter & Bélanger (2005). The measurement of *trust* was adapted from the studies of Carter & Bélanger (2005) and Van Slyke et al. (2004). Each item was rated on a 1 to 7 Likert-type scale ranging from Strongly Disagree through

Neutral to Strongly Agree. A list of the items is provided in the Appendix. Note that the questionnaire was originally designed in English and then translated into Khmer (the Cambodian Language) to let those who understand only Khmer complete the questionnaire. The accuracy of the translation was verified by using back-translation (Zikmund, 2003). We tested the questionnaire in a pilot survey among government officers in the public service secretariat to determine whether there were any ambiguities in the questionnaire items. Based on

Table 3. Reliability analysis

Construct	No. Items	Cronbach's Alpha
Intention to Use	2	.926
Perceived Ease of Use	4	.957
Perceived Usefulness	4	.935
Subjective Norm	2	.764
Image	3	.877
Job Relevance	2	.768
Output Quality	2	.710
Relative Advantage	4	.929
Trust	2	.861
Compatibility	4	.867

their comments, we rephrased some of the questionnaire items for clarity. All items in Khmer were rephrased to make them understandable and clear in the context of Cambodia.

We examined the reliability of each item using the Cronbach's alpha (Cronbach, 1970). Table 3 lists the reliability of each construct. All of the items are above the acceptance level of 0.7 (Hair et al., 2006).

We evaluated construct validity with factor analysis (Hair et al., 2006). Validity is concerned with how well the concept is defined by the measure, whereas reliability relates to the consistency of the measure (Hair et al., 2006). We used Principal Components Analysis (PCA) as the extraction method and Varimax as a rotation technique (Hair et al., 2006).

Table 4. Factor analysis

Construct	Item	Factor Loading								
		1	2	3	4	5	6	7	8	9
Perceived Ease of Use	PEOU1	.926								
	PEOU2	.898								
	PEOU3	.927								
	PEOU4	.948								
Perceived Usefulness	PU1		.848							
	PU2		.840							
	PU3		.897							
	PU4		.743							
Relative Advantage	RA1			.835						
	RA2			.885						
	RA3			.873						
	RA4			.844						
Compatibility	CP1				.853					
	CP2				.791					
	CP3				.782					
	CP4				.757					
Image	IMG1					.790				
	IMG2					.771				
	IMG3					.795				
Trust	TRUST1						.796			
	TRUST2						.846			
Intention to Use	IUSE1							.808		
	IUSE2							.829		
Job Relevance	JR1								.879	
	JR2								.847	
Output Quality	OQ1									.773

Note: SN1, SN2, and OQ2 were not shown because their factor loading values were less than .7 and the threshold value of .7 for factor loading criterion was taken.

As can be seen from Table 4, the items loaded properly on their expected factors. However, we dropped *subjective norm* (SN1 and SN2) and *output quality* (OQ2) from further analysis, as its factor loading was less than .7 and the threshold value of .7 for factor loading criterion was taken (Hair et al., 2006). Hence, we dropped the hypothesis H1a from further analysis as well.

RESULTS

Descriptive Statistics

Table 5 shows the demographic profile of the survey respondents. The table shows that the survey respondents were predominantly male (81.2% male versus 18.8% female). Regarding age distribution, public officer ages between 26 and 35 were dominant (69.6%). In addition to this, regarding education level, public officers with bachelor's and master's degrees were dominant (94.6%). Moreover, most of them used the Internet at the office (65.2%).

We ran the first regression analysis for the hypotheses H1b, H1c, H1d, and H1e. PU is the dependent variable, while IMG, JR, OQ, and PEOU are the independent variables. Table 6 presents these first regression variables.

The results show that the model explains 38.4% of the variance in *perceived usefulness* of the EAS; the adjusted R Square is .355, F=13.199, p<.0001.

Table 5. Demographic profile of respondents

Category		Frequency	Percentage
Gender	Male	91	81.2%
	Female	21	18.8%
Age	18 – 25	13	11.6%
	26 – 35	78	69.6%
	36 – 45	20	17.9%
	46 – 55	1	0.9%
Level of education	TAFE	4	3.5%
	Bachelor	67	59.8%
	Master	39	34.8%
	Doctor	2	1.8%
Position	Top level	5	4.5%
	Middle level	41	36.6%
	Low level	57	50.9%
	Others	9	8%
Place of using the Internet	Office	73	65.2%
	Home	4	3.6%
	Both	15	13.4%
	Internet cafe	20	17.9%
Experience of using the Internet	< 1 year	12	10.7%
	1 – 3 years	30	26.8%
	4 – 5 years	28	25%
	> 5 years	42	37.5%

Table 6. First regression variables

Variable	No. items	Mean	Std. Deviation
PU	4	5.6183	.9562
PEOU	4	5.0737	1.1388
IMG	3	4.8929	1.1575
JR	2	5.0000	.9275
OQ	1	4.9018	1.2463

Note. Variable SN was not shown, since SN1 and SN2 were dropped from further analysis.

Table 7. Hypothesis testing

	Variable	Coeff.	t-value	Sig.	Support
H1a	SN	n/a	n/a	n/a	n/a
H1b	IMG	.322	3.713	.000	Yes
H1c	JR	.123	1.531	.129	No
H1d	OQ	.215	2.530	.013	Yes
H1e	PEOU	.262	3.255	.002	Yes

Multicollinearity among the independent variables is not a problem, since the tolerance value is substantially above .10 (it ranges from .726 to .952), and the variance inflation factor (VIF range from 1.051 to 1.377) is much less than 5 (Hair et al., 2006). Three of the five determinants of *perceived usefulness* (*image* (IMG), *output quality* (OQ), and *perceived ease of use* (PEOU)) were found to be significant in predicting the *perceived usefulness* of the EAS (see Table 7).

We ran the second regression analysis for the hypotheses H1, H2, H3, H4, and H5. IUSE is the dependent variable, while PU, PEOU, TRUST, CP, and RA are the independent variables. Table 8 presents these second regression variables.

The results show that the model explains 30.5% of the variance in user *intention to use* the EAS; the adjusted R Square is .272, F=9.309, p<.0001. Multicollinearity among the independent variables is not a problem, since the tolerance value is substantially above .10 (it ranges from .725 to .966) and the variance inflation factor (VIF range from 1.035 to 1.380) is much less than 5 (Hair et al., 2006). Three of the five determinants of *intention to use* (*perceived usefulness* (PU), *trust* (TRUST), and *relative advantage* (RA)) were

Table 8. Second regression variables

Variable	No. items	Mean	Std. Deviation
IUSE	2	5.5759	.9959
PEOU	4	5.0737	1.1388
PU	4	5.6183	.9562
RA	4	5.6763	1.0508
TRUST	2	4.8839	1.1230
CP	4	4.7790	1.0082

Table 9. Hypothesis testing

	Variable	Coeff.	t-value	Sig.	Support
H1	PU	.347	3.650	.000	Yes
H2	PEOU	-.146	-1.670	.098	No
H3	TRUST	.257	3.125	.002	Yes
H4	CP	.094	1.017	.311	No
H5	RA	.212	2.275	.025	Yes

found to be significant in predicting the *intention to use* the EAS (see Table 9).

DISCUSSION

H1 is supported. This indicates that an increase in perceived usefulness positively influences users' intention to use the EAS in the public sector: that is, public officers will use it if they perceive its efficiency and effectiveness with respect to their job or work. The EAS's web portal, for example, is an important tool that allows public officers to search for information or administrative procedures they want quickly and accurately. In addition to this, the Web portal needs to be updated on a regular basis in order to prevent the proliferation of inaccurate information, broken links, and incorrect email contact information. By maintaining the portal sites and placing more materials online, governments could encourage public officers to go online and use e-Government resources (West, 2008). Furthermore, each government agency should concentrate on how delivering their services online could save users time and money.

Moreover, each government agency could help its own public officers understand the importance of the EAS by providing further training to make the system attractive to them. Training programs should stress the potential of the EAS rather than concentrating on only basic skills (such as typing skills), especially because some public officers do not need to type documents by themselves.

H1b, H1d, and H1e are supported: that is, the three main determinants of the perceived usefulness in the model (*image output quality*, and *perceived ease of use*) affect the perceived usefulness of the EAS directly. This implies that as public officers perceive the EAS as a status symbol of their organization, they consider it to be important. Furthermore, they perceive it to be useful when it does the required tasks adequately or when the quality of the output they get from the system is high. Therefore, each department or agency within a government organization that provides services through an electronic channel needs to ensure that the information they display on the Web site is useful, relevant, accurate, and up-to-date, in order to provide a high level of information quality.

H3 is supported. This result reveals that *trust* in the EAS affects user *intention to use* the EAS significantly. This result is consistent with previous studies (Carter and Bélanger, 2005). Public officers' acceptance of the EAS will increase if they perceive it to be trusted and secure, because they are concerned about the level of security present when performing administrative transactions or providing sensitive information online. They are only willing to participate in these interactions if a certain level of trust is present. Hence, trust and enforcement security mechanisms for the EAS should be developed. In addition to this, a legal framework for the EAS should be set up which includes laws for acceptance of documents in electronic format (such as downloaded documents), laws that protect against unauthorized access, and laws to enable electronic authentication.

H5 is also supported. This indicates that higher levels of perceived relative advantage are associated with increased user acceptance of the EAS. This result is consistent with previous studies (Carter & Bélanger, 2005). This implies that the users will use the EAS if it helps them work more efficiently (for example, gathering information from government agencies).

CONCLUSION

The purpose of this study was to assess and test the factors influencing user acceptance of the EAS in Cambodia. The contributions of this study have both theoretical and practical implications. From a theoretical point of view, the study proposes a comprehensive theoretical framework to identify what influences user adoption of the EAS. This increases our understanding of the factors influencing user acceptance of the EAS in the public sector. At the same time, the study not only introduces new additions to existing technology acceptance research but also provides empirical support and validation for the findings of previous research.

From a practical point of view, the results of this study revealed that the main factors that influence user acceptance of the EAS are *perceived usefulness, relative advantage,* and *trust.* This finding help government policymakers and government agencies design and implement policies and strategies to promote and increase the use of the EAS by public officers: that is, they should implement policies and strategies that emphasize the usefulness, efficiency, and user trust of the EAS. They should conduct awareness campaigns to inform public officers about the real benefits they would be gained from the system. For developers of the EAS, they should implement a system to protect information and system resources with respect to confidentiality and integrity.

Though the results can be considered statistically significant in most parts, the study has some limitations. The first is that, though the research model in this study explains some of the variance in public officers' *perceived usefulness, relative advantag*e, and *trust*, much of the variance remains unexplained. Therefore, identifying the independent variables that account for the remaining variance is an important direction for future research. Additional variables may include other important factors such as information quality, service quality, user satisfaction, risk, culture, and other socioeconomic constraints. The second limitation is that the sample is limited to users in Cambodia. Their perspective may differ from that of users in other countries. Thus, the results may be limited to this specific location.

REFERENCES

Adams, D. A., Nelson, R. R., & Todd, P. A. (1992). Perceived usefulness, ease of use, and usage of information technology: A replication. *Management Information Systems Quarterly, 16,* 227–247. doi:10.2307/249577

Agarwal, R., & Prasad, J. (1997). The role of innovation characteristics and perceived voluntariness in the acceptance of information technologies. *Decision Sciences, 28*(3), 557–582. doi:10.1111/j.1540-5915.1997.tb01322.x

Agarwal, R., & Prasad, J. (1998). A conceptual and operational definition of personal innovativeness in the domain of information technology. *Information Systems Research, 9*(2), 204–215. doi:10.1287/isre.9.2.204

Bélanger, F., & Carter, L. (2008). Trust and risk in e-government adoption. *The Journal of Strategic Information Systems, 17*(2), 165–176. doi:10.1016/j.jsis.2007.12.002

Carter, L., & Bélanger, F. (2005). The utilization of e-government services: Citizen trust, innovation and acceptance factors. *Information Systems Journal, 15*(1), 5–25. doi:10.1111/j.1365-2575.2005.00183.x

Chismar, W. G., & Wiley-Patton, S. (2003). Does the extended technology acceptance model apply to physicians. *Proceedings of the 36th Annual Hawaii International Conference on System Sciences, Vol. 6.* Washington: IEEE Computer Society.

Cronbach, L. (1970). *Essentials of psychology testing.* New York: Harper and Row.

Davis, F. D. (1989). Perceived usefulness, perceived ease of use, and user acceptance of information technology. *Management Information Systems Quarterly, 13*(3), 319–340. doi:10.2307/249008

Davis, F. D., Bagozzi, R. P., & Warshaw, P. R. (1989). User acceptance of computer technology: A comparison of two theoretical models. *Management Science, 35*(8), 982–1003. doi:10.1287/mnsc.35.8.982

Fishbein, M., & Ajzen, I. (1975). *Belief, attitude, intention and behaviour: An introduction to theory and research.* MA: Addision-Wesley.

Gefen, D., Karahanna, E., & Straub, D. W. (2000). Trust and TAM in online shopping: An integrated model. *Management Information Systems Quarterly, 27*(1), 51–90.

Gefen, D., & Straub, D. W. (1997). Gender differences in the perception and use of e-mail: An extension to the technology acceptance model. *Management Information Systems Quarterly, 21,* 389–400. doi:10.2307/249720

Gefen, D., Straub, D. W., & Boudreau, M. (2000). Structural equation modeling and regression: Guidelines for research practice. *Communications of the Association for Information System, 4*(7).

Hair, J. F., Black, W. C., Babin, B. J., Anderson, R. E., & Tatham, R. L. (2006). *Multivariate data analysis.* New York: Pearson Prentice Hall.

Horst, M., Kuttschreuter, M., & Gutteling, J. M. (2007). Perceived usefulness, perceived experiences, risk perception and trust as determinants of adoption of e-government services in the Netherlands. *Computers in Human Behavior, 23*(4), 1838–1852. doi:10.1016/j.chb.2005.11.003

Legris, P., Ingham, J., & Collerette, P. (2003). Why do people use information technology? A critical review of the technology acceptance model. *Information & Management, 40*(3), 191–204. doi:10.1016/S0378-7206(01)00143-4

Mathieson, K. (1991). Predicting user intentions: Comparing the technology acceptance model with the theory of planned behavior. *Information Systems Research, 2*(3), 173–191. doi:10.1287/isre.2.3.173

Moore, G. C., & Benbasat, I. (1991). Development of an instrument to measure the perceptions of adopting an information technology innovation. *Information Systems Research, 2*(3), 192–222. doi:10.1287/isre.2.3.192

Pavlou, P. (2003). Consumer acceptance of electronic commerce: Integrating trust and risk with the Technology Acceptance Model. *International Journal of Electronic Commerce, 7*(3), 69–103.

Phu, L. (2003). *Cambodia: The road to e-Governance,* Phnom Penh: National ICT Development Authority (NiDA).

Rogers, E. M. (2003). *Diffusion of innovations.* New York: The Free Press.

Rotter, L. B. (1971). Generalized expectations for interpersonal trust. *The American Psychologist, 26*(5), 443–452. doi:10.1037/h0031464

Rousseau, D. M., Sitkin, S. B., Burt, R. S., & Camerer, C. (1998). Not so different after all: Across discipline view of trust. *Academy of Management Review, 23*(3), 393–404. doi:10.5465/AMR.1998.926617

Sang, S. (2008). The Influential factors and challenges in implementing e-Government in Cambodia. *Proceeding of the 2008 International Conference on Convergence and Hybrid Information Technology (ICCIT08), Vol. II.* Busan: IEEE Computer Society.

Straub, D. W., Limayem, M., & Karahanna, E. (1995). Measuring system usage: Implications for IS theory testing . *Management Science, 41*(8), 1328–1342. doi:10.1287/mnsc.41.8.1328

Thompson, R. L., Higgins, C. A., & Howell, J. M. (1991). Personal computing: Toward a conceptual model of utilization . *Management Information Systems Quarterly, 15*(1), 125–142. doi:10.2307/249443

Tornatzky, L., & Klein, K. (1982). Innovation characteristics and innovation adoption implementation: A meta analysis of findings. *IEEE Transactions on Engineering Management, 29*(1), 28–45.

Van Slyke, C., Bélanger, F., & Comunale, C. (2004). Factor influencing the adoption of web-based shopping: The impacts of trust. *The Data Base for Advances in Information Systems, 35*(2), 32–49.

Venkatesh, V., & Bala, H. (2008). Technology acceptance model 3 and a research agenda on interventions. *Decision Sciences, 39*(2), 273–315. doi:10.1111/j.1540-5915.2008.00192.x

Venkatesh, V., & Davis, F. D. (2000). A theoretical extension of the technology acceptance model: Four longitudinal field studies. *Management Science, 46*(2), 186–204. doi:10.1287/mnsc.46.2.186.11926

Wang, Y., & Liao, Y. (2008). Assessing e-government systems success: A validation of the DeLone and McLean model of information system success. *Government Information Quarterly, 25*(4), 717–733. doi:10.1016/j.giq.2007.06.002

Warkentin, M., Gefen, D., Pavlou, P., & Rose, G. (2002). Encouraging citizen adoption of e-Government by building trust. *Electronic Markets, 12*(3), 157–162. doi:10.1080/101967802320245929

West, D. M. (2008). *Improving technology utilization in electronic government around the world.* Washington: The Brookings Institution.

Wu, J., Wang, S., & Lin, L. (2007). Mobile computing acceptance factors in the healthcare industry: A structural equation model. *International Journal of Medical Informatics, 76*(1), 66–77. doi:10.1016/j.ijmedinf.2006.06.006

Zikmund, W. G. (2003), *Business research method,* Mason: Thomson South-Western.

APPENDIX

Intention to Use (IUSE)

- Assuming I have access to the Electronic Approval System (EAS), I intend to use it.
- Given that I have access to the Electronic Approval System (EAS), I predict that I would use it.

Perceived Ease of Use (PEOU)

- My interaction with the Electronic Approval System (EAS) would be clear and understandable.
- Interacting with the Electronic Approval System (EAS) would not require a lot of my mental effort.
- I find the Electronic Approval System (EAS) would be easy to use.
- I find it would be easy to get the Electronic Approval System (EAS) to do what I want to do.

Perceived Usefulness (PU)

- Using the Electronic Approval System (EAS) would improve my performance in my job.
- Using the Electronic Approval System (EAS) in my job would increase my productivity.
- Using the Electronic Approval System (EAS) would enhance my effectiveness in my job.
- I find the Electronic Approval System (EAS) would be useful in my job.

Subjective Norm (SN)

- People who influence my behavior (work) think that I should use the Electronic Approval System (EAS).
- People who are important to me think that I should use the Electronic Approval System (EAS).

Image (IMG)

- People in my organization who use the Electronic Approval System (EAS) would have more prestige than those who do not.
- People in my organization who use the Electronic Approval System (EAS) would have a high profile.
- Having the Electronic Approval System (EAS) would be a status symbol in my organization.

Job Relevance (JR)

- In my job, usage of the Electronic Approval System (EAS) would be important.
- In my job, the use of the Electronic Approval System (EAS) would be relevant.

Output Quality (OQ)

- The quality of the output I get from the Electronic Approval System (EAS) would be high.
- I would have no problem with the quality of the Electronic Approval System (EAS)'s output.

Relative Advantage (RA)

- Using the Electronic Approval System (EAS) would enhance my efficiency in gathering information from government agencies as well as conducting administrative procedure transactions.
- Using the Electronic Approval System (EAS) would enhance my efficiency in interacting with government agencies.
- Using the Electronic Approval System (EAS) would make it easier to interact with government agencies.
- Using the Electronic Approval System (EAS) would give me greater control over my interaction with government agencies.

Trust (TRUST)

- The Electronic Approval System (EAS) system could be trusted to carry out online transactions faithfully.
- In my opinion, the Electronic Approval System (EAS) is trustworthy.

Compatibility (CP)

- I think using the Electronic Approval System (EAS) would fit well with the way that I like to gather information from government agencies as well as the way I conduct administrative procedure transactions.
- I think using the Electronic Approval System (EAS) would fit well with the way that I like to interact with government agencies.
- Using the Electronic Approval System (EAS) to interact with government agencies would fit into my lifestyle.
- Using the Electronic Approval System (EAS) to interact with government agencies would be compatible with how I like to do things.

Chapter 15
Perusing E-Readiness and Digital Divide:
From a Critical View

Mohammad Reza Hanafizadeh
Islamic Azad University, Iran

Payam Hanafizadeh
Allameh Tabataba'I University, Iran

Abbas Saghaei
Islamic Azad University, Iran

ABSTRACT

With the advent and evolution of information and communication technologies (ICTs) in general, the Internet, in particular, throughout the world, new terms such as "information society," "digital divide," and "e-readiness" were added to terminologies. Due to the rapid diffusion of the Internet in different aspects of human life, these concepts have attracted many scholars, practitioners, and policy-makers. In addition to much academic research done in these fields, nearly all countries have assessed their e-readiness and compared their digital divide with that of other countries, at least once. Consequently, there have been numerous e-readiness and digital divide models oriented towards certain objectives in recent years. The findings show (1) tremendous importance of the digital divide and e-readiness and (2) their complex and multi-faceted natures. Thus, effective examination and development of digital divide and e-readiness research requires a foundation in several rich literatures. Examining the e-readiness and digital divide literature in terms of their definitions and methodologies, in the current chapter, their strengths and weaknesses were recognized. Moreover, after an extensive literature survey, an integrated model was proposed for assessing e-readiness of small and medium-sized enterprises (SMEs) that can be used as the basis and standard for developing comprehensive models and frameworks in these enterprises. Finally, this chapter contributes to scarce literature on e-readiness/digital divide at micro level and creates additional pool of resources that practitioners and theorists could use to further enrich and extend their analysis of this construct.

DOI: 10.4018/978-1-60960-597-1.ch015

INTRODUCTION

Thus far, information and communication technology (ICT) has developed considerably among countries and organizations and brought them many benefits. Even though ICTs have provided tremendous opportunities, it is generally acknowledged that they have also potential pitfalls, such as the digital divide. The origin of the term digital divide goes back to an unknown American source in the mid 1990s and this concept initially emerged in media and government reports, e.g., "Falling Through the Net", "A Nation Online" and by "US Department of Commerce's National Telecommunications and Information Administration" (NTIA, 1995, 1997, 1999, 2000, 2002, 2004; Vehovar et al., 2006; van Dijk, 2006). The first scholarly papers on such a topic appeared around 1997 (Vehovar et al., 2006). As the information revolution has turned out to be a significant driver of the global economy, the digital divide has increasingly attracted researchers and policy-makers (Dewan et al., 2004). But the first step in any approach to the digital divide problem is to consider a country's ability or "readiness" to integrate information technology (IT) and e-commerce, in order to provide a baseline that can be used for global and regional comparisons and planning. It is essential to understand what it means for a country or economy to be "e-ready" and conduct an evaluation based on objective criteria to establish basic benchmarks. Therefore, if a country is to narrow the digital divide, an understanding of where that country currently stands vis-à-vis the information society must be achieved, which is called "e-readiness". Until now, various academic institutions, private organizations, and commercial publishers have put forward models for assessing and measuring e-readiness and the digital divide. These earlier measurements should be implemented for providing solid foundations for next stages of digital divide analysis and narrowing the gap. This paper addresses current widely diffused measurement instruments with the purpose of measuring e-readiness and the digital divide and their strengths and weaknesses.

DEFINING THE DIGITAL DIVIDE

There has been widespread debate about the definition of the digital divide and of the empirical analyses of its components (Barzilai-Nahon, 2006). The Organization for Economic Co-operation and Development (OECD) (2001) defined the digital divide as differences between individuals, households, companies, or regions related to the access to and use of ICT (Vehovar et al., 2006). The various factors may cause such a divide such as historical, socioeconomic, geographic, educational, behavioral, generation factors, or the physical incapability of individuals. There are a myriad of studies that address the factors influencing the digital divide and the plentiful models that measure it in terms of different factors widening inequalities including income, occupation, gender and age, education, geographic centrality, ethnicity and race, religion, language, family structure, physical capacity, frequency, time online, purpose, skills and experience, autonomy, affordability, competitive market structure, ownership and density of computers and web sites, communication infrastructure, equipment, social support, policy structure. In this paper, a brief focus is centered on some of the efforts that are more popular (for more information, see also Barzilai-Nahon, 2006).

In one study, DiMaggio & Hargittai (2001) pointed out that there are at least five factors of digital inequality: equipment, autonomy of use, skill, social support, and the purpose of using the Internet. Another framework, the MOSAIC model, was built as part of the "Global Diffusion of the Internet (GDI) Project" by Wolcott and his colleagues (2001). They examined the digital divide in terms of the diffusion of the Internet in a country based on six discrete valued factors: pervasiveness, geographic dispersion, sectoral absorption, connectivity infrastructure, organizational infrastructure, and sophistication of use. In addition, Corrocher and Ordanini (2002) quantified the digital divide as a multidimensional construct by combining multiple socio-economic factors into one. Their composite digitization index is based on six factors: markets, diffusion, infrastructures, human resources, competitiveness, and competition. Similarly, Mossberger et al. (2003) distinguished between an access divide, a skills divide, an economic opportunity divide, and a democratic divide. Orbicom (2005), the Network of United Nations Educational, Scientific and Cultural Organization (UNESCO) Chairs in Communications, advocated a framework for measuring the digital divide that develops concepts such as information density (info-density) and information use (info-use) (Sciadas, 2005). Finally, based on the TAI (UNDP) and the Industrial Development Scoreboard, Archiburgi and Coco (2005) developed the ArCo Index, which consists of eight indicators that depend on three main factors: the creation of technology, infrastructure, and human development skills.

DEFINING E-READINESS

E-readiness can be viewed and defined from two perspectives: macro-level and micro-level[1]. The concept of e-readiness from macro perspective, originated as a result of an attempt to provide a unified framework to evaluate the breadth and depth of the digital divide between the developed and developing countries during the later part of the 1990s. This concept from micro perspective has been given impetus by the rapid rate of Internet penetration throughout the world, and the dramatic advances in IT applications in business and industry (Mutula & van Brakel, 2006a).

The first efforts in defining e-readiness were undertaken from a macro perspective in 1998 by the Computer Systems Policy Project (CSPP). CSPP defined e-readiness as the degree to which a community is prepared to participate

in the networked world (CSPP, 1998). Since the development of the first e-readiness definition, Centre for International Development (CID) at Harvard University (2000) with the support of International Business Machines (IBM) (CID, 2000) and the INSEAD, the World Bank and the World Economic Forum (WEF) (Kirkman et al., 2002) developed the same definition as the CSPP. From the same perspective and in contrast to these measures that focus on community's readiness for participating in the networked world, Asian Pacific Economic Cooperation (APEC) in 2000, McConnell International (MI) in 2001 and Association of Southeast Asian Nations (ASEAN) in 2001 defined e-readiness as the degree to which an economy or community is prepared to participate in the digital economy (for more definitions see Hanafizadeh et al., 2009b). Providing general insights into the countries' e-readiness, macro studies at the same time suffer from a major drawback: the choice of factors and their relative weights may vary from one country to country. Relative measures and country rankings may ignore internal variations within a country, as such could be misleading. Micro studies are therefore recommended as they capture many of the factors that may escape macro analysis, and hence offer a more accurate picture (Rizk, 2004). From the latter perspective, e-readiness can be defined as "the level of preparedness pertaining to the ability of exploiting Internet technology for economic purposes through the rapid adoption of e-business" (Jutla et al., 2002). Most studies carried out from a micro perspective are associated with e-readiness assessment of SMEs in a country (e.g., in Egypt, India, Korea, Canada, Malaysia, Iran, etc.) and there are others which are pertinent to companies and financial organizations' e-readiness assessment. In the study of Hartman et al. (2000), net readiness is measured as a company's preparedness to exploit the enormous opportunities in the e-economy landscape. Grant (1999) asserted in his maturity model where a business is "ready" to implement e-business and e-commerce strategy, with the business plans and expectations clear, with no insurmountable obstacles impeding progress, and have identified any needed partners or professional support. Another report by Parker (2000) described e-readiness as "preparedness" to operate in an e-business and e-commerce marketplace.

METHODOLOGIES OF DIGITAL DIVIDE AND E-READINESS MEASURMENT

The construction of a digital divide and e-readiness model is not unsophisticated; besides, the methodological challenges raise a series of technical issues that, if not addressed adequately, can lead to models being misinterpreted or manipulated. Hence, we will focus on these essential methodological issues that are associated with any empirical research on the digital divide and e-readiness. Examining the efforts made to identify the digital divide and e-readiness, it points out that the most widespread methodology that has been used by scholars and practitioners to measure and analyze the digital divide and e-readiness is to construct a composite index from indicators e.g. the Internet Connectedness Index (Jung, Qiu, & Kim, 2001), the Technology Achievement Index (TAI) (United Nations Development Programme (UNDP), 2001), the Information Society Index (ISI) (IDC, 2001), the Global Digital Internet (GDI) (Wolcott et al., 2001), the synthetic index of digitalization presented by Corrocher & Ordanini (2002), the Digital Access Index (DAI) (International Telecommunication Union (ITU), 2003), the Network Readiness Index (NRI) (Dutta & Jain, 2004), the ArCo Index (Archibugi & Coco, 2004), the Digital Divide Index (DIDIX) (Husing & Selhofer, 2004), the Info-state (Sciadas, 2005), the Digital Opportunity Index (DOI) (ITU, 2005), and two telecommunication and ICT infrastructure indices developed recently by Hanafizadeh et al. (2009e) and Al-mutawkkil et al. (2009). A composite index integrates different kinds of indicators, that is, qualitative parameters with quantitative parameters, and hard data with soft data. Therefore, central to the construction of a composite index is the need to combine different indicators and dimensions measured on different scales in a meaningful way. This implies a decision as to which weighting model will be used and which procedure will be applied to aggregate the information (Nardo et al., 2005).

A few modelers such as Sciadas never used any weights for aggregation of their indicators and dimensions. He introduced the notion of a country's "ICTization" or Info-state, as the aggregation of Info-density and Info-use. The Info-state was developed based on an unweighted geometric average of 21 indicators that assessed 192 countries for nine years (Sciadas, 2005). In contrast to this index, most researchers have employed weighted aggregations to build their indices.

In many composite indices, all variables are given the same weight when there are no statistical or empirical grounds for choosing a different scheme. Equal weighting could imply the recognition of an equal status for all indicators (e.g., when policy assessments are involved). Alternatively, it could be the result of insufficient knowledge of causal relationships, or ignorance about the correct model to apply, or even stem from the lack of consensus on alternative solutions. The DOI is an example that used this methodology for constructing its model. The DOI was devised, as the United Nations (UN) World Summit on the Information Society (WSIS) (2003) recognized an urgent need for improving the measurement capabilities for ICT investment, adoption, and impact (ITU, 2005). This composite index utilized a set of eleven indicators and assigned an equal weight to create a single value that can be compared to other countries. Another example of these indices is the NRI, which includes three dimensions, and each dimension is further disaggregated into equally weighted sub-indices and variables. The TAI, which was proposed in a recent Human Development Report by the UNDP (2001), also assigned equal weight to its dimensions. Moreover, Archibugi & Coco (2004) constructed a new indicator (ArCo) of technological capabilities based on the equal weighting of its three dimensions. Likewise, The Bulgarian e-readiness assessment model (index) (2002) was defined as an average value of the four dimensions. In this model, each dimension was defined as an average value of several indicators and each indicator was quantified based on an average value of hard data and soft data. However, when using equal weighting, a variable might occur to be double counted in the composite index by combining variables with high degree of correlation. For example, indicators of the telephone lines and the percentage of households that have a phone line installed in the Bulgarian e-readiness assessment model, indicators of (fixed) broadband Internet subscribers and (mobile) broadband Internet subscribers in the DOI, indicators of internet penetration and telephone penetration in the ArCo index and finally indicators of mean years of schooling and gross enrolment ratio of tertiary students enrolled in science, mathematics and engineering in the TAI, highly correlated but were assigned equal weight. In addition to the aforementioned problems, in most cases it is not advisable to assign the same weight to the indicators which are not of equal importance, e.g., 'teledensity' is more important than 'ISDN connectivity'.

Sometimes modelers have utilized experts' opinions that are aware of policy priorities and theoretical backgrounds, to reflect the multiplicity of stakeholders' viewpoints and weight indicators and dimensions. For example, in July 2001, the Ministry of the Information Industry of the People's Republic of China built the national informatization quotient (NIQ) (Jin & Chengyu, 2002) based on the opinions of the experts. The NIQ is a composite index based on twenty indicators in six dimensions that were weighted based on experts' opinions. In other words, the NIQ uses a subjective expert evaluation for determining the weights of the different dimensions, which

are summed to give the final index value. Bui et al. (2003) applied the same weight for calculating the e-readiness value for each country. In this index, the weight assigned to each indicator reflects the analyst's view of how important or influential that criterion is relative to the entire set of 52 indicators for a particular country based on its overall economy. Therefore, in this case, assigning weights is also a subjective process. Moreover, the Economist Intelligence Unit (EIU) (2010) that has developed a composite index to rank e-readiness in 60-70 countries annually since 2000 and has applied this method to determine how each of its six dimensions influences overall e-readiness of countries. Another ICT readiness index measure, the DAI, was developed by the ITU (2003), around five main factors that were weighted based on the same method as the EIU. One of the main drawbacks of this method is that modelers may not have access to the experts. Even, in some cases, there are a few experts, that is, fewer than 30; accordingly, the outcome of a composite index and countries ranking in a benchmarking exercise is not robust. It is worth mentioning that such a method is of limited use when the number of variables of the model, in turn, the number of questions rises. For instance, in the case of Bui's et al. composite index, they calculated e-readiness values for the various countries by assigning the equal weight to each indicators in their paper since the number of indicators, those the experts should weight was high (52 indicators), despite the fact the equal weight method was proposed in their methodology (Bui et al., 2003). Finally, owing to the fact that this weighing process is based on individuals' perceptions, it may be dubious.

To avoid these limitations, modelers use regression approach that is suitable for a host of variables of different types. In such models, (usually linear) multiple regression models are estimated to retrieve the relative weights of indicators. If we divide the literature of digital divide into two groups, some studies focus mostly on measuring and quantifying digital divide, its magnitude, evolution, and the speed at which it is happening (Corrocher & Ordanini, 2002; OECD, 2005) while others concentrate on explaining the determinants of ICT diffusion (Chinn &Fairlie, 2007; Hargittai, 1999; Kiiski & Pojhola, 2002). There are enormous endeavors from latter group that have been made by using regression approach such as studies done by Hargittai (1999), Norris (2001), Dasgupta et al. (2001), Oxley & Yeung (2001), Robison & Crenshaw (2001), Guillen & Suarez (2001), Caselli & Coleman (2001), Kiiski & Pojhola, 2002, Wallsten (2003), Beilock & Dimitrova (2003), Shih et al. (2003), Quibria et al. (2003), Pohjola (2003), Chinn & Fairlie (2007), Dewan et al. (2004), to name but a few. This approach, although lends itself to numerous variables, implies the assumption of linear behavior and requires the independence of explanatory variables. Indeed, if these variables are correlated, estimators will have high variance; as a result, parameters estimates will not be precise and hypothesis testing will not be powerful. In the extreme case of perfect collinearity among regressors, the model will not even be identified. This problem arises specifically about ICT indicators, which are very likely to lead to overlapping information. Such indicators would be hard to reconcile in the context of econometric models and their estimations for the purposes of associational and causal explanations would not of practical use.

Nearly in all studies listed above, unfortunately the authors apply correlated explanatory variables to evaluate IT penetration and digital divide, so the obtained validity and accuracy results decline. Examining a dataset of OECD countries in 1998, Hargittai (1999) concludes that, while GDP is a large driver of Internet connectivity, telecommunications policy can also have a large effect that is correlated with the telephone density level. Similarly, Oxley & Yeung (2001) studied 30 countries in the same year and found out that Internet host penetration was positively associated with physical communication infrastructure, rule of law and credit card use, while negatively correlated with

telephone service costs. What was neglected in this model is the high correlation between variables of communication infrastructure and telephone service costs, which calls the results into question. Robison & Crenshaw (2001) examine the level of economic development, political openness/ democracy, mass education, the presence of a sizeable tertiary/services sector as drivers of Internet diffusion. They do a cross-sectional analysis of 74 countries over 1995-1999, using the number of Internet hosts per ten thousand people as their dependent variable. They deduced that Internet penetration is driven most significantly by development level, political freedom, and education. But education and level of economic development are closely related, so the presence of both of these variables in the model without considering their correlations may bias the findings.

Beilock & Dimitrova (2003) examined the impact of GNP, including the log and exponential forms, the level of civil liberties, infrastructure and regional variables on internet use in a sample of 105 countries from a dataset published in 2000. They noticed that GNP is "by far" the most important determinant and that the relationship appears to be non-linear, and that increasing civil liberties have a positive and significant impact even in the presence of infrastructure advantages. Hanafizadeh et al. (2009e) state that "a close correlation exists between ICT infrastructure and GDP per capita". This finding can demonstrate high correlation between variables used in the model presented by Beilock & Dimitrova. Wallsten (2003) used a 45-country data set from 2001 to conduct a cross sectional analysis of similar variables as mentioned in the previous studies on two dependent variables, the number of Internet users and the number of Internet hosts per capita. He focused on variables of regulatory regime characteristics and price regulation, and found out that the more formal and controlled a country's regulatory system, the fewer Internet users and hosts. Similarly, Guillen & Suarez (2001) studied the number of Internet hosts and the number of Internet users per capita, using a matched set of independent variables in a cross section of 141 countries in 1998/1999. They incorporated variables associated with telecommunications policy and infrastructure, as well as two predictable policymaking indices and a democracy index that are indicative of an environment conducive to entrepreneurship. They came to the conclusion that policy variables have an impact when the entrepreneurship variables aren't taken into account, but lose their effect when they are. Dasgupta et al. (2001) examined Internet use in a sample of 44 countries from 1990-1997, but used the measure of Internet hosts/telephone mainlines as the dependent variable. They conducted a log-log regression against measures of the baseline (1990) value of the ratio, the urban population, income per capita, and an index of competition policy and some regional dummies. They concluded that the ratio is significantly and positively related to policy and percentage urban population, and negatively related to the baseline value. Despite other studies, income per capita was not found to be significant. Using a different and novel approach to the problem, Norris (2001) examined the dispersion of Internet use by grouping the information on Internet use in over 100 countries into a "New Media Index," and comparing it with an "Old Media Index" representing the distribution of radio, TV sets, and newspaper readership in each nation. She inferred that the two are highly correlated, and concluded that the basic non-technology problems of access to earlier communications technologies, such as illiteracy and government policy controls, are also applied with respect to Internet access. In this model, also, radio, TV sets, and newspaper readership are correlated variables that should be considered. There are a few studies that examine more than one technology concurrently. Quibria et al. (2003) examined a data set of more than 100 countries in 1999 that included counts of personal computer (PC) and Internet use per capita. They found that GDP, education levels, and infrastructure play critical roles in the levels of these and other information technologies. Chinn & Fairlie (2007) used the same two dependent variables with a panel of 161 countries over the 1999-2001 periods. They deduced that GDP, telephone density, and regulatory quality (as measured by index assessing market friendly policies) are important determinants of PC and Internet density. In the two recent models, GDP is highly correlated with education levels, infrastructure and telephone density; if such a fact is not taken into consideration, it may harm the accuracy of findings. Another stream of research has used approaches akin to economic growth models to study the problem at hand. Pohjola (2003) examined a data set over the years 1993-2000 that included measures of income per capita, the relative price of IT equipment, human capital measures, the share of agriculture and openness to international trade. He stated that IT investment is tightly related to income measures and human capital, and inversely related to the importance of agriculture in the economy. Caselli & Coleman (2001) undertook an extensive longitudinal cross-country study of IT use, examining 89 countries from 1970-1990. They used a measure of computer imports/worker ratio as a proxy for the investment in IT, and regressed a large set of explanatory variables on the measure in a cross-sectional regression. They observed that openness to imports from OECD countries, the level of educational attainment, and the index of property rights are statistically significant. Using a flexible accelerator investment model, Shih et al. (2003) studied 39 countries from 1985-1999. They found that there is a positive correlation with the existing stock levels of IT capital, GDP, and education levels, and a negative correlation with interest rates.

Dewan et al. (2004) examined the determinants of the digital divide as closest to the analysis of Chinn & Fairlie (2007) described above. While the Chinn & Fairlie (2007) study is restricted to data on PC's and Internet over the 1999-2001 period, they considered three generations of IT (mainframes, PC's and Internet), and tracked the evolution of the divide, using suitable metrics, over the substantially longer period of 1985-2001. Further, they considered multiple measures of IT penetration, defined on the basis of both per capita and per income, whereas the earlier study just considers the former construct. Finally, they went beyond the panel regression analyses of Chinn & Fairlie (2007) to conduct quantile regressions, in order to gain a more complete understanding of the sometimes-complex relationship between IT penetration and its determinants.

As it can be seen, in the works studying the determinants of digital divide and e-readiness, the dependent variables most commonly considered are Internet users (Beilock & Dimitrova, 2003; Chinn & Fairlie, 2007; Guillen & Suarez, 2005; Norris, 2001; Quibria et al., 2003; Robison & Crenshaw, 2001; Tanner, 2003; Wallsten, 2003) and hosts (Dasgupta et al., 2001; Guillen & Suarez, 2005; Hargittai, 1999; Kiiski & Pohjola, 2002; Oyelaran & Lal, 2005; Oxley & Yeung, 2001; Robison & Crenshaw, 2001; Wallsten, 2003), mobile telephones (Bagchi, 2005; Quibria et al., 2003; Wong, 2002), PCs, (Quibria et al., 2003; Chinn & Fairlie, 2007) and telephone main lines (Hargittai, 1999; Dasgupta et al. 2001) as indicators of infrastructure. Other authors also include secure e-commerce hosts (Gibbs & Kraemer, 2004; Wong, 2002). In summary, the findings are consistent: national income/GDP and infrastructure are important factors in IT penetration levels, and depending on the countries examined, education and policies are also of significance.

In later models (ones developed by Dewan et al and Caselli & Coleman), also, we can see variables such as GDP per capita, density of main telephone lines and telephone subscription cost that have correlations together and applied in the regression model for analyzing IT penetration.

One approach similar to regression, particularly logistic regression, is the Discriminant Analysis for analyzing digital divide. Discriminant Analysis is the appropriate statistical technique when the dependent variable is qualitative and the independent variables are metric (Çilan et al., 2009). The single dependent qualitative variable in Discriminant Analysis turns into an independent variable in MANOVA (Hair et al., 1998). The objective of the analysis is to determine the variables which significantly define the groups and to describe the functions of these discriminating variables. In the analysis, the ability of the variables to discriminate between the groups is determined through the tests and by considering the question of "whether the predicted discriminant function classifies properly the cases to their own groups" (Tacq, 1999). In this method also, the correlations of variables is used to analysis of the digital divide.

As it was mentioned before, the use of the correlated variables in regression models and Discriminant Analysis or some methods like those reduces the validity of the findings; to tackle such a problem, a useful method for is to use factor analysis (FA) to determine the key constructs and to identify the redundant indicators. Another remedy can be found associating principle components analysis (PCA) with regression analysis. The FA and the PCA were found to be a useful technique for exploring the underlying dimensions of the digital divide, as well as for dealing with the complexity of this issue (Cuervo & Mene´ndez, 2006; Hanafizadeh et al., 2009e). The weaknesses and strengths of countries in terms of access to and use of ICT can be analyzed by extracting these dimensions. One of the famous studies in this case is the composite index of digitalization presented by Corrocher & Ordanini (2002). They used the PCA to combine factors influencing digitization into an index of digitization. Also, Hanafizadeh et al. (2009e) and Al-mutawkkil et al. (2009) constructed a composite index using Multi-Stage FA and Common FA, respectively, for measuring and analyzing the divide among countries in the area of telecommunication and ICT infrastructure. Also, some researchers apply a cluster analysis after the FA to obtain a classification of the levels of digital development (Cuervo & Menendez, 2006). The cluster analysis is performed on the identified factors by the FA to look for groups of countries with similar levels of digital development.

As you saw, digital divide and e-readiness indices are often presented as static measures. However, static measures of disparities (e.g., percentage difference, ratio, Gini coefficient, Theil index, coefficient of variation, etc.) are insensitive to changes in the corresponding absolute magnitude of the indicator growth rates. In order to overcome such a problem, an advanced time distance methodology was developed at conceptual and applied levels (Vehovar et al., 2006). This is a new statistical measure in dynamic gap analysis (Sicherl, 2004) where the levels of variable(s) are used as identifiers and time is the focus of comparison. For instance, Selhofer and Husing (2002) used a time-and-distance method for integrating different factors to respond to this question that whether the effect of women's participation in the economy is additive to the density of installed base of telephones or to the "brain drain." Similarly, in 2006, Vehovar et al. (2006) demonstrated how the use of a specific time-distance measure could result in a meaningful representation of the relative dynamics in ICT deployment. Lee et al. (2005) used time series analysis to examine the nexus between the ICT and the economic growth. The study showed that the significance of ICT contribution to economic growth is only "in many developed countries and Newly Industrialized Economies (NIEs), but not in developing countries" (Lee et al., 2005). Generally, the works done on digital divide and e-readiness that used this method can be divided into two groups. First group, the researches that used cross-sectional time series for developing countries (Oyelaran & Lal, 2005; Tanner, 2003), second group, studies that applied it for a combination of developing and developed countries (Bagchi, 2005; Chinn & Fairlie,2007; Guillen &Suarez, 2005; Kiiski &Pohjola, 2002; Kraemer et al., 2005).

In described static measures, models and indices were constructed based on correlations between variables. However, correlations among variables reflect the past behavior of a system—construct that we want to study and measure it (Sterman, 2000). Correlations do not represent the structure of the system. If circumstances change, if previously dormant feedback loops become dominant, if new policies are tried, previously reliable correlations among variables may break down. Modelers found system dynamic models (causal models) as a valuable tool to tackle this limitation (Sterman, 2000). In these models, relationships among variables are causal, no matter how strong the correlation, how high the R^2 (determinate coefficient), or how great the statistical significance of the coefficients in a regression may be. Among the dynamic models, the logistic model is widely used to explain and predict the diffusion of new products and innovations, and the Internet, in particular. A study in which a logistic model was used is that of Kiiski and Pohjola (2001). They, using a Gompertz model of technology diffusion that is a special case of the logistic model, examined the diffusion of the Internet from 60 countries over the years 1995-2000. Likewise, Wolcott ct al. (2001) presented a comprehensive framework for describing the diffusion of the Internet in a country by using this model (Wolcott et al., 2001). Moreover, the Index of the Massachusetts Innovation Economy that measures progress of three key components of the Massachusetts Innovation Economy—results, innovation process, and resources—is based on a dynamic conceptual framework that links resources to economic results through an innovation process (Massachusetts Technology Collaborative, 2003).

Finally, some researchers such as Mutula & van Brakel (2006a), Barzilai-Nahon (2006) and Hanafizadeh et al. (2009a, 2009c, 2009d) using an extensive literature survey of digital divide and e-readiness models, constructed integrated models. These models can be exploited as a basis and a standard for developing comprehensive models and frameworks.

WHAT IS THE GAP OF DIGITAL DIVIDE MEASURES?

Studies conducted on digital divide can be classified into three main groups according to geographical condition. The first group, composing the greatest number of studies, are the studies that have been conducted on measuring and analyzing digital divide between developed and developing countries (Chen & Wellman, 2003; Roller & Waverman 2001, IDATE, 2000; Kenny, 2001; Dewan et al., 2004; Dewan & Kraemer 2000; Norris, 2001; Kiiki and Pohjola, 2002; Beilock & Dimitrova, 2003). The second group, which are less in number than the first group, include some researches that have used cross-sectional data for a specific group of developed countries (Ricci 2000; Corrocher & Ordanini, 2002; Selhofer & Mayringer, 2001; Cuervo & Menendez 2006; Çilan et al. 2009, Hargittai, 1999). The last group, lowest in number compared to two other groups, are very few studies that have been conducted to identify the factors mostly contributing to the assessment of digital divide in developing countries (Al-Solbi & Mayhew, 2005; Al-Kinani & Al-Besher, 2008; Dasgupta, Lall & Wheeler, 2001; Quibria, Shamsun, Tschanh & Reyes-Macasaquit, 2003; Wong, 2002).

In contrast to the progress in the developed world, the digital divide is widening and deepening within developing countries, in spite of efforts at bridging it (Kubicek, 2004). Although developing economies (middle and low income) have increased ICT access and use in recent years, the gap among income groups still remains remarkable and varies according to the type of technology, with newer technologies (such as broadband Internet) being the most unequally distributed (Billon et al.,2009). Digital divide is widening in the sense that few people actively use the Internet,

and deepening in the sense that the consequences of not being online may be greater when moving beyond a subsistence level. Therefore, considering digital divide between these countries is an essential demand for the policy makers and an attractive issue for the researchers.

Furthermore, even among these scarce endeavors related to evaluate digital divide between developing countries, most studies focus on African countries (Center for International Development and Conflict Management (CIDCM), 2001; Lall & Pietrobelli, 2002; Oyelaran & Lal, 2005; Masalu, 2005; Fuchs & Horak, 2008; Oyelaran-Oyeyinka & Nyaki Adeya, 2004; Gebremichael & Jackson, 2006; Mutume, 2003; James, 2009) and international organizations and researches pay less attentions to other developing regions such as the Middle East and Eastern Europe.

Another problem of digital divide measures concerns the determination of appropriate variables for measuring the digital divide. In order to compare the countries and measure the digital divide between them, as a first step, there should be a consensus on the set of indicators that can properly measure the differences in the level of digitalization (Hanafizadeh et al., 2009b; Çilan et al., 2009). At this stage, lack of a theoretical framework describing information society and digital divide is problematic. Far from an established concept, the digital divide has gone from a binary definition of access (have/have not) to being defined as a multidimensional and more complex concept. This new perspective has produced a lively debate on the criteria necessary to measure it (DiMaggio et al., 2001; Warschauer, 2003; Bruce, 1999; de Haan, 2004; Livingstone & Helsper, 2007; Valadez and Duran, 2007). Several research studies have focused on identifying the factors that would facilitate or discourage access to and the use of ICT and the Internet for certain social groups, as well as on describing its distribution throughout the population and among different global regions (Castells, 2000; Norris, 2001; DiMaggio et al., 2001, Hanafizadeh et al.,

2009c; 2009d, 2009e). The most conspicuous fact is that the digital divide has not been discussed against the background of a general theory of social inequality, other types of inequality, or even a concept of human inequality in general (van Dijk, 2006). Therefore, it is required to identify a set of indicators that cover inequality in different aspects, such as social, income, cultural, infrastructure, and are able to highlight the inequalities in access to and use of ICT.

WHAT IS THE GAP OF E-READINESS ASSESSMENTS?

The literature on e-readiness assessments discloses the fact while numerous studies have been conducted on assessing countries' e-readiness–a macro perspective-, few have attempted to evaluate it from a micro perspective (Barzilai-Nahon, 2006; Hanafizadeh et al., 2009b; Rizk, 2004; Mutula and van Brakel, 2006b). Further, the construction of the most of the models (and the choice of the indicators behind it) is not driven by sound theoretical and policy concerns, but rather driven by the simple willingness to provide an empirical measure for e-readiness (Ramayah et al., 2005; Rizk, 2004). In other words, in the development of the models, the modelers often confuse "what is needed" with "what is available" in terms of data. They start their design process with variables and indicator levels and thereby enter the "loop of decision makers"; they are trying to come up with factors that are measurable, and they overlook what is truly meaningful in any particular context.

To overcome mentioned problems, we proposed an integrated model that measure e-readiness and digital divide of SMEs –one of the most important of (in many countries the most important of) economic sectors—based on defining and conceptualizing the e-readiness and digital divide at the micro level and subsequently operationalize this definition.

The definition of SMEs varies in different countries. For the purposes of the research, we adopt the new SME definition published by European Commission in 2005 (Table 1).

WHY FOCUS ON SMES?

Involvement in a networked economy is one of the new challenges that are encountered by SMEs today and has unfortunately left many them behind in the race towards a networked economy. While big organizations can generally muster the resources needed for the networked economy, the challenge is in getting SMEs to work around their resource and skills shortages in ICT. Since it is expensive for SMEs to train and retain ICT workforce, they are suffering from lack of ICT technically staff. Resources needed for investment in ICT must compete with demands from the shop floor and the rate at which technology changes tends to make any investment in ICT un-remunerative from an SME perspective. Yet, in the age of globalization, the leveraging of ICT by SMEs remains crucial.

Although limited resources are a distinguishing characteristic of SMEs and thus as a barrier,

Table 1. SME thresholds

Enterprise category	Headcount: Annual Work Unit (AWU)	Annual turnover	Annual balance sheet total
Medium-sized enterprise	< 250	≤ € 50 million	≤ € 43 million
Small enterprise	< 50	≤ € 10 million	≤ € 10 million
Micro enterprise	< 10	≤ € 2 million	≤ € 2 million

to many, they offer counter-balancing advantages as well. An obvious advantage is that small and medium sized companies are usually more entre-preneurial and willing to experiment and innovate in terms of business models and operations than larger organizations with established hierarchies. Thus, government initiatives aimed at increasing the e-readiness of SMEs can result in a higher level of national competitiveness in this crucial sector.

Since SMEs fulfill an important role in economic growth and in campaign against un-employment in countries[2], various endeavors have been channeled to ensure that they remain globally competitive. In this intensely changing and competitive market, the decision-makers, particularly the chief executive officers and chief financial officers in SMEs, have difficulties in evaluating and adopting Internet strategies. Many factors affect decision-making in the adoption of Internet and managers' awareness of the SMEs' level of e-readiness that can help them make bet-ter decisions. In the next section, we will build a model included various factors that can be used to assess their SME's capacity to participate in the networked world and make the necessary preparations to involve in a networked economy.

TOWARDS AN INTEGRATED SME E-READINESS/ DIGITAL DIVIDE MODEL

In this paper, we would like to propose a way to conceptualize the factors influencing SMEs e-readiness/digital divide— one of the most im-portant sectors relating to literature of e-readiness and digital divide at micro level—and devise an integrated model that can be used as the basis for their measurement. To do so, 56 international and reputable e-readiness and digital divide models were selected with regard to the three following criteria:

- Scientific backing of the model: There have been several models that assess e-readiness and digital divide. Some of them were constructed exclusively for assessing a sector of the economy of a specific coun-try (e.g., Bulgaria, Romania, etc.) and have been not used and referred to by any other books, conference papers, working pa-pers, White papers, journal papers, or any other scholarly and official reports. Since these models have been not supported by any scientific references, in this paper, we eliminated these models from selected models for drawing factors and indicators influencing e-readiness.

- The use of the models that measure e-readiness and digital divide at micro level: Since the purpose of the present article is to develop a model for assessing SMEs' e-readiness/digital divide that are one of sectors at micro level, we discards models that measure e-readiness/digital divide of countries—those assess e-readiness/digi-tal divide at macro level—and confine to those which focus on e-readiness/digital divide of a sector of the economy i.e. busi-nesses, organizations, institutions, etc.

- Access to the model information: In this study, access to the information of the model is used as one of the main crite-ria for selecting a proper model. In some cases, there is not enough information on indicators or factors of the model (e.g., Davidrajuh, 2007; Davidrajuh & Tvedteras, 2006); therefore, we discard these models from the selected models.

The literature on micro e-readiness/digital divide assessment reveals some common factors (factors on which the majority of researchers have consensus) influencing e-readiness/digital divide of micro perspective. Table 2 illustrates these factors and their sources drawn from the numerous theoretical, empirical, and summary attempts at defining and measuring the e-readiness at micro level.

Using common factors in Table 2, an integrated model is constructed shown in Figure 1.

Each and every of the factors presented in Figure 1 is an index by itself and was chosen after an extensive literature survey. In order to measure each factor through benchmarking the studies presented in Table 2, some common indicators are extracted.

In the literature of e-readiness/digital divide, modelers and theorists have selected indicators and variables to map onto their models using the previous studies or their own opinions. However, due to the high number of extracted indicators, it

is not practical here to employ experts' opinion. In this study, the knowledge and the information of e-readiness/digital divide models is exploited as experts' (modelers') opinions. To this end, first all indicators proposed by the models indicated in Table 2 are extracted. Then, content analysis, a quantitative approach taken by counting the frequency of phenomena within a case in order to gauge its importance comparing to other cases (Walliman, 2001), is used; indicators that have been presented at least in two models (at least with the frequency two) were selected as common indicators for assessing SME e-readiness/digital divide. It is noteworthy that the frequency of indicators in the models was identified based

Table 2. The common factors of measures and sources of them

Factors	Sources
Infrastructure and Connectivity	Rizk (2004), Mutula & van Brakel (2006a), Jutla et al. (2002), Ramayah et al. (2005), Keen (1991), APEC (1999), Macintyre & Ramnarine (2003), Mehrtens et al. (2001), World Bank (2004), Fink (1998), Kleindl (2000), Moodley (2001), Kotler (2003), Van Belle & Vosloo (2005), Kasraian (2007), Aminali (2007), Mutula & van Brakel (2006b), Fathian et al. (2008), Jerman-Blaz'ic' (2008)
Human Resources	Ramayah et al. (2005), Fink (1998), Doukidis et al. (1994), Attaran (2001), Hong (2002), Kwon & Zmud (1987), Jutla et al. (2002), Mutula & van Brakel (2006a), Minton (2003), Kasraian (2007), Aminali (2007), Fathian et al. (2008), Horrocks, & Haines (2004)
Networked World Enablers	Norazah (2001), Goodwin (1991), Gupta (1995), Janes et al. (1997), Tan & Teo (1998), Dr Sankaran (1999), Ainin & Rohana (2000), Jutla et al. (2002), World Bank (2004), Mutula & van Brakel (2006a), Grant (1999), Ramayah et al. (2005), Lawrence et al. (1998), Van Belle & Vosloo (2005), Kasraian (2007), Aminali (2007), Mutula & van Brakel (2006b), Fathian et al. (2008)
IT Applications	Evans & Wurster (1997), Barua et al. (2000), Barua & Lee (1997), Clark & Stoddard (1996), Drury & Farhoomand (1996), Hart & Saunders (1998), Iacovou et al. (1995), Massetti & Zmud (1996), Mukhopadhyay et al. (1995), Premkumar & Ramamurthy (1995), Riggins & Mukhopadhyay (1994), Srinivasan et al. (1994), Zaheer & Venkatraman (1994), Jain (2005), Hashem (2001), World Bank (2004), Mutula & van Brakel (2006a), Kasraian (2007), Aminali (2007), Mutula & van Brakel (2006b), Fathian et al. (2008), Jerman-Blaz'ic' (2008)
ICT Use	Payne (1996), Jain (2005), Minton (2003), Macintyre & Ramnarine (2003), Rizk (2004), Gray & Lawless (2000), Ramsey et al. (2003), World Bank (2004), Engler (1999), Fink (1998), Moodley (2001), Kotler (2003), APEC (1999), Van Belle & Vosloo (2005), Aminali (2007), Fathian et al. (2008); Jerman-Blaz'ic' (2008)
Barriers to ICT Use	Khader (2005), OECD (2000), Rizk (2004), World Bank (2004), Ramayah et al. (2005), Sulaiman & Jani (2001), Attaran (2001), Lawrence et al. (1998), APEC (1999), Moodley (2001), Mutula & van Brakel (2006b)
External Environment Readiness	APEC (1999), Mutula & van Brakel (2006a), Kasraian (2007), Jutla et al. (2002), Macintyre & Ramnarine (2003), Hong (2002), Fink (1998), Barua et al. (2000), Fathian et al. (2008)

Figure 1. The conceptual model for assessment of SME e-readiness/digital divide

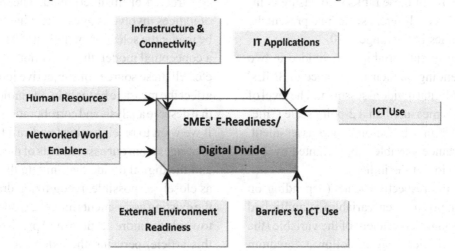

on their definitions, that is, two indicators with different titles but the same definition were assumed as one indicator. In view of adopting the criterion of the existence of the indicator in at least two models, first of all, there is no need for data to extract indicators; second, some models have been built for measuring e-readiness/digital divide of organizations of a specific country or region (e.g., see Van Belle & Vosloo, 2005; Al-Solbi & Mayhew). Since the selected indicators exist in at least two models and were not limited to a specific model, indicators assessing a certain country or region were not selected as common indicators. Therefore, selected indicators are appropriate to assess e-readiness and measure digital divide between all countries and regions. The full list of e-readiness/digital divide indicators for each factor is presented in Appendix.

METHOD OF COMPUTATION E-READINESS/DIGITAL DIVIDE INDICES

The e-readiness/digital divide indices are a system of synthetic indicators. The main objective in constructing these indices is to reduce the multiple dimensions of the information society to a limited set of synthetic measures. The advantages of such an approach are at least the following:

- the employment of synthetic indicators is a prerequisite for establishing time series and respectively for analyzing and assessing change;
- synthetic indicators facilitate the public presentation of the results of the assessment, thus making analysis easier to perceive.

The method used to construct the e-readiness/ digital divide indices involves a number of steps:

First, the value of each indicator is measured on a 4- or 5-point scale[3]

Second, a rank is assigned to each indicator value using the following procedure:

A. **With 5-point scales:** a rank of 1 is assigned to the first value, a rank of 3 to the second value, a rank of 5 to the third value, a rank of 7 to the fourth value and a rank of 10 to the fifth value.

B. **With 4-point scales:** a rank of 1 is assigned to the first value, a rank of 4 to the second, a rank of 7 to the third and a rank of 10 to the fourth value.

The purpose of these ranks is to ensure compatibility between different scales and present the indicator values in the range 1-10.

Third, different variables are divided in two groups depending on their importance to SMEs' e-readiness/digital divide assessment. The level of importance is measured on a 2-point scale ("medium" and "high") based on expert assessment. High-importance variables are weighted by 2 in the computation of the indices.

Fourth, the respective ranks (depending on the real value of a given variable) is multiplied by the importance coefficient of the variable (the weighted coefficients are as follows: "medium importance" w=1 and "high importance" w=2).

Fifth, the values are aggregated in synthetic indicators in several factors. The value of each index is computed as a sum of the weighted ranks of the respective variables included in a given factor. Each index summarizes the values of several variables and is presented in a statistically normalized form: from zero to 10. Values closer to zero indicate a "low level" of e-readiness in the respective factor, and those closer to 10 a "high" state of e-readiness.

Finally, the composite e-readiness/digital divide index is computed as an average value of the indices for different factors (see Appendix).

CONCLUSION

On the one hand, the rapid rate of ICT penetration throughout the world, coupled with dramatic advance in its use in business and society, has created an extensive literature on various aspects of digital divide and e-readiness. Consequently, plentiful models and tools were constructed to measure these aspects. Appreciating the significance of evaluating these concepts on the part of researchers and policy-makers, there continues to be more and more research on this topic. On the other hand, the models and indices can send misleading or non-robust policy messages if they are poorly

constructed or misinterpreted. The construction of indices involves stages where judgment has to be made: the selection of indicators, the choice of a conceptual model, the weighting of indicators, etc. All these sources of subjective judgment will affect the message brought by the indices in a way that deserve analysis and corroboration. Therefore, if we want to receive robust and valid results and messages from our assessments of the e-readiness and the digital divide that imitate the real world as closely as possible, recognizing drawbacks of the existing assessments models, we need to move towards the more accurate and precise models. In this article, perusing the extensive literature of digital divide and e-readiness assessments, their strengths and weaknesses from conceptualization and methodological standpoints were identified. Recognizing and classifying these strengths and weaknesses is handy, since it can make valuable contribution to researchers and top-level decision-makers to use or construct e-readiness and digital divide model.

One of the most challengeable gaps in literature of e-readiness and digital divide is that most these studies have been confined to macro (national) assessments and ignored sectoral-level environments. But even these few studies neglect the stage of the definition and specification of e-readiness and digital divide at this level. Decision makers often fall into the trap of seeking data that exist, instead of putting in the effort to first systematically conceptualize the digital divide and e-readiness, operationalize it as appropriate to the context, and only then collect data. In the present paper, reviewing the literature of e-readiness/digital divide at micro level, we extracted the common factors influencing e-readiness/digital divide one of the main sectors of this level that is SMEs and presented a conceptual model for assessing e-readiness/digital divide it.

It is acknowledged that the contribution of the paper is currently restricted to a theoretical construct because empirical studies have yet to be carried out with various SMEs that have agreed to collaborate in the research. Empirical testing of the proposed model is expected to demonstrate how fieldwork data can be used to support the indicators and the indices that have been presented here. By using case studies in SMEs to test and ultimately formulate a new research base, further questioning and debate can take place around the framework. Future work on this research includes the need to empirically validate the presented framework and develop more indices for SMEs e-readiness/digital divide assessment. Last but not the least, this article contributes to scarce e-readiness/digital divide literature at micro level and the presented model can be used as a basis and a standard for developing a comprehensive model of SMEs e-readiness/digital divide assessment.

REFERENCES

Ainin, S., & Rohana, J. (2000). *E-commerce implementation in Malaysian manufacturing sector.* International Conference on Electronic Commerce. Kuala Lumpur, Malaysia.

Al-Kinani, A. N., & Al-Besher, B. M. N. (2008). Analysis study of culture's impact on e-readiness assessments in developing countries. *Communications of the IBIMA, 6,* 154–164.

Al-mutawkkil, A., Heshmati, A., & Hwang, J. (2009). Development of telecommunication and broadcasting infrastructure indices at the global level. *Telecommunications Policy, 33,* 176–199. doi:10.1016/j.telpol.2008.12.008

Al-Solbi, A., & Mayhew, P. (2005). Measuring e-readiness assessment in Saudi organizations: Preliminary results from a survey study. The *Proceedings of the First European Conference on Mobile Government,* 10-12 July 2005, University of Sussex Brighton, UK.

Aminali, P. (2007). *E-readiness assessment within Iran's automotive Industry: Case of Iran Khodro Industrial Group.* Master Thesis, Luleå University of Technology, Sweden.

Archibugi, D., & Coco, A. (2004). A new indicator of technological capabilities for developed and developing countries (ArCo). *World Development, 32*(4), 629–654. doi:10.1016/j.worlddev.2003.10.008

Asian Pacific Economic Corporation (APEC). (1999). *SME electronic commerce study.* (TEL09/97T) Final Report, September 24.

Asian Pacific Economic Corporation (APEC). (2000). *E-commerce readiness assessment guide.* Hong Kong, China: APEC. Retrieved from http://www.ecommerce.gov/apec/

Association of Southeast Asian Nations (ASEAN). (2001). *E-ASEAN readiness assessment.* Retrieved from http://www.unpan1.un.org

Attaran, M. (2001). The coming age of online procurement. *Industrial Management & Data Systems, 101*(4), 177–180. doi:10.1108/02635570110390080

Bagchi, K. (2005). Factors contributing to global digital divide: Some empirical results. *Journal of Global Information Technology Management, 8*(1), 47–65.

Barua, A., Konana, P., Whinston, A., & Yin, F. (2000). *Assessing Internet enabled business value: An exploratory investigation.* Working paper. Austin, TX: Center of Research in Electronic Commerce, the University of Texas at Austin.

Barua, A., & Lee, B. (1997). An economic analysis of the introduction of an electronic data interchange system. *Information Systems Research, 8*(4), 321–341. doi:10.1287/isre.8.4.398

Barzilai-Nahon, K. (2006). Gaps and bits: Conceptualizing measurements for digital divide/s. *The Information Society, 22*)5), 269–278.

Beilock, R., & Dimitrova, D. V. (2003). An exploratory model of inter-country Internet diffusion. *Telecommunications Policy, 27*(3-4), 237–252. doi:10.1016/S0308-5961(02)00100-3

Billon, M., Lera-Lopez, L., & Marco, R. (2010). Differences in digitalization levels: A multivariate analysis studying the global digital divide. *Rev World Econ, 146,* 39–73. doi:10.1007/s10290-009-0045-y

Bruce, B. (1999). Speaking the unspeakable about 21st century technologies. In Hawisher, G. E., & Selfe, C. L. (Eds.), *Passions, pedagogies, and 21st century technologies. Logan, UT/Urbana.* IL: Utah State University Press and NCTE.

Bui, T., Sankaran, S., & Sebastian, I. M. (2003). A framework for measuring national e-readiness. *International Journal of Electronic Business, 1*(1), 3–22. doi:10.1504/IJEB.2003.002162

Caselli, F., & Coleman, W. J. (2001). *Cross-country technology diffusion: The case of computers.* Cambridge, MA: National Bureau of Economic Research.

Castells, M. (2001). *The Internet galaxy: Reflections on the Internet, business, and society.* New York, NY: Oxford University Press.

Center for International Development and Conflict Management (CIDCM). (2001). *CIDCM at the University of Maryland.* Retrieved from http://www.bsos.umd.edu/cidcm/projects/neo.html/

Center for International Development (CID) at Harvard University. (2000). *Readiness for the networked world, a guide for developing countries.* Cambridge, MA: Harvard University. Retrieved from http://www.cid.harvard.edu/ciditg

Chen, W., & Wellman, B. (2003). *Charting and bridging digital divides: Comparing socio-economic, gender, life stage and rural-urban Internet access and use in eight countries. AMD Global Consumer Advisory Board.* GSAB.

Chinn, M. D., & Fairlie, R. W. (2007). The determinants of the global digital divide: A cross-country analysis of computer and Internet penetration. *Oxford Economic Papers, 59,* 16–44. doi:10.1093/oep/gpl024

Çilan, C. A., Bolat, B. A., & Coşkun, E. (2009). Analyzing digital divide within and between member and candidate countries of European Union. *Government Information Quarterly, 26,* 98–105. doi:10.1016/j.giq.2007.11.002

Clark, T. H., & Stoddard, D. B. (1996). Inter organizational business process redesign: Merging technological and process innovation. *Journal of Management Information Systems, 13*(2), 9–28.

Computer Systems Policy Project. (CSPP). (1998). *Readiness guide for living in the networked world.* Retrieved from http://www.cspp.org

Corrocher, N., & Ordanini, A. (2002). Measuring the digital divide: A framework for the analysis of cross country differences. *Journal of Information Technology, 17,* 9–19. doi:10.1080/02683960210132061

Cuervo, M. R. V., & Menendez, A. J. L. (2006). A multivariate framework for the analysis of the digital divide evidence for the European Union -15. *Information & Management, 43,* 56–766.

Dasgupta, S., Lall, S., & Wheeler, S. (2001). *Policy reform, economic growth, and the digital divide: An econometric analysis.* Development Research Group, World Bank, Washington, DC, Working paper.

Davidrajuh, R. (2007). Fuzzy logic based model of a new tool for measuring e-readiness. *Proceedings of the First Asia International Conference on Modelling & Simulation* (AMS'07), (IEEE Computer Society).

Davidrajuh, R., & Tvedteras, J. E. (2006). *Fuzzy approach for measuring e-readiness*. International Conference on Computational Intelligence for Modelling Control and Automation, and International Conference on Intelligent Agents, Web Technologies and Internet Commerce (CIMCA-IAWTIC'06), (IEEE Conference).

de Haan, J. (2004). *Theorizing the digital divide*. Paper presented at the Conference Papers Annual Meeting of The American Sociological Association, 2004 Annual Meeting, San Francisco.

Dewan, S., Ganley, D., & Kraemer, K. L. (2004). *Across the digital divide: A cross-country analysis of the determinants of IT penetration*. Personal Computing Industry Center.

Dewan, S., & Kraemer, K. L. (2000). Information Technology and productivity: Evidence from country-level data. *Management Science, 46*(4), 548–562. doi:10.1287/mnsc.46.4.548.12057

Dewan, S., & Riggins, F. J. (2005). The digital divide: Current and future research directions. *Journal of the Association for Information Systems, 6*(2), 298–337.

DiMaggio, P., & Hargittai, E. (2001). *From the digital divide to digital inequality: Studying Internet use as penetration increases*. Working Paper 15. Princeton, NJ: Center for Arts and Cultural Policy Studies, Princeton University.

Doukidis, G. I., Smithson, S., & Lybereas, T. (1994). Trends in Information Technology in small businesses. *Journal of End User Computing, 6*(4), 15–25.

Drury, D. H., & Farhoomand, A. (1996). Innovation adoption of EDI. *Information Resources Management Journal, 9*(3), 5–13.

Dutta, S., & Jain, A. (2004). *The networked readiness index 2003-2004: Overview and analysis framework*. Retrieved from http://www.developmentgateway.org/download/222656/Networked Readiness Index.pdf

Economist Intelligence Unit (EIU). (2009). *The 2009 e-readiness rankings*. London, UK/New York, NY/ Hong Kong: EIU. Retrieved from http://www.eiu.com

Engler, N. (1999). Small but Nimble. *Information., 18*, 57–62.

European Commission. (2005). *The new SME definition. User guide and model declaration*. Retrieved from http://ec.europa.eu/enterprise/.../sme_definition/sme_user_guide.pdf

Evans, P., & Wurster, T. S. (1997). Strategy and the new economics of information. *Harvard Business Review, 75*(5), 70–83.

Fathian, M., Akhavan, P., & Hoorali, M. (2008). E-readiness assessment of non-profit ICT SMEs in a developing country: The case of Iran. *Technovation, 28*, 578–590. doi:10.1016/j.technovation.2008.02.002

Fink, D. (1998). Guidelines for the successful adoption of Information Technology in small and medium enterprises. *International Journal of Information Management, 18*(4), 243–253. doi:10.1016/S0268-4012(98)00013-9

Fuchs, C., & Horak, E. (2008). Africa and the digital divide. *Telematics and Informatics, 25*, 99–116. doi:10.1016/j.tele.2006.06.004

Gebremichael, M. D., & Jackson, J. W. (2006). Bridging the gap in Sub-Saharan Africa: A holistic look at information poverty and the region's digital divide. *Government Information Quarterly, 23*, 267–280. doi:10.1016/j.giq.2006.02.011

Gibbs, J., & Kraemer, K. L. (2004). Across-country investigation of the determinants of scope of e-commerce use: An institutional approach. *Electronic Markets, 14*, 124–137. doi:10.1080/10196780410001675077

Goodwin, C. (1991). Privacy: Recognition of a consumer right. *Journal of Public Policy & Marketing, 10*(Spring), 149–166.

Grant, S. (1999). *E-commerce for small businesses*. IEC'99 Conference, September.

Gray, C., & Lawless, N. (2000). *Innovations in the distance development of SME management skills*. Retrieved from http://www.eurodl.org/materials/contrib/2000/gray.html

Guillen, M. F., & Suarez, S. L. (2001). Developing the Internet: Entrepreneurship and public policy in Ireland, Singapore, Argentina, and Spain. *Telecommunications Policy*, *25*(3-4), 349–371. doi:10.1016/S0308-5961(01)00009-X

Gupta, S. (1995). HERMES: A research project on the commercial uses of the World Wide Web. Retrieved from http://www.umich.edu/~sgupta/hermes/

Hair, J. F. Jr, Anderson, R. E., Tatham, R. L., & Black, W. C. (1998). *Multivariate data analysis* (5th ed.). New Jersey: Prentice-Hall.

Hanafizadeh, M. R., Hanafizadeh, P., & Saghaei, A. (2009c). The pros and cons of digital divide and e-readiness assessments. *International Journal of E-Adoption*, *1*(3), 1–29. doi:10.4018/jea.2009092901

Hanafizadeh, M. R., Saghaei, A., & Hanafizadeh, P. (2009e). An index for cross-country analysis of ICT infrastructure and access. *Telecommunications Policy*, *33*(7), 385–405. doi:10.1016/j.telpol.2009.03.008

Hanafizadeh, P., Hanafizadeh, M. R., & Khodabakhshi, M. (2009a). Extracting core ICT indicators using entropy method. *The Information Society*, *25*(4), 236–247. doi:10.1080/01972240903028490

Hanafizadeh, P., Hanafizadeh, M. R., & Khodabakhshi, M. (2009b). Taxonomy of e-readiness assessment measures. *International Journal of Information Management*, *29*(3), 189–195. doi:10.1016/j.ijinfomgt.2008.06.002

Hanafizadeh, P., Khodabakhshi, M., & Hanafizadeh, M. R. (2009d). A methodology to extract a new set of core indicators of the information society. *Journal of Information Technology Research*, *2*(3), 70–94. doi:10.4018/jitr.2009070105

Hargittai, E. (1999). Weaving the Western Web–Explaining differences in Internet connectivity among OECD countries. *Telecommunications Policy*, *23*(10-11), 701–718. doi:10.1016/S0308-5961(99)00050-6

Hart, P., & Saunders, C. (1997). Power and trust: Critical factors in the adoption and use of electronic data interchange. *Organization Science*, *8*(1), 23–42. doi:10.1287/orsc.8.1.23

Hartman, A., Sifonis, J. G., & Kador, J. (2000). *Net ready: Strategies for success in the e-economy*. USA: McGraw-Hill.

Hashem, S. (2001). E-*readiness assessment: Case of Egypt*. Cairo, Egypt: Ministry of Communications and Information Technology. Retrieved from http://www.itu.int/osg/spu/ni/digitalbridges/presentations/07-Hashem.pdf

Hong, Y. S. (2002). *Narrowing the digital gap in the APEC region*. Korea: Institute for International Economic Policy. Working Paper. Retrieved from unpan1.un.org/intradoc/groups/public/documents/APCITY/UNPAN00867.pdf

Horrocks, G., & Haines, M. (2004). *Health information literacy and higher education: The King's College London approach*. Paper presented at the World and International Congress: 70th IFLA General Conference and Council, 22–27 August 2004, Buenos Aires, Argentina.

Husing, T., & Selhofer, H. (2004). DIDIX: A digital divide index for measuring social inequality in IT diffusion. *IT & Society*, *1*(7), 26–42.

Iacovou, C. L., Benbasat, I., & Dexter, A. S. (1995). Electronic data interchange and small organizations: Adoption and impact of technology. *Management Information Systems Quarterly, 19*(4), 465–485. doi:10.2307/249629

IDATE. (2000). *Prioritising countries for assistance to overcome the digital divide.* IDATE, Montepellier.

IDC. (2001). *The IDC/world times information society index: The future of the information society.* Framingham, MA: IDC.

International Telecommunication Union (ITU). (2003). *ITU digital access index: World's first global ICT ranking.* Geneva, Switzerland: ITU. Retrieved from http://www.itu.int/newsarchive/press releases/2003/30.html

International Telecommunication Union (ITU). (2005). *Measuring digital opportunity.* Paper presented at the WSIS Thematic Meeting on Multi-Stakeholder Partnerships for Bridging the Digital Divide, Seoul, Republic of Korea, June. Retrieved from http://www.itu.int/itu-wsis/2005/DOI%20V2.pdf.

Jain, P. (2005). *E-readiness assessment for SMEs in India.* New Delhi, India: Ministry of Small Scale Industries, Government of India. Retrieved from http://www.annualmeeting2005.insme.org/documents

James, J. (2009). From the relative to the absolute digital divide in developing countries. *Technological Forecasting and Social Change, 76,* 1124–1129. doi:10.1016/j.techfore.2009.01.004

Janes, L. Pollett, & Reid. (1997). *The growth of electronic commerce: A critique.* Retrieved from http://www.geocities/Colsseum/7542

Jerman-Blaz̆ic̆, B. (2008). Web-hosting market development status and its value as an indicator of a country's e-readiness. *Telecommunications Policy, 32,* 422–435. doi:10.1016/j.telpol.2008.04.007

Jin, J., & Chengyu, X. (2002). The digital divide in terms of national informatization quotient (NIQ): The perspective of mainland China. *Proceedings of the International Conference on Digital Divides: Technology and Politics in the Information Age,* Hong Kong, Baptist University, Hong Kong, SAR, China.

Jung, J.-Y., Qiu, J. L., & Kim, Y.-C. (2001). Internet connectedness and inequality: Beyond the "Divide." *Communication Research, 28*(4), 507–535. doi:10.1177/009365001028004006

Jutla, D., Bodorik, P., & Dhaliwal, J. (2002). Government support for the e-readiness of small and medium sized enterprises. *Proceedings of the 35th Hawaii International Conference on System Sciences* (IEEE Conference), USA.

Kasraian, L. (2007). *The impact of e-readiness on EC success in public sector in Iran: The case of KWPA.* Khouzestan Water & Power Authority, Ministry of Energy. Master Thesis, Luleå University of Technology, Sweden.

Keen, P. G. W. (1991). *Shaping the future: Business design through Information Technology.* Boston, MA: Harvard Business School Press.

Kenny, C. (2001). Prioritising countries for assistance to overcome the digital divide. *Communications and Strategies, 41,* 17–36.

Khader, M. T. (2005). *The impact of adoption electronic commerce in small to medium enterprises Jordanian companies.* Retrieved from http://medforist.grenobleem.com/ Contenus/ Conference% 20Amman% 20EBEL% 2005/ pdf/ 26.pdf

Kiiski, S., & Pohjola, M. (2001). *Cross-country diffusion of the Internet.* United Nations University, World Institute for Development Economic Research.

Kirkman, G. S., Osorio, C. A., & Sachs, J. D. (2002). *The networked readiness index: Measuring the preparedness of nations for the networked world.* Cambridge, MA: Center for International Development (CID), Harvard University.

Kleindl, B. (2000). Competitive dynamics and new business models for SMEs in the virtual marketplace. *Journal of Developmental Entrepreneurship, 5*(1), 73–85.

Kotler, P. (2003). *Marketing management.* USA: Prentice-Hall International, Inc.

Kubicek, H. (2004). Fighting a moving target. *IT & Society, 1*(6), 1–19.

Kwon, T. H., & Zmud, R. W. (1987). Unifying the fragmented models of Information Systems implementation. In Boland, R. J., & Hirscheim, R. A. (Eds.), *Critical issues in Information Systems research.* New York, NY: John Wiley & Sons.

Lall, S., & Pietrobelli, C. (2002). *Failing to compete: Technology development and technology systems in Africa.* Cheltenham, UK: Edward Elgar.

Lawrence, E., Corbitt, B., Tidwell, A., Fisher, J., & Lawrence, J. (1998). *Internet commerce: Digital models for business.* Australia: John Wiley & Sons Australia, Ltd.

Lee, S. T., Gholami, R., & Tong, T. Y. (2005). Time series analysis in the assessment of ICT impact at the aggregate level—Lessons and implications for the new economy. *Information & Management, 42*, 1009–1022. doi:10.1016/j.im.2004.11.005

Livingstone, S., & Helsper, E. (2007). Gradations in digital inclusion: Children, young people and the digital divide. *New Media & Society, 9*(4), 671–696. doi:10.1177/1461444807080335

Macintyre, G., & Ramnarine, D. (2003). *National ICT strategy development e-readiness assessment report.* Trinidad and Tobago: Ministry of Public Administration & Information. Retrieved from http://unpan1.un.org/intradoc/groups/public/documents/UN/UNPAN015505.pdf

Masalu, D. C. P. (2005). Evolution of information and communication technology in Tanzania and its impact on ocean data and information management. *Ocean and Coastal Management, 48*, 85–95. doi:10.1016/j.ocecoaman.2004.11.001

Massachusetts Technology Collaborative. (2003). *Executive index of the Massachusetts innovation economy.* Westborough, MA. Retrieved from http:64.233.167.104/search?q=cache:fQiIBz61YPUJ:www.cityofboston.gov/bra/gbtf/documents/MTC%2520IndexInnovEconomy2003.pdf

Massetti, B., & Zmud, R. W. (1996). Measuring the extent of EDI usage in complex organizations: Strategies and illustrative examples. *Management Information Systems Quarterly, 20*(3), 331–345. doi:10.2307/249659

McConnell International (MI). (2001). *Ready, net, go!* Retrieved from http://www.mcconnellinternational.com/ereadiness/ereadinessreport2.htm

Mehrtens, J., Cragg, P. B., & Mills, A. M. (2001). A model of Internet adoption by SMEs. *Information & Management, 39*, 165–176. doi:10.1016/S0378-7206(01)00086-6

Moodley, S. (2001). Impact of electronic commerce and small exporting firms in the South African wooden furniture manufacturing sector. *Journal of Information Technology Impact, 2*(3), 89–104.

Mossberger, K., Tolbert, C. J., & Stansbury, M. (2003). *Virtual inequality: Beyond the digital divide.* Washington, DC: Georgetown University Press.

Mukhopadhyay, T., Kekre, S., & Kalathur, S. (1995). Business value of Information Technology: A study of electronic data interchange. *Management Information Systems Quarterly, 19*(2), 137–156. doi:10.2307/249685

Mutula, S. M., & van Brakel, P. (2006a). An evaluation of e-readiness assessment tools with respect to information access: Towards an integrated information rich tool. *International Journal of Information Management, 26,* 212–223. doi:10.1016/j.ijinfomgt.2006.02.004

Mutula, S. M., & van Brakel, P. (2006b). E-readiness of SMEs in the ICT sector in Botswana with respect to information access. *The Electronic Library, 24*(3), 402–417. doi:10.1108/02640470610671240

Mutume, G. (2003). Africa takes on the digital divide: New Information Technologies change the lives of those in reach. *Africa Renewal, 17*(3).

Nardo, M., Saisana, M., Saltelli, A., & Tarantola, S. (2005). *Tools for composite indicators building.* European Communities. Retrieved from http://farmweb.jrc.cec.eu.int/ci/bibliography.htm

Norazah, M. S. (2001). Malaysian Internet users' motivations and concerns on shopping online. *Malaysian Journal of Library & Information Sciences, 6*(2), 21–33.

Norris, P. (2001). *The digital divide: Civic engagement. Information poverty & the Internet worldwide.* Cambridge, UK: Cambridge University Press.

NTIA. (1995). *Falling through the Net: A survey of the 'have nots' in rural and urban America.* U.S. Department of Commerce, Washington DC, 1995. Retrieved from http://www.ntia.doc.gov/ntiahome/fallingthru.html

NTIA. (1998). *Falling through the Net II: More data on the digital divide.* U.S. Department of Commerce, Washington DC, 1998. Retrieved from http://www.ntia.doc.gov/ntiahome/net2

NTIA. (1999). *Falling through the Net III: Defining the digital divide.* U.S. Department of Commerce, Washington DC, 1999. Retrieved from http://www.ntia.doc.gov/ntiahome/fttn99/contents.html

NTIA. (2000). *Falling through the Net IV: Towards digital inclusion.* U.S. Department of Commerce, Washington DC, 2000. Retrieved from http://www.ntia.doc.gov/ntiahome/fttn00/contents-00.html

NTIA. (2002). *A nation online.* Washington, DC: U.S. Department of Commerce.

Organization for Economic Co-operation and Development (OECD). (2000). *Realizing the potential of electronic commerce for SMEs in the global economy.* Issues Paper, Bologna, SME Conference Business Symposium, 2000.

Organization for Economic Co-operation and Development (OECD). (2001). *Understanding the digital divide.* Paris, France: OECD. Retrieved from http://www.oecd.org/dataoecd/38/57/1888451.pdf

Oxley, J. E., & Yeung, B. (2001). E-commerce readiness: Institutional environment and international competitiveness. *Journal of International Business Studies, 32*(4), 705–723. doi:10.1057/palgrave.jibs.8490991

Oyelaran-Oyeyinka, B., & Lal, K. (2005). Internet diffusion in sub-Saharan Africa: A cross-country analysis. *Telecommunications Policy, 29*(7), 507–527. doi:10.1016/j.telpol.2005.05.002

Oyelaran-Oyeyinka, B., & Nyaki Adeya, C. (2004). Internet access in Africa: Empirical evidence from Kenya and Nigeria. *Telematics and Informatics, 21*(1), 67–81. doi:10.1016/S0736-5853(03)00023-6

Parker, S. (2000). *A survey of small business in Colorado.* CCCOES, April.

Payne, J. E. (1996). *E-commerce readiness for SMEs in developing countries: A guide for development professionals*. Washington, D.C., USA: Academy for Educational Development.

Pohjola, M. (2003). The adoption and diffusion of ICT across countries: Patterns and determinants. In Jones, D. C. (Ed.), *The new economy handbook*. San Diego, CA: Academic Press.

Premkumar, G., & Ramamurthy, K. (1995). The role of inter-organizational and organizational factors on the decision mode for adoption of inter organizational systems. *Decision Sciences, 26*(3), 303–336. doi:10.1111/j.1540-5915.1995.tb01431.x

Quibria, M. G., Ahmed, S. N., Tschang, T., & Reyes-Macasaquit, M.-L. (2003). Digital divide: Determinants and policies with special reference to Asia. *Journal of Asian Economics, 13*, 811–825. doi:10.1016/S1049-0078(02)00186-0

Ramanathan, S. (1999). *Internet in Malaysia*. Retrieved from http://www.interasia.org/malaysia/ramanantha.html

Ramayah, T., Yan, C. L., & Sulaiman, M. (2005). SME e-readiness in Malaysia: Implications for planning and implementation. *Sasin Journal of Management, 11*(1), 103–120.

Ramsey, E., Ibbotson, P., Bell, J., & Gray, B. (2003). E-opportunities of service sector SMEs: An Irish cross-border study. *Journal of Small Business and Enterprise Development, 10*(3), 250–264. doi:10.1108/14626000310489709

Ricci, A. (2000). Measuring information society dynamics of European data on usage of information and communication technologies in Europe since 1995. *Telematics and Informatics, 17*, 141–167. doi:10.1016/S0736-5853(00)00002-2

Riggins, F. J., & Mukhopadhyay, T. (1994). Interdependent benefits from interorganizational systems: Opportunities for business partner reengineering. *Journal of Management Information Systems, 11*(2), 37–57.

Rizk, N. (2004). *E-readiness assessment of small and medium enterprises in Egypt: A micro study*. Cairo, Egypt: American University. Retrieved from http://www.sba.luc.edu/orgs/meea/volume6/Rizk.htm

Robison, K. K., & Crenshaw, E. M. (2001). *Post-industrial transformations and cyber-space: A cross-national analysis of Internet development*. Columbus, OH: The Ohio State University.

Roller, L., & Waverman, L. (2001). Telecommunication infrastructure and economic development: A simultaneous approach. *The American Economic Review, 91*(4), 909–923. doi:10.1257/aer.91.4.909

Sciadas, G. (Ed.). (2005). *From the digital divide to digital opportunities: Measuring infostates for development*. Montreal, Canada: NRC Press. Retrieved from http://www.orbicom.uqam.ca/projects/ddi2005/index ict opp.pdf

Selhofer, H., & Husing, T. (2002). *The digital divide index—A measure of the social inequalities in the adoption of ICT*. Paper presented at the IST 2002 Conference, Copenhagen.

Selhofer, H., & Mayringer, H. (2001). Benchmarking the information society. Development in European countries. *Communications and Strategies, 43*, 17–55.

Shih, E., Kraemer, K. L., & Dedrick, J. (2003). *An extended accelerator model of country level investment in Information Technology*. Irvine, CA: Center for Research on Information Technology and Organization (CRITO).

Sicherl, P. (2004). *A new generic statistical measure in dynamic gap analysis. The European E-Business Report*. Luxembourg: European Commission.

Srinivasan, K., Kekre, S., & Mukhopadhyay, T. (1994). Impact of electronic data interchange technology on JIT shipments. *Management Science, 40*(10), 1291–1304. doi:10.1287/mnsc.40.10.1291

Sterman, J. D. (2000). *Business dynamic system thinking and modeling for a complex world. Irwin.* CA: McGraw-Hill.

Sulaiman, A., & Jani, R. (2001). *E-commerce implementation in Malaysian manufacturing sector*. Malaya: Faculty of Business and Accountancy, University of Malaya. White Paper

Tacq, J. (1999). *Multivarate technique in social sciences*. Great Britain: Sage Publications.

Tan, M., & Teo, T. S. H. (1998). Factors influencing the adoption of the Internet. *International Journal of Electronic Commerce, 2*(3), 5–18.

Tanner, E. (2003). Bridging Latin America's digital divide: Government policies and Internet access. *Journalism & Mass Communication Quarterly, 80*(3), 646–665.

United Nations Development Programme. (UNDP). (2001). *Human development report 2001*. New York, NY: UN. Retrieved from http://www.undp.org/

U.S. Department of Commerce, Bureau of the Census. (2002). *Falling through the net: Defining the digital divide, economics & statistics administration. National Telecommunications and Information Administration*. NTIA.

Valadez, J. R., & Duran, R. (2007). Redefining the digital divide: Beyond access to computers and the Internet. *High School Journal, 90*, 31–44. doi:10.1353/hsj.2007.0013

Van Belle, J. P., & Vosloo, S. (2005). E-government and the e-readiness of non-profit organizations in the Western Cape, South Africa. *Proceedings of the 2nd Annual Conference of the Community Informatics Research Network*, Cape Town, 24-26 August 2005.

van Dijk, J. (2006). Digital divide research, achievements and shortcomings. *Poetics, 34*, 221–235. doi:10.1016/j.poetic.2006.05.004

Vehovar, V., Sicherl, P., Husing, T., & Dolnicar, V. (2006). Methodological challenges of digital divide measurements. *The Information Society, 22*(5), 279–290. doi:10.1080/01972240600904076

Walliman, N. (2001). *Your research project* (1st ed.). London, UK: SAGE Publications.

Wallsten, S. (2003). *Regulation and Internet use in developing countries*. Washington, DC: AEI and Brookings Institution. doi:10.1596/1813-9450-2979

Warschauer, M. (2003). *Technology and social inclusion: Rethinking the digital divide*. Cambridge, MA: MIT Press.

Wolcott, P., Press, L., McHenry, W., Goodman, S. E., & Foster, W. (2001). A framework for assessing the global diffusion of the Internet. *Journal of the Association for Information Systems, 2*(6), 1–50.

Wong, P. K. (2002). ICT production and diffusion in Asia: Digital dividends or digital divide? *Information Economics and Policy, 14*(2), 167–187. doi:10.1016/S0167-6245(01)00065-8

World Bank. (2004). *SME E-Readiness Questionnaire*. Korea.

Zaheer, A., & Venkatraman, N. (1994). Determinants of electronic integration in the insurance industry: An empirical test. *Management Science, 40*(5), 549–566. doi:10.1287/mnsc.40.5.549

ENDNOTES

[1]   E-readiness assessment at the macro-level means assessment at the international and national level or country, government, policy levels and at the micro level denotes assessment of levels of sectors, community, public systems, enterprises, organizations, institutions, and individual levels (consumers) (Barzilai-Nahon, 2006; Corrocher & Ordanini, 2002; Dewan & Riggins, 2005Mutula & van Brakel, 2006a; Rizk, 2004)

[2]   In the United Nations Conference on Trade and Development (UNCTAD), SME's account for 60 to 70 percent of all employment in developing countries (UNCTAD, 2002). Ninety nine percent of all businesses in North America and Europe are SMEs (Jutla et al., 2002). In the enlarged European Union of 25 countries, some 23 million SMEs provide around 75 million jobs and represent 99 percent of all enterprises (European Commission, 2005).

[3]   The scales were created with the following approach in mind: the most developed enterprises were studied and their approximate level was taken as the highest possible; then, the interval was split into five thus giving a linear scale. Most commonly two types of scales are used: one with top level of 100 percent (for long-time available service such as telephone lines) and one with top level of 40 percent (for newer services such as EDI). In some occasions custom scales were used, mainly for high-tech issues.

APPENDICES

Definitions of SME e-readiness / digital divide assessment model and indexes.

The SME E-readiness Assessment Model is defined as an average value of the following indexes: *Infrastructure and Connectivity, Human Resources, Networked World Enablers, IT Applications, ICT Use, Barriers to ICT Use, External Environment Readiness.*

APPENDIX A

Infrastructure and Connectivity is defined as follows: Infrastructure and Connectivity = average of survey data

Survey data

1. Value of IT investment. (World Bank, 2004; Jutla et al., 2002; Macintyre and Ramnarine, 2003)
2. Value of investment in ICT infrastructure (Rizk, 2004; Jutla et al., 2002)
3. How many PCs do you have? Please classify by type of microprocessor. (World Bank, 2004; Rizk, 2004; Macintyre and Ramnarine, 2003; Keen, 1991; Vosloo and Van Belle, 2005; Mutula and van Brakel, 2006b; Jerman-Blazˇicˇ, 2008)
4. Do you have network access? If yes, please answer Questions 4-12. If no, please go to Question 13. (World Bank, 2004; Macintyre and Ramnarine, 2003; Keen, 1991; APEC, 1999; Vosloo and Van Belle, 2005)
5. What types of network access facilities do you have? (Mutula and van Brakel, 2006a; World Bank, 2004; Rizk, 2004; Mehrtens et al., 2001; Ramsay et al., 2003; Kleindl, 2000; Keen, 1991; Vosloo and Van Belle, 2005; Kasraian, 2007; Jerman-Blazˇicˇ, 2008)
   a. Internet;
   b. Intranet;
   c. EDI;
   d. Extranet access to other enterprises.
6. If you have access to Internet, then which of the following access methods do you use? (Mutula and van Brakel, 2006a; World Bank, 2004; Rizk, 2004; Macintyre and Ramnarine, 2003; Mehrtens et al., 2001; Keen, 1991; APEC, 1999; Mutula and van Brakel, 2006b; Jerman-Blazˇicˇ, 2008)
   a. Dial-up modem;
   b. ISDN;
   c. DSL;
   d. Cable modem;
   e. Leased line;
   f. Others.
7. If you have internal communication, then which of the following access means do you use? (Rizk, 2004; Macintyre and Ramnarine, 2003; Kleindl, 2000; Keen, 1991; APEC, 1999; Vosloo and Van Belle, 2005; Aminali, 2007; Mutula and van Brakel, 2006b)

a.   E-mail;

b.   Fax;

c.   Telephone;

d.   Others.

8.   If you have external communication, then which of the following access means do you use? (Rizk, 2004; Macintyre and Ramnarine, 2003; Kleindl, 2000; Keen, 1991; APEC, 1999; Vosloo and Van Belle, 2005; Aminali, 2007; Kasraian, 2007; Mutula and van Brakel, 2006b)

a.   E-mail;

b.   Fax;

c.   Telephone;

d.   Others.

9.   Do you have a website or home page? If yes, please answer questions 10 and 11. (World Bank, 2004; Vosloo and Van Belle, 2005; Rizk, 2004; Barua et al., 2000, Jutla, 2002; Kasraian, 2007; Mutula and van Brakel, 2006b)

10.   Please provide the following information about your home page: (World Bank, 2004; Macintyre and Ramnarine, 2003; Barua et al., 2000; Jerman-Blazˇicˇ, 2008)

a.   What is the URL?

b.   Who designed and commissioned your website?

c.   Who and how maintains your website?

d.   Who hosts your website?

e.   What security arrangements are in place to prevent unauthorized access or modification of your website?

f.   How many people visit your website per day?

11.   What activities are possible by visiting your home page and web site? (World Bank, 2004; Barua et al., 2000; Macintyre and Ramnarine, 2003; Kasraian, 2007; Jerman-Blazˇicˇ, 2008)

a.   Obtain information about your products;

b.   Obtain financial and operating information about your enterprise;

c.   Place and modify orders on your enterprise;

d.   Track status of orders, production and shipment;

e.   Exchange delivery and payment data;

f.   Identify and research our suppliers;

g.   Others.

12.   How often is the content on your website of enterprise updated? (Aminali, 2007; Kasraian, 2007)

13.   If you do not have a home page or network access, please tick all the reasons for not having a home page or network access: (World Bank, 2004; Aminali, 2007)

a.   Not useful for doing business with major suppliers and buyers;

b.   Cannot afford development and maintenance costs;

c.   Technology is complex;

d.   Internal business procedures are not ready for effective use of network enabled business processes.

14.   Ability to generate local content (Mutula and van Brakel, 2006a; Jutla et al., 2002; Barua et al., 2000; Macintyre and Ramnarine, 2003; Vosloo and Van Belle, 2005; Fathian et al., 2008)

15. Allocating adequate resources in terms of time, staff and budget to the development of ICT strategy projects and for information management functions (Mutula and van Brakel, 2006a; Macintyre and Ramnarine, 2003; Aminali, 2007; Kasraian, 2007; Fathian et al., 2008; Jerman-Blazˇicˇ, 2008)
16. How much of the expenditure is allocated to (World Bank, 2004, Moodley, 2001; Aminali, 2007)
    a. In-house activities;
    b. External purchases.
17. Current ICT and Information infrastructure is adequate for supporting the functions of e-commerce tools (Aminali, 2007; Fathian et al., 2008)
18. ICT networks use standard interchange protocols and industry standard information syntax and semantics to connect, and navigate and manage our shared information assets (Kasraian, 2007; Fathian et al., 2008).
19. Flexibility of organization network to engage in electronic commerce (Aminali, 2007; Kasraian, 2007).

APPENDIX B

Human Resources is defined as follows: Human Resources = average of survey data

Survey data

1. Ability to evaluate information and its sources (Mutula and van Brakel, 2006a; Horrocks, and Haines, 2004)
2. Ability to organize information (Mutula and van Brakel, 2006a; Horrocks, and Haines, 2004)
3. Ability to manage and maintain information (Mutula and van Brakel, 2006a; Barua et al., 2000)
4. Ability to access, analyze, and use information (Mutula and van Brakel, 2006a; Barua et al., 2000)
5. The employees have the necessary levels of IT literacy, functional expertise and skills to use e-commerce tools (Vosloo and Van Belle, 2005; Aminali, 2007; Fathian et al., 2008)
6. Employees recognize the benefits of the use of e-commerce applications, trends, options and models and well organized and managed information (Mutula and van Brakel, 2006a; Aminali, 2007; Kasraian, 2007)
7. Diversity of staff ICT educational qualifications and skills (Mutula and van Brakel, 2006a; Macintyre and Ramnarine, 2003; Fink, 1998; Attaran, 2001, Kwon and Zmud, 1987)
8. Senior management levels of awareness towards ICTs (Mutula and van Brakel, 2006a; Doukidis et al., 1994; Aminali, 2007)
9. Ability of management to determine the organization's IT needs and communicate the organization's IT needs to internal or external IT resources (Mutula and van Brakel, 2006a; Kasraian, 2007)
10. Chief executive ICT educational qualifications and prior ICT experience (Mutula and van Brakel, 2006a; Macintyre and Ramnarine, 2003; Doukidis et al., 1994; Aminali, 2007)
11. Information management skills available in the enterprise (Mutula and van Brakel, 2006a; Macintyre and Ramnarine, 2003; Kwon and Zmud, 1987)

12. Life long education and training programmes (Mutula and van Brakel, 2006a; Macintyre and Ramnarine, 2003; Doukidis et al., 1994; Kasraian, 2007)

13. Employees are flexible and adaptable to continuously changing business and technological environments, opportunities and challenges. (Aminali, 2007; Kasraian, 2007)

14. Percentage of enterprise's staffs using of following applications and services: (Jutla et al., 2002; Doukidis et al., 1994; Kasraian, 2007; Fathian et al., 2008)
    a. Knowledge management applications;
    b. Supply chain applications;
    c. Customer relationship management applications;
    d. Online government services;
    e. Stripped-down ERP-type applications (e.g. MS White Plains);
    f. Security applications;
    g. Human resource applications.

APPENDIX C

Networked world enablers is defined as follows: Networked world enablers = average of survey data

Survey data

1. E-readiness/information strategy, policy and action plan (Mutula and van Brakel, 2006a; Grant, 1999; Aminali, 2007; Kasraian, 2007; Mutula and van Brakel, 2006b; Fathian et al., 2008)

2. Information /ICT strategy revision plans (Mutula and van Brakel, 2006a; Grant, 1999)

3. Information security and disaster recovery plans (Mutula and van Brakel, 2006a; Grant, 1999; Kasraian, 2007; Mutula and van Brakel, 2006b)

4. Capacity building strategies incorporating information management (Mutula and van Brakel, 2006a; Kasraian, 2007)

5. Security, privacy and reliability of network to support e-commerce (Mutula and van Brakel, 2006a; Barua et al., 2000; Macintyre and Ramnarine, 2003; Ainin and Rohana, 2000; Norazah, 2001; Goodwin, 1991; Gupta, 1995; Janes et al., 1997; Tan and Teo, 1998; Dr Sankaran, 1999; Lawrence et al., 1998; Kasraian, 2007; Fathian et al., 2008)

6. Consumer protection policy commerce (Mutula and van Brakel, 2006a; Barua et al., 2000; Ainin and Rohana, 2000)

7. Top management commitment in developing and implementing enterprise's e-business strategy. (Mutula and van Brakel, 2006a; Fink, 1998; Ramayah et al., 2005; Aminali, 2007; Kasraian, 2007).

8. Organizational culture is well suited for e-commerce adoption and use (Aminali, 2007; Macintyre and Ramnarine, 2003).

APPENDIX D

IT applications is defined as follows: IT applications = average of survey data

Survey data

1. Adoption and deployment of Electronic Data Interchange (EDI),Internet-based procurement and other e-commerce tools to improve our overall business and project performance (Barua and Lee, 1997, Clark and Stoddard 1996; Drury and Farhoomand 1996; Hart and Saunders 1998; Iacovou, Benbasat and Dexter 1995; Massetti and Zmud 1996 ; Mukhopadhyay, Kekre and Kalathur 1995; Premkumar and Ramamurthy 1995; Riggins and Mukhopadhyay 1999; Srinivasan, Kekre and Mukhopadhyay 1994; Zaheer and Venkatraman 1994; Aminali, 2007)

2. For which of the following applications do you use digital technology? (World Bank, 2004; Ramayah et al., 2005; Barua et al., 2000; Jain, 2005; Hashem, 2001; Aminali, 2007; Kasraian, 2007; Mutula and van Brakel, 2006b; Fathian et al., 2008; Jerman-Blazˇicˇ, 2008)
   a. Word Processing
   b. Network related activities
   c. Accounting and Budgeting
   d. Financial Planning, Management and Control
   e. Production Planning, Management and Control
   f. Billing and invoicing
   g. CAD/CAM
   h. Marketing and Customer Relations Management (CRM)
   i. Logistics and Supply Chain Management (SCM)
   j. Enterprise Resource Planning (ERP)
   k. Inventory management
   l. Group collaboration
   m. Scheduling
   n. Outsourcing activities
   o. Call centre systems

3. Please list the main operating systems and software packages used by you and for what purpose (please also include customized software packages) (World Bank, 2004; Barua et al., 2000)

4. Mechanism and standards formats to organize, collect, store and retrieve information (Mutula and van Brakel, 2006a; Barua et al., 2000; Jutla et al., 2002)

5. Means of sharing and disseminating information within and outside the enterprise (Mutula and van Brakel, 2006a; Mutula and van Brakel, 2006b)

6. Mechanism for information systems analysis, design and implementation (Mutula and van Brakel, 2006a)

7. Diversity of computer technology and information system used and their ease of use (Mutula and van Brakel, 2006a; Jerman-Blazˇicˇ, 2008)

8. Percent of new Web-enabled and automated processes in the business (Jutla et al., 2002; Aminali, 2007)

APPENDIX E

ICT use is defined as follows: ICT use = average of survey data

Survey data

1. For which of the following purposes do you use the network access facilities? (World Bank, 2004; Barua et al., 2000; Macintyre and Ramnarine, 2003; Moodley, 2001; Aminali, 2007; Kasraian, 2007; Jerman-Blazˇicˇ, 2008)
    a. E-mail;
    b. Business information and business research;
    c. Place orders;
    d. Make payments;
    e. Receive orders;
    f. Receive payments;
    g. Send a bill;
    h. Exchange business process data with suppliers and buyers;
    i. Submit requests and applications to government agencies;
    j. Receive approval from government agencies.
2. Are there Transactions involving ICT? If yes please answer below Questions. (Rizk, 2004; Evans and Wurster, 1997; Fathian et al., 2008)
3. What are these Transactions? (Rizk, 2004; Barua et al., 2000; Evans and Wurster, 1997; Kotler, 2003; Jerman-Blazˇicˇ, 2008)
    a. E-Procurement;
    b. Sales;
    c. Maintenance, Repair and Operations (MRO);
    d. Order Tracking;
    e. Quality Control;
        h. Others.
4. Which of the following purpose do you use of ICTs (especially Internet) (Mutula and van Brakel, 2006a; Ramayah et al. 2005; Rizk, 2004; Barua et al., 2000; Macintyre and Ramnarine, 2003; Jain, 2005; Ramsay et al., 2003; Gray and Lawless, 2000; Engler, 1999; Minton, 2003; Moodley, 2001; Payne, 1996; APEC, 2000; Jerman-Blazˇicˇ, 2008):
    ◦ In marketing
        a. Marketing/Advertisement (e.g., Catalog, Product Description, Detailed Specifications, Price, Discount, etc.);
        b. Sales;
        c. Pitches;
        d. Offers;
        e. Research & Development (R&D);
        f. Receive Purchases;
        g. Other.
    ◦ In production

       a.   Ware-Housing;
       b.   Sampling;
       c.   Quality Control;
       d.   Production Tracking;
       e.   Assembling Operations;
       f.   Planning Line Loading;
       g.   Markers (Plotter Printing);
       h.   Pattern Making and Grading;
       i.   Design and Creation;
       j.   Research & Development (R&D).

- In management and staffs

       a.   Production Planning and Control;
       b.   Internal & External Communication;
       c.   Financial and Administrative Activities;
       d.   Human Resources;
       e.   Communication with Consumer or Supplier;
       f.   Order Processing and Follow Up;
       g.   Identifying, Storage and Retrieval of Information;
       h.   Human Resources (HR) Management;
       i.   General Management;
       j.   Training.

5. Frequency of the use of ICT systems (Mutula and van Brakel, 2006a; Jerman-Blaẑiĉ, 2008)

6. What percent of your sales can be classified as e-commerce sales? (An E-commerce sale in this context means that all the steps of order fulfillment --- order booking, processing, shipping, payment is done via Internet or EDI). (World Bank, 2004; Rizk, 2004; Barua et al., 2000; Macintyre and Ramnarine, 2003; Kotler, 2003)

7. What types of IT services do you outsource? (World Bank, 2004; Jerman-Blaẑiĉ, 2008)

       a.   Systems Design;
       b.   Hardware Acquisition;
       c.   Software Design (including pre-packaged software);
       d.   Hardware Maintenance;
       e.   Systems and Software Maintenance;
       f.   Data Processing;
       g.   Web Development and Web-Hosting;
       h.   Services Provided by Application Service Providers (ASPs).

8. Impact of use of ICT on for example productivity, profitability, and cost reduction (Mutula and van Brakel, 2006a; Engler, 1999)

APPENDIX F

Barriers to ICT use is defined as follows: Barriers to ICT use = survey data

Survey data

1. Please rank the following barriers to developing ICT and ICT use in decreasing order of importance: (World Bank, 2004; Rizk, 2004; Macintyre and Ramnarine, 2003; Fink, 1998; Khader, 2005; Sulaiman and Jani, 2001; Attaran, 2001; OECD, 2000; Lawrence et al., 1998; APEC, 1999; Moodley, 2001; Mutula and van Brakel, 2006b)
    a. Lack of in-house technological and business expertise to identify and develop IT and network applications;
    b. Cost of adapting and integrating existing business processes to IT and networked enabled processes;
    c. Technical difficulty in adapting and integrating existing business processes to IT and networked enabled processes;
    d. Cost of running a dual system: paper-based system and an e-commerce system;
    e. Limited use of e-commerce among your major customers;
    f. Lack of finance to deploy new technologies;
    g. Concern about security and privacy/ Lack of secure payments settlement mechanisms;
    h. High cost of third party technology and consulting services;
    i. Uncertainty about authentication mechanisms;
    j. Shortages of trained and skilled IT personnel;
    k. Unwilling Personnel;
    l. Lack of standards;
    m. Difficulty to plan / Choose Application;
    n. Shortage of local community and business Web content;
    o. Lack of understanding of electronic commerce techniques and the technology needed to use it;
    p. The high cost of computers;
    q. Lack of adequate e-commerce infrastructures (e.g., Limited and poor-quality bandwidth, Limited quality telecommunication access);
    r. High cost of internet connectivity;
    s. Inadequate legislative framework;
    t. Frequent internet downtime;
    u. High taxation;
    v. Inadequate technical support.

APPENDIX G

External Environment Readiness is defined as follows: External Environment Readiness = 5/27 Hard Data + 22/27 Survey data.

Hard data

1. Maximum broadband transmission speeds (Jutla et al., 2002; Macintyre and Ramnarine, 2003; APEC, 1999)
2. Number of Internet hosts (Jutla et al., 2002; APEC, 1999)
3. Internet access costs (Jutla et al., 2002; Hong, 2002; Macintyre and Ramnarine, 2003; APEC, 1999)
4. Wireless access costs (Jutla et al., 2002; Macintyre and Ramnarine, 2003; APEC, 1999)
5. Broadband access costs (Jutla et al., 2002; Macintyre and Ramnarine, 2003; APEC, 1999)

Survey data

6. Broadband penetration (Jutla et al., 2002; Macintyre and Ramnarine, 2003; APEC, 1999; Fathian et al., 2008)
7. Cable penetration (Jutla et al., 2002; Macintyre and Ramnarine, 2003; APEC, 1999)
8. Telephone penetration (Jutla et al., 2002; Macintyre and Ramnarine, 2003; APEC, 1999)
9. Quality of cable connection (Jutla et al., 2002; Macintyre and Ramnarine, 2003; APEC, 1999; Fathian et al., 2008)
10. Quality of Telephony (Jutla et al., 2002; Macintyre and Ramnarine, 2003; APEC, 1999)
11. Quality of broadband connection (Jutla et al., 2002; Mutula and van Brakel, 2006a; Macintyre and Ramnarine, 2003; APEC, 1999; Fathian et al., 2008)
12. Availability of cable service (Jutla et al., 2002; Macintyre and Ramnarine, 2003, Fink, 1998; APEC, 1999)
13. Availability of hardware and software (Jutla et al., 2002, Fink, 1998; APEC, 1999; Fathian et al., 2008)
14. Availability of online service (Jutla et al., 2002; Barua et al., 2000; Macintyre and Ramnarine, 2003, Fink, 1998; Fathian et al., 2008)
15. Adequacy and affordability of bandwidth (Internet) (Mutula and van Brakel, 2006a; Jutla et al., 2002; Macintyre and Ramnarine, 2003; APEC, 1999; Fathian et al., 2008)
16. Affordability of hardware and software (Jutla et al., 2002; Macintyre and Ramnarine, 2003; APEC, 1999; Fathian et al., 2008)
17. Scalability of network infrastructure (Jutla et al., 2002; Macintyre and Ramnarine, 2003; APEC, 1999)
18. ICTs affordability from the service providers (Mutula and van Brakel, 2006a; Macintyre and Ramnarine, 2003)
19. Enabling legislative and regulatory frameworks (Mutula and van Brakel, 2006a; Jutla et al., 2002; Macintyre and Ramnarine, 2003)

20. Legal and regulatory framework to address information management issues such as (Mutula and van Brakel, 2006a; Jutla et al., 2002; Hong, 2002; Kasraian, 2007; Fathian et al., 2008)
    a. Intellectual property rights
    b. Legal and regulatory mechanism for e-commerce
    c. Freedom of information legal and regulatory framework
21. Adequacy and reliability of national power grid (Mutula and van Brakel, 2006a; Kasraian, 2007)
22. Government support (Mutula and van Brakel, 2006a; Macintyre and Ramnarine, 2003; Kasraian, 2007)
    d. Government Education system can provide adequately trained personnel to engage in e-commerce;
    e. Awareness rising by planning Government demonstration programs and public profile of electronic commerce misrepresented the dynamics of ecommerce and raised dubious expectations;
    f. Government provision of online electronic services had a positive effect in drawing our customers and suppliers into the e- commerce environment.
23. Financial supports for R&D, diffusion or uptake were sufficient to encourage the organization to engage in electronic commerce. (Mutula and van Brakel, 2006a; Kasraian, 2007)
24. National information and ICT policy (Mutula and van Brakel, 2006a; Macintyre and Ramnarine, 2003)
25. National ICT network security for business transactions (Mutula and van Brakel, 2006a; Macintyre and Ramnarine, 2003)
26. Taxation regime (Mutula and van Brakel, 2006a; Jutla et al., 2002; Macintyre and Ramnarine, 2003)
27. Competition policy in ICT areas (Mutula and van Brakel, 2006a; Macintyre and Ramnarine, 2003)

Chapter 16
From "S" to "J":
A Theoretical Technology Adoption Rate Model

Jeanne C. Samuel
Tulane University School of Medicine, USA

ABSTRACT

This article proposes a hypothetical model for determining rate of diffusion of an innovation in a system. The model modifies Everett Rogers' S-curve using an index created from Gartner's hype cycle phases. Rogers' model for technology innovation adoption demonstrates that cumulative technology diffusion in a system from zero through the late majority adopters' phase forms a curve resembling the letter "S". Hype cycles analyze the five emotional stages technology adopters go through from over-enthusiasm (hype) though disappointment until it plateaus (beginning of mainstream adoption). When numbers assigned to the phases of adoption from the hype cycle are used as multipliers and applied to the cumulative adoption data of an innovation (Rogers' S-curve), the "S" becomes a "J". With the J-curve you can determine the rate of innovation diffusion in an organization.

INTRODUCTION

Everett M. Rogers' S-curve has been the vanguard as an innovation diffusion indicator for over 40 years. The S-curve is the foundation upon which the J-curve is built. The hypothesis of this article is that creating an index by assigning values to the phases of Gartner's hype cycle and applying this index to Rogers' stages of innovation adoption reveals the adoption rate. In rapid adoption events, the product of applying this index to an S-curve data is a J-curve. The S-curve is the representation of innovation diffusion in an organization. The J-curve represents the rate of innovation diffusion

DOI: 10.4018/978-1-60960-597-1.ch016

in the same organization. The J-curve combines the two models, the S-curve and the hype cycle to help organizations determine the best adoption pace to maximize their return on investment. The aim of this article is to present the J-curve as an extension of the S-curve to assist organizations with innovation adoption planning and evaluation. The J-curve can be used to help organizations set reasonable innovation adoption timelines. After diffusion, the resulting J-curve can be analyzed to determine whether the anticipated adoption pace was met.

The next section of this article describes the S-curve innovation adoption model and presents the literature review for Rogers' model. The third section describes the hype cycle model and presents the literature review for Gartner's model. The fourth section, the J-curve, describes the hype cycle index, compares the S-curve and the hype cycle, details how to create an index from the hype cycle, and describes how to apply the hype cycle index to create a J-curve. The last section of the article is the conclusion and future work section. The research questions guiding this manuscript are:

- Is there a relationship between Rogers' S-curve and Gartner's hype cycle?
- If there is a relationship between Rogers' S-curve and Gartner's hype cycle, can this relationship be used to determine the pace of innovation adoption?

THE S-CURVE

This section describes innovation adoption within the context of Rogers' S-curve. According to Rogers (2003), the rate innovations diffuse in an organization "usually follows a normal, bell-shaped curve when plotted over time on a frequency basis" (p. 272). Initially, a few innovators in an organization adopt the innovation, followed by early adopters, followed by the bulk of the

adopters, and finally by the few who lag behind the rest. Specifically, the bell is formed by 68 percent of the adopters - early and late majority. The leading tail is formed from data representing the innovators and early adopters. The lagging tail is formed from data representing laggard adoption (p. 282). It is the textbook model for creating frequency distribution classes. He states that a set of categories should be "exhaustive", "mutually exclusive", and "derived from a single classificatory principle" (p. 280). Rogers identified five types of innovation adopters (p. 280). His adopter type classifications meet these criteria. The five adopter categories defined by Rogers are Innovators [I], Early Adopters [EA], Early Majority [EM], Late Majority [LM], and Laggards [L]. The percentage of adoption by adopter type for new adopters forms a bell curve (2.5% for innovators, 13.5% for early adopters, 34% for early majority, 34% late majority, and 16% for laggards). Rogers' classification is based on the adopter characteristic of innovativeness (p. 267). In *Diffusion of Innovations,* Rogers describes the process for standardizing adopter categories and his criteria. For innovators (I) the characteristic is venturesome. The other characteristics described by Rogers by adopter type are early adopters (EA) are respectful, early majority (EM) are deliberate, late majority (LM) are skeptical, and laggards (L) are traditional (pp. 282-285).

In Rogers' model, the five adopter categories are created from the innovativeness variable by "laying off standard deviations from the average time of adoption" (Rogers, 2003, p. 281). The category delimiters from left to right (over time) are the mean minus two times the standard deviation (innovators/early adopters), the mean minus the standard deviation (early adopters/early majority), the mean (early majority/late majority), and the mean plus the standard deviation (laggards). Rogers felt that laggards are a homogenous group and did not require division (p. 281). The delimiters create the normal innovation diffusion category percentage boundaries (2.5%,

13.5%, 34%, 34%, and 16%). Adopter distributions "approach normality" over time forming a "bell-shaped curve" (p. 275). According to Rogers, after an innovation reaches between the 10% and 20% adoption mark, the diffusion requires less promotion. He states that after that point, "it is often impossible to stop further diffusion of a new idea, even if one wished to do so" (p. 274). Malcolm Gladwell calls this the "tipping point" (2000, p. 9). Geoffrey Moore, author of *Crossing the Chasm: Marketing and Selling High-Tech Products to Mainstream Customers,* states that the largest gap to cross is the one between Rogers' early adopters and early majority (Moore, 1999, as cited in Celik 2007). Moore has the gap starting after 16 percent cumulative adoption. All adoption (cumulative) over time in a system when plotted, according to Rogers, forms an S-curve (p. 272). The cumulative percentages are 2.5%, 16%, 50%, 84%, and 100%. Rogers' S-curve demonstrates the diffusion of cases of successfully adopted innovations. Rogers excludes non-adopters from the data analysis (p. 281). Successful denotes diffusion; the innovation was adopted throughout the system (p. 275). Additionally, Rogers states that the S-curve is "innovation specific and system specific" (p. 275). Therefore, not all bell shapes and S-curves are exactly alike.

THE HYPE CYCLE

This section describes the hype cycle model and presents the literature review for Gartner's model. In 1995, Gartner, Inc. introduced the hype cycle. The term was created by analyst Jackie Fenn to help Gartner graphically present the company's views regarding emerging technologies (Hansen, 2002). "The hype cycle reflects the full range of human response to an innovation – the rational and irrational, hype and reality, imagination and plodding thought, excitement and sober assessment, right brain and left brain" (Fenn & Raskino, 2008, pp. 45-46). The hype cycle identifies the phases of technology adoption from Technology Trigger through Plateau of Productivity. Fenn describes the hype cycle as, "a good snapshot of where technologies are at a certain point in time" (Hansen, 2002). "A hype cycle is a graphical representation of the maturity, adoption and business application of specific technologies" (Fenn, 2007). The hype cycle according to Fenn and Raskino (2008) represents emotional reaction to "positive and negative hype" plus an S-curve representing slow then steady growth followed by "diminishing returns" (P. 26).

The hype cycle stages are: (1) the Technology Trigger during which there is significant buzz and interest about the innovation, (2) the Peak of Inflated Expectations where the degree of "unrealistic expectations" is similar to the "degree of over-enthusiasm" despite more failures than successful applications, (3) the Trough of Disillusionment which is marked by significantly diminished press coverage and where the innovation is no longer in vogue, (4) the Slope of Enlightenment where some businesses continue to experiment with the innovation to "understand the benefits and practical application of the technology", and (5) Plateau of Productivity during which wide-acceptance and recognition of the stable innovation endure (Fenn, 2007). In their book, *Mastering the Hype Cycle,* Fenn and Raskino (2008) include two stages to complete an innovation's life cycle (p.60). They add The Swamp of Diminishing Returns (legacy) and The Cliff of Obsolescence (obsolete). These final stages are not generally included in hype cycle data and are not considered in the analysis for the J-curve.

J-CURVE ADOPTION RATE MODEL

The Hype Cycle Index

This section compares the two models, the S-curve and the hype cycle to determine what if any relationship exists between the models. This section of the manuscript also includes details about how to create an index from the hype cycle and describes how to apply the hype cycle index to create a J-curve. Included at the end of this section is an example of how to use the J-curve to determine the pace of an innovation adoption event. Although this is not a strict comparison, there are many commonalities between Rogers' S-curve and Gartner's hype cycle. Both track innovation adoption over time, are centered around behaviors or adoption philosophies, and are influenced or motivated by communication. Both track different variables (y-axis) over the same variable, time (x-axis).

Rogers' time represents a constant, real time - for example, months or years. In other words, the S-curve indicates the percent of adoption in a system over real time until the innovation is completely diffused. The hype cycle tracks innovation maturation. Innovation maturation is defined by the time until the hype returns to more positive reports in the hype cycle model. Hype cycle time is variable in that it is innovation-specific. Each innovation may stay in a cycle phase for different, actual time periods. Furthermore, time on the hype cycle may not be linear and is not constant. An innovation may fall off the chart only to reappear again in a different phase/point on the hype cycle. Look for example, at tablet pcs adoption. The tablet pc was on the 2003 *Hype Cycle for Emerging Technologies* at the peak (Linden et al., 2003). In 2004, the tablet pc was sliding into the trough (Fenn et al., 2004). The 2005 and 2006 *Hype Cycle for Emerging Technologies* again placed tablet pcs sliding into the trough (Linden et al., 2005; Fenn et al., 2006). The tablet pc fell off the chart in 2007 (Fenn et al., 2007). It was back on the chart in 2008 climbing the slope (Fenn et al., 2008).

In both Rogers' model and the hype cycle, events are unique. Rogers' innovation adoption event is unique within a system. In other words, it may take 9 months for an innovation to diffuse in one organization while it takes the same in-

novation 2 years in another organization. In the hype cycle, the duration for an innovation to pass through the cycle within a specific realm pertains specifically to the innovation - each cycle is different. According to Fenn and Raskino (2008), an innovation can spend as little as 6-9 months in the trough or as long as a decade (p. 76).

Rogers' work centers around individual adoption behavior within a system while the hype cycle centers around innovation diffusion behavior of multiple systems in multiple realms. Rogers' adopters were classified by innovativeness. Gartner's organizations differ by innovation adoption philosophies and strategies. In the 1999 Gartner article titled, *When to Leap on the Hype Cycle*, Fenn describes business enterprises as one of three types: (1) Technologically aggressive, type A, (2) Competitive but low risk, type B, and (3) Cost-focused and cautious, type C. The business model of an organization influences adoption decisions. Rogers' late adopters are similar to Fenn's Type C business. Rogers' laggards put off adopting until they are certain the innovation is not a fad. Businesses with Type C personalities also hold off on adoption until they are certain the innovation is entering the mainstream.

Both Rogers' diffusion of innovations model and the hype cycle model describe ways in which something spreads within a population. Both are stage-based analyses which consider communication, relationships, and users' perceptions of the innovation characteristics. For Rogers, diffusion takes place as word spreads from one group to the next within a system. For example, innovators talk to early adopters during a school's adoption of clicker technology in the classroom. In Gartner's hype cycle, the media sparks the early enthusiasm as well as the gloom and doom product or technology scenarios. Hype cycle communication is global, reporting about numerous innovation categories to many realms (communities) including consumer, corporate, and education. The communication triggers community behaviors which are tracked by the hype cycle analysts.

Rogers identifies adopter characteristics which contribute to the different individual innovation adoption rates. Gartner identifies three adopter rate characteristics for enterprises. Rogers' S-curve is the result of a successful innovation diffusion within a system while a hype cycle is the result of data for specific innovations at a point in time. The innovations may be conceptual, rising, falling, mainstream, legacy, or even obsolete at the time of the snapshot.

Microblogging is an example of an innovation on the rise. Mark Raskino (2009) of Gartner stated on the *Mastering the Hype Cycle* book blog that the microblogging [Twitter] makes for a "particularly clear [hype cycle] reference example, as it passes through the early stages of the Hype Cycle". Microblogging joined two charts at the peak, the Hype Cycle Emerging Technologies 2008 (Fenn et al., 2008) and the Hype Cycle for Social Software 2008 (Drakos et al., 2008). Interestingly, Twitter, a microblogging application was in the news so much in early 2009 that Comedy Central's The Daily Show presented a Twitter news montage on March 2, 2009 (Albanese, 2009). Oprah Winfrey joined Twitter, http://twitter.com/Oprah, creating a Twitter frenzy, followed by a Twitter backlash (George-Cosh, 2009). It will be interesting to follow the pace of long-term adoption of microblogging by individuals, schools, and corporations.

Creating the Hype Cycle Index

The hype cycle index (HCI) represents hype influence on potential adopters throughout the entire adoption period (Rogers' complete diffusion). Some readers may wonder what the index value assignments mean or perceive the assignments as arbitrary. The values represent positive and negative motivation. Young (2006) suggests that adoption diffusion is a learning model which positively correlates "with the potential gains from adoption" (p.34). People in the system are more likely to adopt as they see the benefit from earlier adoptions. He uses this to explain Rogers'

adoption distribution. Young suggests that adoption models demonstrate "linear and decreasing" acceleration rates when adoption is motivated by contagion and conformity (pp. 33-34). The hype cycle could be divided into contagion and conformity phases. Hypothetically, early reaction to hype both peak and trough map strongly to contagion. Type A companies may respond to pre-innovation release and early media hype, while Type B and C companies are more cautious and appear to perceive adoption safety in numbers (conformity). The hype cycle index is the linear and decreasing representation of the hype cycle phases. The index employs a 1-5 scale which correlate with Gartner hype cycle phases: Technology Trigger (value 5), Peak of Inflated Expectations (value 4), Trough of Disillusionment (value 1), Slope of Enlightenment (value 3), and Plateau of Productivity (value 2). Note that the index values are not sequential with respect to the hype cycle phases. In other words, where the order of hype cycle phases is Technology Trigger, Peak of Inflated Expectations, Trough of Disillusionment, Slope of Enlightenment, and Plateau of Productivity, the index hype/enthusiasm order is 5, 4, 1, 3, and 2. The index number assignment reflects the positive hype quantity per phase (or potential to motivate an adopter). The values do not represent the likelihood that adopters would jump on the innovation adoption bandwagon regardless of their business model or degree of individual innovativeness trait. Those factors influence the resultant S-curve which is the foundation of the J-curve. The Technology Trigger phase index is assigned a value of 5 to denote boundless enthusiasm while the Trough of Disillusionment is assigned an index of 1 to reflect the depths of disappointment. Fenn and Raskino (2008) describe the trigger phase as the period where the "innovation is all possibility unencumbered by real experience" (p. 27). The stages which may have the most effect on creating a "J" are the Trough of Disillusionment and the Slope of Enlightenment. Fenn and Raskino state that the trough stage is one of the most variable parts of the hype cycle. Shorter time in the trough should better enable institutions and suppliers to endure human reaction to negative hype and enable faster pace innovation diffusion (p. 76). It is important to note that Fenn and Raskino (2008) state that adoption numbers as an "innovation slides into the trough do not drop" (p. 75). When hype changes from positive to negative, they say people adopt gradually during a longer period. Adoption escalation does not occur as quickly as anticipated. By the end of the trough and the start of the slope, Fenn and Raskino note that innovation adoption by the "target audience" "may be less than 5% and no more than 10%" (p. 81). "Often only 20% to 30% of the target market has adopted" from the Slope of Enlightenment to the Plateau of Possibility (p. 82). This places the adoption tipping point in the slope. Furthermore, sometimes the slope resembles a second peak, a minipeak, sometimes mistaken for the first peak (pp. 80-81). These factors lend one to hypothesize that rapid adoption is most likely to occur where the negative hype period is short and is followed by high, positive hype. Fenn and Raskino refer to the minipeak as the "Second Peak of Reflated Expectations" (p. 81).

To use the index, a matrix was created mapping multipliers per indexes 5-1 to Rogers' innovator type segments (innovators though laggards - See Table 1).

The first column in Table 1, the Index column, lists the index values in descending order (5 to 1) from most to least amount of potential hype surrounding the innovation. In emotional terms, these values represent emotions ranging from expectant to despairing. For instance, innovators are the first to adopt. They contribute to the early hype if they find merit in what they learn and encourage early adopters to adopt the innovation. A product adopted while hype is high is assigned a hype cycle index of 5. In the second column, Multipliers per Innovator Type, the multipliers are weights to represent the amount of motivation needed to influence adoption by type. The weights are numerical placeholders representing quantity ranging from very much to a little. The multipliers for index 5 are 1, 2, 3, 4, and 5 from Innovators to Laggards. Innovators require little motivation (1) and Laggards much (5). Laggards are not positively influenced by hype. Rogers (2003) describes laggards as "the last in a social system to adopt an innovation" they "tend to be suspicious of innovation" and are "extremely cautious" (p. 284).

Making the J-Curve (Applying the Hype Cycle Index to Determine Adoption Rate)

Innovations adopted during the first hype cycle phase, Technology Trigger (Index 5), have a curve which resembles a "J" while innovations adopted by the third hype curve phase, Trough of Disillusionment (Index 1), still resemble an "S". When comparing adoption curves resulting from indexes 1 to 3, the foot of the "J" is the adoption rate visual indicator. For any normal to rapid adoption of an

Table 1. J-curve index multipliers

Index			Multipliers per Innovator Type		
Hype Cycle Stages	**Innovator**	**Early Adopter**	**Early Majority**	**Late Majority**	**Laggards**
5– Technology trigger	1	2	3	4	5
4 – Peak of inflated expectations	1	2	3	4	4
3 – Slope of enlightenment	1	2	3	3	3
2 – Plateau of productivity	1	2	2	2	2
1 – Trough of disillusionment	1	1	1	1	1

Figure 1. Cumulative adoption curve comparison (Index 5)

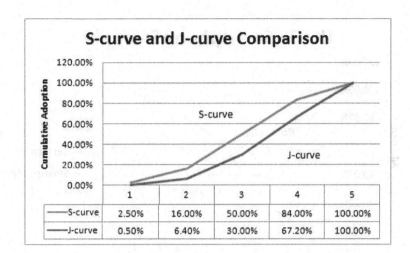

innovation, the indexed cumulative result should produce a J-curve. Figure 1 compares the resultant curves from Rogers' adopter categorization data (Rogers, 2003, p. 281), the S-curve and the J-curve resulting from applying the hype cycle index of 5 to Rogers' data indicates a rapid adoption of an innovation. (See Figure 1).

To calculate the J-curve from Rogers' S-curve, refer to Table 2. Column 1, Innovator Type, contains Rogers' innovator types: innovator (I), early adopter (EA), early majority (EM), late majority (LM), and laggards (L). The second column, Frequency Basis, contain the percentage of adoption over time: 2.5%, 13.5%, 34%, 34%, and 16%. The next column is the data used to plot the S-curve, Cumulative Basis (s), contains the cumulative adoption data: 2.5%, 16%, 50%, 84%, and 100%. The next column, Index Multiplier (m)

contains the index multipliers which will be applied to the cumulative basis data. These multipliers are: 1, 2, 3, 4, and 5 for hype cycle index 5. The final column data, when plotted, forms the J-curve. Each cell in this column, Result/Index, is the product of the cumulative basis (s) times the index multiplier (m), by innovator type (row), divided by the index value. The formula for plotting the J-curve is $(s*m)/i$. The s represents the variables per adopter type of the cumulative adoption data. The i represents the index corresponding with the hype cycle phase during which the innovation was adopted, and the m represents the multiplier which corresponds with the index.

In Table 2 for example, the last column field in the first row contains the result of $(2.5*1)/5$ which equals .50. The last column field, second row, corresponding with the innovator type early

Table 2. J-curve analysis of index 5 adoption

Innovator Type	Frequency Basis	Index(i)	Cumulative Basis (s)	Index Multiplier (m)	Result (s*m)/i
IN	2.5	5	2.5	1	(2.5*1)/5 = .50
EA	13.5	5	16	2	(16*2)/5 = 6.40
EM	34	5	50	3	(50*3)/5 = 30
LM	34	5	84	4	(84*4)/5 = 67.2
LA	16	5	100	5	(100*5)/5 = 100

Figure 2. Reference J-curve from Smartphone data compared with S-curve

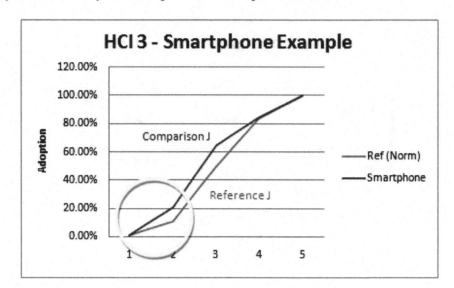

Table 3. J-curve analysis of index 3 adoption

Innovator Type	Frequency Basis	Index (i)	Cumulative Basis (s)	Index Multiplier (m)	Result (s*m)/i
IN	2.5	3	2.5	1	(2.5*1)/3 = .83
EA	13.5	3	16	2	(16*2)/3 = 10.67
EM	34	3	50	3	(50*3)/3 = 50
LM	34	3	84	3	(84*3)/3) = 84
LA	16	3	100	3	(100*3)/3 = 100

adopter, contains the product of (16*2)/5 or 6.40. The rest of the products are 30, 67.2, and 100 respectively. The resultant curve is labeled "J-curve" in Figure 1. Figure 2 is an example of calculating Smartphone adoption. This example will track the adoption of Smartphones by an organization in 2006. The 2006 Hype Cycle for Emerging Technologies place Smartphones on the cycle climbing the slope (Fenn et al., 2006). Therefore, assign a hype cycle index of 3 to this adoption example.

The first step in analyzing the adoption of Smartphones in this organization is to create a baseline or reference J-curve. Table 3 contains the data for calculating a J-curve for an innovation with an index of 3.

No hype cycle multiplier may be higher in value (weight) than the hype cycle stage index value. For example, adoption during the slope of enlightenment is assigned index 3 and the index multipliers are applied to Rogers' cumulative adoption data: 2.5% (I), 13.5% (EA), 34% (EM), 34% (LM), and 16% (L) respectively in ascending rank 1-3 as 1, 2, 3, 3, and 3. (See Index Multiplier Column, Table 3). Next, for each adopter type, multiply the cumulative basis (s) by the index multiplier (m). The next step is to divide each product from the preceding step by the hype cycle index (i). The hype cycle index will be the same for all calculations in this example. The results from the last step are displayed in the Result column in Table 3. The results in order by type starting with innovators are: .83, 10.67, 50,

84, and 100. Figure 2 shows the Result column data plotted as the Reference J (normal). The Reference J-curve is what an anticipated normal-paced adoption of Smartphones during 2006 would look like in an organization. The comparison J-curve is plotted from data from the actual installation. In this example the data used simulated a rapid installation. The final step is to compare the curves. Questions you may ask when evaluating the results are (1) Did the "S" become a "J", (2) How steep is the foot of the "J", and (3) How straight is the ascending slope of the "J"? If the resultant (comparison) J-curve resembles a "J", then the diffusion was rapid. If not, compare the foot of the comparison J-curve with the foot of the reference J-curve. This concept is similar to the "hockey stick" Fenn and Raskino (2008) reference in their book (p. 75). If the foot of the comparison J-curve is steeper (more vertical) than the reference J-curve foot, then the adoption was rapid. Note that in this example, Figure 2, the hype cycle index was 3 and the J-curve still resembles an S-curve. But, note the foot of the comparison J-curve (the "actual" adoption) is steeper than the reference J-curve (baseline). This indicates that the innovation adoption was at a more rapid pace than normal. The steeper the foot of the "J", the more rapid the adoption.

In theory, an organization can create a baseline (reference) J-curve from adoption projections to determine the anticipated pace of adoption. After the innovation is fully adopted, the organization can compare the actual (comparison) adoption J-curve with the anticipated (reference) J-curve to determine the success of the adoption. The steps to creating a comparison J-curve is similar to creating the reference J-curve. First you create an S-curve, next apply the index (s*m)/i, and finally plot the J-curve.

CONCLUSION

The S-curve is comprised of action data within a system. The S-curve is a representation of the aggregate data of a specific innovation adoption event. The hype cycle data show on a large scale, at which enthusiasm point and generation an innovation is. The J-curve uses hype cycle data to enhance the S-curve. Where the S-curve is useful in determining that innovation diffusion has occurred in a system, the J-curve is useful in determining the rate of diffusion.

There are still some lingering questions about the relationship between the S-curve and the hype cycle to be pursued at a later date. For instance, there may be a stronger correlation between Rogers' early adopters and adoption behavior during the slope of enlightenment. Perhaps there even might be a closer correlation between all stages of Rogers' model and hype cycle phases. Future research should also answer the following questions. Does crossing the chasm early create a J? In other words if more people became early adopters what would the plotted data look like?

ACKNOWLEDGMENT

Thank you to Dr. Janice Hinson, my mentor, who supported and advised me from concept to completion of this article. My endless appreciation also goes to Dr. Jennifer Gibson for her SPSS assistance crunching data to demonstrate that the "S" to "J" hypothesis is viable.

REFERENCES

Albanese, R., Lieb, J., & Stewart, J. (Producers). (2009, March 2). The Daily Show with Jon Stewart [Episode #14029]. *Twitter frenzy*. Podcast retrieved on May 3, 2009, from http://www.thedailyshow.com/video/index.jhtml?videoId=2195 19&title=twitter-frenzy

Celik, A. (2007, December 25). *Crossing the chasm* (Geoffrey A. Moore). Message posted to http://celikalper.wordpress.com/2007/12/25/crossing-the-chasm-geoffrey-a-moore/

Drakos, N., Mann, J., Cain, M., Andrews, W., Knox, R., Valdes, R., et al. (2008). *Hype cycle for social software, 2008* (Report No. G00158239). Retrieved May 1, 2009, from http://www.gartner.com/DisplayDocument?id=735719

Fenn, J. (1999). *When to leap on the hype cycle* (Report No. DF-08-6751). Retrieved March 4, 2008, from http://www.cata.ca/files/PDF/Resource_Centres/hightech/reports/indepstudies/Whentoleaponthehypecycle.pdf

Fenn, J. (2007). *Understanding Gartner's hype cycles, 2007* (Report No. G00144727). Retrieved December 8, 2007, from http://www.digeratimarketing.co.uk/gartnershypecycle.pdf

Fenn, J., Cearley, D., Valdes, R., Tully, J., Basso, M., Uzureau, C., et al. (2006). *Hype cycle for emerging technologies, 2006* (Report No. G00141901). Retrieved October 21, 2008, from http://www.gartner.com/DisplayDocument?doc_cd=141901

Fenn, J., Drakos, N., Andrews, W., Knox, R., Tully, J., Ball, R., et al. (2008). *Hype cycle for emerging technologies, 2008* (Report No. G00159496). Retrieved from May 1, 2009, from http://www.gartner.com/DisplayDocument?doc_cd=159496&ref= g_homelink

Fenn, J., Linden, A., Tully, J., Davidson, J., Smith, S., Margevicius, M., et al. (2004). *Hype cycle for emerging technologies, 2004* (Report No. G00121844). Retrieved October 21, 2008, from http://www.gartner.com/DisplayDocument?doc_cd=121844

Fenn, J., & Raskino, M. (2008). *Mastering the hype cycle: How to choose the right innovation at the right time*. Boston, MA: Harvard Business Press.

Fenn, J., Raskino, M., Basso, M., Phifer, G., Lundy, J., Gilbert, M., et al. (2007). *Hype cycle for emerging technologies, 2007* (Report No. G00149712). Retrieved October 21, 2008, from http://www.gartner.com/DisplayDocument?id=509710

Gartner, Inc. (2006, August 9). *Gartner's 2006 emerging technologies hype cycle highlights key technology themes: 2006* [Press release]. Retrieved October 21, 2008, from http://www.gartner.com/it/page.jsp?id=495475

George-Cosh, D. (2009, April 29). Has the Twitter backlash begun? Message posted to http://blogs.thenational.ae/beep_beep/2009/04/has-the-twitter-backlash-begun.html

Gladwell, M. (2000). *The tipping point: How little things can make a big difference*. New York, New York, NY: Little, Brown and Company.

Hansen, P. (2002, August, 2). Electronics and the Gartner hype cycle - opinion & analysis electronics - vehicle telematics - brief article. *Automotive Industries*, Retrieved February 18, 2008, from http://goliath.ecnext.com/coms2/gi_0199-1995351/Electronics-and-the-Gartner-Hype.html

Linden, A., Fenn, J., McCoy, D., Cearley, D., Drakos, N., Tully, J., et al. (2005). *Hype cycle for emerging technologies, 2005* (Report No. G00129853). Retrieved October 21, 2008, from http://www.gartner.com/DisplayDocument?doc_cd=129853

Linden, A., Fenn, J., Redman, P., Pescatore, J., Ball, R., Tully, J., et al. (2003). *Hype cycle for emerging technologies, 2003* (Report No. R-20-4160). Retrieved October 21, 2008, from http://www.gartner.com/DisplayDocument?doc_cd=115998

Raskino, M. (2009, April 17). Classic hype cycle turn signal: 'Twitter Backlash' reported. Message posted to http://blogs.gartner.com/hypecycle-book/2009/04/17/classic-hype-cycle-turn-signal-twitter-backlash-reported/

Rogers, E. (2003). *Diffusion of innovations*. New York, NY: Free Press.

Young, P. (2006, March). *The Spread of Innovations by Social Learning*. Working paper. Retrieved April 30, 2009 from http://www.santafe.edu/events/workshops/images/0/0a/Spread21march.pdf

This work was previously published in International Journal of E-Adoption, Volume 1, Issue 2, edited by Sushil Sharma, pp. 55-68, copyright 2009 by IGI Publishing (an imprint of IGI Global).

Section 5
E–Learning

Chapter 17
E–Learning Methods and the Factors Hindering Their Usage:
An Empirical Exploration

Chengbo Wang
Edge Hill University, UK

Baomin Qi
University of Bolton, UK

ABSTRACT

In recent years, e-learning technology has been widely used in the academic institutes for supporting the effectiveness and efficiency of the students' learning and the educators' teaching, as a favored approach. However, regarding the student community, the extent to which e-learning technology is used, types of e-learning methods are being mainly used, as well as the barriers for enjoying the advantages of e-technology, remain interesting topics for the educators to explore. This chapter focuses on these issues through an investigation among the students within a higher education institute. The findings give an understanding regarding the usage of e-learning methods and the factors hindering the efficacy of their usage among the students. Also, a primary analysis on the usage difference between undergraduate and postgraduate students is presented.

INTRODUCTION

E-learning, brought about by the development of information technology and network systems, as a type of information and communication technology (ICT), has become a very popular method in

DOI: 10.4018/978-1-60960-597-1.ch017

facilitating the educational processes (Siritongtha-worn and Krairit, 2006; Bennet & Bennet, 2008; Wang, et al., 2009; Owens and Price, 2010) in many academic institutes as well as in other industries (Little, 2010). Academic instructors use e-leaning methods as a powerful complementary tool to enhance their class teaching effectiveness and the effect of students learning. Furthermore many institutes currently offer distance learning courses and rely heavily on the e-leaning methods as the teaching mechanism.

Researchers have argued that the e-learning methods have a positive effect on learning process (e.g., Alexander, 2001; Bose, 2003; Duffy & Cunningham, 1996). However, according to the authors' observation in their daily teaching, e-learning methods (hereafter simplified as e-methods, referring to the concrete methods contained in the major e-learning systems currently applied in the academic institutes) seem having not realized the expected benefits to all students. In order to understand the most frequently used e-methods by the students, and the frequency of these e-methods' usage as well as the barriers (hindering factors) for students using e-methods in their learning process, the authors conducted a survey among the students in an education institute. This paper presents the findings from this research.

The paper is structured in the following way. The next section describes the methodology employed in this research. This is followed by a brief description of e-learning and its related issues; investigation scenarios and the primary analysis are then considered and the paper ends with the conclusions and further research.

RESEARCH METHODOLOGY

In order to achieve the research objectives, namely to find the most frequently used e-methods by the students, the frequency of these e-methods' usage as well as the hindering factors for students using e-methods in their learning process, three steps were followed.

Step 1, investigating the relevant literature, and based on the findings and understanding from literature, summarising the e-methods and possible hindering factors affecting the usage of them.

Step 2, a survey was conducted among current students, to find the most frequently used e-methods and evaluate the hindering factors found from the literature through the users' (students') judgement. A further interview with students was also conducted for a further comprehensive understanding and triangulation of the survey findings.

Step 3, following the previous two steps, generalising the findings regarding the frequently used e-methods and the hindering factors of their usage, as well as the countermeasures to resolve the identified problems.

E-TECHNOLOGY IN FACILITATING LEARNING

E-learning refers to the application and deployment of the network and digital technologies to facilitate and conduct learning and communication processes (Bose, 2003; Siritongthaworn & Krairit, 2006; Roffe, 2002; Henry, 2001) in different types of organizations. Among these organizations, educational institutes are taken as representative.

With the advance of the information technology, the conduction of instruction has been improved (Shim, et al., 2007), which gives the education institutes a powerful approach in helping the students' learning process. Within recent years, many higher education institutes have employed e-technology in their academic work (Siritongthaworn & Krairit, 2006; Bose, 2003; Alexander, 2001; Hadengue, 2005). The most popular e-learning technologies include WebCT, Blackboard and Moodle, etc. (Qi, et al., 2009). The e-methods, such as email, instant chatting, etc., commonly contained by them are the focused elements of this paper. In many institutes, e-methods are also used as a new strategy to enrich the learning effect obtained from long existing teaching approaches, namely face to face communication, etc.

It has been argued by academics that e-methods as a flexible approach (Bose, 2003; Siritongthaworn & Krairit, 2006) have advantageous aspects in enhancing learning effectiveness. By following the contention from Alexander (2001), Bose (2003) and Roffe (2002), the main benefits of e-learning methods include: 1) Better usage of resources like classrooms, teachers, etc., improvement of the quality of teaching and learning, as well as easing the access of the learners to a wider range of knowledge resources; concurrent with this is the increase in the cost-effectiveness ratio of education, namely reducing the cost in education operations and improve the productivity of the learning/teaching process; 2) Through e-medium instantly update course contents and provide recent development of knowledge within the course focused fields; 3) With the opportunity to communicate with others internationally, to gain more insights in the relevant learning areas, and meanwhile increase the skill level and understanding of the application of ICT tools; 4) Indirectly promote the information communication technology (ICT)'s application and further development by deploying the relevant software/hardware and providing corresponding feedback for the ICT developers to make further improvement on their products; 5) Provide more flexibility to the learners regarding the availability of time and places of learning, which better suits the various individual learners' learning style and resource availability. This may also improve students' attitude towards learning more positively; 6) A strong approach to enhance and enrich the learning through face-to-face communication in classroom lectures to improve the student-centered learning and teaching strategy; also to provide a complementary format of communication between learners and between learners and teachers.

These advantages are not exhaustive, people can still identify more benefits of learning through e-technology.

Even though the importance and usefulness of e-technology have been recognized, and it has also been widely used in higher education institutes, there are still existing challenging factors. If these are not properly considered and tackled they can hinder the full play of its function with

regarding to the learners. These factors are termed as hindering factors. Following the understanding and comprehension from the contentions of the researchers like Alexander (2001), Hart & Rush (2007), Roffe (2002), Packham, et al. (2004), etc., the main factors can be summarized as follows:

- Speed (Anonymous, 2003): Low speed of the IT system. This is a common phenomenon existing in many institutes, which can be caused by the network systems and computers' CPU speed.
- Accessibility: Lack of access to the IT system. This is a frequently raised issue by the students, due to opening hours of IT facilities or insufficient facilities' provision, can also be due to some students having a part-time job which restricts their use of the facility at the opening hours.
- IT infrastructure (Siritongthaworn & Krairit, 2006; Packham, et al., 2004; Hadengue, 2005): Low dependability of IT system. This problem can be caused by the issues related to updating and maintenance of software and hardware of the IT systems.
- Technical support (Siritongthaworn & Krairit, 2006): Insufficient support from the IT administration department. This is mainly due to the staffing issue of the institutes' IT department and can be resolved through management policy.
- Ease usability (Shim, et al., 2007; Roffe, 2002): Computer-user interface is not sufficiently designed user friendly (uneasiness of usage). This is an issue of selection of appropriate package of e-learning.
- Appropriateness of content (Siritongthaworn & Krairit, 2006): Lack of usefulness/usability of the content. The elements within the e-learning system should provide opportunities to accommodate what are needed by the user (mainly students and educators).

- Course content attractiveness (Packham, et al., 2004): Lack of attractiveness of the content. This issue requires the educators using e-learning system to fully understand the function and carefully prepare the materials uploaded to the system.
- Time availability (Alexander, 2001; Packham, et al., 2004; Hadengue, 2005; Swain, 2010): Lack of the availability of time. This challenges the students themselves on how to manage their own schedule, to balance the study with other activities.
- IT skills (Packham, et al., 2004; Hadengue, 2005; Owens and Price, 2010): Insufficient skill level for using the e-methods. Some students (also educators) do not have sufficient knowledge and skills to use the IT system in order to enjoy the benefits from it. Thus training is always a necessity.
- Buy-in of the technology (Alexander, 2001; Owens and Price, 2010): Lack of recognition of the usefulness of the e-methods. This is a mindset issue, can be resolved through training and demonstration of the benefits of e-methods.
- Direct communication: need for face to face communication with the tutors/peer students. Face to face communication can ensure a higher performance (Williams and Castro, 2010); it is also a necessary part in the teaching/learning process, cannot be replaced by e-methods. However, the percentage of time taken by this direct communication, compared to e-methods is always an interesting topic to be argued.

With the aforementioned advantages of e-methods in learning process, keeping in mind the factors hindering the learners' usage, the authors conducted research, with the intention to investigate: 1) the most frequently used e-methods by the students and the reasons; 2) the factors currently affecting the thorough usage of e-methods, and 3)

the factors potentially could hinder the full usage of e-methods by the students.

RESEARCH INVESTIGATION SCENARIOS AND ANALYSIS

The following sub-sections introduce the research conducted and its outcomes.

Questionnaire Content and Survey Conduction

This investigation was conducted by use of a student questionnaire. Due to resources limitation, this survey was implemented in only one selected institute in UK. This institute has a student population including undergraduates and postgraduates. To facilitate learning and teaching, this institute has deployed Blackboard system as e-learning technology. The survey questionnaire has three sections; questions are based on the literature and the authors' understanding of the practical daily application of e-methods, which was obtained through debriefing/discussion with a focus group of students/tutors during the design stage of the questionnaire:

Section A investigates the main e-methods used by the students for facilitating their learning and the rate (percentage) and reasons of usage of the chosen methods, from a group of options: Email, Discussion area (forum/board) on Blackboard, Documents downloading site on Blackboard, Instant chatting. They were also given the opportunity to specify their own methods if different from the provided options.

Section B investigates the factors which are currently hindering the students' usage of the e-methods, from the multiple choices of: Low speed of the IT system (Speed), Lack of access to the IT system (Accessibility), Low dependability of IT system (IT infrastructure), Insufficient support from the IT administration department (Technical support), an insufficiently designed user-friendly computer-user interface [uneasiness of usage (Ease usability)], Lack of usefulness/usability of the content (Appropriateness of content), Lack of attractiveness of the content (Course content attractiveness), Lack of the availability of time (Time availability), Insufficient skill level for using the e-methods (IT skills), Lack of recognition of the usefulness of the e-methods (Buy-in of the technology), Need for face to face communication with the tutors/peer students (Direct communication).

Section C based on the same multiple choices from Question B, but with focus on the factors, which might not be hindering the usage of the e-methods currently, but potentially could become barriers in the future. The feedback in this section can give some in advance warning to the tutors to prepare certain countermeasures for prevention.

To avoid biased understanding/finding from the research, based on the understanding of the characteristics and the availability of the sample groups, the purposive sampling (Jankowicz, 2005) concept was followed to select the sample groups. The sample groups answering the questions in this questionnaire are from postgraduate and undergraduate students in business/management and engineering related courses, who account for the biggest portion of the student population in this institute. These undergraduates and postgraduates have already been well informed and familiarised with the availability and functionality of the e-learning methods in the university; the majority of the undergraduates are British students, while the postgraduates consist of students from different countries.

Due to the availability of resources, the sample group is rather small, however, as a primary stage exploratory study, this research can provide insight and the basis for a further wider scale investigation.

In total 41 questionnaires have been distributed to the students (25 postgraduates, 16 undergraduates) within the institute, with a total effective feedback rate of 73% (postgraduate 72%, undergraduate 75%), which is a very satisfactory outcome for a survey study, based on the pre-condition that the students were informed that answering these questionnaires is not compulsory. The reason of such a return rate is due to the students' enthusiasm in helping the tutors for further understanding of the e-methods' usage in supporting learning process.

RESEARCH FINDINGS

In order to have a thorough understanding of the e-methods and their usage from the students, based on the descriptive summarisation on the collected data, the analysis focused on two aspects: the sample students as a whole, and a comparison between undergraduate and postgraduate students.

Findings from the Sample Group as a Whole

Figure 1 is the main e-methods used by the students, as well as the reasons for usage of the cho-

Figure 1. The main e-methods used

Method used	Percentage of usage among the students	Reason (and its percentage of proposition) for using this method
Email	100%	1) Up-to-date information; 2) Flexible, convenient and quickest for information communication; 3) Easy usage; 4) Easily available.
Documents downloading site on Blackboard	80%	1) Lecture notes printing; 2) Relevant information;
Discussion area (forum/board) on Blackboard	57%	1) Flexible for communication; 2) Support understanding of lectures; 3) Direct communication with relevant groups of people; 4) Check course information.
Instant chatting	23%	1) Convenient/ relaxed communication; 2) Knowledge sharing.

sen methods. Based on the summarized outcome from the survey in this table, one can identify that students in the sample group all use email, the reasons for using email include obtaining up-to-date information, convenient and quick communication, ease of usage, etc. 80% of the sample group use document downloading function for obtaining lecture notes and relevant course information, as well as some further knowledge facilitating the learning in lectures and seminars. Around 57% of the sample group use the discussion board/forum, with the supporting arguments on choosing this method as: flexible for communication, facilitation of the understanding of the teaching content, direct communication with relevant people, etc. Around 23% of the sample group students use instant chatting function, they feel this method can

ensure a convenient and relaxed communication, and provide a better chance for knowledge sharing.

Figure 2 illustrates the recognised importance level (reflected by the percentage of propositions among the sample group) of the factors currently hindering the usage of the e-methods. Figure 3 illustrates the recognized importance level of the factors potentially hindering the usage of the e-methods.

From Figure 2, we can find that the majority of the previously proposed factors have been proposed as more or less currently hindering the usage of e-methods, the leading factors include Accessibility (73%), Speed (60%), and Time availability (40%).

Figure 3 illustrates that all the proposed factors are considered by the sample group students as

Figure 2. Factors currently hindering the usage of e-methods

Current hindering factors	Percentage of proposition from the feedback
Accessibility	73%
Speed	50%
Time availability	40%
Direct communication	20%
IT infrastructure	10%
Technical support	10%
IT skills	10%
Buy-in of the technology	10%

Figure 3. Factors potentially hindering the usage of e-methods

Potentially hindering factors	Percentage of proposition from the feedback
Accessibility	63%
Appropriateness of content	43%
Speed	27%
IT infrastructure	27%
Course content attractiveness	27%
Buy-in of the technology	27%
Direct communication	27%
Ease usability	20%
Time availability	20%
Technical support	10%
IT skills	10%

having the possibility to affect the usage of the e-methods in the future. Among them the leading factors proposed by more than 40% of the sample group students are Accessibility and Appropriateness of content.

In-Depth Interview on the Summarised Findings

After the above findings were summarised, three undergraduate and three postgraduate students external to the sample group were selected (voluntary basis) to participate in an in-depth interview, focusing on the elements in the findings, to check if there are any possible disagreements and/or concerns with regard to the coverage of the hindering factors and their respective importance indicated by the percentage of propositions from the sample group's feedback.

The investigation outcome confirmed the meaningfulness of the findings and the interviewees proposed no doubt or questioning on the mentioned issues.

Comparison Between the Feedback from Undergraduate and Postgraduate Students

Taking into consideration that the University is divided into undergraduate and postgraduate levels, for a further insight into the differences and similarities of the e-methods' usage between these two types of students, the data has been further summarized and sorted. Figure 4 is a comparison of the e-methods' usage rates by the two types of students; Figure 5 is a comparison on factors currently hindering the e-methods usage; Figure 6 visualizes the comparison on factors potentially hindering the usage. Meanwhile, the authors have tried to identify the underlying reasons for the difference, through further discussion/communication with the students.

Due to the convenience and ease of usage, etc. of email, all postgraduates and undergraduates use it as an information obtaining and communication approach, compared with the other methods that show a difference in the usage rate between postgraduate and undergraduate students. For Discussion area (forum/board) on Blackboard and

Figure 4. Comparison of the e-methods' usage rates

Usage rate of different e-methods

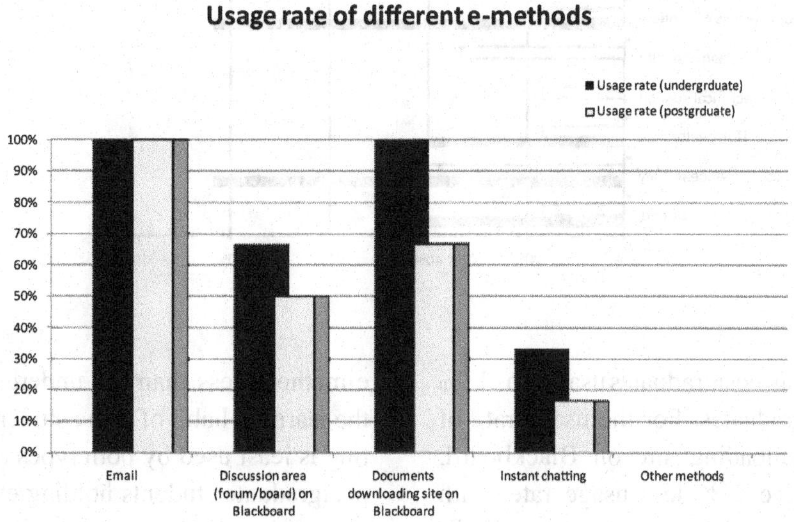

Figure 5. Comparison on factors currently hindering the e-methods usage

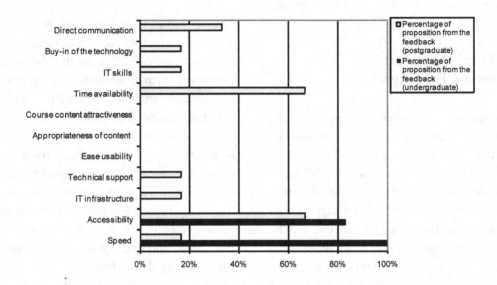

Figure 6. Comparison on factors potentially hindering the usage

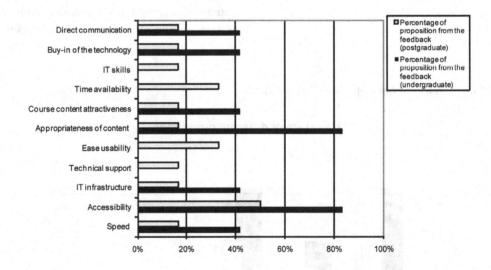

the Instant chatting, postgraduates usage was 17% less than undergraduates. For the usage rate of Documents downloading site on Blackboard, postgraduates have 33% less usage rate, with 100% usage rate from the undergraduates. It illustrates that the postgraduates in general use the

e-methods less than the undergraduates, due to the learning habit of some students. Instant chatting is least used by both types of students, with postgraduate students holding even lower usage rate.

According to observation, there are more postgraduates failing to prepare their lectures in advance through checking lecture notes and relevant information from the e-learning system.

For the factors that can currently hinder the usage of e-methods, undergraduates only proposed Speed (100%) and Accessibility (83%) as the barriers to their usage of e-methods in learning. For postgraduates, they have proposed Speed (17%), Accessibility (67%), IT infrastructure (17%), Technical support (17%), Time availability (67%), IT skills (17%), Buy-in of the technology (17%), Direct communication (33%), namely the majority of the factors can affect their usage of the e-methods, with Accessibility (Lack of access to the IT system) as the leading one. This phenomenon is a reflection of student cohorts' composition and relevant knowledge/skill background. The undergraduates are all local students in UK, they have been using the e-learning system for years, while some of the international postgraduates are relatively new to this country and the e-learning systems, their skills, awareness, etc. of e-methods application need further improvement. Meanwhile, some of the students have part-time jobs, which may have conflicts with the opening schedule of the computer systems in the university and thus cause less accessibility to IT facilities, especially for those having no network connections at home.

For the factors that can potentially hinder the usage of e-methods in the future, undergraduates chose fewer factors compared with that from the postgraduates, postgraduates in fact selected all factors as potential barriers. Undergraduates have chosen: Speed (42%), Accessibility (83%), IT infrastructure (42%), Appropriateness of content (83%), Course content attractiveness (42%), Buy-in of the technology (42%), Direct communication (42%). Postgraduates have a rather scattered choice reflected by the factors' respective recognized importance level: Speed (17%), Accessibility (50%), IT infrastructure (17%), Technical support (17%), Ease usability (33%), Appropriateness of content (17%), Course

content attractiveness (17%), Time availability (33%), IT skills (17%), Buy-in of the technology (17%), Direct communication (17%). Both undergraduates and postgraduates give the first priority to the Accessibility to IT system, this is a phenomenon can be observed in any institute with IT facilities shared by all the students. There are three possible means to resolve the problem: 1) increase the numbers of computers (with network connections); 2) extend the opening hours of the IT facilities; 3) from students' own aspect, they need to have their computers and network connections at home.

A very interesting point must be highlighted here is that regardless of factors currently or potentially hindering the usage of e-methods, the undergraduates have emphasized much more than postgraduates on Speed. With regard to the background skills/knowledge foci, it seems that the undergraduates have a more critical requirement on the efficiency of IT system itself.

CONCLUSION AND FUTURE RESEARCH

With consideration of the main targets of this research, namely to find the most frequently used e-methods by students in the case institute, the factors that currently and potentially could impede the full usage of e-methods, as found by the survey, allow the following primary conclusions to be drawn:

- The most frequently used e-methods include Email, Document downloading function, Discussion board/forum, due to their characteristics of convenient/quick support on communication, obtaining information and knowledge, and ease of usage. However, except for Email, postgraduate students have less usage of the e-methods than the undergraduate students.

- Among the factors currently affecting the usage of e-methods, for the students as a whole, Accessibility, Speed, Time availability are the leading ones according to the proposed percentage from the students responses. However, with the exception of Ease of usability, Appropriateness of content and Course content attractiveness, the remaining factors have all been proposed, though not from a high percentage of the sample group students.

- For the factors potentially affecting the usage of e-methods, besides that all having been proposed from the sample group as a whole, Accessibility and Appropriateness of content are the two leading critical ones being selected. Both undergraduates and postgraduates give the first priority to the Accessibility to IT system. There are three possible means to resolve the problem: 1) increase the numbers of computers (with network connections); 2) extend the opening hours of the IT facilities; 3) suggest students to have their own computers/network connections at home.

- The undergraduates illustrate a higher level of skills and appreciation of the e-methods usage. This provides a reminder to the educators that relevant e-learning technology training is necessary to increase the IT application knowledge/competence of those students who do not have deep IT system application background knowledge.

- The heavy emphasis of the undergraduates on Speed illustrates that with high level of e-technology application knowledge, students tend to place a more critical requirement on the IT system's performance.

This research has provided a primary understanding of the main e-methods and the barriers of their usage in learning process; however, due to the limitation regarding the rather small sample size, there is still a need for further research to enrich the current findings and conclusions. If time and resources are available, a further investigation at a wider scale of sample groups should be carried out, with more participants and more importantly with more institutes involved, to enhance and refine the findings regarding the previously described research objectives.

A longitudinal study following a time series survey investigation could also be conducted, to follow up the possible changes on the main e-methods used and the hindering factors of their application/usage.

Meanwhile, a future survey study should also be conducted by focusing on the appropriate countermeasures for tackling the hindering factors, to assure an efficient and effective learning process.

REFERENCES

Alexander, S. (2001). E-learning developments and experience. *Education + Training, 43*(4/5), 240-248.

Anonymous. (2003). Canon creates a successful blend with e-learning-Ignoring the hype and focusing on the method. *Development and Learning in Organizations, 17*(1), 23–26. doi:10.1108/14777280310795711

Bennet, A., & Bennet, D. (2008). E-learning as energetic learning. *The Journal of Information and Knowledge Management Systems, 38*(2), 206–220.

Bose, K. (2003). An e-learning experience – A written analysis based on my experience in an e-learning pilot project. *Campus-Wide Information Systems, 20*(5), 193–199. doi:10.1108/10650740310507399

Duffy, T., & Cunningham, D. (1996). Constructivism: Implications for the design and delivery of instruction. In Jonassen, D. H., & Driscoll, M. P. (Eds.), *Handbook of research for educational telecommunications and technology* (pp. 170–190). New York, NY: MacMillan.

Hadengue, V. (2005). E-learning for information literacy-A case study. *Library Review, 54*(1), 36–46. doi:10.1108/00242530510574147

Hart, M., & Rush, D. (2007). E-learning and the development of "voice" in business studies education. *International Journal of Educational Management, 21*(1), 68–77. doi:10.1108/09513540710716830

Henry, P. (2001). E-learning technology, content and services. *Education + Training, 43*(4/5), 249-255.

Jankowicz, A. D. (2005). *Business research projects* (4th ed.). Thomson Learning.

Little, B. (2010). E-learning flowers in the UK. *Industrial and Commercial Training, 42*(3), 135–138. doi:10.1108/00197851011049158

Owens, J. D., & Price, L. (2010). Is e-learning replacing the traditional lecture? *Education + Training, 52*(2), 128-139.

Packham, G., Jones, P., Miller, C., & Thomas, B. (2004). E-learning and retention: Key factors influencing student withdrawal. *Education + Training, 46*(6/7), 335-342.

Qi, B., Lu, L., Oliver, S., Wang, C., & Zhang, R. (2008). *Can ICT replace the traditional teaching and learning model? A case study.* ECS 2009, March, Wuhan, China.

Roffe, I. (2002). E-learning: Engagement, enhancement and execution. *Quality Assurance in Education, 10*(1), 40–50. doi:10.1108/09684880210416102

Shim, J. P., Shropshire, J., Park, S., Harris, H., & Campbell, N. (2007). Podcasting for e-learning, communication, and delivery. *Industrial Management & Data Systems, 107*(4), 587–600. doi:10.1108/02635570710740715

Siritongthaworn, S., & Krairit, D. (2006). Satisfaction in e-learning: The context of supplementary instruction. *Campus-Wide Information Systems, 23*(2), 76–91. doi:10.1108/10650740610654465

Swain, D. K. (2010). Students' keenness on use of e-resources. *The Electronic Library, 28*(4), 580–591. doi:10.1108/02640471011065391

Wang, Q., Zhu, Z., Chen, L., & Yan, H. (2009). E-learning in China. *Campus-Wide Information Systems, 26*(2), 77–81. doi:10.1108/10650740910946783

Williams, E. A., & Castro, S. L. (2010). The effects of teamwork on individual learning and perceptions of team performance: A comparison of face-to-face and online project settings. *Team Performance Management, 16*(3-4), 124–147. doi:10.1108/13527591011053232

Chapter 18

Costs of E–Learning Support:
A Hong Kong Study of Costs for Supplemental E–Learning and Impact on Institutional Planning

Paul Lam
The Chinese University of Hong Kong, China

Josephine Csete
The Hong Kong Polytechnic University, China

Carmel McNaught
The Chinese University of Hong Kong, China

ABSTRACT

Understanding e-learning costs informs decision making on support for the development and implementation of teaching and learning technologies in higher education. This chapter describes costs and processes in a central e-learning support service that is especially applicable to face-to-face universities that use e-learning in a blended or supplemental mode. We differentiate three types of costs: infrastructure costs that are less sensitive to variation in the complexity of e-learning strategies, and e-development and e-delivery costs that are directly related to the nature of the strategies used. Using actual data from a three-year e-learning support project (e3Learning) with 139 sub-projects, the chapter illustrates how the calculations promoted an understanding of e-learning in the following four aspects: 1) total cost of running an e-learning support service, 2) individual costs attributable to each of the sub-projects, 3) 'price-tags' of e-learning strategies, and 4) initial exploration of the cost-effectiveness issue. Institutional decisions made as a consequence of this study are described.

DOI: 10.4018/978-1-60960-597-1.ch018

THE ISSUE OF E-LEARNING COSTS

Teaching and learning technology is resource-intensive. Schechter (2009) warned that it involves considerable initial costs as well as ongoing costs. Bowles (2004) described the early phase of e-learning development as being characterized by rapid adoption of the technology, followed by a mature phase of reflection on practice, including examination of issues such as determining costs and benefits. Even some years ago, there were concerns about the value of e-learning in supporting learning and justifying continued investment. Lytras and Pouloudi (2001), for example, stated that many e-learning strategies in practice are not as effective for learning as they were initially hoped to be. Nicol and Coen (2003) reported the challenges that university administrators and funding bodies have in collecting systematic information about costs and benefits of e-learning to inform decision making. Higgins and Prebble (2008) noted that finance questions, including cost-effectiveness of e-learning, are the responsibilities of educational leaders.

As Bates (2005) noted, any educational technology is not intrinsically good or bad; its effectiveness depends on how well it is used. Hence, studying the costs of e-learning does not imply that we should base all educational decisions purely on monetary considerations. Cost is only one aspect to consider. Nicol and Coen (2003) commented that knowing the expenses is not the final solution; it only represents a guide for decision making: "It helps users to 'reflect upon and structure their thought processes' while making decisions in areas of professional practice" (p. 55). Knowing more about the costs in e-learning will increase our ability to figure out ways to maximize effects while minimizing costs (Twigg, 1999; Boettcher, 2004; Pätzold, 2005).

When empirical evidence is lacking, cost-effectiveness judgments must necessarily be speculative. In this spirit, the present paper, through analyzing actual expenses of a central support service on e-learning, aims to provide insights to the question "How much does e-learning cost?" (Ash & Bacsich, 2000).

STUDIES OF COSTS IN DIFFERENT MODES OF E-LEARNING USE

Twigg (2003) described e-learning modes using three classifications. The substantially online mode represents cases where teaching is mainly conducted online, and e-learning is the sole mode of delivery; this applies most often to distance-education institutions. The replacement mode represents cases where the technology is intended to substitute for at least some of the traditional classroom activities. In the supplemental mode, e-learning is used to assist the traditional face-to-face teaching, and very often there is little change to the class activities. There have been studies of costs in each of the three modes of e-learning use and their approaches tend to differ.

In the substantially online mode, e-learning costs are relatively easy to identify as a substantial portion of the institution's costs are related to the development and maintenance of the e-learning environment. Typically, these costs may include staff expenses, administration expenses, and preparation and delivery of online materials and activities. Bassi (2000) suggested grouping these costs into fixed costs (costs that tend to stay the same regardless of student size), and marginal costs (costs that increase per student head multiplied by the number of learners served). There is also a distinction between direct and indirect costs among these fixed and marginal costs. The direct costs are money paid for services and equipment: trainers' compensation, material development, material production and material distribution. The indirect costs are opportunity costs that teachers and departments, for example, pay through sacrificing some other revenue-generating activities because of their engagement in e-learning. In a professional training context, the indirect costs can also include opportunity costs of learners or compensation paid to them by their organizations in supporting them to study.

The benefits of e-learning in this mode also are readily identifiable. As all of the instruction is occurring through e-learning, measurements such as the number of courses held, the number of students served, and the turnover rates of courses, etc. can be construed as benefits. Wentling and Park (2002) conducted an empirical study of balancing costs and benefits in a fully online mode. They added up costs such as 'faculty salary and benefit', 'TA and tech support', 'equipment and software updates', and 'coordination expense'; these costs were balanced by the revenue which was the 'total revenue from tuition'.

In the replacement mode, researchers tend to focus on comparing innovations with traditional methods and seek to justify the use of the new technologies when more learning is achieved with the same or fewer resources. In order to make comparisons, a rather limited set of cost-and-benefit indicators is usually considered. For example, costs may involve the time and effort spent by teachers in both situations. Variation in administrative costs is often ignored in this mode. In order to make direct comparison of 'benefits' possible, often quantifiable measurements are collected such as the number of courses or students involved and/or student drop-out rates. Moonen (1997) described these measurements as "tangible efficiency indicators" and presents the rationale that "the system with the largest effects is the most efficient … when the effects are the same for both alternatives, the system with the smallest costs is the most efficient" (p. 70). Geith and Cometa (1999) conducted a study of costs in the replacement mode that focused on time as a major unit of measure. There were courses using various degrees and forms of the technology. On the one end of the spectrum, there were courses that ran in the traditional manner with no e-components. On the other end, there were anytime/ anywhere courses in which students were told to access learn-

ing resources online, or attend lecturers through teleconferencing means. They monitored the staff time spent in developing and delivering the courses and then converted the time into monetary terms. The comparison was done by calculating the cost per credit hour, and balancing that with the students' number of hours actually spent in the course using the different methods. In other words, the interest is on 'Return on Investment' (ROI). Huddlestone and Pike (2008) regarded ROI as "the total cost savings from conversion to e-learning divided by the additional one-off course design and development costs incurred with producing e-learning" (p. 243).

In the supplemental mode, an estimation of costs and benefits is perhaps the most complicated to calculate. There are challenges in identifying costs, identifying benefits, and balancing costs against benefits (Nicol & Coen, 2003). Costs of e-learning in the supplemental mode are hard to distinguish as the resources and the personnel often are engaged in both face-to-face teaching and online activities. There are no easy ways to distinguish the portions of resources and staff effort paid to each of these two types of activities. Institutions generally lack a sophisticated activity-based costing (ABC) system which can provide costing information at the level of the specific activities (Moonen, 1997). Teaching staff are also not used to keeping records of how their time is spent and so "cost data [are] not available at the task level" (Geith & Cometa, 1999, p. 7).

Further complicating the issue, benefits are often non-quantifiable in the supplemental mode. It is very difficult to isolate the additional learning benefits that e-learning might bring to the face-to-face component of the courses (Draper, 1997) as learning outcomes are usually influenced by many factors in the learning environment. In addition, there are benefits external to course-level teaching and learning enhancement such as advantages at the level of "changes in organizational processes (e.g. improved communication)", and "external standing of the institution (e.g. its public image)"

(Nicol & Coen, 2003, p. 48). Though recognizably important as benefits, there seems to be no effective way to turn these into quantifiable numbers. Moreover, benefits of different e-learning cases cannot be easily compared as evaluation methodologies are often tailor-made to fit the specific teaching context, and the value assigned to benefits varies from one case to another (Anderson et al., 2002). Of course, even if costs and benefits can both be clearly identified, the judgment about whether the benefits are worth the costs is still difficult to make. Thus, "it is almost impossible to assess the effects of an educational process in a reliable monetary amount, the cost-benefit analysis is practically not applicable in an educational context" (Moonen, 1997, p. 70).

Also, to date, most empirical studies on e-learning costs are conducted at a departmental level (Nicol & Coen, 2008). A wider scope of analysis would be beneficial.

COMPONENTS OF COSTING IN THE SUPPLEMENTAL MODE

In order to study costing in the supplemental mode, careful formulation of the costing components is the first step. Costs seem to be attributable to two major components: the e-learning tasks and their agents.

Regarding the e-learning tasks, we follow the suggestions made by Rumble (2001) who classified the following tasks as contributing to e-learning costs:

- **Online materials development:** Developing e-materials and interactive activities.
- **E-delivery:** Facilitating (and assessing) students' learning online, accessing the website, and administering the course online.
- **Infrastructure:** Providing the infrastructure and support within which e-education

can operate; planning and managing e-education at the macro-level.

Regarding the e-learning agents, the work of Nicol and Coen (2003) serves as our starting point and we propose the following three types of agents as involved in the development, e-delivery and infrastructure tasks:

- E-learning-related tasks are carried out by teachers and local support staff. Teachers write the content for the online materials and propose suitable learning interactions. The teachers monitor and supervise the creation of the materials and interactions (development work). There are also e-delivery activities/ tasks in which teachers and teaching assistants plan and implement the e-learning strategies in their courses (e-delivery). Collective effort at the level of department or faculty may also be involved. In addition, local-level infrastructural support is involved, including the provision and maintenance of department-based computers and network. Normand, Littlejohn and Falconer (2008) were correct in stressing that staff effort should not be underestimated. For example, extra time is needed for teaching staff to adjust to new ways of teaching. Underestimating workload in this area may result in excessive work pressure which in turn leads to teachers' resistance to innovations.
- Central services provided by the university. Information and technology service units are usually involved at this level, providing the institution-wide network and learning platforms to facilitate online learning (infrastructure). The library may also be involved in e-learning by providing access to online learning resources such as e-journals and e-books (e-delivery).
- Support units in the institution provide technical and pedagogical support. The

range of support from these central units can vary, ranging from merely providing consultations on learning designs, to actually developing the materials (development) and systems needed for e-learning, and supporting the evaluation of the strategies for the teachers (e-delivery). The administrative and managerial system within which the services operate need to be included in the infrastructural aspect.

McNaught and Vogel (2006) examined the diversity of e-learning support services that evolve within different university cultures. There are two extremes. At one extreme is the decentralized service in which teachers bid for funding and then act entirely independently, including contracting out their e-learning development. The other extreme is represented by a centralized service where a well funded e-learning support unit is present to provide a range of services (including, but not limited to development) to teaching staff who wish to use technology in their teaching.

Previous empirical studies on e-learning costs in the supplemental mode reflect this diversity in university e-learning support. Maher, Sommer, Acredolo, and Matthews (2005), for example, examined the additional efforts expended by teachers and local support staff in technology-assisted situations in a decentralized context where the acquisition and/or development of the content materials were supported by, or funded by, resources at the departmental level; a separate e-learning support team was not involved. Similarly, Geith and Cometa (1999), and Rumble (2001) also focused on costs related to teachers and local support staff, and subsumed the development of the learning materials under this cost category. Taking a different approach, Green, Smallen, Leach, and Hawkins (2005) described three projects, the Campus Computing Project, the COSTS Project and the EDUCAUSE Core Data Service, which focused on more centralized expenses such as IT budgets, percentage of IT

budget in total institutional budget, and central IT staffing, etc. These studies and reports in general confirmed that e-learning can be very costly and thus the issue of costing is important.

OUR STUDY

The present study is based on an e-learning support service which was essentially a centralized process supporting supplemental e-learning. The support service was a little unusual in that it worked across three universities in an Asian context. The data from this three-year multi-university e-learning support project (described below) will be used to examine the following four costing issues:

- The **total cost** of running an e-learning support service;
- The **individual costs** attributable to each of the sub-projects served;
- The '**price-tags**' of e-learning strategies; and
- An initial exploration of **cost-effectiveness analyses in the supplemental mode**.

The e3Learning project (in which the three 'e's stand for enriching, extending, and evaluating learning) was designed to assist teachers to better exploit the possibilities of web-assisted teaching. It offered a range of design, development and evaluation services. For each sub-project, a team was formed so that teachers had access to educational and technical support. Full details of the design of this project are in James et al. (2003) and the project website (http://e3learning.edc.polyu.edu.hk/). Descriptions and working exemplars of many of e3L sub-projects exist on the website. The e3L project operated across three universities in Hong Kong from 2003 to 2006.

The centralized processes in the project resulted in three advantages that allowed for this study of costs. First, the project treated each teacher's request for e-learning development as a sub-project. Each sub-project had its own lifecycle which included planning, design and development, implementation, and evaluation. Thus the e3Learning project was not just an IT technical support project, but offered a comprehensive service that covered activities related to infrastructure, e-material development and e-delivery and therefore allowed for the collection of data across a wide range of activities to build a more comprehensive understanding of costs. Second, the project was able to collect data across a relatively large number of teachers and projects. A total of 139 sub-projects were supported. Third, the nature of sub-projects ranged widely. Projects were created for many different disciplines in three different universities. Sub-projects also varied widely in terms of size and the nature of support requested. For example, 70 out of these 139 sub-projects had a strong evaluation component. These 70 evaluated sub-projects were all supplemental course websites for actual courses. The existence of a rich set of evaluation data from multiple sources enables us to get some sense of the effectiveness. Lam, McNaught and Cheng (2008) described the evaluation process and a summary of the evaluation data for all 70 evaluated sub-projects. The diversity of the sub-projects enables the present study to look at costs at two levels: overall costs

as well as costs in relation to the nature of the e-learning strategies used.

The funding came from a project grant assigned to the investigators in the three universities. The project followed on from an earlier e-learning service project called "Megaweb" (http://mega-web.polyu.edu.hk/) which had served only one university. The previous project handed over to the new project a considerable amount of start-up equipment and software. A significant portion of staff employed on the earlier project continued in the new project. The fact that the overall project was able to begin with personnel experienced in supporting e-learning would have an impact on the costs. Transfers of existing equipment would also artificially depress the costs in this area.

A breakdown of the agents and the tasks attributable to e-learning costs in the present context are presented in Table 1. The shaded area indicates the main sources of data investigated. In other words, while we acknowledge that the total e-learning costs are in reality shared by many parties and units in a university, the present study has a limited scope and focuses on costs that fall under the central e-learning support service.

The support team members described in this study were located in a central service unit, and were in roles dedicated to supporting e-learning. However, many of the types of support also re-

Table 1. The e-learning agents and their e-learning activities

Agent \ Task	Teacher and local support staff	Central IT services	e3L support
E-material development	Creating content Converting content into e-format	--	Converting content into e-format Developing activities and interactions
E-delivery	Planning e-strategies Implementing the strategies	Training on learning platforms Training on information literacy Maintenance of the e-learning platforms	Consultation on strategies Implementing/ monitoring the strategies Evaluation
Infrastructure	Administration Computer and networking in department/ faculty	Administration Network and e-learning platform Links to learning resources Macro-level e-learning decisions	Administration Self-development Accumulation of experiences and reusable objects

quired are not included in this study. Personnel (such as technicians) in the departments and faculties who may have a part of their role to support e-learning are not included. Staff members who look after learning management systems (LMSs, e.g. WebCT) and train teachers and learners to use them have also been regarded as central services in this study and were not included in the calculation. Similarly, the costs paid by the central services to buy the licenses necessary to host LMSs were excluded as well. Lastly, the time and effort three professors spent on the project were chargeable to the accounts of the respective centres and teaching departments at three different universities and were not counted as expenses in the study.

COST CALCULATION METHOD

Expenses were carefully kept by the project. In the present study, these expenses were retrieved and categorized into expenditure relating to one of the following types.

The infrastructure expenses were the general expenses that were required to start the project and keep the project running. They are further classified and recorded as below.

- **Resources spent on administration**: mainly the cost of the administrative staff, and the time spent on administrative work (such as student-helper applications and claims);
- **Equipment/ office expenses**: money spent on computers, media production equipment, computer software, and costs on stationery and paper;
- **Resources spent on professional development**: time identified to be spent by staff members not directly on specific sub-projects but on reading, attending or presenting at workshops and conferences that

prepared them to work more efficiently in the field; and

- **Costs of investigation ofnew technologies**: the costs spent on preparatory work such as investigation of the readiness of the mobile technology in facilitating teaching and learning. The costs included the time the researchers spent on these issues.

These costs were equally shared among all sub-projects when the costs of the individual teacher sub-projects were calculated. Each sub-project was apportioned an equal split share of the fixed cost.

The development work was done by the technical team which was composed of 1) full-time staff and 2) part-time student helpers. Staff and helpers reported the number of hours they spent on each sub-project. The reported hours led to the calculation of the specific development costs for each individual sub-project. The technical team, however, also found that not all their time should be accountable to development work. About 20% of their time was used in self-improvement, giving and attending workshops, learning new hardware and software, and self-reflection. As previously mentioned, these 'professional development' activities were counted as infrastructure expenses.

E-delivery support related to the pedagogy-oriented services of the project. Consultation services were provided by instructional designers. If evaluation support was required, evaluation officers were available. Full-time technical staff who had been involved in the development work were also available to assist in e-delivery. The team then followed each sub-project and gave timely advice at the planning stage, during the implementation, at the evaluation stage, and even at the post-implementation stage. The instructional designers and evaluation officers reported the number of hours spent, also attributable to the individual sub-projects. The hours were then converted into monetary terms to represent the costs of the individual sub-projects for the pedagogical component. As with the development staff, about

20% of their time was spent on self-improvement, giving and attending workshops, and reflection. This was interpreted as 'professional development' expenses under the infrastructure category. The conversion of hours into dollars was based on the actual salaries of the staff employed by the e3L project. [Note: inflation is low and salaries are quite stable in Hong Kong.]

Data concerning the outcomes came from two sources. First, project completion data (completion rate close to 95%) tracked whether the projects were successfully handed over to the teachers who had requested service. Second, towards the end of the project in August 2006, a questionnaire was sent to all teachers who had requested services as a means of evaluating the project. Sixty-five out of the 139 sub-projects returned the survey (response rate of 47%). In one question, the teachers were asked to report on the number of students who had used the developed website in each year. The number of students who had experience with (and potentially benefited from) the e-learning strategies in the last year of the project was the second source of data. Neither of these two types of data is an accurate measure of the benefits of the e-learning strategies. However, as discussed earlier, e-learning benefits are not easily distinguishable, quantifiable and comparable. Our simple strategy for beginning to understand e-learning benefits was quite useful as a preliminary endeavour at finding empirical data to compare costs and effectiveness. In addition, a number of evaluation studies were carried out using e3Learning date; details of many of these are at http://e3learning.edc.polyu.edu.hk/EvaluateRes.htm and summarized in Lam, McNaught and Cheng (2008).

FINDINGS

The calculations allow us to analyze the costs of e-learning in the following four dimensions:

1) Total cost of running an e-learning support service;
2) Individual costs attributable to each of the sub-projects served;
3) 'Price-tags' of e-learning strategies; and
4) Initial exploration of the cost-effectiveness issue.

Overall Costs

The infrastructure, e-development and e-delivery costs are illustrated in Figure 1, in US dollars (USD). The cost of infrastructure was a major component of the overall expenses, occupying more than 40% of the total cost. As mentioned earlier, the project was not completely "created from scratch" as much of the equipment purchased in a previous project was reused. The expenses allocated to 'equipment/ office expenses' thus are considerably lower than a typical support service that would require more purchases. In addition, some programming of templates was reused. However, there was little reuse of previously constructed materials.

It should be noted that a single staff position would perform multiple roles – especially between e-delivery and the infrastructure areas of project development and administration. In our analysis, the project staff were asked to allocate their time spent on each type of work.

Figure 1. Overall costs of the project in US dollars.

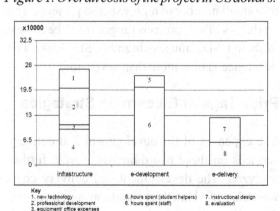

Key
1. new technology
2. professional development
3. equipment/ office expenses
4. administration
5. hours spent (student helpers)
6. hours spent (staff)
7. instructional design
8. evaluation

The costs spent on the actual development work comprised the second largest component, just below 40% of the total expenses. The majority of the resources were paid to full-time programmers while a comparatively small proportion was used to employ student helpers.

The expenses spent on delivering the e-learning strategies that are accountable as costs paid by the support project were comparatively lower, occupying about 20% of the total expenditure. The money was found to be equally spent on instructional design and evaluation support.

Sub-Project Costs

The second level of expenditure analysis identifies the costs in the individual sub-projects. The 139 sub-projects equally shared the infrastructural costs. The e-development and e-delivery costs were calculated depending on the actual usage of services of the various sub-projects, based on the actual time spent on the sub-projects by our project members for various development and delivery tasks. As a result, each sub-project had the same shared infrastructural cost (about USD2,200 per share) but varied in the cost in the development and delivery dimensions. Also, the total expenses of the individual sub-projects were quite different from one another.

The sub-project costs are illustrated in monetary terms in Figure 2. The distribution of the costs assumed a bell-shape curve which is skewed by a small number of high-expense projects. The total costs of sub-projects ranged from the lowest of about USD2,500 to as high as USD19,000. The difference is thus more than seven-fold.

Price Tags of E-Learning Strategies

The expenses of the development and delivery services on these two dimensions were further analyzed. The development and delivery costs were classified into high, medium, and low costs depending on how far they ranged from the aver-

age expenses. The classification was done with a certain degree of subjectivity. The sub-projects with development costs lower than USD770 were considered as 'Development Low' sub-projects (e.g. simple enhancements to an existing WebCT course); while the sub-projects with development costs higher than USD3,850 were regarded as 'Development High' sub-projects (e.g. the development of complex animations or simulations). 'Development Medium' sub-projects were those where development costs were between USD700–3,850 (e.g. mounting multimedia case-study material). Based on this classification, it turned out that there were 60 development-low sub-projects, 63 development-medium sub-projects and 16 development-high sub-projects.

The sub-projects with e-delivery that had costs lower than USD640 were considered 'Low' sub-projects; while the sub-projects with e-delivery costs higher than USD1,280 were regarded as 'High' sub-projects. 'Medium' sub-projects were those which cost USD640–1,280. After applying the above criteria, 69 sub-projects were classified as delivery-low, 56 as delivery-medium and 14 as delivery-high. Please note that the e-delivery component was a smaller portion of the sub-project's cost than the development; so, the delivery-high costs were no match against the amount payable to high-development.

Figure 2. The range of sub-project costs

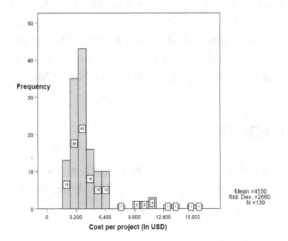

Table 2. Number of sub-projects (out of 139) of different combinations of technological and pedagogical costs

e-delivery e-development	Low	Medium	High	(sub-total)
Low	32	24	4	60
Medium	28	27	8	63
High	9	5	2	16
(sub-total)	69	56	14	139

Table 2 summarizes the distribution of the sub-projects. Most of the sub-projects fell in the low–low and medium–medium range.

One hundred and eleven of the 139 sub-projects (80%) could be classified as low to medium e-delivery and e-development support. A fairly typical pattern for their progress is as follows. Average to low delivery usually involved brief discussion and planning of the pedagogical issues beforehand between the teacher(s) involved and the support-team members. Teachers involved in this type of project would become most familiar with three team members: the instructional designer, the evaluation officer and the technical development support staff. Teachers would not require much help in writing and revising instructions and content of online materials as they would do that themselves, but would usually welcome assistance in conducting simple evaluations at the end of the course to collect students' feedback on the innovation (through student surveys and often focus-group interviews as well). The development costs were spent on building relatively simple learning materials and/or the building of a simple course website usually through using the functions of the existing LMS.

The remaining 28 non-typical sub-projects are interesting. Vignettes of a representative case in each of these categories are described below to explain how the strategies can lead to different patterns of expenses.

The following analysis (Boxes 1, 2, and 3) in general shows that e-learning strategies, depend-ing on the nature and design of the strategies, can vary a great deal in the resources needed in the development and delivery stages.

Some Comments on Cost-Effectiveness

Seven of the 139 sub-projects were recorded as incomplete at the end of the overarching project. This relatively low rate of non-completion was a positive feature of this overall project. The overall economy of the e3Learning project was very satisfactory (on average spending only less than USD4,500 a sub-project).

Considering the seven less successful cases, four were in the high-development category, two in the medium-development category, and one in the low-development category. They were all low-delivery because they had never reached the implementation stage and the costs spent on evaluating the strategies were minimal. The low-development sub-project might have needed at least a medium level of development cost if the teacher had been more enthusiastic about the development and provided the developers with the necessary course content.

Table 3 represents the range of costs of the 65 sub-projects that returned the project-end survey, together with the reported number of students (in brackets) using the materials in the year 2005–06.

It should be noted that the four high-development sub-projects took up nearly 17% of the expenditure for 65 courses. The 32 medium-de-

Box 1.

A high-development and low-delivery sub-project
The teacher created two simulations to show dynamic phenomena, two games to test students' understanding and two activities to illustrate problem-solving processes. Student helpers were employed during the summer to help the teacher develop and improve the materials. The students provided fresh ideas on how to better represent (with pictures, animations, simulations, and short quizzes) the various important ideas in the course. The students also designed a few exercises that assisted students to solve problems in this subject.
The development cost was high since creating games and multimedia online materials takes a great deal of time. There were also needs for reviewing and further revising the games and materials during the production stage. The delivery cost was low since despite initial consultation with the teacher concerning instructional design, there was not much work associated with the evaluation of the final materials.

Box 2.

A low-development and high-delivery sub-project
The teacher in this sub-project prepared self-learning materials for students to prepare for a government-required language examination. The development cost was low because the teacher made use of ready-made materials provided by a third-party content provider and the cost was not chargeable to the support team. A great deal of effort was expended by the support team to evaluate the effectiveness of the package and the learning activities as requested by the teacher. The evaluation was done in two consecutive years with students in four cohorts.

Box 3

A high-development and high-delivery sub-project
This project involved revamping an existing website. A special feature in this course site was the abundance of course-related materials – the scope of this subject was broad, but the lecturer tried hard to include as many resources in the site as possible to help students enjoy and learn. The teacher put up lecture notes, PowerPoints, quizzes, video clips, links and references, and past papers with answer keys. The high development costs induced were mainly because of a few multimedia and interactive resources. They included a quiz system (written in Flash; not using the existing function provided by the LMS), video clips, animated explanations of key concepts with Cantonese voice-overs, and an online role-play game. Evaluation of this course site focused on the changes of learning approach before and after access to the online self-learning materials. Students' examination scores were also collected and analyzed. The team supported the evaluation in four cohorts of the course. Even towards the end of the project, the revisions of the materials were still ongoing, mostly on correcting bugs in the quiz system and the games. The problems with the game were more than just technical. There were also design problems as the teacher and the students who assisted him were novices in designing educational games.

Table 3. The 65 sub-projects and student use in 2005–06 academic year

e-delivery e-development	No. of sub-projects and students involved				Actual cost
	Low	Medium	High	Sub-total	Cost (USD, rounded to the nearest 100)
Low	16 (615)	10 (962)	3 (277)	29 (1854=~41%)	91,400 (32%)
Medium	13 (664)	13 (1321)	6 (265)	32 (2251=~50%)	147,400 (51%)
High	1 (149)	2 (125)	1 (100)	4 (374=~8%)	48,700 (17%)
(sub-total)	30 (1428)	25 (2408)	10 (642)	**65 (4478)**	**287,500 (100%)**

velopment sub-projects cost 51%, while the 29 low-development sub-projects used 32%.

It is interesting to compare the costs of these 65 sub-projects with the number of students they supported. The expensive sub-projects were little used (8%), the medium sub-projects supported 50% of the students while the inexpensive strategies were used with 41% of the students. Care must be taken though in interpreting these numbers as the analysis involves only a very limited numbers of sub-projects (especially in the high-development category).

DISCUSSION

The setting up and maintenance of a support service requires the allocation of a large amount of resources. The administration costs and the resources needed to continuously train staff and prepare them for the latest technology should not be underestimated. Thus, there seems to be an argument for e-learning support that is centralized rather than decentralized as the costs of running multiple teams will almost certainly be substantial.

As in the case of the project reported on in this paper, the overall cost amounted to approximately USD640,000 but the sum supported 139 sub-projects. This amounts to about USD4,500 a project on average. The sub-projects in this study involve teaching and learning strategies used in specific courses, and thus are different from the extremely high-cost development projects that cost millions and intended for use by thousands or tens of thousands.

The costing method in this study has enabled a way to calculate the costs of the individual sub-projects, and the calculation revealed that e-learning strategies can have widely different costs. The variance mainly comes from the fact that e-learning strategies can have a large range of development needs. Some of the variance can also be caused by the expenses related to delivering the strategies.

The study reviewed some sub-projects that used exceedingly high or low amounts of development and delivery services. The experiences in these few sub-projects tend to show that the costs and the returns do not have a simple proportional relationship. This seems to be especially true in the high-development sub-projects.

The expectation of high benefits from high investment does not seem to be borne out. On the contrary, we found that the more expensive projects are often in danger of lengthened development even to a point of incompletion. The numbers of students who are able to benefit from these expensive strategies tend to be inversely proportional to the amount of money spent on their development. There are many factors that may have influenced the success of such materials. For example, the building of complex e-learning materials need to have very carefully compiled instructions, a high level of cooperation between the teacher and the development team, good mechanisms for developing and evaluating the products, and a high demand of expertise from the support team, etc. McNaught et al. (2009) provided more reflections of the challenges met in complex e-learning sub-projects.

The implication seems to be that the support team should conduct detailed feasibility studies concerning both the technical and pedagogical aspects of a complex e-learning strategy before the project commences. The team should also consider whether there are other alternatives to the strategy. For example, can the key functions being sought after be fulfilled by any existing e-learning tools? Also, rather than creating the materials from scratch, can the content be met by reusing some existing e-learning objects or packages, or by making modifications to ready-made materials? However, reuse of 'learning objects' has not been very successful in Hong Kong (McNaught, 2007).

This discussion on cost-effectiveness, however, is inevitably preliminary and indicative. We are clearly aware of the fact that actual benefits should be measured in terms of the real learning benefits students obtained rather than merely through a head count. Cohen and Nachmias (2009), for example, discussed 44 different benefits under main areas such as 'increasing efficiency of teaching and learning processes', 'improving instruction quality', 'improving affective aspects' and 'knowledge management improvement'. This framework is beyond the scope of the present study. Thus, an obvious counter-argument to our statement above can easily be: students who used the complex and expensive strategies had such an improvement in learning that it is still worth the costs. More research certainly is needed.

Impact on Institutional Planning for E-Learning

Usually one reports a study but its subsequent impact is often left unreported. This revision of our original paper (Lam, Csete, & McNaught, 2009) provides us with an opportunity to report on the impact on our respective institutions of the e3L project and the data we collected on the e3L sub-projects.

The experience and findings of the e3L project have had direct influence on the e-learning support services that resulted after the project formally ended. The high completion rate and the general positive tenor of the evaluation data compares favorably with similar outcomes from other individually funded and organized projects in Hong Kong. In addition, the costs appear to be lower that costs from other previous funding arrangements. While these comparisons are somewhat anecdotal, the evidence has been sufficient to persuade internal funding managers that centralized e-learning support services are the best arrangement for us to pursue. The positive report on institutional advantages for e-learning by the Joint Information Systems Committee (2008) in the UK complements the decisions made in our universities in Hong Kong.

In two of the universities involved in the e3L project centralized e-learning support structures were established and the design of these services can, at least partially, be attributed to the experience of the project outlined in this paper. In the third university there were a number of staffing changes and the connections are less clear.

In the case of one of the universities (University A), shortly after the project closed, the University decided to create and provide recurrent funding for a central support unit, named the eLearning Development and Support and Section (eLDSS). The eLDSS has been tasked with providing a pedagogically led 'one-stop-shop' service to support e-learning through projects, and professional and organizational development. Substantial attention has been paid to limiting indirect costs to teachers and departments. An analysis of the costs, motivators and barriers to successfully implementing e-learning was considered when developing a position paper on e-learning which guides the work of the established unit (http://eldss.edc.polyu.edu.hk/position). The composition of the unit includes technical staff possessing a range of skills to meet the needs of a wide variety of projects and university-wide initiatives (e.g. programming, multimedia development, web design, etc.) and professional staff to provide training, learning design, project management and evaluation assistance. There are currently ten full-time staff in the eLDSS.

Recent data indicates good uptake of eLDSS services. In May 2009 over 90% of students reported use of e-learning technologies to help them access or download course materials in at least half of their academic subjects in the 2008–2009 academic year. However, percentages are lower for other kinds of activities such as engaging in electronic practice and quizzes outside of class time (67.5%) and further reduces to just over 50% reporting that at least half of their subjects required them to engage in online learning activities.

In the second university to organize a central service (University B), a somewhat different strategy was adopted. The Centre for Learning Enhancement And Research (CLEAR) and the

Information Technology Services Centre (ITSC) have worked closely and collegially together since 2002 to support pedagogical and technical aspects of e-learning. University B decided to capitalize on an existing successful arrangement and, in 2006, allocated ~ USD130,000 to formalize the eLearning Service. This Service is now ongoing and has recurrent funding for a range of services, shared between staff in the two Centres, including:

- Streamlining of the University's eLearning system;
- Consultation services for teachers, the most notable of which is the eLearning Assistant service where a number of part-time and full-time helpers work directly with teachers (Lam, Au Yeung, Cheung, & McNaught, 2009);
- Seminars and workshops;
- Support for courseware development – involving another internal grant scheme;
- Promotion of e-learning, including an annual conference, the Teaching and Learning Innovation Expo (http://www.cuhk.edu.hk/eLearning/expo/); and
- Research on new strategies and technologies.

These services are detailed in McNaught and Lam (2009). At University B, there has also been a significant growth in e-learning; the percentage of supplementary online course websites has grown from ~45% in 2003–04 to over 80% in 2008–09. A formal eLearning Strategy, including a detailed action plan, was adopted in 2009 (http://www.cuhk.edu.hk/english/documents/teaching/elearning-strategy.pdf).

Staff in both the eLDSS in University A and the eLearning Service in University B recognize that we have a long way to go, especially in terms of having more interactive online teaching and learning, but we believe that our evidence-based approach has provided university administration with data that has given them the confidence to invest in e-learning services.

CONCLUSION

The main focus of this paper has been on the expenses of e-learning strategies in traditional campus-based universities: i.e. the supplemental mode of e-learning use. We have used the records of the expenses used and the activities undertaken in a centralized support project to explore the overall cost components of e-learning support and services, and also to examine the range of expenses in the individual teacher sub-projects we have supported. Even though understanding the costs of sub-projects cannot give us a direct and simple answer to the question of whether e-learning strategies are cost-effective, the analysis so far is very useful in at least two ways.

First, the discussion drew attention to the major costing components in e-learning services and may enable better consideration in the future regarding the allocation of resources in subsequent e-learning support projects. Second, the discussion highlighted the broad range of sub-project costs and the fact that costs and learning benefits are not necessarily proportionate. Care, thus, has to be paid in order to ensure high pedagogical benefits especially from the sub-projects that demand high costs. Because of obvious practical limitations, however, our insights are mainly about the support expenses, and much of the time and effort paid by teachers, local support staff and the central services are not examined in this study.

While we cannot claim that the costing data alone had tremendous impact, it was part of a suite of data and institutional experiences arising from the e3L project that has changed the e-learning landscape in at least two of our universities in Hong Kong.

ACKNOWLEDGMENT

Funding support from the University Grants Committee in Hong Kong is gratefully acknowledged, as is the collaborative support of many colleagues in our three universities. This is an updated and extended version of the paper by Lam, Csete and McNaught (2009).

REFERENCES

Anderson, C., Day, K., Haywood, D., Heywood, J., Land, R., & Macleod, H. (2002). Evaluating networked learning: Developing a multi-disciplinary, multi-method approach. In Steeples, C., & Jones, C. (Eds.), *Networked learning: Perspectives and issues* (pp. 169–192). London, UK: Springer-Verlag.

Ash, C., & Bacsich, P. (2000). A new cost analysis model for networked learning. Proceedings of the European Distance Education Network (EDEN) Conference (pp. 208–210). Prague, Czech Republic, 16–17 March.

Bassi, L. (2000). How much does e-learning cost? Retrieved September 15, 2010, from http://www.linezine.com/2.1/features/lbhmec.htm

Bates, A. W. (2005). *Technology, open learning and distance education* (2nd ed.). London, UK: Routledge.

Boettcher, J. V. (2004). Online course development: What does it cost? Campus Technology. Retrieved September 15, 2010, from http://connect.educause.edu/Library/Abstract/OnlineCourseDevelopmentWh/35735?time=1204536851

Bowles, M. S. (2004). *Relearning to e-learn: Strategies for electronic learning and knowledge*. Victoria, Australia: Melbourne University Press.

Cohen, A., & Nachmias, R. (2009, October, 6). Implementing a cost effectiveness analyzer for Web-supported academic instruction: A campus wide analysis. European Journal of Open, Distance and E-Learning, 3, Article 369. Retrieved September 15, 2010, from http://www.eurodl.org/?p=current=363&article=369

Draper, S. (1997). Prospects for summative evaluation of CAL in higher education. *ALT-J, 5*(1), 33–39. doi:10.1080/0968776970050106

Geith, C., & Cometa, M. (1999). Cost analysis results: Comparing distance learning and on-campus courses. Teaching, Learning, Technology Group. Retrieved September 15, 2010, from http://www.tltgroup.org/resources/F_Eval_Cases/Geith_Cometa.htm

Green, K. C., Smallen, D., Leach, K., & Hawkins, B. L. (2005). Data: Roads traveled, lessons learned. EDUCAUSE Review, 40(2), 14–25. Retrieved September 15, 2010, from http://www.educause.edu/ir/library/pdf/ERM0520.pdf

Higgins, A., & Prebble, T. (2008). Taking the lead: Strategic management for e-learning. Retrieved September 15, 2010, from http://www.caudit.edu.au/educauseaustralasia09/assets/papers/monday/Andrew-Higgins.pdf

Huddlestone, J., & Pike, J. (2008). Seven key decision factors for selecting e-learning. *Cognition Technology and Work, 10*(3), 237–247. doi:10.1007/s10111-007-0102-z

James, J., McNaught, C., Csete, J., Hodgson, P., & Vogel, D. (2003). From MegaWeb to e³Learning: A model of support for university academics to effectively use the Web for teaching and learning. In D. Lassner & C. McNaught (Eds.), ED-MEDIA 2003, Proceedings of the 15th annual World Conference on Educational Multimedia, Hypermedia & Telecommunications, (pp. 3303–3310). Honolulu, Hawaii, USA, 23–28 June. Norfolk, VA: Association for the Advancement of Computers in Education.

Joint Information Systems Committee. (2008). Exploring tangible benefits of e-learning: Does investment yield interest? Retrieved September 15, 2010, from http://www.jiscinfonet.ac.uk/publications/camel-tangible-benefits.pdf

Lam, P., Au Yeung, M., Cheung, E., & McNaught, C. (2009). Using the development of eLearning material as challenging and authentic learning experiences for students. In R. Atkinson & C. McBeath (Eds.), Same places, different spaces. Proceedings of the 26th annual Australasian Society for Computers in Learning in Tertiary Education Conference (pp. 548–556). (ASCILITE), University of Auckland, 6–9 December. Retrieved September 15, 2010, from http://www.ascilite.org.au/conferences/auckland09/procs/lam.pdf

Lam, P., Csete, J., & McNaught, C. (2009). Costs of e-learning support: An investigation across 139 small projects. [IJEA]. *International Journal of E-Adoption, 1*(1), 61–75. doi:10.4018/jea.2009010105

Lam, P., McNaught, C., & Cheng, K.-F. (2008). Pragmatic meta-analytic studies: Learning the lessons from naturalistic evaluations of multiple cases. *Association of Learning Technologies Journal ALT-J, 16*(2), 61–79. doi:10.1080/09687760802315879

Lytras, M. D., & Pouloudi, A. (2001). E-learning: Just a waste of time. In D. Strong, D. Straub, & J. I. DeGross (Eds.), Proceedings of the Seventh Americas Conference on Information Systems AMCIS (pp. 216–222). Boston, Massachusetts. Retrieved September 15, 2010, from http://citeseerx.ist.psu.edu/viewdoc/download?doi=10.1.1.21.5012&rep=rep1&type=pdf

Maher, M. W., Sommer, B., Acredolo, C., & Matthews, H. R. (2005). What are the relevant costs of online education? In Groccia, J. E., & Miller, J. E. (Eds.), *On becoming a productive university: Strategies for reducing costs and increasing quality in higher education* (pp. 196–204). Bolton, MA: Anker Publishing Company.

McNaught, C. (2007). Developing criteria for successful learning repositories. In Filipe, J., Cordeiro, J., & Pedrosa, V. (Eds.), *Web Information Systems and Technologies* (pp. 8–18). Dordrecht, The Netherlands: Springer. doi:10.1007/978-3-540-74063-6_2

McNaught, C., & Lam, P. (2009). Institutional strategies for embedding blended learning in a research-intensive university. Proceedings of the elearn2009 Conference, Bridging the development gap through innovative eLearning environments, The University of the West Indies, St Augustine, Trinidad and Tobago, 8-11 June 2009.

McNaught, C., Lam, P., Cheng, K.-F., Kennedy, D. M., & Mohan, J. B. (2009). Challenges in employing complex e-learning strategies in campus-based universities. *International Journal of Technology Enhanced Learning, 1*(4), 266–285. doi:10.1504/IJTEL.2009.030778

McNaught, C., & Vogel, D. (2006). The fit between e-learning policy and institutional culture. *International Journal of Learning Technology, 2*(4), 370–385. doi:10.1504/IJLT.2006.011341

Moonen, J. (1997). The efficiency of telelearning. *Journal of Asynchronous Networked Learning, 1*(2), 68–77.

Nicol, D., & Coen, M. (2003). A model for evaluating the institutional costs and benefits of ICT initiatives in teaching and learning in higher education. *ALT-J, 11*(2), 46–60. doi:10.1080/0968776030110205

Nicol, D., & Coen, M. (2008). Getting from here to there - Strategies for change. In Boys, J., & Ford, P. (Eds.), *The e-revolution and post-compulsory education: Using e-business models to deliver quality education* (pp. 103–115). London, UK & New York, NY: Routledge.

Normand, C., Littlejohn, A., & Falconer, I. (2008). A model for effective implementation of flexible programme delivery. *Innovations in Education and Teaching International*, *45*(1), 25–36. doi:10.1080/14703290701757351

Pätzold, H. (2005). Increasing value without increasing effort? The use of WebCT in accompanying face-to-face lectures. Journal of Distance Education Revue De L'Éducation À Distance, 20(2), 78–84. Retrieved September 15, 2010, from http://www.jofde.ca/index.php/jde/article/viewFile/83/62

Rumble, G. (2001). The costs and costing of networked learning. *Journal of Asynchronous Learning Networks*, *5*(2), 75–96.

Schechter, H. B. (2009). The cost of e-learning. eLearn, 7(5). Retrieved September 15, 2010, from http://www.elearnmag.org/subpage.cfm?section=articles&article=86-1

Twigg, C. A. (1999). Improving learning & reducing costs: Redesigning large-enrollment courses. Rensselaer Polytechnic Institute: Center for Academic Transformation.

Twigg, C. A. (2003) Improving quality and reducing costs: New models for online learning. EDUCAUSE Review, 38(5), 28–38. Retrieved September 15, 2010, from http://www.educause.edu/ir/library/pdf/ERM0352.pdf

Wentling, T. L., & Park, J. (2002). Cost analysis of e-learning: A case study of a university program. 2002 Academy of Human Resource Development Annual Conference (AHRD '02), Hawaii. Retrieved September 15, 2010, from http://citeseerx.ist.psu.edu/viewdoc/download?doi=10.1.1.86.5844&rep=rep1&type=pdf

Section 6
E–Adoption and Knowledge Management

Chapter 19
The Different Key Processes in the Implementation of Knowledge Management Among IC Designers, Distributors and Manufacturers

Pei-Di Shen
Ming Chuan University, Taiwan

Tsang-Hsiung Lee
National Chengchi University, Taiwan

Chia-Wen Tsai
Yuanpei University, Taiwan

Yi-Fen Chen
Chung Yuan Christian University, Taiwan

ABSTRACT

This study is an exploratory investigation of the enabling roles of knowledge management for integrated circuit (IC) Designers, Distributors, and Manufacturers. This study explores the different enabling roles in terms of knowledge creation, storage/retrieval, transfer and application when businesses implement knowledge management in upstream, midstream, and downstream firms in the IC industry. Three cases, Winbond, Worldpeace, and Taiwan Semiconductor Manufacturing Company (TSMC) were studied and analyzed systemically to illustrate the findings and insights in this study. The findings in this study point out that IC designers may focus more on knowledge storage, while IC distributors pay more attention to knowledge application and IC Manufacturers emphasize knowledge creation. The necessity to implement knowledge management in the distribution industry is also emphasized in this study. Moreover, the reasons for the different enabling roles are presented in the 'Insights from Case Studies' section of the paper.

INTRODUCTION

Today a 'Third Industrial Revolution' is under way; knowledge will replace land and a firm's physical or financial resources as the most important asset (Thurow, 1999). Even Drucker (1993) argues that in the new economy, knowledge is not just another resource alongside the traditional factors of production - labor, capital and land, but is the only meaningful resource today. Tangible assets will be decreased or consumed because of use, but intangible assets — knowledge, information and technology will grow through sharing and application. In many industries, firms can sustain their competitive advantage if their abilities in learning and evolution progress faster than their competitors. Thus, organizations should learn to survive in the fast changing and intensely competitive environment, continually redesigning themselves into learning organizations (Parker & Nitse, 2005; Daft, 1998).

Knowledge is a limitless resource in the knowledge-based economy; therefore, organizations should learn, store, transfer and apply knowledge to add value or gain competitive advantage (Sveiby, 1997). Knowledge management (KM) refers to identifying and leveraging the collective knowledge within the organization to help in competing (von Krogh, 1998). Discussions amongst policy makers, industry representatives and academics about KM are in fashion (Lange, 2006). KM is usually discussed and implemented in high-tech industries (e.g., Texas Instruments (TI) and TSMC) and the software industry (e.g., Microsoft and Oracle), where it is the basis for competitive advantage. However, it remains unclear whether the implementations of KM in upstream, midstream, and downstream firms focus on the same key process in the related industries. For example, do the designers (upstream firms), distributors (midstream firms) and manufacturers (downstream firms) in the IC industry all focus on the creation of knowledge? Should all firms pay the same attention to every process when imple-

menting knowledge management? Unfortunately, there are no research findings yet to indicate the key processes of knowledge management in the upstream, midstream, and downstream firms of the supply chain. This study illustrates how knowledge management is implemented in high-tech related industry - IC designer, distributor, and manufacturer, as those play the roles of upstream, midstream, and downstream firms in this supply chain. Reasons for the different enabling roles of knowledge management in these three types of firms are also discussed.

LITERATURE REVIEW

KM is based on applying the fullness of an organization's knowledge and this requires representing it, transferring it, making it accessible and encouraging its use (Metaxiotis & Psarras, 2006). In addition, KM is concerned with systematic, effective management and utilization of an organization's knowledge resources (Demarest, 1997). It consists of the creation, storage, arrangement, retrieval and distribution of an organization's knowledge (Demarest, 1997; Saffady, 2000). Alavi and Leidner (2001) classified the processes of KM into four steps: knowledge creation, knowledge storage/retrieval, knowledge transfer and knowledge application, representing a detailed process framework of organizational KM with a focus on the role of Information Technology. This systematic framework is shown as Figure 1 and each process is interpreted clearly in the following sections.

Knowledge Creation

Organizational knowledge creation involves developing new content or replacing existing content within the organization's tacit and explicit knowledge (Pentland, 1995). In today's rapidly changing environment, organizations have to focus on the creation of knowledge, instead of relying

Figure 1. Four processes of knowledge management

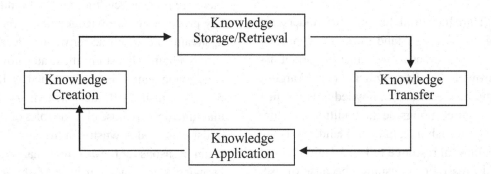

on quickly obsolescent existing knowledge. When organizations innovate, they do not simply process information from the outside in, but use information to solve existing problems and adapt to the dynamic environment. They actually create new knowledge and information from the inside out, in order to redefine both problems and solutions and, in the process, to re-create their environment (Nonaka & Takeuchi, 1995). New knowledge is a necessary raw material for innovation and the creation of knowledge; both are closely tied to new products and services (Hauschild, Licht & Stein, 2001). When a firm starts to develop new products or services, or when organizational knowledge is antiquated or insufficient, a firm should innovate and create new knowledge by means of organizational learning activities to face the challenges.

Knowledge Storage/Retrieval

While new knowledge is developed by individuals, organizations play a critical role in articulating and amplifying that knowledge (Nonaka, 1994). Actually, the storage, organization, and retrieval of organizational knowledge are referred to as organizational memory (Stein & Zwass, 1995; Malhotra, 2000). An organizational memory includes knowledge residing in various component forms, including structured information stored in electronic databases, written documentation, expert systems, documented organizational proce-

dures and processes and tacit knowledge acquired by individuals and networks of individuals (Tan, Teo, Tan, & Wei, 1998). Some companies store the knowledge; however, it seems the knowledge is lost as employees can not find or retrieve it. Advanced computer storage technology and sophisticated retrieval techniques, such as multimedia databases, and database management systems (DBMS) can be effective tools in improving organizational memory and helping employees retrieving knowledge (Alavi & Leidner, 2001).

Since the organizational knowledge is at company-level, it should be identified or shared by the organization members and recorded in a knowledge system. Two strategies are being used for storing knowledge (Hansen, Nohria & Tierney, 1999):

1. Codification: Provide high-quality, reliable, rapid information-systems implementation by reusing codified knowledge;
2. Personalization: Provide creative, analytically rigorous advice on high-level strategic problems by channeling individual expertise.

Knowledge Transfer

The distribution and transfer of knowledge is an important process in knowledge management (Alavi & Leidner, 2001; Huber, 1991). Knowledge must go through a re-creation process in the mind of the receiver (EI Sawy, Eriksson, Raven

& Carlsson, 2001) that depends on the cognitive capacity of the individual to process incoming stimuli (Vance & Eynon, 1998). Research has shown that inter-firm cooperative agreements provide opportunities for knowledge transfer (Soekijad & Andriessen, 2003) and knowledge access (Grant & Baden-Fuller, 2004; Jolly, 2005; Khamseh & Jolly; 2008). For the level of intra-firm, knowledge should be particularly shared and generalized within the organization. Generalization occurs not only when single ideas are moved, but also when the entire process of moving ideas becomes institutionalized within an organization (Yeung, Ulrich, Nason, & von Glinow, 1999). The institutional process embedded in a firm and the capability of generalizing ideas consistently are important elements to meet the real goal of KM.

For shared knowledge to be meaningfully used, the knowledge needs to be coupled with mechanisms for organization, retention, maintenance, search and retrieval of the information (Stein & Zwass, 1995). Such mechanisms are often computer-based, ranging from simple keyword organizing principles to complex intelligent agents and neural networks that grow with the expansion of knowledge repositories (Ellis, Gibbs & Rein, 1991; Johansen, 1988; Maes, 1994). Facing external pressures, organizations today are almost compelled to use virtual teams (Pauleen, 2004). Communication processes and information flows drive knowledge transfer in an organization (Alavi & Leidner, 2001). The use of collaborative technologies (CT) is fundamental to make virtual teams work. A collaborative technology, also referred to as a virtual workplace, should be able to record, at a minimum, the process of the group, an agenda, libraries of solutions and practices, different forms of interaction, meta-information, and provide shared information storage, access and retrieval (Ellis *et al.*, 1991; Ishii, Kobayashi & Arita, 1994; Kling, 1991; Nunamaker, Briggs & Mittleman, 1995; Romano, Nunamaker, Briggs & Vogel, 1998; Thornton & Lockhart, 1994). For optimum knowledge sharing and reuse, CTs include

not only a mechanism for exchanging knowledge (such as E-mail), but also a mechanism for creating a knowledge repository and a mechanism for accessing the knowledge repository (Majchrzak, Rice, King, Malhotra & Ba, 1999).

Knowledge transfer success requires that both parties to a knowledge transfer develop an understanding of where the desired knowledge resides within the source, and that they both participate in the processes by which the knowledge is made accessible (Dixon, 1994). In addition to the technology-based channels, organizations should provide other mechanisms to transfer and distribute knowledge to ensure unrestricted collaboration. For example, knowledge that is more or less explicit can be embedded in procedures or represented in documents, databases, or CTs, then transferred accurately. Besides, transfer of tacit knowledge generally requires extensive personal contacts (Davenport & Prusak, 1998). Organization members tend to use face-to-face or phone for the more ambiguous tasks of managing external relationships and conflicts, brainstorming, and strategic direction-setting. Nonetheless, the members tend to use the synchronous CTs for the more routine tasks of analysis, and project statusing (Majchrzak et al., 1999). Webster and Trevino (1995) suggested that rational and social factors should be included in comprehensive models of media choice that address both traditional and new media. In conventional communications environments, individuals' behavior choice was found to be largely underpinned by so-called rational determinants. Conventional media such as the telephone, facsimile, and printed documentation have been in use for extensive periods, during which views of what are effective, and then rational decisions of choice have grown over time and been validated by experience, and are implicitly shared by the user community (Breu, Ward & Murray, 2000). In newly implemented IT-enabled communications environments, individual media choice was found to be overwhelmingly informed by so-called social determinants of how these technologies might most adequately and effectively be used (Webster & Trevino, 1995; Fulk & Boyd, 1991).

Knowledge Application

Knowledge application means making knowledge more active and relevant for firms in creating value since organizational knowledge needs to be employed into a company's products, processes and services (Bhatt, 2001; Demarest, 1997). Employees use all available resources, including the corporate knowledge base, to improve their chance of reaching the goals of the organization (Hauschild et al., 2001). The source of competitive advantage resides in the application of the knowledge rather than in the knowledge itself (Alavi & Leidner, 2001). As stated by Prokesch (1997), using knowledge more powerfully than your competitors is a key to battling it out in the global information era. Learning from the experience of others and reusing materials that have been effective elsewhere improves the quality and speed of problem solving (Cross & Baird, 2000). Knowledge should really be used to create value for the company, and when it is applied, the company can judge the validity and suitability.

RESEARCH METHODOLOGY

Case Selection and Data Collection

This study attempts to explore the key processes in the implementation of KM in upstream, midstream, and downstream firms in the IC industry. The development of the IC industry in Taiwan has been ongoing for more than 30 years. Based on the government's support and the whole industry's effort, Taiwan is playing a critical role in the global IC industry, particularly as IC designers. Thus, the implementation of KM in these firms may provide important reference for those who are planning to implement, or are currently engaged in, KM. In

this regard, the case study is applied to illustrate how high-tech firms put KM into practice, and how they pay differing degrees of attention to the four processes of KM.

Case selection is very important; the cases in this study were selected for their implementations of KM and their financial performance. Each firm in this study is selected from high-tech related industries in Taiwan. The first case, Winbond, is selected from the IC design industry; the second case, WorldPeace, is selected from semiconductor distribution industry; and the last case, TSMC, is selected from among semiconductor manufacturers. We selected these cases from upstream, midstream, and downstream firms in the IC industry in order to compare and analyze if different enabling roles existed in related industries. This case study contributes to the validity and transferability of qualitative findings (Lincoln & Guba, 1985).

As to the reason for case selection, Winbond and TSMC were selected because of their reputation for KM practice. Winbond is the largest IC designer in Taiwan's IC industry, while TSMC is the world's largest and most successful dedicated independent semiconductor foundry. The case in the IC distribution sector, WorldPeace, was selected because it is one of a tiny minority in the sector that really puts KM into practice and gains competitive advantage from this implementation. WorldPeace was ranked as top electronics components distributor and recognized for outstanding service by Micro Electronics, one of the key electronics-oriented trade media in Taiwan. We had three interviews at WorldPeace, with the Corporate Vice President, Associate Vice President of Corporate Marketing and Communication Office, and Assistant Manager of Knowledge Management, respectively. Each of the interviews took about two hours. The interviews were tape-recorded, transcribed, and analyzed. The three interviews were conducted over a two-month period.

The sources of evidence for case studies could be documentation, archival records, interviews, direct observations, participant-observation, and physical artifacts (Yin, 1994). As the research began, the authors wrote to Winbond, World-Peace, and TSMC for interviews. However, as is known to all, the engineers and managers in this industry are extremely busy, too much so to provide interviews. Though the authors tried to arrange interviews many times; nevertheless, the managers in Winbond and TSMC were not available to be interviewed. In personal interviewing, it often occurs that researchers can not locate the persons whom they are supposed to study (Cooper & Schindler, 2001). In this regard, case data about Winbond and TSMC was collected from multiple resources, including journals, chapters in published books, doctoral dissertations, company profiles, documents from the firms, information on the websites and knowledge portals, books published in Taiwan, and internal documents.

A chain of evidence was formed to keep track of the processes of implementing KM in Winbond, Worldpeace, and TSMC to control the construct validity of the study. Data and content was collected and analyzed systematically. The case study protocol and database were applied in this study to control the reliability. The case study protocol consists of the following sections: overview of the case study project, field procedures, case study questions, and guide for the case study report. It is a major tactic in increasing the reliability of case study research and is intended to guide the researchers in carrying out a case study. Moreover, the application of a case study database could help other investigators review the evidence directly and not be limited to the written reports. In this regard, a case study database could increase the reliability of the entire case study (Yin, 1994).

CASE STUDY: WINBOND, WORLDPEACE, AND TSMC

Three cases, Winbond, Worldpeace, and TSMC were used to illustrate how they implement KM, showing the different enabling roles of KM in the

upstream, midstream, and downstream firms in the IC supply chain. We adopted the model modified from Alavi and Leidner (2001) to describe and analyze the implementations of KM in terms of knowledge creation, storage/retrieval, transfer and application.

Winbond:Company Overview

Winbond Electronics Corporation, established in 1987 in the Hsin-Chu Science-based Industrial Park, Taiwan, is the largest brand name IC designer in search of excellence in process technology, worldwide marketing networks and wafer processing. Their products include PC and peripheral ICs, micro-based consumer ICs, Network Access ICs, Memory ICs, etc. Winbond, on the average, invests more than 10 percent of annual revenue into R&D and has built on its extensive technical knowledge and technological experiences. For the past few years, Winbond investment in R&D has yielded substantial growth in technology and helped it to forge strategic alliances, combining R&D with leading global companies. R&D centers have been setup in China and the United States, both tasked with aggressively absorbing new market trends. Winbond's depth in design IP, combined with skilled production capability, allows the company to effectively leverage its efforts in a number of growing markets.

Winbond: Knowledge Management Practices

1. Knowledge Creation: Since 1991, Winbond has been honored annually with the receipt of 'R&D Investment Award' from the Hsinchu Science-Based Park. The company has a long history of KM and patent production worldwide; already surpassing one thousand patents. In 1999, Winbond became the winner of the Gold Medal of National Invention by the Taiwan Intellectual Property Office, Ministry of Economic Affairs. Winbond

has been named 'Outstanding Electronics Component Supplier' for two years in a row, and was also selected as the best performing desing/manufacturing company in Taiwan. Dr. Tauso, the manager of Knowledge Management, implied that company does emphasize the storage, transfer and application of knowledge rather than the creation of knowledge. This does not mean that Winbond ignores the importance of knowledge creation; in fact, Winbond is checking and counting its intangible assets first and foremost. If the knowledge is incorrect, out of date, or not suitable for use, the company may be compelled to engage in knowledge creation (Lu & Tsai, 2004).

2. Knowledge Storage/Retrieval: With the rapid change in the electronics industry, Winbond tends to collect and check knowledge, then store it in Winbond's knowledge bank after investigation and refinement by the technical board. As the invention of IC is highly specialized in varied fields of knowledge, the invention of new product designs requires clear standard interfaces and technical definitions within the IC framework. Thus, it is easy to transfer individual knowledge to codified knowledge, and accumulate it systematically. This crucial knowledge is standardized and stored in Winbond's knowledge systems for those who request it.

The knowledge systems comprise patents databases, learning materials and technical information, etc. Technical information is subdivided into debug/design reports, IP code and IP Map. Some IP and debug/design contents are designed to be online training courses to reduce the training time for newcomers. Most patent information is classified into company patents and market patents and is provided for administrators and executives as reference in making decisions. The evidence shows that Winbond pays much attention to knowledge storage/retrieval (Lu & Tsai, 2004).

3. Knowledge Transfer: Winbond's technical information and learning materials are full of explicit knowledge through which workers obtain knowledge and peers' experience through the Intranet at any time. Moreover, senior engineers' experiences can also be transferred to new employees through IP Map or Yellow Pages, when they are vague about the knowledge or need to check it out. The knowledge department plays a mediating role for workers to search for knowledge sources. As to knowledge that is unclear or of undefined value, Winbond provides an online forum to facilitate sharing implicit knowledge. This online forum is divided into two kinds – public and nonpublic – with some confidential issues reserved for qualified members only.

4. Knowledge Application: Winbond set up the Knowledge Management Center to advance product technology and improve service innovation for its core competence by applying knowledge. According to the statistics in the Knowledge Management Center, most engineers encountered similar problems in their work before; but now engineers need not waste time in solving the same problems or recommitting the same errors due to the functions of the center, which has reduced product defect rate to 2~3% and reduced the cycle time by 25%. This implies that Winbond takes advantage of organizational knowledge to improve the quality of products, lower defect rate and decrease cycle time of production, and utilizes organizational knowledge to lead the firm (Lu & Tsai, 2004).

Worldpeace: Company Overview

WorldPeace Group, established in Taipei, Taiwan in 1981, became an OTC listed-company in

1987 and a TSE-listed company (Taiwan Stock Exchange) in June 2000. Its capital was 0.97 billion USD in 2004, and its group sales in 2006 were 20 billion USD with over 40% growth rate. It is the largest, leading electronic component distributor in the Asia Pacific region; moreover, it was ranked the sixth-largest among top global semiconductor distributors worldwide by EBN (a dedicated semiconductor website) in its yearly selections in 2003. Worldpeace is building a solid distribution and service channel to grow with its customers. Its ultimate value resides in customers' satisfaction with its industry-leading services, such as technical support, logistic management and e-services.

Worldpeace was awarded No. 11 of top 500 service industry companies by Taiwan Common Wealth Magazine and was No. 1 in the information, communication, and IC distribution industry in 2005. Worldpeace builds close relationships with its suppliers, to reliably provide customers' IC components with high quality service at competitive prices. Worldpeace's primary products are ASSP, Central Processing Unit (CPU) / Micro Processing Unit (MPU), Memories, Logic Components, Linear Components, and Discrete Components.

Worldpeace: Knowledge Management Practice

1. Knowledge Creation: In the IC distribution industry, firms have to keep their knowledge consistent with their supply chain; that is, when their upstream firms or suppliers innovate or create new knowledge about IC products, the distributors must get that new knowledge instantly. However, many innovations occur and much new knowledge is created in the IC design industry, so, distributors have to work hard to keep up with their suppliers even though they seldom create knowledge by themselves. In order to provide the newest information and knowledge for

customers, Worldpeace keeps knowledge consistent with suppliers by being a so-called "mirror" of the knowledge creation of their suppliers. This means that the knowledge will be transferred by the IC designer to the distributor as it is created or devised. The distributor acts the same as the designer in knowledge creation; therefore, this way of learning from suppliers is called "mirror". On the other side, when new requirements from customers or information about market demand are generated, the distributor also has to acquire the knowledge. Besides acquiring the knowledge from suppliers and customers, Worldpeace plays an important role in transferring knowledge between upstream and downstream firms whenever knowledge is created.

In addition to the technical knowledge from suppliers, Worldpeace also creates market intelligence from customers. Worldpeace regards customers' suggestions and complaints as the material of knowledge creation. As a distributor, information regarding customers' status and propositions is extremely valuable to Worldpeace. Therefore, both suppliers and customers are critical sources of knowledge to Worldpeace.

2. Knowledge Storage/Retrieval: As distributors, they do not produce, but transfer manufacturers' products or services to customers, so they make profit by managing knowledge and information about products. In Worldpeace, knowledge and information are well stored in their database, and employees can retrieve it via intranet. Worldpeace will become a distributor for B2B e-commerce based on the KM platform of its self-developed information system that is named EIP (Enterprise Internal Portal). It established E-service for Customer Relationship Management (CRM) to greatly improve the transaction process. The information on status of order, accounts receivable, and customers' status is recorded in EIP.

A report must be completed when any project closes. The new knowledge, findings, specifics, and experiences in the case must be recorded. In particular, a "standard knowledge" mechanism is implemented before the knowledge or information is stored in EIP. For effective knowledge sharing and understanding, the knowledge in Worldpeace should be standardized. So, the engineers, salesmen and the employees of Worldpeace are educated to write a standard document when they store knowledge that they have learned or discovered. The policy of "standardized knowledge" is critical when implementing KM.

3. Knowledge Transfer: There are two approaches to transfer knowledge in Worldpeace. Explicit knowledge is stored in the EIP system in the standard format. Managers, engineers, salesmen, and employees can access the knowledge that they need according to their priority. Worldpeace, headquartered in Taipei, Taiwan, has a solid and complete Asia-Pacific service network. It has over 20 sales offices in Hong Kong, China, Singapore, Malaysia, Thailand, Philippines, Japan, and India, etc. around the greater China and Asia Pacific region. Employees everywhere can access the EIP system via Internet. This EIP system is divided into four sections presented in four colors: blue, green, red, and orange. The colors represent the headquarters, branches in Taiwan, branches in China, and branches in throughout the Asia Pacific, respectively. That is, employees can store and access the information and knowledge within the same color section.

The second approach is for implicit knowledge transfer. In the distribution industry, implicit knowledge could be the experience of sealing a business deal. The salesmen or managers, who are masters in making deals or marketing, are invited to give a lecture or speech for employees. Besides, some special or excellent cases will be studied to discover their characteristics, called "Worldpeace DNA". Associate Vice President of Corporate Marketing and Communication Office will study and decide which cases are worth publicizing. The case study will proceed, and Assistant Manager of Knowledge Management will interview the salesman or manager to complete this case study. After it is completed, it will be stored in the EIP system for Worldpeace employees' reference (Shen & Tsai, 2005).

4. Knowledge Application: There are three kinds of domain knowledge in the distribution industry: first, knowledge about products, meaning the nature of IC chips; second, knowledge about application, meaning the purpose, function and application of the products; finally, knowledge about system integration, which means how to integrate IC chips in a module or system. Therefore, distributors build the knowledge base of products first, then understand how and where to apply them. Then, they try to discover how to integrate different IC chips in a module.

Being distributors, they create value for customers by integrating chips from different suppliers in a module and providing total solutions that add value for their customers. Moreover, they emphasize the reuse and flow rate of knowledge. The margin cost will decrease progressively if they reuse their knowledge and intellectual property more frequently. Therefore, knowledge application is emphasized more in the distribution sector than other KM processes.

TSMC: Company Overview

TSMC, founded in 1987 and located in the Hsin-Chu Science-Based Industrial Park of Taiwan, is listed on the New York Stock Exchange as TSM.

As the first "pure play" foundry company, TSMC has experienced strong growth by being a true partner with its customers by manufacturing IC products for them. The evolution of advanced IC technology over the past decade has been so rapid that it has changed the ways that companies do business. Demands for faster time-to-market and design cycles have increased, as well as demands for higher speed and product quality. TSMC enhances its ability to serve its customers by operating, expanding and developing many new facilities.

TSMC: Knowledge Management Practice

1. Knowledge Creation: TSMC maintains stable relationships with their customers, has extended their production, innovated their service in eFoundry via the Internet, owns the most advanced process technologies and leads the market. The main reason for the constant growth is its positive investments in the innovation of technologies and the development of value innovation ability that enables TSMC to be the leader. To be more competitive, TSMC has concentrated its attention on the modification and the coordination of various technologies to decrease production costs, reduce its defect rate, cut down product cycle time, and improve productivity (Hung, 2001). TSMC is not only devoted to technical innovation but also to the innovation of customer service. Morris Chang, TSMC chairman, announced that TSMC is a customer-oriented service business, and he stresses the importance of service innovation. In July 2000, TSMC proposed the idea of eFoundry that allows their customers to be served via the Internet. The vision of eFoundry is to offer the best services for customers; that they can gain benefits from eFoundry without paying a lot for establishment and management. TSMC

offers customers a highly integrated supply chain management system with reliability, security, speed and transparency through strategic use of Information Technology. This innovative strategy has enabled TSMC to maintain its superior position and more competitive edge. TSMC continues to boost its learning capabilities and create new knowledge, such that its organizational learning occurs not necessarily because of the shortage of knowledge, but out of the desire to maintain its superior market position.

2. Knowledge Storage/Retrieval: Dr. Tsai, the President and Chief Operating Officer, drives the KM activities in TSMC and founded eight technical boards that are categorized according to the processes in the semiconductor industry. The workers have to join relevant technical boards to share information and knowledge. The manager of IC Design, Dr. Kao, indicates that TSMC should translate the records of the best machines, equipment and technical processes into know-how that can be shared, and then transfer that knowledge to the new foundry. He said, "The best knowledge in the world on building foundries is filed in our technical board." Every employee in each foundry would like to share the best technique and knowledge with others on the technical board. The technical board checks and reviews records, in which the experience of work will be encoded, stored and shared (Lu & Tsai, 2004).

3. Knowledge Transfer: TSMC promotes two approaches for knowledge transfer, sharing and collaboration. (a) Sharing: The experiences of engineers are codified and stored in the knowledge system. As the production process can be scientifically measured, it's easy to translate into explicit knowledge and to accumulate it. Besides the technical knowledge, information about decision-

making is also stored in the Documentation Center after review by the managers. Then, that information can be shared and referred to by the relevant workers. (b) Collaboration: TSMC builds communities among its departments to help the knowledge seeker track down the knowledge provider and request support. This is a social mechanism in which all workers can seek support from those experienced workers through the TSMC Yellow Pages (Hung, 2001). The effect of knowledge transfer in such a dynamic sharing mechanism is better than the static knowledge system. Through the combination of active knowledge network and static knowledge system, working knowledge is shared continuously. Sharing and collaboration improve the knowledge transfer in TSMC and help to create more new knowledge. It also enables the positive cycle of knowledge creation, storage and transfer.

4. Knowledge Application: TSMC's employees are urged to apply knowledge to their work and benefit from this. Owing to efficient KM, TSMC grew rapidly over the past 12 years, and there are five new factories still in the process of construction. As to process technology, TSMC developed 0.18 micron logic, copper process technology and the embedded process technology applied in sys-on-a-chip. TSMC provides support to the process technology and design of semiconductors to satisfy customers' needs. The primary process technology is 0.35 micron, but it will expand that technology from 0.25 micron to the advanced 0.18 micron at the same time for mass production. The advanced process technologies significantly cut down the production costs, so that TSMC has made great profit and gained competitive advantage in the world. The abilities of continuous improvement, learning and innovation lead to high efficiency in inte-

grating and coordinating the varied process technologies, and reduce the production cost, while achieving high product quality, low defect rate and short cycle time. The main reason for TSMC superiority is the concentration on technological evolution and innovation of new knowledge and process technology (Lu & Tsai, 2004).

DISCUSSION ABOUT THE DISTINCTNESS AMONG THE THREE CASES

Winbond's human resources are an important asset for the company to go from strength to high quality. It provides suitable working environment, competitive salaries and bonuses for its employees to keep talent in Winbond. In addition, Winbond provides 1200 training programs and more than 20 web-based training courses for employees to pursue further upgrades and learning. Winbond has formed a continuous-learning culture and many channels (like IP Map, Expert Yellow Pages) through which workers can solve their problems or seek for help based on their Knowledge Portal.

The president of Worldpeace attaches great importance to new technologies that enable or help their operation. For example, Worldpeace announced 2000 to be the first year of the e-commerce era, and started their electronic customer service system. The next year, they announced the first year of e-Group. Worldpeace has invested a lot of money in information systems and technologies. They developed their Management Information System (MIS) by themselves, and imported a knowledge management system in 2002. This proved that they are generous in technologies to serve customers and cooperate with suppliers.

TSMC's technological innovation is the wellspring of its growth and is vital to all sectors of the company, from strategic planning to management of technology and production. TSMC regards employees and shareholders as important constituents and its goal is to provide better benefits and salaries for employees. TSMC has implemented an open-style management system designed to keep all lines of communication free in the working environment. Employees should treat one another sincerely, honestly and cooperatively.

Winbond, Worldpeace and TSMC are famous high-tech companies in the world. Their implementation of knowledge management and the way they learn, serves as valuable references for other (IC-related) companies to consult regarding transforming into learning organizations. Their implementation of KM, the systems they apply, and the different enabling roles of KM among these related industries are important issues for both academicians and practitioners. This study provides practical implications and insights for business and research.

Insights from Case Studies

With the stiff global competition, high-tech companies face the challenge of shorter product life cycle, the rapid depreciation of tangible assets and discontinuous changes. It is essential for firms to put KM into practice positively and actively. Based on the literature and cases studies of Winbond, Worldpeace and TSMC, this study has found three *insights*. Table 1 shows the *comparison* of the case studies in terms of an enabling role of KM management in these organizations.

Insight 1. The enabling roles of KM processes may be different as they are implemented in the different but related sectors. That is, the firms in the IC design sector may focus more on knowledge storage/retrieval; then, they may place more attention on the knowledge creation process. Firms engaged in IC distributor may emphasize knowledge application and integration to create value-added service for customers while IC manufacturers may still focus on knowledge creation to innovate the newest and best technologies and manufacturing. Therefore, the emphases of KM processes may be different in different industries, despite them being related (See Table 2).

Insight 2. The strategies for knowledge management and practices probably differ because of different implementation stages; for example, Winbond does not focus mainly on creating knowledge but on checking and reviewing existent intangible assets because they are still in the early stage of implementing KM. However, TSMC has

Table 1. The comparison of case studies: Winbond, Worldpeace, and TSMC

Item comparison	Winbond	Worldpeace	TSMC
Industry	IC design	Semiconductor distributor	IC manufacturer
Enabling role of KM	Focus more on knowledge storage/retrieval (on knowledge checking)	Focus more on knowledge application, (on knowledge integration)	Focus more on knowledge creation, (on knowledge innovation)
Purposes of KM	Facilitate checking and counting the intangible asset of IC know-ledge by refinements	Integrate IC knowledge and technology, and provide value-added service for customers	Facilitate faster design cycle, time-to-market and high quality of product/ service
Competitive advantage via KM practices	Lower defect rate and shorten cycle time to cut down IC product cost. Reduce training cost and retain experience with added value	Provide value-added knowledge and information for customers, and market information for suppliers	Move toward customer-oriented service business via the eFoundry with advanced process technologies

Table 2. The comparison of the enabling roles in IC Designer, Distributor, and Manufacturer

		Knowledge Creation	Knowledge Storage / Retrieval	Knowledge Transfer	Knowledge Application
IC Designer	Winbond		✓		
IC Distributor	Worldpeace				✓
IC Manufacturer	TSMC	✓			

been implementing KM since 1999, so it makes much effort to create more technology knowledge in order to safeguard its leading advantage in the world marketplace.

Insight 3. People outside the IC distribution industry may consider that distributors just transact business; they do not have their own products, even though the scale of IC distributors has become greater. So an inaccurate notion exists that it is not necessary to innovate or put KM into practice in the distribution industry. The upstream and downstream firms of the IC industry have been implementing KM in their organizations for several years. However, there is still no research to discuss whether KM could be applied in the midstream firms. In this study, Worldpeace, indicates that KM is suitable to be implemented in the distribution industry to help firms to apply knowledge strategically and keep robust relationships with their suppliers and customers. The results of putting KM into practice also accelerated the products' time to market. Distributors have to implement KM more urgently than designers and manufacturers because they need to face the rapidly changing technologies of upstream firms and the different, changing requirements of downstream customers. A supply chain could profit and grow greater by implementing KM and applying knowledge efficiently in every link.

CONCLUSION AND SUGGESTIONS

This study indicated the different enabling roles in terms of knowledge creation, storage/

retrieval, transfer and application when businesses implement KM in upstream, midstream, and downstream firms in the IC industry. Three cases, Winbond, Worldpeace and TSMC were studied to suggest the different enabling role of KM processes in different sectors. Findings in this investigation indicate that IC designers may focus more on knowledge storage, while IC distributors pay more attention to knowledge application and IC manufacturers emphasize knowledge creation. Furthermore, the stages of the implementation may also affect the strategies and practices of KM. For example, Winbond focuses on the storage and retrieval of knowledge to check their intangible assets because they are still in the early stage of implementation of KM.

This article also points out the suitability for distributors to put KM into their practices. Distributors need to implement KM even more because they have to change and learn faster than their suppliers and customers to face the drastically changing and intensely competitive environment. To maximize the impact of KM processes, the implementation of work-flow design and information systems should reflect an understanding of the vital role that knowledge plays in contributing to improving the firm's performance and profitability and anticipating customers' intentions.

However, overall findings are difficult to infer from just a few cases and the generalization of the findings is limited to the context (Yin, 1994; Huberman and Miles, 2002). Future research may apply quantitative methods to consider or calculate the weight of KM processes when implementing KM in different industries. Besides, researchers could investigate the enabling roles of KM in other industries, even though it is usually discussed and implemented positively in high-tech industries.

REFERENCES

Alavi, M. & Leidner, D.E. (2001). Review: Knowledge management and knowledge management systems: Conceptual foundations and research issues. *MIS Quarterly*, *25*(1), 107-136.

Bhatt, G.D. (2001). Knowledge management in organizations: examining the interaction between technologies, techniques, and people. *Journal of Knowledge Management*, *5*(1), 68-75.

Breu, K., Ward, J. & Murray, P. (2000). Success factors in leveraging the corporate information and knowledge resource through internets. in Y. Malhotra (eds.), *Knowledge Management and Virtual Organizations*, pp. 306-320. USA: Idea Group Publishing.

Cooper, D.R. & Schindler, P.S. (2001). *Business Research Methods*, 7th edition, New York: McGraw-Hill.

Cross, R. & Baird, L. (2000). Technology is not enough: Improving performance by building organizational memory. *Sloan Management Review*, *41*(3), 69-78.

Daft, R.L. (1998). *Organization Theory and Design*, Ohio: South-Western.

Davenport, T.H. & Prusak, L. (1998). *Working knowledge: How organizations manage what they know*, Boston: Harvard Business School Press.

Demarest, M. (1997). Understanding knowledge management. *Long Range Planning*, *30*(3), 374-384.

Dixon, N.M. (1994). *The Organizational Learning Cycle: How We Can Learn Collectively*. New York: McGraw-Hill.

Drucker, P.F. (1993). *Post-Capitalist society*, Oxford: Butterworth Heinemann.

EI Sawy, O. A., Eriksson, I., Raven, A., & Carlsson, S. A. (2001). Understanding the nature of shared knowledge creation spaces around business processes: Precursors to process innovation implementation. *Journal of Technology Management*, *22*(1-3), 149-173

Ellis, C. A., Gibbs, S. J. & Rein, G. (1991). Groupware: Some issues and experiences. *Communications of the ACM*, *34*(1), 39-58.

Fulk, J. & Boyd, B. (1991). Emerging theories of communication in organizations. *Journal of Management*, *17*(2), 407-446.

Grant, R. & Baden-Fuller, C. (2004). A knowledge accessing theory of strategic alliances. *Journal of Management Studies*, *41*(1), 61-84.

Hansen, M.T., Nohria, N. & Tierney T. (1999). What's your strategy for managing knowledge? *Harvard Business Review*, *77*(2), 106-116.

Hauschild, S., Licht, T. & Stein, W. (2001). Creating a knowledge culture. *The McKinsey Quarterly*, *1*, 74-81.

Huber, G. (1991). Organizational learning: The contributing processes and the literatures. *Organization Science 2*(1), 88-115.

Huberman, A. M. & Miles, M. B. (2002). *The Qualitative Researcher's Companion*. Thousand Oaks, London: New Delhi: Sage Publications.

Hung, K.Y. (2001). *Knowledge Management Mechanisms and Enterprise's Innovation Ability: An Exploratory Study to Build A Positive Research Model*, unpublished doctoral dissertation, Graduate Institute of Business Administration, National Taiwan University.

Ishii, H., Kobayashi, M. & Arita, K. (1994). Iterative design of seamless collaboration media. *Communications of the ACM*, *37*(8), 83-97.

Johansen, R. (1988). *Groupware: Computer Support for Business Teams*, New York: Free Press.

Jolly, D. (2005). The exogamic nature of sino-foreign joint ventures. *Asia Pacific Journal of Management, 22* (3), 285-306.

Khamseh, H.M. & Jolly, D.R. (2008). Knowledge transfer in alliances: Determinant factors. *Journal of Knowledge Management, 12*(1), 37-50.

Kling, R. (1991). Cooperation, Coordination, and Control in Computer-Supported Work. *Communications of the ACM, 34*(12), 83-88.

Lange, T. (2006). The creation and management of knowledge: What can we learn from applying the principles of economics? *International Journal of Knowledge Management Studies, 1,* 7–17.

Lincoln, Y. & Guba, E. (1985). Designing a Naturalistic Inquiry. *Naturalistic Inquiry.* London: Sage Publications

Lu, J.C. & Tsai, C.W. (2004) An Investigation to an enabling role of knowledge management between learning organization and organizational learning. in Gupta, J. N. D. and Sharma, S. K. (eds.), *Creating Knowledge Based Organizations,* Idea Group Press, 278-297.

Maes, P. (1994). Agents that reduce work and information overload. *Communications of the ACM, 35*(11), 30-40.

Majchrzak, A., Rice, R.E., King, N., Malhotra, A. & Ba, S. (1999). Computer-mediated inter-organizational knowledge-sharing: Insights from a virtual team innovating using a collaborative tool. *Information Resources Management Journal, 13*(1), 44-53.

Malhotra, Y. (2000). Knowledge management & new organization forms: a framework for business model innovation. *Information Resources Management Journal, 13*(1), 5-14.

Metaxiotis, K. & Psarras, J. (2006). Analysing the value of knowledge management leading to innovation. *International Journal of Knowledge Management Studies, 1,* 79–89.

Nonaka, I. (1994). A dynamic theory of organizational knowledge creation. *Organization Science, 5*(1), 14-37.

Nonaka, I. & Takeuchi, H. (1995). *The Knowledge-Creating Company,* New York: Oxford University Press.

Nunamaker, J., Briggs, R. & Mittleman, D. (1995). Electronic meeting systems: Ten years of lessons learned. in D. Coleman and R. Khanna (eds) *Groupware: Technology and Applications*, pp. 149-193. Englewood Cliffs, NJ: Prentice-Hall.

Parker, K.R. & Nitse, P.S. (2005). Improving competitive intelligence for knowledge management systems. *International Journal of Internet and Enterprise Management, 3*(1), 24–45.

Pauleen, D. (2004). *Virtual teams: Projects, protocols and processes.* Hershey: PA., Idea Publishing Group.

Pedler, M., Boydell, T. & Burgoyne, J. (1988). *Learning company project report*, Train Lund, Sweden.

Pentland, B.T. (1995). Information systems and organizational learning: The social epistemology of organizational knowledge systems. *Account, Management and Information Technologies, 5*(1), 1-21.

Prokesch, S.E. (1997) Unleashing the power of learning: An interview with British Petroleum's John Browne. *Harvard Business Review, 75*(5), 5-19.

Romano, N. Jr., Nunamaker, J., Briggs, R. & Vogel, D. (1998). Architecture, design, and development of an html/javascript web-based group support system. *Journal of the American Society for Information Science, 49*(7), 649-667.

Saffady, W. (2000). Knowledge management: An overview. *Information Management Journal, 34*(3), 4-8.

Shen, P.D. & Tsai, C.W. (2005) A case study on the web-based knowledge management model – The EIP in Worldpeace. in Dasgupta, S. (eds.), *Encyclopedia of Virtual Communities and Technologies*, Idea Group Press, 278-297.

Soekijad, M. & Andriessen, M. (2003). Conditions for knowledge sharing in competitive alliances. *European Management Journal, 21*(5), 578-587.

Stein, E.W. & Zwass, V. (1995). Actualizing organizational memory with information systems. *Information Systems Research, 6*(2), 85-117.

Sveiby, K.E. (1997). *The New Organizational Wealth: Managing & Measuring Knowledge-based Assets*, San Francisco, Calif.: Berrett-Koehler Publishes.

Tan, S.S., Teo, H.H., Tan, B.C., & Wei, K.K. (1998). Developing a preliminary framework for knowledge management in organizations. in *Proceedings of the Fourth Americas Conference on Information Systems*, Hoadley, E. and Benbasat I. (eds) Baltimore, MD, 14 to 16 August, pp. 629-631.

Thornton, C. & Lockhart, E. (1994). Groupware or electronic brainstorming. *Journal of Systems Management, 45*(10), 10-12.

Thurow, L.C. (1999). *Building Wealth: The New Rules for Individuals, Companies, and Nation in A Knowledge-based Economy*, New York: Harper Collins.

Vance, D. & Eynon, J. (1998). On the requirements of knowledge-transfer using is: A schema whereby such transfer is enhanced. In *Proceeding of the Fourth Americas Conference on Information Systems*, E. Hoadley and I. Benbasat (eds.), Baltimore, MD, 632-634.

von Krogh, G. (1998). Care in knowledge creation. *California Management Review, 40*(3), 133-153.

Webster, J. & Trevino, L.K. (1995). Rational and social theories as complementary explanations of communication media choices: Two policy-capturing studies. *Academy of Management Journal, 38*(6), 1544-1572.

Yeung A.K., Ulrich D. O., Nason S.W., & von Ginow M.A. (1999). *Organizational Learning Capability*, New York: Oxford University Press.

Yin, R.K. (1994). *Case Study Research Design and Methods*, 2nd. Thousand Oaks, CA: Sage.

This work was previously published in International Journal of E-Adoption, Volume 1, Issue 1, edited by Sushil Sharma, pp. 47-61, copyright 2009 by IGI Publishing (an imprint of IGI Global).

Compilation of References

Ab Hamid, N. R. (2005). E-CRM: Are we there yet? *The Journal of American Academy of Business*, *6*(1), 51–57.

Ab Hamid, N. R., & Kassim, N. (2004). Internet technology as a tool in customer relationship management. *The Journal of American Academy of Business*, *4*(1/2), 103–108.

Acar, E., Koçak, I., Sey, Y., & Arditi, D. (2005). Use of information and communication technologies by small and medium-sized enterprises (SMEs) in building construction. *Construction Management and Economics*, *23*(7), 713–722. doi:10.1080/01446190500127112

Acquisti, A., Gritzalis, S., Lambrinoudakis, C., & De Capitani di Vimercati, S. (2007). *Digital Privacy: Theory, Technologies, and Practices*. New York: Auerbach Publications, Taylor and Francis Group.

Adams, D. A., Nelson, R. R., & Todd, P. A. (1992). Perceived usefulness, ease of use, and usage of information technology: A replication. *MIS Quarterly*, *16*(2), 227–247. doi:10.2307/249577

Adebanjo, D. (2003). Classifying and selecting e-CRM applications: An analysis-based proposal. *Management Decision*, *41*(6), 570–577. doi:10.1108/00251740310491517

Agarwal, R., & Karahanna, E. (2000). Time flies when you're having fun: Cognitive absorption and beliefs about information technology usage. *MIS Quarterly*, *24*(4), 665–694. doi:10.2307/3250951

Agarwal, R., & Prasad, J. (1999). Are individual differences germane to the acceptance of new Information Technologies? *Decision Sciences*, *30*(2), 361–391. doi:10.1111/j.1540-5915.1999.tb01614.x

Agarwal, R., & Prasad, J. (1997). The role of innovation characteristics and perceived voluntariness in the acceptance of information technologies. *Decision Sciences*, *28*(3), 557–582. doi:10.1111/j.1540-5915.1997.tb01322.x

Agarwal, R., & Prasad, J. (1998). A conceptual and operational definition of personal innovativeness in the domain of information technology. *Information Systems Research*, *9*(2), 204–215. doi:10.1287/isre.9.2.204

Ainin, S., & Rohana, J. (2000). *E-commerce implementation in Malaysian manufacturing sector*. International Conference on Electronic Commerce. Kuala Lumpur, Malaysia.

Ajzen, I. (1991). The theory of planned behavior. *Organizational Behavior and Human Decision Processes*, *50*, 179–211. doi:10.1016/0749-5978(91)90020-T

Ajzen, I. (2001). Nature and operation of attitudes. *Annual Review of Psychology*, *52*, 27–58. doi:10.1146/annurev.psych.52.1.27

Ajzen, I., & Fishbein, M. (1980). *Understanding attitudes and predicting social behavior*. Englewood Cliffs, NJ: Prentice-Hall.

Akhter, S. H. (2003). Digital divide and purchase intention: Why demographic psychology matters? *Journal of Economic Psychology*, *24*(3), 321–327. doi:10.1016/S0167-4870(02)00171-X

Alam, S. S., Khatibi, A., Sayyed Ahmad, M. I., & Ismail, H. (2007). Factors affecting e-commerce adoption in the electronic manufacturing companies in Malaysia. *International Journal of Commerce and Management*, *17*(1/2), 125–139. doi:10.1108/10569210710776503

Alam, S. S., & Ahsan, M. N. (2007). ICT adoption in Malaysian SMEs from services sectors: Preliminary findings. *Journal of Internet Banking and Commerce, 12*(3). Retrieved May 12, 2009, from http://www.arraydev.com/commerce/jibc/2007-12/ Syed_accepted.pdf

Alam, S. S., Ahmad, I., Abdullah, Z., & Ishak, N. A. (2007). ICT usage in SMEs: Empirical study of service sectors in Malaysia. In *Proceedings of the 4th SMEs in a Global Economy Conference,* Shah Alam, Malaysia.

Alba, J. W., Lynch, J., Weitz, B., Janiszewski, C., Lutz, R., & Sawyer, A. (1997). Interactive home shopping: Consumer, retailer, and manufacturer incentives to participate in electronic marketplaces. *Journal of Marketing, 61*(3), 38–53. doi:10.2307/1251788

Albanese, R., Lieb, J., & Stewart, J. (Producers). (2009, March 2). The Daily Show with Jon Stewart [Episode #14029]. *Twitter frenzy.* Podcast retrieved on May 3, 2009, from http://www.thedailyshow.com/video/index.jhtml?videoId=219519&title=twitter-frenzy

Albers-Miller, N., & Gelb, B. (1996). Business advertising appeals as mirror of cultural dimensions: A study of eleven countries. *Journal of Advertising, 25*(Winter), 57–70.

Alexander, S. (2001). E-learning developments and experience. *Education + Training, 43*(4/5), 240-248.

Al-Kinani, A. N., & Al-Besher, B. M. N. (2008). Analysis study of culture's impact on e-readiness assessments in developing countries. *Communications of the IBIMA, 6,* 154–164.

Allinson, G., Braidford, P., Grewer, N., Houston, M., Orange, R., Leigh Sear, R., & Stone, I. (2004) *Ethnic minority businesses and ICT, focus group research.* Durham Business School for SBS. Retrieved May 2, 2008, from http://www.sbs.gov.uk/SBS_Gov_files/researchandstats/EMB_and_ICT.pdf

Al-mutawkkil, A., Heshmati, A., & Hwang, J. (2009). Development of telecommunication and broadcasting infrastructure indices at the global level. *Telecommunications Policy, 33,* 176–199. doi:10.1016/j.telpol.2008.12.008

Alonso Mendo, F., & Fitzgerald, G. (2005a). A multidimensional framework for SME e-business progression. *Journal of Enterprise Information Management, 18*(6), 678–696. doi:10.1108/17410390510628382

Alonso Mendo, F., & Fitzgerald, G. (2005b). Theoretical approaches to study SMEs e-business progression. *Journal of Computing and Information Technology, 13*(2), 123–136. doi:10.2498/cit.2005.02.04

Alsajjan, B., & Dennis, C. (2010). Internet banking acceptance model: Cross-market examination. *Journal of Business Research, 63*(9-10), 957–963. doi:10.1016/j.jbusres.2008.12.014

Al-Solbi, A., & Mayhew, P. (2005). Measuring e-readiness assessment in Saudi organizations: Preliminary results from a survey study. The *Proceedings of the First European Conference on Mobile Government,* 10-12 July 2005, University of Sussex Brighton, UK.

Al-Somali, S. A., Gholami, R., & Clegg, B. (2009). An investigation into the acceptance of online banking in Saudi Arabia. *Technovation, 29*(2), 130–141. doi:10.1016/j.technovation.2008.07.004

Alzougool, B., & Kurnia, S. (2008). Electronic commerce technologies adoption by SMEs: A conceptual study. In *proceedings of the 19th Australasian Conference on Information Systems,* Christchurch, New Zealand.

Aminali, P. (2007). *E-readiness assessment within Iran's automotive Industry: Case of Iran Khodro Industrial Group.* Master Thesis, Luleå University of Technology, Sweden.

AMI-Partners. (2004). The SMB Global Model [Electronic Version] from http://www.ami-partners.com.

Amoroso, D. (2002). Successful penetration into the e-business environment: An empirical study. In *Proceedings of the 36th Annual Hawaii International Conference on System Sciences,* Kona-Kailua, HI (vol. 8, pp. 257). Washington, DC: IEEE Computer Society.

Amoroso, D., & Gardner, C. (2003, January). Development of an instrument to measure the acceptance of Internet technology by consumers. In *Proceedings of the 37th Annual Hawaii International Conference on System Sciences,* Big Island, HI (vol. 8, pp. 80260c). Washington, DC: IEEE Computer Society.

Analoui, F., & Karami, A. (2003). *Strategic Management in SMEs.* London: Thomson Learning.

Anderson, R., & Huang, W.-Y. (2006). Empowering salespeople: Personal, managerial, and organizational perspectives. *Psychology and Marketing, 23*(2), 139–159. doi:10.1002/mar.20104

Anderson, R., & Srinivasan, S. S. (2003). E-satisfaction and e-loyalty: A contingency framework. *Psychology and Marketing, 20*(2), 123–138. doi:10.1002/mar.10063

Anderson, C., Day, K., Haywood, D., Heywood, J., Land, R., & Macleod, H. (2002). Evaluating networked learning: Developing a multi-disciplinary, multi-method approach. In Steeples, C., & Jones, C. (Eds.), *Networked learning: Perspectives and issues* (pp. 169–192). London, UK: Springer-Verlag.

Anderson, J. E., & Schwager, P. H. (2003). *SMEs Adoption of Wireless LAN Technology: Applying UTAUT Model.* Proceedings of the 7th Annual Conference of the Southern Association for Information Systems.

Andries, P., & Debackere, K. (2006). Adaptation in new technology-based ventures: Insights at the company level. *International Journal of Management Reviews, 8*(2), 91–112. doi:10.1111/j.1468-2370.2006.00122.x

Anonymous. (2003). Canon creates a successful blend with e-learning-Ignoring the hype and focusing on the method. *Development and Learning in Organizations, 17*(1), 23–26. doi:10.1108/14777280310795711

Arbore, A., & Ordanini, A. (2006). Broadband divide among SMEs: The role of size, location and outsourcing strategies. *International Small Business Journal, 24*(1), 83–99. doi:10.1177/0266242606059781

Archibugi, D., & Coco, A. (2004). A new indicator of technological capabilities for developed and developing countries (ArCo). *World Development, 32*(4), 629–654. doi:10.1016/j.worlddev.2003.10.008

Arnott, D. C., & Bridgewater, S. (2002). Internet interaction and implications for marketing. *Marketing Intelligence & Planning, 20*(2), 86–95. doi:10.1108/02634500210418509

Ash, C., & Bacsich, P. (2000). A new cost analysis model for networked learning. Proceedings of the European Distance Education Network (EDEN) Conference (pp. 208–210). Prague, Czech Republic, 16–17 March.

Asian Pacific Economic Corporation (APEC). (1999). *SME electronic commerce study.* (TEL09/97T) Final Report, September 24.

Asian Pacific Economic Corporation (APEC). (2000). *E-commerce readiness assessment guide.* Hong Kong, China: APEC. Retrieved from http://www.ecommerce.gov/apec/

Asokan, N. Janson, Phillipe A., Steiner, Michael, Waidner, Michael (1997). The State of the Art in Electronic Payment Systems, from http://www.semper.org/sirene/publ/AJSW_97PayOver.IEEE.pdf

Association of Southeast Asian Nations (ASEAN). (2001). *E-ASEAN readiness assessment.* Retrieved from http://www.unpan1.un.org

Athiyaman, A. (2002). Internet users' intention of purchase air travel online: An empirical investigation. *Marketing Intelligence & Planning, 20*(3-4), 234–243. doi:10.1108/02634500210431630

Attaran, M. (2001). The coming age of online procurement. *Industrial Management & Data Systems, 101*(4), 177–180. doi:10.1108/02635570110390080

Audretsch, D. B., & Thurik, A. R. (2001). What is new about the new economy? Sources of growth in the managed and entrepreneurial economies. *Industrial and Corporate Change, 10*(1), 17–34. doi:10.1093/icc/10.1.267

Bagchi, K. (2005). Factors contributing to global digital divide: Some empirical results. *Journal of Global Information Technology Management, 8*(1), 47–65.

Baggozi, R., & Lee, K. H. (1999). Consumer resistance to, and acceptance of, innovations. *Advances in Consumer Research. Association for Consumer Research (U. S.), 26*, 218–225.

Baker & McKenzie. (2001). *Doing E-Commerce in Europe.* Hong Kong: Baker and McKenzie.

Ballantine, J., Levy, M., & Powell, P. (2005). Evaluation Information Systems in small and medium-sized enterprises: Issues and evidence. *European Journal of Information Systems, 7*(4), 241–251. doi:10.1057/palgrave.ejis.3000307

Bandura, A. (1977). Self-efficacy: Toward a unifying theory of behavioral vhange. *Psychological Review*, *84*, 191–215. doi:10.1037/0033-295X.84.2.191

Bandura, A. (1982). Self-efficacy mechanism in human agency. *The American Psychologist*, *37*(2), 122–147. doi:10.1037/0003-066X.37.2.122

Banks, E. (2000). *e-Finance: The electronic Revolution.* New York: Wiley.

Bantel, K. A., & Jackson, S. E. (1989). Top management and innovations in banking: Does the composition of the top management team make a difference? *Strategic Management Journal*, *10*, 107–124. doi:10.1002/smj.4250100709

Barabasi, A. L., & Bonabeay, E. (2003, May). Scale-free networks. *Scientific American*, *288*(5), 60–70. doi:10.1038/scientificamerican0503-60

Barclay, D. W., Thompson, R., & Higgins, C. (1995). The partial least squares (PLS) approach to causal modeling: Personal computer adoption and use-An illustration. *Technology Studies*, *2*(2), 285–309.

Barnett, R. R., & Mackness, J. R. (1983). *An Action Research Study of Small Firm Management Journal of Applied Systems*, *10*, 63–83.

Baronas, A. K., & Louis, M. R. (1998). Restoring a Sense of Control during Implementation: How Users Involvement Leads to System Acceptance. *Management Information Systems Quarterly*, *12*(1), 111–124. doi:10.2307/248811

Barry, H., & Milner, B. (2002). SME's and Electronic Commerce: A Departure from the Traditional Prioritisation of Training? *Journal of European Industrial Training*, *25*(7), 316–326. doi:10.1108/03090590210432660

Barua, A., & Lee, B. (1997). An economic analysis of the introduction of an electronic data interchange system. *Information Systems Research*, *8*(4), 321–341. doi:10.1287/isre.8.4.398

Barua, A., Konana, P., Whinston, A., & Yin, F. (2000). *Assessing Internet enabled business value: An exploratory investigation.* Working paper. Austin, TX: Center of Research in Electronic Commerce, the University of Texas at Austin.

Barzilai-Nahon, K. (2006). Gaps and bits: Conceptualizing measurements for digital divide/s. *The Information Society, 22*)5), 269–278.

Bassellier, G., Benbasat, I., & Reich, B. H. (2003). The influence of business managers' IT competences on championing IT. *Information Systems Research*, *14*(4), 317–336. doi:10.1287/isre.14.4.317.24899

Bassi, L. (2000). How much does e-learning cost? Retrieved September 15, 2010, from http://www.linezine.com/2.1/features/lbhmec.htm

Bates, A. W. (2005). *Technology, open learning and distance education* (2nd ed.). London, UK: Routledge.

Bauer, H. H., Gretner, M., & Leach, M. (2002). Building customer relations over the Internet. *Industrial Marketing Management*, *31*(2), 155–163. doi:10.1016/S0019-8501(01)00186-9

Baumeister, H. (2002, October). Customer Relationship Management for SMEs, e2000 e-business & e-work. *Proceedings of the E2002 Conference*, Prague.

Bayo-Moriones, A., & Lera-López, F. (2007). A firm-level analysis of determinants of ICT adoption in Spain. *Technovation, 27*(6/7), 352–366. doi:10.1016/j.technovation.2007.01.003

Beaver, G. (2007). The strategy payoff for smaller enterprises. *The Journal of Business Strategy*, *28*(1), 11–17. doi:10.1108/02756660710723161

Beckinsale, M. J. J., Levy, M., & Powell, P. (2006). Exploring Internet adoption drivers in SMEs. *Electronic Markets – International Journal (Toronto, Ont.)*, *16*(4), 361–370.

Beckinsale, M. J. J., & Ram, M. (2006). Delivering ICT to ethnic minority businesses: An action research approach. *Environment and Planning. C, Government & Policy*, *24*(6), 847–867. doi:10.1068/c0559

Beckinsale, M. J. J., & Levy, M. (2002). *Hi-tech entrepreneurs and the Internet.* Paper presented at the 10th Annual International Conference High Technology Small Firms Conference, Twente University, 10-11 June 2002, Netherlands.

Beckinsale, M. J. J., & Ram, M. (2008). *SME/EMB action research: A framework for ICT policy driven initiatives* ®. Paper presented at the 31st Institute for Small Business and Entrepreneurship, Nov 5th-Nov 7th, Belfast, Ireland.

Beekhuyzen, J. P., & Von Hellens, L. A. (2006), An actor-network theory perspective of online banking in Australia, Proceedings of the American Conference on Information Systems

Beethika, S. K. (2004). Consumers Adoption of Online Banking: Does Distance Matters? Economic University of California, Berkeley, Working Paper E04-338

Beilock, R., & Dimitrova, D. V. (2003). An exploratory model of inter-country Internet diffusion. *Telecommunications Policy*, 27(3-4), 237–252. doi:10.1016/S0308-5961(02)00100-3

Bélanger, F., & Carter, L. (2008). Trust and risk in e-government adoption. *The Journal of Strategic Information Systems*, 17(2), 165–176. doi:10.1016/j.jsis.2007.12.002

Bengtsson, M., Boter, H., & Vanyushyn, V. (2007). Integrating the Internet and marketing operations: A study of antecedents in firms of different size. *International Small Business Journal*, 25(2), 27–48. doi:10.1177/0266242607071780

Bennet, A., & Bennet, D. (2008). E-learning as energetic learning. *The Journal of Information and Knowledge Management Systems*, 38(2), 206–220.

Berry, L. L. (1995). Relationship marketing of services – Growing interest, emerging perspectives. *Journal of the Academy of Marketing Science*, 23, 236–245. doi:10.1177/009207039502300402

Berthon, P., Pitt, L., & Watson, R. (1996). The World Wide Web as an advertising medium: Toward an understanding of conversion efficiency. *Journal of Advertising Research*, 36(1), 43–54.

Beynon-Davies, P. (2004). *E-business*. New York, NY: Palgrave Macmillan. Blackburn, R., & McClure, R. (1998). *The use of Information Communication Technologies (ICTs) in small business service firms*. Small Business Research Centre, Kingston Business School.

Bhagwat, R., & Sharma, M. K. (2007). Information System architecture: A framework for a cluster of small and medium-sized enterprises (SMEs). *Production Planning and Control*, 18(4), 283–296. doi:10.1080/09537280701248578

Bhatnagar, A., Misra, S., & Rao, H. R. (2000). On risk, convenience, and Internet shopping behavior. *Communications of the ACM*, 43(11), 98–105. doi:10.1145/353360.353371

Bhattacherjee, A. (2000). Acceptance of e-commerce services: The case of electronic brokerages. *IEEE Transactions on Systems, Man, and Cybernetics. Part A, Systems and Humans*, 30(4), 411–420. doi:10.1109/3468.852435

Bhattacherjee, A., & Pregmkumar, G. (2004). Understanding changes in belief and attitude toward information technology usage: A theoretical model and longitudinal test. *MIS Quarterly*, 28(2), 229–254.

Billon, M., Lera-Lopez, L., & Marco, R. (2010). Differences in digitalization levels: A multivariate analysis studying the global digital divide. *Rev World Econ*, 146, 39–73. doi:10.1007/s10290-009-0045-y

Bitner, M. J., Brown, S. W., & Meuter, M. L. (2000). Technology infusion in service encounters. *Journal of the Academy of Marketing Science*, 28(1), 138–149. doi:10.1177/0092070300281013

Blackburn, R., & Athayde, R. (2000). Making the connection: The effectiveness of Internet training in small business. *Education and Training*, 42(4/5), 289–299. doi:10.1108/00400910010373723

Blankson, C., & Stokes, D. (2002). Marketing practices in the UK small business sector. *Marketing Intelligence & Planning*, 20(1), 49–61. doi:10.1108/02634500210414774

Boettcher, J. V. (2004). Online course development: What does it cost? Campus Technology. Retrieved September 15, 2010, from http://connect.educause.edu/Library/Abstract/OnlineCourseDevelopmentWh/35735?time=1204536851

Bolongkikit, J., Obit, J. H., Asing, J. G., & Tanakinjal, G. H. (2006). An exploratory research of the usage level of E-commerce among SMEs in the West Coast of Sabah, Malaysia. *Journal of Internet Banking and Commerce*, 11(2).

Borreguero, F. J. M., & Pelaez, J. C. (2005), Spanish mobile banking services: an adoption study, International Conference on Mobile Business, 2005. ICMB 2005. 274- 280

Bose, K. (2003). An e-learning experience – A written analysis based on my experience in an e-learning pilot project. *Campus-Wide Information Systems, 20*(5), 193–199. doi:10.1108/10650740310507399

Boulding, W., Staelin, R., Ehret, M., & Johnston, W. J. (2005). A customer relationship management roadmap: What is known, potential pitfalls, and where to go. *Journal of Marketing, 69*(4), 155–166. doi:10.1509/jmkg.2005.69.4.155

Bowles, M. S. (2004). *Relearning to e-learn: Strategies for electronic learning and knowledge*. Victoria, Australia: Melbourne University Press.

Bradshaw, D., & Brash, C. (2001). Managing customer relationships in the e-business world: How to personalise computer relationships for increased profitability. *International Journal of Retail & Distribution Management, 29*(11/12), 520. doi:10.1108/09590550110696969

Brandley, L., & Stewart, K. (2003). A Delphi Study of the Drivers and Inhibitors of Internet Banking. *International Journal of Bank Marketing, 20*(6), 250–260. doi:10.1108/02652320210446715

Briedenhann, J., & Wickens, E. (2004). Tourism routes as a tool for the economic development of rural areas – Vibrant hope or impossible dream? *Tourism Management, 25*(1), 71–79. doi:10.1016/S0261-5177(03)00063-3

Brock, J. K. (2000). Information and Communication Technology in the Small Firm. In Jones-Evans, D., & Carter, S. (Eds.), *Enterprise and Small Business: Principles, Practice and Policy* (pp. 384–408). Harlow, England: FT - Prentice Hall.

Brodie, R. J., Winklhofer, H., Coviello, N. E., & Johnston, W. J. (2007). Is E-marketing coming of age? An examination of e-marketing and firm performance. *Journal of Interactive Marketing, 21*(1), 3–21. doi:10.1002/dir.20071

Brown, D. H., & Lockett, N. (2001). Engaging SMEs in EBusiness: The Role of Intermediaries within eClusters. *Electronic Markets, 11*(1), 52–58. doi:10.1080/10196780151105429

Brown, D. H., & Lockett, N. (2004). Potential of Critical e-Applications for Engaging SMEs in e-Business: A Provider Perspective. *European Journal of Information Systems, 13*(1), 21–34. doi:10.1057/palgrave.ejis.3000480

Bruce, B. (1999). Speaking the unspeakable about 21st century technologies. In Hawisher, G. E., & Selfe, C. L. (Eds.), *Passions, pedagogies, and 21st century technologies. Logan, UT/Urbana*. IL: Utah State University Press and NCTE.

Brunner, C., & Bennett, D. (1998). Technology perceptions by gender. *Education Digest*, (February): 56–58.

Bruque, S., & Moyano, J. (2007). Organisational determinants of Information Technology adoption and implementation in SMEs: The case of family and cooperative firms. *Technovation, 27*(5), 241–253. doi:10.1016/j.technovation.2006.12.003

Buck, P. S. (1996). Electronic commerce – would, could and should you use current Internet payment mechanisms. *Internet Research, 6*, 5–18. doi:10.1108/10662249610127283

Buck, P. S. (1997). From Electronic money to electronic cash: payment on the Net. *Logistic Information Management., 10*(6), 289–299. doi:10.1108/09576059710187429

Bui, T., Sankaran, S., & Sebastian, I. M. (2003). A framework for measuring national e-readiness. *International Journal of Electronic Business, 1*(1), 3–22. doi:10.1504/IJEB.2003.002162

Bull, C. (2003). Strategic issues in customer relationship management (CRM) implementation. *Business Process Management Journal, 9*(5), 592–602. doi:10.1108/14637150310496703

Bunker, D. J., & MacGregor, R. C. (2000). *Small Generation of Information Technology (IT) Requirements for Small/Medium Enterprises (SME's) - Cases from Regional Australia*. Proceedings of SMEs in a Global Economy, Wollongong, Australia.

Buonanno, G., Faverio, P., Pigni, F., Ravarini, A., Sciuto, D., & Tagliavini, M. (2005). Factors Affecting ERP System Adoption: A Comparative Analysis Between SMEs and Large Companies *Journal of Enterprise Information Management, 18*(4), 384-426.

Burke, R. R. (2002). Technology and the customer interface: What consumers want in the physical and virtual store. *Academy of Marketing Science, 30*(4), 411–432. doi:10.1177/009207002236914

Burnham, B. (1996). *The Internet's impact on retail banking* (Booz-Allen Hamilton 3ʳᵈ Quarter Rep.). Retrieved from http://www.strategy-business.com /briefs/96301/

Buttle, F. (2004). *Customer relationship management, concepts and tools*. Oxford, UK: Elsevier, Butterworth, Heinemann.

Caldeira, M. M., & Ward, J. M. (2003). Using resource-based theory to interpret the successful adoption and use of Information Systems and Technology in manufacturing small and medium-sized enterprises. *European Journal of Information Systems, 12*(2), 127–141. doi:10.1057/palgrave.ejis.3000454

Carey, J. M., & Day, D. (2005). *Cultural aspects for technology acceptance: Asian perspectives and research techniques*. Paper presented at the Americas Conference on Information Systems, Omaha, NE.

Carree, M., van Stel, A., Thurik, R., & Wennekers, S. (2002). Economic development and business ownership: An analysis using data of 23 OECD countries in the period 1976-1996. *Small Business Economics, 19*(3), 271–290. doi:10.1023/A:1019604426387

Carson, D., Cromie, S., McGowan, P., & Hill, J. (1995). *Marketing and entrepreneurship in SMEs*. Englewood Cliffs, NJ: Prentice-Hall.

Carson, D., & Gilmore, A. (2000). Marketing at the interface: Not 'what' but 'how.' *Journal of Marketing Theory and Practice, 8*(2), 1–8.

Carter, N. M., & Allen, K. R. (1997). Size determinants of women-owned businesses: Choice or barriers to resources? *Entrepreneurship and Regional Development, 9*(3), 211–220. doi:10.1080/08985629700000012

Carter, L., & Bélanger, F. (2005). The utilization of e-government services: Citizen trust, innovation and acceptance factors. *Information Systems Journal, 15*(1), 5–25. doi:10.1111/j.1365-2575.2005.00183.x

Carter, S., & Bennett, D. (2006). Gender and entrepreneurship. In Carter, S., & Jones-Evans, D. (Eds.), *Enterprise and small business: Principles, practice and policy*. London, UK: FT Prentice-Hall.

Caselli, F., & Coleman, W. J. (2001). *Cross-country technology diffusion: The case of computers*. Cambridge, MA: National Bureau of Economic Research.

Castells, M. (2001). *The Internet galaxy: Reflections on the Internet, business, and society*. New York, NY: Oxford University Press.

CEEDR. (2001). *Researching business support needs of ethnic minority owned businesses in Coventry and Warwickshire*. Coventry and Warwickshire Chamber of Commerce, Training and Enterprise, Centre for Enterprise and Economic Development Research, Middlesex University.

Celik, A. (2007, December 25). *Crossing the chasm* (Geoffrey A. Moore). Message posted to http://celikalper.wordpress.com/2007/12/25/crossing-the-chasm-geoffrey-a-moore/

Celuch, K., Taylor, S. A., & Goodwin, S. (2004). Understanding insurance salesperson Internet information management intentions: A test of competing models. *Journal of Insurance Issues, 27*(1), 22–40.

Cenfetelli, R. T. (2004). *An empirical study of the inhibitors of technology usage*. Paper presented at the International Conference on Information Systems, Washington, DC.

Center for International Development and Conflict Management (CIDCM). (2001). *CIDCM at the University of Maryland*. Retrieved from http://www.bsos.umd.edu/cidcm/projects/neo.html/

Center for International Development (CID) at Harvard University. (2000). *Readiness for the networked world, a guide for developing countries*. Cambridge, MA: Harvard University. Retrieved from http://www.cid.harvard.edu/ciditg

Chaffey, D. (2007). *E-business and e-commerce management* (3rd ed.). London, UK: Pearson Education.

Chakraborty, I., Hu, P. J.-H., & Cui, D. (2005). *Examining effects of cognitive style on technology acceptance decisions*. Paper presented at the Pacific Asia Conference on Information Systems, Bangkok, Thailand.

Chan, S. C., & Lu, M. T. (2004). Understanding internet banking adoption and use behavior: A Hong Kong perspective. *Journal of Global Information Management,* *12*(2), 21–43.

Chanston, I., & Mangles, T. (2003). Relationship marketing in online business-to-business markets: A pilot investigation of Small UK manufacturing firms. *European Journal of Marketing, 37*(5/6), 753–773. doi:10.1108/03090560310465134

Chau, P. Y. K., & Hu, P. J. (2001). Information Technology acceptance by professionals: A model comparison approach. *Decision Sciences, 32*(4), 699–719. doi:10.1111/j.1540-5915.2001.tb00978.x

Chau, P. (1996). An empirical assessment of a modified technology acceptance model. *Journal of Management Information Systems, 13,* 185–204.

Chau, P., & Hu, P. (2001). Information Technology acceptance by individual professionals: A model of comparison approach. *Decision Sciences, 32*(4), 699–719. doi:10.1111/j.1540-5915.2001.tb00978.x

Checchi, R. M., Sevcik, G. R., Loch, K. D., & Straub, D. D. (2002). An instrumentation process for measuring ICT policies and culture. *Proceedings of International Conference on Information Technology, Communications and Development* (pp. 1-17). Kathmandu, Nepal.

Chen, J., & Bernard, C. W. (1993). The Impact of Microcomputer Systems on Small Businesses: England, 10 Years Later. *Journal of Small Business Management, 31*(3), 96–102.

Chen, L.-D., Haney, S., Pandzik, A., Spigarelli, J., & Jesseman, C. (2003). Small business Internet commerce: A case study. *Information Resources, 16*(3), 17–41. doi:10.4018/irmj.2003070102

Chen, I. J., & Popovich, K. (2003). Understanding customer relationship management (CRM) people, process and technology. *Business Process Management Journal, 9*(5), 672–688. doi:10.1108/14637150310496758

Chen, Q., & Chen, H. (2004). Exploring the success factors of e-CRM strategies in practice. *Database Marketing & Customer Strategy Management, 11*(4), 333–343. doi:10.1057/palgrave.dbm.3240232

Chen, W., & Wellman, B. (2003). *Charting and bridging digital divides: Comparing socio-economic, gender, life stage and rural-urban Internet access and use in eight countries. AMD Global Consumer Advisory Board.* GSAB.

Cheng, T. C. E., Lam, D. Y. C., & Yeung, A. C. L. (2006). Adoption of internet banking: An empirical study in Hong Kong. *Decision Support Systems, 42*(3), 1558–1572. doi:10.1016/j.dss.2006.01.002

Chetty, S., & Campbell-Hunt, C. (2003). Paths to internationalisation among small- to medium-sized firms: A global versus regional approach. *European Journal of Marketing, 37*(5/6), 796–820. doi:10.1108/03090560310465152

Cheung, C. M. K., & Lee, M. K. O. (2010). A theoretical model of intentional social action in online social networks. *Decision Support Systems, 49*(1), 24–30. doi:10.1016/j.dss.2009.12.006

Cheung, W., Chang, M. K., & Lai, V. S. (2000). Prediction of internet and world wide web usage at work: A test of an extended Triandis model. *Decision Support Systems, 30,* 83–100. doi:10.1016/S0167-9236(00)00125-1

Chin, W. W. (1998a). Issues and opinions on structural equation modeling. *Management Information Systems Quarterly, 22*(1), 7–16.

Chin, W., & Todd, P. (1995). On the use, usefulness, and ease of use of structural equation modeling in MIS research: A note of caution. *Management Information Systems Quarterly, 19*(2), 237–246. doi:10.2307/249690

Chin, W. W. (1998). The partial least squares approach to structural equation modeling. In G. A. Marcoulides (Ed.), *Modern methods for business research* (pp. 295-336). Mahway, NJ: Lawrence Erlbaum.

Chinn, M. D., & Fairlie, R. W. (2007). The determinants of the global digital divide: A cross-country analysis of computer and Internet penetration. *Oxford Economic Papers, 59,* 16–44. doi:10.1093/oep/gpl024

Chismar, W. G., & Wiley-Patton, S. (2003). Does the extended technology acceptance model apply to physicians. *Proceedings of the 36th Annual Hawaii International Conference on System Sciences, Vol. 6.* Washington: IEEE Computer Society.

Chuang, T. T., Nakatani, K., Chen, J. C. H., & Huang, I. L. (2007). Examining the impact of organisational and owner's characteristics on the extent of e-commerce adoption in SMEs. *Int. J. Business and Systems Research*, *1*(1), 61–80. doi:10.1504/IJBSR.2007.014770

Chuang, T. T., Rutherford, M. W., & Lin, B. (2007). Owner/manager characteristics, organisational characteristics and IT adoption in small and medium enterprises. *International Journal of Management and Enterprise Development*, *4*(6), 619–634. doi:10.1504/IJMED.2007.014985

Chuang, T.-T., Nakatani, K., Chen, J. C. H., & Huang, I.-L. (2007). Examining the impact of organisational and owner's characteristics on the extent of ecommerce adoption in SMEs. *International Journal of Business and Systems Research*, *1*(1), 61–80. doi:10.1504/IJBSR.2007.014770

Çilan, C. A., Bolat, B. A., & Coşkun, E. (2009). Analyzing digital divide within and between member and candidate countries of European Union. *Government Information Quarterly*, *26*, 98–105. doi:10.1016/j.giq.2007.11.002

Clark, T. H., & Stoddard, D. B. (1996). Inter organizational business process redesign: Merging technological and process innovation. *Journal of Management Information Systems*, *13*(2), 9–28.

CLES (Centre for Local Economic Strategies) Consulting. (2003). *EMBs and ICT services*. Retrieved June 14, 2005, from http://cles.live.poptech.coop/C2B/document_tree/ViewACategory.asp?CategoryID=1

Coghlan, D., & Brannick, T. (2004). *Doing action research in your own organization* (2nd ed.). London, UK: Sage Publications.

Cohen, S., & Kallirroi, G. (2006). E-commerce investments from a SME perspective: Costs, benefits and processes. *Electronic Journal of Information Evaluation*, *9*(2), 45–56.

Cohen, B. J. (2001). Electronic Money: new day or false dawn. *Review of International Political Economy*, *8*(2), 197–225. doi:10.1080/09692290010033376

Cohen, A., & Nachmias, R. (2009, October, 6). Implementing a cost effectiveness analyzer for Web-supported academic instruction: A campus wide analysis. European Journal of Open, Distance and E-Learning, 3, Article 369. Retrieved September 15, 2010, from http://www.eurodl.org/?p=current=363&article=369

Collinson, E., & Shaw, E. (2001). Entrepreneurial marketing- A historical perspective on development and practice. *Management Decision*, *39*(9), 761–766. doi:10.1108/EUM0000000006221

Compeau, D. R., & Higgins, C. A. (1995). Computer self-effcacy: Development of a measure and initial test. *MIS Quarterly*, *18*(2), 189–211. doi:10.2307/249688

Compeau, D., Higgins, C., & Huff, S. (1999). Social cognitive theory and individual reactions to computing technology: A longitudinal study. *Management Information Systems Quarterly*, *23*(2), 145–158. doi:10.2307/249749

Computer Systems Policy Project. (CSPP). (1998). *Readiness guide for living in the networked world*. Retrieved from http://www.cspp.org

Cooper, R., & Zmud, R. (1990). Information Technology implementation research: A technological diffusion approach. *Management Science*, *36*(2), 123–139. doi:10.1287/mnsc.36.2.123

Corrocher, N., & Ordanini, A. (2002). Measuring the digital divide: A framework for the analysis of cross country differences. *Journal of Information Technology*, *17*, 9–19. doi:10.1080/02683960210132061

Coviello, N., & Munro, H. (1997). Network relationships and the internationalisation process of the small software firm. *International Business Review*, *6*(4), 361–386. doi:10.1016/S0969-5931(97)00010-3

Cragg, P. B., & King, M. (1993). Small-Firm Computing: Motivators and Inhibitors. *Management Information Systems Quarterly*, *17*(1), 47–60. doi:10.2307/249509

Cragg, P., & Zinatelli, N. (1995). The evolution of IS in small firms. *Information & Management*, *29*(1), 1–8. doi:10.1016/0378-7206(95)00012-L

CREME. (2009). *The Minority Ethnic Enterprise Centre of Expertise*. Retrieved February 25, 2009, from http://www.dmu.ac.uk/faculties/business_and_law/business/research/creme/meecoe/index.jsp

Crespi, G., Mahdi, S., & Patel, P. (2004). *Adoption of e-commerce technology: Do network and learning externalities matter? Draft Final Report for the Department of Trade and Industry.* London, UK: HMSO.

Cronbach, L. (1970). *Essentials of psychology testing.* New York: Harper and Row.

Crone, R. (2003). The Future of Electronic Billing lies in "electronic" payments. *ProQuest,* from http://proquest. umi.com/pqdweb?did=283552781&sid=2&Fmt=3&clie ntId=24792&RQT=309&VName=PQD

Cuervo, M. R. V., & Menendez, A. J. L. (2006). A multivariate framework for the analysis of the digital divide evidence for the European Union -15. *Information & Management, 43,* 56–766.

Culnan, M. J., & Armstrong, P. K. (1999). Information privacy concerns, procedural fairness and impersonal trust: An empirical investigation. *Organization Science, 10,* 104–115. doi:10.1287/orsc.10.1.104

Curran, J., & Blackburn, R. (2001). *Researching the Small Enterprise.* Sage Publications.

Curran, J., & Blackburn, R. A. (2001). *Researching the Small Enterprise.* SAGE Production, London.

Cyr, D., & Lew, R. (2003). Emerging challenges in the software localization industry. *Thunderbird International Business Review, 45*(3), 337–358. doi:10.1002/tie.10077

Cyr, D., & Trevor-Smith, H. (2004). Localization of Web design: An empirical comparison of German, Japanese and United Stats Web site characteristics. *Journal of the American Society for Information Science and Technology, 55*(13), 1199–1208. doi:10.1002/asi.20075

Dahlan, N., Ramayah, T., & Koay, A. H. (2002). Data mining in the banking industry: An exploratory study. In *Proceedings of the International Conference, Internet Economy and Business,* Kuala Lumpur, Malaysia.

Damanpour, F. (1991). Organizational innovation: A meta-analysis of effects of determinants and moderators. *Academy of Management Journal, 34*(3), 555–590. doi:10.2307/256406

Dandridge, T., & Levenburg, N. M. (2000). High-tech Potential? An exploratory study of very small firms' usage of the Internet. *International Small Business Journal, 18*(81), 81–91. doi:10.1177/0266242600182004

Daniel, E. M., & Grimshaw, J. (2002). An Exploratory Comparison of Electronic Commerce Adoption in Large and Small Enterprises. *Journal of Information Technology, 17*(3), 133–147. doi:10.1080/0268396022000018409

Daniel, E. M., Wilson, H., & Myers, A. (2002). Adoption of E-commerce by SMEs in the UK: towards a stage model. *International Small Business Journal, 20*(3), 253–270. doi:10.1177/0266242602203002

Daniel, E., & Wilson, H. (2002). Adoption intentions and benefits realised: A study of e-commerce in UK SMEs. *Journal of Small Business and Enterprise Development, 9*(4), 331–348. doi:10.1108/14626000210450522

Daniel, E., Wilson, H., & Myers, A. (2002). Adoption of e-commerce by SMEs in the UK: Towards a stage model. *International Small Business Journal, 20*(3), 253–270. doi:10.1177/0266242602203002

Darch, H., & Lucas, T. (2002). Training as an e-commerce enabler. *Journal of Workplace Learning, 14*(4), 148–155. doi:10.1108/13665620210427276

Dasgupta, S., Agarwal, D., Ioannidis, A., & Gopalakrishnan, S. (1999). Determinants of Information Technology adoption: An extension of existing models to firms in a developing country. *Journal of Global Information Management, 7*(3), 30–40.

Dasgupta, S., Granger, M., & McGarry, N. (2002). User acceptance of e-collaboration technology: An extension of the technology acceptance model. *Group Decision and Negotiation, 11,* 87–100. doi:10.1023/A:1015221710638

Dasgupta, S., Lall, S., & Wheeler, S. (2001). *Policy reform, economic growth, and the digital divide: An econometric analysis.* Development Research Group, World Bank, Washington, DC, Working paper.

Datamonitor. (2004). CRM For Small to Medium Business [Electronic Version] from http://www.datamonitor.com

Davidrajuh, R. (2007). Fuzzy logic based model of a new tool for measuring e-readiness. *Proceedings of the First Asia International Conference on Modelling & Simulation (AMS'07),* (IEEE Computer Society).

Davidrajuh, R., & Tvedteras, J. E. (2006). *Fuzzy approach for measuring e-readiness*. International Conference on Computational Intelligence for Modelling Control and Automation, and International Conference on Intelligent Agents, Web Technologies and Internet Commerce (CIMCA-IAWTIC'06), (IEEE Conference).

Davis, F. D. (1989). Perceived usefulness, perceived ease of use, and user acceptance of information technology. *MIS Quarterly*, *13*(3), 319–339. doi:10.2307/249008

Davis, F. D., Bagozzi, R. P., & Warshaw, P. R. (1989). User acceptance of computer technology: A comparison of two theoretical model. *Management Science*, *35*(8), 982–1003. doi:10.1287/mnsc.35.8.982

Davis, C., & Vladica, F. (August 2004). *Adoption of Internet Technologies and e-Business Solutions by Small and Medium Enterprises (SMEs) in New Brunswick*. Saint John, Canada: University of New Brunswick Saint John, Electronic Commerce Centre.

Davis, C., Lin, C., & Vladica, F. (2005). *State of e-Business in SMEs in Atlantic Canada in 2005*. Paper presented at the annual Atlantic Schools of Business conference, Halifax, N.S., Canada.

Davis, F. (1986). *A technology acceptance model for empirically testing new end-user information systems: theory and results*. Unpublished doctoral dissertation, Massachusetts Institute of Technology.

Day, G. S., & Bens, K. F. (2005). Capitalizing on the Internet opportunity. *Journal of Business and Industrial Marketing*, *20*(4/5), 160–168. doi:10.1108/08858620510603837

Day, G. S., & Hubbard, J. K. (2003). Customer relationships go digital. *Business Strategy Review*, *14*(1), 17–26. doi:10.1111/1467-8616.00240

de Búrca, S., Fynes, B., & Marshall, D. (2005). Strategic technology adoption: Extending ERP across the supply chain. *Journal of Enterprise Information Management*, *18*(4), 427–440. doi:10.1108/17410390510609581

de Haan, J. (2004). *Theorizing the digital divide*. Paper presented at the Conference Papers Annual Meeting of The American Sociological Association, 2004 Annual Meeting, San Francisco.

Deakins, D., & Freel, M. (2006). *Entrepreneurship and small firms* (4th ed.). Berkshire, UK: McGraw-Hill Education.

Deakins, D., Ram, M., & Smallbone, D. (2003). Addressing the business support needs of ethnic minority firms in the United Kingdom. *Environment and Planning. C, Government & Policy*, *21*(6), 843–859. doi:10.1068/c0305

Deakins, D. a&nd Freel, M. (2009). Entrepreneurship and small firms, 5th edition. Berkshire, UK: McGraw-Hill Education.

Del Aguila-Obra, A. R., & Padilla-Meléndez, A. (2006). Organizational factors affecting Internet technology adoption. *Internet Research*, *16*(1), 94–110. doi:10.1108/10662240610642569

Delone, W. H., & Mclean, E. R. (1992). Information Systems success: The quest for dependent variable. *Information Systems Research*, *3*(1), 60–95. doi:10.1287/isre.3.1.60

Deng, Z., Lu, Y., & Chen, Z. (2010). Exploring Chinese user adoption of mobile banking. *International Journal of Information Technology and Management*, *9*(3), 289–301. doi:10.1504/IJITM.2010.030945

Dennis, C. (2000). Networking for Marketing Advantage. *Management Decision*, *38*(4), 287–292. doi:10.1108/00251740010371757

Dennis, C., Harris, L., & Sandhu, B. (2002). From bricks to clicks: Understanding the e-consumer. *Qualitative Market Research*, *5*(4), 281–290. doi:10.1108/13522750210443236

DePalma, D., & Beninatto, R. (2006). Language services 2006: Supply-side outlook. *Research Report by Common Sense Advisory*. Retrieved July 28 2008, from www.commonsenseadvisory.com

Department for Business Enterprise & Regulatory Reform of UK. (2007). *Small and Medium Enterprise Statistics for the UK and Regions*. Retrieved May 8, 2009, from http://stats.berr.gov.uk/ed/sme/

Department of Justice Canada and Solicitor General Canada, (1997). Electronic money laundering: An environmental scan. 1-22

Department of Statistics Malaysia. (2005). *Census of Establishments and Enterprises 2003*. The Secretariat, Research & Development Division, Department of Statistics, Federal Government Administrative Centre, Putrajaya, Malaysia.

Dev, C. S., & Schultz, D. E. (2005, January/February). In the Mix: A Customer Focused Approach Can Bring the Current Marketing Mix into the 21st Century. *Marketing Management, 14*(1).

Dewan, S., Ganley, D., & Kraemer, K. L. (2004). *Across the digital divide: A cross-country analysis of the determinants of IT penetration*. Personal Computing Industry Center.

Dewan, S., & Kraemer, K. L. (2000). Information Technology and productivity: Evidence from country-level data. *Management Science, 46*(4), 548–562. doi:10.1287/mnsc.46.4.548.12057

Dewan, S., & Riggins, F. J. (2005). The digital divide: Current and future research directions. *Journal of the Association for Information Systems, 6*(2), 298–337.

Dewar, R. D., & Dutton, J. E. (1986). The adoption of radical and incremental innovations: An empirical analysis. *Management Science, 32*(11), 1422–1433. doi:10.1287/mnsc.32.11.1422

Dholakia, R. R., & Kshetri, N. (2004). Factors impacting the adoption of the Internet among SMEs. *Small Business Economics, 23*(4), 311–322. doi:10.1023/B:SBEJ.0000032036.90353.1f

DiMaggio, P., & Hargittai, E. (2001). *From the digital divide to digital inequality: Studying Internet use as penetration increases*. Working Paper 15. Princeton, NJ: Center for Arts and Cultural Policy Studies, Princeton University.

Dishaw, M. T., Strong, D. M., & Bandy, D. B. (2004). *The impact of task-technology fit in technology acceptance and utilization models*. Paper presented at the Americas Conference on Information Systems, New York.

Doherty, N., & Lockett, N. (2008). Mind the gap: Exploring the links between the expectations of Relationship marketing and the reality of electronic-CRM. *International Journal of e-Business Management, 2*(2), 1-17.

Doukidis, G. I., Smithson, S., & Lybereas, T. (1994). Trends in Information Technology in small businesses. *Journal of End User Computing, 6*(4), 15–25.

Downie, G. (2003). Internet marketing and SMEs. *Management Services, 47*(7), 8–11.

Drakos, N., Mann, J., Cain, M., Andrews, W., Knox, R., Valdes, R., et al. (2008). *Hype cycle for social software, 2008* (Report No. G00158239). Retrieved May 1, 2009, from http://www.gartner.com/DisplayDocument?id=735719

Draper, S. (1997). Prospects for summative evaluation of CAL in higher education. *ALT-J, 5*(1), 33–39. doi:10.1080/0968776970050106

Drennan, J., & McColl-Kennedy, J. R. (2003). The relationship between Internet use and perceived performance in retail and professional service firms. *Journal of Services Marketing, 17*(3), 295–311. doi:10.1108/08876040310474837

Drew, S. (2003). Strategic uses of e-commerce by SMEs in the East of England. *European Management Journal, 21*(1), 79–88. doi:10.1016/S0263-2373(02)00148-2

Drury, D. H., & Farhoomand, A. (1996). Innovation adoption of EDI. *Information Resources Management Journal, 9*(3), 5–13.

DTI (2004). *Business in the Information Age: International Benchmarking Study 2004*. London: Department of Trade & Industry. Retrieved January, 2005

DTI. (2004). *International bench marking survey for ICT use*. UK Department of Trade and Industry. Retrieved July 28, 2006, from http://www2.bah.com/dti2004/main/mr_86.htm

Duffy, T., & Cunningham, D. (1996). Constructivism: Implications for the design and delivery of instruction. In Jonassen, D. H., & Driscoll, M. P. (Eds.), *Handbook of research for educational telecommunications and technology* (pp. 170–190). New York, NY: MacMillan.

Duhan, S., Levy, M., & Powell, P. (2001). Information Systems strategies in knowledge-based SMEs: The role of core competencies. *European Journal of Information Systems, 10*(1), 25–40. doi:10.1057/palgrave.ejis.3000379

Dutt, A., & Srite, M. (2005). *A cultural perspective on technology acceptance*. Paper presented at the Americas Conference on Information Systems, Omaha, NE.

Dutta, S., & Evrard, P. (1999). Information Technology and organisation within European small enterprises. *European Management Journal, 17*(3), 239–251. doi:10.1016/S0263-2373(99)00003-1

Dutta, S., & Jain, A. (2004). *The networked readiness index 2003–2004: Overview and analysis framework*. Retrieved from http://www.developmentgateway.org/download/222656/Networked Readiness Index.pdf

Dwivedi, Y. K., Selamat, M. H., Abd Wahab, M. S., Mat Samsudin, M. A., & Lal, B. (2008). Examining factors influencing the behavioral intention to adopt broadband in Malaysia. In León, G., Bernardos, A., Casar, J., Kautz (Eds), *Open IT-based innovation: Moving towards cooperative IT transfer and knowledge diffusion* (pp. 325-342). Boston: Springer.

Dyerson, R., & Harindranath, G. (2007). ICT adoption & use by SMEs in the UK: A survey of South East. *Management of Engineering and Technology, 5*(9), 1756–1770.

Dyerson, R., & Spinelli, R. (2010). The evaluation and impact of ICT readiness in SMEs: Constructing a new framework. Paper presented at the 33rd Institute of Small Business and Enterprise Conference, 3rd-4th November, 2010, London.

Ebusiness Engineering. (2003). *Making sense of US B2C e-commerce findings*. Retrieved from http://www.ebusinessteam.com/

EC. (2003). SME User Guide Explaining the New SME Definition [Electronic Version] from http://ec.europa.eu/enterprise/ enterprise_policy/sme_definition /index_en.htm.

EC. (2005). The European e-Business Report 2005 [Electronic Version] from http://www.ebusiness-watch.org /key_reports/ synthesis_reports.htm.

EC. (2007). The European e-Business Report 2006/07 [Electronic Version] from http://www.ebusiness-watch.org /key_reports/ synthesis_reports.htm.

Economist Intelligence Unit (EIU). (2009). *The 2009 e-readiness rankings*. London, UK/New York, NY/ Hong Kong: EIU. Retrieved from http://www.eiu.com

Eden, C., & Huxham, C. (1996). Action research for the study of organisations. In Clegg, S., Hardy, C., & Nord, W. (Eds.), *Handbook of organisation studies* (pp. 526–542). London, UK: Sage.

Egan, T., Clancy, S., & O'Toole, T. (2003). The integration of e-commerce tools into the business processes of SMEs. *Irish Journal of Management, 24*(1), 139–153.

Elbeltagi, I. (2007). E-commerce and globalization: An exploratory study of Egypt. *Cross Cultural Management: An International Journal, 14*(3), 196–201. doi:10.1108/13527600710775748

Electronic Commerce Research & Training Centre (ECRTC). (2008). *Marketing on the Internet Training Program*. University of New Brunswick Saint John, Saint John, N.B., Canada.

Elliot, S., & Fowell, S. (2000). Expectations versus reality: A snapshot of consumer experiences with Internet retailing. *International Journal of Information Management, 20*(5), 323–336. doi:10.1016/S0268-4012(00)00026-8

Engler, N. (1999). Small but Nimble. *Information., 18*, 57–62.

Eriksson, K., Kerem, K., & Nilsson, D. (2004). Customer Acceptance of Internet Banking in Estonia. *International Journal of Bank, 23*(2), 200–216. doi:10.1108/02652320510584412

ESRC. (2008). Society today – Business engagement scheme for ESRC centres. Retrieved June 25, 2008, from http://www.esrcsocietytoday.ac.uk/ESRCInfoCentre/opportunities/current_funding_opportunities/business_engagement.aspx?ComponentId=18191&SourcePageId=15428

Esselink, B. (2000). *A practical guide to localization (Language International world directory)*. Philadelphia: John Benjamins Publishing Co.

Eun, J. L. (2001). *Customer Adoption and Diffusion of Technological Innovations: A case of E-banking Technologies*. International Journal of Bank Marketing. Emerald Group Publishing Limited.

European Commission. (2007). *ICT- Information and Communication Technologies – Work programme 2007-8*. Cordis. Retrieved May 3, 2008, from ftp://ftp.cordis.europa.eu/pub/fp7/ict/docs/ict-wp-2007-08_en.pdf

European Commission. (2005). *The new SME definition. User guide and model declaration.* Retrieved from http://ec.europa.eu/enterprise/.../sme_definition/sme_user_guide.pdf

European Strategic Program on Research in Information Technology. (1997). *ESPRIT and ACTS projects related to Electronic Commerce.* Retrieved May 8, 2009, from http://cordis.europa.eu/ esprit/src/ecomproj.htm

Eurostat.(1996). *Enterprises in Europe,* 4th report.

Evans, P., & Wurster, T. S. (1997). Strategy and the new economics of information. *Harvard Business Review,* 75(5), 70–83.

Fallon, M., & Moran, P. (2000). Information Communications Technology (ICT) and manufacturing SMEs. In *Proceedings of the 2000 Small Business and Enterprise Development Conference,* University of Manchester (pp. 100–109).

Fariselli, P., Oughton, C., Picory, C., & Sugden, R. (1999). Electronic commerce and the future for SMEs in a global market-place: Networking and public policies. *Small Business Economics,* 12(3), 261–275. doi:10.1023/A:1008029924987

Fathian, M., Akhavan, P., & Hoorali, M. (2008). E-readiness assessment of non-profit ICT SMEs in a developing country: The case of Iran. *Technovation,* 28, 578–590. doi:10.1016/j.technovation.2008.02.002

Featherman, M. S. (2001). *Extending the technology acceptance model by inclusion of perceived risk.* Paper presented at the Americas Conference on Information Systems, Waltham, MA.

Feinberg, R., & Kadam, R. (2002). E-CRM Web service attributes as determinants of customer satisfaction with retail Web sites. *International Journal of Service Industry Management,* 13(5), 432–451. doi:10.1108/09564230210447922

Fenn, J., & Raskino, M. (2008). *Mastering the hype cycle: How to choose the right innovation at the right time.* Boston, MA: Harvard Business Press.

Fenn, J. (1999). *When to leap on the hype cycle* (Report No. DF-08-6751). Retrieved March 4, 2008, from http://www.cata.ca/files/PDF/Resource_Centres/hightech/reports/indepstudies/Whentoleaponthehypecycle.pdf

Fenn, J. (2007). *Understanding Gartner's hype cycles, 2007* (Report No. G00144727). Retrieved December 8, 2007, from http://www.digeratimarketing.co.uk/gartnershypecycle.pdf

Fenn, J., Linden, A., Tully, J., Davidson, J., Smith, S., Margevicius, M., et al. (2004). *Hype cycle for emerging technologies, 2004* (Report No. G00121844). Retrieved October 21, 2008, from http://www.gartner.com/DisplayDocument?doc_cd=121844

Ferranti, M. (1999). From global to local. *InfoWorld,* 21(41), 36–37.

Fichman, R. G., & Kemerer, C. F. (1997). The assimilation of software process innovations: An organizational learning perspective. *Management Science,* 43(10), 1345–1363. doi:10.1287/mnsc.43.10.1345

Fillis, I., Johannson, U., & Wagner, B. (2004). Factors impacting on e-business adoption and development in the smaller firm. *International Journal of Entrepreneurial Behaviour and Research,* 10(3), 178–191. doi:10.1108/13552550410536762

Fink, D. (1998). Guidelines for the successful adoption of Information Technology in small and medium enterprises. *International Journal of Information Management,* 18(4), 243–253. doi:10.1016/S0268-4012(98)00013-9

Fishbein, M., & Ajzen, I. (1975). *Belief, attitude, intention and behaviour: An introduction to theory and research.* MA: Addision-Wesley.

Fleet, G. (November 2008). *Export and the role of the Internet for SMEs in Atlantic Canada.* Paper presented at the International Council for Small Business (ICSB) 2008 World Conference, Halifax, N.S., Canada.

Fletcher, R., Bell, J., & McNoughton, R. (2004). *International e-business marketing.* London, UK: Thomson.

Fletcher, R. (2006). The impact of culture on Web site content, designs, and structure: An international and a multicultural perspective. *Journal of Communication Management,* 10(3), 259–273. doi:10.1108/13632540610681158

Fock, H. (2000, September). *Cultural influences on marketing communication on the World Wide Web.* Paper presented at the Multicultural Marketing Conference, Hong Kong.

Foley, P., Watts, H. D., & Wilson, B. (1993). New technology, skills shortages and training strategies. In Swann, P. (Ed.), *New technology and the firm* (pp. 279–289). London, UK: Routledge.

Foley, P., & Ram, M. (2002). *The use of online technology by ethnic minority businesses: A comparative study of the West Midlands and UK.* De Montfort University monograph. Retrieved February 3, 2008, from http://www.sbs.gov.uk/contents/research/EMB-IT.pdf

Fornell, C., & Larcker, D. F. (1981). Evaluating structural equation models with unobservable variables and measurement error. *JMR, Journal of Marketing Research, 18*(1), 39–50. doi:10.2307/3151312

Fornell, C., & Bookstein, F. L. (1982). Two structural equation models: LISREL and PLS applied to consumer exit-voice theory. *JMR, Journal of Marketing Research, 19*, 440–452. doi:10.2307/3151718

Fornell, C., & Cha, J. (1994). Partial least squares. In Bagozzi, R. P. (Ed.), *Advanced methods of marketing research* (pp. 52–78). Oxford, UK: Blackwell.

Frambach, R., & Schillweaert, N. (2002). Organizational innovation adoption: A multi-level framework of determinants and opportunities for future research. *Journal of Business Research, 55*(2), 163–176. doi:10.1016/S0148-2963(00)00152-1

Freidlein, A. (2001, February). *CRM meets E-CRM: An executive briefing.* Wheel Consultancy. Retrieved 4th February, 2008, from www.e-consultancy.com

Friedman, T. (2005, April). The World is Flat: A Brief [*st* Century. New York: Farrar, Straus & Giroux.]. *Histoire (Paris)*, 21.

Fuchs, C., & Horak, E. (2008). Africa and the digital divide. *Telematics and Informatics, 25*, 99–116. doi:10.1016/j.tele.2006.06.004

Fuller-Love, N. (2006). Management development in small firms. *International Journal of Management Reviews, 8*(3), 175–190. doi:10.1111/j.1468-2370.2006.00125.x

Galloway, L. (2006). Information and Communications Technologies and e-business. In Deakins, D., & Freel, M. (Eds.), *Entrepreneurship and small firms* (4th ed., pp. 139–156). Berkshire, UK: McGraw-Hill.

Galloway, L., Deakins, D., & Sanders, J. (2008). *The use of Internet portals by Scotland's rural business community.* Paper presented at the 31st Institute for Small Business and Entrepreneurship (ISBE) Conference, Belfast, Northern Ireland. November.

Gammack, J., & Hodkinson, C. (2003). Virtual reality, involvement and the consumer interface. *Journal of End User Computing, 15*(4), 78–96. doi:10.4018/joeuc.2003100105

Gartner, Inc. (2006, August 9). *Gartner's 2006 emerging technologies hype cycle highlights key technology themes: 2006* [Press release]. Retrieved October 21, 2008, from http://www.gartner.com/it/page.jsp?id=495475

Gebremichael, M. D., & Jackson, J. W. (2006). Bridging the gap in Sub-Saharan Africa: A holistic look at information poverty and the region's digital divide. *Government Information Quarterly, 23*, 267–280. doi:10.1016/j.giq.2006.02.011

Gefen, D., Karahanna, E., & Detmar, W. S. (2003). Trust and TAM in online shopping: An integrated model. *Management Information Systems Quarterly, 27*(1), 51–90.

Gefen, D. (2002). Customer loyalty in e-commerce. *Journal of the Association for Information Systems, 3*, 27–51.

Gefen, D. (2003). TAM or just plain habit: A look at experienced online shoppers. *Journal of End User Computing, 15*(3), 1–13. doi:10.4018/joeuc.2003070101

Gefen, D., & Straub, D. (1997). Gender differences in the perception and use of e-mail: An extension to the technology acceptance model. *Management Information Systems Quarterly, 21*(4), 389–400. doi:10.2307/249720

Gefen, D., & Straub, D. W. (1997). Gender differences in the perception and use of e-mail: An extension to the technology acceptance model. *Management Information Systems Quarterly, 21*, 389–400. doi:10.2307/249720

Gefen, D., Straub, D. W., & Boudreau, M. (2000). Structural equation modeling and regression: Guidelines for research practice. *Communications of the Association for Information System, 4*(7).

Geiger, S., & Martin, S. (1999). The Internet as a relationship marketing tool – Some evidence from Irish companies. *Irish Marketing Review, 12*(2), 24–35.

Geith, C., & Cometa, M. (1999). Cost analysis results: Comparing distance learning and on-campus courses. Teaching, Learning, Technology Group. Retrieved September 15, 2010, from http://www.tltgroup.org/resources/F_Eval_Cases/Geith_Cometa.htm

Geller, K. (1998). The Internet: The ultimate relationship marketing tool. *Direct Marketing, 61*(5), 36–39.

George-Cosh, D. (2009, April 29). Has the Twitter backlash begun? Message posted to http://blogs.thenational.ae/beep_beep/2009/04/has-the-twitter-backlash-begun.html

Giaglis, G. M., Klein, S., & O'Keefe, R. M. (2002). The role of intermediaries in electronic marketplaces: Developing a contingency model. *Information Systems Journal, 12*(3), 231–246. doi:10.1046/j.1365-2575.2002.00123.x

Gibbs, J., & Kraemer, K. L. (2004). Across-country investigation of the determinants of scope of e-commerce use: An institutional approach. *Electronic Markets, 14*, 124–137. doi:10.1080/10196780410001675077

Giglio, V. (2002). Privacy in the World of Cyberbanking: Emerging Legal Issues and How You Are Protected, The secured lender, March/April 2002, 48-60

Gil-Garcia, J. R. (2008). Using partial least squares in digital government research. In Garson, G. D., & Khosrow-Pour, M. (Eds.), *Handbook of research on public Information Technology* (pp. 239–253). Hershey, PA: Idea Group. doi:10.4018/9781599048574.ch023

Gillian, C., Graham, S., Levitt, M., McArthur, J., Murray, S., & Turner, V. (1999). *The ASPs' Impact on the IT Industry*. IDC Corporation.

Gilmore, A., & Carson, D. (1999). Entrepreneurial marketing by networking. *New England Journal of Entrepreneurship, 2*(2), 31–38.

Gilmore, A., Carson, D., & Grant, K. (2001). SME marketing in practice. *Marketing Intelligence & Planning, 19*(1), 6–11. doi:10.1108/02634500110363583

Gilmore, A., Carson, D., Grant, K., O'Donnell, A., Laney, R., & Pickett, B. (2006). Networking in SMEs: Findings from Australia and Ireland. *Irish Marketing Review, 18*(1/2), 21–29.

Gilmore, A., Carson, D., O'Donnell, A., & Cummins, D. (1999). Added value: A qualitative assessment of SME marketing. *Irish Marketing Review, 12*(1), 27–36.

Gilmore, A., Gallagher, D., & Henry, S. (2007). E-marketing and SMEs: Operational lessons for the future. *European Business Review, 19*(2), 234–247. doi:10.1108/09555340710746482

Girard, T., Korgaonkar, P., & Silverblatt, R. (2003). Relationship of type of product, shopping orientations, and demographics with preference for shopping on the Internet. *Journal of Business and Psychology, 18*(1), 101–119. doi:10.1023/A:1025087021768

Gladwell, M. (2000). *The tipping point: How little things can make a big difference*. New York, New York, NY: Little, Brown and Company.

Globalization Industry Primer (LISA). (2007). Globalization industry primer. *LISA*. Retrieved April 3, 2009, from http://www.lisa.org/ Globalization-indust.468.0.html#c261.

Goi, C. L. (2005). E-banking in Malaysia: Opportunity and challenges. *Journal of Internet Banking and Commerce, 10*(3). Retrieved June 25, 2006, from http://www.arraydev.com/ commerce/JIBC/2006-02 /GOI.htm

Goode, A., & Stevens, K. (2000). An analysis of the business characteristics of adopters and non-adopters of World Wide Web technology. *Information Technology and Management, 1*, 129–154. doi:10.1023/A:1019112722593

Goodhue, D. L., & Thompson, R. L. (1995). Task-technology fit and individual performance. *Management Information Systems Quarterly, 19*(2), 213–236. doi:10.2307/249689

Goodwin, C. (1991). Privacy: Recognition of a consumer right. *Journal of Public Policy & Marketing, 10*(Spring), 149–166.

Google Investor Relations – Financial Tables. (2008). Retrieved March 18, 2009, from http://investor.google.com /fin_data.html

Gorton, M. (1999). Spatial variations in markets served by UK-based small and medium sized enterprises (SMEs). *Entrepreneurship and Regional Development, 11*(1), 39–55. doi:10.1080/089856299283281

Grandon, E. E., & Pearson, J. M. (2004). Electronic commerce adoption: An empirical study of small and medium US businesses. *Information & Management, 42*(1), 197–216.

Grandon, E. E. (2005). *Extension and validation of the theory of planned behavior: The case of electronic commerce adoption in small and medium-sized businesses in Chile.* Ph.D. thesis Southern Illinois University at Carbondale, 2005, 213 pages.

Grant, J., & Davis, L. (1997). Selection and use of content experts for instrument development. *Research in Nursing & Health, 20,* 269–274. doi:10.1002/(SICI)1098-240X(199706)20:3<269::AID-NUR9>3.0.CO;2-G

Grant, S. (1999). *E-commerce for small businesses.* IEC'99 Conference, September.

Gray, C., & Lawless, N. (2000). *Innovations in the distance development of SME management skills.* Retrieved from http://www.eurodl.org/materials/contrib/2000/gray.html

Green, K. C., Smallen, D., Leach, K., & Hawkins, B. L. (2005). Data: Roads traveled, lessons learned. EDUCAUSE Review, 40(2), 14–25. Retrieved September 15, 2010, from http://www.educause.edu/ir/library/pdf/ERM0520.pdf

Gribbins, M., & King, R. (2004). Electronic retailing strategies: A case study of small businesses in the gifts & collectibles industry. *Electronic Markets, 14*(2), 138–152. doi:10.1080/10196780410001675086

Gribbins, M. L., Shaw, M. J., & Gebauer, J. (2003). *An investigation into employees' acceptance of integrating mobile commerce into organizational processes.* Paper presented at the Americas Conference on Information Systems, Tampa, FL.

Grimm, C. M., & Smith, K. G. (1991). Management and organizational change: a note on the railroad industry. *Strategic Management Journal, 12,* 557–562. doi:10.1002/smj.4250120708

Gritzalis, S., Katsikas, S. K., & Gritzalis, D. (2003). *Network Security: Technologies and Services.* Athens, Greece: Papasotiriou Pubs.

Grönroos, C. (1994). From marketing mix to relationship marketing: Towards a paradigm shift in marketing. *Management Decision, 32*(2), 4–22. doi:10.1108/00251749410054774

Grönroos, C. (2004). The relationship marketing process: Communication, interaction, dialogue, value. *Journal of Business and Industrial Marketing, 19*(2), 99–113. doi:10.1108/08858620410523981

Guillen, M. F., & Suarez, S. L. (2001). Developing the Internet: Entrepreneurship and public policy in Ireland, Singapore, Argentina, and Spain. *Telecommunications Policy, 25*(3-4), 349–371. doi:10.1016/S0308-5961(01)00009-X

Gummesson, E. (1994). Making relationship marketing operational. *International Journal of Service Industry Management, 5*(5), 5–20. doi:10.1108/09564239410074349

Gummesson, E. (2004). Return on relationships (ROR): The value of relationship marketing and CRM in business-to-business contexts. *Journal of Business and Industrial Marketing, 19*(2), 136–146. doi:10.1108/08858620410524016

Gupta, M., Rao, R., & Upadhyaya, S. (2004). Electronic banking and information assurance issues: survey and synthesis. *Journal of Organizational and End User Computing, 16*(3), 1–21. doi:10.4018/joeuc.2004070101

Gupta, S. (1995). HERMES: A research project on the commercial uses of the World Wide Web. Retrieved from http://www.umich.edu/~sgupta/hermes/

Guru, B. K., Vaithilingam, S., Ismail, N., & Prasad, R. (2000). Electronic banking in Malaysia: A note on evolution of services and consumer reactions. *Journal of Internet Banking and Commerce, 5*(1). Retrieved June 27, 2006, from http://www.arraydev.com /commerce/jibc/ 0001-07.htm

Hackbarth, G., Grover, V., & Mun, Y. Y. (2003). Computer playfulness and anxiety: Positive and negative mediators of the system experience effect on perceived ease of use. *Information & Management, 40*(3), 221–232. doi:10.1016/S0378-7206(02)00006-X

Hadengue, V. (2005). E-learning for information literacy-A case study. *Library Review, 54*(1), 36–46. doi:10.1108/00242530510574147

Hair, J. F., Black, W. C., Babin, B. J., & Anderson, R. E. (2010). *Multivariate data analysis*. Upper Saddle River, NJ: Prentice-Hall.

Hair, J. F. Jr, Anderson, R. E., Tatham, R. L., & Black, W. C. (1998). *Multivariate data analysis* (5th ed.). New Jersey: Prentice-Hall.

Håkansson, H., & Snehota, I. (1995). *Developing relationships in business networks*. London, UK: Routledge.

Hall, E. T. (1976). *Beyond culture*. Garden City, NY: Doubleday & Company.

Hambrick, D. C., & Mason, P. A. (1984). Upper echelons: The organization as a reflection of it's top managers. *Academy of Management Review*, *9*, 193–206. doi:10.2307/258434

Hamlet, C., & Strube, M. (2000). Community Banks go Online, ABA Banking journal's 2000 White paper/ Banking on the Internet, March, 61-65

Hampton-Sosa, W., & Koufaris, M. (2005). The effect of Web site perceptions on initial trust in the owner company. *International Journal of Electronic Commerce*, *10*(1), 55–81.

Han, S. P., & Shavitt, S. (1994). Persuasion and culture: Advertising appeals in individualistic and collectivistic societies. *Journal of Experimental Psychology*, *30*, 8–18.

Hanafizadeh, M. R., Hanafizadeh, P., & Saghaei, A. (2009c). The pros and cons of digital divide and e-readiness assessments. *International Journal of E-Adoption*, *1*(3), 1–29. doi:10.4018/jea.2009092901

Hanafizadeh, M. R., Saghaei, A., & Hanafizadeh, P. (2009e). An index for cross-country analysis of ICT infrastructure and access. *Telecommunications Policy*, *33*(7), 385–405. doi:10.1016/j.telpol.2009.03.008

Hanafizadeh, P., Hanafizadeh, M. R., & Khodabakhshi, M. (2009a). Extracting core ICT indicators using entropy method. *The Information Society*, *25*(4), 236–247. doi:10.1080/01972240903028490

Hanafizadeh, P., Hanafizadeh, M. R., & Khodabakhshi, M. (2009b). Taxonomy of e-readiness assessment measures. *International Journal of Information Management*, *29*(3), 189–195. doi:10.1016/j.ijinfomgt.2008.06.002

Hanafizadeh, P., Khodabakhshi, M., & Hanafizadeh, M. R. (2009d). A methodology to extract a new set of core indicators of the information society. *Journal of Information Technology Research*, *2*(3), 70–94. doi:10.4018/jitr.2009070105

Hansemark, O. C. (1998). The effects of an entrepreneurship programme on need for achievement and locus of control of reinforcement. *International Journal of Entrepreneurial Behaviour and Research*, *4*(1), 28–50. doi:10.1108/13552559810203957

Hansen, P. (2002, August, 2). Electronics and the Gartner hype cycle - opinion & analysis electronics - vehicle telematics - brief article. *Automotive Industries*, Retrieved February 18, 2008, from http://goliath.ecnext.com/coms2/gi_0199-1995351/Electronics-and-the-Gartner-Hype.html

Hargittai, E. (1999). Weaving the Western Web–Explaining differences in Internet connectivity among OECD countries. *Telecommunications Policy*, *23*(10-11), 701–718. doi:10.1016/S0308-5961(99)00050-6

Harrigan, P., Ramsey, E., & Ibbotson, P. (2008). E-CRM in SMEs: An exploratory study in Northern Ireland. *Marketing Intelligence & Planning*, *26*(4), 385–404. doi:10.1108/02634500810879296

Harrison, A. D., Mykytyn, P. P. Jr, & Riemenschneider, K. C. (1997). Executive Decision About Adoption of Information Technology in Small Business: Theory and Empirical Tests. *Information Systems Research*, *8*(2), 171–195. doi:10.1287/isre.8.2.171

Hart, P., & Saunders, C. (1997). Power and trust: Critical factors in the adoption and use of electronic data interchange. *Organization Science*, *8*(1), 23–42. doi:10.1287/orsc.8.1.23

Hart, M., & Rush, D. (2007). E-learning and the development of "voice" in business studies education. *International Journal of Educational Management*, *21*(1), 68–77. doi:10.1108/09513540710716830

Hartman, A., Sifonis, J. G., & Kador, J. (2000). *Net ready: Strategies for success in the e-economy*. USA: McGraw-Hill.

Hashem, S. (2001). E-*readiness assessment: Case of Egypt*. Cairo, Egypt: Ministry of Communications and Information Technology. Retrieved from http://www.itu.int/osg/spu/ni/digitalbridges/presentations/07-Hashem.pdf

Hashim, N. A. (2006). E-commerce adoption issues in Malaysian SME. In *Proceedings of International Conference on E-commerce (ICoEC)*, Penang, Malaysia.

Haynes, P. J., Becherer, R. C., & Helms, M. M. (1998). Small and mid-sized businesses and Internet use: unrealized potential? *Internet Research: Electronic Networking Applications and Policy*, 8(3), 229–235. doi:10.1108/10662249810217786

Heckman, J. J. (1979). Sample selection bias as a specification error. *Econometrica*, 47(1), 153–161. doi:10.2307/1912352

Heijden, H., Verhagan, T., & Creemers, M. (2001, January). Predicting online purchase behavior: Replications and tests of competing models. In *Proceedings of the 34th Hawaii International Conference on Systems Sciences*, Maui, Hawaii (vol. 7, pp.7068). Washington, DC: IEEE Computer Society.

Helen, A. (2003). Innovation in retail payments: e-payments. From http://www.findarticles.com/p/articles/mi_qa3774/is_200301/ai_n9180494

Henry, P. (2001). E-learning technology, content and services. *Education + Training*, 43(4/5), 249-255.

Hermeking, M. (2005). Culture and Internet consumption: Contributions from cross-cultural marketing and advertising research. *Journal of Computer-Mediated Communication*, 11(1). Retrieved April 3, 2009, from http://jcmc.indiana.edu/ vol11/issue1/ hermeking.html.

Higgins, A., & Prebble, T. (2008). Taking the lead: Strategic management for e-learning. Retrieved September 15, 2010, from http://www.caudit.edu.au/educauseaustralasia09/assets/papers/monday/Andrew-Higgins.pdf

Hill, J. (2001). A multidimensional study of the key determinants of effective SME marketing activity: Part 1. *International Journal of Entrepreneurial Behaviour & Research*, 7(5), 171–204. doi:10.1108/EUM0000000006006

Hill, J., & McGowan, P. (1996). Marketing development through networking: A competency based approach for small firm entrepreneurs. *Journal of Small Business and Enterprise Development*, 3(3), 148–157. doi:10.1108/eb020974

Ho, S.M., & Simon, T.F.Ng Victor. (1994). Customers' risk perceptions of Electronic payment systems. *International Journal of Bank Marketing*, 12(8), 26–38. doi:10.1108/02652329410069029

Hoffman, D. L., Novak, T. P., & Schlosser, A. E. (2000). The evolution of the digital divide: How gaps in Internet access may impact Electronic commerce. *Journal of Computer-Mediated Communication*, 5(3).

Hoffman, D. L., & Novak, T. P. (1997). A new paradigm for electronic commerce. *The Information Society*, 13, 43–54. doi:10.1080/019722497129278

Hoi, J., Shim, J. P., & Yin, A. (2003). Current Progress of E-commerce adoption: SMEs in Hong Kong. *Communications of the ACM*, 46(9).

Holland, J., & Baker, S. M. (2001). Customer participation in creating site brand loyalty. *Journal of Interactive Marketing*, 15(4), 34–45. doi:10.1002/ dir.1021

Holsapple, C. W., & Sasidharan, S. (2005). The dynamics of trust in online B2C e-commerce: A research model and agenda. *Information Systems and E-business Management*, 3(4), 377–403. doi:10.1007/s10257-005-0022-5

Hong, Y. S. (2002). *Narrowing the digital gap in the APEC region*. Korea: Institute for International Economic Policy. Working Paper. Retrieved from unpan1.un.org/intradoc/groups/public/documents/APCITY/UNPAN00867.pdf

Hoppe, R., Newman, P., & Mugera, P. (2001). *Factors affecting the adoption of internet banking in South Africa: A comparative study* (University of Cape Town working paper). Cape Town, South Africa: University of Cape Town.

Horrocks, G., & Haines, M. (2004). *Health information literacy and higher education: The King's College London approach*. Paper presented at the World and International Congress: 70th IFLA General Conference and Council, 22– 27 August 2004, Buenos Aires, Argentina.

Horst, M., Kuttschreuter, M., & Gutteling, J. M. (2007). Perceived usefulness, perceived experiences, risk perception and trust as determinants of adoption of e-government services in the Netherlands. *Computers in Human Behavior*, *23*(4), 1838–1852. doi:10.1016/j.chb.2005.11.003

Howcroft, B., Hamilton, R., & Hewer, P. (2002). Consumer Attitude and the Usage and Adoption of Home-based Banking in the United Kingdom. *International Journal of Bank Marketing*, *20*(3), 111–121. doi:10.1108/02652320210424205

Howcroft, D. (2001). After the goldrush: Deconstructing the myths of the dot.com market. *Journal of Information Technology*, *16*(4), 195–204. doi:10.1080/02683960110100418

Howcroft, J. B., & Durkin, M. (2000). Reflections on bank-customer interactions in the new millennium. *Journal of Financial Services Marketing*, *5*(1), 9–20. doi:10.1057/palgrave.fsm.4770002

Huddlestone, J., & Pike, J. (2008). Seven key decision factors for selecting e-learning. *Cognition Technology and Work*, *10*(3), 237–247. doi:10.1007/s10111-007-0102-z

Hung, S. Y. (2003). Expert versus novice use of the executive support systems: An empirical study. *Information & Management*, *40*(3), 177–189. doi:10.1016/S0378-7206(02)00003-4

Hunt, S. D., & Morgan, R. M. (1994). Relationship marketing in the era of network competition. *Marketing Management*, *3*(1), 18–28.

Hunter, K., & Kemp, S. (2004). The personality of E-commerce investors. *Journal of Economic Psychology*, *25*(4), 529–537. doi:10.1016/S0167-4870(03)00050-3

Husing, T., & Selhofer, H. (2004). DIDIX: A digital divide index for measuring social inequality in IT diffusion. *IT & Society*, *1*(7), 26–42.

Hussin, H., & Mohamad Noor, R. (2005). Innovating business through E-commerce: Exploring the willingness of Malaysian SMEs. Retrieved: March 3, 2009, from http://www.it-innovations.ae/iit005/proceedings/articles/I_4_IIT05_Hussin.pdf

Huy, L. V., & Filiatrault, P. (2006). The adoption of E-commerce in SMEs in Vietnam: A study of users and prospectors. *In Proceedings of the 10th Pacific Asia Conference on Information Systems*, Kuala Lumpur, Malaysia (pp. 1335-44).

Hwang, Y. (2005). *An empirical study of online trust and consumer behavior: Cultural orientation, social norms, and personal innovativeness in Information Technology*. Paper presented at the International Conference on Information Systems, Las Vegas, NV.

Iacovou, C. L., Benbasat, I., & Dexter, A. S. (1995). Electronic data interchange and small organizations: Adoption and impact of technology. *Management Information Systems Quarterly*, *19*(4), 465–485. doi:10.2307/249629

Ian, D., & Christie, G.-S. (1999). E-cash is more interesting than you think: what are the key issues. *European Business Review*, *99*(4), 207–210. doi:10.1108/09555349910281379

Ibeh, K. I., Luo, Y., & Dinnie, K. (2005). E-branding strategies of Internet companies: Some preliminary insights from the UK. *The Journal of Brand Management*, *12*(5), 355–373. doi:10.1057/palgrave.bm.2540231

IDATE. (2000). *Prioritising countries for assistance to overcome the digital divide*. IDATE, Montepellier.

IDC. (2001). *The IDC/world times information society index: The future of the information society*. Framingham, MA: IDC.

Igbaria, M., Zinatelli, N., Cragg, P., & Cavaye, A. (1997). Personal computing acceptance factors in small firms: A structural equation model. *MIS Quarterly*, *21*(3), 279–305. doi:10.2307/249498

Igbaria, M., Guimaraes, T., & Davis, G. (1995). Testing the determinants of microcomputer usage via a structural equation model. *Journal of Management Information Systems*, *11*(2), 87–114.

Igbaria, M., Parasuraman, S., & Baroudi, J. (1996). A motivational model of microcomputer usage. *Journal of Management Information Systems*, *13*(2), 127–143.

Igbaria, M., Zinatelli, N., Cragg, P., & Cavaye, A. (1997). Personal computing acceptance factors in small firms: A structural equation model. *Management Information Systems Quarterly*, *21*(3), 279–305. doi:10.2307/249498

International Telecommunication Union (ITU). (2003). *ITU digital access index: World's first global ICT ranking.* Geneva, Switzerland: ITU. Retrieved from http://www.itu.int/newsarchive/press releases/2003/30.html

International Telecommunication Union (ITU). (2005). *Measuring digital opportunity.* Paper presented at the WSIS Thematic Meeting on Multi-Stakeholder Partnerships for Bridging the Digital Divide, Seoul, Republic of Korea, June. Retrieved from http://www.itu.int/itu-wsis/2005/DOI%20V2.pdf.

Internet World Stats. (2008). World Internet users and population stats. *Internet World Stats.* Retrieved July 28, 2008, from http://www.internetworldstats.com/stats.htm.

Irani, Z., Ezingeard, J.-N., & Grieve, R. J. (1997). Integrating the costs of a manufacturing IT/IS infrastructure into the investment decision-making process. *Technovation, 17*(11/12), 695–362. doi:10.1016/S0166-4972(97)00060-6

Iyer, R., & Bejou, D. (Eds.). (2003). *Customer relationship management in electronic markets.* Binghamton, NY: Hawthorne Press.

Jain, P. (2005). *E-readiness assessment for SMEs in India.* New Delhi, India: Ministry of Small Scale Industries, Government of India. Retrieved from http://www.annualmeeting2005.insme.org/documents

James, J. (2009). From the relative to the absolute digital divide in developing countries. *Technological Forecasting and Social Change, 76,* 1124–1129. doi:10.1016/j.techfore.2009.01.004

James, J., McNaught, C., Csete, J., Hodgson, P., & Vogel, D. (2003). From MegaWeb to e³Learning: A model of support for university academics to effectively use the Web for teaching and learning. In D. Lassner & C. McNaught (Eds.), ED-MEDIA 2003, Proceedings of the 15th annual World Conference on Educational Multimedia, Hypermedia & Telecommunications, (pp. 3303–3310). Honolulu, Hawaii, USA, 23–28 June. Norfolk, VA: Association for the Advancement of Computers in Education.

Janes, L. Pollett, & Reid. (1997). *The growth of electronic commerce: A critique.* Retrieved from http://www.geocities/Colsseum/7542

Jankowicz, A. D. (2005). *Business research projects* (4th ed.). Thomson Learning.

Jantan, M., Ismail, N., Ramayah, T., & Mohamed Salehuddin, A. H. (2001). The CEO and AMT adoption in Malaysian small and medium scale manufacturing industries. In *Proceedings of the International Conference on Information Technology,* Lausanne, Switzerland.

Jarboe, G. (March 16, 2007). *Boosting PR results with SEO and RSS.* Retrieved March 18, 2009 from www.ipressroom.com/pr/ SchwartzmanPR/info/document/JarboeBulldogChicago2007.ppt

Jarvenpaa, S. L., Tractinsky, N., & Vitale, M. (2000). Consumer trust in an Internet store. *Information Technology Management, 1*(1-2), 45–71. doi:10.1023/A:1019104520776

Javenpaa, S., & Todd, P. (1997). Consumer reactions to electronic shopping on the World Wide Web. *International Journal of Electronic Commerce, 1*(2), 59–88.

Jaw, Y.-L., & Chen, C.-L. (2006). The influence of the Internet in the internationalization of SMEs in Taiwan. *Human Systems Management, 25*(3), 167–183.

Jaworski, B. J., & Kohli, A. J. (1993). Marketing orientation: Antecedents and consequences. *Journal of Marketing, 57,* 53–70. doi:10.2307/1251854

Jerman-Blazˇicˇ, B. (2008). Web-hosting market development status and its value as an indicator of a country's e-readiness. *Telecommunications Policy, 32,* 422–435. doi:10.1016/j.telpol.2008.04.007

Jeyaraj, A., Rottman, J. W., & Lacity, M. C. (2006). A Review of the Predictors, Linkages, and Biases in IT Innovation Adoption Research. *Journal of Information Technology, 21*(1), 1–23. doi:10.1057/palgrave.jit.2000056

Jin, J., & Chengyu, X. (2002). The digital divide in terms of national informatization quotient (NIQ): The perspective of mainland China. *Proceedings of the International Conference on Digital Divides: Technology and Politics in the Information Age,* Hong Kong, Baptist University, Hong Kong, SAR, China.

Johanson, J., & Vahlne, J.-E. (1977). The internationalization process of the firm - A model of knowledge development and increasing foreign market commitments. *Journal of International Business Studies, 8*(1), 23–32. doi:10.1057/palgrave.jibs.8490676

Johnson, M. D., & Selnes, F. (2004). Customer portfolio management: Toward a dynamic theory of exchange relationships. *Journal of Marketing, 68*, 1–17. doi:10.1509/jmkg.68.2.1.27786

Joint Information Systems Committee. (2008). Exploring tangible benefits of e-learning: Does investment yield interest? Retrieved September 15, 2010, from http://www.jiscinfonet.ac.uk/publications/camel-tangible-benefits.pdf

Jones, T., & Ram, M. (2003). South Asian businesses in retreat? The case of the United Kingdom. *Journal of Ethnic and Migration Studies, 29*(3), 485–500. doi:10.1080/13691830305611

Jung, J.-Y., Qiu, J. L., & Kim, Y.-C. (2001). Internet connectedness and inequality: Beyond the "Divide.". *Communication Research, 28*(4), 507–535. doi:10.1177/009365001028004006

Jupiter Research. (2008). Jupiter research. *Jupiter Research*. Retrieved July 28, 2008, from http://www.jupiterresearch.com /bin/item.pl/home/.

Jutla, D., Bodorik, P., & Dhaliwal, J. (2002). Government support for the e-readiness of small and medium sized enterprises. *Proceedings of the 35th Hawaii International Conference on System Sciences* (IEEE Conference), USA.

Kadlec, P., & Mareš, M. (2003). B2B e-commerce opportunity for SMEs. In *Proceedings of the 11th International Conference on Systems Integration,* Prague, Czech Republic (pp. 537-544).

Kai-Uwe Brock, J. (2000). Information and technology in the small firm. In Carter, S., & Jones-Evans, D. (Eds.), *Enterprise and the small business* (pp. 384–408). Prentice Hall, Pearson Education.

Kalapesi, C., Willersdorf, S., & Zwillenberg, P. (2010). *The connected kingdom: How the Internet is transforming the U.K. economy*. Boston, MA: Boston Consulting Group.

Karahanna, E., Straub, D. W., & Chervany, N. L. (1999). Information Technology adoption across time: A cross-sectional comparison of pre-adoption and post-adoption beliefs. *Management Information Systems Quarterly, 23*(2), 183–213. doi:10.2307/249751

Karjaluoto, H., Mattila, M., & Pento, T. (2002). Electronic Banking in Finland Consumer Beliefs and Reactions to a New Delivery Channel. *Journal of Financial Services Marketing, 6*(4), 346–360. doi:10.1057/palgrave.fsm.4770064

Karvonen, K. (1999). Enhancing Trust Online. Proccedings of PhDIT'99: Ethics in Information Technology Design. Second International Workshop on Philosophy of Design and Information technology, 16-17 December, 1999, Saint-Ferreol, Toulouse, France

Kasraian, L. (2007). *The impact of e-readiness on EC success in public sector in Iran: The case of KWPA.* Khouzestan Water & Power Authority, Ministry of Energy. Master Thesis, Luleå University of Technology, Sweden.

Kasteler, J. M., Gay, R. M., & Caruth, M. J. (1968). Involuntary relocation of the elderly. *The Gerontologist, 8*(4), 276–279.

Kau, A. K., Tang, Y. E., & Ghose, S. (2003). Typology of online shoppers. *Journal of Consumer Marketing, 20*(2), 139–156. doi:10.1108/07363760310464604

Keen, P. G. W. (1991). *Shaping the future: Business design through Information Technology*. Boston, MA: Harvard Business School Press.

Kelley, J. R., & Edward, W. (1997). The future of Electronic money: a regulator's perspective. *IEEE Spectrum, 34,* Issue: 2, from http://140.98.193.112/xpls/abs_all.jsp?isnumber=12295&arnumber=570822&count=17&index=5

Kennedy, A. (2006). Electronic customer relationship management, (e-CRM): Opportunities and challenges in a digital world. *Irish Marketing Review, 18*(1/2), 58–69.

Kenny, C. (2001). Prioritising countries for assistance to overcome the digital divide. *Communications and Strategies, 41*, 17–36.

Khader, M. T. (2005). *The impact of adoption electronic commerce in small to medium enterprises Jordanian companies*. Retrieved from http://medforist.grenobleem.com/Contenus/Conference%20Amman%20EBEL%2005/pdf/26.pdf

Kiiski, S., & Pohjola, M. (2001). *Cross-country diffusion of the Internet*. United Nations University, World Institute for Development Economic Research.

Kim, G., Shin, B., & Lee, H. G. (in press). Understanding dynamics between initial trust and usage intention of mobile banking. *Information Systems Journal*.

Kim, D. (2003). The internationalization of US Internet portals: Does it fit the process model of internationalization? *Marketing Intelligence & Planning*, *21*(1), 23–36. doi:10.1108/02634500310458126

Kim, E., Nam, D.-I., & Stimpert, J. L. (2004). Testing the applicability of Porter's generic strategies in the digital age: A study of Korean cyber malls. *The Journal of Business Strategy*, *21*(1), 19–45.

Kim, H., Chan, H., & Gupta, S. (2007). Value-based adoption of mobile Internet: An empirical investigation. *Decision Support Systems*, *43*(1), 111–126. doi:10.1016/j.dss.2005.05.009

Kim, H. W., & Xu, Y. (2004). *Internet shopping: Is it a matter of perceived price or trust?* Paper presented at the International Conference on Information Systems, Washington, DC.

Kirkman, G. S., Osorio, C. A., & Sachs, J. D. (2002). *The networked readiness index: Measuring the preparedness of nations for the networked world*. Cambridge, MA: Center for International Development (CID), Harvard University.

Kleindl, B. (2000). Competitive dynamics and new business models for SMEs in the virtual marketplace. *Journal of Developmental Entrepreneurship*, *5*(1), 73–85.

Kobsa, A. (2002). Personalized Hypermedia and International Privacy. *Communications of the ACM*, *45*(5), 64–67. doi:10.1145/506218.506249

Kobsa, A. (2001). Tailoring Privacy to Users' Needs (invited keynote) in Bauer, M., Gmytrasiewicz, P.J. and Vassileva, J.(Eds), Proccedings of the User Modeling 2001: 8th International Conference, Springer Verlag, Berlin and Heidelberg, 303-13

Kolodinsky, J.M, Hogarth, J.M., & Hilger, M.A (2004). The Adoption of Electronic Banking Technologies by US Customers. The International journal of Bank, 22(4), 238-256

Korea Institute for Electronic Commerce. (2005). *Korea e-business white paper*. Retrieved from http://www.kiec.or.kr

Kotler, P. (2003). *Marketing management*. USA: Prentice-Hall International, Inc.

Koufaris, M., Kambil, A., & LaBarbera, P. A. (2002). Consumer behavior in web-based commerce: An empirical study. *International Journal of Electronic Commerce*, *6*(2), 115–138.

Koufaris, M. (2002). Applying the technology acceptance model and flow theory to online consumer behavior. *Information Systems Research*, *13*(2), 205–223. doi:10.1287/isre.13.2.205.83

Krishnamurthy, S. (2002). An empirical study of the causal antecedents of customer confidence in e-tailers. *First Monday*, *6*(1), 1–13.

Kuan, K. K. Y., & Chau, P. Y. K. (2001). A Perception-Based Model for EDI Adoption in Small Businesses Using a Technology-Organization-Environment Framework. *Information & Management*, *38*(8), 507–521. doi:10.1016/S0378-7206(01)00073-8

Kubicek, H. (2004). Fighting a moving target. *IT & Society*, *1*(6), 1–19.

Kula, V., & Tatoglu, E. (2003). An exploratory study of Internet adoption by SMEs in an emerging market economy. *European Business Review*, *15*(5), 324–333. doi:10.1108/09555340310493045

Kuo, Y. F., Wu, C. M., & Deng, W. J. (2009). The relationships among service quality, perceived value, customer satisfaction, and post-purchase intention in mobile value-added services. *Computers in Human Behavior*, 887–896. doi:10.1016/j.chb.2009.03.003

Kwintessential (2009). Culture and Web site localization. *Kwintessential*. Retrieved April 3, 2009, from http://www.kwintessential.co.uk /translation/articles/ culture-Website-localization.html.

Kwon, T. H., & Zmud, R. W. (1987). Unifying the fragmented models of Information Systems implementation. In Boland, R. J., & Hirscheim, R. A. (Eds.), *Critical issues in Information Systems research*. New York, NY: John Wiley & Sons.

Lafferty Ltd. (2005). Payments industry facing a rapidly growing menace from online criminals, from http://proquest.umi.com/pqdweb?did=862647621&sid=12&Fmt=3&clientId=24792&RQT=309&VName=PQD

Lai, V. S., & Li, H. (2005). Technology acceptance model for internet banking: An invariance analysis. *Information & Management*, *42*(2), 373–386. doi:10.1016/j.im.2004.01.007

Lal, K. (2002). E-business and manufacturing sector: A study of small and medium-sized enterprises in India. *Research Policy*, *31*, 1199–1211. doi:10.1016/S0048-7333(01)00191-3

Lall, S., & Pietrobelli, C. (2002). *Failing to compete: Technology development and technology systems in Africa*. Cheltenham, UK: Edward Elgar.

Lam, P., Csete, J., & McNaught, C. (2009). Costs of e-learning support: An investigation across 139 small projects. [IJEA]. *International Journal of E-Adoption*, *1*(1), 61–75. doi:10.4018/jea.2009010105

Lam, P., McNaught, C., & Cheng, K.-F. (2008). Pragmatic meta-analytic studies: Learning the lessons from naturalistic evaluations of multiple cases. *Association of Learning Technologies Journal ALT-J*, *16*(2), 61–79. doi:10.1080/09687760802315879

Lam, P., Au Yeung, M., Cheung, E., & McNaught, C. (2009). Using the development of eLearning material as challenging and authentic learning experiences for students. In R. Atkinson & C. McBeath (Eds.), Same places, different spaces. Proceedings of the 26th annual Australasian Society for Computers in Learning in Tertiary Education Conference (pp. 548–556). (ASCILITE), University of Auckland, 6–9 December. Retrieved September 15, 2010, from http://www.ascilite.org.au/conferences/auckland09/procs/lam.pdf

Lang, J. R., & Calantone, R. J. (1997). Small Firm Information Seeking as a Response to Environmental Threats and Opportunities. *Journal of Small Business Management*, *35*(1), 11–23.

Langston, C. M., & Teas, R. K. (1976). *Export commitment and characteristics of management*. Paper presented at the Annual Meeting of the Midwest Business Association, St Louis, MO.

Lassar, W. M., Manolis, C., & Lassar, S. S. (2005). The relationship between consumer innovativeness, personal characteristics, and online banking adoption. *International Journal of Bank Marketing*, *23*(2), 176–199. doi:10.1108/02652320510584403

Laudon, K. C., & Laudon, J. P. (2007). *Management Information Systems* (10th ed.). New Jersey: Pearson Prentice Hall.

Laudon, K. C., & Traver, C. G. (2008). *E-commerce business, technology, society* (4th ed.). London, UK: Pearson.

Laukkanen, T. (2007). Internet vs mobile banking: Comparing customer value perceptions. *Business Process Management*, *13*(6), 788–797. doi:10.1108/14637150710834550

Lawrence, E., Corbitt, B., Tidwell, A., Fisher, J., & Lawrence, J. (1998). *Internet commerce: Digital models for business*. Australia: John Wiley & Sons Australia, Ltd.

Lawson, R., Alcock, C., Cooper, J., & Burgess, L. (2003). Factors affecting adoption of electronic commerce technologies by SMEs: An Australian study. *Journal of Small Business and Enterprise Development*, *10*(3), 265–276. doi:10.1108/14626000310489727

Lederer, A. L., & Mendelow, A. L. (1988). Convincing top management of the strategic potential of information systems. *MIS Quarterly*, *12*(4), 526–536. doi:10.2307/249127

Lee, M.-C. (2009). Factors influencing the adoption of Internet banking: An integration of TAM and TPB with perceived risk and perceived benefit. *Electronic Commerce Research and Applications*, *8*(3), 130–141. doi:10.1016/j.elerap.2008.11.006

Lee, J. (2004). Discriminant analysis of technology adoption behaviour: A case of Internet technologies in small businesses. *Journal of Computer Information Systems*, *44*(4), 57–66.

Lee, S. T., Gholami, R., & Tong, T. Y. (2005). Time series analysis in the assessment of ICT impact at the aggregate level—Lessons and implications for the new economy. *Information & Management*, *42*, 1009–1022. doi:10.1016/j.im.2004.11.005

Lee, B. L. (2005). *Factors influencing e-mail usage: Applying the UTAUT Model*. Unpublished MBA dissertation, Universiti Sains Malaysia, Penang.

Lee, L. Z. (2005). Evolving localization and its brand extension. *Galaxy Newsletter, Q4*. Retrieved April 3, 2009, from http://www.gala-global.org/ newsletters/newsletter_3516.html.

Legris, P., Ingham, J., & Collerette, P. (2003). Why do people use information technology? A critical review of the technology acceptance model. *Information & Management, 40*(3), 191–204. doi:10.1016/S0378-7206(01)00143-4

Levy, M., & Powell, P. (2003). Exploring SME Internet adoption: Towards a contingent model. *Electronic Markets, 13*(2), 173–181. doi:10.1080/1019678032000067163

Levy, M., Powell, P., & Yetton, P. (2002). The dynamics of SME information systems. *Small Business Economics, 19*(4), 341–354. doi:10.1023/A:1019654030019

Levy, M., Powell, P., & Worrall, L. (2005). Strategic intent and e-business in SMEs enablers and inhibitors. *Information Resources Management Journal, 18*(4), 1–20. doi:10.4018/irmj.2005100101

Levy, M., Powell, P., & Yetton, P. (1998). SMEs and the gains from IS: From cost reduction to value added. In Larsen, T., Levine, L., & DeGross, J. (Eds.), *Information Systems: Current issues and future changes* (pp. 377–392). Amsterdam, The Netherlands: Kluwer Academic Publishers.

Levy, M., & Beckinsale, M. J. J. (2004). *SMEs and Internet adoption strategy: Who do SMEs listen to?* Paper presented at the 12th European Conference on Information Systems, June 14-16, 2004, Turku, Finland.

Levy, M., Powell, P., & Yetton, P. (2002). SMEs: The dynamics of IS development, small business economics.

Liao, S., Shao, Y. P., Wang, H., & Chen, A. (1999). The adoption of virtual banking: An empirical study. *International Journal of Information Management, 19*(1), 63–74. doi:10.1016/S0268-4012(98)00047-4

Liao, Z., & Cheung, M. T. (2002). Internet-based e-banking and consumer attitudes: An empirical study. *Information & Management, 39*, 283–295. doi:10.1016/S0378-7206(01)00097-0

Liaw, S. S., & Huang, H.-M. (2003). An investigation of user attitudes toward search engines as an information retrieval tool. *Computers in Human Behavior, 19*(6), 751–766. doi:10.1016/S0747-5632(03)00009-8

Liew, V. K. (2002). *The Prospect of E-commerce for the Small and Medium Enterprises in Malaysia*. Kuala Lumpur, Malaysia: University of Malaya.

Lim, T. M. (2006). *Outsourcings to ensure successful ICT systems implementation and maintenance*. School of Information Technology, Monash University. Retrieved March 20, 2008, from http://www.infotech.monash.edu.my /news/media.html

Lin, C., Huang, Y.-A., & Tseng, S.-W. (2007). A study of planning and implementation stages in electronic commerce adoption and evaluation: The case of Australian SMEs. *Contemporary Management Research, 3*(1), 83–100.

Lin, C., Lin, K., Huang, Y., & Kuo, N. (2006). Evaluation of electronic customer relationship management: The critical success factors. *Business Review (Federal Reserve Bank of Philadelphia), 6*(2), 206–212.

Linden, A., Fenn, J., McCoy, D., Cearley, D., Drakos, N., Tully, J., et al. (2005). *Hype cycle for emerging technologies, 2005* (Report No. G00129853). Retrieved October 21, 2008, from http://www.gartner.com/DisplayDocument?doc_cd=129853

Little, B. (2010). E-learning flowers in the UK. *Industrial and Commercial Training, 42*(3), 135–138. doi:10.1108/00197851011049158

Lituchy, T. R., & Rail, A. (2000). Bed and breakfasts, small inns, and the Internet: The impact of technology on the globalization of small business. *Journal of International Marketing, 8*(2), 86–97. doi:10.1509/jimk.8.2.86.19625

Liu, C., & Arnett, K. P. (2000). Exploring the factors associated with Web site success in the context of electronic commerce. *Information & Management, 38*(1), 23–33. doi:10.1016/S0378-7206(00)00049-5

Liu, C., Marchewka, J., & Ku, C. (2004). American and Taiwanese perceptions concerning privacy, trust, and behavioral intentions in electronic commerce. *Journal of Global Information Management, 12*(1), 18–40. doi:10.4018/jgim.2004010102

Livingstone, S., & Helsper, E. (2007). Gradations in digital inclusion: Children, young people and the digital divide. *New Media & Society*, *9*(4), 671–696. doi:10.1177/1461444807080335

Localization Program at California State University. Chico, College of Business (2008). What is localization? *The Localization Program*. Retrieved November 26, 2008, from http://www.csuchico.edu/localize/ whatislocalization.html.

Lockett, N., Brown, D. H., & Kaewkitipong, L. (2006). The Use of Hosted Enterprise Applications by SMEs: A Dual Market and User Perspective. *Electronic Markets*, *16*(1), 85–96. doi:10.1080/10196780500491444

Lockett, N., & Brown, D. H. (2006). Aggregation and the role of trusted third parties in SME e-business engagement: A regional policy issue. *International Small Business Journal*, *24*(4), 379–404. doi:10.1177/0266242606065509

Lockett, N. (1999). Legal Perspective on Digital money in Europe. *European Business Review*, *99*(4), 235–241. doi:10.1108/09555349910281423

Lohse, G., & Spiller, P. (1998). Electronic shopping. *Communications of the ACM*, *41*(7), 81–86. doi:10.1145/278476.278491

Lommel, A. (2003). LISA, The localization industry primer, 2nd edition. *LISA*. Retrieved July 28, 2008, from http://www.lisa.org/ Globalization-Indust.468.0.html?&no_cache=1&sword_list[]= industry&sword_list[]= localizatio&sword_list[]=primer.

Long, K. (2004). Customer loyalty and experience design. *Design Management Review*, *15*(2), 60–67. doi:10.1111/j.1948-7169.2004.tb00163.x

Love, P. E. D., & Irani, Z. (2004). An exploratory study of Information Technology evaluation and benefits management practices for SMEs in the constructing industry. *Information & Management*, *42*(1), 227–242.

Love, P. E. D., Irani, Z., Li, H., Cheng, E. W. L., & Tse, R. Y. C. (2001). An empirical analysis of the barriers to implementing e-commerce in small-medium sized construction contractors in the state of Victoria, Australia. *Construction Innovation*, *1*(1), 31–41.

Luarn, P., & Lin, H. H. (2005). Toward an understanding of the behavioral intention to use mobile banking. *Computers in Human Behavior*, *21*(6), 873–891. doi:10.1016/j.chb.2004.03.003

Luna, D., Peracchio, L. A., & de Juan, M. D. (2002). Cross-cultural and cognitive aspects of Web site navigation. *Journal of the Academy of Marketing Science*, *30*(4), 397–410. doi:10.1177/009207002236913

Lunati, M. (2000). *SMEs and electronic commerce: An overview*. OECD, Directorate for Science, Presented to the Technology and Industry Committee, DST/IND/PME.

Luo, X., Li, H., Zhang, J., & Shim, J. P. (2010). Examining multi-dimensional trust and multi-faceted risk in initial acceptance of emerging technologies: An empirical study of mobile banking services. *Decision Support Systems*, 222–234. doi:10.1016/j.dss.2010.02.008

Lytras, M. D., & Pouloudi, A. (2001). E-learning: Just a waste of time. In D. Strong, D. Straub, & J. I. DeGross (Eds.), Proceedings of the Seventh Americas Conference on Information Systems AMCIS (pp. 216–222). Boston, Massachusetts. Retrieved September 15, 2010, from http://citeseerx.ist.psu.edu/viewdoc/download?doi=10.1.1.21.5012&rep=rep1&type=pdf

Ma, Q., & Liu, L. (2003). *The role of internet self-efficacy in accepting Web-based medical records*. Paper presented at the Americas Conference on Information Systems, Tampa, FL.

MacGregor, R. C. (2004). The role of small business strategic alliances in the adoption of E-commerce in small-medium enterprises (SMEs). Retrieved June 6, 2008, from http://ro.uow.edu.au/cgi/ viewcontent.cgi?article=1303&context=theses

MacGregor, R. C., & Vrazalic, L. (Eds.). (2008). *E-commerce in regional Small to Medium Enterprises*. Hershey, PA: IGI Publishing.

Macintyre, G., & Ramnarine, D. (2003). *National ICT strategy development e-readiness assessment report*. Trinidad and Tobago: Ministry of Public Administration & Information. Retrieved from http://unpan1.un.org/intradoc/groups/public/documents/UN/UNPAN015505.pdf

Maguire, S., Koh, S. C. L., & Magrys, A. (2007). The adoption of e-business and knowledge management in SMEs. *Benchmarking: An International Journal, 14*(1), 37–58. doi:10.1108/14635770710730928

Maher, M. W., Sommer, B., Acredolo, C., & Matthews, H. R. (2005). What are the relevant costs of online education? In Groccia, J. E., & Miller, J. E. (Eds.), *On becoming a productive university: Strategies for reducing costs and increasing quality in higher education* (pp. 196–204). Bolton, MA: Anker Publishing Company.

Mahinda, E., & Whitworth, B. (2005). *The Web of system performance: Extending the TAM model.* Paper presented at the Americas Conference on Information Systems, Omaha, NE.

Malhotra, N., Kim, S., & Agarwal, J. (2004). User's information privacy concerns (IUIPC): The construct, the scale, and a causal model. *Information Systems Research, 15*(4), 336–355. doi:10.1287/isre.1040.0032

Mansor, N., & Abidin, A. F. A. (2010). The application of e-commerce among Malaysian small medium enterprises. *European Journal of Scientific Research, 41*(4), 591–605.

Martin, L. (2005). Internet adoption and use in small firms: Internal processes, organisational culture and the roles of the owner-manager and key staff. *New Technology, Work and Employment, 20*(3), 190–204. doi:10.1111/j.1468-005X.2005.00153.x

Martin, L., & Matlay, H. (2001). "Blanket" approaches to promoting ICT in small firms: Some lessons from the DTI ladder adoption model in the UK. *Internet Research, 11*(5), 399–410. doi:10.1108/EUM0000000006118

Martin, L., & Matlay, H. (2003). Innovative use of the Internet in established small firms: The impact of knowledge management and organisational learning in accessing new opportunities. *Qualitative Market Research: An International Journal, 6*(1), 18–26. doi:10.1108/13522750310457348

Masalu, D. C. P. (2005). Evolution of information and communication technology in Tanzania and its impact on ocean data and information management. *Ocean and Coastal Management, 48*, 85–95. doi:10.1016/j.ocecoaman.2004.11.001

Massachusetts Technology Collaborative. (2003). *Executive index of the Massachusetts innovation economy.* Westborough, MA. Retrieved from http:64.233.167.104/search?q=cache:fQiIBz61YPUJ:www.cityofboston.gov/bra/gbtf/documents/MTC%2520IndexInnovEconomy2003.pdf

Massetti, B., & Zmud, R. W. (1996). Measuring the extent of EDI usage in complex organizations: Strategies and illustrative examples. *Management Information Systems Quarterly, 20*(3), 331–345. doi:10.2307/249659

Mathieson, K. (1991). Predicting user intentions: Comparing the technology acceptance model with the theory of planned behavior. *Information Systems Research, 2*(3), 173–191. doi:10.1287/isre.2.3.173

Mathwick, C. (2002). Understanding the online consumer: A typology of online relational norms and behavior. *Journal of Interactive Marketing, 16*(1), 40–55. doi:10.1002/dir.10003

Matlay, H., & Westhead, P. (2005). Virtual teams and the rise of e-entrepreneurship in Europe. *International Small Business Journal, 23*(6), 279–302. doi:10.1177/0266242605052074

Matlay, H. (2000). Training in the small business sector of the British Economy. In S. Carter & D. Jones (Eds.), *Enterprise and small business: Principles, policy, and practice.* London: Addison Wesley Longman.

Mattila, M., Karjaluoto, H., & Pento, T. (2003). Internet Banking Adoption Among Mature Customers: Early Majority or Laggards. *Journal of Services Marketing, 17*(5), 514–526. doi:10.1108/08876040310486294

Mazzarol, T., Volery, T., Doss, N., & Thein, V. (1999). Factors influencing small business start-ups. *International Journal of Enterpreneurial Behaviour and Research, 5*(2), 48–63. doi:10.1108/13552559910274499

McCarthy, E. J. (1960). *Basic Marketing: A Managerial Approach.* Homewood, IL: Irwin.

McCole, P., & Ramsey, E. (2004). Internet-enabled technology in knowledge-intensive business services: A comparison of Northern Ireland, the Republic of Ireland and New Zealand. *Marketing Intelligence & Planning, 22*(7), 761–779. doi:10.1108/02634500410568

McConnell International (MI). (2001). *Ready, net, go!* Retrieved from http://www.mcconnellinternational.com/ereadiness/ereadinessreport2.htm

McConville, A. (2009). *Impact of ICT on SMEs in the South East: Report prepared for the South East of England Development Agency*. Birmingham, UK: BMG Research.

McDougall, P. P., & Oviatt, B. M. (2000). International entrepreneurship: The intersection of two research paths. *Academy of Management Journal, 43*(5), 902–906. doi:10.2307/1556418

McEntee, E. C. (2000). Connecting e-payment to e-commerce, from http://www.bankingmm.com/e-Commerce/e-payments.htm

McGowan, P., & Durkin, M. (2002). Toward an understanding of Internet adoption at the marketing/entrepreneurship interface. *Journal of Marketing Management, 18*, 361–377. doi:10.1362/0267257022872451

McGowan, P., Durkin, M., Allen, L., Dougan, C., & Nixon, S. (2001). Developing competencies in the entrepreneurial small firm for the use of the Internet in the management of customer relationships. *Journal of European Industry Training, 25*(2/3/4), 126-36.

McNaught, C., Lam, P., Cheng, K.-F., Kennedy, D. M., & Mohan, J. B. (2009). Challenges in employing complex e-learning strategies in campus-based universities. *International Journal of Technology Enhanced Learning, 1*(4), 266–285. doi:10.1504/IJTEL.2009.030778

McNaught, C., & Vogel, D. (2006). The fit between e-learning policy and institutional culture. *International Journal of Learning Technology, 2*(4), 370–385. doi:10.1504/IJLT.2006.011341

McNaught, C. (2007). Developing criteria for successful learning repositories. In Filipe, J., Cordeiro, J., & Pedrosa, V. (Eds.), *Web Information Systems and Technologies* (pp. 8–18). Dordrecht, The Netherlands: Springer. doi:10.1007/978-3-540-74063-6_2

McNaught, C., & Lam, P. (2009). Institutional strategies for embedding blended learning in a research-intensive university. Proceedings of the elearn2009 Conference, Bridging the development gap through innovative eLearning environments, The University of the West Indies, St Augustine, Trinidad and Tobago, 8-11 June 2009.

McQuade, S., Waitman, R., Zeisser, M., & Kierzkowski, A. (1996). Marketing to the digital consumer. *The McKinsey Quarterly, 3*, 5–21.

Mehrtens, J., Cragg, P. B., & Mills, A. M. (2001). A model of Internet adoption by SMEs. *Information & Management, 39*(3), 165–176. doi:10.1016/S0378-7206(01)00086-6

Methlie, L. B., & Nysveen, H. (1999). Loyalty of online bank customers. *Journal of Information Technology, 14*, 375–386. doi:10.1080/026839699344485

Migration Policy Group. (2002). *Supplier diversity: The case of immigrant and ethnic minority enterprise.* Background paper prepared for the Transatlantic Round Table, Brussels, 15 January 2002.

Mingers, J. (2002). Realizing Information Systems: Critical realism as an underpinning philosophy for Information Systems. *Proceedings from the International Conference on Information Systems*, (pp. 295-303). Association of Information Systems, Barcelona.

Mirchandani, D. A., & Motwani, J. (2001). Understanding small business e-commerce adoption: An empirical analysis. *Journal of Computer Information Systems, 41*(3), 70–73.

Misra, S. K. Rajshekhar (Raj) G.Javalgi and Robert F.Schere (2004), "Global Electronic Money and Related Issue" http://www.findarticles.com/p/articles/mi_go2233/is_200403/ai_n6545665

Miyazaki, A. D., & Fernadez, A. (2001). Consumer perceptions of privacy and security risks for online shopping. *The Journal of Consumer Affairs, 35*(1), 27–44. doi:10.1111/j.1745-6606.2001.tb00101.x

Mols, N. P. (1998). The Behavioural Consequences of PC Banking. *International Journal of Bank Marketing, 16*(5), 195–201. doi:10.1108/02652329810228190

Moodley, S. (2001). Impact of electronic commerce and small exporting firms in the South African wooden furniture manufacturing sector. *Journal of Information Technology Impact, 2*(3), 89–104.

Mooij, M. D. (1998). *Global marketing and advertising. Understanding cultural paradox*. Thousand Oaks, CA: Sage Publications.

Moonen, J. (1997). The efficiency of telelearning. *Journal of Asynchronous Networked Learning, 1*(2), 68–77.

Moore, G., & Benbasat, I. (1991). Development of an instrument to measure the perceptions of adopting new Information Technology innovation. *Information Systems Research, 2*(3), 192–222. doi:10.1287/ isre.2.3.192

Morris, M., & Ventakesch, V. (2000). Age differences in technology adoption decisions: Implications for a changing work force. *Personnel Psychology, 53*(2), 375–403. doi:10.1111/j.1744-6570.2000.tb00206.x

Morris, M. B., Schindehutte, M., & Laforge, R. W. (2002). Entrepreneurial marketing: A construct for integrating emerging entrepreneurship and marketing perspectives. *Journal of Marketing Theory and Practice, 10*(4), 1–19.

Morrisette, S., McQuivey, J., Maraganore, N., & Lampher, G. (1999). *Are net shoppers loyal?* Boston, MA: Forrester.

Mossberger, K., Tolbert, C. J., & Stansbury, M. (2003). *Virtual inequality: Beyond the digital divide*. Washington, DC: Georgetown University Press.

Moutinho, L., & Smith, A. (2000). Modeling bank customer satisfaction through mediation of attitudes towards human and automated banking. *International Journal of Bank Marketing, 18*(3), 124–134. doi:10.1108/02652320010339699

Mukhopadhyay, T., Kekre, S., & Kalathur, S. (1995). Business value of Information Technology: A study of electronic data interchange. *Management Information Systems Quarterly, 19*(2), 137–156. doi:10.2307/249685

Muthitacharoen, A., & Palvia, P. C. (2003). *Explaining alternative behaviors of online consumers: An integration of the technology acceptance model to preferential decision*. Paper presented at the Americas Conference on Information Systems, Tampa, FL.

Mutula, S. M., & van Brakel, P. (2006a). An evaluation of e-readiness assessment tools with respect to information access: Towards an integrated information rich tool. *International Journal of Information Management, 26*, 212–223. doi:10.1016/j.ijinfomgt.2006.02.004

Mutula, S. M., & van Brakel, P. (2006b). E-readiness of SMEs in the ICT sector in Botswana with respect to information access. *The Electronic Library, 24*(3), 402–417. doi:10.1108/02640470610671240

Mutume, G. (2003). Africa takes on the digital divide: New Information Technologies change the lives of those in reach. *Africa Renewal, 17*(3).

Napier, H. A., Rivers, O. N., Wagner, S. W., & Napier, J. B. (2005). *Creating a winning e-business*. Boston, MA: Thompson Course Technology.

Nardo, M., Saisana, M., Saltelli, A., & Tarantola, S. (2005). *Tools for composite indicators building*. European Communities. Retrieved from http://farmweb.jrc.cec.eu.int/ ci/bibliography.htm

National SME Development Council of Malaysia. (2005). *Definitions for small and medium enterprises in Malaysia*. Secretariat to National SME Development Council, Bank Negara Malaysia, Kuala Lumpur. Retrieved May 3, 2009, from http://www.smeinfo.com.my/ pdf/sme_definitions _ENGLISH.pdf

Ndubisi, N. O., & Jantan, M. (2003). Evaluating IS usage in Malaysian small and medium-sized firms using the technology acceptance model. *Logistics Information System, 16*(6), 440–450. doi:10.1108/09576050310503411

Nicol, D., & Coen, M. (2003). A model for evaluating the institutional costs and benefits of ICT initiatives in teaching and learning in higher education. *ALT-J, 11*(2), 46–60. doi:10.1080/0968776030110205

Nicol, D., & Coen, M. (2008). Getting from here to there - Strategies for change. In Boys, J., & Ford, P. (Eds.), *The e-revolution and post-compulsory education: Using e-business models to deliver quality education* (pp. 103–115). London, UK & New York, NY: Routledge.

Nolan, P., & O'Donnell, K. (1991). Restructuring and the Politics of Renewal: The Limits of Flexible Specialisation. In Pollert, A. (Ed.), *Farewell to Flexibility?* (pp. 158–178). Oxford: Blackwell.

Noor, N. L. M., Hashim, M., Haron, H., & Sriffin, S. (2005). *Community acceptance of knowledge sharing system in the travel and tourism Web sites: An application of an extension of TAM*. Paper presented at the European Conference on Information Systems, Regensburg, Germany.

Norazah, M. S. (2001). Malaysian Internet users' motivations and concerns on shopping online. *Malaysian Journal of Library & Information Sciences, 6*(2), 21–33.

Normah, M. A. (2006). *SMEs: Building blocks for economic growth*. Paper presented at the National Statistical Conference, Kuala Lumpur, Malaysia.

Normand, C., Littlejohn, A., & Falconer, I. (2008). A model for effective implementation of flexible programme delivery. *Innovations in Education and Teaching International, 45*(1), 25–36. doi:10.1080/14703290701757351

Norris, P. (2001). *The digital divide: Civic engagement. Information poverty & the Internet worldwide*. Cambridge, UK: Cambridge University Press.

Novak, T., Hoffman, D., & Yung, Y. (2000). Measuring the customer experience in online environments: A structural modeling approach. *Marketing Science, 19*(1), 22–42. doi:10.1287/mksc.19.1.22.15184

NTIA. (2002). *A nation online*. Washington, DC: U.S. Department of Commerce.

NTIA. (1995). *Falling through the Net: A survey of the 'have nots' in rural and urban America*. U.S. Department of Commerce, Washington DC, 1995. Retrieved from http://www.ntia.doc.gov/ntiahome/fallingthru.html

NTIA. (1998). *Falling through the Net II: More data on the digital divide*. U.S. Department of Commerce, Washington DC, 1998. Retrieved from http://www.ntia.doc.gov/ntiahome/net2

NTIA. (1999). *Falling through the Net III: Defining the digital divide*. U.S. Department of Commerce, Washington DC, 1999. Retrieved from http://www.ntia.doc.gov/ntiahome/fttn99/contents.html

NTIA. (2000). *Falling through the Net IV: Towards digital inclusion*. U.S. Department of Commerce, Washington DC, 2000. Retrieved from http://www.ntia.doc.gov/ntiahome/fttn00/contents-00.html

Nunnally, J., & Berstein, I. (1994). *Psychometric theory*. New York, NY: McGraw-Hill.

O'Donnell, A. (2004). The nature of networking in small firms. *Qualitative Market Research: An International Journal, 7*(3), 206–217. doi:10.1108/13522750410540218

O'Farrell, P. N., Hitchens, D. M., & Moffat, L. A. R. (1995). Business service firms in two peripheral economies: Scotland and Ireland. *Tijdschrift voor Economische en Sociale Geografie, 86*(2), 115–128. doi:10.1111/j.1467-9663.1995.tb01351.x

O'Keefe, R. M., O'Connor, G., & Kung, H.-J. (1998). Early adopters of the Web as a retail medium: Small company winners and losers. *European Journal of Marketing, 32*(7/8), 629–643. doi:10.1108/03090569810224038

O'Toole, T. (2001). E-relationships – Emergence and the small firm. *Marketing Intelligence & Planning, 21*(2), 115–122. doi:10.1108/02634500310465434

OECD. (2005). SME and entrepreneurship outlook. Retrieved November 6th, 2007, from www.oecd.org

Office for National Statistics. (2009). *E-commerce and information and communication Technology (ICT) activity, 2008*. Newport, UK: ONS.

Ogunlana, E. A. (2004). The technology adoption behavior of women farmers: The case of alley farming in Nigeria. *Renewable Agriculture and Food Systems, 19*, 57–65. doi:10.1079/RAFS200057

Ordanini, A. (2006). *Information Technology and Small Businesses: Antecedents and Consequences of Technology Adoption*. Cheltenham, UK: Edwaed Elgar.

Organisation for Economic Co-operation and Development. (1997). *Globalisation and Small and Medium Enterprises (SMEs)*. Paris, France: OECD Publications Service.

Organisation for Economic Co-operation and Development. (2004). *SME Statistics: Towards a more systematic statistical measurement of SME behaviour*. Background report for the 2nd OECD Conference of Ministers Responsible for Small and Medium Enterprises (SMEs), Istanbul, Turkey. Retrieved May 3, 2009, from http://www.oecd.org/dataoecd /6/6/31919286.pdf

Organisation for Economic Co-operation and Development. (2005). *OECD SME and Entrepreneurship Outlook - 2005 Edition*. Paris, France: OECD Publications Service. Retrieved May 3, 2009, from http://www.oecd.org/document /15/0,2340,en_2649_33956792 _35096847_1_1_1_1,00.html

Organization for Economic Co-operation and Development (OECD). (2001). *Understanding the digital divide.* Paris, France: OECD. Retrieved from http://www.oecd.org/dataoecd/38/57/1888451.pdf

Oviatt, B. M., & McDougall, P. P. (1999). Accelerated internationalization: Why are new and small ventures internationalizing in greater numbers and with increasing speed? In Wright, R. (Ed.), *Research in global strategic management* (pp. 23–40). Stamford, CT: JAI Press.

Ovum, "E-payments are the way to E-commerce success" URL: http://techtalk.appssolutions.com/viewcontent.asp?article_id=56

Owens, J. D., & Price, L. (2010). Is e-learning replacing the traditional lecture? *Education + Training, 52*(2), 128-139.

Oxley, J. E., & Yeung, B. (2001). E-commerce readiness: Institutional environment and international competitiveness. *Journal of International Business Studies, 32*(4), 705–723. doi:10.1057/palgrave.jibs.8490991

Oyelaran-Oyeyinka, B., & Lal, K. (2005). Internet diffusion in sub-Saharan Africa: A cross-country analysis. *Telecommunications Policy, 29*(7), 507–527. doi:10.1016/j.telpol.2005.05.002

Oyelaran-Oyeyinka, B., & Nyaki Adeya, C. (2004). Internet access in Africa: Empirical evidence from Kenya and Nigeria. *Telematics and Informatics, 21*(1), 67–81. doi:10.1016/S0736-5853(03)00023-6

Packham, G. (2002). Competitive advantage and growth: The challenge for small firms. *International Journal of Management and Decision-Making, 3*(2), 165–179. doi:10.1504/IJMDM.2002.002471

Packham, G., Brooksbank, D., Miller, C., & Thomas, B. (2005). Climbing the mountain: Management practice adoption in growth oriented firms in Wales. *Small Business and Enterprise Development, 12*(4), 482–497. doi:10.1108/14626000510628171

Packham, G., Jones, P., Miller, C., & Thomas, B. (2004). E-learning and retention: Key factors influencing student withdrawal. *Education + Training, 46*(6/7), 335-342.

Pan, S. L., & Lee, J. (2003). Using e-CRM for a unified view of the customer. *Communications of the ACM, 46*(4), 95–99. doi:10.1145/641205.641212

Papazafeiropoulou, A., Pouloudi, A., & Doukidis, G. (2002). A framework for best practices in electronic commerce awareness creation. *Business Process Management Journal, 8*(3), 233–245. doi:10.1108/14637150210428943

Park, C.-H., & Kim, Y.-G. (2003). Identifying key factors affecting consumer purchase behavior .in an online shopping context. *International Journal of Retail & Distribution Management, 31*(1), 16–29. doi:10.1108/09590550310457818

Parker, C., & Castleman, T. (2007). New directions for research on SME-eBusiness: Insights from an analysis of journal articles from 2003-2006. *Journal of Information Systems and Small Business, 1*(1), 21–40.

Parker, S. (2000). *A survey of small business in Colorado.* CCCOES, April.

Parsons, A. G. (2002). Non-functional motives for online shoppers: Why we click. *Journal of Consumer Marketing, 19*(4-5), 380–392. doi:10.1108/07363760210437614

Pätzold, H. (2005). Increasing value without increasing effort? The use of WebCT in accompanying face-to-face lectures. Journal of Distance Education Revue De L'Éducation À Distance, 20(2), 78–84. Retrieved September 15, 2010, from http://www.jofde.ca/index.php/jde/article/viewFile/83/62

Pavic, S., Koh, S. C. L., Simpson, M., & Padmore, J. (2007). Could e-business create a competitive advantage in UK SMEs? *Benchmarking: An International Journal, 14*(3), 320–351. doi:10.1108/14635770710753112

Pavlou, P. A. (2003). Consumer acceptance of electronic commerce: Integrating trust and risk with the technology acceptance model. *International Journal of Electronic Commerce, 7*(3), 69–103.

Pavlou, P. A., & Gefen, D. (2004). Building effective online marketplaces with institution-based trust. *Information Systems Research, 15*(1), 37–59. doi:10.1287/isre.1040.0015

Pavlou, P. A., Lie, T., & Dimoka, A. (2007). An integrative model of mobile commerce adoption. *JMR, Journal of Marketing Research*, 1–18.

Pavlou, P. (2003). Consumer acceptance of electronic commerce: Integrating trust and risk with the Technology Acceptance Model. *International Journal of Electronic Commerce, 7*(3), 69–103.

Payne, J. E. (1996). *E-commerce readiness for SMEs in developing countries: A guide for development professionals*. Washington, D.C., USA: Academy for Educational Development.

Peppers, D., Rodgers, M., & Dorf, B. (1999). Is your company ready for one-to-one marketing? *Harvard Business Review, 77*(1), 151–160.

Petersen, B., Welch, L. S., & Liesch, P. (2002). The Internet and foreign market expansion by firms. *Management International Review, 42*(2), 207–221.

Peterson, R., Balasubramanian, S., & Bronnenberg, B. (1997). Exploring the implications of the Internet for consumer marketing. *Academy of Marketing Sciences Journal, 25*(4), 329–346. doi:10.1177/0092070397254005

Phu, L. (2003). *Cambodia: The road to e-Governance*, Phnom Penh: National ICT Development Authority (NiDA).

Pikkarainen, T., Pikkarainen, K., Karjaluoto, H., & Pahnila, S. (2004). Consumer acceptance of online banking: An extension of the technology acceptance model. *Internet Research, 14*(3), 224–235. doi:10.1108/10662240410542652

Pikkarainen, T., Pikkarainen, K., Karjaluoto, H., & Pahnila, S. (2004). Consumer acceptance of online banking: An extension of the technology acceptance model. *Internet Research, 14*(3), 224–235. doi:10.1108/10662240410542652

Pitt, L., Berthon, P., & Watson, R. (1996). From surfer to buyer on the WWW: What marketing managers might want to know. *Journal of General Management, 22*(1), 1–13.

Pohjola, M. (2003). The adoption and diffusion of ICT across countries: Patterns and determinants. In Jones, D. C. (Ed.), *The new economy handbook*. San Diego, CA: Academic Press.

Polatoglu, V. N., & Ekins, S. (2001). An Empirical Investigation of the Turkish Consumers' Acceptance of Internet Banking Services. *International Journal of Bank Marketing, 19*(4), 156–165. doi:10.1108/02652320110392527

Pollach, I. (2005). Corporate self-presentation on the WWW: Strategies for enhancing usability, credibility and utility. *Corporate Communications, 10*(4), 285–301. doi:10.1108/13563280510630098

Pollman, A., W., & Johnson, A. C. (1974). Resistance to change, early retirement and managerial decisions. *Industrial Gerontology, 1*(1), 33–41.

Poon, S., & Swatman, P. M. C. (1999). An exploratory study of small business Internet commerce issues. *Information & Management, 35*(1), 9–18. doi:10.1016/S0378-7206(98)00079-2

Poon, S. (2000). Business environment and Internet commerce benefit- Small business perspective. *European Journal of Information Systems, 9*(2), 72–81.

Porter, M. E. (2001). Strategy and the Internet. *Harvard Business Review, 79*(3), 62–78.

Premkumar, G. (2003). A Meta-Analysis of Research on Information Technology Implementation in Small Business. *Journal of Organizational Computing and Electronic Commerce, 13*(2), 91–121. doi:10.1207/S15327744JOCE1302_2

Premkumar, G., & King, W. R. (1994). Organizational Characteristics and Information Systems Planning: An Empirical Study. *Information Systems Research, 5*(2), 75–109. doi:10.1287/isre.5.2.75

Premkumar, G., & Roberts, M. (1999). Adoption of New Information Technologies in Rural Small Businesses. *Omega: The International Journal of Management Science, 27*(4), 467–484. doi:10.1016/S0305-0483(98)00071-1

Premkumar, G., & Ramamurthy, K. (1995). The role of inter-organizational and organizational factors on the decision mode for adoption of inter organizational systems. *Decision Sciences, 26*(3), 303–336. doi:10.1111/j.1540-5915.1995.tb01431.x

Pricewaterhousecoopers (1999). *Asia Pacific Economic Cooperation (APEC): SME Electronic Commerce Study - Final Report September 24, 1999*. Retrieved May 12, 2009, from http://www.apec.org/apec/ publications/ free_downloads/ 1999.MedialibDownload.v1.html ?url=/ etc/medialib/ apec_media_library/downloads /working-groups/telwg/pubs /1999.Par.0001.File.v1.1

Qi, B., Lu, L., Oliver, S., Wang, C., & Zhang, R. (2008). *Can ICT replace the traditional teaching and learning model? A case study.* ECS 2009, March, Wuhan, China.

Quibria, M. G., Ahmed, S. N., Tschang, T., & Reyes-Macasaquit, M.-L. (2003). Digital divide: Determinants and policies with special reference to Asia. *Journal of Asian Economics*, *13*, 811–825. doi:10.1016/S1049-0078(02)00186-0

Ragins, J. E., & Greco, J. A. (2003). Customer relationship management and e-business: More than a software solution. *Review of Business, Cambridge*, *24*(1), 25–30.

Ram, M., Gilman, M., Arrowsmith, J., & Edwards, P. (2003). Once more into the sunset? Asian clothing firms after the national minimum wage. *Environment and Planning. C, Government & Policy*, *21*, 71–88. doi:10.1068/c0136

Ram, M., & Smallbone, D. (2002). Ethnic minority business support in the era of the small business service. *Environment and Planning. C, Government & Policy*, *20*(2), 235–249. doi:10.1068/c0050

Ram, M., & Smallbone, D. (2003). Policies to support ethnic minority enterprise: The English experience. *Entrepreneurship and Regional Development*, *15*(2), 151–166. doi:10.1080/0898562032000075177

Ram, M., & Jones, T. (2008). Ethnic minority business: An overview. Retrieved February 26, 2009, from http://www.oi.acidi.gov.pt/docs/Revista_3_EN/Migr3_Sec1_Art3_EN.pdf

Ram, M., & Smallbone, D. (1999). *Ethnic minority enterprises in Birmingham*. Paper presented to the 2nd Ethnic Minority Enterprise Seminar, London, November 1999.

Ramanathan, S. (1999). *Internet in Malaysia*. Retrieved from http://www.interasia.org/malaysia/ramanantha.html

Ramayah, T., Jantan, M., Mohd Noor, M. N., Razak, R. C., & Koay, P. L. (2003). Receptiveness of Internet banking by Malaysian consumers: The case of Penang. *Asian Academy of Management Journal*, *8*(2), 1–29.

Ramayah, T., Oh, S. M., & Omar, A. (2008). Behavioral determinants of online banking adoption: Some evidence from a multicultural society. *Journal of Management*, *2*(3), 29–37.

Ramayah, T., Yan, C. L., & Sulaiman, M. (2005). SME e-readiness in Malaysia: Implications for planning and implementation. *Sasin Journal of Management*, *11*(1), 103–120.

Ramayah, T., Dahlan, N., Mohamad, O., & Siron, R. (2002). Technology usage among owners/managers of SME's: The role of demographic and motivational variables. In *Proceedings of the 6th Annual Asian-Pacific Forum for Small Business on Small and Medium Enterprises Linkages, Networking and Clustering*, Kuala Lumpur, Malaysia.

Ramayah, T., Taib, M. F., & Koay, P. L. (2006). Classifying users and non-users of Internet banking in Northern Malaysia. *Journal of Internet Banking and Commerce*, *11*(2). Retrieved November 25, 2006, from http://www.arraydev.com /commerce/JIBC/2006-08/ Thurasamy.asp.htm

Ramdani, B., & Kawalek, P. (2007b). SMEs & IS Innovations Adoption: A Review & Assessment of Previous Research. [Latin American Journal of Management]. *Revista Latinoamericana de Administración*, *39*(1), 47–70.

Ramdani, B., & Kawalek, P. (2007a). *SME Adoption of Enterprise Systems in the Northwest of England: An Environmental, Technological and Organizational Perspective.* Paper presented at the IFIP - Organizational Dynamics of Technology-Based Innovation: Diversifying the Research Agenda, Boston.

Ramdani, B., & Kawalek, P. (2008). *Predicting SMEs Willingness to Adopt ERP, CRM, SCM & E-Procurement Systems.* Paper presented at the 16th European Conference on Information Systems.

Ramsey, E., Ibbotson, P., Bell, J., & Gray, B. (2003). E-opportunities of service sector SMEs: An Irish cross-border study. *Journal of Small Business and Enterprise Development*, *10*(3), 250–264. doi:10.1108/14626000310489709

Rao, S. S., Metts, G., & Monge, C. A. M. (2003). Electronic commerce development in small and medium sized enterprises: A stage model and its implications. *Business Process Management Journal*, *9*(1), 11–32. doi:10.1108/14637150310461378

Raskino, M. (2009, April 17). Classic hype cycle turn signal: 'Twitter Backlash' reported. Message posted to http://blogs.gartner.com/hypecyclebook/2009/04/17/classic-hype-cycle-turn-signal-twitter-backlash-reported/

Raymond, L. (2001). Determinants of Website Implementation in Small Businesses. *Internet Research, 11*(5), 411–422. doi:10.1108/10662240110410363

Raymond, L., Bergeron, F., & Blili, S. (2005). The assimilation of e-business in manufacturing SMEs: Determinants and effects on growth and internationalization. *Electronic Markets, 15*(2), 106–118. doi:10.1080/10196780500083761

Reich, B. H., & Benbasat, I. (1990). An Empirical Investigation of Factors Influencing the Success of Customer Oriented Strategic Systems. *Information Systems Research, 1*(3), 325–347. doi:10.1287/isre.1.3.325

Reichheld, F. F., & Sasser, J. W. E. (1990). Zero defections: Quality comes to services. *Harvard Business Review, 68*(5), 105–111.

Reichheld, F. F., & Schefter, P. (2000). E-loyalty: Your secret weapon on the Web. *Harvard Business Review*, 105–113.

Rensel, A. D., Abbas, J. M., & Rao, H. R. (2006). Private transactions in public places: An exploration of the impact of the computer environment on public transactional Web site use. *Journal of the Association for Information Systems, 7*(1), 19–51.

Report, J. M. M. B. *US Advertising Forecast*. (November 2007). Retrieved November 2008 from http://www.jackmyers.com

Reynolds, W., Savage, W., & Williams, A. (1994). *Your own business: A practical guide to success*. New York: Thomson Learning Nelson.

Ricci, A. (2000). Measuring information society dynamics of European data on usage of information and communication technologies in Europe since 1995. *Telematics and Informatics, 17*, 141–167. doi:10.1016/S0736-5853(00)00002-2

Richard, H. (1997). New Electronic Payment Technologies: A Look at Security Issues. *Journal of Retail Banking Services., XIX*(3), 41.

Riemenschneider, C. K., Harrison, D. A., & Mykytyn, P. P. (2003). Understanding IT adoption decisions in small business: Integrating current theories. *Information & Management, 40*(4), 269–287. doi:10.1016/S0378-7206(02)00010-1

Riemenschneider, C. K., Harrison, D. A., & Mykytyn, P. P. Jr. (2003). Understanding IT adoption decisions in small business: Integrating current theories. *Information & Management, 40*, 269–285. doi:10.1016/S0378-7206(02)00010-1

Rigby, D. K., Reichheld, F. F., & Schefter, P. (2002). Avoid the four perils of customer relationship marketing. *Harvard Business Review, 80*(2), 101–199.

Riggins, F. J., & Mukhopadhyay, T. (1994). Interdependent benefits from interorganizational systems: Opportunities for business partner reengineering. *Journal of Management Information Systems, 11*(2), 37–57.

Rigopoulos, G., & Askounis, D. (2007). A TAM framework to evaluate users' perception towards online electronic payments. *Journal of Internet Banking and Commerce, 12*(3).

Rizk, N. (2004). *E-readiness assessment of small and medium enterprises in Egypt: A micro study*. Cairo, Egypt: American University. Retrieved from http://www.sba.luc.edu/orgs/meea/volume6/Rizk.htm

Robertson, A., Lockett, N. J., Brown, D. H., & Crouchley, R. (2007). *Entrepreneur attitude towards the computer and its effect on e-business adoption*. Paper presented at the 30th Institute for Small Business and Entrepreneurship (ISBE) Conference, Glasgow. November.

Robertson, T. S. (1971). *Innovative behavior and communication*. New York: Holt, Rinehart and Winston, Inc.

Robinson, T. (2000). Internet banking: Still not a perfect marriage. *Information Week, 17*(782), 104–106.

Robison, K. K., & Crenshaw, E. M. (2001). *Post-industrial transformations and cyber-space: A cross-national analysis of Internet development*. Columbus, OH: The Ohio State University.

Roffe, I. (2002). E-learning: Engagement, enhancement and execution. *Quality Assurance in Education, 10*(1), 40–50. doi:10.1108/09684880210416102

Rogers, E. (2003). *Diffusion of innovations*. New York, NY: Free Press.

Roller, L., & Waverman, L. (2001). Telecommunication infrastructure and economic development: A simultaneous approach. *The American Economic Review, 91*(4), 909–923. doi:10.1257/aer.91.4.909

Romano, N. C. Jr, & Fjermestad, J. (2003). Electronic commerce customer relationship management: A research agenda. *Information Technology Management, 4*, 233–258. doi:10.1023/A:1022906513502

Rothwell, R. (1992). Successful industrial innovation: Critical factors for the 1990s. *R & D Management, 22*(3), 221–239. doi:10.1111/j.1467-9310.1992.tb00812.x

Rotter, L. B. (1971). Generalized expectations for interpersonal trust. *The American Psychologist, 26*(5), 443–452. doi:10.1037/h0031464

Roush, W. (2003, October). The Internet Reborn. [from BCA database.]. *Technology Review*, 10. Retrieved March 08, 2008.

Rousseau, D. M., Sitkin, S. B., Burt, R. S., & Camerer, C. (1998). Not so different after all: Across discipline view of trust. *Academy of Management Review, 23*(3), 393–404. doi:10.5465/AMR.1998.926617

Rowley, J. (2004). Partnering paradigms? Knowledge management and relationship marketing. *Industrial Management & Data Systems, 104*(2), 149–157. doi:10.1108/02635570410522125

Rumble, G. (2001). The costs and costing of networked learning. *Journal of Asynchronous Learning Networks, 5*(2), 75–96.

Runyan, R., Droge, C., & Swinney, J. (2008). Entrepreneurial orientation versus small business orientation: What are their relationships to firm performance? *Journal of Small Business Management, 46*(4), 567–588. doi:10.1111/j.1540-627X.2008.00257.x

Sadowski, B. M., Maitland, C., & van Dongen, J. (2002). Strategic use of the Internet by small-and medium-sized companies: An exploratory study. *Information Economics and Policy, 14*, 75–93. doi:10.1016/S0167-6245(01)00054-3

Sagi, J. (2004). ICT and business in the new economy: Globalization and attitudes towards eCommerce. *Journal of Global Information Management, 12*(3), 44–65.

Samiee, S. (1998). Exporting and the Internet: A conceptual perspective. *International Marketing Review, 15*(5), 413–426. doi:10.1108/02651339810236452

Sánchez-Franco, M. J., & Roldán, J. L. (2005). Web acceptance and usage model: A comparison between goal-directed and experiential Web users. *Internet Research, 15*(1), 21–48.doi:10.1108/10662240510577059

Sander, Ta-Shma, Tomas, Amnon (1999).On Anonymous Electronic Cash and Crime. 202-206.

Sanderson, I. (2002). Evaluation, policy learning and evidence-based policy making. *Public Administration, 80*(1), 1–22. doi:10.1111/1467-9299.00292

Sands, M. (2003). Integrating the Web and e-mail into a push-pull strategy. *Qualitative Market Research, 6*(1), 27–37. doi:10.1108/13522750310457357

Sang, S., Lee, J. D., & Lee, J. (2010). E-government adoption in Cambodia: A partial least squares approach. *Transforming Government: People, Process, and Policy, 4*(2), 138–157. doi:10.1108/17506161011047370

Sang, S. (2008). The Influential factors and challenges in implementing e-Government in Cambodia. *Proceeding of the 2008 International Conference on Convergence and Hybrid Information Technology (ICCIT08), Vol. II.* Busan: IEEE Computer Society.

Sarosa, S., & Zowghi, D. (2003). Strategy for adopting information technology for SMEs: Experience in adopting email within an Indonesian furniture company. *Electronic Journal of Information Systems Evaluation, 6*(2), 165–176.

Sarosa, S., & Underwood, J. (2005). Factors affecting IT adoption within Indonesian SMEs: manager's perspectives. In *Proceedings of the 9th Pacific Asia Conference on Information Systems*, Bangkok, Thailand.

Sathye, M. (1999). Adoption of internet banking by Australian consumers: An empirical investigation. *International Journal of Bank Marketing, 17*(7), 324–334. doi:10.1108/02652329910305689

Sathye, M. (1999). Adoption of Internet Banking by Australian Consumers: An Empirical Investigation. *International Journal of Bank*, 324- 331

Sato, S., & Hawkins, J. (2001). Electronic Finance: an overview of the issues, from http://www.paris-europlace. net/files/dossier059034.pdf

SBS (Small Business Service). (2004). *SBS booster survey*. Retrieved July 7, 2005, from http://www. sbs.gov.uk/sbsgov/action/layer?r.l2=7000000243&r. l1=7000000229&r.s=tl&topicId=7000011759

Schaupp, L. C., & Belanger, F. (2005). A Conjoint Analysis of Online Consumer Satisfaction. *Journal of Electronic Commerce Research*, *6*(2), 95–111.

Schechter, H. B. (2009). The cost of e-learning. eLearn,*7*(5). Retrieved September 15, 2010, from http:// www.elearnmag.org/subpage.cfm?section=articles&article=86-1

Schindehutte, M., & Morris, M. H. (2001). Understanding strategic adaptation in small firms. *International Journal of Entrepreneurial Behaviour and Research*, *7*(3), 84–107. doi:10.1108/EUM0000000005532

Sciadas, G. (Ed.). (2005). *From the digital divide to digital opportunities: Measuring infostates for development.* Montreal, Canada: NRC Press. Retrieved from http://www. orbicom.uqam.ca/projects/ddi2005/index ict opp.pdf

Scullin, S. S., Fjermestad, J., & Romano, N. C. Jr. (2004). E-relationship marketing: Changes in traditional marketing as an outcome of electronic customer relationship management. *The Journal of Enterprise Information Management*, *17*(6), 410–415. doi:10.1108/17410390410566698

Scupola, A. (2003). The adoption of Internet commerce by SMEs in the South of Italy: An environmental, technological and organizational perspective. *Journal of Global Information Technology Management*, *6*(1), 52–71.

Selhofer, H., & Mayringer, H. (2001). Benchmarking the information society. Development in European countries. *Communications and Strategies*, *43*, 17–55.

Selhofer, H., & Husing, T. (2002). *The digital divide index—A measure of the social inequalities in the adoption of ICT*. Paper presented at the IST 2002 Conference, Copenhagen.

Sellitto, C., Wenn, A., & Burgess, S. (2003). A review of the websites of small Australian wineries: Motivations, goals and success. *Information Technology Management*, *4*(2/3), 215–232. doi:10.1023/A:1022954429432

Sexton, R. S., Johnson, R. A., & Hignite, M. A. (2002). Predicting internet/EC use. *Internet Research: Electronic Networking Application and Policy*, *12*(5), 402–410. doi:10.1108/10662240210447155

Seyal, A. H., & Rahman, M. N. A. (2003). A preliminary investigation of E-commerce adoption in small & medium enterprises in Brunei. *Journal of Global Information Technology Management*, *6*(2), 6–26.

Shaw, E. (1999). Networks and their relevance to the entrepreneurial/marketing interface: A review of the evidence. *Journal of Research in Marketing & Entrepreneurship*, *1*(1), 24–40. doi:10.1108/14715209980001554

Sheppard, B. H., Hartwick, J., & Warshaw, P. R. (1988). The theory of reasoned action: A meta-analysis of past research with recommendations for modifications and future research. *Journal of Consumer Behaviour*, *15*(3), 325–343.

Shergil, G. S., & Bing, L. (2005). An Empirical Investigation of Customers' Behaviour for Online Banking in New Zealand. Journal of E-business Sheshunoff, A.(2000). Internet Banking –An Update Form the Frontlines. *ABA Banking Journal*, (January): 51–53.

Shih, Y., & Fang, K. (2004). The use of a decomposed theory of planned behavior to study Internet banking in Taiwan. *Internet Research*, *14*(3), 213–223. doi:10.1108/10662240410542643

Shih, Y., & Fang, K. (2006). Effects of network quality attributes on customer adoption intentions of Internet banking. *Total Quality Management & Business Excellence*, *17*(1), 61–77. doi:10.1080/14783360500249661

Shih, Y. Y. (2006). The effect of computer self-efficacy on enterprise resource planning usage. *Behaviour & Information Technology*, *25*(5), 407–411. doi:10.1080/01449290500168103

Shih, E., Kraemer, K. L., & Dedrick, J. (2003). *An extended accelerator model of country level investment in Information Technology*. Irvine, CA: Center for Research on Information Technology and Organization (CRITO).

Shim, J. P., Shropshire, J., Park, S., Harris, H., & Campbell, N. (2007). Podcasting for e-learning, communication, and delivery. *Industrial Management & Data Systems, 107*(4), 587–600. doi:10.1108/02635570710740715

Shrader, C., Mulford, C., & Blackburn, V. (1989). Strategic and operational planning, uncertainty, and performance in small firms. *Journal of Small Business Management, 27*(4), 45–60.

Shukla, S., & Fui-Hoon, N. (2005, August). Web Browsing and Spyware Intrusion. [from BCA database.]. *Communications of the ACM, 8*. Retrieved March 03, 2008.

Sicherl, P. (2004). *A new generic statistical measure in dynamic gap analysis. The European E-Business Report.* Luxembourg: European Commission.

Simmons, G., Armstrong, G. A., & Durkin, M. G. (2008). A conceptualization of the determinants of small business website adoption: Setting the research agenda. *International Small Business Journal, 26*(3), 351–389. doi:10.1177/0266242608088743

Simmons, G. (2008). Marketing to postmodern consumers: Introducing the Internet chameleon. *European Journal of Marketing, 42*(3/4), 294–310. doi:10.1108/03090560810852940

Simon, S. J. (2001). The impact of culture and gender on Web sites: An empirical study. *The Data Base for Advances in Information Systems, 32*(1), 18–37.

Simpson, M., & Docherty, A. J. (2004). E-commerce adoption support and advice for UK SMEs. *Journal of Small Business and Enterprise Development, 11*(3), 315–328. doi:10.1108/14626000410551573

Simpson, C. L. Jr, & Kujawa, D. (1974). The export decision process: An empirical inquiry. *Journal of International Business Studies, 5*(1), 107–117. doi:10.1057/palgrave.jibs.8490815

Singh, N., & Boughton, P. (2002). *Measuring Web site globalization: A cross-sectional country and industry level analysis. Proceedings from American Marketing Association Educators' Conference (Winter), Austin, TX.* Chicago: American Marketing Association.

Singh, N., & Boughton, P. (2005). Measuring Web site globalization: A cross-sectional country and industry level analysis. *Journal of Website Promotion, 1*(3), 3–20. doi:10.1300/J238v01n03_02

Singh, N., Furrer, O., & Ostinelli, M. (2004). To localize or to standardize on the Web: Empirical evidence from Italy, India, Netherlands, Spain, and Switzerland. *Multinational Business Review, 12*(1), 69–88.

Singh, N., & Matsuo, H. (2004). Measuring cultural adaptation on the Web: A study of U.S. and Japanese Web sites. *Journal of Business Research, 57*(8), 864–872. doi:10.1016/S0148-2963(02)00482-4

Singh, N., & Pereira, A. (2005). *The culturally customized Web site: Customizing Web sites for the global marketplace.* Burlington, MA: Elsevier.

Singh, N., Toy, D. R., & Wright, L. K. (2009). A diagnostic framework for measuring Web site localization. *Thunderbird International Business Review, 51*(3), 281–295. doi:10.1002/tie.20265

Singh, N., & Little, J. (2009). Culturally customizing international Web sites. In Shareef, M. A., Dwivedi, Y. K., Williams, M. D., & Singh, N. (Eds.), *Proliferation of the Internet economy: E-commerce for global adoption, resistance, and cultural evolution.* Hershey, PA: IGI Global.

Sinkovics, R. R., & Penz, E. (2005). Empowerment of SME websites – Development of a Web-empowered scale and preliminary evidence. *Journal of International Entrepreneurship, 3*(4), 303–315. doi:10.1007/s10843-006-7858-8

Siritongthaworn, S., & Krairit, D. (2006). Satisfaction in e-learning: The context of supplementary instruction. *Campus-Wide Information Systems, 23*(2), 76–91. doi:10.1108/10650740610654465

Slovic, P. (1966). Risk-taking in children: Age and sex difference. *Child Development, 37*, 169–176. doi:10.2307/1126437

Smallbone, D., Lyon, F., & Li, X. (2006). Trust, cooperation and networking in an immigrant business community: The case of Chinese-owned businesses in the UK. In Hohmann, H. H., & Welter, F. (Eds.), *Trust and entrepreneurship: A West-East perspective.* Cheltenham, UK/ Brookfield, USA: Edward Elgar.

Smith, J. A. (1998). Strategies for start-ups. *Long Range Planning, 31*(6), 857–872. doi:10.1016/S0024-6301(98)80022-8

Sohal, A. S., & Ng, L. (1998). The role and impact of Information Technology in Australian Business. *Journal of Information Technology, 13*, 201–217. doi:10.1080/026839698344846

Southern, A., & Tilley, F. (2000). Small firms and information and communication technologies (ICTs): Toward a typology of ICT usage. *New Technology, Work and Employment, 15*(2), 138–154. doi:10.1111/1468-005X.00070

Sparling, L., Toleman, M., & Cater-Steel, A. (2007). SME Adoption of e-Commerce in the Central Okanagan Region of Canada. *In Proceedings of the 18th Australasian Conference on Information Systems*, Toowoomba, Australia (pp. 1046-1059).

Speier, C., & Poston, R. (2001). *Web site acceptance: The effects of task type.* Paper presented at the Americas Conference on Information Systems, Waltham, MA.

Srinivasan, K., Kekre, S., & Mukhopadhyay, T. (1994). Impact of electronic data interchange technology on JIT shipments. *Management Science, 40*(10), 1291–1304. doi:10.1287/mnsc.40.10.1291

Srirojanant, S., & Cresswell-Thirkell, P. (1998). Relationship marketing and its synergy with Web-based technologies. *Journal of Market Focused Management, 3*, 23–46. doi:10.1023/A:1009790421951

Stafford, T. F., Turan, A., & Raisinghani, M. S. (2004). International and cross-cultural influences on online shopping behavior. *Journal of Global Information Technology Management, 7*(2), 70–87.

Sterman, J. D. (2000). *Business dynamic system thinking and modeling for a complex world. Irwin.* CA: McGraw-Hill.

Stevens, E. (2002). Electronic money and the future of Centrals Banks. From http://www.clevelandfed.org/research/com2002/0301.pdf

Stockdale, R., & Standing, C. (2004). Benefits and barriers of electronic marketplace participation: An SME perspective. *Journal of Enterprise Information Management, 17*(4), 301–311. doi:10.1108/17410390410548715

Stokes, D. (2000). Entrepreneurial marketing: A conceptualisation from qualitative research. *Qualitative Market Research: An International Journal, 3*(1), 47–54. doi:10.1108/13522750010310497

Storey, D. J. (1994). *Understanding the small business sector.* London, UK: Routledge.

Straub, D. W., Loch, K. D., Evaristo, R., Karahanna, E., & Strite, M. (2002). Toward a theory-based measurement of culture. *Journal of Global Information Management, 10*(January), 13–23. doi:10.4018/jgim.2002010102

Straub, D., Limayem, M., & Karahanna-Evaristo, E. (1995). Measuring system usage: Implications for IS theory testing. *Management Science, 41*(8), 1328–1342. doi:10.1287/mnsc.41.8.1328

Straub, D. W., Limayem, M., & Karahanna, E. (1995). Measuring system usage: Implications for IS theory testing. *Management Science, 41*(8), 1328–1342. doi:10.1287/mnsc.41.8.1328

Subba Rao, S., Metts, G., & Monge, C. A. M. (2003). Electronic commerce development in small and medium sized enterprises. *Business Process Management Journal, 9*(1), 11–33. doi:10.1108/14637150310461378

Suh, B., & Han, I. (2002). Effects of trust on customer acceptance of Internet banking. *Electronic Commerce Research and Applications, 1*(3/4), 247–263. doi:10.1016/S1567-4223(02)00017-0

Suh, B., & Han, I. (2003). The impact of customer trust and perception of security control on the acceptance of electronic commerce. *International Journal of Electronic Commerce, 7*(3), 135–161.

Sulaiman, A., & Jani, R. (2001). *E-commerce implementation in Malaysian manufacturing sector.* Malaya: Faculty of Business and Accountancy, University of Malaya. White Paper

Sun, H. (2003). *An integrative analysis of TAM: Toward a deeper understanding of technology acceptance model.* Paper presented at AMCIS '03, Tampa, FL.

Sun, H., & Zhang, P. (2003). *A new perspective to analyze user technology acceptance.* (Working paper).

Swain, D. K. (2010). Students' keenness on use of e-resources. *The Electronic Library, 28*(4), 580–591. doi:10.1108/02640471011065391

Swanson, E. B. (1994). Information Systems Innovation Among Organisations. *Management Science, 40*(9), 1069–1092. doi:10.1287/mnsc.40.9.1069

Swatman, P. (2000). Internet for SMEs: A new Silk Road? *International Trade Forum, 3*, 22–24.

Szajna, B. (1994). Software evaluation and choice: Predictive validation of the technology acceptance instrument. *Management Information Systems Quarterly, 18*(3), 319–324.doi:10.2307/249621

Szmigin, I. T. D., & Humphrey, B. (1999). Electronic Cash: A qualitative assessment of its adoption. *International Journal of Bank Marketing, 17*(4), 192–202. doi:10.1108/02652329910278888

Tabor, S. W. (2005). Achieving significant learning in E-Commerce education through small business consulting projects.*Journal of Information Systems Education,16*(1).

Tacq, J. (1999). *Multivarate technique in social sciences.* Great Britain: Sage Publications.

Tan, M., & Teo, T. S. H. (2000). Factors influencing the adoption of internet banking. *Journal of Association for Information Systems, 1*(5), 1–42.

Tan, K. S., & Chong, S., C., Lin, B., & Eze, U. C. (2009). Internet-based ICT adoption: Evidence from Malaysian SMEs. *Industrial Management & Data Systems, 109*(2), 224–244. doi:10.1108/02635570910930118

Tan, M., & Teo, T. S. H. (1998). Factors influencing the adoption of the Internet. *International Journal of Electronic Commerce, 2*(3), 5–18.

Tanner, E. (2003). Bridging Latin America's digital divide: Government policies and Internet access. *Journalism & Mass Communication Quarterly, 80*(3), 646–665.

Taylor, S., & Todd, P. A. (1995a). Understanding Information Technology usage: A test of competing models. *Information Systems Research, 6*(2), 144–174. doi:10.1287/isre.6.2.144

Taylor, S., & Todd, P. A. (1995). Assessing IT usage: The role of prior experiences. *MIS Quarterly, 19*(3), 561–570. doi:10.2307/249633

Taylor, M., & Murphy, A. (2004). SMEs and E-Business. *Journal of Small Business and Enterprise Development, 11*(3), 280–289. doi:10.1108/14626000410551546

Taylor, S., & Todd, P. (1995a). Assessing IT usage: The role of prior experience. *Management Information Systems Quarterly, 19*(2), 561–570.doi:10.2307/249633

Taylor, S., & Todd, P. (1995b). Understanding Information Technology usage: A test of competing models. *Information Systems Research, 6*(4), 144–176.doi:10.1287/isre.6.2.144

Teo, T. S. H. (2001). Demographic and motivational variables associated with Internet usage activities. *Internet Research: Electronic Networking Applications and Policy, 11*(2), 125–137. doi:10.1108/10662240110695089

Teo, T. S. H., & Lim, V. K. G. (2000). Gender differences in Internet usage and task preferences. *Behaviour & Information Technology, 19*(4), 283–295. doi:10.1080/01449290050086390

Teo, T. S. H., & Tan, M. (1998). An Empirical Study of adopters and non-adopters of Internet in Singapore. *Information & Management, 34*, 339–345. doi:10.1016/S0378-7206(98)00068-8

Tetteh, E., & Burn, J. (2001). Global strategies for SME-business: Applying the SMALL framework. *Logistics Information Management, 14*(1-2), 171–180. doi:10.1108/09576050110363202

Thatcher, J. B., & Perrewe, P. L. (2002). An empirical examination of individual traits as antecedents to computer anxiety and computer self-efficacy. *MIS Quarterly, 26*(4), 381–396. doi:10.2307/4132314

The Localization Industry Standards Association. (2008). What is globalization? *The Localization Industry Standards Association.* Retrieved July 28, 2008, from http://lisa.org/ What-Is-Globalization.48.0.html.

Thomas, D. (2002). Retailers and Card Issuers step up fight against online fraud. *Computer Weekly*, from http://www.computerweekly.com/Articles/2002/10/17/190338/Retailersandcardissuersstepupfightagainstonlinefraud

Thompson, R. L., Higgins, C. A., & Howell, J. M. (1991). Personal computing: Toward a conceptual model of utilization. *Management Information Systems Quarterly, 15*(1), 125–142. doi:10.2307/249443

Thompson, P., Williams, R., Thomas, B. C., & Packham, G. (2010). *Shortages of IT Skills in UK SMEs*. Paper presented at the 33rd Institute for Small Business and Entrepreneurship (ISBE) Conference, London. November.

Thong, J. Y. L. (1999). An integrated model of information systems adoption in small businesses. *Journal of Management Information Systems, 15*(4), 187–214.

Thong, J. Y. L., & Yap, C. S. (1995). CEO characteristics, organisational characteristics and Information Technology adoption in small businesses. *International Journal of Management Science, 23*(4), 429–442.

Thorbjornsen, H., & Supphellen, M. (2004). The impact of brand loyalty on Web site usage. *The Journal of Brand Management, 11*(3), 199–209. doi:10.1057/palgrave.bm.2540166

Tiessen, J., Wright, R., & Turner, I. (2001). A model of E-commerce use by internationalizing SMEs. *Journal of International Management, 7*, 211–233. doi:10.1016/S1075-4253(01)00045-X

Torkzadeh, G., Chang, J., & Demirhan, D. (2006). A contingency model of computer and Internet self-efficacy. *Information & Management, 43*(4), 541–550. doi:10.1016/j.im.2006.02.001

Torkzadeh, G., & Dhillon, G. (2002). Measuring factors that influence the success of Internet commerce. *Information Systems Research, 13*(2), 187–204. doi:10.1287/isre.13.2.187.87

Tornatzky, L., & Klein, K. (1982). Innovation characteristics and innovation adoption implementation: A meta analysis of findings. *IEEE Transactions on Engineering Management, 29*(1), 28–45.

Triandis, H. C. (1979). Values, attitudes and interpersonal behavior. In *Proceedings of the Nebraska Symposium on Motivation, Beliefs, Attitudes and Values,* Lincoln, NE (pp. 195-259). University of Nebraska Press.

Turban, E., King, D., Lee, K. J., & Viehland, D. (2004). *Electronic Commerce: A Managerial Perspective*. New Jersey: Pearson Prentice Hall.

Turban, E., McLean, E., & Wetherbe, J. (2004). *Information Technology for management: Transforming organizations in the digital economy*. Hoboken, NJ: John Wiley & Sons.

Twigg, C. A. (1999). Improving learning & reducing costs: Redesigning large-enrollment courses. Rensselaer Polytechnic Institute: Center for Academic Transformation.

Twigg, C. A. (2003) Improving quality and reducing costs: New models for online learning. EDUCAUSE Review, 38(5), 28–38. Retrieved September 15, 2010, from http://www.educause.edu/ir/library/pdf/ERM0352.pdf

U.S. Department of Commerce, Bureau of the Census. (2002). *Falling through the net: Defining the digital divide, economics & statistics administration. National Telecommunications and Information Administration*. NTIA.

Uhl, K., Anrus, R., & Poulson, L. (1970). How are laggards different? An empirical inquiry. *JMR, Journal of Marketing Research, 7*, 51–54. doi:10.2307/3149506

United Nations Development Programme. Malaysia. (2007). *Small and Medium Enterprises: Building an enabling environment*. Retrieved May 12, 2009, from http://www.undp.org.my/uploads /UNDP_SME_Publication.pdf

United Nations Development Programme. (UNDP). (2001). *Human development report 2001*. New York, NY: UN. Retrieved from http://www.undp.org/

Uzoka, F. M. E., Seleka, G. G., & Khengere, J. (2007). E-commerce adoption in developing countries: A case analysis of environmental and organizational inhibitors. *International Journal of Information Systems and Change Management, 2*(3), 232–260. doi:10.1504/IJISCM.2007.015598

Uzzi, B. (1997). Social structure and competition in interfirm networks: The paradox of embeddedness. *Administrative Science Quarterly, 42*(1), 35–67. doi:10.2307/2393808

Valadez, J. R., & Duran, R. (2007). Redefining the digital divide: Beyond access to computers and the Internet. *High School Journal, 90*, 31–44. doi:10.1353/hsj.2007.0013

Van Akkeren, J. K., & Cavaya, A. L. M. (2000). Factors affecting entry-level Internet technology adoption by small firms in Australia – Evidence from three cases. *Journal of Systems and Information Technology, 3*(2), 33–47. doi:10.1108/13287269980000747

Van Belle, J. P., & Vosloo, S. (2005). E-government and the e-readiness of non-profit organizations in the Western Cape, South Africa. *Proceedings of the 2nd Annual Conference of the Community Informatics Research Network*, Cape Town, 24-26 August 2005.

Van de Ven, W. P. M. M., & Van Praag, B. M. S. (1981). The demand for deductibles in private health insurance: a probit model with sample selection. *Journal of Econometrics, 17*(2), 229–252. doi:10.1016/0304-4076(81)90028-2

Van der Heijden, H. (2000). *Using the technology acceptance model to predict Web site usage: Extensions and empirical test*. Series Research Memoranda.

Van der Heijden, H. (2003). Factors influencing the usage of Web sites: The case of the generic portal in the Netherlands. *Information & Management, 40*, 541–549. doi:10.1016/S0378-7206(02)00079-4

Van der Heijden, H. (2004). User acceptance of hedonic Information Systems. *Management Information Systems Quarterly, 28*(4), 695–704.

Van der Heijden, H., Verhagen, T., & Creemers, M. (2003). Understanding online purchase intentions: Contributions from technology and trust perspectives. *European Journal of Information Systems, 12*, 41–48. doi:10.1057/palgrave. ejis.3000445

Van der Veen, M. (2004). *Explaining e-business adoption: Innovation and entrepreneurship and in Dutch SMEs*. Unpublished doctoral dissertation, University of Twente, Holland.

van Dijk, J. (2006). Digital divide research, achievements and shortcomings. *Poetics, 34*, 221–235. doi:10.1016/j. poetic.2006.05.004

Van Slyke, C., Bélanger, F., & Comunale, C. (2004). Factor influencing the adoption of web-based shopping: The impacts of trust. *The Data Base for Advances in Information Systems, 35*(2), 32–49.

Vehovar, V., Sicherl, P., Husing, T., & Dolnicar, V. (2006). Methodological challenges of digital divide measurements. *The Information Society, 22*(5), 279–290. doi:10.1080/01972240600904076

Venkatesh, V., & Davis, F. D. (2000). A theoretical extension of the technology acceptance model: Four longitudinal studies. *Management Science, 46*(2), 186–204. doi:10.1287/mnsc.46.2.186.11926

Venkatesh, V., & Morris, M. G. (2000). Why don't men stop to ask for directions? Gender, social influence, and their role in technology acceptance and usage behavior. *Management Information Systems Quarterly, 24*(1), 115–139. doi:10.2307/3250981

Venkatesh, V., Morris, M. G., Davis, G. B., & Davis, F. D. (2003). User acceptance of information technology: Toward a unified view. *Management Information Systems Quarterly, 27*(3), 425–478.

Venkatesh, V. (2000). Determinants of perceived ease of use: Integrating control, intrinsic motivation, and emotion into the technology acceptance model. *Information Systems Research, 11*(4), 342–365. doi:10.1287/ isre.11.4.342.11872

Venkatesh, V., & Davis, F. D. (2000). A theoretical extension of the technology acceptance model: Four longitudinal field studies. *Management Science, 46*(2), 186–204. doi:10.1287/mnsc.46.2.186.11926

Venkatesh, V., Morris, M. G., Davis, G. B., & Davis, F. D. (2003). User acceptance of information technology: Toward a unified view. *MIS Quarterly, 27*(3), 425–478.

Venkatesh, V. (2000). Determinants of Perceived Ease of Use: Integrating Control, Intrinsic Motivation, and Emotion into the Technology Acceptance Model. *Information Systems Research, 11*(4), 342–365. doi:10.1287/ isre.11.4.342.11872

Venkatesh, V., & Morris, M. G. (2000). Why don't men ever stop to ask for directions? Gender, social influence, and their role in technology acceptance and usage behavior. *MIS Quarterly, 24*(1), 115–139. doi:10.2307/3250981

Venkatesh, V., & Davis, F. (2000). A theoretical extension of the technology acceptance model: Four longitudinal field studies. *Management Science, 46*(2), 186–204. doi:10.1287/mnsc.46.2.186.11926

Venkatesh, V., & Morris, M. (2000). Why don't men ever stop to ask for directions? Gender, social influence, and their role in technology acceptance and usage behavior. *Management Information Systems Quarterly, 24*(1), 115–139.doi:10.2307/3250981

Venkatesh, V., Morris, M., Davis, G., & Davis, F. (2003). User acceptance of Information Technology: Toward a unified view. *Management Information Systems Quarterly, 27*(3), 425–478.

Venkatesh, V., & Bala, H. (2008). Technology acceptance model 3 and a research agenda on interventions. *Decision Sciences, 39*(2), 273–315. doi:10.1111/j.1540-5915.2008.00192.x

Venkatesh, V., & Davis, F. D. (2000). A theoretical extension of the technology acceptance model: Four longitudinal field studies. *Management Science, 46*(2), 186–204. doi:10.1287/mnsc.46.2.186.11926

Vijayasarathy, L. R. (2004). Predicting consumer intentions to use on-line shopping: the case for an augmented technology acceptance model. *Information & Management, 41*(6), 747–762. doi:10.1016/j.im.2003.08.011

Vijayasarathy, L. R. (2003). Shopping orientations, product types and Internet shopping intentions. *Electronic Markets, 13*(1), 67–79.doi:10.1080/1019678032000039903

Violino, B. (2001). E-business lurches abroad. *Internet Week, March 19ᵗʰ*. Retrieved July 28, 2008, from http://www.internetweek.com.

Wade, W. (2004). Government's New Stance on E-Payments. *American Banker, 169*(Iss. 165), 1–4.

Waite, K., & Harrison, T. (2002). Consumer Expectations of Online Information Provided by Bank Websites. *Journal of Financial Services Marketing, 6*(4), 309–322. doi:10.1057/palgrave.fsm.4770061

Walczuch, R., Van Braven, G., & Lundgren, H. (2000). Internet Adoption Barriers for Small Firms in The Netherlands. *European Management Journal, 18*(5), 561–572. doi:10.1016/S0263-2373(00)00045-1

Walker, E., & Brown, A. (2004). What success factors are important to small business owners? *International Small Business Journal, 22*(6), 577–594. doi:10.1177/0266242604047411

Walliman, N. (2001). *Your research project* (1st ed.). London, UK: SAGE Publications.

Wallsten, S. (2003). *Regulation and Internet use in developing countries*. Washington, DC: AEI and Brookings Institution. doi:10.1596/1813-9450-2979

Wang, Y.-S., Wang, Y.-M., Lin, H.-H., & Tang, T.-I. (2003). Determinants of user acceptance of Internet banking: An empirical study. *International Journal of Service Industry Management, 14*(5), 501–519. doi:10.1108/09564230310500192

Wang, Y., & Liao, Y. (2008). Assessing e-government systems success: A validation of the DeLone and McLean model of information system success. *Government Information Quarterly, 25*(4), 717–733. doi:10.1016/j.giq.2007.06.002

Wang, Q., Zhu, Z., Chen, L., & Yan, H. (2009). E-learning in China. *Campus-Wide Information Systems, 26*(2), 77–81. doi:10.1108/10650740910946783

Wang, W., & Benbasat, I. (2004). *Trust and TAM for online recommendation agents*. Paper presented at the Americas Conference on Information Systems, New York.

Ward, J., & Peppard, J. (2002). *Strategic Planning for Information Systems* (3rd ed.). West Sussex: John Wiley & Sons.

Warkentin, M., Gefen, D., Pavlou, P., & Rose, G. (2002). Encouraging citizen adoption of e-Government by building trust. *Electronic Markets, 12*(3), 157–162. doi:10.1080/101967802320245929

Warschauer, M. (2003). *Technology and social inclusion: Rethinking the digital divide*. Cambridge, MA: MIT Press.

Weiss, T. J. (1999). Cyber-relationships and brand building. *Integrated Marketing Communications Research Journal, 5*, 19–22.

Weltevreden, J. W. J., & Boschma, R. A. (2008). The influence of firm owner characteristics on Internet adoption by independent retailers: A business survey. *International Journal of Internet Science, 3*(1), 34–54.

Wen, H. J., Chen, H. G., & Hwang, H. G. (2001). E-commerce web site design: Strategies and models. *Information Management & Computer Security, 9*(1), 5–12. doi:10.1108/09685220110366713

Wen, H. J., Chen, H.-G., & Hwang, H.-G. (2001). E-commerce Web site design: Strategies and models. *Information Management & Computer Security*, 9(1), 5–12. doi:10.1108/09685220110366713

Wentling, T. L., & Park, J. (2002). Cost analysis of e-learning: A case study of a university program. 2002 Academy of Human Resource Development Annual Conference (AHRD '02), Hawaii. Retrieved September 15, 2010, from http://citeseerx.ist.psu.edu/viewdoc/download?doi=10.1.1.86.5844&rep=rep1&type=pdf

West, D. M. (2008). *Improving technology utilization in electronic government around the world*. Washington: The Brookings Institution.

Westhead, P., & Story, D. J. (1996). Management Training and Small Firm Performance: Why is the Link so Weak? *International Small Business Journal*, 14(4), 13–24. doi:10.1177/0266242696144001

Wiersema, M. F., & Bantel, K. A. (1992). Top management team demography and corporate strategic change. *Academy of Management Journal*, 35, 91–121. doi:10.2307/256474

Williams, E. A., & Castro, S. L. (2010). The effects of teamwork on individual learning and perceptions of team performance: A comparison of face-to-face and online project settings. *Team Performance Management*, 16(3-4), 124–147. doi:10.1108/13527591011053232

Williams, R., Packham, G. P., Thomas, B. C., & Thompson, P. (2010). Small business sales growth and internationalization links to Web site functions in the United Kingdom. In Thomas, B., & Simmons, G. (Eds.), *E-commerce adoption and small business in the global marketplace: Tools for optimization* (pp. 139–173). Hershey, PA: Business Science Reference. doi:10.4018/978-1-60566-998-4.ch008

Wilson, H., & Daniel, E. (2007). The multi-channel challenge: A dynamic capability approach. *Industrial Marketing Management*, 36(1), 10–20. doi:10.1016/j.indmarman.2006.06.015

Wilson, E. V., Mao, E., & Lankton, N. K. (2005). *Predicting continuing acceptance of IT in conditions of sporadic use*. Paper presented at the Americas Conference on Information Systems, Omaha, NE.

Windrum, P., & de Berranger, P. (2003). The adoption of e-business technology by SMEs. In Jones, O., & Tilley, F. (Eds.), *Competitive advantage in SMEs: Organising for innovation and change* (pp. 177–201). England: Wiley.

Wolcott, P., Press, L., McHenry, W., Goodman, S. E., & Foster, W. (2001). A framework for assessing the global diffusion of the Internet. *Journal of the Association for Information Systems*, 2(6), 1–50.

Wolfinbarger, M., & Gilly, M. C. (2001). Shopping online for freedom, control, and fun. *California Management Review*, 43(2), 34–55.

Wong, P. K. (2002). ICT production and diffusion in Asia: Digital dividends or digital divide? *Information Economics and Policy*, 14(2), 167–187. doi:10.1016/S0167-6245(01)00065-8

World Bank. (2004). *SME E-Readiness Questionnaire*. Korea.

Wu, J. H., Hsia, T. L., & Heng, M. S. H. (2006). Core Capabilities For Exploiting Electronic Banking. *Journal of Electronic Commerce Research*, 7(2), 111–122.

Wu, F., Mahajan, V., & Balasubramanian, S. (2003). An analysis of e-business adoption and its impact on business performance. *Academy of Marketing Science Journal*, 31(4), 425–448. doi:10.1177/0092070303255379

Wu, S.-L. (2003). The relationship between consumer characteristics and attitude toward online shopping. *Marketing Intelligence & Planning*, 21(1), 37–44. doi:10.1108/02634500310458135

Wu, J., Wang, S., & Lin, L. (2007). Mobile computing acceptance factors in the healthcare industry: A structural equation model. *International Journal of Medical Informatics*, 76(1), 66–77. doi:10.1016/j.ijmedinf.2006.06.006

Wu, J.-H., & Wang, S.-C. (2005). What drives mobile commerce? An empirical evaluation of the revised technology acceptance model. *Information & Management*, 42(5), 719–729. doi:10.1016/j. im.2004.07.001

Xia, L., & Sudharshan, D. (2000). *An examination of the effects of cognitive interruptions on consumer online decision processes*. Paper presented at the 2nd Marketing Science Internet Conference, Los Angeles.

Xiao, J. J., Alhabeeb, M. J., Hong, G. S., & Haynes, G. W. (2001). Attitude toward risk and risk-taking behavior of business-owning families. *The Journal of Consumer Affairs, 35*(2), 307–325.

Yao, J. D., Liu, C., Xu, X., & Lu, J. (2003). Organizational size: a significant predictor of IT innovation and adoption. *Journal of Computer Information Systems, 43*(2), 76–82.

Yap, C. S. (1990). Distinguishing characteristics of organizations using computers. *Information & Management, 18*(2), 97–107. doi:10.1016/0378-7206(90)90056-N

Yap, C. S., Soh, C. P. P., & Raman, K. S. (1992). International systems success factors in small business. *Omega International of Management Science, 5*(6), 597–609. doi:10.1016/0305-0483(92)90005-R

Yap, C. S., Soh, C. P. P., & Raman, K. S. (1992). Information Systems success factors in small businesses. *Omega International Journal of Management Science, 20*(5), 597–609. doi:10.1016/0305-0483(92)90005-R

Yeung, W. L., & Lu, M.-T. (2004). Functional characteristics of commercial Web sites: A longitudinal study in Hong Kong. *Information & Management, 41*(4), 483–495. doi:10.1016/S0378-7206(03)00086-7

Yi, M. Y., Jacson, J. D., Park, J. S., & Probst, J. C. (2006). Understanding Information Technology acceptance by individual professionals: Toward an integrative view. *Information & Management, 43*, 350–363. doi:10.1016/j.im.2005.08.006

Yoon, S. J. (2002). The antecedents and consequences of trust in online-purchase decisions. *Journal of Interactive Marketing, 16*(2), 47–63. doi:10.1002/ dir.10008

Yoonhee, T. C. (2005). Dynamics of Internet Banking Adoption MIS Quarterly, 413-443

Young, P. (2006, March). *The Spread of Innovations by Social Learning.* Working paper. Retrieved April 30, 2009 from http://www.santafe.edu/events/workshops/images/0/0a/Spread21march.pdf

Yu, L., Suojapelto, K., Hallikas, J., & Tang, O. (2008). Chinese ICT industry from supply chain perspective - A case study of the major Chinese ICT players. *International Journal of Production Economics, 115*(2), 374. doi:10.1016/j.ijpe.2008.03.011

Yu, J. L. C.-S., Liu, C., & Yao, J. E. (2003). Technology acceptance model for wireless internet. *Internet Research, 13*(3), 206–233. doi:10.1108/10662240310478222

Zaheer, A., & Venkatraman, N. (1994). Determinants of electronic integration in the insurance industry: An empirical test. *Management Science, 40*(5), 549–566. doi:10.1287/mnsc.40.5.549

Zhang, M. J., & Lado, A. A. (2001). Information Systems and competitive advantage: A competency-based view. *Technovation, 21*(3), 147–156. doi:10.1016/S0166-4972(00)00030-4

Zhuang, Y., & Lederer, A. L. (2006). A resource-based view of electronic commerce. *Information & Management, 43*(2), 251–261. doi:10.1016/j.im.2005.06.006

Zikmund, W. G. (2003), *Business research method*, Mason: Thomson South-Western.

Zineldin, M. (2000). Beyond relationship marketing: Technological ship marketing. *Marketing Intelligence & Planning, 18*(1), 9–23. doi:10.1108/02634500010308549

Zmud, R. W. (1982). Diffusion of modern software practices: Influence of centralization and formalization. *Management Science, 28*(12), 1421–1431. doi:10.1287/mnsc.28.12.1421

Zontanos, G., & Anderson, A. R. (2004). Relationships, marketing and small business: An exploration of links in theory and practice. *Qualitative Market Research: An International Journal, 7*(3), 228–236. doi:10.1108/13522750410540236

About the Contributors

Sushil K. Sharma is a Professor and Chairperson of the Department of Information Systems and Operations Management at Ball State University, Muncie, Indiana. He has the distinction of having earned two doctoral degrees— Management Information Systems (MIS) and Management. Prior to joining the faculty at Ball State, Dr. Sharma held the Associate Professor position at the Indian Institute of Management (India) and a Visiting Research Associate Professor at the Department of Management Science at the University of Waterloo (Canada). He was chair of the Quantitative Systems Group and Information Technology and Systems Department at Indian Institute of Management. Dr. Sharma has travelled worldwide and lectured in several business schools around the globe in England, Europe, Australia, Asia, and North America.

* * *

Donald L. Amoroso is currently Professor and Department Chair of Information Systems at Kennesaw State University serves as executive director for Kennesaw State University's research center on Innovation in Technologies . He received his Bachelors degree in accounting and finance from Old Dominion University and his MBA and PhD from the University of Georgia. He has conducted seminars in the areas of leadership and strategy, corporate governance, marketing, technology investment, supply chain, Six Sigma, procurement, information modeling and information quality. In the area of marketing, Amoroso has taught marketing strategies, international marketing, new product development, customer engagement, aligning marketing and sales, pricing strategies, Internet marketing and advertising, global distribution, and marketing research. He also works with consumer-based research, customer business planning, and metrics related to marketing and sales strategies. He has worked in the aerospace, retail, banking, and government industry spaces. His current areas of research include strategy and leadership, Internet adoption, understanding consumer behavior using the Internet, online shopping, and music downloading. He has authored 67 articles and proceedings, written 5 books, presented at over 52 professional conferences and venues. He is under contract with Prentice-Hall to write a textbook due out 2010 entitled Strategy Development. He is an associate editor for the Journal of Electronic Commerce in Organizations, International Journal of E-Adoption, and the Journal of Information Systems Management.

Martin Beckinsale is a Senior Lecturer & Researcher in Strategy and Management at Leicester Business School (DMU). As a module leader, his teaching focus relates to e-business, service operations, and business research issues and analysis. He is a research team member of CREME (Centre for Research in Ethnic Minority Entrepreneurship). His academic background began in strategic technology management, small firms, and innovation. Currently, he specializes in Information Communication Technology (ICT), e-business, Ethnic Minority Businesses (EMBs), and SMEs. Recent funding, through the ESRC Business Placement Fellows Scheme, sees his research focusing on the development of Ethnic Minority Business support. The primary objective is in the area of ICT and e-procurement capacity building amongst Ethnic Minority Businesses. A critical aspect of his research focus is the development of the "action research methodology" assisting and enabling policy development and delivery.

Rui Chen is an Assistant Professor of Information Systems. He previously served on the faculty of Medaille College at Buffalo, New York. He holds a Bachelor's and Master's degree in Computer Science and a PhD degree in Management Science and Systems from State University of New York at Buffalo. His research focuses on information assurance, technology enabled emergency management, and Information Technology outsourcing.

Yi-Fen Chen is currently an assistant professor in the department of International Trade at the Chung Yuan Christian University, Chung Li, Taiwan. Her research interests include Internet marketing, consumer behavior, electronic commerce, and information management. Her papers have appeared in Psychology & Marketing, Computers in Human Behavior, Cyberpsychology, Behavior, and Social Networking, and others.

Namho Chung is an Assistant Professor at Kyung Hee University, Korea. He received his PhD in MIS from Sungkyunkwan University, Seoul, Korea. His research focuses on decision support in electronic commerce, decision analysis of management problems, and human computer interface design for electronic business. His articles have been published in Computers In Human Behavior, Behaviour & Information Technology, Interacting With Computers, Expert Systems With Applications, and Online Information Review, among others.

Josephine M. Csete has a PhD in educational systems development and more than 15 years experience in designing, developing, and implementing educational innovations as well as teaching others to do so. She has been working at Hong Kong Polytechnic University since 1995 in a department charged with "improving the quality of teaching and learning" on a campus of over 1,000 full-time teaching staff and over 25,000 undergraduate and graduate students. She is Section Leader of the e-Learning Development and Support Section (eLDSS) at the Hong Kong Polytechnic University. She believes the Web has the potential to redefine what and how we learn, as well as broaden the definition of "learner."

Daniel Doiron is a Professor in the Faculty of Business at the University of New Brunswick Saint John, Canada, where for the past six years he has been teaching in the areas of management Information Systems, new venture development, small business management, competitive strategy, and managing innovation at both the undergraduate and graduate levels. He also serves as the director of the Electronic Commerce Research and Training Centre. Doiron has been involved in founding four technology startups, the most recent of which is a company which provides a GIS based Marine Electronics solution to the global in-shore fisheries market. Doiron began his career in the telecommunications industry in 1984 following graduation from the University of New Brunswick where he received a Bachelor's degree in electrical engineering. In 1991, Doiron received a Master's degree in the Management of Technology from the Sloan School of Management at MIT.

Mohammad Reza Hanafizadeh holds a B.Sc. in Applied Mathematics from Teacher Training University, Tehran, Iran, and a Master's degree in Social and Economic Systems Engineering from Science and Research Branch, Islamic Azad University, Iran. He is a member of Young Researchers Club. He has published papers in *Telecommunications Policy, The Information Society, International Journal of Information Management, Journal of Information Technology Research, International Journal of Value Chain Management, International Journal of E-Adoption,* and in international conference of European and Mediterranean Conference on Information Systems 2008 (EMCIS 2008) and in some Iranian scientific journals. His research interests include digital divide measurement and analysis, e-readiness assessment, and evaluating the diffusion of ICT in businesses and higher education institutions.

Payam Hanafizadeh is an Assistant Professor of Industrial Management at Allameh Tabataba'i University in Tehran, Iran and a member of the Design Optimization under Uncertainty Group at the University of Waterloo, Canada. He was a visiting research fellow at the University of Canberra, Australia in 2010 and a visiting scholar at the University of Waterloo, Canada in 2004. He received his MSc and PhD in Industrial Engineering from Tehran Polytechnic University and pursues his research in Information Systems and decision-making under uncertainty. He has published in such journals as the Information Society, Systemic Practice and Action Research, Management Decision, Journal of Global Information Management, Telecommunications Policy, Mathematical and Computer Modeling, Expert Systems with Applications, International Journal of Information Management, and Energy Policy, to name only a few. Meanwhile, he has been serving on the editorial review board for the International Journal of Enterprise Information Systems, the Journal of Information Technology Research, the Journal of Electronic Commerce in Organizations, and the International Journal of Decision Support System Technology. In addition, he is the author of e-Commerce (2nd edition), and Internet Advertising New Opportunity for Promotion (2nd edition).

Scott Hunsinger is Assistant Professor of Computer Information Systems in the Walker College of Business at Appalachian State University in Boone, North Carolina. He holds a PhD in Information Technology from The University of North Carolina at Charlotte. His research interests include IT certification, IT adoption, and IS education. He has published articles in journals including Journal of Information Technology Management, Journal of Information Technology Education, Journal of Information Systems Applied Research, and Journal of Organizational and End User Computing.

Harilaos Koumaras was born in Athens, Greece in 1980. He received his BSc degree in Physics in 2002 from the University of Athens, Physics Department, his MSc in Electronic Automation and Information Systems in 2004, being scholar of the non-profit organization Alexander S Onassis, from the University of Athens, Computer Science Department and his PhD in 2007 at Computer Science from the University of Athens, Computer Science Department, having granted the four-year scholarship of National Centre of Scientific Research "Demokritos". He has received twice the Greek State Foundations (IKY) scholarship during the academic years 2000-01 and 2003-04. He has also granted with honors the classical piano and harmony degrees from the classical music department of Attiko Conservatory. Since 2004 he is a principal lecturer at the Business College of Athens (BCA) teaching modules related to Information Technology and Mathematics and Logic. From 2009, he has been elected as the Head of the Computer Science Department of BCA and Course leader of the respective franchised course of

London Metropolitan University. He also joined the Digital Communications Lab at the National Centre of Scientific Research "Demokritos" in 2003 and since then he has participated in numerous EC-funded and national funded projects with presentations and publications at international conferences, scientific journals and book chapters. His research interests include objective/subjective evaluation of the perceived quality of multimedia services, video quality and picture quality evaluation, video traffic modeling, digital terrestrial television and video compression techniques. Currently, he is the author or co-author of more than 45 scientific papers in international journals, technical books and book chapters, numbering 112 non-self citations. He is an editorial board member of the Telecommunications Systems Journal and a reviewer of the IEEE Network magazine, the EURASIP Journal of Applied Signal Processing, the IEEE Transactions on image processing and the IEEE Transactions on Broadcasting. Dr. Koumaras is a member of IEEE, SPIE, NGS and ECPMA.

Vaios Koumaras received his BSc degree in Business Administration with major in Computer Information Systems from the American College of Greece and his MBA in Project Management from the City University. Since 1997, he has worked in several positions as Computer Analyst and Software Developer, participating in major IT projects. Currently, he holds the position of senior R&D software engineer, with participation and collaboration in R&D IT projects of numerous companies worldwide. In parallel, he has more than ten years teaching experience of Business and IT courses in various grades. Currently, as part of his teaching activities, he is a lecturer at the Business College of Athens (BCA), at the Departments of Computer Science and Business Administration, teaching modules related to Information Technology, Business Administration and Mathematics. Additionally, he is part of the research team of the Computer Science Department at the Business College of Athens. He also participates, as associate R&D consultant and researcher, in several business and EC-funded projects and tasks related to business planning, marketing analysis and strategy development.

Paul Lam is an Assistant Professor at the Centre for Learning Enhancement And Research (CLEAR) at The Chinese University of Hong Kong. He is involved in many teaching and learning (T&L) research studies and services such as promotion of outcomes-based approaches to T&L, the enhancement of T&L spaces, and the use of technology for T&L. Additional research interests include case-based T&L, learners' characteristics, self and peer assessment, and English language teaching (ELT). Prior to joining CLEAR, he worked in a number of language-education projects in Hong Kong universities, and before that he was a secondary school teacher in Hong Kong.

Bee Theng Lau is a Lecturer in the School of Computing and Design at Swinburne University of Technology, Sarawak Campus, Malaysia. She received a PhD in Computer Science and Information Technology from the University Malaysia Sarawak. Her research interests include e-commerce; face image processing, facial expressions pattern recognition, and communication application for disabled children and adults. She has presented at a number of national and international conferences and published numerous papers in international journals.

Jeong-Dong Lee is a Professor at the Department of Industrial Engineering, Seoul National University and also a Professor at the Technology Management, Economics, and Policy Program (TEMEP) of Seoul National University. Lee served as the director of TEMEP until 2007. He published more than

30 papers in peer reviewed international journals including Journal of Productivity Analysis, Technovation, Scientometrics, Small Business Economics, Technological Forecasting and Social Change, Energy Economics, Applied Economics, Journal of Environmental Management, International Journal of Industrial Organization, etc. He published two books in 2008 as edited by Springer Verlag and NOVA Science regarding productivity and competitiveness of industries in various countries. He was the chief coordinator of Asia-Pacific Productivity Conference (APPC) in 2006. He has been a Vice President of Education of ETMERC (Engineering and Technology Management Education and Research Council), which is a global forum in the field of technology management since 2006. He is also very active in working with consulting bodies for competiveness enhancement of various private and public sectors.

Jongsu Lee is currently an Associate Professor of the Department of Industrial Engineering, and Technology Management, Economics, and Policy Program (TEMEP) of Seoul National University. He received the PhD degree in Engineering in 2001 from Seoul National University. His main research interest is oriented on demand forecasting for new products/technologies/services, which includes discrete choice analysis, diffusion of innovation theory, panel data analysis, and high-technology marketing.

Kun Chang Lee is a full Professor of MIS and Creativity Engineering at Sungkyunkwan University in Seoul, Korea. He holds a joint appointment at the SKK Business School and Department of Interaction Science. He received his PhD in MIS from Korea Advanced Institute of Science and Technology (KAIST), a Master of Sciences in MIS from KAIST, and a BA in Business Administration from Sungkyunkwan University, Seoul, Korea. His recent research interests lie in the interaction science issues among human and devices, creativity engineering, and artificial intelligence-based approach to understanding human perception and cognition. His research works have been published in several leading journals including Journal of Management Information Systems, Decision Support Systems, IEEE Transactions on Engineering Management, and Information & Management, among others.

Tsang-Hsiung Lee has a Ph.D. degree in the MIS area at the Katz Graduate School of Business at the University of Pittsburgh. His primary interest areas are management of information technology, organizational aspects of MIS, strategic use of information technology in small business, information systems development and implementation, and case study method.

Joseph P. Little is a PhD student with a concentration in Marketing and International Business at the John Cook School of Business, Saint Louis University. He earned his MBA from Indiana University Southeast. Little's research interests include cross-cultural consumer behavior focusing on consumer animosity and consumer ethnocentrism, international e-commerce, ethics, and international marketing strategy. Little's research has been published in Proliferation of the Internet Economy: E-Commerce for Global Adoption, Resistance, and Cultural Evolution and the Journal of Applied Business Research (forthcoming). Little has also presented his work at the Academy of International Business Annual Meeting, the American Marketing Association Educators' Conference, and the International Business and Economics Research Conference.

Fiona McMahon is a Lecturer in Advertising at the University of Ulster. She has 10 years experience working in advertising and marketing from both a client and agency perspective. Her research interests include online advertising, e-marketing, and e-business adoption, and she is currently undertaking doctoral research into how small firms can optimise their Internet use to create competitive advantage. She has also worked on e-marketing consultancy projects with small firms. She is a member of the Chartered Institute of Marketing, The Chartered Management Institute, The Institute of Small Business and Entrepreneurship, and the Publicity Association of Northern Ireland.

Carmel McNaught is the Director and Professor of Learning Enhancement in the Centre for Learning Enhancement And Research (CLEAR) at The Chinese University of Hong Kong (CUHK). She has had extensive experience in secondary and higher education in Australasia and southern Africa in chemistry, science education, second language learning, e-learning, and higher-education curriculum and policy matters. She has been involved in numerous design and implementation projects for e-learning and associated systems. She is a well-known international speaker, is actively involved in several e-learning professional organizations, and is a Fellow of the Association for the Advancement of Computers in Education. She is on 12 international editorial boards and has ~300 academic publications. Further details can be found at http://www.cuhk.edu.hk/clear/people/Carmel.html

Kamel Rouibah is an Associate Professor of Information Systems, College of Business Administration (CBA), Kuwait University. He holds a PhD in Information Systems from Ecole Polytechnique of Grenoble, France. Before joining CBA, he worked at the Faculty of Technology Management at Eindhoven (Netherlands) and Institut National de la Recherche Scientifique (France).

Aodheen O'Donnell is a Lecturer in Communication and Advertising. Her PhD research is in the area of small firm marketing, with a particular focus on how small firm owner-managers build networks and use the process of networking to further their businesses. In addition, Aodheen has engaged in research within the tourism and financial services sectors. A particular research interest is the relationship between face-to-face communication and remote, technologically based communication in a financial services context. She hopes to build upon this sector specific research to explore how businesses generally have embraced new technology in their marketing and advertising.

Oh Sook May graduated with a Master of Business Administration from School of Management, Universiti Sains Malaysia in the year 2005. Her research work has focused on technology adoption among individual users in Penang, Malaysia. Upon her graduation she joined a multinational company in Penang. Her research work has been published in numerous international conferences and also journals of repute.

Gary Packham is Professor and Director for Enterprise for the University of Glamorgan and Head of Programmes for the Glamorgan Business School. He recently managed the prestigious Federation of Small Business' Lifting the Barriers Survey and acts as the Institute of Small Business and Entrepreneurship's regional champion for Wales. Previously, Professor Packham was Head of Division for Enterprise and Economic Development and was academic delivery manager for the circa £14 million ESF project - e-College Wales. He has published widely in the areas of enterprise and small business management and has extensive experience in developing and delivering enterprise and management education. Professor Packham is a Member of the Chartered Management Institute, the Institute for Leadership and Management and a Fellow of the Higher Education Academy. He is also a director of Age Concern Morgannwg Ltd.

Baomin Qi (PhD) is senior lecturer of business logistics and information systems at the University of Bolton. Her research focuses on the topics of development of e-business strategy, e-supply chain management, systems integration, and e-learning. Her research work has been published in a range of international refereed conferences and Journals. She is currently supervising three PhD students. Her teaching focuses on the innovative e-business, e-marketing, and projects management, and she has supervised over 50 Master's theses. Prior to pursue her academic career, she had worked within manufacturing industry for ten years as senior engineer, and gained firsthand experience in engineer design and innovation.

Modapothala Jashua Rajesh is a lecturer in the School of Business and Enterprise at Swinburne University of Technology, Sarawak Campus, Malaysia. He received a PhD in Commerce from Sri Krishnadevaraya University, India. His research interests include strategic use of Information Technologies/Systems, data mining, corporate social responsibility, and environmental related studies. He has presented at a number of national and international conferences (inclusive of IEEE) and has a good publishing record.

Boumediene (Ben) Ramdani is Senior Lecturer in Strategy and Operations Management at Bristol Business School (UK). He has experience through different roles and contributions in Manchester Business School (UK), King's College London (UK), WMG – University of Warwick (UK), and IE Business School (Spain). His research investigates how senior managers can most effectively select, implement, and deploy Information Technology (IT) to achieve their business goals. He has published papers in leading journals including California Management Review. His current research falls in two categories. The first is to investigate how firms can build capabilities to deliver incremental business value from IT. The second is to explore disruptive change and how businesses that may be well managed, customer-friendly, and technologically advanced - are still susceptible to failure or to being overtaken by upstart competitors. Professionally, he has worked for a number of private and public sector organisations including Datamonitor.com, CA Technologies, Expertia Consulting Group and UK Government. His consulting activities focus on advising firms on strategy-related matters.

Kamel Rouibah has directed many funded research projects, and has served as the program committee member of various international conferences (Australasian Conference of Information Systems-ACIS, Information System Development-ISD; ACM Symposium on Applied Computing on e-Business Applications; IADIS, etc.) and reviewer for various international journals (IT & People, Journal of Global Information Management, Industrial Management & Data System, Journal of Electronic Commerce in Organization, International Journal of e-Adoption, International Journal of Computer Integrated Manufacturing, International Journal of Production Research, The Australasian Journal of Information System, Arab Journal of Administrative Sciences, Journal of Global Information Technology Management, Asian Academy of management Journal, Information Management & Computer Security, Communication of the IIMA.). Dr. Rouibah sits on the Editorial Board of several IS journals: Journal of Global Information Management; Journal of Electronic Commerce in Organizations (JECO); International Journal of e-Adoption; The Australasian Journal of Information System, International Journal of Handheld Computing Research, International Journal of Advanced Pervasive and Ubiquitous Computing (IJAPUC).

T. Ramayah has an MBA from Universiti Sains Malaysia (USM). Currently he is an Associate Professor at the School of Management in USM. He teaches mainly courses in Research Methodology and Business Statistics. Apart from teaching, he is an avid researcher, especially in the areas of technology management and adoption in business and education. His publications have appeared in *Computers in Human Behavior, Resources, Conservation and Recycling, Turkish Online Journal of Education Technology, Journal of Research in Interactive Marketing, Information Development, Journal of Project Management (JoPM), IJITDM, International Journal of Services and Operations Management (IJSOM), Engineering, Construction and Architectural Management (ECAM) and North American Journal of Psychology. He* is constantly invited to serve on the editorial boards and program committees of many international journals and conferences of repute. His full profile can be accessed from http://www.ramayah.com

Abbas Saghaei is an Associate Professor at Islamic Azad University, Science & Research branch. He received his Ph.D. in Industrial Engineering from Iran Science and Technology University. His research interest includes statistical quality control, time series analysis, and numerical analysis. He is a member of the board of the Iranian Quality Management Society. He is also a certified quality engineer and reliability engineer.

Jeanne Samuel is an Instructional Technologist for the Office of Medical Education in the Tulane University School of Medicine in New Orleans, LA. Her current responsibilities include exploring ways to make faculty, student, and staff tasks easier through technology. She explored the pedagogical applications of Web 2.0 technology while exiled from New Orleans during Hurricane Katrina in 2005. During her twenty plus years as a computer analyst/consultant, certified technical trainer, and educator, she has been an advocate of innovation in education. Samuel now is shifting gears to focus on publishing, collaborative learning, digital knowledge management, and innovation diffusion. To that end, she is working toward a Doctorate in Educational Technology at Louisiana State University.

Sinawong Sang has been working as a Deputy Director of the department of ICT policy and strategy for the National ICT Development Authority (NiDA) since 2002. In his role in the department, he is responsible for the ICT policy and strategy, particularly e-government. Sang received his Bachelor's degree in Computer Sciences & Engineering from the Royal University of Phnom Penh in Cambodia in 2001. He got his Master's degree in Management from Charles Sturt University, Australia, in 2006. Currently he is a PhD candidate at International IT Policy Program (ITPP), Technology Management, Economics and Policy (TEMEP), College of Engineering, Seoul National University. His research interests include: e-government acceptance and adoption, issues of e-government implementation in developing countries, and Partial Least Squares (PLS) and related methods.

Pei-Di Shen now works as Director of the Teacher Education Center and professor of Graduate School of Education, Ming Chuan University, Taipei, Taiwan. Professor Shen is one of the Editors-in-Chief of International Journal of Online Pedagogy and Course Design. Her primary interest areas are E-learning, Knowledge Management, Virtual Community, and Management Information Systems. Her research focus is the distance education in higher education.

Chia Hua Sim is a Lecturer in the School of Business and Enterprise at Swinburne University of Technology, Sarawak Campus, Malaysia. Her research interests include entrepreneurship, small businesses research, and e-commerce. She has presented at national and international conferences on topics related to ICTs and e-commerce.

Nitish Singh is an Assistant Professor of International Business at the Boeing Institute of International Business, St. Louis University. His research emphasis is in the area of international e-business, cross-cultural research, and emerging markets. He has publishing activity in a variety of journals including the Journal of International Business Studies, Journal of Business Research, Psychology & Marketing, International Marketing Review, European Journal of Marketing, Journal of Advertising Research, and Journal of Electronic Commerce Research, Journal of Global Information Management, Journal of Computer Mediated Communication, Multinational Business Review, Thunderbird International Business Review, and others. He is also a co-author of the book The Culturally Customized Website, and the book, Proliferation of Internet Economy.

John E. Spillan serves as an Associate Professor of Business Administration at the University of North Carolina at Pembroke. His articles have appeared in the International Journal of Marketing and Marketing Research, Journal of Business in Developing Nations, Journal of East West Business, European Management Journal, Journal of Teaching in International Business, Journal of Small Business Strategy, International Small Business Journal, Journal of Crisis and Contingency Management, Journal of Small Business Management, Journal of Marketing Theory and Practice, Journal of Asia-Pacific, Journal of Global Marketing and Journal of World Business, Latin American Business Review, International Journal of Sustainable Strategic Management, Journal of International Business Systems Research, Journal for Advancement of Marketing Education, and European Management Journal, among others.

Reima Suomi is a Professor of Information Systems Science at University of Turku, and a part-time Professor at Huazhong Normal University, Wuhan, Hubei, China. He has been a Professor at Turku School of Economics and Business Administration, Finland since 1994. He is a Docent for the universities of Turku and Oulu, Finland. Years 1992-93 he spent as a "Vollamtlicher Dozent" in the University of St. Gallen, Switzerland, where he led a research project on business process re-engineering. Currently, he concentrates on topics around management of networked activities, including issues such as management of telecommunication networks, electronic and mobile commerce, virtual organizations, telework, and competitive advantage through telecommunication-based Information Systems. His research agenda includes different governance structures applied to the management of IS, enabled by IS, as well as application of Information Systems in healthcare. Reima Suomi has over 500 publications, and has published in journals such as Communications of the Association for Information Systems, CIN: Computers, Informatics, Nursing, Information & Management, Information Services & Use, Technology Analysis & Strategic Management, The Journal of Strategic Information Systems, Behaviour & Information Technology, Journal of Management History, Orthopaedic Nursing and Information Resources Management Journal. For the academic year 2001-2002, he was a senior researcher "varttunut tutkija" for the academy of Finland. With Paul Jackson he published the book "Virtual Organization and workplace development" with Routledge, London.

Brychan Thomas is a Senior Research Fellow in Small Business and Innovation and Deputy Leader of the Welsh Enterprise Institute at the University of Glamorgan Business School, UK. He has a science degree and an MSc in the Social Aspects of Science and Technology from the Technology Policy Unit at Aston University and a PhD in Science and Technology Policy, CNAA/University of Glamorgan. He has produced over 280 publications in the area of science communication, innovation, and small business policy, including the books "Triple Entrepreneurial Connection" and "E-Commerce Adoption and Small Business in the Global Marketplace: Tools for Optimization," and is on the Editorial Advisory and Review Board of the International Journal of E-Business Management, the Editorial Review Board of the International Journal of E-Entrepreneurship and Innovation and the Editorial Advisory Board of IMJ – International Management Journals. During the academic year 2008/2009 he was on secondment as a Fellow of the Advanced Institute of Management at the Centre for Technology Management, University of Cambridge.

Piers Thompson is a Lecturer in Economics at the Cardiff School of Management within the University of Wales Institute, Cardiff (UWIC). Prior to this he worked on the Welsh component of the Global Entrepreneurship Monitor (GEM) project, the world's largest international study of entrepreneurial activity and attitudes. His research interests are in small firm finance, ethnic entrepreneurship, and macroeconomic investment patterns. His work on topics relating to small business and firm start-up activity has been published in a number of international journals including: Regional Studies, the International Journal of Entrepreneurial Behaviour & Research, and the International Small Business Journal. He has also recently worked on the UK Competitiveness Index for 2010, a study benchmarking the competitiveness of localities across the United Kingdom. His current research integrates his earlier work on entrepreneurial activity, attitudes, and technological development and diffusion in the digital age within the framework of regional and local development.

Chia-Wen Tsai is an assistant professor in the Department of Information Management, Ming Chuan University. Dr. Tsai is one of the Editors-in-Chief of International Journal of Online Pedagogy and Course Design, and International Journal of Technology and Human Interaction. He is also the Associate Editor of Cyberpsychology, Behavior, and Social Networking, and International Journal of Information Communication Technologies and Human Development. He is interested in online teaching methods and knowledge management.

Chengbo Wang is a Senior Lecturer in the Business School of Edge Hill University. He had been working for nine years in industry, with an extensive experience of industrial engineering, supply chain management, project management, and the application research of academic theories into real world operations. After he joined the academic world, he keeps doing research and publishing papers, besides other academic activities. His academic foci include: logistics management/supply chain management, retailing operations, green issues in operations and logistics, operations management, knowledge management, case-based reasoning, quality management, manufacturing strategy, and educational issues within operations and supply chain management. Besides cooperation network in academia, Dr. Wang also has extensive links and collaboration with industries both in UK and other countries.

Robert Williams is a researcher based at NEO. Previous assignments include working on the Welsh element of the Global Entrepreneurship Monitor (GEM) project, which is recognised as the world's largest international study of entrepreneurial activity. His research interests are in small rural firms' entrepreneurial capabilities and their interactions with government rural development policy. His more recent work has focused on the role and impact of social enterprise in deprived areas of Wales. His work on topics relating to small rural business, social enterprise activity and enterprise education as been presented and published in the proceedings of a number of international and national conferences. He is also the author of a number of book chapters and journal articles on topics such as e-commerce in small and medium enterprises, and rural entrepreneurship. His latest research concentrates on bringing his existing areas of expertise together to examine the usage of e-commerce in rural SMEs and the social impacts of greater e-commerce diffusion.

Index

A

application ontology 307
application programming interface (API) 81, 216, 231, 241-242, 248-249, 255, 348
assertional reasoning 108
authoritative sources 131, 147

B

Berlin SPARQL Benchmark (BSBM) 81-86, 89-92, 94-95, 97, 101-102
British Broadcasting Corporation (BBC) 209, 213, 217, 226, 291, 301
Browsing Concept Groups 247
business semantics management (BSM) 252

C

ClashDetect 189, 202-203
Class hierarchy 116, 118, 125, 259, 262, 272
clickthrough data 66-67, 74, 77-78
Cohen's Kappa 350, 357
collaborative idea development 303
collaborative working environments 317
compound noun candidate list (CNLc) 50-51
compound noun (NNS) tag 49
compound proper noun (NNPS) tag 49
computational feasibility (CF) 108, 112, 115-116, 125-126, 132, 136-137, 145-146, 148, 177, 263-264, 310, 313
Concept Cloud 245
concept distances 67
Concise Bound Descriptions (CBD) 112, 130
consolidated attributes 240, 243-244, 249
constituent concepts 240-241, 249
Content Management System (CMS) 232
Core Idea 303-304, 309-310
corpus-based methods 343-344, 349-350, 354, 356
Creative Commons 222

D

cross-organizational communication 1
cutoff value (CV) 349, 354-356

D

D2R Server 81, 92-93, 96-98, 100-101, 211-212, 224
database-oriented system 316
Data Bookmarking 232
Data Exploration 205
Data Fusion 221, 224
data generator 82-84, 101
data-linking 234, 253
data publishing 212, 234, 253, 256
Data Sharing 205, 251
DBpedia 91, 102, 104-105, 114-115, 118-125, 128, 207, 210, 213, 216-217, 223-224, 226, 237-238, 254, 285-289, 295-299, 301
DERI pipes 217-218, 221
Description Logics (DLs) 106, 325
Distributed Description Logics (DDLs) 252
DL Implementation Group (DIG) 109, 128, 184, 207, 299
DOGMA approach 244, 252, 256
Dopplr 280
Drupal module 290
Dusty Springfield 118

E

Ease of use and freedom 232
e-commerce 81-83, 85, 101
e-government 1-3, 7-9, 11-12, 29, 36-37, 41-46
Enterprise 2.0 256, 279, 283, 291-292, 301
Enterprise 2.0 ecosystem 279, 283
e-services 1-2
European Union (EU) 7, 9, 12, 35, 42, 44
Extensible Markup Language (XML) 7, 44, 173, 177, 184, 201, 205, 211, 223, 234, 236, 264, 290